Women Writing Across Cultures

This collection brings together an international, multicultural, multilingual, and multidisciplinary community of scholars and practitioners in different media seeking to question and re-theorize the contested terms of our title: "woman," "writing," "women's writing," and "across." "Culture" is translated into an open series of interconnected terms and questions. How might one write across national cultures; or across a national and a minority culture; or across disciplines, genres, and media; or across synchronic discourses that are unequal in power; or across present and past discourses or present and future discourses?

The collection explores and develops recent feminist, queer, and transgender theory and criticism, and also aesthetic practice. "Writing across" assumes a number of orientations: posthumanist; transtemporal; transnationalist; writing across discourses, disciplines, media, genres, genders; writing across pronouns – he, she, they; writing across literature, non-literary texts, and life.

This book was originally published as a special issue of *Angelaki: Journal of the Theoretical Humanities.*

Pelagia Goulimari teaches feminist theory, feminist writing and women's writing at the English Faculty, University of Oxford, UK. She is Co-Convenor of the interdisciplinary Oxford M.St. in Women's Studies. Her books include *Literary Criticism and Theory: From Plato to Postcolonialism* (2015), *Toni Morrison* (2011), and the edited collection *Postmodernism. What Moment?* (2007). She is co-founder and co-editor of *Angelaki: Journal of the Theoretical Humanities.*

Women Writing Across Cultures

Present, Past, Future

Edited by

Pelagia Goulimari

LONDON AND NEW YORK

First published 2018 by Routledge

2 Park Square, Milton Park, Abingdon, Oxfordshire OX14 4RN
52 Vanderbilt Avenue, New York, NY 10017

Routledge is an imprint of the Taylor & Francis Group, an informa business

First issued in paperback 2019

British Library Cataloguing in Publication Data
A catalogue record for this book is available from the British Library

ISBN 13: 978-1-138-29576-6 (hbk)
ISBN 13: 978-0-367-33665-3 (pbk)

Typeset in TimesNewRomanPSMT
by diacriTech, Chennai

Publisher's Note
The publisher accepts responsibility for any inconsistencies that may have arisen during the conversion of this book from journal articles to book chapters, namely the possible inclusion of journal terminology.

Contents

Citation Information

The chapters in this book were originally published in the *Angelaki: Journal of the Theoretical Humanities*, volume 22, issue 1 (March 2017). When citing this material, please use the original page numbering for each article, as follows:

Introduction
Women Writing Across Cultures: Present, Past, Future
Pelagia Goulimari
Angelaki: Journal of the Theoretical Humanities, volume 22, issue 1 (March 2017) pp. 1–10

Chapter 1
A Symbiological Approach to Sex, Gender, and Desire in the Anthropocene
Regenia Gagnier
Angelaki: Journal of the Theoretical Humanities, volume 22, issue 1 (March 2017) pp. 11–22

Chapter 2
Is there Such a Thing as "Woman Writing"? Julia Kristeva, Judith Butler and Writing as Gendered Experience
Sylvie Gambaudo
Angelaki: Journal of the Theoretical Humanities, volume 22, issue 1 (March 2017) pp. 23–34

Chapter 3
From Symptom to the Symbolization of Receptivity: A Girl's Psychoanalytic Journey
Louise Gyler
Angelaki: Journal of the Theoretical Humanities, volume 22, issue 1 (March 2017) pp. 35–48

Chapter 4
Theorizing Closeness: A Trans Feminist Conversation
Talia Bettcher and Pelagia Goulimari
Angelaki: Journal of the Theoretical Humanities, volume 22, issue 1 (March 2017) pp. 49–60

Chapter 5
Spreading the Word: The "Woman Question" in the Periodicals A Voz Feminina *and* O Progresso *(1868–69)*
Cláudia Pazos-Alonso
Angelaki: Journal of the Theoretical Humanities, volume 22, issue 1 (March 2017) pp. 61–76

Chapter 6
Encounter with the Mirror of the Other: Angela Carter and her Personal Connection with Japan
Natsumi Ikoma
Angelaki: Journal of the Theoretical Humanities, volume 22, issue 1 (March 2017) pp. 77–92

Chapter 7
Transnational Theatrical Representation of the Aging: Velina Hasu Houston's Calligraphy
Eriko Hara
Angelaki: Journal of the Theoretical Humanities, volume 22, issue 1 (March 2017) pp. 93–102

Chapter 8
Tracing Back Trauma: The Legacy of Slavery in Contemporary Afro-Brazilian Literature by Women
Claire Williams
Angelaki: Journal of the Theoretical Humanities, volume 22, issue 1 (March 2017) pp. 103–122

Chapter 9
To be or Not to be Métis*: Nina Bouraoui's Embodied Memory of the Colonial Fracture*
Mona El Khoury
Angelaki: Journal of the Theoretical Humanities, volume 22, issue 1 (March 2017) pp. 123–136

Chapter 10
Constructing Selfhood through Re-voicing the Classical Past: Bernardine Evaristo, Marlene NourbeSe Philip, and Robin Coste Lewis
Tessa Roynon
Angelaki: Journal of the Theoretical Humanities, volume 22, issue 1 (March 2017) pp. 137–152

Chapter 11
Faith, Family, and Memory in the Diaries of Jane Attwater, 1766–1834
Cynthia Aalders
Angelaki: Journal of the Theoretical Humanities, volume 22, issue 1 (March 2017) pp. 153–162

Chapter 12
Women's Voices of Renewal within Tradition: The Women of the Wall of Jerusalem
Kim Treiger-Bar-Am
Angelaki: Journal of the Theoretical Humanities, volume 22, issue 1 (March 2017) pp. 163–182

Chapter 13
Attitudes to Futurity in New German Feminisms and Contemporary Women's Fiction
Emily Spiers
Angelaki: Journal of the Theoretical Humanities, volume 22, issue 1 (March 2017) pp. 183–196

Chapter 14
"Aulinhas de Sedução" [Small Lessons in Seduction]: Clarice Lispector on How (Not) to be a Woman
Mariela E. Méndez
Angelaki: Journal of the Theoretical Humanities, volume 22, issue 1 (March 2017) pp. 197–206

Chapter 15
"Does Feminism Have a Generation Gap?": Blogging, Millennials and the Hip Hop Generation
Alison Winch
Angelaki: Journal of the Theoretical Humanities, volume 22, issue 1 (March 2017) pp. 207–222

Chapter 16
Feminist to Postfeminist: Contemporary Biofictions by and about Women Artists
Julia Novak
Angelaki: Journal of the Theoretical Humanities, volume 22, issue 1 (March 2017) pp. 223–230

Chapter 17
Practice and Cultural Politics of "Women's Script": Nüshu *as an Endangered Heritage in Contemporary China*
Fei-wen Liu
Angelaki: Journal of the Theoretical Humanities, volume 22, issue 1 (March 2017) pp. 231–246

Chapter 18
"My main job is to translate / pain into tales they can tolerate // in another language": Women's Poetry and the Health Humanities
Jane Dowson
Angelaki: Journal of the Theoretical Humanities, volume 22, issue 1 (March 2017) pp. 247–260

Chapter 19
Love in the Novels of Toni Morrison
Jean Wyatt
Angelaki: Journal of the Theoretical Humanities, volume 22, issue 1 (March 2017) pp. 261–270

Chapter 20
Ethical Ways of Seeing the Female Nude in Spanish Cinema
María Donapetry
Angelaki: Journal of the Theoretical Humanities, volume 22, issue 1 (March 2017) pp. 271–278

Chapter 21
On or about December 1930: Gender and the Writing of Lives in Virginia Woolf
Morag Shiach
Angelaki: Journal of the Theoretical Humanities, volume 22, issue 1 (March 2017) pp. 279–288

Chapter 22
Writing as a "sie": Reflections on Barbara Köhler's Odyssey Cycle Niemands Frau
Georgina Paul
Angelaki: Journal of the Theoretical Humanities, volume 22, issue 1 (March 2017) pp. 289–296

Chapter 23
They
Aliki Krikidi
Angelaki: Journal of the Theoretical Humanities, volume 22, issue 1 (March 2017) pp. 297–310

Chapter 24
Gendered Expectations: Writing Counter to my Gender
Lauren Grodstein
Angelaki: Journal of the Theoretical Humanities, volume 22, issue 1 (March 2017) pp. 311–314

Chapter 25
Writing Men Imagining Women
Kirsty Gunn
Angelaki: Journal of the Theoretical Humanities, volume 22, issue 1 (March 2017) pp. 315–320

Notes on the Contributors

Cynthia Aalders has recently completed doctoral studies at the University of Oxford, where her research focused on the spiritual lives and manuscript cultures of eighteenth-century British women. She is the author of *To Express the Ineffable: The Hymns and Spirituality of Anne Steele* (Paternoster, 2008), and her doctoral thesis is forthcoming from Oxford University Press. Currently the Library Director at Regent College in Vancouver, Canada, she is also beginning a new research project on religious children in the eighteenth century.

Talia Bettcher is a Professor of Philosophy at California State University, Los Angeles, and she currently serves as Chair. Some of her articles include "Evil Deceivers and Make-Believers: Transphobic Violence and the Politics of Illusion" (*Hypatia*, 2007), "Trapped in the Wrong Theory: Re-thinking Trans Oppression and Resistance" (*Signs*, 2014), and "When Selves Have Sex: What the Phenomenology of Trans Sexuality Can Teach about Sexual Orientation" (*Journal of Homosexuality*, 2014). With Susan Stryker, she co-edited the *Transgender Studies Quarterly* special double issue *Trans/Feminisms* (2016). She is currently at work on the monograph *Personhood as Intimacy: A Trans Feminist Philosophy* (under contract with Minnesota UP).

María Donapetry has taught cinema at Pomona College (California) and at the University of Oxford to both graduate and undergraduate students. Most of her publications are devoted to women and film, including *Imagi/naci♀n: feminización de la nación en el cine español y de América Latina* (Fundamentos, 2006), *Sola ante el peligro: la maternidad imperfecta* (<www.39ymas.com>, 2003), and *Toda ojos* (KRK, 2001). For the past ten years she has been lecturing and writing on the interrelation between ethics and film.

Jane Dowson is Reader in Twentieth-Century Literature at De Montfort University, Leicester, UK. She has written broadly on twentieth-century and contemporary poetry. Her publications include *A History of Twentieth-Century British Women's Poetry* (Cambridge UP, 2005; coauthored), *The Cambridge Companion to Twentieth-Century British and Irish Women's Poetry* (Cambridge UP, 2011), and *Carol Ann Duffy: Poet for our Times* (Palgrave, 2016).

Mona El Khoury is an Assistant Professor in French at Tufts University. She has published on contemporary Francophone literature and film, and is currently working on a book manuscript on memory and Franco-Algerian identities. Her research interests include postcolonial cultural productions, trauma, migration, and the diaspora phenomenon.

Regenia Gagnier is Professor of English at the University of Exeter, editor of *Literature Compass*'s Global Circulation Project, and Senior Research Fellow in Egenis, the

Centre for the Study of Life Sciences. Her single-authored books include *Idylls of the Marketplace: Oscar Wilde and the Victorian Public* (Stanford UP, 1986), *Subjectivities: A History of Self-Representation in Britain* (Oxford UP, 1991), *The Insatiability of Human Wants: Economics and Aesthetics in Market Society* (University of Chicago Press, 2000), and *Individualism, Decadence and Globalization: On the Relationship of Part to Whole* (Palgrave, 2010). Her current research is on the global circulation of literatures of liberalization.

Sylvie Gambaudo is Lecturer in Philosophy at the University of Durham. Her research interests focus on gender theory, feminist philosophy, and marginal narratives. She has recently published on menopause theory, on Julia Kristeva, and on Janet Frame.

Pelagia Goulimari has been teaching feminist theory, women's writing, and feminist writing for the English Faculty, University of Oxford, and for the interdisciplinary Oxford M.St. in Women's Studies. Her books include *Literary Criticism and Theory: From Plato to Postcolonialism* (Routledge, 2015), *Toni Morrison* (Routledge, 2011), and the edited collection *Postmodernism: What Moment?* (Manchester UP, 2007). She is co-founder and co-editor of *Angelaki: Journal of the Theoretical Humanities.*

Lauren Grodstein is the author of the *New York Times'* bestselling *A Friend of the Family* and the *Washington Post* Book of the Year *The Explanation for Everything*, among other novels. Her essays have been widely anthologized, and her writing has been translated into languages including French, Turkish, and Hebrew. She directs the creative writing program at Rutgers University, Camden.

Kirsty Gunn is the author of eight works of fiction, the most recent of which, a short story collection, *Infidelities*, was shortlisted for the Frank O'Connor International Short Story Award, and was winner of the Edge Hill Short Story Prize. An essay about Katherine Mansfield was published by Notting Hill Editions and was launched in America by New York Review Books in November 2016. She is published in the United Kingdom by Faber & Faber and is Professor of Writing Practice and Study at the University of Dundee. She lives in London and Scotland with her husband and two daughters.

Louise Gyler is a Child and Adult Training Analyst of the Australian Psychoanalytical Society and a member of the International Psychoanalytic Association. She gained her Ph.D. in Gender Studies from the University of Sydney and is the author of *The Gendered Unconscious: Can Gender Discourses Subvert Psychoanalysis?* (Routledge, 2010). She is currently working on the problem of empathy and imagination as a member of an international interdisciplinary network (INSEI). She has a psychoanalytic private practice in Sydney.

Eriko Hara is Professor of English Communication at Tokyo Kasei University. Her research fields include contemporary American drama, gender studies, and cultural studies. She is the editor of *Gender and American Literature* (Keisoshobo, 2002) and co-editor of *Haunting Past: Trauma, Memory, Regeneration in Asian American Literature* (Kinsei-do, 2014).

Natsumi Ikoma (Ph.D., University of Durham) is a Professor of Literature at the International Christian University in Tokyo, Japan. Her research interests include representations of the grotesque body, monstrosity, Gothic literature, gender studies, and feminist theories.

She is currently working on gender performativity in Angela Carter's works, focusing especially on the influence of Japan on her literature.

Aliki Krikidi is an artist. She studied at the Athens School of Fine Art before completing an MA in Fine Art at Goldsmiths, University of London. Aliki currently lives and works in Oxford and Berlin. Her practice is mainly painting based and orbits around various phenomenological and existential themes including, amongst others, the nature of time and being, affect, speed, and physicality as they are experienced in the artistic process itself. In other aspects of her work, she brings into play the antithetical juxtaposition of the ethereal narrative of text alongside the physicality of painting. She has also worked with text as a proxy tool for a potential performative reconfiguration.

Fei-wen Liu is Research Fellow at the Institute of Ethnology, Academia Sinica, Taiwan. She has conducted fieldwork in southern rural China on the world's only "women's script," known as *nüshu*, since 1992. Her research explores the dynamics of expression, depths of sentiments, and women's voices. Her recent publication *Gendered Words: Sentiments and Expression in Changing Rural China* was published by Oxford University Press in 2015.

Mariela E. Méndez is an Assistant Professor of Latin American and Iberian Studies and of Women, Gender and Sexuality Studies at the University of Richmond, in Richmond, VA, USA. She is coeditor of *Un libro quemado* (Excursiones, 2014) and *Nosotras … y la Piel* (Alfaguara, 1998), two collections of chronicles by Argentinean writer Alfonsina Storni, as well as of *Escrituras a ras de suelo: Crónica latinoamericana del siglo XX* (U Finis Terrae, 2014), an anthology of scholarly essays on Latin American chronicle writing between 1930 and 1970. Her book *Crónicas travestis: El periodismo transgresor de Alfonsina Storni, Clarice Lispector y Marıá Moreno* is forthcoming with Beatriz Viterbo, one of Latin America's premier academic presses. In it, she uses the concept of transvestism to trace a genealogy between the transgressive reappropriation of women's pages staged by Alfonsina Storni (Argentina, 1892–1938), Clarice Lispector (Brazil, 1920– 77), and Marıá Moreno (Argentina, 1947–).

Julia Novak is a Marie Andessner Research Fellow at King's College London and the Department of English, University of Salzburg, working on a book on biographical novels about historical women artists. She has written a book on reading groups, *Gemeinsam Lesen* (Lit, 2007), and a book entitled *Live Poetry: An Integrated Approach to Poetry in Performance* (Rodopi, 2011).

Georgina Paul is Associate Professor in German at the University of Oxford and Fellow and Tutor in German at St Hilda's College, Oxford. She has published widely on post-1990 German literature, including on contemporary poetry, and has a particular interest in literary representations of gender. She is the author of *Perspectives on Gender in Post-1945 German Literature* (Camden, 2009) and editor of *An Odyssey for Our Time: Barbara Köhler's* Niemands Frau (Rodopi, 2013).

Cláudia Pazos-Alonso is Associate Professor in Portuguese and Brazilian Studies, University of Oxford, and a Fellow of Wadham College. Her research interests range widely across nineteenth- and twentieth-century Lusophone literature and are informed by a gender studies perspective. Her main book publications include *Antigone's Daughters?*

Gender, Genealogy, and the Politics of Authorship in 20th-Century Portuguese Women's Writing (Bucknell UP, 2011; coauthored with Hilary Owen), *Imagens do Eu na Poesia de Florbela Espanca* (Imprensa Nacional-Casa da Moeda, 1997), and co-edited volumes such as *Reading Literature in Portuguese: Commentaries in Honour of Tom Earle* (Legenda, 2013), *A Companion to Portuguese Literature* (Tamesis, 2009), and *Closer to the Wild Heart: Essays on Clarice Lispector* (Legenda/EHRC, 2002). She is currently Co-Convener of the M.St. in Women's Studies at Oxford, and Vice President of the International Association of Lusitanists.

Tessa Roynon is a Teaching and Research Fellow at the Rothermere American Institute, University of Oxford. She has published widely on Toni Morrison, and her monograph *Toni Morrison and the Classical Tradition* (Oxford University Press, 2013) was awarded the Toni Morrison Society Prize for best single-authored book in 2015. She is currently researching the intellectual formation of Ralph Ellison.

Morag Shiach is Professor of Cultural History in the School of English and Drama, Queen Mary University of London. Her publications include *Modernism, Labour and Selfhood, 1890–1930* (Cambridge: Cambridge University Press, 2004) and *The Cambridge Companion to the Modernist Novel* (Cambridge: Cambridge University Press, 2007). She has published widely on modernism and cultural history, and has also edited texts by Virginia Woolf. Her current research focuses on cultural policy, on modernism and language reform, and on marginal modernisms.

Emily Spiers is Lecturer in Creative Futures at Lancaster University, UK. She is currently revising the final draft of her monograph *The Making of Pop-Feminist Narratives: A Comparative Study*, for publication with Oxford University Press in 2017. She has co-edited, with Birgit Mikus, a 2016 special issue of *Oxford German Studies*, on *Fractured Legacies: Historical, Cultural and Political Perspectives on German Feminism*. She is contributing a chapter on Kate Tempest to the forthcoming Oxford University Press volume *Homer and Contemporary Women's Writing* (eds. Fiona Cox and Elena Theodorakopoulos). Further recent articles on digital performances of authorship have appeared in the journals *Feminist Media Studies* and *Women: A Cultural Review*.

Kim Treiger-Bar-Am has published widely in law on freedom of expression and copyright, as well as Kantian theory, feminist theory, and Jewish thought. Her forthcoming work explores Kantian and Jewish views of positive freedom and expression. She teaches at Bar Ilan University, Israel, and lives in Israel with her husband and two daughters.

Claire Williams is Associate Professor of Brazilian Literature and Culture at the University of Oxford and a Fellow of St Peter's College. Her research focuses on women's writing and minority writing from the Lusophone world and she collaborates with a number of research groups working on, for example, contemporary Brazilian literature, Goan literature, and short story writing. Her publications include the volume co-edited with Cláudia Pazos-Alonso *Closer to the Wild Heart: Essays on Clarice Lispector* (Oxford: Legenda/EHRC, 2002) and the monograph *The Encounter Between Opposites in the Works of Clarice Lispector* (HiPLAM, 2006). She has recently co-edited, with Maria José Blanco, a volume entitled *Feminine Singular: Life-Writing by Women in the Luso-Hispanic World* (Lang, 2016).

Alison Winch is Lecturer in Media Studies at the University of East Anglia, UK. She is the author of *Girlfriends and Postfeminist Sisterhood* (Palgrave, 2013). She has published on intergenerational feminisms, as well as wedding culture, branding, the chick flick, and feminine conduct books. Her current project is on generation, intimacy, and popular culture.

Jean Wyatt is Professor of English at Occidental College. She is the author of *Love and Narrative Form in Toni Morrison's Later Novels* (University of Georgia Press, 2017). Her recent articles include essays on Louise Erdrich's *The Painted Drum* and Toni Morrison's *Tar Baby*.

build bridges, not walls

EDITORIAL INTRODUCTION

pelagia goulimari

WOMEN WRITING ACROSS CULTURES

present, past, future

The reader will swiftly conclude – having glanced through the Contents, the names of contributors, and essay titles – that this is a thoroughly international, multicultural, multilingual collection. Nevertheless, the reader is no doubt aware that the terms comprising the title of the collection are highly contested, their meaning far from obvious or descriptive. Indeed, it is the aim of this collection and of my Introduction to ask what these terms might mean and how they might be used. We are seeking to question and retheorize "woman," "writing," "women's writing" and "across." And we will be translating "culture" into an open series of interconnected terms and questions. For example, how might one write across national cultures or across a national and a minority culture or across disciplines, genres and media or across synchronic discourses that are unequal in power or across present and past discourses or present and future discourses?

Let's begin with "woman," particularly in the context of feminist, queer and transgender theory and criticism, but also aesthetic practice. Back in 1993 Judith Butler proposed that "it remains politically necessary to lay claim to 'women,'" and other such terms, "precisely because of the way these terms, as it were, lay their claim on us" – for example, in their "deployments in racist and misogynist discursive regimes" (20).[1] In 2009 Toril Moi argued that the claim "I am not a woman writer" is "always in *response* to a provocation, usually to someone who has tried to use her sex or gender against her [...] a specific kind of *defensive* act [...] *once someone has been taken to be a woman*" (7).[2] But she added that "it is simply wrong to believe that the word "woman" always and without exception has the same, conventional, conservative meaning, regardless of who is speaking and in what context" (8). In 2016, during the US presidential election campaign, far too many voters seemed more comfortable with women as the object of abusive "locker room talk" than with women as politicians.

In the ongoing effort to democratize and pluralize "woman," it is neither necessary nor desirable to assume the priority of gender over race, class, ethnicity, sexuality, etc. In response to Wendy Brown, I suggest that feminist scholarship does not require the priority of gender as its "firm foundation" or its "core" (30).[3] Does scholarship require a core at all? Robyn

Wiegman called for a feminist scholarship that embraces "contingency and unknowability": willingness to denaturalize its object, "women" – "that there might be 'no there there'" – interdisciplinarity, self-reflexivity, openness to the future.[4] Rejecting a facile pluralism that multiplies "definable categories" of women and assumes "recognizability," Afsaneh Najmabadi called for "unavailable intersections."[5] Najmabadi proposed names that defy definition, such as "secular Muslim feminist."[6] Back in 1984 Chandra Mohanty famously rejected the essentialism of the category "Third World Woman."[7] But while the critique of essentialism dominated feminist debates for decades, contemporary debates in feminist, queer and transgender theory are moving beyond the false dilemma or double bind of essentialism vs. social constructionism. Continuing anti-essentialism goes hand-in-hand with what I would call a friendly critique of social constructionism, for example in Rosi Braidotti's *The Posthuman*[8] or in research biologist and feminist theorist Julia Serano's *Whipping Girl*.[9] The background for Regenia Gagnier's essay in this collection is indeed the "loop of nature, culture, and technology," as she calls it. Her innovative "symbiological approach" to literature, outlined in her piece, emerged in the context of a collective interdisciplinary research project across the humanities and the life sciences. It is indebted to, among others, the work of biologist and gender theorist Anne Fausto-Sterling.

In literary studies, my own discipline, academic feminist literary criticism since the late 1960s has endowed us with "women's writing" and "literature by women" as legitimate scholarly terms and fields. See, for example, journals such as *Women's Writing* and *Contemporary Women's Writing*;[10] or the 2007 two-volume third edition of the *Norton Anthology of Literature by Women: The Traditions in English*, compiled by pioneers Sandra M. Gilbert and Susan Gubar; or the monumental ten-volume, multi-editor book series *The History of British Women's Writing*, which began publishing in 2010.[11] This collection includes scholarship on the following women novelists, playwrights and poets, writing in a variety of languages, some of them "greats" of the literary canon, most of them contemporary and emerging: Antonia Baum, Eavan Boland, Nina Bouraoui, Angela Carter, Hélène Cixous, Robin Coste Lewis, Julia Darling, Bernardine Evaristo, Conceição Evaristo, U.A. Fanthorpe, Janice Galloway, Ana Maria Gonçalves, Velina Hasu Houston, Helene Hegemann, Jackie Kay, Barbara Köhler, Gwyneth Lewis, Adriana Lisboa, Clarice Lispector, Toni Morrison, Sharona Muir, Marlene NourbeSe Philip, Priya Parmar, Charlotte Perkins Gilman, Tatiana Salem Levy, Carol Satyamurti, Jo Shapcott, and Virginia Woolf.

Research in women's writing in the last fifty years has been largely organized by national context or by language. Partly to address the limitations of these approaches, recent scholarship has been strongly transnationalist in orientation. To capture transnational networks and identities more fully and sensitively, a theoretical/methodological shift has been taking place – towards theorizing linguistic and cultural "translation," and the relation between cultural "centre" and "periphery" or "margin," but also towards theorizing mixed-race identities that do not fit into existing identity-categories and that question the very process of categorization itself. In this collection, many contributors develop transnational perspectives – focusing on France and Algeria (Mona El Khoury), the United States and Japan (Eriko Hara), Japan and the United Kingdom (Natsumi Ikoma), Portugal and the United Kingdom (Cláudia Pazos-Alonso), and the black diaspora (Tessa Roynon). Pazos-Alonso examines, for the first time, the "pioneer early feminism" of progressive Portuguese periodicals *A Voz Feminina* and *O Progresso* (1868–69) in relation to transnational women's networks and transnational debates on women's suffrage. She reconstructs the connections between Principal Editor Francisca Wood and her collaborators with "key radical figures such as Lydia Becker in England, Marie Goegg in Switzerland and André Léo in France." She suggests that Francisca Wood "may have been behind [...] the (unsigned and incomplete) first translation of *Jane Eyre* into Portuguese" from 1877 onwards. Countering Wood's "invisibility at the point of her death," Pazos-Alonso reappraises Wood's role in transnational cultural history. Natsumi Ikoma, in the midst of recent strongly renewed interest in Angela Carter, investigates a gap in Carter scholarship, Carter's years in Japan (1969–72). With "original information drawn from interviews with Carter's former Japanese boyfriend, combined with the examination of [Carter's] unpublished journal entries," Ikoma reconstructs the impact of Carter's close encounter with all aspects of Japanese life and culture – from her love life to her readings in Japanese literature – on her work, especially on the evolution of her feminist thinking and experimental novelistic practice. Eriko Hara focuses on the transnationalism of Asian-American playwright Velina Hasu Houston and her explorations of "cultural collision and coalescence in transnational communities." Discussing Houston's work since *Tea* (1987), especially *Calligraphy* (2010), Hara highlights Houston's insights into "women's memories," old age, dementia, and processes of "aging from both Japanese and American perspectives." Houston's transnationalist feminist "politics of life," argues Hara, thus creates an innovative "viewpoint through which to look at Japan, the United States and the world" – that of the "transformative nature of cultural identity and change" – and "inspires [Houston] to re-envision women's writing."

However, what is "women's writing" after all? Is it (great) literature by those assigned female at birth or by those who identify as women? Or addressed primarily to those assigned female at birth or those who identify as women? Or influenced by "women" or situated within women's literary traditions? Or feminist in the broadest sense? Or necessarily one of the above? This collection certainly advocates an inclusive understanding of "writing," in keeping with the poststructuralist theorization of "text" and "intertextuality" by Roland Barthes and Julia Kristeva. The collection places (great) literature within a continuum of "texts" of all sorts: film (María Donapetry) and painting (Aliki Krikidi); women's pages (Mariela E. Méndez) and blogs (Alison Winch); manuscript Chinese women s writing, *nüshu* (Fei-wen Liu); manuscript diaries (Cynthia Aalders); talking in the psychoanalytic encounter (Louise Gyler); and group singing (Kim Treiger-Bar-Am). But this collection also strongly endorses literature as having a vital role within the continuum (see Jane Dowson), including difficult, experimental literature (see Georgina Paul), and invites literary practitioners to reflect on their practice (see Lauren Grodstein and Kirsty Gunn). Yet it insists on making connections between "great" literature, non-literary texts and life (see Morag Shiach). So what I have described as a writing continuum can alternatively be described as a *writing-across*.

Before going on to discuss the idea of "across" that is in the title of this collection and running through it, let me ask once again: (how) can women's writing be theorized? In this collection, philosophers Sylvie Gambaudo and Talia Bettcher and psychoanalyst Louise Gyler offer ways to pose the question. Gambaudo eschews established terms such as "women's writing" in favour of her neologism "woman writing." Aiming to formulate a non-essentialist definition of "woman writing," she turns to the work of Kristeva and Butler for the tools to understand what a "woman writing" practice might be. Continuing her feminist critique of psychoanalysis, Gyler here challenges the idea of a "simple linear progression from the pre-Oedipal to the Oedipal" and the "centrality given to the Oedipus complex and the associated paternal function" in the psychoanalytic account of the "processes involved in entering the symbolic realm." She goes on to outline what might be described as a maternal-symbolic function – what Gyler calls the "symbolization of an inner receptive space" as a precondition for thought. Bettcher, in conversation with Pelagia Goulimari, discusses her substantial contributions to transgender theory and theorizes "woman" and "writing" from a trans feminist perspective. In the context of wider debates in feminist, queer and transgender theory, Bettcher and Goulimari ask how (not) to theorize "woman," "trans woman" and "trans woman of colour" but also how (not) to theorize "experience," "local knowledge," and communication across worlds. They explore aesthetic experiments crossing the boundaries between theory, literature and life-writing, and their connection to an intersectional ethics of closeness. Bettcher goes on to outline her concept of intimacy and "interpersonal spatiality," developing the work of philosopher María Lugones on communication across "worlds."

I will now turn to "across," as theorized and practised in this collection. I will begin by situating it in relation to contemporary feminist theory, particularly the so-called New Materialist feminisms. The word "across" points to a cluster of concepts developed in this field: the transversal, the nomadic, the rhizomatic, the in between, assemblage, entanglement, intra-action. I am alluding to the evolving work of Karen Barad, Rosi Braidotti, Claire Colebrook, Elizabeth Grosz, Donna Haraway, Dorothea Olkowski and others, since the 1980s.[12] In this body of work, the emphasis is often on the "posthuman" crossing of the boundaries between the human and the non-human natural world, and between nature, culture and technology – as addressed by Gagnier in this collection. But the collection develops the idea of "across" in a number of other directions. Transnationalism, as discussed above, is one of them, suggesting a spatial understanding of "across."

Yet another direction is a temporal understanding of "across" that I call transtemporal, distinguishing somewhat artificially between: present & past and present & future. To begin with the former, several pieces in this collection pursue the connection between present & past in innovative ways. One of the strongest themes in postcolonial and African-American literature by women has been that of *traumatic memory*, and the pieces here by Claire Williams, Mona El Khoury and Jean Wyatt contribute to its ongoing theorization. Tessa Roynon focuses on another strong theme in these fields: the reconstruction of black female subjectivity and retrieval of agency through intertextual "revoicing" of the past. In particular, Williams analyses four contemporary novels by Brazilian women writers, which "trace back" historical "trauma" to the "impact and legacy of slavery on contemporary society." The four texts by Adriana Lisboa, Conceição Evaristo, Ana Maria Gonçalves and Tatiana Salem Levy return to "shockingly brutal events which seem to prove wrong the myths of gentle colonization and harmonious racial democracy." Williams analyses how, narrating "from the point of view of the most vulnerable member of colonial society: the enslaved African woman," these writers "claim justice for their characters and remind readers that those excluded from official histories had names, faces and voices." Highlighting "women's history, visibility, individuality, legacy and heroism" will "enable healing from trauma in the present." El Khoury, on the other hand, highlights the intractable intergenerational transmission of trauma. El Khoury focuses on Nina Bouraoui's *métis* (mixed-race) Franco-Algerian identity "as presented in her autobiographical novels," *Garçon manqué* [*Tomboy*] and *Mes mauvaises pensées* [*My Bad/Evil Thoughts*]. El Khoury's psychoanalytic reading draws synthetically on Marianne Hirsch's concept of "postmemory," Teresa Brennan on the transmission of affect, psychiatrist Judith Herman, psychiatrist and psychoanalyst Vamik Volkan, psychoanalyst Didier Anzieu, critic Nadine Fresco and others. El Khoury explores a "contradiction at work" in Bouraoui's texts: "while reclaiming the existence of a Franco-Algerian *métis* identity, Bouraoui represents the *métis* as the incarnated perpetuation of the historical tensions that divided France and Algeria." Close reading shows Bouraoui's "embodied memory of the colonial fracture": for example, how "traumatic memories of asphyxiation are a metaphor for Bouraoui's difficult relationship with her French self." Rather than healing, Bouraoui thus provides a "problematic acceptance" of her *métis* identity. Roynon's essay compares and evaluates three texts by black women writers whose "strategies for rewriting the past include a revisionary engagement with the cultural legacies of Ancient Greece and Rome": Bernardine Evaristo, Marlene NourbeSe Philip and Robin Coste Lewis. Each text "protests the historic oppression" of women of colour and "asserts a black female agency" which is predicated on a "transnational conception of black identity" and the interconnections between Africa, Europe and the Americas. Each text invokes "the cultures of Ancient Greece and Rome, the legacies of which underpinned" colonialism. However, Roynon argues, "those by Evaristo and Lewis (in part through their strategy of engaging with the traditions of Ancient Egypt, Nubia and Sudan) ultimately constitute works of greater subversive power than does that of Philip."

Continuing with the transtemporal connection between present & past developed in this collection, historian Cynthia Aalders and legal theorist Kim Treiger-Bar-Am focus their essays on women's religious experience and active, dynamic participation in religious traditions. Braidotti and others have described the "post-secular" turn in feminism[13] and, in this field, Saba Mahmood's feminist theorizing – in her essay "Feminist Theory, Embodiment, and the Docile Agent" – has been hugely influential, particularly in reconceptualizing and retrieving female agency and subjectivity.[14] Aalders examines Jane Attwater's manuscript diary between 1766 and 1834, the most extensive diary written by a Nonconformist woman in the eighteenth and nineteenth centuries. Aalders's piece contributes to the methodologically innovative field of women's history: retrieving the archivist role of women's often manuscript texts in the construction of historical memory beyond "official" history.[15] This field is interconnected with the feminist questioning of the private–public distinction, and Aalders describes the intergenerational dialogue of women addressing each other across four generations of their extended family. While also contributing to current work in the new field of Material Text, Aalders describes the text of Attwater's diaries as a palimpsest with embedded fossils. (In this collection, Mariela E. Méndez and Cláudia Pazos-Alonso also contribute to Material Text scholarship with their archival work, attending to the more material aspects of their texts – newspapers and periodicals respectively.) Treiger-Bar-Am sets out to theorize what she calls "renewal within tradition" in relation to the Women of the Wall in Jerusalem, who have been praying collectively in song, in spite of thirty years of hostility. Treiger-Bar-Am builds her defence of the Women through recourse to Kantian democratic theory and Jewish thought. Jewish and Kantian thought are compared and "seen to conceptualize the essence of freedom as obligation, from which arise duties of respect for the other. Duties of respect indeed are owed" to the Women. Further, she demonstrates the radical pluralism and openness to interpretation of Jewish thought – a pluralism that is open to the future, and effectively met halfway by the Women's rejuvenation of Jewish traditions.

In developing transtemporal perspectives that rethink temporality, queer theory has made an enormous contribution in the last decades, theorizing a queer temporality against "patrilinearity" – see especially the work of Sara Ahmed, Lee Edelman, J. Jack Halberstam and others.[16] This work is especially asking us to rethink inheritance, succession, success and failure, and the connection between present & future. In this collection, the piece by Emily Spiers contributes to this field. Spiers explores the temporality of four recent German-language texts by women writers: two "pop-feminist" texts and two "complex first-person novels." Spiers argues that the former texts – *Wir Alpha-Mädchen* [*We Alpha-Girls*] and *Neue deutsche Mädchen* [*New German Girls*] – deploy a temporality of "linear progress" to "consign second-wave feminism to the past in the name of a normative future." By contrast, the latter – Helene Hegemann's *Axolotl Roadkill* and Antonia Baum's *Vollkommen leblos, bestenfalls tot* [*Completely Lifeless, Preferably Dead*] – convey "disorientation" (as theorized by Sara Ahmed in *Queer Phenomenology*) and a queer "asynchronous temporality." Their "queer disruptions [...] throw doubt on the figure of the coherent sovereign subject who lurks persistently behind [...] the self-empowered 'individual'" of the pop-feminist texts. Spiers contends that their "queer refusal of normative futures," as theorized by Halberstam, "allows the opportunity to imagine alternative modes of being that are potentially politically transformative." Of course, to praise queer temporality for its unprecedented novelty and originality in relation to previous theories of temporality would be to repeat the very pattern of progressive linearity that queer theory has so strongly criticized. Indeed, Morag Shiach's discussion of temporality in Virginia Woolf, in this collection, shows that a theory and practice of queer temporality has been with us at least since modernism. Similarly, Mariela E. Méndez examines Clarice Lispector's women's pages in Brazilian newspapers between 1959 and 1961, "crafted under a pseudonym," which have "hardly received any critical attention." Méndez argues that "through their nuanced parody" of "comparable discursive spaces" that commodify gender and their "overemphasis on what is culturally constructed as feminine," Lispector's women's pages "perform a transvestite gesture that unsettles normative models of femininity and dislodges a heteronormative temporality predicated upon birth, marriage, reproduction, and death." (Méndez's discussion of "transvestism" draws on Marjorie Garber.)

Developing the transtemporal connection between present & future, Alison Winch's piece, on the other hand, pursues a post-Marxist orientation to theorize temporality, proposing the concept of "conjuncture" and a "conjunctural" analysis as developed by Antonio Gramsci, and in a contemporary British context by Stuart Hall and Doreen Massey, recently towards an understanding of neoliberalism.[17] Winch proposes a conjunctural analysis of intergenerational feminism and intergenerational conflict, focusing on blogging, Millennials and the Hip Hop generation in the United States and the United Kingdom. Winch's conjunctural analysis insistently includes a feminist intersectional approach, proposing a "conjunctural and intersectional" understanding of generation – one that explores how feminist "generational identity intersects with categories of race, gender, class, sexuality and place." Julia Novak's contribution to this volume is asking how to think the relation between feminism and postfeminism, particularly in the context of biographical novels about historical women artists, which "have been experiencing a veritable boom in recent years." Comparing Janice Galloway's *Clara* (2002) and Priya Parmar's *Exit the Actress* (2011), Novak argues that they "differ markedly in the biographical and fictional subgenres in which they participate, and, hence, in their gender politics."

Yet another understanding of "across" in this collection has to do with moving across distinct discourses, e.g., distinct disciplines. It is obvious that this collection is interdisciplinary or multidisciplinary. It includes work in: anthropology, film theory, history, legal theory, literary criticism, philosophy, psychoanalytic theory, and visual art. Essays also engage with disciplines outside the Arts and Humanities: biology, the life sciences, medicine, neuroscience, and quantum physics. But some pieces specifically explore or reflect on the space in between discourses. Anthropology, having been the discipline perhaps most obviously tainted by colonialism and power inequalities in the relationship between researchers and research participants – and therefore inequalities in the interaction between the discourses of researcher and participant – has had to develop an acute self-reflexivity to address this legacy. Here, feminist anthropology has made an important contribution.[18] Fei-wen Liu's piece in this collection is exemplary in its ethics of self-reflexivity, as an inextricable part of Liu's ethnographic research into southern rural Chinese women's unique "expressive tradition," written in their own women's script, *nüshu*. Based on twenty-five years of fieldwork, Liu "traces the trajectory of *nüshu*'s evolving function and social meanings" from "communication platform" and transformative "social forum" to "academic property" and "government-supervised profession," calling for a "rethinking of where *nüshu*," now multiply endangered, "might be heading." Jane Dowson's piece addresses power inequalities in the relationship between doctor and patient and their respective discourses, and the role of women's (experimental) poetry – in its very polysemy – in voicing the patient's experience of illness. Discussing poems by women about cancer and depression over the last fifty years, Dowson claims that their "non-verbal features," particularly "metaphors and symbols, mark the space of what a patient cannot fully articulate," but also remind "the reader – or health professional – that interiority can never be fully presented." Dowson thus contributes to the new field of Medical Humanities.

While critiquing power inequalities between discourses, this volume also takes part in the search for *ethical* alternatives. Bettcher and Goulimari's discussion of recent experiments, in feminist writing, that cross the boundaries between life-writing, theory and literature, focuses on the ethics of these genre-crossing aesthetic experiments. Jean Wyatt outlines the evolution of Toni Morrison's work towards a more participatory role for the reader and enhanced collaboration between writer and reader. Wyatt shows how Morrison's later novels use formal and structural means to "draw out a reader's assumptions" and "prompt the reader to examine and re-evaluate them." The engagement with "a reader's own values in an ethical dialogue with the text" is Morrison's "variation on the tradition of call-and-response central to African American art forms." This is mirrored in the way in which Morrison theorizes love in the later novels: as a "disruptive force that produces profound change" or as "something you innovate and recreate each moment," Wyatt writes. María Donapetry's piece focuses on three feminist Spanish films – by Dunia Ayaso and Félix Sabroso, Icíar Bollaín, and Isabel Coixet – which construct scenes of female nudes that self-reflexively address the representation of the female nude in film and other art forms. These are films "precisely about the relationship between art and the living woman, between the creative exercises of film, painting and photography and their ethical engagement with the individual," and Donapetry "elucidates the ethical rules of engagement with the spectators the directors propose, particularly in regard to the commodification of the female body." Donapetry goes on to outline and advocate a feminist ethical perspective built on ambiguity and the spectator's freedom, developing the work of Spanish philosopher Fernando Savater. One of the major themes in this collection is the interaction, the *in between* writer or speaker or analysand and reader or audience or analyst as well as the in between writing or speaking and active reading or listening: see also the pieces by Cynthia Aalders, Louise Gyler, Fei-wen Liu, and Georgina Paul.

Student representatives of the Oxford M.St. in Women's Studies recently proposed a policy of asking students which pronouns they use – he, she or they? (Feminist) protocols of respectful social interaction seem to be moving towards self-identification, uncoupled from gender presentation and (any assumptions about) the gender one was assigned at birth. In literature and literary criticism in the aftermath of the women's movements of the 1960s and 1970s, there were calls to prioritize female characters and audiences. For example, Alice Walker called for dark-skinned black women characters, traditionally underrepresented, even in African-American literature.[19] Most of Toni Morrison's novels return to her theme of friendship among black women and girls, while she has been programmatically addressing primarily an audience of black women, and has criticized the beginning of her novel, *Sula*, for failing to do so.[20] The project of articulating marginalized female subjectivities and identities is far from complete and, in this collection, Claire Williams cites research to show how seriously underrepresented Afro-Brazilian women are in contemporary Brazilian literature.[21] This does not mean at all that women writers should be *limited to* writing female characters or writing from a female perspective or through a female focalizer. Indeed, in this collection, Lauren Grodstein and Kirsty Gunn discuss their practice of writing male characters or writing from a male perspective. Grodstein describes the clash between her writing experience and critics' assumptions. Grodstein's own writing experience has been that "the success of creating a thoroughly constructed fictional human being often resides in that character's otherness"; writing from a male perspective has freed her to "fully imagine [...] another human being," thus "rendering the whole enterprise of creating a fictional character more possible." By contrast, critics have been commenting on the "unlikelihood" of her decision to write about a man in the first person, labelling her "ventriloquist." That no one questioned her authority and credibility in writing parenting scenes or scenes of medical consultation simply highlighted for Grodstein the undue, unreflective and "stifling" critical attention to her gender, "as though the imagining of a young woman couldn't approach middle-aged male truth." The intractability of such critical attitudes after more than a century of modernist literary experiments with voice (e.g., going back to Emily Dickinson) is difficult to ignore; as is some publishers' crude stereotyping of femininity – in the colour palette of book covers for some literature by women, for example.

Morag Shiach's piece in this collection details Woolf's experiments with gender and life-writing "on or about" 1930, and Woolf's efforts to rethink their intersection with wider political problems. Shiach's interdisciplinary attention to a "diverse range of texts" in a "cultural moment" is indebted to Woolf's own experiments with temporality and critique of progressive linearity but also resonates, in my view, with the recent critique of patrilinearity in favour of the queer moment in queer theory (discussed above). Shiach studies *pronominal* "tension," "ambiguity" and "strain" in Woolf: discontinuous shifts from "his" to "her" to "their" in *Orlando*; the "unstable and precarious subjectivity" of the first-person singular "I" in *The Waves* where "one moment does not lead to another" (Woolf), challenging "any notion of life-writing"; and especially Woolf's lesser-known Preface to a collective publication by the Women's Co-operative Guild, *Life As We Have Known It*. In this Preface in the form of a letter, Woolf oscillates between a "very tentative" first-person "I" and the "gender-neutral and class-specific" pronoun "one"; she also juxtaposes temporalities to further destabilize "the letter writer's subjectivity" and to perform a "failure" of identification.[22] Georgina Paul's piece in this collection discusses an intensification of such modernist experiments, Barbara Köhler's 2007 poem-cycle *Niemands Frau* [*Nobody's Wife*]. Köhler not only re-accents Homer's *Odyssey* away from Odysseus and towards a "web" of women characters, she also, argues Paul, performs a pronominal shift:

> from the masculine singular pronoun "er" to the polyvalent pronoun "sie" that denotes the feminine singular, the gender-unmarked plural and the formal "you." "Sie" acts as the "quantum linguistic particle" that transports the reader [...] into a quantum universe of plural probabilities.

Köhler's practice of polysemy – deviating from the "sovereign individual subject and his linear modes of narration, inheritance, calculation and grammatical proposition" – generates "intriguing ways of reconceiving subjectivity, relationality, rationality, and authorship." Kirsty Gunn theorizes her own evolving literary practice of writing male protagonists who are looking at women who are looking at them, as a "breaking open (of) the gaze": the "fracturing of a singular point of view into a multiple one, a seeing and a being seen [...] energizing and transforming the roles of both male and female characters." In Gunn's work traditional male protagonists are "at the centre of texts that are actually female in perspective, so allowing for the reader to have the experience of a sort of inversion of reading." In this process, "the traditional male becomes someone else, the male gaze transported to another kind of looking" that prioritizes "female agency." We might perhaps read Gunn as D.H. Lawrence's undutiful feminist daughter.

This collection started its life as part of University of Oxford research networks. Early versions of many essays were initially delivered as papers in three contexts: the ongoing Gender, Literature and Culture research seminar which I have been co-convening since 2011;[23] the Oxford TORCH Interdisciplinary Research Group, "Reopening the Question: 'What is Women's Writing?'";[24] and an international three-day conference, "Women Writing Across

Cultures: Past, Present, Future" at St Hilda's College, University of Oxford, 26–28 September 2014.[25] The pieces I selected for inclusion in this collection are intended to capture or allude to broader tendencies in current research, as sketched out in this Introduction. But in order to point to as many directions in emerging research as possible, some of the essays were especially commissioned. The collection is an assemblage whose essays are mobile parts each putting ambiguously, tentatively, uncertainly *in process* a number of terms: woman, writing, across ... But these terms are also produced by creative intersections, conjunctions and collisions between the essays. In this Introduction I have suggested ways to put the mobile parts together. It is now up to the reader to take over and reassemble the collection and its terms anew.

December 2016
Oxford, UK and Xanthi, Greece

notes

I am grateful to Gerard Greenway and James Hypher for their generous editorial support of this volume.

1 Judith Butler, "Critically Queer," *GLQ: A Journal of Lesbian & Gay Studies* 1 (1993): 17–32.

2 Toril Moi, "'I am not a woman writer': About Women, Literature and Feminist Theory Today," *Eurozine* (2009): 1–8, available <http://www.eurozine.com/articles/2009-06-12-moi-en.html> (accessed 10 Sept. 2015). See also Moi, "What is a Woman?" in Moi, *What is a Woman? And Other Essays* (Oxford: Oxford UP, 1999) 3–120.

3 Wendy Brown, "The Impossibility of Women's Studies" in *Women's Studies on the Edge*, ed. Joan Wallach Scott (Durham, NC and London: Duke UP, 2008) 30.

4 Robyn Wiegman, "The Possibility of Women's Studies" in *Women's Studies for the Future: Foundations, Interrogations, Politics*, eds. Elizabeth Lapovsky Kennedy and Agatha Beins (New Brunswick, NJ and London: Rutgers UP, 2005) 42, 54.

5 Afsaneh Najmabadi, "Teaching and Research in Unavailable Intersections" in *Women's Studies on the Edge* 70–71.

6 Ibid. 77.

7 Chandra Talpade Mohanty, "Under Western Eyes: Feminist Scholarship and Colonial Discourses," *boundary 2* 12.3/13.1 (1984): 333–58.

8 Rosi Braidotti, *The Posthuman* (Cambridge: Polity, 2013).

9 Julia Serano, *Whipping Girl: A Transsexual Woman on Sexism and the Scapegoating of Femininity* (Emeryville, CA: Seal, 2007).

10 Published by Taylor & Francis and Oxford University Press respectively.

11 Published by Palgrave Macmillan.

12 Karen Barad, *Meeting the Universe Halfway: Quantum Physics and the Entanglement of Matter and Meaning* (Durham, NC and London: Duke UP, 2007); and Interview with Karen Barad in *New Materialism: Interviews & Cartographies*, eds. Rick Dolphijn and Iris van der Tuin (Ann Arbor: Open Humanities, 2012), available <http://dspace.library.uu.nl:8080/handle/1874/256718> (accessed 17 Aug. 2016). Rosi Braidotti, *The Posthuman*; and Interview with Rosi Braidotti in *New Materialism: Interviews & Cartographies*. Claire Colebrook, *Death of the PostHuman: Essays on Extinction* vol. 1 (Ann Arbor: Open Humanities, 2015); and Colebrook, *Sex After Life: Essays on Extinction* vol. 2 (Ann Arbor: Open Humanities, 2015). Elizabeth Grosz, *Chaos, Territory, Art: Deleuze and the Framing of the Earth* (New York: Columbia UP, 2008); Grosz, *Becoming Undone: Darwinian Reflections on Life, Politics, and Art* (Durham, NC: Duke UP, 2011); Grosz, *The Incorporeal: Ontology, Ethics, and the Limits of Materialism* (New York: Columbia UP, 2017). Donna Haraway, *The Companion Species Manifesto: Dogs, People, and Significant Otherness* (Chicago: Prickly Paradigm, 2003); Haraway, *Staying with the Trouble: Making Kin in the Chthulucene* (Durham, NC: Duke UP, 2016). Dorothea Olkowski, *The Universal (In the Realm of the Sensible): Beyond Continental Philosophy* (New York: Columbia UP, 2007).

13 Rosi Braidotti, "In Spite of the Times: The Postsecular Turn in Feminism," *Theory, Culture & Society* 25.6 (2008): 1–24.

14 Saba Mahmood, "Feminist Theory, Embodiment, and the Docile Agent: Some Reflections on

the Egyptian Islamic Revival," *Cultural Anthropology* 16.2 (2001): 202–36.

15 See, for example, Selma Leydesdorff, Luisa Passerini, and Paul Thompson, eds., *Gender & Memory* (Oxford: Oxford UP, 2009).

16 Sara Ahmed, *Queer Phenomenology: Orientations, Objects, Others* (Durham, NC: Duke UP, 2006). Lee Edelman, *No Future: Queer Theory and the Death Drive* (Durham, NC and London: Duke UP, 2004). Judith Halberstam, *In a Queer Time and Place: Transgender Bodies, Subcultural Lives* (New York: New York UP, 2005); and Halberstam, *The Queer Art of Failure* (Durham, NC: Duke UP, 2011). Elizabeth Freeman, *Time Binds: Queer Temporalities, Queer Histories* (Durham, NC: Duke UP, 2010).

17 Doreen Massey, "Ideology and Economics in the Present Moment" in *The Neoliberal Crisis*, eds. Sally Davison and Katharine Harris (London: Lawrence, 2015) 102–12.

18 See, for example, Ellen Lewin, ed., *Feminist Anthropology: A Reader* (Oxford: Blackwell, 2006).

19 Alice Walker, *In Search of Our Mothers' Gardens: Womanist Prose* (San Diego: Harcourt, 1983).

20 Toni Morrison, "Unspeakable Things Unspoken: The Afro-American Presence in American Literature" in *The Black Feminist Reader*, eds. Joy James and T. Denean Sharpley-Whiting (Oxford: Blackwell, 2000) 46ff.

21 See Claire Williams n. 7.

22 On "failure," see Halberstam's *The Queer Art of Failure*. Woolf seems to be anticipating and approaching Muñoz's concept of "(dis)identification." José Esteban Muñoz, *Disidentifications: Queers of Color and the Performance of Politics* (Minneapolis and London: U of Minnesota P, 1999).

23 I was sole convenor in 2011–12; my co-convenors were Dr Stephanie Clare and Prof. Tim Whitmarsh in 2012–13, Prof. Ros Ballaster and Prof. Cláudia Pazos-Alonso in 2013–16, and Prof. Ros Ballaster in 2016–17. Since 2015–16 the students of the Oxford M.St. in Women's Studies have also been actively involved. The seminar has been funded by the Faculties of English Language and Literature, Classics, and Medieval & Modern Languages since 2011 and Philosophy since 2014.

24 I was Co-ordinator – with Prof. Ros Ballaster, Prof. Cláudia Pazos-Alonso and Prof. Tim Whitmarsh – of this 2013–14 research programme. We organized nine seminars and three workshops in 2013–14.

25 My conference co-organizers were Prof. Ros Ballaster and Prof. Cláudia Pazos-Alonso. We were helped by Sarah Gabriel, Kathleen Lawton-Trask, Clare Morgan, Emily Spiers and Eve Worth. The conference was funded by TORCH.

Pelagia Goulimari

regenia gagnier

A SYMBIOLOGICAL APPROACH TO SEX, GENDER, AND DESIRE IN THE ANTHROPOCENE

Recent developments in molecular biology imply that classic distinctions between nature and nurture or biology and culture are not applicable to the human ecological niche. Research in epigenetics shows that the effects of culture on nature go all the way down to the gene and up to the stratosphere, and the effects of biology on culture are similarly inextricable (Gilbert and Epel; Griffiths and Stotz; Meloni and Testa). Living systems almost invariably involve the interaction of many kinds of organisms with a diversity of technologies. The Anthropocene – the age of human cultures and technologies impacting on natural environments – changes rapidly, and to understand and manage its functioning requires perspectives from each domain. Symbiology is the study of such relations-in-process. The kinds of relations we study include mutualism, parasitism, domination, recognition, separation, solubility, symmetric mutuality (relations among equals in power or status), asymmetric mutuality (relations among unequals – parents/offspring, teacher/pupil, human/nonhuman animals), reciprocity, alienation, isolation, autonomy, and so forth, and these relations are discernible throughout nature and all cultures, implying a politics.[1]

The first part of this essay will describe a symbiological approach to gender and sexuality; the second, a symbiological approach to literature and some examples of gender and sexuality in symbiological literature. Both are intended to provide more intimate accounts of the Anthropocene than the typical big pictures of global warming and climate change. While grand and world-historical, to be sure, the Anthropocene also affects the most intimate aspects of our lives.

I sex, gender, desire

The nature of sex and its relation to gender are questions that fall centrally within the remit of biophilosophy. Both sex and gender should be understood as the outcomes of developmental processes more or less stabilized by a wide variety of more or less variable factors. Understanding the nature of these processes and their social and biological causes is essential for comprehending the nature of gender, its relation to sex, and the extent to which these are mutable.

Within the symbiological approach, we do not ask what percentage of our sex or gender or sexuality is due to nature (biology) and what to nurture (culture). Because symbiology denotes a loop of continuous interrelated developments between nature, culture, and technology, it is better to understand sex, gender, and sexuality as dynamic, developmental systems, as processes rather than fixed entities or identities. For complex multicellular organisms, development is not predetermined "in the genes" but is rather a continuous process of interaction between the developing organism and its environment or niche (Odling-Smee, Laland, and Feldman). Although the normal paradigm of a human animal tends to be an adult in the so-called prime of life, we could as easily think of a foetus, a child, or an old person: what is fundamental, biologically, is a life cycle, a process, or a development.

This symbiological approach to sex and gender contradicts a popular biological "big picture" that assumes that different evolutionary pressures led to sexually specific genes, which led to sexually differentiated brains, which led to gender-specific behaviours. Our genomic loop, rather, describes the genome as neither static nor fixed, not a programme that directs development of the organism but rather one participant in a dynamic process highly sensitive to a range of the external influences that make up its particular niche. Parents provide genomes for their offspring, but they also provide the sequence of environments that channel development in particular directions.

Whereas reductionist methodologies tend to analyse a thing into its (usually smaller and smaller) parts, a process is naturally analysed into stages, although in neither case can we assume that the divisions are clear or unambiguous. Even before birth, in the maternal pre-natal niche, each of the four stages of sexual differentiation is permeable to environmental interference.[2] However, the following provides a sufficiently clear series of stages for present purposes:

(1) *Chromosomal sex.* Most women have two X chromosomes, and most men have an X and a Y chromosome; and they originated from a fertilized egg with those chromosomes. The word "most" is very important, however. First, not all humans have either an XX or an XY genotype. There are people with XYY, XXY and XO chromosomes (or karyotypes), of which the first are generally assigned a male gender, and the last two are generally treated as female. Second, for various reasons, now including elective reassignment, later stages in gender development do not always coincide with chromosomal sex.

(2) *Foetal gonadal sex.* By twelve weeks most foetuses have embryonic gonads, irreversibly committed to becoming either testes or ovaries. The development of testes appears to be triggered by a gene on the Y chromosome, the product of which binds to a gene on chromosome 17, and triggers a cascade of events involved in the production of the testes. A different sequence of genetic events pushes the as yet undifferentiated gonad in the direction of becoming an ovary. The Y chromosome gene just mentioned is known as the SRY gene (SRY for humans and Sry for mammals generally), which stands for Sex Reversal on the Y chromosome, echoing the curious idea, dating from Aristotle, that being female is a default. The persistence and untenability of this idea is noted by two experts on the relevant genetics:

> The discovery that gonads develop as ovaries in the absence of the Y-chromosome (or, more specifically, the Sry gene) supported the prevailing view that the testis pathway is the active pathway in gonad development. However, as Eicher and others have emphasized, the ovarian pathway must also be an active genetic pathway. (Brennan and Capel citing Eicher and Washburn)

Of course, if the Sry gene is indeed the relevant "switch" it might equally well be described as preventing ovary development. In neither case is the ensuing genetic cascade fully understood.

(3) *Foetal hormonal sex.* As the gonads develop they begin to produce their characteristic mix of hormones. The reproductive system, under the influence of these hormones, begins to differentiate towards characteristically male or female physiologies. Again, this depends not only on the production of hormones but also on the proper functioning of receptors that recognize these hormones. So, for example, occasionally XY foetuses carry a mutation that hinders androgen recognition and produces children born with highly feminized external genitalia. If everything follows the standard path, however, this leads us, finally, to

(4) *Genital sex*, the standard criterion that is used to distinguish the sex of babies at birth.

The process of foetal differentiation, then, is complex and multifactorial. While most babies will be born either with an XY genotype and typical male physiology, or with an XX genotype and female physiology, there are many ways in which these typical outcomes can be altered. It is no surprise that there are a significant number of atypical outcomes, sometimes described as intersexed, or, more normatively, moralistically, "Disorders of Sex Development."

The next crucial point in human development is, of course, birth. This is the point at which the wider community decides whether a baby is a boy or a girl. In the cases where this decision is difficult, standard medical practice has been to attempt to adjust the baby to one or other of the standard kinds. This often involves surgical reshaping of the external genitalia and treatment with hormones. The *exhaustive* division of people into two sexes is not a reflection of how things are in the world but of a social policy that everyone must be assigned to one or other of these categories. Very recently Germany, Australia and New Zealand have allowed babies to be registered at birth as of indeterminate sex, though this move is highly controversial, and has been criticized by some advocates for intersex people as maintaining a fixed and determinate set of categories.

To a rough approximation, gender begins at birth, though techniques of foetal surveillance such as ultrasound may rapidly be changing this. And the countless institutions that enforce gender – Fausto-Sterling calls them gender fortifications (*Sex/Gender* 10) – require that it be decided on which side of this fundamental dichotomy every individual falls. On endless forms we must say whether we are male or female – a question generally framed as a request for our sex, though more accurately it should ask for our gender. As noted above, however, in some places this dichotomy is being challenged, and the effects of this on the gendered organization of social life are as yet impossible to predict.

At any rate, after birth development moves on. Developmental processes tend to be very stable for good and obvious reasons. Indeed, life would be impossible if there were not developmental processes that fairly reliably reproduced in offspring the characteristics of parents. Parents not only provide genomes, they provide for their offspring the sequence of environments that channel development in the typical direction. This may be no more than providing exactly the right place to deposit an egg, or it may involve creating a complex built environment such as a bird's nest, a beaver's dam, or a termite mound (Odling-Smee, Laland, and Feldman). It will often also involve imparting behaviour through imitation or other kinds of training; and the training imparted will typically be that to which the parent, in its development, was exposed.

Humans have taken the complexity of these developmental processes far beyond anything else in the natural world. The environments, or epigenetic niches as biologists call them, in which we place our children have reached a bewildering complexity, parenting is an often frighteningly difficult skill, and socially provided institutions from maternity wards to universities are designed to contribute to the development of our offspring. Because so much of the developmental matrix in which humans grow is constructed by us, it follows that we have unparalleled abilities to change the developmental trajectories of our children. As with everything else in the Anthropocene, it is not easy to change these institutions, still less is it easy to predict the consequences of changes that we make; but it is possible. Feminist scholars have for decades been pointing to the variety of gender systems found in different places and at different times, and we have consequently inferred that the presence of a particular system is always contingent. Our critics, committed to a biologically reductive view of gender development, have claimed that this diversity is largely illusory. But given the symbiological approach to development there is no reason to suppose that things are not as they so clearly seem. The institutions and norms surrounding gender development have diverged in different places and over time, and the gender system has changed too. Gender is thoroughly norm-ridden. We teach our children how boys and girls, men and women ought to behave, and often that they ought to behave differently from each other.

We are now in the position to turn from sex and gender development to the development or evolution of *desire*. Being gay, lesbian, straight, bisexual or pansexual is a developmental outcome. Like all human developmental outcomes it results from a complex interaction between internal, including genetic, and external causes. Fausto-Sterling's research on the development of desire is probably the clearest to date. She asks: how do events in the social sphere become events taking place in an individual? How does information cross the border from outside to inside an organism (Fausto-Sterling, *Sex/Gender* 14)? Sexual desire has a neurophysiological component that individuals interpret as pleasure and attraction. Over time, an underlying neurophysiology develops in response to specific experiences of pleasure/attraction and perhaps aversion. To study the development of adult sexuality and desire we must start by understanding the physiology and embodiment of pleasure from infancy – Fausto-Sterling says parenthetically "Freud – are you still there?" (93) – through childhood, adolescence, young adulthood, into middle and old age, through all the stages of a life cycle. Dopamine, a chemical made in the human midbrain by nerve cells with a reputation for responding strongly to rewards, may also incite aversive responses to non-rewarding situations. Erotic tastes, like tastes for fast food or slow death, *develop* over time; desires evolve through inner and outer events (Berlant).

A final striking perspective on the ontogeny of desire, the developmental process that leads to the orientation towards one object of desire rather than another, is provided by the much-debated issue of pornography. Prominent feminists have suggested that pornography, or certain forms of pornography, may promote violence against women or normalize various demeaning treatments of women. This may well be so. Psychiatrist Norman Doidge (Doidge) provides a compelling argument that pornography can, at any rate, radically reshape sexual desire. He describes patients becoming increasingly addicted to pornography and simultaneously increasingly unable to become sexually excited by their live partners. He also describes the evolution of pornography from the relatively uncomplicated depiction of sexual intercourse to the growing menu of violent, abusive, or simply Other genres currently available on the internet. As an example of the outside coming in, of neuroplasty or the brain altering due to external environment, Doidge reports that consumers of internet pornography may reach a state where they are sexually aroused not just by thinking about the activities performed in pornography but by thinking of the computer itself, so that boys become aroused by the sound of the operating system when the computer is switched on.

Desire, it appears, is malleable, and can be shaped in the most unexpected ways. Fausto-Sterling concludes that bodies are not bounded: to understand sex, gender, and sexuality we have to study how sensory, emotional, and motor experience becomes embodied. We should accept the complexity and contextual nature of desire.

The picture I have sketched is one in which sex, gender, and sexuality point to the most typical outcomes of developmental processes, but outcomes from which many individual trajectories diverge. At birth, or perhaps sooner as prenatal surveillance becomes more and more routine, the male/female dichotomy of sex is normatively enforced, with medical intervention common in response to atypical individuals. This dichotomy is then the basis for a more systematically normative dichotomous gender fortification. While it is still commonly supposed that the stages of this process are determined largely by genes, the growing understanding of the complexity of human development, and of the deep entanglement of internal and external influences that development involves, makes this kind of genetic determinism wholly implausible. Essentialist perspectives on sex, gender, and sexuality are misguided.

So what of the future? Sexual differentiation is no more immune to external, epigenetic influences than are other aspects of physiological development within the Anthropocene. The system of gender differentiation may act causally on physiological articulations of sex. As many individuals fall in the gaps between male and female, hetero- and homosexuality, there is much to be said for relaxing the normative dichotomies. Rather, we might see male and female pathways within a wider range of possibilities, perhaps ever widening as we increase our tolerance of diversity. Recently I have begun to write references using the gender-neutral pronoun "they" at the applicant's request ("as they prefer") and we would expect this to become more widespread in future. Exceptions to sex/gender/sexuality dichotomies should be welcomed as reminders of the flexibility and open texture of the developmental process.

II sex, gender and sexual desire in symbiological literature

A symbiological approach to modern literatures might consider how global processes criss-cross local niches with their particular mixes of nature, culture, and technology. Because they tend to represent total environments of nature, culture, and technology, novels may be especially productive sites to explore biological, cultural, and technological relations-in-process, including the processes of gendering and desire. (After a lifetime of literary engagement, I cannot think of a novel that does not include gender, even if only, as in some science fiction, through its negation or sublation.) Elsewhere I have considered certain geopolitical commodities linking the production and reproduction of life: water, cotton, tea, rice, petroleum, coffee, tobacco, sugar, bananas, opium, or other commodities around which lives and literatures are built. I have considered literatures about total environments, such as novels called *Yeast*, *Oil*, *Water*, *Salt*, *Men of Maize*, *Wolf Totem*, *Rickshaw Boy*, *Opium Family*, and so forth. Here I use Su Tong's novel *Rice* (1992), as an example of how a symbiological approach can make sense of literature that might otherwise seem to be merely decadent, or even pornographic, in superficial senses.

Because of the preoccupation of "worrying about China" (Davies) that was central to modern Chinese literature before the founding of the People's Republic, the extreme forms of Decadent literatures that appeared in transitions from traditional to modern societies throughout the globe were infrequent in Chinese literature (Gagnier). There is one author, however, whom reviewers typically brand as decadent. Here are some typical quotations from Su Tong's novel *Rice*:

> The subtle fragrance of raw rice and the strong scent of a woman's sex achieved a wondrous unity on the palms of his grimy hands. (78)

> Rice enveloping feminine flesh, or feminine flesh wrapped around rice, always drove him into a state of uncontrollable sexual desire. (129)

> Whoring was his great pleasure. And wherever he went he carried a small cloth bag filled with raw rice; at the critical moment, he would take out a handful and cram it inside the woman. (159)

Reviews of *Rice* in both the Asian and anglophone press – here selected randomly from the internet – responded with condemnations of its decadence: "Disgusting"; "Graphic perspective on the psyche of cruelty"; "Sadistic"; "extreme egotism"; "There is no reprieve, no justice and no individual triumph. At the end, the reader is just left exhausted; as having gone through a dark tunnel of despair and wickedness only to perversely yearn for more"; "All of his peasants are ignoble; all of his capitalists are corrupt; and there's no redemption in sight." Yet one review, in the *New York Times* (20 Nov. 1995), makes the novel sound like Dostoevsky. Although Dostoevsky is much more than Decadent, his readers will know that he also frequently exhibits the concerns and characteristics of Decadent writers of the later nineteenth century, during which Russia, like Europe generally, was undergoing massive change in response to the processes we associate with modernization (Gagnier). The *Times* reviewer could be writing of *The Brothers Karamazov* (1878–80) transposed to 1930s Shanghai: "The Great Swan Rice Emporium is turned into a minor sort of hell. There are loose women, gangsters, sexual predators, gamblers, weaklings, tyrants, prostitutes – the whole ill-favored, deformed human family."

Yet in our symbiological view, in *Rice*, Su Tong was following the events of China in the 1930s and showing typical Decadent patterns of distorted relations of part to whole: civil war between communists and nationalists; war with Japan, in which torture was rampant and many were betrayed by collaborators; catastrophic flood and famine; widespread venereal disease; and the Food Problem around rice, the traditional symbol of Chinese civilization and Heaven's bounty. In the novel, rice is food, rice is wine and vinegar to drink and bathe in (as relief from syphilis), rice is a bed to sleep and have sex on. Rice fills the vaginas of wives and prostitutes and is a murder weapon to smother children. Rice gives people their names like Rice Boy, and it is the only source of wealth.

For those of us interested in the relation of literary forms like Decadence to social formations, it is significant that rice is the geopolitical commodity par excellence. Providing 23 per cent of the world's calories, in the 1930s it manifested itself as the Food Problem and the nationalists tried desperately to regulate its balance of trade, while, partly in response to the Food Problem, Chairman Mao conceived of the Great Leap Forward of the 1950s. The 1930s were an era of war and modernization, in which China arguably became a modern national economy through a regime of social surveys and quantification, in part in response to the Food Problem (Lee). The response to the Food Problem was so intense that high-ranking members of the Guomindang proposed that Chinese universities should stop admitting students of humanities and law for a decade in order to promote science and technology exclusively. Rice was in every sense of the theoretical terms, a geopolitical *actant* and an *event*.

My point is that rice, the decadent fetish in the novel – Freud also defined fetishism in 1927 as a repressed relation between part and whole (Freud) – is the geopolitical commodity as decadent fetish, representing the protagonist's lost home and lost mother, the only source of consolation/compensation for extreme loss and subsequent lives of humiliation; "Settling finally on the storeroom, he rolled up his mat and fell asleep naked on a mound of rice. It was rice, and rice alone, that had a calming, cooling effect on him; all his life it had comforted him" (241). The last lines of the novel show the relation of part to whole at that moment in China's history:

> RICE – His head moved toward the mound of rice as he uttered one last word [. . .] He knew only that he had been an orphan ever since he could remember, and that he had fled Maple-Poplar Village during a catastrophic flood. The last image he ever saw was of himself floating on the surface of a boundless expanse of water, moving farther and farther away, like an uprooted rice plant. (266)[3]

Rice represents the whole that is lost as the uprooted, abject, migrant individual must find his way in a shattered world. Rice was a geopolitical actant and an event, but it was also a psychological actant and event in the individual:

a well-documented case of the outside coming inside, the macro becoming micro.

Sharona Muir's *Invisible Beasts* (2014) is, more explicitly than Su Tong's, fiction grounded in the life sciences that illuminates the interdependence of living things and their natural and technological environments. The protagonist Sophie is an amateur naturalist with the rare ability to see invisible, sentient creatures that share a symbiotic relationship with humankind. She composes a bestiary and records her meditations on sex, evolution, extinction, truth, and self-knowledge. A typical passage reads:

> Cities are growing all the time, and animals evolve with them. Rats chew through lead and cement; songbirds add the sounds of car alarms and construction equipment to their repertoires. Cliff swallows are evolving shorter wings for faster takeoffs from roadways to their nests in overpasses. (73)

In another passage, Muir develops the idea of species co-evolution, through the very literary character of the wolf (for lupine literariness, see Jiang Rong's [Lü Jiamin] *Wolf Totem*; the Big Bad Wolf of "Little Red Riding Hood" and fairy tale; the proverbial Wolf at the door; Freud's "Wolf Man"; Werewolves; and so forth). The wolf is the untamed antecedent (the Unconscious?) of the domesticated dog, and just as humans have both untamed and domestic capacities, both are with us today:

> Thousands of years before humans began domesticating livestock, wolves domesticated humans. Enjoying our garbage heaps, wolves who were bold and friendly set out to make us share the warm, safe spots at our firesides where cooking went on, and the choicest scraps were to be had. They learned our body language better than any other nonhuman species [...] and became dogs. Since then, we have evolved in intimate mutuality. Anyone who thinks that dogs are mere servile pets may learn from the following tale how our consciousness is controlled by those whom we think we have mastered. (79)

Muir emphasizes that uniquely for humans it is a *choice* to see the interdependent, symbiological picture, and this concurs with my original account of symbiology at the beginning of this essay. I surmised that the relations of co-production and co-evolution "are discernible throughout nature and all cultures, implying a politics." Although all species are affected by the Anthropocene, only humans can reverse, stabilize, or sustain it. Only humans have the power to alter the ecosphere irrevocably and therefore only humans have the responsibility to manage it:

> The present, or Holocene, mass extinction is not the only one in life's history. It is the only one caused by a single organism capable of seeing the big picture, understanding its own destructive role, and changing that [...] If I saw the big picture [...] it was because I had to make a choice. (153)

The Epilogue to *Invisible Beasts* has Sophie the Naturalist reading a love letter "with Plato and a Dog":

> Aristophanes said, "Love is the desire and pursuit of the whole." The desire and pursuit of wholeness lead us to embrace [...] a mystery too great to encompass, as unending as nature because it is nature, the endlessness of the universe itself in which we are born and die, that haunts every intimacy [...] Love remains unknowable. Knowing that, the smile of Cupid deepens [...] And a naturalist, having sought truth, is satisfied with observation and hypothesis. (251–52)

There is a rise in symbiological literature and it is curious that as it dwells on species' interdependence, co-evolution, extinction – on species' dying and being born, on sex and death – it so often returns to love. *Love in the Anthropocene* (2015), by the environmental philosopher Dale Jamieson and writer Bonnie Nadzam, has chapters on places, things, activities, and events. The stories are set in a future time, though one often overlapping with our own, when Nature is entirely an artefact, when the rivers, as well as the fishes, are artificial ("Flyfishing"). (Already today, more seafood that people consume is produced by aquaculture (fishfarming) than by fishing (Jamieson and Nadzam 12).) In "Carbon" the poor are removed from model cities on shorelines rapidly disappearing into the sea. Milk, steak, grapes are all artificial; dating is "off-grid" with robotic fucking machines or virtual partners ("Holiday"). As the authors say, "technology and the Anthropocene are joined at the hip" (24). In "Shanghai," families are no more, having been relegated either to a sentimental or an oppressive past. Domed cities keep lethal climates at bay. In the final story, "Zoo," the zookeeper is caretaker of the last of species, and he cannot tell whether women are attracted to him for himself or for his last remaining tiger. He also does not know whether he himself knows/loves the tiger more than the woman.

Interestingly, like *Invisible Beasts*, *Love in the Anthropocene* also ends with a Coda on "Love." Jamieson and Nadzam ask: "How will love arise in a world without nature as we have known it?" (212). They cite Iris Murdoch that "love is the extremely difficult realization that something other than oneself is real" (202). As the ravenous ego blocks out everything else and prevents us from seeing or knowing others, love is the antidote to narcissism.

> The Anthropocene threatens to give us a narcissist's playground – a nature that is only the extension of ourselves and our desires, without independent meaning or sustenance. Love relationships are not possible in a world that consists only of oneself and one's projections [...] In many ways the task before us in the Anthropocene is the same task that has always been before us: to get the dear self out of the way enough to be able to really see and come to know – in relationship – the world of other people, plants, animals, oceans and rivers around us. But there may be more at stake, now, as well. (205–07)

The authors draw our attention to how inextricable our love lives, our desires, have been with nature and natural scenes: holidays in the country or at the seaside, walks in the park and on rivers and cliffs, swimming together, "make-out point" (208), campfires, cookouts, until sometimes nature itself is the beloved: the Sahara sands, the Bitterroot Mountains, Five Flower Lake, Point Lobos. Then they say:

> Imagine a world of endless drought: no rain, no tin roofs, no soaked flowers, and a lot more from our familiar world missing besides. Will experiences like this or the art that expresses them be accessible to us? Will we even be able to understand the loves of our parents or grandparents? [...] [R]each into your real or imagined memory and recover those feelings of joy and wonder as you were careering down [ski] runs [...] It was just you and the mountain, you and the wind; no condos and no snow-making machines. Now imagine that Monsanto has brought you "Ice-9," a nano-particle that forms the nucleus for fluffy snowflakes that don't melt and stick. The snow-making machines are gone, and every day is a powder day. Is this better: Do you love the experience more? Or has the object of your love slipped away? (209–10)

As with Doidge's example above of boys who desire their computers more than their live partners, *Love in the Anthropocene* shows that Nature was never simply a background or static context against which humans acted out their ambitions. Rather, the loop between human culture, Nature and technology is mutually constitutive. The Frankfurt School called this the Dialectic of Enlightenment, when humans created technologies that came back to recreate them (Adorno). Like our sex and our gender, our desires will change with our technologies until past loves may be as unrecognizable as our grandparents' old photographs:

> We may once have thought of nature as the backdrop against which we lived our lives – pretty scenery to be sometimes plundered for its resources, or to write songs about – but the Anthropocene throws into stark relief that nature is not a "background" and never has been. It has always been a part of our lives – a part of us as we are part of it. (210–11)

The danger is that our instrumentalism, encoded in our technological languages of efficiency, management, finance, governance, command and control, will have wiped out the obscure object of desire before we know it:[4]

> The languages of sciences, technology, and economics dominate the discourse: can it be done? How much will it cost? But there are other questions that the Anthropocene will ask and other languages in which they must be discussed: should it be done? What will we become if we follow that path? The Anthropocene will challenge not just our science and technology, but also the human heart in ways that are difficult to predict but which we're already beginning to experience. (211–12)

Love in the Anthropocene concludes: "The question we ask may seem simple but is fundamental: how will love arise in a world without nature as we have known it?" (212).[5] The same can be asked of a world of sex, gender and erotic mutability.

We may conclude that, having sought truth, a symbiological approach is satisfied with observation and hypothesis. What we observe is that the enhanced use of technology in human niche-construction distinguishes humans from other animals. While many animals use technology – beavers build dams, bees build hives, birds build nests – humans are the (most) technological animals. What is universal is our biological evolution as humans and our exceptional ability to transform nature through our use of technology, which in turn transforms us. Genomic ecology tells us that the mutual effects of biology and environment go all the way down into the gene and up to the stratosphere, and that it is not what is in your genes, but what your genes are in, that makes the difference. Developmentally plastic, creative or destructive, rational or irrational, multisexed and polyamorous, humans are the protean life forms par excellence, the creatures whose nature is not to have a nature, as Giovanni Pico della Mirandola put it in the fifteenth century (Pico della Mirandola). Reflection on this natural history of change and difference tells us that things can and will change. Therefore, hope is the natural consequence of the genetic under-determination of the human phenotype, but resentment and despair are ever in the wings for when we fail to live up to the promise of our freedoms.

disclosure statement

No potential conflict of interest was reported by the author.

notes

1 This manifesto of a symbiological approach has much in common with process biology, actor-network-theory, and object-oriented ontologies, and may be considered a fellow traveller with the positions of Bruno Latour on actants and matters of concern, Isabelle Stengers on events and causes of thinking, and Andrew Pickering on the mangle of practice (see Latour; Stengers, "Including Nonhumans in Political Theory: Opening Pandora's Box?" in Braun and Whatmore; Pickering). It also has some sympathy with the "thing theory" of Jane Bennett and Bill Brown and the treatment of circulation in Arjun Appadurai (Bennett; Brown; Appadurai). However, the symbiology manifesto has actually evolved out of years of interdisciplinary research and administration, most recently at Egenis, the Centre for the Study of Life Sciences, at the University of Exeter, and out of a life-long study of the kinds of total environments that are presented in world literatures. I am also grateful to Dr Jos Smith, British Academy Postdoctoral Research Fellow, and Exeter's ECLIPSE Environmental Humanities Group, for comments on a draft of this essay.

2 The following section is indebted to the work of biologist and gender theorist Anne Fausto-Sterling. Her *Myths of Gender* (1985) pioneered biologically informed criticism of purportedly scientific accounts of gender difference, a project developed in new directions in *Sexing the Body* (2000). The outline of the stages of sexual differentiation here closely follows her *Sex/Gender* (2012). What follows is also indebted to the work of my long-time collaborator John Dupré. (See Barnes and Dupré; Dupré, *Human Nature*; idem, *Processes*;

Fausto-Sterling, *Myths*; idem, *Sexing*; idem, *Sex/ Gender*.)

3 This image of the protagonist's identification with the rice plant is striking for more than one reason. Professional biologists anecdotally advise that one cannot claim to be seriously engaged with a crop until one has dreamt that one is embodied as a crop plant in the ground. Symbiology is a biological process, but it is also a natural sympathy (see Hughes; Bray et al.).

4 For an operationalized study of how the language of global processes can become codified, self-referential, and detached from everyday language, concreteness, and human participants, with world-historical effects, see Moretti and Pestre on the World Bank.

5 One answer may well have been predicted in that very early breviary of Decadence, J.K. Huysmans's *A Rebours* (1884), frequently translated as *Against Nature*:

> [A]rtifice was considered by Des Esseintes to be the distinctive mark of human genius. Nature, he used to say, has had her day; she has finally and utterly exhausted the patience of sensitive observers by the revolting uniformity of her landscapes and skyscapes. After all, what platitudinous limitations she imposes, like a tradesman specializing in a single line of business; what petty-minded restrictions, like a shopkeeper stocking one article to the exclusion of all others; what a monotonous store of meadows and trees; what a commonplace display of mountains and seas!
>
> In fact, there is not a single one of her inventions, deemed so subtle and sublime, that human ingenuity cannot manufacture; no moonlit Forest of Fontainebleau that cannot be reproduced by stage scenery under floodlighting; no cascade that cannot be imitated to perfection by hydraulic engineering; no rock that papier-mâché cannot counterfeit; no flower that carefully chosen taffeta and delicately coloured paper cannot match! (22)

Yet *A Rebours* would lead Huysmans, as his contemporary Barbey d'Aurevilly put it, either to the foot of the cross or to the muzzle of a pistol, i.e., to religion or to suicide (in Huysmans, loc. 3768: Barbey, "Le Roman Contemporain," *Constitutionel* (28 July 1884)). And others in their different ways, such as the Futurists or Walter Benjamin, have also observed that the love of technology for its own sake typically leads to war (see "The Work of Art in the Age of Mechanical Reproduction: Epilogue" in Benjamin).

bibliography

Adorno, Theodor W., and Max Horkeimer. *Dialectic of Enlightenment*. 1947. London: Verso, 1997. Print.

Appadurai, Arjun. *The Social Life of Things*. Cambridge: Cambridge UP, 1986. Print.

Barnes, Barry, and John Dupré. *Genomes and What to Make of Them*. Chicago: U of Chicago P, 2008. Print.

Benjamin, Walter. *Illuminations*. 1955. Trans. Harry Zohn. New York: Schocken, 1976. Print.

Bennett, Jane. *Vibrant Matter: A Political Ecology of Things*. Durham, NC: Duke UP, 2010. Print.

Berlant, Lauren. "Slow Death: Sovereignty, Obesity, Lateral Agency." *Critical Inquiry* 33.4 (2007): 754–80. Print.

Braun, Bruce, and Sarah J. Whatmore, eds. *Political Matter: Technoscience, Democracy, and Public Life*. Minneapolis: U of Minnesota P, 2010. Print.

Bray, Francesca, Peter A. Coclanis, Edda L. Fields Black, and Dagmar Schafer, eds. *Rice: Global Networks and New Histories*. New York: Cambridge UP, 2015. Print.

Brennan, Jennifer, and Blanche Capel. "One Tissue, Two Fates: Molecular Genetic Events That Underlie Testis versus Ovary Development." *Nature Reviews Genetics* 5 (1 July 2004): 509–21. Print.

Brown, Bill. "Thing Theory." *Critical Inquiry* 28.1 (2002): 1–22. Print.

Davies, Gloria. *Worrying About China: The Language of Chinese Critical Inquiry*. Cambridge, MA: Harvard UP, 2007. Print.

Doidge, Norman. *The Brain That Changes Itself: Stories of Personal Triumph from the Frontiers of Brain Science*. London: Penguin, 2007. Print.

Dupré, John. *Human Nature and the Limits of Science*. Oxford: Oxford UP, 2003. Print.

Dupré, John. *Processes of Life: Essays in the Philosophy of Biology*. Oxford: Oxford UP, 2012. Print.

Eicher, E.M., and L.L. Washburn. "Genetic Control of Primary Sex Determination in Mice." *Annual Review of Genetics* 20.1 (1986): 327–60. Print.

Fausto-Sterling, Anne. *Myths of Gender*. New York: Basic, 1985. Print.

Fausto-Sterling, Anne. *Sex/Gender: Biology in a Social World*. New York: Routledge, 2012. Print and Web.

Fausto-Sterling, Anne. *Sexing the Body: Gender Politics and the Construction of Sexuality*. New York: Basic, 2000. Print.

Freud, Sigmund. "Fetishism." 1927. *Miscellaneous Papers, 1888–1938. Vol. 5 of Collected Papers*. 5 vols. London: Hogarth and Institute of Psycho-Analysis, 1924–50. 198–204. Print.

Gagnier, Regenia. "Global Literatures of Decadence." *The Fin-de-Siècle World*. Ed. Michael Saler. London: Routledge, 2015. 11–28. Print.

Gilbert, Scott R., and David Epel. *Ecological Developmental Biology: Integrating Epigenetics, Medicine, and Evolution*. Sunderland, MA: Sinauer, 2009. Print.

Griffiths, Paul, and Karola Stotz. *Genetics and Philosophy: An Introduction*. Cambridge: Cambridge UP, 2013. Print.

Hughes, Steve. "Review of *Rice: Global Networks and New Histories*." *Food Security: The Science, Sociology and Economics of Food Production and Access to Food* 8.1 (2016): 301–03. Print.

Huysmans, Joris-Karl. *Against Nature* [*A Rebours*]. 1884. Trans. Robert Baldick. Appendices trans. Patrick McGuinness. London: Penguin, 2003. E-book.

Jamieson, Dale, and Bonnie Nadzam. *Love in the Anthropocene*. New York: OR, 2015. Print.

Latour, Bruno. *Reassembling the Social: An Introduction to Actor-Network-Theory*. New York: Oxford UP, 2005. Print.

Lee, Seung-Joon. "Taste in Numbers: Science and the Food Problem in Republican Guangzhou, 1927–1937." *Twentieth-Century China* 35.2 (2010): 81–103. Print.

Meloni, Maurizio, and Giuseppe Testa. "Scrutinizing the Epigenetics Revolution." *BioSocieties* 9.4 (2014): 431–56. Print and Web.

Moretti, Franco, and Dominique Pestre. "Pamphlet 9: Bankspeak: The Language of World Bank Reports, 1946–2012." *Stanford Literary Lab* (2015). Web. 9 Jan. 2017.

Muir, Sharona. *Invisible Beasts*. New York: Bellevue, 2014. Print.

Odling-Smee, F. John, Kevin N. Laland, and Marcus W. Feldman. *Niche Construction: The Neglected Process in Evolution*. Princeton: Princeton UP, 2003. Print.

Pickering, Andrew. *The Mangle of Practice: Time, Agency, and Science*. Chicago: U of Chicago P, 1995. Print.

Pico della Mirandola, Giovanni. *On the Dignity of Man; on Being and the One; Heptaplus*. Trans. Charles Wallis, Paul Miller, and Douglas Carmichael. Indianapolis: Bobbs-Merrill, 1965. Print.

Rong, Jiang [Lü Jiamin]. *Wolf Totem*. 2004. Trans. Howard Goldblatt. London: Penguin, 2008. Print.

Su, Tong. *Rice*. 1992. Trans. Howard Goldblatt. London: Scribner, 1995. Print.

Regenia Gagnier

sylvie gambaudo

IS THERE SUCH A THING AS "WOMAN WRITING"?

julia kristeva, judith butler and writing as gendered experience

In 1898 Charlotte Perkins Gilman warned us that "There is no female mind. The brain is not an organ of sex. Might as well speak of a female liver" (*Women and Economics* 149). Yet today we still find that research in neuroscience of sex difference argues that "some brain structures are sexually dimorphic" (Cahill; Ruigrok et al.). Some studies show that brain dimorphism is evidenced in both structure ("male brains are optimized for intrahemispheric and female brains for interhemispheric communication" (Ingalhalikar 823)) and functioning ("male brains are structured to facilitate connectivity between perception and coordinated action, whereas female brains are designed to facilitate communication between analytical and intuitive processing modes" (ibid.)). Structural and functional dimorphism is deemed responsible for an array of behavioural differences between men and women, from cognitive aptitude to sexual orientation. Explanations for differences range from evolutionary needs (for example, females needing to maximize their chances of impregnation and the survival of their offspring developed more sophisticated perception of social cues and better recall of vital information such as location of food) to hormonal stimulation during brain development (Cahill). My aim is not to put evolutionary and biological motivations for gender differences of the brain on trial[1] but to use scientific findings as a starting point to revisit the idea that writing might indeed be a gendered activity.

Since feminists have put gender on the political map, the very experience of writing has been intimately enmeshed with the experience of gender. There are few who would reject the idea that gender is a political category of meaning. But to say categorically that there is such a thing as gendered writing is trickier. In this piece, I am focusing on the possibility of "woman writing" which, by default, suggests there is also such a thing as "man writing." I use terms like "woman" and "man" as the expression of a social experience, founded on one's engagement with one's biological gender (being female or male) and on one's culturally contingent gender (being feminine or masculine). I am using the phrase "woman writing" to point to a philosophical discussion on what writing the experience of "woman" might entail. I have intentionally avoided the use of established phrases (women's writing, poetic language, *écriture féminine*, queer writing, etc.), which belong to particular moments in academic understandings of what it is to write as a woman. Today, feminist work on epistemic bias is, to say the least, ambiguous and inconclusive. Let us start with second-wave feminists. The work of feminist academics and activists, such as Kate Millett, Betty Friedan, Germaine Greer or Gloria Steinem, has profoundly altered our perception of gendered experience from the late 1960s onwards. For reasons of space, I am synthesizing here the wonderfully diverse positions these authors have taken over years of academic and popular engagement. These feminists have all agreed that in a patriarchal world there is necessity to build equal status for women within culture, lest women carried on being denied the specificity of their gendered experience. For example, the creation of British publisher Virago in 1973 aimed to publish, revive and/or rehabilitate work written by women until then neglected by traditionally male-oriented publishing houses. To allow the specificity of women's experience to come forth, second-wave feminism argued for two things: the importance of one's confrontation with a phenomenology of femaleness in writing material and the importance of having female authors. So, in their eyes, gendered writing is not solely about the stuff that writing is made of but also about the reader's experience of "woman stuff"; the reader is necessary to validate that it is indeed woman's stuff (or not) they are being presented with. Gendered writing is about harmony between author and her text, between her being and her telling of being. Indeed, from the Brontës to J.K. Rowling, the absence of female gender markers presupposes the author is expressing the experience of man. It would then appear that second-wave feminists were right to insist that female authors write in the name of woman and about female experience, to disambiguate gendered writing.

The rise of poststructuralist thought both confirmed and challenged this view. It confirmed it by positing omniscience and authority of writers as a declarative effect; woman writing is the writing of woman's experience because she indeed declares her sex and asserts the content, and in some cases the form of text, as exclusive to female experience. Poststructuralism also challenges "woman writer" by pronouncing the death of the author, but also the death of the totalized, meaningful subject of enunciation. The death of the author signals the end of the authorial pretence to omniscience and control over interpretation of text. The death of the subject establishes a critical theory of writing whereby the presentation of literary heroes as fully formed, totalized beings immediately raises suspicion of political malpractice. To avoid accusations of collaboration with bourgeois values, narrators now need to present characters with less defined identities, and this includes gender.

While the death of the author has had negative repercussions on the facilitation of female authorship, it has also opened new debates and possibilities for gendered writing. To evaluate a philosophy of the writing experience, two authors spring to my mind for their invaluable contribution to poststructuralist feminist thinking. They are Julia Kristeva and Judith Butler. Grouping these two may seem controversial given Butler's critique of Kristeva's framework, and given Kristeva's doubt regarding the possibility of Butlerian "queer" to become anything socially significant. Yet their common interest in repositioning gender away from a strictly biological body has opened the door to interesting possibilities regarding one's experience of gender, including experiences once thought to belong strictly to the "opposite" sex. Let us look at this more closely.

Kristeva has argued that gendered experience is really a positioning along a masculine–feminine spectrum of practices, whose gender markers are dependent on particular cultural moments in history. In a world where cultural organization is by and large founded upon patriarchal experience, the ordering of meaning is necessarily mediated by patriarchal rule. Hence, in Kristeva's model, we are born into a rule that informs us as to what signifying practices we might choose or dissent against. The representative of patriarchal rule, which conveys meaning and closure to textual practices, remains ultimately "the father," a term that does not so much refer to the flesh-and-blood person but rather to a function of fatherhood, a paternal function that Kristeva openly borrows from Jacques Lacan and makes her own (Gambaudo, *Kristeva*). The creative legacy of Kristeva possibly lies here: she takes the omnipotent, omniscient, untouchable and ultimately unchangeable father of Lacanian/Freudian psychoanalytic models to change "him" into a more human and fallible agency, a father with whom one may engage more creatively, precisely because "he" is fallible. We will return to the issue of paternal fallibility below. For now, beyond the more humane face of the Kristevan father, however innovative she hopes her psychoanalytic model will be, explaining human experience is always for her an act of positioning in relation to what comes to signify paternal rule. Hence, the father, however approachable he has become, remains the representative of rule, *before* I even attempt to make my experience meaningful to others. So, in a father-mediated masculine–feminine spectrum, what does woman writing look like for Kristeva?

Defining woman writing would amount to seeking out in women's experience the material that typifies them and that Kristeva calls "the feminine" (Kristeva, "Unes femmes"). "The feminine" in Kristeva's work is not the popular understanding of feminine, like wearing make-up, having long hair or being gentle and caring. Rather, the feminine is that material that typifies females as women in their own right. In a patriarchy where recognized experience is mediated by male bodies (and the masculinist binary structure of Western thought), the feminine remains obscured by the difficulty in reconciling female experience with male bodies/sensitivities. This does not mean it is impossible, but that feminine experience is to be found where phallus-centred experience breaks down.[2] For example, in her novella *The Yellow Wallpaper* (1892), Charlotte Perkins Gilman initially proposed to denounce the medical practice she was subjected to as a woman suffering with neurasthenia, a practice that had not cured her but had led her to more psychosis. Her work has been one of the most celebrated and studied pieces of woman writing in Anglo-American feminist studies. However, her work has not gone down feminist literary history because of its critique of late nineteenth-century medical practices, as Perkins Gilman planned. Instead, the text is still fascinating readers for its ability to convey feminine experience, in spite and through the fabric of American *fin-de-siècle* literary conventions. So, while the essence of feminine may be by definition unintelligible, we are in no doubt as to what the experience of "feminine" looks like in Perkins Gilman's account. How does Perkins Gilman achieve this?

First, she proposes a narrator who agrees with everything she is told while injecting her text with doubt. The unnamed narrator strives to obey social order but uses words connoting negation, thus giving an image of her experience as that which is not what she says it is (Ford). In other words, what she says she is is the learnt narrative of woman's experience mediated by phallocentric (marital/medical) experience telling her how she should talk about herself. The insertion of negation has the effect of making this well-rehearsed narrative negate itself to the point of saying that what the narrator is telling us she is is really what she is not. What she may positively be is not spelt out, except in terms of contradictions and metaphors. Contradiction is conveyed primarily through discrepancy between form and content (Crewe): her husband expresses his love and care for the narrator. The form of address is correct linguistically and morally. Yet we work out that behind linguistic decorum what he says he does and what he actually does are two different things: he locks her up in her room, has put bars on the window and screwed the furniture to the floor. Hence, behind correct form we see a different content: abusive and morally reprehensible. The narrator herself is a clumsy speaker when it comes to explaining her condition using learnt medical terms (Treichler). Her awkwardness becomes the awkwardness of the medical profession at truly "getting her." As phallocentric narratives fail under her pen, woman-centred texts emerge at the same time in the form of contradictions, awkwardness, images and metaphors that mirror her experience. The metaphor of the wallpaper being ripped off the wall to reveal the woman trapped behind its crazy-making pattern is graphic enough to need no further rational elaboration and gains meaning through its imaginary strength. Hence, in *The Yellow Wallpaper*, strong repression of woman's authorship and of female experience is no barrier to woman writing. Many critiques (Mills et al.; Clark) have objected that the narrator's salvation is indeed in the margin, even outside the realm of normal experience, and while the mad text may be her triumph and liberation by literary standards, the narrator's evident psychosis is hardly the sign of a socially viable woman. Perhaps, but this is too limiting a conclusion.

Returning to Kristeva, woman writing is a positioning of writing on the side of the feminine. In the case of *The Yellow Wallpaper*, it would be the positioning of the narrator on the side of insanity that would evoke the narrator's feminine experience. Admittedly, the narrator's insanity is true only in the context of late nineteenth-century medical narratives. Today, *The Yellow Wallpaper* could not be written to the same effect, given new understandings of the narrator's experience as post-natal depression (although we might today see patiency, especially in relation to hormonal disarray, as a figure of feminine experience, but I do not have the space to develop this here). The text is more likely to end up on the reading list of trainee doctors, as the place where they might study a phenomenology of post-natal depression. But given the nineteenth-century context, the narrator's insanity becomes the vehicle for woman writing. Indeed, Kristeva has spoken about psychosis, woman's primary homosexuality[3] and maternity as overarching forms of feminine experience. But the narrating of feminine *experience* is not enough to warrant calling a piece "woman writing." Kristeva also insists that it is the manner in which the narrator attempts to stabilize (or not) chaotic experience through narrative strategies that conveys "feminine" to textual practice. This requires the writer's engagement with paternal mediation and the "father" needs to remain relatively stable in the writer's imagination for meaning to be possible. It is this stability that confers the paternal function its power to hold the writer while s/he ventures on the edge of signification. Hence, in Kristeva's understanding, woman writing is dependent on a signifying practice that precedes its telling. The writer in search of a narrative of marginal experience can only hope to navigate the edge of that practice, but not to cross its borders towards a pure "woman writing" realm. Or at least not if that writing seeks to convey some semblance of coherence. We saw how the sensical text, informed by phallocentric narratives, can be the vehicle of a form of woman writing, in the example of *The Yellow Wallpaper*. More contemporary writers have tried to purposefully create a truer version of woman writing.

In a text entitled *Inside*, Hélène Cixous attempted to capture the moment before the individual is born, before separation, before there is a distinction between self and other. In other words, she attempted to represent the very margin that has come to be regarded as the privileged terrain of *écriture féminine*. Here is one extract:

> A mouth with a firm line is speaking to the bowl of undelineated night. The mouth is speaking to me, inside me however, I see its firm lips forming speech, I do not see myself, I am black, filled with a soft pliable substance, an unlimited mass, silent, vibrant. The lips in profile articulate vigorously: their color? a young man's lips, full, carmine perhaps, though shaded, warm, a living man, young, eloquent: they persuade me. He's right, thinks my black pasty mass kneaded to attention. Fibers stretch me taut, pulling on invisible ends of myself – am I contractile? I must have an end. (*Hélène Cixous Reader* 20)

Cixous's text is, by rational standards, fairly nonsensical. However, if we use a Kristevan approach, then meanings emerge. As we saw, the father confers meaning to experience, as the holder of a law that enables the separation of meaning into distinct categories. *Inside* evokes the experience of transformation of one's being, at two (at least) moments of individual experience: parturition is physical transformation of one body that becomes two, a physical movement from inside the mother's body to a space outside of her. The second moment is castration when the individual experiences psychical transformation from unintelligible, shapeless mind to separated, contained, meaningful consciousness. The narrator appears caught in defining moments where s/he will either refuse transformation and stay unintelligible or forsake present experience against the promise of another way of being. But Cixous goes further. Faced with tension and choice she challenges established (patriarchal) narratives of castration and loss whereby maternal, feminine experience must be forsaken and lost in order to make room for paternal, masculine experience. Instead, she suggests another form of experience when one may let contradictory (feminine *and* masculine) experiences cohabit within one single yet multiple experience.

The understanding of such a text still requires some regulatory intervention that is borrowed from traditional narratives of self. Void of adopting some form of pre-existing framework of human development, we could not gain any insight into the world that Cixous presents us with. This would then go some way towards agreeing with Kristeva that outside the paternal framework no woman writing is possible. Woman cannot make herself intelligible away from patriarchal presence as paternal rules of meaning help us decipher her experience by comparison or in relation to established narratives. So, while authors such as Kristeva or Cixous grant power of creation to one's challenge of the father, in the form of woman writing for example, this is only conditional upon a pre-existing paternal agency effectively remaining stable and secure beyond the personal history of the speaker. Yet it is rarely the case that such a strong and unproblematically stable father figure actually exists. Kristeva proposes that the individual does find such a "good father"[4] somewhere other than in the encounter with the imperfect flesh-and-blood father figure. The good father would be an imagined, idealized father. This ideal father does not come from direct experience with the actual father but rather from experiences with the mother who herself has an interest in that more perfect paternal agency. The young child learns about this more perfect father because the mother sometimes turns her attention away from the child and towards something else: her work, an activity, a partner, etc., in short what ties her to the social contract. The child imagines this something else to be better than itself (since it captures the mother's attention better than the child does) and desires to emulate it to recapture maternal focus onto itself. While still tied to the biological body, the child's desire to identify with the something else located in the social contract is the blueprint for future identifications. In Kristeva's work, experience with the good father marks the moment one begins to become a consciousness, and will affect future identifications. The Oedipal father will intervene later and replay the same scenario but with a more tangible force, given that the Oedipal father takes form in the social contract, for example, the actual father, the school teacher, the driving instructor, etc. The failure of primitive experience with the father bodes badly for the individual's future social viability, as the blueprint for identification with social things outside of the individual is truncated. All experiences are founded on resembling the original blueprint of experience, and on the "success" of that primitive experience depends the possibility of future identifications.

Before turning to Butler's critique of the Kristevan model and contribution to the possibility of woman writing, I would like to recapitulate Kristeva's position. For Kristeva no woman writing is possible outside the symbolic framework. The aim of woman writing is to explore the relationship between something we call "woman" and phallocentric intelligibility; it is this exploration that produces literary features we may read as woman writing. Both texts given as illustrations of woman writing present us with a similar strategy. In the case of Perkins Gilman's text, the aim is clearly to respect phallocentric rules of writing and make oneself intelligible within that framework. Perkins Gilman succeeds (albeit unintentionally, given the text was published in 1892) in creating an example of woman writing by tapping into some form of psychology of the reading experience. The injection of negation or hesitancy on the one hand and of metaphor on the other is mirrored in the reading experience. The reader's mind is eased into agreeing to negate or at least doubt phallocentric experience. It is also readily caught in the play of metaphor: as Freud explained, with its condensed and displaced meanings, metaphor is a figure of speech that bypasses defences we would expect with the presentation of blunter meanings. Cixous resorts to similar strategies with the advantage of late 1960s interest in psychoanalytic and poststructuralist theories (*Inside* was first published in French as *Dedans* in 1969). She is thus able to more self-consciously create a text that speaks about the difficulty of writing woman's experience and preserving phallocentric clarity. In both cases, woman writing is dependent upon its positioning vis-à-vis phallocentric experience. Hence, for Kristeva, woman writing per se cannot exist. But if woman writing does not exist strictly, Kristeva's work opens another door that is radical in its own right. Her contribution to woman writing is found in her work on the feminine. I said above that the feminine is that material that typifies female experience. This was a rather quick definition of the feminine and not quite complete and I can now flesh out further what feminine writing entails. In Kristevan theory, the formation of the feminine happens when the individual, whether male or female, learns to relinquish certain materials in favour of more coherent ones. As we saw above, the child wants to become something other than itself, hoping to recapture the maternal interest temporarily lost when she turned her attention to things other than the child. This is the moment phallocentric content and the feminine become separated. As s/he is drawn towards becoming meaningful to the mother, the individual also leaves the fragmented, unintelligible experience of the baby world. The feminine is thus associated with early, pre-Oedipal experience. While the experience of Oedipus will be played out differently for each sex, both sexes retain a memory of feminine experience, or rather, both retain the memory of the separation from the maternal that brought about the formation of the feminine/phallocentric separation. Feminine writing is, then, the recalling of that experience in the moment of writing, and is open to both sexes. But at the risk of repeating myself, feminine writing cannot be found independently of phallocentric experience because the phallus precedes and moderates significations. This is what Judith Butler criticizes Kristeva for.

In her most famous contribution to gender theory, *Gender Trouble* (1990/2008), Judith Butler vehemently refutes the possibility of a father existing a priori. On the one hand she notes that Kristeva's "theory appears to depend upon the stability and reproduction of precisely the paternal law that she seeks to displace" (108); on the other, she accurately describes the modalities of maternal experience as a "prediscursive libidinal economy which occasionally makes itself known in language, but which maintains an ontological status prior to language itself" (109). Butler critiques the way Kristeva imagines maternal experience not as a modality in its own right with its own pre-paternal causality but as "a closed concept, indeed, a heterogeneity confined by a teleology both unilinear and univocal" (122). Instead of being an origin of signification, maternal experience, where we might hope to find one source, if not "the" source of feminine writing, becomes the outcome of paternal regulation of meaning:

> The law that is said to repress the semiotic [maternal experience] may well be the governing principle of the semiotic itself, with the result that what passes as "maternal instinct" may well be a culturally constructed desire. (123)

This is quite a damning conclusion. Kristeva proposed feminine writing as a possibility, partly hidden behind the prism of phallocentric interpretation, but nevertheless palpable. Butler sweeps the prospect of feminine writing as an effect of that interpretation. Applied to our purpose, if there is no pre-discursive maternal experience to speak of, there is then no woman writing that is not already an intrinsic part of the construction of phallocentric narratives.

> Whereas Kristeva posits a maternal body prior to discourse that exerts its own causal force in the structure of drives, [...] the discursive production of the maternal body as prediscursive is a tactic in the self-amplification and concealment of those specific power relations by which the trope of the maternal body is produced. (125)

So what is woman writing for Butler? Like Kristeva, she also envisions writing as an experience dependent on social forces within which the writing is taking place. Short of being able to disengage from the regulatory forces of phallocentric discourse, Butler proposes to challenge them from within. Identity is not to be discovered in searching ways to better express some biological being, for there is no biological gender waiting to be discovered, outside its expression. Rather, Butler draws a novel way of thinking about identity with what she calls *re-iterated performativity*. Its definition is that identity would be "performatively constituted by the very expressions that are said to be its results" (34). For example, if in the process of wanting to tell the world who I am I come to understand that raising my left arm signifies "woman," then that is what I will do. The repetition of left-arm-raising over time gives me and others an illusion of constancy of being which, soon enough, is understood as the origin of my being. Seeking to capture who I might be, others notice that I raise my left arm and conclude that I am a woman: left-arm-raising has become the origin of my identity. Butlerian theory asks that we critically engage with identity politics by being aware of, if not exposing, the inversion of meaning by which we become meaningful to others. To explain this further, we need to turn to Butler's work on melancholia.

In *The Psychic Life of Power* (1997), Butler takes up Freud's theory of grief and melancholia to put "loss" forward as an essential element formative of identity. Freud had suggested that loss of a loved object generates either grief or melancholia. Grief would be achieved when the individual disengages his/her attachment to the lost object to invest it in other existing objects. Melancholia, on the other hand, would be loss that does not achieve grief because the individual cannot let go of the object lost. Instead, attachment to loss, with all its emotional force, becomes the site where the lost object is retained. In short, melancholia is attachment to loss following attachment to the object lost. Butler proposes that there is "a peculiar turning of a subject against itself that takes place in acts of self-reproach, conscience, and melancholia that work in tandem with processes of social regulation" (*Psychic Life* 18–19). In the Freudian model of development, the relinquishing of the individual's pre-history in favour of paternal regulation is accompanied by strong repression of those contents that are undesirable under paternal rule. Although she does not name her sources, Butler pitches that part of Freud's work that posits undesirable contents as *repressed* against Lacan's re-reading of Freudian repression as sometimes *foreclosed*. Lacan introduced the term "foreclosure" to account for the difference between grieved and melancholic contents during castration. In Freud, repression marks the moment the individual's psyche becomes divided into conscious and unconscious. During castration, some experiences of pleasure are rejected into a part of the psyche the individual will not be conscious of, and replaced by more acceptable and pleasurable formations, for example, for their power to confer intelligibility, belonging or personal worth. Foreclosure distinguishes itself from repression in the way the repressed elements "are not integrated into the subject's unconscious" (Laplanche and Pontalis 166), that is in the way they are not strictly speaking "repressed." Instead, they reappear as psychotic episodes, that is pre-discursive, pre-imaginary contents, having bypassed repression on the way, as in the experience of hallucinations, for instance.

Returning to Butler, she is interested in those foreclosed elements as they are by definition capable of bursting forth unchanged into citational narratives, where their presence undoes the work done by paternal repression and opens speech to new possibilities. A big part of her work has been and still is to bring forward those experiences that manifest foreclosed contents: homosexuality or warfare, for example. To remain close to our topic, woman writing, I find interesting the way Butler magnifies the presence of melancholia in expression as that which "grounds the subject" and "threatens to unsettle and disrupt that ground" (*Psychic Life* 23). Grounding and unsettling are generated by the presence of melancholic content and, for Butler, melancholia is thus

> the limit to the subject's sense of *power* [...] Because the subject does not, cannot, *reflect* on that loss, that loss marks the limit of reflexivity, that which exceeds (and conditions) its circuitry. Understood as foreclosure, that loss inaugurates the subject and threatens it with dissolution. (Ibid.)

But while foreclosure prevents reflection on the object of loss, thus limiting the writer's agency and condemning her to circular, paternally mediated expression, it also constitutes excess. Excess, then, represents that which dissolves circularity and potentially permits new possibilities of expression. Hence, in melancholic loss we find the matter out of which the writer may challenge paternally mediated expression, if not undo paternal narratives and formulate the content of woman writing. We are, of course, far from second-wave feminist visions of woman writing as that which typifies female experience and bears the name of female authors. But we are closer to an understanding of woman writing as textual and subjective practice. I would like to bring back Kristeva into the picture and recapitulate our discussion, and offer conclusions on what a Kristevan and Butlerian approach to woman writing practice might entail.

If we compare Butler and Kristeva, there is no doubt the latter proposes a more embodied model of gendered writing, anchored in some form of physiological event. Maternal experience acts as a form of blueprint of pre-discursive experience, out of and from which the writer draws psychical material. Pre-paternal time is psychically imprinted on the individual's mind. Out of those psychical impressions the individual will be able to draw memories of archaic being that Kristeva sees as the mark of the feminine. Those memories are not the organized narratives that we usually refer to as memory. Instead, they are closer to embodied memory, made of sensations and proto-representations of the world. So, in this sense, maternal time is closer to a physiological state of being. Yet Kristeva does not offer pre-paternal experience as purely physiological. Indeed, parental desire, and especially maternal desire, already inscribes the future individual into a matrix that is always already social, before the child is even conceived. Kristeva's work on maternal experience is undoubtedly the closest we get to a theory of pre-discursive experience, and that is, in my mind at least, its force. Maternal experience is, then, that pre-discursive experience where woman writing can be located. But Kristeva has particular views about what "woman" might be in the experience of woman writing. In her theoretical and critical work, she acknowledges the possibility of woman writing, but only on the condition that it is not bound to a biological category. In other words, woman writing is not the privilege of females. For that matter, we need to remember that phallocentric writing is not the privilege of males either. Instead, abiding by phallocentric rules of writing is man writing and any attempt to recapture the experience of pre-paternal time typifies woman writing, whether the writer is male or female. Woman writing then tries "to put the neutral surface of abstract words into contact with a whole dynamic of recollection that leads us at once to recall traumas, the pains or the pleasures, and the most archaic sensations" (*Julia Kristeva Interviews* 55).

More tangibly, woman writing is an opportunity to convey two things. First, it seeks to recapture what psychoanalytic theory describes as "the repressed," that is experiences evoking one's personal pre-history. In agreement with Freud, these repressed contents can return on the condition they are disguised (condensation and displacement), for instance as metaphors as we saw with *The Yellow Wallpaper*. But Kristeva goes further. Woman writing also testifies to the individual's encounter with the maternal and in particular what Kristeva calls "the semiotic." The semiotic refers to those contents that belong to the early relationship with the mother and that the baby perceives as her "language": its rhythm, pitch, musicality, etc. Early in her career (*La Révolution du langage poëtique*), Kristeva proposes a theory of subjectivity that challenges Freud and Lacan (*Révolution*). In addition to Freud's Oedipal model of repression/return of repressed contents, she adds the semiotic as a modality of language that can be heard in communication and typifies woman writing (Kristeva herself refers to it sometimes as "poetic language," sometimes as "*écriture féminine*") (Kristeva, *Révolution*; "Unes femmes"). If we return to Cixous's text, the reading aloud of *Inside* echoes the musicality of human speech that a baby would hear: the rhythms, repetitions, alliterations, and so on participate in creating the experience of hearing this strange speech, more efficiently than if the author had spelt out her intention. Hence, in Kristeva's work, the experience of maternity, or of woman's primary homosexuality, or of psychosis are all incidences where we might find materials for woman writing; through them, the individual has the opportunity to recall and make intelligible maternal contents, and to mimic semiotic experience linguistically.

For Butler, such historicizing of the content of one's speech is highly problematic. Indeed, there can be no such thing as woman writing if by woman writing we understand the telling of experience that pertains to something we could trace back to an original experience. For Butler, there is no "woman" to be (re)discovered in maternal experience. In a Butlerian world where mimicry and repetition of experience is everything, that original blueprint cannot exist. Instead, woman writing would be that experience co-dependent with phallocentric writing. But it does not mean that phallocentric writing is any more authentic or essential than woman writing either. Again, in Butler, we find that there is no such thing as phallocentric writing, if by this we mean experience that would typify the experience of man as universal subject. There is no phenomenology of gender that we may discursively discover and describe, because it is always preceded by the terms by which we are meant to discover it.

This is where I find that Butler strangely joins Kristeva. She decried Kristeva's body politics for its selective ignorance of the political motivations hiding behind the creation of ontological categories such as "symbolic" or "semiotic," or its fabrication of a historically feasible speaking subject. Yet, like Kristeva, she denies the possibility of intelligible discourse outside paternal regulation of meaning. "[T]he terms that make up one's own gender are, from the start, outside oneself, beyond oneself in a sociality that has no single author (and that radically contests the notion of authorship itself)" (Butler, *Undoing Gender* 1). Whether we call it paternal or sociality, the function of that regulating force amounts to the same thing. The next best thing, then, is challenge to the pressure to perform identity correctly in order to retain some semblance of agency. In Butler, the misalignment between the performance I wish to copy and my performance is the source of differentially constituted agency. It may not be intentional, but that differential is where resistance is at, and so it is where woman-writing-like practice could be found.

So, we are left with two approaches to defining woman writing. We can either locate woman writing in the historicizing of individual development in a time that precedes the acquisition of language, as Kristeva does. We have distinguished earlier the mark of woman writing in texts that either openly (Cixous) or unintentionally (Perkins Gilman) seek to make intelligible a distinctive experience that women would share. In both cases, the manner in which the narrator magnifies elements marginal to signification constitutes the idiosyncrasies of woman writing. These marginal elements suggest that, at least for those narrators, being themselves is not solely here-and-now experience but arches back and beyond to a time when marginality was their true being.

Or, we can agree with Butler that there never was a time when individuals were any more real or true to some natural state of themselves. And so the narrative search for this pre-historical individual is futile. All writing is regulated by normative forces outside the writer's control. To critically engage with such forces would mean decoding the rules by which the telling of experience is made acceptable while recognizing that these rules are also what make such telling unviable. So, what is the point? For Butler, critical engagement with the terms that constitute *and* undo the individual is the way to open up possibilities. Her politics thus rejects a founding moment of resistance and anchors resistance in the moment of enunciation itself.

While it would seem that the two thinkers are in disagreement, their differing positions can be reconciled. Kristeva and Butler have in common an understanding of marginal experience (queer for Butler, semiotic for Kristeva) as encompassing the experience of loss. For Kristeva, loss is a founding moment and that which one must let go of. But in letting go, loss also becomes the material of woman writing. Kristeva does not envision woman writing in melancholic experience. Melancholic experience, for her, signals the inability of the individual to situate him/herself on the side of the father and his linguistic rule. In melancholia, there is no confrontation between the paternal symbolic and the feminine, since the individual is unable to let go of the object of loss in favour of other objects (loss that would be "metaphorized," for instance). Without the transformation of loss, through writing, there can be no critique of established narratives of experience. Hence, the idea of a type of writing that would be, say, entirely psychotic, is not possible. When Kristeva speaks of privileged experiences, like maternal, homosexual or psychotic, to generate woman writing material, it is always with the understanding that the writing occurs from a symbolic position, that is that the writer is aiming to bring to intelligibility the experience obscured by the absence of symbol. In other words, woman writing tells of the experience of pre-Oedipal maternal time and of the moment that narrative pre-history is relinquished in favour of a paternally regulated narrative. Woman writing is a tool empowering the writer to confront (phallocentric) claims to writer omniscience and rationality. That confrontation with one's own desire for omniscience is, then, where a woman writing practice is found. For Butler too, loss is the site of a revolt of expression. But her work makes more of melancholia because she rejects the historicizing of identity formation. Instead, melancholic elements come to constitute *and* undo identities *at the same time*. Even if regulation closes off the possibilities offered to make myself socially viable, those closed-off possibilities are nevertheless present through the very terms I "choose" when I re-iterate who I might be. Woman writing, seen through the Butlerian prism, can thus be situated in an intentional, re-iterated and performative writing practice of individual experience.

disclosure statement

No potential conflict of interest was reported by the author.

notes

1 I refer the reader to my article "The Regulation of Gender in Menopause Theory" for further critical discussion on this matter.

2 In what follows, I shall use the Derridean term "phallocentric" to mean the privileging of masculine experience in the construction of meaning.

3 For an explanation of why we should talk about woman's primary homosexuality rather than

lesbianism, see my "Julia Kristeva, 'Woman's Primary Homosexuality' and Homophobia."

4 Kristeva terms the good father "loving father" to differentiate him from the stern and punishing Oedipal father (Kristeva, *Le Génie féminin*).

Bibliography

Butler, Judith. *Gender Trouble*. 1990. Abingdon and New York: Routledge, 2008. Print.

Butler, Judith. *The Psychic Life of Power*. Stanford: Stanford UP, 1997. Print.

Butler, Judith. *Undoing Gender*. Abingdon and New York: Routledge, 2004. Print.

Cahill, Larry. "Why Sex Matters for Neuroscience." *Nature Reviews Neuroscience* 7.6 (2006): 477–84. Print.

Cixous, Hélène. *The Hélène Cixous Reader*. Ed. Susan Sellers. Trans. Hélène Cixous. London: Routledge, 1994. Print.

Cixous, Hélène. *Inside*. Trans. Carol Barko. New York: Schocken, 1986. Print.

Clark, Hilary. *Depression and Narrative: Telling the Dark*. New York: State U of New York P, 2008. Print.

Crewe, Jonathan. "Queering the Yellow Wallpaper: Charlotte Perkins Gilman and the Politics of Form." *Tulsa Studies in Women's Literature* 14.2 (1995): 273–93. Print.

Ford, Karen. "*The Yellow Wallpaper* and Women's Discourse." *Tulsa Studies in Women's Literature* 4.2 (1985): 309–14. Print.

Gambaudo, Sylvie. "Julia Kristeva, 'Woman's Primary Homosexuality' and Homophobia." *European Journal of Women's Studies* 20.1 (2011): 8–20. Print.

Gambaudo, Sylvie. *Kristeva, Psychoanalysis and Culture*. Aldershot: Ashgate, 2007. Print.

Gambaudo, Sylvie. "The Regulation of Gender in Menopause Theory." *Topoi: An International Review of Philosophy* (2015). 29 Oct. 2015. Web. 28 Sept 2016. <http://link.springer.com/article/10.1007/s11245-015-9351-2>. doi:10.1007/s11245-015-9351-2.

Ingalhalikar, Madhur. "Sex Differences in the Structural Connectome of the Human Brain." *Proceedings of the National Academy of Sciences of the United States of America* 111.2 (2013): 823–28. Print.

Kristeva, Julia. *Le Génie féminin. Melanie Klein*. Paris: Fayard, 2000. Print.

Kristeva, Julia. *Julia Kristeva Interviews*. Ed. Ross Mitchell Guberman. Trans. Suzanne Clark and Kathleen Hulley. New York: Columbia UP, 1996. Print.

Kristeva, Julia. *La Révolution du langage poétique*. Paris: Seuil, 1974. Print.

Kristeva, Julia. "Unes femmes." *Les Cahiers du Grif* 7 (1975): 22–27. Print.

Laplanche, Jean, and Jean-Bertrand Pontalis. *The Language of Psychoanalysis*. Trans. Donald Nicholson-Smith. London: Karnac, 1988. Print.

Mills, Sara, et al. *Feminist Readings/Feminists Reading*. Ed. Sara Mills and Lynne Pierce. New York and London: Harvester, 1989. Print.

Perkins Gilman, Charlotte. *Women and Economics: A Study of the Economic Relation between Men and Women as a Factor in Social Evolution*. Boston: Small, 1898. Print.

Perkins Gilman, Charlotte. *The Yellow Wallpaper*. 1892. London: Virago, 1981. Print.

Ruigrok, Amber, et al. "A Meta-analysis of Sex Differences in Human Brain Structure." *Neuroscience & Biobehavioral Reviews* 39 (2014): 34–50. Print.

Treichler, Paula. "Escaping the Sentence: Diagnosis and Discourse in *The Yellow Wallpaper*." *Tulsa Studies in Women's Literature* 3.1–2 (1984): 61–77. Print.

Sylvie Gambaudo

louise gyler

FROM SYMPTOM TO THE SYMBOLIZATION OF RECEPTIVITY

a girl's psychoanalytic journey

> Dinner was ready. It was a plain gravy soup. There was nothing to stir the fancy in that. One could have seen through the transparent liquid any pattern that there might have been on the plate itself. But there was no pattern. The plate was plain.
>
> *Woolf 18*

In the psychoanalytic encounter, the analysand tells her inchoate story through projection, displacement, silence and enactment. This communicative journey interlaces words, affects, relationship and action to bring about moments of meaning and understanding. The "as if" nature of the relationship, the transference/countertransference encounter, is crucial to the production of meaning and thought. Of the transference, Freud said:

> we may say that the patient does not *remember* anything of what he has forgotten and repressed, but *acts* it out. He reproduces it not as a memory but as an action; he *repeats* it, without, of course, knowing that he is repeating it. (Freud, "Remembering" 150; emphasis in the original)

Melanie Klein extended the understanding of transference to the total situation where a dynamic constellation of emotions, defences and object relations is transferred from the past into the present. Transference then comes to be understood not just as direct references to the figure of the analyst but as the entire orientation to the analyst and the analysis. Subsequent developments based on Klein's concept of projective identification allow for countertransference to be seen as a promising resource in the process of meaning making. Meaning making or the work of representing the unrepresented and/or "unrepresentable" is the aim of most contemporary psychoanalytic models – rather than uncovering repressed memories or "making conscious the unconscious" central to the classical Freudian model. The work of representation relies on the analysand's free associative speech and the psychoanalyst's dual task of experiencing and analysing. The first task involves the psychoanalyst's work of listening, experiencing and "taking in" the patient with "free-floating attention" and the second concerns interpretation, limits and boundaries. The latter task is supported by a psychoanalytic encounter with fixed appointments of a specified time limit (the fifty-minute session, although Lacan notoriously disrupted the fixed session time), together with the analyst's speech from her own separate perspective which symbolically introduces the notion of otherness that is a necessary element in the contruction of subjectivity.

Klein's account of negativity (the ongoing internalization of the negation/death of the maternal object and the re-creation of the lost maternal object), destructiveness and phantasy potentially offers a complex and subversive account of the unconscious preconditions of knowledge production and thought (Kristeva, *Melanie Klein*; Jacobus). While the meaning of the maternal object is in the forefront of her theorizing of subjectivity it needs to be stressed that it is not the actual mother – or as Kristeva writes: "the only mother who interests her is the mother who can be thought" (*Melanie Klein* 238). For Klein, the psychic treatment of the maternal object, whether conceived as good or bad, idealized or devalued, is central to the construction of subjectivity. The discourse of the maternal object is connected to the development of the capacity for a freedom of thought or, put another way, the development of a sense of agency. "Real" agency, as we know, requires the representation of aggression. Due to both psychological and socio-cultural factors, this remains, I suggest, complicated and sometimes fraught for women's self-actualization.

In this paper, a psychoanalytic journey is recounted by the analyst. In the clinical vignettes, I have attempted to be faithful to the story as it unfolded but, undoubtedly, my own interests and sensibilities are reflected in memory and selection. Freud wrote: "Nothing takes place between them except they talk to each other" ("Question" 189). We know, however, that this claim is not as simple and innocent as it appears at first glance. Psychoanalytic listening is anything but innocent not only because the analyst listens with a particular ear to that which cannot be thought and spoken but also because the way we listen and observe is influenced explicitly and implicitly by our theoretical frameworks. Julia Kristeva writes of the accumulative violent nature of the psychoanalytic act of listening:

> Analytic listening is in itself a violent act. I appropriate the patient's utterances, I identify with their suffering and pleasure, and I am stirred by their words and hear with them in the same music. There is a part of perverted pleasure in this identification, which inevitably takes the way of part-objects and the ambivalence of the drives and desires in the transference and countertransference. But a further violence is added. I detach myself from this free-floating attention in order to name a meaning. My interpretation, because it is verbal, has to remain limited with regard to tone [...] But it is the more so, because of the "theoretical" choice that stands out unconsciously in my spoken interpretation [...] ("From Symbols" 785)

Our meta-theory "choices" about the representation of gender and sexuality are inherently ambiguous for the interest of women. Notwithstanding Judith Butler's brilliant insight that the meaning of the body is read through culture (*Gender Trouble*), the female's experiential relation to her body is different from the male's relation to his body and from trans and intersexed persons' relation to their body. How it is different is unknown and unknowable and the potential for possible meanings is infinite. Dana Birksted-Breen writes: "The paradox is that there is no one-to-one relationship between mind and body but nor can the body be ignored in the construction of the psyche and of representation" (*Work of Psychoanalysis* 128–29). The question of how we approach theory construction is challenging. The relationships between the body, psychic representations of masculinity and femininity and the maternal and paternal objects are complex and contentious both in psychoanalytic accounts and in the lived experience of our subjective inner and outer worlds. On one side lurks the issue of essentialism and essentializing women's experience that has been historically oppressive for women's interests; on the other side, there is the need to represent the particularity of women's experience, especially of the body and procreativity – the site for envy of women described by Klein, Horney and others. Previously, I have argued that slippage in psychoanalytic theorizing can occur where the unconscious and conscious gendered and sexual imagery used by individual analysands to organize and symbolize experience can be too concretely incorporated into the theory, leading our theories to reflect uncritically socially normative values (Gyler).

My aim in this paper is two-fold: first, to employ a case study to explore, from the clinical perspective, some impediments and disruptions to women's self-actualization. The analysand that I shall discuss below surrendered her potentiality for creativity and agency. In the consulting room, she, like other women, presented without self-definition but self-absorbed, anxiously requiring the other's reassurance of their goodness and, yet, even if love and admiration were forthcoming, it never reassured or satisfied or was internalized. It was "as if" there was no interior space to hold and structure meaning and aliveness. There was only a gaping hole where dread found its resting place. Second, I use the clinical insights to question the relevance of the capacity for thought (the structuring moment of subjectivity) being hinged exclusively to the tale of Oedipus for women. While I agree that struggling and working with the dynamics of triadic relationships is an essential part of the development of mind[1] – a necessary confrontation with one's narcissism and the recognition of otherness, if you like, that facilitates the capacity for both sharing and competition – it is only part of the story. In this paper, I argue that women's symbolic journey involves the representation of an internal receptive space. This representation is a crucial restructuring moment in the girl's psychic economy and contests any simple conceptualization of a linear move from the pre-Oedipal to the Oedipal. The account of the psychic inner space leans on the representation of presence in contrast to the Freudian Oedipus complex which is concerned with loss, absence and incompleteness. This line of thought suggests that there are alternative and more circuitous ways to enter the symbolic realm than the patriarchal rendition of the Oedipus tale would have us believe.

why thinking?

Both following and departing from Klein's account, Bion formulated a theory of thinking, with thinking as a portmanteau concept for thinking and feeling (Bion, *Learning*; "Attacks"; "Theory"). Bion's innovative ideas re-fashioned the approach to Kleinian clinical practice; notably, Bion's work extended the understanding of the transference/countertransference to encompass the possibility that the analyst's subjective responses are reflecting the patient's unconscious communications. In his explication of Bion's theory of thinking, Ogden, with his customary precision and clarity, identifies that this theory is based on four overlapping and interconnected principles of mental functioning. The first principle advances the idea that there is a human need to know the "truth"; that is to know the reality of who one is and what is occurring in one's life. The second principle involves the observation that two minds are needed to think a person's disturbing thoughts. This observation rests on the Kleinian mechanism of projective identification. For Klein, this mechanism is an intrapsychic phenomenon, describing a particular form of identification, which arises when hatred against parts of the self is directed towards the maternal object (m/other), that is, "the prototype of an aggressive object-relation" (8). This idea, conceptualizing an *internal* object-related process, in the hands of Bion is extended to formulate the intersubjective dimension in the construction of subjectivity as it shows how ego mechanisms such as splitting, projection and introjection function in relation to the outer world. The consequences of this mechanism of projective identification for subjectivity are serious: experiences of confusion, fragmentation and fear; the denial of separateness between self and object; a depletion of personal resources; and distorted perception. Bion radically conceived that the deployment of projective identification was an ordinary and necessary part of human life: representing the earliest form of communication.

The third principle is that a capacity for thinking is necessary to manage thoughts and feelings generated from disturbing experience. Bion's model of container/contained, based on the model of the infant/mother dyad, hypothesizes that, if the experience goes well, the infant projects unmanageable, unbearable feelings and impulses into the mother who processes these feelings through her "reverie" (*Learning* 36) and, then, presents them back to the infant in a manageable form. Bion describes a process whereby the infant engages in "learning by experience" (47) to cope with his own inner emotional life through these cycles of projective and introjective identification with a "container," modelled on the mother (90). Conversely, if the experience goes badly (for Bion, either because of the caregiver's incapacity for reverie or because of the infant's excessive envy and sadism), the infant resorts to forceful excessive use of projective identification which then leads, via reintrojection, to the development of an internal world based upon fragile, distorting and/or malignantly misunderstanding internal object relations (disorders of thought). The fourth principle is the work of dreaming, as "a psycho-analytic function of the personality" (89), that occurs unconsciously in sleep and in waking life and allows for working through of emotional issues.

case illustration: emma[2]

When I first met Emma she was twelve and a half years of age and had believed for six months that she was unable to walk. There was no organic pathology to account for her predicament (other attempts at help had all faltered). During the initial interviews, she described sleep problems and an anxious depressed mood but she was not unduly concerned about her apparent inability to walk, not unlike Freud's infamous women at the heart of psychoanalytic theory. She described herself as a "goodie, goodie" who wanted to be "perfect" but found it "very hard to be that all the time." Her sessions overflowed with her disappointment in herself but also complaints about the inadequacies of her family, friends and medical staff caring for her. She also believed that she was the long-suffering victim of others' criticisms. She drew for me a striking picture of her family depicting all family members as the same, that is, the same height, size, shape and dress, and hence, undifferentiated by gender and age.

Emma told her narrative, thin and disembodied, repetitively for months on end. Listening to this grey swirl of sameness, I saw no underlying pattern that might give some traction on transformation and relief to her suffering. There was "nothing to stir the fancy" (Woolf 18) except, on reflection, her "performance" of gender was paradoxical. On the one hand, her drawing conveyed a "unisex" model of gender: is the model blind or transgressive or both? On the other hand, she appeared stuck terrified in some halfway position, literally both in her mind and body "crippled" and put upon. Additionally, I (and those attempting to help Emma) was also left feeling passive, helpless and anxious in a version of massive projective identification with Emma. Yet, of course, this powerful psychic evacuation of her mind cost Emma greatly and, in her own words, she felt "superficial" and "shallow." She appeared to idealize a version of extremely passive femininity or "hyper-femininity," as Lynne Layton puts it. As others have observed, at the margins, our conceptions of a stereotypical version of femininity and hysteria are blurred (Glocer Fiorini; Showalter).

I describe below Emma's four-year psychoanalytic journey from symptom to symbolization through five vignettes; from a frightening and persecuting inner maternal representation to a representation of femininity as receptivity which supports her in beginning to mourn and rework the phantasy of narcissistic completeness.

the beginning

Emma claimed that her mother (the most important figure in her internal and external worlds) saw her as having "only bad thoughts." From the outset, she harboured transferential anxieties that her analyst would see her in this way and she positioned herself as the long-suffering victim of the analyst's complaints about her "badness." In her mind, the other had only two possible positions: one, "for her," that is, accepting her as a helpless invalid or baby who is entitled to abdicate responsibility for herself; two, "against her," that is, criticizing and complaining about her and pushing her to grow up.

Early in her analysis this situation was concretely enacted over and over again. For example, Emma attended her sessions in a wheelchair but there was a problem negotiating the wheelchair along a narrow corridor which led to my consulting room. Emma at the beginning of this corridor would hold out her hand for physical assistance. This gesture placed me in a bind, mirroring Emma's divided and constricted world, as to refuse to assist her positioned me in her mind as uncaring and insensitive to her dilemma but, at the same time, to support her in this practical and physical way would be to collude with her that she was physically incapacitated. Both these positions are, of course, problematic, as the former would appear to judge her and the latter would collude with her passivity. So, from the beginning of her analysis, her mode of relating suggests that, in the transference, she experienced the other as either an extension of herself, not fully recognized as another person, or, on the other hand, as a persecuting other, that is, there was no sense of otherness as difference. There was no third position; there was no alternative position from which to observe these two restricted possibilities of either a narcissistic merger or persecuting opposition.

vignette two

As Emma's analysis proceeded (about six months into the analysis), she began to develop an improved capacity to name and articulate her sense of self. She not only, at times, identified feeling helpless and passive but also active and aggressive. But, for Emma, to be assertive was dangerous and precarious, as she feared she could lose control and murder her mother or me. She said in a session "what will you think of me being angry ... [you will] not like me ... fearful I might murder ... lose control."[3] For Emma, the Law of the Father, the Oedipal moment of separateness and subjectivity, was not only murder but a murder in which the maternal object cannot survive; not a tale of lost and found, as in Freud's *fort da* game, but a tale which is too real with a loss without hope of recovery and reparation. The question can be asked as to why separateness with its promise of development and agency was felt to be dangerous. For Emma, this was not a question but a concrete psychic reality.

Also, Emma was able to speak now of murder because she was finding, or beginning to represent in her mind, the possibility of another: that is, there was another to speak with (Ogden's second Bionic principle). As Emma was able to speak more openly about her aggression and destructiveness, she began to be able to talk more freely about her anxious understanding of family history and the "mothers" that she would have liked to annihilate from her mind. In her mind, she was a member of a "long line of family freaks," that is, there have been generations of women in her family with serious mental health issues associated with pregnancy, childbirth and loss.

Emma talked of her terror in sessions that, if she could not "get control over herself," she believed that she would continue to "crack up" when exposed to any stress, in keeping with her image of her female family members. She described her experience in the following way: she felt "like a jigsaw puzzle, full of cracks, ready to break apart when any pressure is exerted." Pressure, for her, meant separations and losses such as those inherent in giving birth and death. It was not safe to be a woman; for her, women were weak, vulnerable and mad. Emma appeared to attempt to cope by evading her inner "truth," by keeping up an illusion that her "surface" was plain and unmarked by her inner world of phantasies, anxieties and defences. This illusion distracted from the cracks beneath the surface; for Emma, her internal sense of containment was not up to the task of holding the complicated and contradictory anxieties and conflicts linked to her transgenerational history.[4] The maternal object could not survive being the target of matricide; the process of separation had not become symbolized but remained too literal and concrete, leaving Emma in a crippled bind, repudiating her recognition of gender difference and her "feminine dimension."[5]

vignette three

About two years after the commencement of her analysis, Emma appeared to be much more able to recognize the reality of her own emotional life, although she remained terrified of others' judgement, especially of being seen as "stupid," and was easily narcissistically hurt. Her talk was more emotionally alive and she began to report her dreams around this time. The following two dreams seem to reflect a different version of her self than the one represented pictorially by her at the beginning of her therapy (the unisex drawing); she no longer conceives herself as an impenetrable surface unmarked by the experience of difference or by traumatic feminine/maternal identifications. In her dreams we see a modified conception of femininity. First, she dreamed about the subject of "emotions," which were blobs being investigated in a laboratory. The study of the blob required much understanding and patience but, in the dream, just as she began to think that she had discovered it, got hold of it, she found that it had gone inside her. In the second dream, Emma reported that a clear plastic dome-like thing was wrapped around her and, then, the wrapping went inside her. These dreams suggest the process of internalization, of taking in, and the idea that there is a receptive space in her mind to hold her emotions. Further, from Emma's associations, these dreams appear to have reflected her assessment of her development in her analysis. She believed that she started her therapy as an undifferentiated blob, identified with her primary "bad" maternal object, which she murdered again and again, leaving her ashamed and guilty and unable to internalize a helpful object. Emma's experience of receptivity (her analyst as someone who took her in mentally) began a process of identification that permitted the recovery of the lost "good" object (Brenman).

The above transformation came about through her internalization of an aspect of the therapeutic function where in the intersubjective encounter she takes in the receptive, understanding and exploratory stance towards her – this, of course, is "maternal" in the usual way it is understood in the psychoanalytic literature, but it is also, I suggest, something more, as it brings to life an identification with learning and enquiry; animates a space for Klein's epistemological instinct,[6] perhaps. This other element, that is not the usual paternal function, might be akin to what the French psychoanalyst Marilia Aisenstein describes as a virile but non-phallic identification that inculcates an interest, an agency in learning in women – although I would hope we can find terms that do not hinge so closely off our binary language that references and restates the masculine as the privileged site of enculturation. Aisenstein links this identification in her clinical material to the patient's retrieved memory of a helpful male family member. While she does allow for bisexual aspects of the mother, this important representation gets given to the work of "a particular form of paternal identification in women" as she entitles her paper (27). She writes: "I believe in the importance of a symbolic passage in which the father, representing a paternal order or community, is internalised" (36). From my clinical material, I want to suggest that the inculcation of identification with learning and curiosity can also arise from identification with a "taking in" figure (who is elaborated as feminine in the associative chain of binary pairings) and the symbolization of the receptive maternal function which differs from the immersion in the dynamics with the pre-Oedipal maternal object. With symbolization of this function, there develops the capacity to observe and think about the question of "inside"; it opens a space for the representation of a symbolic presence in the mind.

vignette four

In the third year of her analysis, Emma was more aware of the contradictory parts of her personality – aware that she both felt "superior" in one part and "inferior" in another. She described having an "unthinking servant" and a "dictator" in her. For her, the "unthinking servant" represented one of the "line of freaks," that is, a nervous, crazy woman whose aggression and sexuality has to be controlled or quashed by the "dictator." Further, when entertaining the idea of a relationship with a boy, she described feeling unsafe as she felt it was "bad" and "sinful" to flirt. She imagined being "five" or "twenty-five," not "fifteen" (her actual age), as, for her, five meant asexual and twenty-five meant married and also asexual. During this time, she also began to experience my presence differently, saying "I can't expect you to be a shadow of me," that is, a narcissistic extension of her, and began to see her analyst as an "ordinary" person who can manage everyday tasks, for example talking on the telephone and driving. Are these named activities also code for her awareness of the mother/analyst as an ordinary sexual woman? Florence Guignard refers to the "scandal of the mother's sexuality" that can evoke envy and jealousy in relation to the Oedipal mother but also, importantly, "her right to possess her own reproductive organs evokes in every daughter a much deeper sensitivity that brings to mind the splendid term 'memories in feelings' devised by Klein" (116).

vignette five

At the beginning of the fourth year of her analysis, Emma was struggling with feelings of depression which were connected to her recognition of her contradictory states of mind. She said that she both wished and feared going mad: "sometimes I wish I would have a nervous breakdown ... to go into my mind ... no worries ... peace ... walk around in a daze." Emma recalled a fragment of a dream: "a painted Chinese face." Her associations were to a Chinese woman who had served her recently in a shop. Emma remembered that the woman "made a big deal" of obtaining accurate information from another store about the product that she wanted to purchase. Emma would have preferred to take the product without "fuss." A second association was to a figurine with a painted black and white face, which was a valued gift from recent work experience. She talked of not liking black, as it reminded her of the "black blob." Emma's dream fragment gives a helpful insight into her transferential experience, that is, she saw her analyst as offering a rather foreign encounter (the Chinese face[7]) in which care is taken to understand her needs – but the work of understanding is difficult and painful. Emma's experience of care, then, is laced with ambivalence because "fuss" disrupts the "daze" state of mind which is an antidote to mourning with its working through the phantasy of omnipotent completeness. In the dream association of the painted black and white face of the figurine, a valued gift, the opposition between the black uncontained blob and the white "goodie, goodie" light-reflecting pattern-free surface is portrayed. This opposition is now progressively represented in a verbal and symbolic form rather than non-verbally as it was at the beginning of her therapy with her broken physical body and the unisex picture which lacked detail and difference. The "Chinese face" standing for an encounter with otherness (foreignness) represents a third position from which to observe and "face" the "black/white" conflict. Of interest, Emma refers to the idea of "painted" both in the dream fragment and in the association of the figurine. It is as if "painted" captures the analytic representational work of creatively holding the tension between linking thoughts and emotions and the breakdown of thought and value. Perhaps, the possibility of allowing conflicts, anxieties, fears and hopes to stand side by side rather than the need to repudiate one or other side.

case discussion

Emma, angry and distressed about the fragility of her inner and external objects, needed to deny her development as a female along with sexual differentiation (the sameness drawing); it just was not a safe psychic position. At the outset of her psychoanalytic journey, Emma was unable to represent her deeper subjective experience in thought as, I suggest, it was too disturbing for her to "think" about alone. With her "thin" speech and crippled body, she performed her brokenness and her sense that she was not properly human but a passive victim, a freak. She needed to denude herself of her agency and aggression, fearing and wishing to "murder" her objects who would not survive. To hide the "murder" and avoid retaliation, she became the frail helpless sick one that she so hated. Initially, she was trapped in unrelenting cycles of projection and introjection, without another mind to help contain her disturbing emotional experiences.

From the beginning, Emma related to her analyst "as if" she was either an extension of herself (two inadequate broken girls) or she carried Emma's own critical self-judgement. No sense of separateness was possible; no other as other. We see by the third vignette that she is able to find a different way to understand femininity, that is, to represent femininity as receptivity which offers (ambivalently for her) a resource with which to think. The dreams suggest a capacity to take in/internalize and convey the imaginative development of an inner mental space that structures and holds conflicts, sexuality, aggression, ambiguity and ambivalence. We might say she dreams the possibility of Bion's container/contained through the ongoing receptive presence of her analyst. Kristeva writes: "Kleinian negativity, which, as we shall see, guides the drive to intelligence by way of fantasy, chooses the mother as its target: in order to think, one must first lose the mother" (*Melanie Klein* 130).

Emma arrived at her therapy caught in a hysterical impasse. She was unconsciously identified and refusing identification with a (maternal) object/other moulded in phantasy and reality with transgenerational gendered meanings. Her rendering of what it meant to be a woman was disturbing and was unable to be contained in thought. With the development of the capacity for thought through the use of another, a psychoanalyst, to hold and mentally work with her initially projected anxieties, she was able to symbolize her terrors and, in doing so, she re-connected with her desire to learn and to move, to walk and relate with emotion.

Emma's story is told through the action of words; "the talking cure" as Anna O. termed it. The language, however, works to carry affects, action and embodiment, as well as the abstract, symbolic meaning of words. When Emma first spoke, her talk was grey, disembodied and apparently without texture and pattern. Her sense of damage and fear was carried literally in her crippled body. As her analysis progressed, her speech became embodied, evoking feelings and thoughts and reverberating with imagery and meaning. Language, as Vivona describes, carries the dual effects of receptivity to the embodied aspects of communication and the ordering effects of symbolization. In Kristeva's language, the analysand's language becomes both more semiotic and more symbolic, with the semiotic and symbolic linking and relating rather than moving from the semiotic to the symbolic. In telling her story from bodily symptom to the representation of a receptive inner space, Emma's use of language became both expressive and reflective.

memorializing oedipus?

As Charles Hanly writes, notions of the third in philosophy relate to an "outside" position that allows an engagement with the question of rationality. In psychoanalysis, the "third" and its various nomenclatures refers to the third-party role that instigates the separation in the early relationship between parent (usually mother) and child. The third can refer to the structural account (most notably associated with the French psychoanalytic model) that claims the paternal function goes before and eclipses lived experience or it can refer to the more personal lived Oedipal father and be linked to family relationships. Freud argued that the father, and, in his later works, the more abstract paternal function, was at the forefront of the construction of individual subjectivity, permitting entry into the symbolic and cultural realm. The Freudian Oedipus complex takes as its starting point the themes of incest and patricide portrayed in Sophocles' family tragedy, *Oedipus Rex*. As has been well argued, the Oedipal narrative gives a neat explanation of the theory of cultural and symbolic parenthood that restates or reflects, depending on your sensibility, a patriarchal world-view. Freud wrote:

> This turning from the mother to the father points in addition to a victory of intellectuality over sensuality – that is, an advance in civilization, since maternity is proved by the evidence of the senses while paternity is a hypothesis, based on inference and a premise. (Freud, "Moses" 114)

The work of enculturation is given to the representation of the father – the Law, Phallus, the father of personal pre-history and so on. This is an account of the symbolic paternal function, for example Rosine Perelberg's interesting work on differentiating the murdered father and the dead father – and not an account of actual parenting arrangements. But we often get a slippage into the concrete which privileges the masculine (and men) as standing for representation and language – as in, for example, the work of Ron Britton where he offers very helpful clinical accounts but, then, often collapses the distinction between the level of clinico-description and conceptualization – from actual family situations to conceptualizations (see Gyler). Butler (*Undoing Gender*) takes this argument further, suggesting that the distinction between the social and symbolic law cannot be sustained as the symbolic is grounded in social practices. In these accounts, the mother gets to do the work of the pre-symbolic function, as in, for example, Kristeva's *New Maladies of the Soul* (1993) where the inability to represent is associated with the deficient paternal function.

The intervention of the third structuring function (an intervention in the mother–child dyadic relationship that facilitates the development of separateness; the role of otherness to the parent–child dyadic relationship is traditionally given to the "father") inaugurates the loss of a narcissistic sense of completeness in both sexes. In the Freudian account, the place of the girl's developmental moment tied to the recognition of anatomical difference has been even more precarious. Janine Chasseguet-Smirgel, in her influential assessment of Freudian theory of female sexuality, famously wrote of the litany of lacks:

> Female sexuality is therefore a series of lacks: the lack of vagina, lack of a penis, lack of a specific sexuality, lack of adequate erotic object, and finally the lacks which are implied by her being devoid of any intrinsic feminine qualities which she could cathect directly and by her being forced to give up the clitoris, we can add the relative lack of superego and the capacity for sublimation. (281)

Buchberg has recently argued that Freud's account offers a brilliant reflection on melancholia and narcissistic vulnerability in the girl becoming a woman. She deploys Lena Dunham's HBO television series *Girls* to illustrate that the girl's entrance into the positive Oedipus complex is based on unconscious grievance and unmourned loss of infantile relationship with the mother. In his heteronormative narrative of the girl's Oedipal developmental phase, Freud grandly concluded: "This step in development does not involve a simple change of object. The turning away from the mother is accompanied by hostility: the attachment to the mother ends in hate" ("New Introductory Lectures" 121).

In addition to the account of lacks and negativity in the Freudian account, the role of the maternal function is shadowy and, of course, the maternal body is castrated and damaged. The project to recover a more complex and satisfying account of female subjectivity started in the 1920s, for example the work of Klein, Horney, etc., and in recent accounts that juxtapose femininity as lack with a more bodily-based account of femininity (see, for example, Birksted-Breen, "Holding"; Balsam, *Women's Bodies*); nevertheless, this invaluable project has always been problematic. It has struggled to cast off the moorings of biological essentialism, and, as we know, essentialism cuts in all directions for the interests of women.

women's representational journey?

At the outset, Emma appeared to offer a double communication. She repudiated in her unconscious mind any notion of sexual difference and denied the reality of the Oedipal moment with its loss of imaginary completeness. At the same time, her body tells another narrative. She unconsciously enacts through her bodily symptom her sense of inner immobilization founded on her "damaged" maternal and feminine identifications. Her deep sense of the inadequacy and brokenness mimics the Freudian Oedipal resolution for the girl of femininity as lack. So the girl's melancholic journey motivated by shame and envy, as Emma portrayed, produces little of positive value "to stir the fancy." And we see writ large the close theoretical association between hysterical impasse and female development. In the classical psychoanalytic account, the maternal as being discussed belongs to the pre-Oedipal and pre-symbolic realm. Rosemary Balsam cogently argues:

> Calling the early phases of development preoedipal, unfortunately, has turned out to so foreclose and pathologize our knowledge of "unseparated" states with the mother that we have been unable to explore progressive maturation within that relation, rather than simply labelling "mother and child" as necessarily regressive, regressed or pathologically fixated mental states. ("Oedipus Rex" 572)

In the case study, I attempted to track the shifts in Emma's states of mind; from a split one with states of fusion, un-differentiation, fear and persecution to one that reflects separateness, inside and outside and the representation of inner space that holds conflict, ambivalence and ambiguity. This suggests that the girl's development does not entirely rely on, to put it simply, the need to abandon her mother as a love object and to substitute her with the father in order to enter into the symbolic realm. I propose that the symbolic representation of an inner receptive space with the potentiality to contain "something" signifies a significant restructuring moment in the girl's psychic life. This representation of an inner receptive space is a necessary precondition for the development of thinking; it allows an articulation of a symbolic dimension of femininity.

Crucially for women, the nature of their maternal and feminine identification forged in bodily phantasy, transgenerational memory traces and lived experience plays an important role in facilitating and/or impeding representation of inner receptive space. I argue that the representation of inner space with its allusions to the female procreative body allows a psychic resource that supports women's sense of agency and worth. Perhaps the development of agency and worth can sometimes have a more circuitous and hazardous developmental trajectory for women than men whose bodily appearance has historically equated with the phallus in the "have/have not" binary. This line of thinking leads to a series of questions: what is the symbolic status of the representation of the maternal in our psychic and theoretical economies? Can it carry another aspect of the symbolic world that gets overshadowed in our account of the paternal function, standing as it does for limit, boundary and intelligibility? Or, as Jacqueline Schaeffer asks: "Can the female sex be symbolized and be brought into the mental sphere?" (140).

concluding thoughts

It is through the clinical encounter that we can vividly sense the importance of maternal discourse by listening to the unconscious and/or out-of-awareness and sometimes non-verbal communications of our analysands. This case vignette speaks to the production of gendered meanings, commonly specific to women, associated with problems in female agency, creativity and ambition (Elise; Harris, "Aggression, Envy"; "Aggression"; "Mothers"). Emma's aggression ultimately collapses back in on herself. This problem, too, is associated with the meaning of the maternal object. The symbolized maternal object rests upon Klein's understanding of mourning and Kristeva's notion of femininity as receptivity. I am also asking whether the necessary separation from the archaic mother constitutes a more nuanced process than the move to the father (however conceptualized). If we conceive a less linear approach to pre-Oedipal and Oedipal desire, as

Klein did, with heterogeneous desires folding into one another, can we represent a more complex version of the mother and of femininity as receptivity? Does the maternal always need to be located as pre-Oedipal, as a pre-symbolic function, in our psychic and theoretical economies? Can, for example, the internalization of the analytic function through the transference and countertransference experience which symbolizes the receptive interior space that holds ambiguity, uncertainty, loss and mourning, complicate the discourse of the maternal? Would this bring a different approach to intelligibility?

disclosure statement

No potential conflict of interest was reported by the author.

notes

I am grateful to Pelagia Goulimari, Louise Braddock, Sylvia Martin and Gill Straker for their helpful comments on an earlier version of this paper.

1 I don't use "resolving" here as I believe these struggles are continually required to be reworked.

2 The analysand, Emma, was referred to in *The Gendered Unconscious* (157–59) to highlight issues concerning femininity and aggression.

3 I was to learn from Emma's perspective that she (mis)believed that any angry, "out of control" moments could only be survived by men without risk of breakdown.

4 In discussing the criteria for terminating a psychoanalysis, Klein wrote:

> Two features are usually emphasized in this connection, growth in stability and in the sense of reality, but I hold that expansion in the depth of the ego is essential as well. An intrinsic element of a deep and full personality is wealth of phantasy life and the capacity for experiencing emotions freely. ("On the Criteria" 45–46)

5 While authors use the term "feminine dimension" differently, it usually refers to identification with women's maternal, procreative and sexual aspects.

6 For Bion, the desire for learning and knowledge has comparable importance in the construction of subjectivity as the capacity to love and hate (*Learning*; "Theory").

7 Emma and her analyst are of Caucasian appearance.

bibliography

Aisenstein, Marilia. "A Particular Form of Paternal Identification in Women." *The Psychoanalytic Quarterly* LXXXI.1 (2012): 27–37. Print.

Balsam, Rosemary H. "Oedipus Rex: Where Are We Going, Especially with Females?" *The Psychoanalytic Quarterly* LXXXIV.3 (2015): 555–88. Print.

Balsam, Rosemary H. *Women's Bodies in Psychoanalysis*. New York: Routledge, 2012. Print.

Bion, Wilfred R. "Attacks on Linking." 1959. *Second Thoughts: Selected Papers on Psychoanalysis*. London: Maresfield, 1967. 93–109. Print.

Bion, Wilfred R. *Learning from Experience*. London: Heinemann, 1962. Print.

Bion, Wilfred R. "A Theory of Thinking." 1962. *Second Thoughts: Selected Papers on Psychoanalysis*. London: Maresfield, 1967. 110–119. Print.

Birksted-Breen, Dana. "Holding the Tension." *Female Sexuality: Contemporary Engagements*. Ed. D. Bassin. Northvale, NJ: Aronson, 1999. 281–86. Print.

Birksted-Breen, Dana. *The Work of Psychoanalysis: Sexuality, Time and the Psychoanalytic Mind*. London: Routledge, 2016. Print.

Brenman, Eric. *Recovery of the Lost Good Object*. Ed. and intro. G.F. Spoto. London: Routledge, 2006. Print.

Britton, Ron. *Belief and Imagination: Explorations in Psychoanalysis*. London: Routledge, 1998. Print.

Buchberg, Lisa. "Oedipus in Brooklyn: Reading Freud on Women, Watching Lena Durham's Girls." *The Psychoanalytic Quarterly* LXXXIII.1 (2014): 121–50. Print.

Butler, Judith. *Gender Trouble: Feminism and the Subversion of Identity*. New York: Routledge, 1990. Print.

Butler, Judith. *Undoing Gender*. New York: Routledge, 2004. Print.

Chasseguet-Smirgel, Janine. "Freud and Female Sexuality: Blind Spots in the 'Dark Continent.'" *International Journal of Psychoanalysis* 57.2 (1976): 275–86. Print.

Elise, Diane. "Sex and Shame: The Inhibition of Female Desire." *Journal of the American Psychoanalytic Association* 56.1 (2008): 73–98. Print.

Freud, Sigmund. "Moses and Monotheism." 1939. *The Standard Edition of the Complete Psychological Works of Sigmund Freud*. Vol. XXIII. London: Hogarth and Institute of Psycho-Analysis, 1953–74. 1–138. Print.

Freud, Sigmund. "New Introductory Lectures on Psychoanalysis." 1933. *The Standard Edition of the Complete Psychological Works of Sigmund Freud*. Vol. XXII. London: Hogarth and Institute of Psycho-Analysis, 1953–74. 1–182. Print.

Freud, Sigmund. "The Question of Lay Analysis." 1926. *The Standard Edition of the Complete Psychological Works of Sigmund Freud*. Vol. XX. London: Hogarth and Institute of Psycho-Analysis, 1953–74. 177–250. Print.

Freud, Sigmund. "Remembering, Repeating and Working-Through (Further Recommendations on the Technique of Psycho-Analysis II)." 1914. *The Standard Edition of the Complete Psychological Works of Sigmund Freud*. Vol. XII. London: Hogarth and Institute of Psycho-Analysis, 1953–74. 145–56. Print.

Glocer Fiorini, Leticia. "The Analyst's Meta-theories Concerning Sexual Difference and the Feminine." Glocer Fiorini and Abelin-Sas Rose 79–96. Print.

Glocer Fiorini, Leticia, and Graciela Abelin-Sas Rose, eds. *On Freud's "Femininity."* London: Karnac, 2010. Print.

Guignard, Florence. "Envy in Western Society: Today and Tomorrow." *Envy and Gratitude Revisited*. Ed. P. Roth and A. Lemma. London: International Psychoanalytic Association, 2008. 109–23. Print.

Gyler, Louise. *The Gendered Unconscious: Can Gender Discourses Subvert Psychoanalysis?* London: Routledge, 2010. Print.

Hanly, Charles. "The Third Position: A Brief Historical Analysis of an Idea." *The Psychoanalytic Quarterly* LXXIII.1 (2004): 267–90. Print.

Harris, Adrienne. "Aggression, Envy and Ambition: Circulating Tensions in Women's Psychic Life." *Gender and Psychoanalysis* 2.3 (1997): 291–325. Print.

Harris, Adrienne. "Aggression: Pleasures and Dangers." *Psychoanalytic Inquiry* 18 (1998): 31–44. Print.

Harris, Adrienne. "Mothers, Monsters, Mentors." *Studies in Gender and Sexuality* 3.3 (2002): 281–95. Print.

Horney, Karen. "The Flight from Womanhood: The Masculinity Complex in Women, as Viewed by Men and Women." 1925. *Female Sexuality: The Early Psychoanalytical Controversies*. Ed. R. Grigg, D. Hecq, and C. Smith. London: Rebus, 1999. 107–21. Print.

Jacobus, Mary. *First Things*. New York and London: Routledge, 1995. Print.

Klein, Melanie. *Envy and Gratitude and Other Works 1946–1963*. London: Karnac, 1993. Print.

Klein, Melanie. "Notes on Some Schizoid Mechanisms." 1946. Klein, *Envy and Gratitude* 1–24. Print.

Klein, Melanie. "On the Criteria for the Termination of a Psycho-Analysis." 1950. Klein, *Envy and Gratitude* 43–47. Print.

Kristeva, Julia. "From Symbols to Flesh: The Polymorphous Destiny of Narration." *International Journal of Psychoanalysis* 61.4 (2000): 771–87. Print.

Kristeva, Julia. *Melanie Klein*. New York: Columbia UP, 2001. Print.

Kristeva, Julia. *New Maladies of the Soul*. 1993. New York: Columbia UP, 1995. Print.

Layton, Lynne. *Who's That Girl? Who's That Boy? Clinical Practice Meets Postmodern Gender Theory*. Northvale, NJ: Aronson, 1998. Print.

Ogden, Thomas H. "Bion's Four Principles of Mental Functioning." *Fort Da* 14 (2008): 11–35. Print.

Perelberg, Rosine J. *Murdered Father, Dead Father: Revisiting the Oedipus Complex*. London: Routledge, 2015. Print.

Schaeffer, Jacqueline. "The Riddle of the Repudiation of Femininity: The Scandal of the Feminine Dimension." Glocer Fiorini and Abelin-Sas Rose 129–43. Print.

Showalter, Elaine. *The Female Malady: Women, Madness and English Culture, 1830–1980*. London: Virago, 1985. Print.

Vivona, Jeanine M. "Introduction: How Does Talking Cure?" *Journal of the American Psychoanalytic Association* 62.6 (2014): 1025–27. Print.

Woolf, Virginia. *A Room of One's Own*. 1929. St Albans: Triad Panther, 1977. Print.

Louise Gyler

talia bettcher
pelagia goulimari

THEORIZING CLOSENESS

a trans feminist conversation

Pelagia Goulimari: The title of this edited collection is Women Writing Across Cultures *so I want to start with "woman." Beauvoir emphasized the constructed nature of "woman" and the weight of "situation." More recently Foucault-inspired archaeological and genealogical critiques of "woman" explored implicit presuppositions and rules for the discursive production of "woman": for example, Hortense J. Spillers ("Mama's Baby") and Ellen K. Feder (*Family Bonds, *2007) focused on the role of race, Judith Butler on compulsory/normative heterosexuality and genders as polar opposites. The main aim of such critiques is, it seems to me, to contribute to the democratizing, pluralizing, opening-up of the meanings of "woman" and the gender practices involved. What is announced – as a tendency rhizomatically connecting some feminist, queer and transgender theory and practice – is an ontological and epistemological pluralism boldly legitimizing and constellating local, "disqualified" or "subjugated" knowledges. Here your work on the "existence of multiple worlds of sense," developing the work of María Lugones, has been very fruitful.*

In "Trapped in the Wrong Theory: Rethinking Trans Oppression and Resistance" (2014) you wrote: "I simply found friendship and love in the activist trans subcultures of Los Angeles. There we had developed alternative ways of living gender that felt far more safe and healthy" (384). You affirmed "the resistance inherent in the self-identities of trans people, particularly for those who claim to be men and women [...] [W]hen a trans woman says 'I'm a woman' and her body is precisely the kind of body taken to invalidate a claim to womanhood in mainstream culture, the claim is true in some trans subcultures because the meaning of the word 'woman' is different; its very meaning is under contestation" (388–89). You argued that "it is precisely" the "foreclosure of the multiplicity of interpretations [of 'woman' and 'trans'] that allows for abstraction from the multiplicity of oppressions" (401). You insisted on "the existence of multiple worlds of sense, worlds in which terms such as 'woman' have different, resistant meanings; worlds in which there exist different, resistant gender practices" (403). You concluded that this is "analogous to the use of political expressions such as [...]

'women of color' – expressions invested with meanings or perhaps potentials for meaning that are both lived in resistant opposition to dominant meanings and at the same time open ended and multiple" (403–04). I should add that your discussion of "resistance" has been inextricable from your analysis of sexism, transphobia and what you call "reality enforcement" – especially the "maximal intermeshing of oppressions" targeting "trans women of color" (395) (also discussed by Muñoz, Halberstam, Shakhsari, DarkMatter and others). Would you agree that using these terms does not mean *subscribing to the priority of gender over race, class, ethnicity, sexuality?*

Talia Bettcher: I don't think using expressions like "woman" and "trans woman" *has to* mean subscribing to the priority of gender. But it could mean that. So much depends upon who is using the terms, how they are using the terms, and why they are using the terms. The expressions are *English* expressions. So there's already the issue of linguistic hegemony. Must English expressions always have English meanings? Not when they are used in resistance to such hegemony in a US context. They might be used to carry both English and Spanish meanings at once, that is, hegemonic meaning, plus what Lugones calls "a second order meaning" (*Pilgrimages/Peregrinajes*). For those of us who don't always see the *English* in our English expressions, we may mistakenly believe we are dealing with fixed and entirely transparent meanings.

I certainly reject any view that sees "woman" as merely naming a category that applies to individuals based upon perceived sexual (i.e., reproductive) capacities, oppressed on the basis of their being so categorized as *women.* It's clear that the term "woman" is implicated in *multiple* oppressions. Consider, for example, Lugones's view that "woman" (and "man") functioned to locate non-white, non-European peoples outside of the realm of the human – that is, as female (or male), but not necessarily women or men (i.e., humans) ("Toward a Decolonial Feminism"). Or consider the ways in which the meaning of "woman" can centralize white or straight as paradigm. Given the multiple ways in which the deployment of "woman" can function to oppress or marginalize, there are invariably multiple resistant resignifications of the term – reclaimings that contest various modes of oppression and marginalization. This suggests that taking terms like "woman" as the firm starting point for a feminist analysis, with the meaning fully fixed, is a questionable move. Given the multiplicity of meaning, what is the meaning one is presupposing?

In my view, the endorsement of a multiple-meanings model is essential to understanding trans oppression/resistance. Trans oppression/resistance simply *cannot* be well formulated in a categorical model of oppression. Typically, trans people are *not* oppressed because they are placed into the category "trans." On the contrary, trans men are oppressed in having their existential identities annihilated through placement within the category "woman" and trans women are oppressed in having their existential identities annihilated through placement in the category "man." In such instances of transphobia the term "trans" may not even be salient. To put it crudely, it doesn't usually go down like this: "Hey, look, a transgender person! Let's go harass them!" It typically goes down like this: "Hey, look, a man in a dress! Let's go harass him!" Indeed, the very interpretation of "trans woman" and "trans man" is up for grabs in instances of transphobia and resistance. To some they may mean "man who lives as a woman" and "woman who lives as a man." To trans people, of course, the expressions will mean something entirely different. But the point is this: once interpretation becomes so central to an account of oppression and resistance, category-based accounts of oppression/resistance can't get off the ground.

I see the "categorical gesture" – the move to fix the meaning of expressions like "woman," "trans," "person of color," and so forth – as a gesture of control. If you think about it, it's a bizarre thought that one can fix the meaning of terms once and for all – declare that this is what they mean or ought to mean. To be sure, if one's meanings are backed up with institutions, if one has the cultural capital, one can certainly guarantee one's meaning will be hegemonic. But it's delusional to think that one can control meanings absolutely. Political terms will always be used differently, resistantly, in contestation to hegemonic meaning.

Lugones sees this impulse to control (what I'm calling the categorical gesture) as dogging attempts to frame intersectionality itself in terms of overlapping categories (*Pilgrimages/Peregrinajes*; "Toward a Decolonial Feminism"). If we proceed to outline vectors of oppression that target people belonging to specific categories and then attempt to formulate a genuinely intersectional account based upon that starting point, we have already foreclosed some possibilities of resistance ("Toward a Decolonial Feminism"). In so far as "woman" centralizes white women and "black" centralizes black men, no room has been provided for a locus of resistance for black women. Only resistant meaning that contests the purity of the categories can allow that "black woman" can be posited in resistant response to the fragmentation effected by the categories.

This makes it all very complicated. Resistant deployments of the term "woman" typically involve second-order meanings that are closely wedded to a specific, concrete history of oppression. As a consequence, they may also perpetuate other forms of oppression. The resistant claiming of black womanhood, the response to racist marginalization or outright denial of personhood, can replicate a deployment that excludes trans women. The resistant claiming of (black) trans womanhood, then, may intervene in the oppressive denial of trans identities not merely at the level of racist and transphobic deployments of woman but also at the level of racially resistant reclamations of womanhood. One of the things this means is that some (white) trans deployments of "woman" that resist only an (apparently) non-racially inflected form of trans oppression can elide the complex resistant work that other trans deployments of "woman" (as in "trans woman of color") are doing while simultaneously deploying a racially hegemonic meaning of "woman." This suggests the importance of meaning openness, that is to say, the willingness to break up one's own possibly hardened, petrified resistant significations, the recognition that these terms may not always mean what one supposes they mean.

Rather than viewing "woman" as a category (of gender), I prefer to think of various discursive practices in which "woman" is deployed with some significance. I see such practices as implicated in complex extra-linguistic social practices, both oppressive and resistant. Terms like "banker" and "fashion model," for example, cannot be extricated from the extra-linguistic practices that effectively constitute bankers and fashion models. Much of my work has been an attempt to get a handle on some of the abusive extra-linguistic practices that help constitute "woman" and "man" – the practices that provide the context for the linguistic deployments that are interwoven with this. I see such a project as operating at a different level of analysis ("one level down") since it does not proceed with a more abstract formulation of category-based oppression. Instead, it examines such practices in terms of structures of violence and abuse.

For me, one of the most important forms of structural violence against trans people (reality enforcement) is the consequence of the way in which gender presentation is taken to communicate genital status. I see this communicative feature as inherently abusive as it compels euphemistic disclosures of intimate information. I see "trans" as a potentially resistant intervention into this practice – a refusal to disclose.

You're right that, for me, it has been important to situate this representational relation within a broader context of oppressions (e.g., sexism, racism). One must begin with the facts: In the United States, for example, trans women of color are at the greatest risk for the gravest forms of reality enforcement. One can, of course, correctly point to the multiplicity of oppressions in such cases (sexism, racism, classism, transphobia) that converge to create such a state of affairs. But I am also interested in a more integrated account. In what sense are the conditions for reality enforcement the same conditions for (hetero)sexist forms of sexual violence and racist violence? Is there an account of reality enforcement which exposes any characterization of it in terms of transphobia, sexism, or racism as already relying on illicit abstraction? For example, I have argued that the system whereby gender presentation communicates genital status is the same non-verbal communicative system that facilitates (hetero-) sexual manipulation and that justifies (hetero-) sexual violence. So to call the conditions of reality enforcement *sexist and transphobic* is to miss the way in which such description involves an abstract separation into aspects of something that isn't separate in that way.

PG: Let me now turn to the question of trans feminism. Your work seems to explore the interconnectedness and irreducibility of different forms of oppression, also the dialogue *and* interaction *between non-trans feminism, queer theory and transgender theory, while they remain distinct (see, for example, your Introduction, co-written with Ann Garry, to the* Hypatia *special issue* Transgender Studies and Feminism *in 2009). What are the main issues involved, in your view?*

TB: "Trans feminism" is going to mean different things and do different work depending upon the local histories of oppression to which it is a response. The work that "transfeminismo" does in Spain and in some Latin American contexts cannot be easily reduced to the work that "trans feminism" does in the United States and the United Kingdom, for example.

Most of my own work on the topic is situated in the US context. In my opinion, the most important issue is the considerable harassment, abuse, and violence to which trans women, particularly trans women of color, poor trans women, trans women who do sex-work, are subject. Now your question, I think, concerns negotiating the tension between *interconnectedness* and *dialogue*. So I'd like to distinguish between the historical, genealogical realities which underlie the development of different theories and politics, on the one hand, and the deeper difficulties negotiating the intersections and divergences of multiple oppressions, on the other. I've already discussed the latter, so I'll say a little bit about the former.

Historically, transgender theory and politics arose in the United States in the nineties in direct response to the exclusionary and outright transphobic nature of (non-trans) feminism – particularly lesbian separatist feminism. Of course, these days the tensions between trans feminists and anti-trans feminists are simply through the roof. While I have no faith that one can convince the virulent transphobe, feminist or otherwise, I do worry about the gap between political visions. Some of my dear friends were pioneers in the lesbian feminist movement way back in the day when Beth Elliott's presence caused such an uproar at the West Coast Lesbian Conference in 1973. I have benefited from long conversations which have helped sharpen my worries about the current state of trans feminism in the United States. I have worried about the monolithic representation of lesbian feminists. And I have worried about possible foreclosures of insight and historical amnesia.

Because it was imperative that trans oppression be characterized as a mode of gender-based oppression distinct from sexist oppression, it is perhaps not surprising that the "beyond-the-binary" view came into prominence (the view that trans people are positioned outside of the gender binaries and oppressed by the insistence on a binary opposition between man and woman). Unfortunately, this led to several consequences.

First, since in this model it is tough to see identification *within* the binary (e.g., *as* a woman) as at all resistant, the possibilities for a genuinely intersectional trans feminism – one that sees trans women as located at the intersection of sexist and transphobic forms of violence – seem entirely foreclosed. In the absence of a theoretical underpinning, it is perhaps unsurprising that we have seen some trans feminisms that seem a tad too individualistic, touting the freedom to gender identify and express without paying much attention to the relational nature of gender and therefore the ethico-political constraints on identification and expression. I'm drawing here on Cressida Heyes's notion of an ethics of self-transformation (Heyes). My own work has been, in part, an attempt to articulate an account of trans oppression/resistance that answers such concerns.

I have also been concerned that the mere inclusion of trans women within the feminist purview by well-meaning non-trans women has not led to a change in their own self-identities. I think this is absolutely necessary for there to be a meaningful trans feminism that brings together trans women, non-trans women, and others. The alternative meanings and the alternative gender practices that underlie trans self-identification as "woman" expose the way dominant deployments of "woman" can invalidate or marginalize trans people. It becomes necessary, then, for all who would be allies to rethink their own self-identifies, rethink their claims on womanhood and the meanings that underlie those claims.

PG: One of the areas of dialogue and interaction across non-trans feminism, queer theory and transgender theory is around local knowledge, local theory, self-theorizing. For example, in "Trapped in the Wrong Theory" you theorize from what you call "my local knowledge" (384). To me this attitude inherits and develops Barbara Christian's insights in her 1987 essay "The Race for Theory," where she reads texts by African-American women writers as self-theorizing, in dialogue with the self-theorizing practice of African-American women writers of her generation, for example Toni Morrison. As a philosopher, what does "local knowledge" mean to you?

TB: If we begin with the thesis of ontological pluralism, then we recognize that there are multiple experiences of *the everyday* (or, rather, *multiple everydays*). By "the everyday" I simply mean the world as it presents itself to us as we try our best to get through the business of life. I see local knowledge as, in part, a knowledge of a specific, local everyday. We have intuitions about what is true and false, we have "know how" in terms of negotiating the social practices of that everyday. There is a "common sense" in that social reality that may be absurd in others.

Traditionally, "local knowledge" and philosophy have not gone very well together. Indeed, local philosophizing seems rather like an oxymoron. Philosophy has, after all, been so interested in making claims about the world that are universal in nature. Once one starts to philosophize from marginalized local knowledge, such pretensions must immediately be relinquished. One's philosophizing can only deliver results that are at best partial and likely distorted. That's okay, I think, once we recognize that this business is a collaborative affair. No one gets to have the final word.

I *do* think that all philosophizing proceeds from some local knowledge of an everyday regardless of whether that is acknowledged. Philosophers typically don't have much to go on. They have the existing literature and they have their capacity for critical analysis and argumentation. But that isn't going to be enough if they want there to be some sort of engagement with the world. I mean, it's not as if most philosophers do a lot of empirical studies. So they invariably rely on their own experiences about how the world works. And that plays a crucial methodological role, recognized or not, in what sort of philosophy they do and what sort of results they get.

In Analytic Philosophy, for example, "philosophical intuitions" play a big role in conceptual analysis – projects that attempt to answer questions like "what is knowledge?" or "what is a woman?" These intuitions often concern the standard or correct deployment of the relevant terms within ordinary contexts. But, of course, if one operates in a resistant subculture where the linguistic practices are different, one's intuitions about what makes sense are going to differ. What philosophical intuitions should we take seriously? This is both a political and a methodological question. Because philosophy doesn't usually ask such questions, it ends up taking for granted the intuitions that arise solely in dominant worlds. It might therefore be worth distinguishing the local knowledge that is invisible to itself as local, and the local knowledge that is well aware of its locatedness precisely because it is a knowledge formed in resistance to dominant and oppressive ways of knowing. In my view, proceeding from the latter sort of located knowledge is going to be a better strategy in getting closer to truth or at least farther away from falsity. And I take that to be an important part of the project of philosophy.

So much has to do with the *relation* between philosophizing, on the one hand, and local knowledge, on the other. Christian asks the central question "for whom are we doing what we are doing when we do literary criticism?" (61). More generally, we can ask: for whom are we theorizing or philosophizing? And what is the aim of that endeavour? Very often it turns out that philosophers are philosophizing for other philosophers. A critique is offered of some existing theory, and that critique is backed up by an alternative account. And so we get a tight circle. Jargon helps make the back-and-forth much smoother, while blocking out those who don't have access to this game. Meanwhile, the role of the philosopher's groundedness in the everyday recedes into the background. We end up with a kind of detached theoretical enterprise that is practiced for the sake of theory itself. This type of philosophy leaves me cold. I am moved by Christian when she writes: "What I write and how I write is done in order to save my own life" (ibid.). Yes. For some of us, philosophizing is about survival, not amusement. And in such cases, as hooks famously argues, there is no distinction between theory and practice.

PG: One of the implications of Christian's "self-theorizing literary text" is the permeability of the boundaries between theory, literature and life-writing, and this resonates with genre-bending experiments crossing these boundaries: Woolf's A Room of One's Own, *Wittig's* Le Corps lesbien, *Kristeva's "Stabat Mater," Lorde's* Zami, *Le Doeuff's* Hipparchia's Choice, *Preciado's* Testo Junkie *(including also Beauvoir, Irigaray, Cixous). How would you describe your own writing?*

TB: I would describe my own work as "getting there." All of my work in trans studies has flowed from my twenty years of life-experiences in LA trans communities. It is unquestionably autobiographical, even if I haven't always made that explicit. For example, "Evil Deceivers and Make-Believers" was inspired by our community response to the erasure of Gwen Araujo's identity through both mainstream media and the strategies deployed by the defense team. We saw clearly that the representation of her as "really a boy dressed as a girl" was what helped get her killed in the first place. We saw and felt the deep violence inherent in that move. My own struggles trying to formulate a theory of oppression/resistance and my dismay with both the "wrong body" and "beyond-the-binary" accounts were grounded in my experience in trans communities. The dissonance between theory and practice was breathtaking.

And it's deeply personal. I didn't start doing trans theory for the fun of it. Trying to theorize transphobic violence is a deeply depressing project. But, for me, I had to confront my own life, my own confusions about being a trans woman in a world that isn't always so friendly. Existential questions abound: Why am I? Who am I? What the heck is going on? And so I faced a choice. I could either "do philosophy" as a theoretical, professional exercise. Or I could do it in order to make sense of my life. I chose the latter.

I describe my work as "getting there" because it is only now that I have become fully prepared to make all of this completely explicit in my work. The book that I'm in the process of writing, *Personhood as Intimacy: Trans Feminist Philosophy*, mixes theory with autobiographical reflections on my experience in LA trans communities. It's important to me to reveal the locatedness of my work, the inspiration for my work, and the personal and interpersonal stakes and contexts that shape my philosophizing.

Part of this is to make explicit the underpinnings of the work, to reveal the everyday that plays such a significant methodological role in my philosophizing. But part of it also has to do with that long-standing question whether philosophy's business is just to *tell* or to also *show*. Judith Butler's "Can the 'Other' of Philosophy Speak?" really got me thinking about this.

A lot of my earliest ideas in trans philosophy emerged through my attempts at performance art. Now this was a kind of "philosophizing in theatrical space" that made good use of that space. Theatrical space is very interesting. There's a liminality between appearance and reality there that I found most useful. What I also found very useful was the way in which I self-consciously *performed* philosophy to an audience of non-philosophers, often self-effacingly. There was a way in which I was *on the spot* as a philosopher when I donned that role. And I now find myself returning to this. I've started to incorporate some more performance-based techniques into my scholarly presentations. But, more than that, I've found that as I write more and more for a multi-disciplinary audience, rather than a purely philosophical one, that I'm *on the spot again*, in this awkwardly self-conscious way. Not only do the methodological questions arise in full force (What on earth do I think I'm doing? How might it be illuminating or at least useful?), but I find myself *performing* the philosopher. I want to play with this. I think that autobiographical narrative and other forms of genre-play will help me accomplish that.

PG: Let's revisit feminist debates on "experience." In her 2010 article "Black Feminism, Poststructuralism and the Constructed Nature of Experience" Diane Perpich discussed critiques of Joan Scott's 1992 essay "Experience" by black, Latina and lesbian feminists such as Paula Moya and Mae Henderson – as well as broader critiques of poststructuralism by Barbara Christian, bell hooks and Patricia Hill Collins. When, for example, black feminists were using "autobiography" towards social theory and calling upon the "authenticity" of their "experience" against dominant/official/academic knowledge (including mainstream feminisms), they were not necessarily theoretically naïve. These calls might be read as political, where "experience" works to question canonical accounts. For example, the ex-slave Harriet Jacobs writes in her 1861 abolitionist slave-narrative: "I want to add my testimony to that of abler pens to convince the people of the Free States what Slavery really is. Only by experience can any one realize how deep, and dark, and foul is that pit of abominations" (1–2). Appeals to "experience" might be read as acts of resistance – adding a perspective that was missing, subjugated, submerged, neglected, silenced. Or they might be read as acts of creative political expression, open to multiple interpretations, including their co-optation by dominant discourses. How would you situate your own work in relation to these debates?

TB: This is a highly complex debate. So I don't think I can do justice to it now. But I do want to say a bit. While I do agree that appeals to experience of this type are often acts of resistance or creative political expressions, I don't think that that's all appeals to experience are, or at least all they can be. Here I'm speaking only of philosophy, but I think this is true of literature as well. Concerns about these appeals may be partially discipline specific. But in philosophy, I think that experience itself has *more* value than something to which one can appeal to make the erased visible, for example. There is a sense in which I would say that experience is, for the better or the worse, a starting-point. I don't know what else there is for me to go on.

Of course, I don't think that my experience gives me direct access to the world "as it really is" or anything remotely close to that. But, as I explained above, my philosophical reflections *begin* with my experience of the world. Such reflections may, of course, require that I go beyond or even rethink my experiences. But they still have to start there. It's not as if I do empirical research. If I did, I would be very interested in the experiences of various trans people. So experience would still be important.

Since I don't do empirical research, I just live my life in trans worlds and reflect on that. I try to be involved. I try my best to "world"-travel, since rather than one "world," in Los Angeles, there is something more like a confluence or constellations of "worlds." In a way, you could say that my philosophy is based on a lot of experiential data shaped in the form of a life. This gives it a first-personal quality. But it's not based on nothing.

Again, much has to do with what the theory is for and to whom it is addressed. My own reflections are personal. They flow from my attempts to orient myself, to figure out what's going on. There's a kind of disorientation that arises when one is forced to inhabit social realities that are hostile to one's very existence. Inevitably, one needs an everyday that is resistant to those realities. But one also needs to think it all through. In this way, philosophical reflection can have a very practical value. Beyond that, there's the question of audience. Is the theory addressed to those who practice hegemonic theorizing? Is it contestatory, in that way, resistantly pointing to erasures? It needn't be. One might say, "I don't care much about intervening in hegemonic theorizing. This is for others who are trying to find their way in realities that are hostile to them. My theorizing is for my *compadres*." In such cases, one does not cite experience to make it visible – it is *already* visible to theorist and reader in case it is shared or at least sufficiently analogous. The appeal to experience is less of an act or move in such cases. Rather, it's the stuff one is trying to make sense of. To be sure, it can be more complex than that. One can do different things with theory simultaneously.

I do think a case can be made that those who are seasoned practitioners of some social practice that is part of some social reality are in a better position to, at least in some sense, *understand* that social practice. After all, it's *their* social practice. To be sure, reflection and analysis may be required. But they're obviously better off than those who don't even know such practices even exist because they're blind to multiple social realities. Moreover, I think a case can be made that those who occupy both resistant and dominant social realities are in a better position to critically and with reflection describe and analyze social practices in dominant social realities. I don't see how any of this commits us to saying that experience always delivers perfect access to reality or that there is a common, homogeneous experience named by some identity-category or that these categories are not historically located.

I think it's crucial to separate these experiences and the identity-categories that are supposed to track them. In the worlds that I have traveled, many of the trans people I know are very careful to specify that they are speaking from their own experience and that they are not speaking for all trans people. Perhaps because one's personal journey is so important to how one understands and explains one's identity in these contexts, such qualifications become necessary. But there certainly isn't any reason why one needs to speak of a homogeneous group experience, let alone naturalize the categories one uses to name such groups. There are commonalities, of course. But that has less to do with shared identities and more to do with a shared social. I mean, our experiences are *of* the social. So it's no surprise that our experiences are socially constructed (given that the social is, well, socially constructed). But it's precisely *experience* that links us to the social. And without this link, theory is at grave risk of becoming unengaged with actual political struggle. And once that happens, what's the point?

PG: I want now to turn to the idea of moving "across cultures," which is in the title of this collection. In "Evil Deceivers and Make-Believers: Transphobic Violence and the Politics of Illusion" (2007) and other texts you describe the "dangerous double bind" that trans people are still confronted with in Western mainstream social contexts: "disclose 'who one is' and come out as a pretender or masquerader, or refuse to disclose (be a deceiver) and run the risk of forced disclosure, the effect of which is exposure as a liar" (50). This seems to me an existential annihilation of trans people; they are denied authenticity and deemed to be in "bad faith" whatever path they take and a priori. This is why, you have been arguing, it is so vitally important for trans people to belong to resistant countercultures and trans-friendlier contexts – and to be able to move between the mainstream world and those other worlds. There is a lot of feminist scholarship on resistant counter-public spaces and, more recently, in queer theory, Muñoz's last work on a "brown undercommons" and Halberstam's work on "wildness." You have been returning to the work of Lugones for inspiration. How have you developed Lugones and what is your current thinking on moving, writing, telling one's story "across cultures"?

TB: I have been deeply inspired by Lugones's work. No other philosopher has so thoroughly transformed me in quite the way that she has. Now Lugones herself is concerned about the possibilities of communication across distinct liminal spaces and this gets to your question about telling one's story "across cultures" ("On Complex Communication"). To put it crudely, for Lugones, there is no reason to believe that members of different resistant social realities will be able to simply understand each other: Histories of oppression and resistance are far too specific for meanings to be readily translatable. Indeed, the assumption that meaning *is* transparent in some idealized, unified "limen" is likely to lead to reiterations of oppression. But what she does recognize is that once different people from different liminal spaces begin to recognize each other as liminal, they can understand that communication is complex and that people may not be meaning what they seem to be meaning and that they may be meaning different things at once. While they may not at first understand the subcultural message, they may understand the form of the speech as resistant in nature. Moreover, Lugones thinks that such communications can be heard as invitations across "worlds" to disrupt the dominant world of meaning.

How have I developed her work? One of the most important themes in my own work is *intimacy*. More generally, I'm focused on the way that all of our interpersonal experiences are mediated by distance or closeness (intimacy). I call this characteristic "interpersonal spatiality." Consider, for example, the way in which trans people accused of deception are sometimes subject to "genital verification." It's an abusive practice that is deeply bound up with intimacy, in this case intimate violation. So I'm interested in how our bodies and our discursive practices are structured by boundaries between the object and subject of access – boundaries which make intimacy possible *as* intimacy, boundaries which make abuse possible *as* abuse. I see these boundaries as morally binding, yet culturally contingent. There are different social realities that have different systems of interpersonal spatiality. Some of these systems are themselves inherently abusive, some are resistant to that abuse. I'm interested in the possibilities for resistant forms of intimacy as well as dignity (taken in terms of interpersonal distance). I guess one way to put this is to say that I'm not focused so much on counter-publics (or counter-privates) but alternative, resistant ways in which we experience each other both from a distance and up-close-and-personal, that is, *as people*. Specifically, I'm interested in how intimacy is possible across different social realities. I'm interested in how new forms of interpersonality spatiality can be created and negotiated across "worlds" given the fact that meaning isn't transparent, given that systems of interpersonal spatiality may differ. The possibilities for harm while opening oneself up for intimate possibilities across worlds are, of course, great. Sharing one's deepest sense of what it means to be a woman can be answered by the question "so have you had the surgery yet?" That's profoundly hostile.

This has quite a lot to do with telling one's story "across cultures." I see telling one's story as an intimate act. Or at least it can be. It can also be a dignifying act, an act that draws a firm boundary and creates a little distance. In general, I see autobiography as negotiating interpersonal space in just this way. One needs to decide just how much one will open oneself up, what kind of story to tell. And these are all ways of presenting ourselves to others, revealing ourselves as "who we are." Reflecting back on some of my early performance work, I see myself as having been interested for a very long time now in how one can both narrate and perform a story in such a way that opens up new possibilities for intimacy.

For me, this is of a piece with theorizing. Certainly as usually practiced, philosophical theorizing is one of the most distant ways of presenting oneself possible. But once philosophizing is grounded in experience, once it flows from one's own life, then there are real possibilities for intimate theorizing. I have found this in Lugones's work. And I guess it's also one of the things I want to *show* in my book. Through sharing my personal experiences and through being *on the spot* as a philosopher, I want to see how a theory of interpersonal spatiality can itself *negotiate* interpersonal spatiality – moving close, then pulling back, then perhaps moving closer. Perhaps I've been trying to do a little bit of that now, too. I mean, we're in this dialogue. It's not in person. It's not in real time. But it's an interview. And I'm showing parts of myself to you and to potential readers that are important to me. We're talking *meta*-theory here. And, yet, I feel *vulnerable* because my philosophy is also a window into who I am.

PG: In "Trans Identities and First-Person Authority" (2009) you call for a "multiplicity of trans-authored narratives" and for "polyvocality" (98). The mainstream world denies trans people's authenticity and treats its own account of them inappropriately as authoritative: namely, that trans people's "truth" is their genital status. In response, you outline what you call "ethical first-person authority": one's self-identifications and self-narratives matter, on grounds that in your eyes are primarily ethical (and perhaps also political) rather than epistemological or ontological. Asserting the "ultimate priority of ethical considerations," you add that one's self-identification and "existential self-identity" may not "necessarily indicate something deep" but may have a political aspect (110, 115). For example, "[w]hen a transperson answers 'I am a woman,'" this may "be understood as a resistant *refusal to disclose genital status [...] It seems that the correct account is one that fails to provide* any *defining feature of category membership and thus leaves it open for cultural dispute" (109–10). Instead, one would give an ethical or political account of oneself, for example one's sense of what is important, what matters, one's reasons for acting, what it means to them to identify as a woman. Can you explain your understanding of ethics and politics in this context?*

TB: I meant a lot of different things. One of the things that I had in mind was intrapolitical disagreement. Trans terminology is often underwritten by political visions. For example, "transgender" has been used as an umbrella term that is closely wedded to a view that posits the binary as a source of oppression. For some trans people who view themselves *within* the binary, such a vision may be politically problematic. Hence, it would be important to disavow self-identification as "transgender" and to take up other terminology, such as "transsexual." By contrast, some trans people have disavowed "transsexual" because of its association with a pathologizing medical model. So while self-identification as "woman" or "man" may concern deep personal resonances, self-identifications as "transsexual," "transgender," "trans," and so forth may be reflections of a political stance. Sometimes such political stances are stable. Sometimes they are strategic – changing, depending upon specific contexts and political necessities. I was also thinking of Heyes's notion of an ethics of self-transformation (Heyes). I have known several trans-masculine individuals who have disavowed self-identification as "man" because they were deeply concerned, as feminists, about the hegemonic meaning of the term as well as the privileges sometimes associated with it. Here both ethics and politics are in play. Such choices can be very difficult, too. Ethical and political considerations may lead one to disavow a term with which one has a strong personal resonance.

Finally, I was thinking about privacy, intimacy, and abuse as moral notions. At the time, I hadn't found my way yet to the concept of interpersonal spatiality. But I was working towards it. I saw the terms "woman" and "man" as implicated in abusive practices that euphemistically communicate private information. For example, sometimes trans people are confronted with questions like "Are you a woman or a man?" Typically, such questions are euphemistic ways of inquiring about genital status. Often "was discovered to be a man" is polite way of saying "was discovered to have a penis." I was also thinking about the fact that when a trans person says "I'm a woman" in trans subcultures, one may have no idea what this means to the person who says it. Such self-identifications are often complex and deep, given content through the trajectory of a life struggle. So, at least in trans subcultures, such statements serve as a locus for possibilities of distance and closeness: how much a person shares about their identity is a question of intimacy. In effect, I was proposing something more radical than the suggestion that terms like "woman" and "man" have different meanings in different worlds. I was proposing that the roles of "man" and "woman" in the linguistic and extra-linguistic practices were very different.

In the mainstream, "I am a woman" is not very different from "she is a woman." In both cases we're apparently dealing with a mere report about a fact in the world on par with "I am six feet tall" or "she is six feet tall." However, in trans subcultures, saying "I am a woman" can be a first-person, present-tense avowal, on par with "I am angry" or "I think I'll go home now." While "she is angry" may report a fact about the world, "I am angry" is doing something more. Philosophers think that the avower has a first-person authority over what they say. For example, while "she is six feet tall" can be contested by another as a factual mistake on the part of the speaker ("No, you're wrong. She's not six feet tall!"), it is generally inappropriate to contest "I am angry" in the same way. "No, you're mistaken. You aren't angry" is usually "out of bounds." (One could accuse the speaker of lying, but that's a different matter.) My idea was that in mainstream contexts, "I am a woman" is like "I am six feet tall" in that one can charge the speaker with having made a mistake, while in trans subcultural spaces, "I am a woman" is like "I am angry" in that suggesting the speaker has made a mistake is typically "out of bounds." I wanted to contrast these discursive practices of providing a putative description and of avowing and situate them within larger extra-discursive practices, such as the communication of genital status through public gender presentation.

I was trying to link the ethical basis for this authority to concerns around privacy or at least the autonomy to negotiate that privacy. I don't think I really succeeded in that. These days, I would say that the ethical basis for this authority derives from the demands of interpersonal spatiality. First-person, present-tense avowals play an important role in making possible and constructing our personas – the appearances of "who we are" to others. I see these appearances as structured and negotiated in the field of interpersonal spatiality. There's far more to say, of course. But I'll leave that for the book.

disclosure statement

No potential conflict of interest was reported by the authors.

bibliography

Bettcher, Talia. "Evil Deceivers and Make-Believers: Transphobic Violence and the Politics of Illusion." *Hypatia* 22.3 (2007): 43–65. Print.

Bettcher, Talia. *Personhood as Intimacy: Trans Feminist Philosophy.* Minneapolis: U of Minnesota P, forthcoming. Print.

Bettcher, Talia. "Trans Identities and First-Person Authority." *You've Changed: Sex Reassignment and Personal Identity.* Ed. Laurie Shrage. Oxford: Oxford UP, 2009. 98–120. Print.

Bettcher, Talia. "Trapped in the Wrong Theory: Rethinking Trans Oppression and Resistance." *Signs* 39.2 (2014): 383–406. Print.

Bettcher, Talia, and Ann Garry, eds. *Transgender Studies and Feminism*. Spec. issue of *Hypatia* 24.3 (2009). Print.

Butler, Judith. "Can the 'Other' of Philosophy Speak?" *Undoing Gender*. By Judith Butler. New York and London: Routledge, 2004. 232–50. Print.

Christian, Barbara. "The Race for Theory." *Cultural Critique* 6 (1987): 51–63. Print.

Feder, Ellen K. *Family Bonds: Genealogies of Race and Gender*. Oxford and New York: Oxford UP, 2007. Print.

Halberstam, Jack. "Wildness, Loss, Death." *Being With: A Special Issue on the Work of José Esteban Muñoz*. Spec. issue of *Social Text* 32.4 (121) (2014): 137–48. Print.

Heyes, Cressida. "Feminist Solidarity After Queer Theory: The Case of Transgender." *Signs* 28.4 (2003): 1093–120. Print.

Jacobs, Harriet. *Incidents in the Life of a Slave Girl. Written by Herself*. Enl. ed. Ed. L. Maria Child. Intro. Jean Fagan Yellin. Cambridge, MA and London: Harvard UP, 2000. Print.

Kristeva, Julia. "Stabat Mater." *The Portable Kristeva*. Updated ed. Ed. Kelly Oliver. New York: Columbia UP, 2002. 310–32. Print.

Le Doeuff, Michèle. *Hipparchia's Choice: An Essay Concerning Women, Philosophy, Etc.* Trans. Trista Selous. New York and Chichester: Columbia UP, 2007. Print.

Lorde, Audre. *Zami: A New Spelling of My Name*. London: Pandora, 1996. Print.

Lugones, María. "On Complex Communication." *Hypatia* 21.3 (2006): 75–85. Print.

Lugones, María. *Pilgrimages/Peregrinajes: Theorizing Coalition Against Multiple Oppressions*. Lanham, MD: Rowman, 2003. Print.

Lugones, María. "Toward a Decolonial Feminism." *Hypatia* 25.4 (2010): 242–57. Print.

Muñoz, José Esteban. "Feeling Brown, Feeling Down: Latina Affect, the Performativity of Race, and the Depressive Position." *Signs* 31.3 (2006): 675–88. Print.

Perpich, Diane. "Black Feminism, Poststructuralism and the Constructed Nature of Experience." *Convergences: Black Feminism and Continental Philosophy*. Ed. Maria del Guadalupe Davidson, Kathryn T. Gines, and Donna-Dale L. Marcano. Albany: State U of New York P, 2010. 13–34. Print.

Preciado, Beatriz. *Testo Junkie: Sex, Drugs, and Biopolitics in the Pharmacopornographic Era*. Trans. Bruce Benderson. New York: Feminist P at City U of New York, 2013. Print.

Scott, Joan W. "Experience." *Feminists Theorize the Political*. Ed. Judith Butler and Joan Wallach Scott. New York and London: Routledge, 1992. 22–40. Print.

Shakhsari, Sima. "Killing me Softly with your Rights." *Queer Necropolitics*. Ed. Jin Haritaworn, Adi Kuntsman, and Silvia Posocco. Abingdon: Routledge, 2014. 93–110. Print.

Spillers, Hortense J. "Mama's Baby, Papa's Maybe: An American Grammar Book." *Diacritics: A Review of Contemporary Criticism* 17.2 (1987): 65–81. Print.

Wittig, Monique. *The Lesbian Body*. Trans. David Le Vay. Boston: Beacon, 1986. Print.

Woolf, Virginia. *A Room of One's Own*. London: Penguin Classics, 2014. Print.

Talia Bettcher

Pelagia Goulimari

cláudia pazos-alonso

SPREADING THE WORD
the "woman question" in the periodicals a voz feminina *and* o progresso *(1868–69)*

On 6 June 1868 *The Athenaeum*, one of the most influential periodicals of the Victorian period, registered in its "Our Weekly Gossip" column the following event:

> The Female Question is making strange progress. From a city so little likely to be stirred by sentiment as Lisbon we have received several numbers of a paper called *A Voz Feminina*, which is written by ladies and devoted to the cause of woman's emancipation. The chief editor is Madame Francisca D'Assis Martinz Wood [*sic*], the Portuguese wife of an English gentleman. Space is given to fiction, poetry, musical history, and fashions; the latter being described in French. *A Voz Feminina* would be useful to persons who are studying Portuguese. (799)

This article will attempt to consider some of the questions prompted by this announcement, namely: who was Francisca Wood and the Englishman to whom she was married? What led *The Athenaeum* to register the appearance of a periodical written in Portuguese? In what ways did *A Voz Feminina* [*The Female Voice*] represent a landmark in women's emancipation? And last but not least, in the late 1860s how topical was the "Woman Question" not only in Portugal but also in England and across the rest of Europe?

border crossings: a portuguese periodical and its transnational editor

As Duby and Perrot indicate, "la presse féministe trouve son troisième souffle à partir de 1868" (the feminist press finds its third wind from 1868 onwards) (501) across several countries, building on scattered instances in the first half of the nineteenth century. What their general overview does not consider is the extent to which the "échanges d'expériences qui s'opèrent à travers la presse" (the exchange of experiences carried out via the press) (504) became relevant that very year too in the Portuguese context, thanks to the launch in January 1868 of *A Voz Feminina*.[1] The periodical, a weekly which claimed to be made up exclusively of female contributors (a statement that was soon dropped), carried on uninterrupted for 102 issues until the very end of 1869 – albeit with a change of title to *O Progresso* [*Progress*] in the last six months when Francisca also began to share the role of Editor with her husband

William. At least in some quarters, it was welcomed for the novelty of its outspoken positions, with particular regard to the education and emancipation of women: we know this for certain because many favourable critical reviews, originating from a variety of newspapers from all over mainland Portugal (and even Madeira), were regularly transcribed in the pages of *A Voz Feminina* itself. Needless to say, the periodical also elicited several negative reactions, perhaps best summarized in the editorial where Francisca announced closure: she cited the covert war waged against her by some Catholic priests, and their indoctrination of Portuguese women as one of the main reasons for being unable to carry on (no. 94, 179). The all-pervasive power and influence of the Catholic Church was undeniable, with frequently adverse consequences for women; this thorny problem would take centre stage shortly after, in *The Crime of Father Amaro*, a monumental realist novel penned by Eça de Queirós, initially serialized in 1875, and subsequently revised and published in book form (1880).

The public visibility of the "Woman Question" had been escalating in Britain ever since Barbara Bodichon, responsible for the first Women's Suffrage Committee, had collected 1,499 signatures in favour of female suffrage within a fortnight in advance of the second Reform Bill in 1867. The petition was presented to parliament by John Stuart Mill.[2] Such a context may help to explain not only why *The Athenaeum* had seen fit to report the launch of *A Voz Feminina* but moreover why, in its footsteps, this news item was widely featured in the regional press: within one week, more than a dozen papers across the British Isles had duly transcribed the *Athenaeum* article.[3] Yet the extent to which Wood's attempt to disseminate progressive ideas concerning the rights of women to a nationwide Portuguese audience may have been informed by a transnational background has, surprisingly, not yet been examined. This is what this article seeks to do, primarily through an analysis of relevant editorials, articles, and correspondence received from abroad (England, France, Switzerland and even the United States). In order to do so, however, we must first consider the unusual trajectory of Francisca Wood herself.

The severe neglect of this remarkable woman from cultural memory has persisted for so long that even her actual dates of birth and death have remained a matter of speculation until now. For the purposes of this article, I was able to establish them with some degree of certainty as being 1802–1900.[4] But nothing is yet known about the circumstances that led a young Francisca d'Assis Martinz, born and raised for the first fourteen years of her life in Lisbon, to move to England, where she lived for some thirty-five years.[5] Archival research, however, enables us to uncover that Francisca and William Wood were married on 17 July 1852 at St Dunstan in the West, a church in Fleet Street, central London. He was indeed a gentleman, as mentioned in *The Athenaeum*, for his mother, Jane, was the daughter of Sir John Thorold, a baronet and a book collector whose family seat was Syston Park in Lincolnshire.[6] William Wood was a musician and composer, and the British Library holds three of his musical compositions, dating from 1840, 1846 and 1848 – the latter setting to music what was at the time an overtly revolutionary hymn, "The Peoples' Anthem."[7]

By the time the wedding took place, unconventionally enough, the couple had probably been living together for one year already, or at least the census of 1851 identifies Francisca as an overnight visitor at William's house (7 Albion Road, Clapham). Seven years later, in 1858, William Wood's name appears on the electoral roll, which confirms that he was living in London (48 Cambridge Street). Presumably so too was Francisca, although as a female and a foreigner her name would not have featured in any electoral roll. Little is known about their relocation to Portugal, likely to have taken place by the early 1860s, since neither of the Woods features on the British census of 1861.[8] By the time *A Voz Feminina* was launched, on 5 January 1868, Francisca was sufficiently well regarded to have been approached to direct the periodical. She penned and signed the inaugural editorial, although she became officially named as "redactora principal" (Principal Editor) only from no. 4 onwards. Her mission statement is tellingly ambitious: "the acquisition of human knowledge; spiritual superiority; in short perfectibility; that grandiose utopia" (no. 1: 1).[9]

Francisca Wood's long residency in England means that she would have lived through the political turmoil surrounding the Great Reform Bill of 1832. She continued to be immersed in a culture of change, particularly when the fight for women's rights started to build momentum in Britain from the 1850s onwards. Significantly, she was still residing in England when the 1857 Divorce Act was passed. To her mind this represented a landmark for women's rights and thus, when *A Voz Feminina* transcribed a news item sent in by a reader that detailed a real-life account of wife-selling as reported in the British press, Wood promptly countered that the reader must have seen it in an old newspaper, since such practice had been outlawed in Britain since the Divorce Act of 1857 (no. 5: 4).

The familiarity of the couple with what *The Athenaeum* referred to as the "Female Question" in Britain set the tone for subsequent issues, and ran through *A Voz Feminina* from beginning to end. In July 1868, William explicitly praised

> sensible men like Mr Stuart Mill who believe that a woman should exercise, in all the breadth of the public sphere, the influence to which her innate faculties are well adapted; who wish to see her analyse the great themes of public good and evil; in short throw the weight of her moral and intellectual influence onto the scales of justice. (no. 25: 1)[10]

For her part, Francisca's own editorials and articles indicated that she was following the debates surrounding women's campaigns during the course of 1868–69 with keen interest.

english women and the right to vote, through portuguese eyes

In September 1868, Francisca spotlighted women's crusades in favour of the vote:

> In the north-east of England 1100 ladies, among whom one finds the names of Lady Elizabeth Drummond, Mrs Berkley [*sic*], and other distinguished ladies, demanded to be admitted on the list of electors for Manchester, claiming that they were legally qualified since as heads of house and property owners they contributed to the state. In other counties, women have demanded similar rights, and in some, civil authorities in the parishes have accepted them onto the list of electors. (no. 35: 1)[11]

Francisca was not the only one to be avidly au fait with the progress of the "Female Question" in England. So too was her close contributor Guiomar Torresão (1844–98) who, on being given the opportunity to contribute an editorial on 1 November 1868, used it to defend women's intellectual ability and their right to equality, citing the ongoing parliamentary debate in England about women's right to vote, specifically in connection with women who were heads of the family. Torresão followed up on this matter a few weeks later in her editorial of 20 December 1868, no. 49, where she alluded specifically to Miss Becker and her bid to collect signatures to revise the law to allow women to vote.[12] Clearly, Torresão had had access to the British press through the mediation of Francisca, as she herself indicated in her article. The last couple of months of 1868 therefore reveal a clever strategy on the part of The Editor, in a bid to keep the "Woman Question" at the forefront of her readers' minds: she proposed editorials penned by a variety of trusted contributors, including men, to give critical mass and ongoing visibility to the debate.

At the beginning of 1869, the visionary rallying cry of the periodical became "A mulher livre ao lado do homem livre" (Free women by the side of free men) from no. 51 onwards.[13] Simultaneously, Francisca's concerted effort to document for her readers what was going on elsewhere in Europe, particularly England, seemed to have become a strategy of choice to legitimize her ongoing commitment to free Portuguese women from the shackles of tradition – or to put it differently, to educate them and raise their aspirations. On 19 January 1869, editorial space was taken up with an introduction to Marie Goegg (1826–99), an early Swiss feminist (no. 55: 1–2).[14] *A Voz Feminina* reproduced firstly a letter addressed by Goegg to Francisca and more importantly the speech delivered by Goegg to the second Congress of the League for Peace and Freedom on 26 September 1868, in her role as president of the newly created International Association of Women. The speech had highlighted the League's unanimous support of women since it "recognises, as a principle, that all human rights, be they economic, civic, social or political, belong to women, and decides to study the most appropriate means to bring closer the time where she may enjoy full use of those rights" (no. 55: 2–3).[15] In other words, very shortly after the formation of the first transnational network of activist women, Goegg had reached out to Wood. The symbolic importance of this fact was not lost on the latter, and it led her to publish a six-page issue, thereby extending the usual format of four pages. As for the explanation of how Francisca's endeavours had come to the attention of the Swiss feminist in the first place, Goegg's letter revealed that she had been given Francisca's contacts by Lydia Becker – a fact which therefore suggests that by then the latter two were already in epistolary contact.

The following month, Francisca penned a series of articles under the title "English Women and the Right to Vote," published in three consecutive issues from February 1869 onwards (nos. 58–60). The first began by tracing a dismal portrayal of women's subjugation until the "forever memorable" Divorce Act of 28 August 1857: mistreatment included lawful wife-beating and wife-selling, as the law

> allowed a man to put a rope round his wife's neck and take her to the market to be sold. Two were thus disgracefully sold between the years of 1830 and 1850 at different points in time, while I was living in England. (no. 58: 3)[16]

Many years later, Hardy would famously open *The Mayor of Casterbridge* (1886) with a wife-selling scene. But nearly two decades before he did so, Francisca's novel *Maria Severn* (1869), initially serialized in the pages of *A Voz Feminina*, featured an instance of wife-selling. Its intention was specifically to push forward her educational agenda: the peasant who believed that purchasing a wife was acceptable was shown to be tragically ignorant and primitive, eliciting either contempt or heartfelt pity from those better placed in society.[17] In her article, Francisca stated that the Divorce Act granted equality between the sexes in matrimonial matters. This was not quite true, but it is understandable that enthusiasm may have got the better of her.

Wood's second article argued cogently that, given British women's already considerable intellectual achievements in a range of fields, legal reform would be the obvious next step for them. To prove the point, Wood invoked distinguished scientists such as Mrs Marcet and Mrs Somerville, as well as Harriet Martineau.[18] She further pointed out that Martineau, whom she described as a political economist, wrote editorials for *Daily News* for sixteen years.[19] She also alluded to the fact that in Britain women writers "occupy a position that is in nothing inferior to that of men" and, to further support her argument, added that Queen Victoria was herself a writer. Francisca clarified that English women were seeking two rights: firstly the vote and secondly for married women to be able to manage their own income. Regarding the first point, she highlighted that there was a non-negligible number of women, either rich or in employment, who were ratepayers – "just in Manchester and Salford there are 13,000 to 14,000" – and felt short-changed. She told her readers that the popular agitation had started two years earlier; although she did not cite the name of Barbara Bodichon, she mentioned committees of ladies in London, Bristol and Manchester (no. 59: 2). Furthermore, she explained that given that in some places the right to vote was recognized while in others it was rejected, a new law was needed urgently.

Her third article brought her readers up to the present. Commenting on the ongoing campaign of women for the vote, she remarked that

> the battle may be long and ferocious but eventually the cause of justice will triumph, just like the cause of the serf against his powerful Lord, who claimed the right to even his life and the honour of his daughters, eventually triumphed.[20]

According to Francisca, Harriet Martineau was the earliest voice in the debate, some thirty years earlier. She attributed to her the following words:

> There may be some who laugh at hearing me say that women should have the right to elect their representatives, but what does that matter! The Old World also laughed when it heard the cry of Washington for the independence of the New World, and yet the New World is now independent.[21]

Wood reported that the general movement had recently become fronted by Lydia Becker, as secretary of the group of women from Manchester. In fact, Wood divulged that Becker had sent to *A Voz Feminina* a report of a meeting held in October 1868, chaired by Mrs Kyllmann as president.[22] This effectively provided a direct source of information about the English context. Becker had also sent in a photograph of herself where, according to Wood, she looked about thirty – it must have been a flattering photograph, since by then Becker, who was born in February 1827, was already in her early forties. Wood concluded by expressing hope that there would be a debate concerning women and the right to vote in the coming parliamentary session, and stressed that signatures for the petition were being sought far and wide, even in Lisbon itself (no. 60: 3).

In other words, as a political commentator, Francisca had her finger on the pulse and was well informed about the progress of the "Woman Question" in England, ensuring that it was closely reported in *A Voz Feminina* as it unfolded. These were indeed exciting times for the first suffragettes and, in March 1869, a short unsigned entry titled "Elections in England" reported the fact that several women were able to vote because their names had been registered before the Supreme Court of Justice decreed that women could not vote. Accordingly "fifteen ladies voted in Finsbury [...] In Manchester nine ladies voted and several in Lancashire." The author of the article, in all likelihood Wood herself, rejoiced that "all but one voted Liberal rather than Conservative" (no. 63: 4).[23] As such, the year of 1869 represented a watershed moment; in the words of Millicent Garrett Fawcett:

> that year deserves to be remembered as one in which the most important step was made in the direction of women's complete political enfranchisement. A municipal reform act was passed which conferred upon women householders the right to take part in municipal elections. (16)

The sense that the subject of women's rights was increasingly sweeping not only Britain but France too (symbolically still the main cultural model for her Portuguese target audience) is conveyed in the same issue where, on the previous page, a short piece of news titled "Associação das Senhoras Francesas" [Association of French Ladies] divulged the creation of a French group for women's rights in Paris, led by Mrs André Léo (no. 63: 3).[24] In practice, then, Wood acted as a cultural mediator, in an attempt to provide up-to-date news on women's movements that were gathering momentum in Europe, in order to encourage her readers to feel that the time was ripe for change at home too. It provided a template for Portuguese women to consider, showing how elsewhere women were increasingly launching associations and coming together to take action.

In this context, it is probably not a coincidence that the most striking serialized prose published between numbers 60 and 64 (running in tandem not only with Francisca's own articles on "English Women and the Right to Vote" but also her serialized novel *Maria Severn*) was a biography of Toussaint L'Ouverture (1743–1803), translated into Portuguese from an unnamed source by João Luís da Silva Viana. In her important study of Victorian serialized fiction, Catherine Delafield observes in connection with *Cranford*: "Gaskell's sketches were set in a completed past which occupied an intertextual place within the issues of the periodical constructed out of the discussion of the present" (93–94). In the context of *A Voz Feminina*, there is a case for suggesting that a biography of the leader of the Haitian Revolution, which may at first appear to be a random item completely unrelated to the "Woman Question," in fact functions as an additional commentary: it subtly complements a series of articles on the march of progress, not least given the analogy made repeatedly by Francisca and her cast of contributors about women being akin to slaves in need of emancipation.

building alliances: internationalization and men's support for women's rights

Francisca had a very clear vision, as outlined in the magazine leitmotif: "free women by the side of free men." In this context, she defended her policy of opening up *A Voz Feminina* to both men and women, by emphasizing that several foreign periodicals were also following a similar practice (no. 64: 3).[25] The titles that she cited, most of them equally radical in outlook, were listed in Portuguese, but can be translated back into their original language as follows: in Geneva, *Journal des femmes*; in England, *The Englishwoman's Review*; and in North America six titles, *The Revolution*, *The Sorosis*, *Women's Advocate*, *The New York Women's Advocate*, *Mother and Home*, and *Hearth and Home* – the latter directed, as she reminded her readers, by the well-known author of *Uncle Tom's Cabin*, Mrs Beecher Stowe. It is worth noting that some of these periodicals had been launched only recently, which provides further proof that Francisca was very much au fait with what was going on elsewhere in the world. We already know the identity of her main contacts in Switzerland (Marie Goegg) and England (Lydia Becker) but, given how well informed she seemed about print culture in the United States, where did her extensive information come from?

A clue comes three months later, in the form of an open letter written in English by William Wood to Theodore Stanton, of *The Revolution* (no. 73: 4). Theodore Stanton (1851–1925) was the son of the well-known American feminist activist Elizabeth Stanton, one of the Editors of the progressive periodical *The Revolution*.[26] His father was the abolitionist Henry Stanton and, in fact, when writing to Theodore, William mistook him for Henry. It is not clear who had approached whom first, nor does it perhaps matter: what is significant is that like-minded revolutionary women and men worldwide were availing themselves of the new opportunities afforded by the press to create international networks to support each other across national boundaries.

In his open letter to Theodore Stanton, William states that

> the English here [i.e., in Lisbon] are perfectly indifferent, or, to speak more correctly, adverse to the cause we advocate. We have only one English subscriber, and have not succeeded in obtaining a single signature to the petition to [the British] Parliament for the political enfranchisement of women. (4)

The petition must be the one that Francisca had alluded to at the close of her series of articles on "English Women and the Right to Vote." A subsequent open letter by William Wood, this time addressed to the Editor of *The Printers' Register*, also dealt with the gradual progress being made in England with regard to the vote for women, and clarified that "following Mr Jacob Bright's amendment to the Municipal franchise […] the petition for women's vote presented to Parliament by Sir Charles Wentworth Dilke, only attracted five signatures from Portugal" (no. 80: 123).[27] It was no doubt rather less than what William or indeed Francisca Wood would naturally have hoped for.

If the Woods' activism deserves to be singled out, so does the contact with Dilke, a man who famously boasted that "I have known everyone worth knowing from 1850 until my death" (Jenkins) and whose network of connections was significantly strengthened by the fact that his family owned *The Athenaeum*. The contact with Dilke, however indirect, may provide an explanation as to why the influential Victorian periodical had publicized the appearance of *A Voz Feminina* one year earlier, in the terms quoted at the beginning of this article – although it was a newsworthy item in its own right, a personal connection may have helped. Certainly the links between the Woods and Dilke did not stop with the parliamentary petition, for when later that year Francisca Wood published her serialized novel *Maria Severn* in book form, she offered a copy to Dilke himself, as can be ascertained from the presence of a handwritten dedication in the copy owned by the British Library. Francisca's offering may have been primarily a gesture of courtesy since, although Dilke had studied Classics, there is no indication that he could read Portuguese. Alternatively, it may also have been prompted by the hope of generating publicity for her novel which, as far as we can ascertain, did not occur.

Be that as it may, *The Athenaeum* is cited explicitly as a source of information in *A Voz Feminina* on more than one occasion. Curiously, it was invoked in an open letter in which Francisca rebuked a male reader, João A. Elliott, for believing that he was entitled to determine how far his younger sister's intellectual aspirations were allowed to go: he deemed culture to be fine but not politics (no. 78: 117).[28] Francisca encouraged him to read the review of John Stuart Mill's work published in *The Athenaeum* on 19 June 1869. This allusion reveals that Francisca was aware of the recent publication of *The Subjection of Women*. Ironically, although Wood thought it expedient to cite the authority of a mainstream and respectable periodical, the anonymous reviewer had in fact expressed misgivings at the likely upheaval if women were granted political power ("Literature" 819–20). Nonetheless, in her bid to incite João A. Elliott to rethink his unprepossessing attitude, Francisca also recommended that he read Professor F.W. Newman's lecture "On Women's Suffrage,"[29] and a report by the committee of the Parliament of Massachusetts about "the advantages of giving women electoral rights" (117) as further evidence of the support of men for women's rights. Once more, then, Francisca was deploying ammunition from England and the United States in order to persuade someone – in the first instance one man in particular, but by extension her entire readership too – about the fairness of women's demands for equality.

These were indeed exciting times of change, as the "Woman Question" appeared to be making visible progress. While Francisca drew repeatedly on the British press, her knowledge of what was going on elsewhere simultaneously remained firmly in evidence. An example of her ongoing connections with French-speaking feminists came in the form of an open letter from Wood to the French activist Mrs André Léo, written in French, where she thanked Léo for sending her a copy of the essay she had published that very year, "La Femme et les moeurs" [Women and Customs] (no. 81: 128). And the same issue also foregrounded the ongoing importance of women's education by featuring an article by C. Hippeau about Vassar College in the United States, transcribed from the *Gazeta Pedagógica*. Vassar had been founded in 1861 to further young women's higher education, as Hippeau's article explained (no. 81: 129–30). The theme of female higher education would be taken up in the next issue, with an article by Guiomar Torresão celebrating the first Portuguese woman doctor "Uma Senhora Portuguesa Médico" (*sic*) [A Portuguese Lady Doctor], while stressing that several other countries already boasted qualified female doctors (no. 82: 134).

In the last three months of the periodical's life, from no. 87 onwards, *O Progresso* started a new rubric entitled "O que se faz lá for a" [What is Happening Abroad]. This offered particularly compelling snippets of information under one prominent heading. For instance, an article transcribed from yet another British source, *The Quarterly Review*, reported that Tennyson, author of *The Princess* (1847) and Poet Laureate, was amongst those who had voted in favour of the foundation of a college for women (no. 87: 153). Although not named, the college in question must have been Girton, the first Oxbridge female college, established in Hitchins (Hertfordshire) in 1869 and subsequently transferred to Cambridge.[30] A couple of issues later, Francisca cited from *The Athenaeum* news about the creation of a Women's Club and Institute, in Newman Street, London. She explained the desirability of ladies' clubs, giving women access to the comforts routinely available to (gentle)men in the numerous and exclusive existing all-male clubs (no. 89: 160). In her view, the availability of a public space was particular attractive given the number of women who could not afford to run their own house and therefore had to rent a room in a lodging-house. She went into detail about the prohibitive financial expenditure involved in keeping a home of one's own; it seems likely that she was speaking from first-hand experience.[31] In between these two pieces of news, in the rubric "O que se faz lá fora," the periodical gave advance notice of the third Congress of the League for Peace and Freedom in Lausanne, highlighting that, thanks to Mme Goegg's intervention, the statutes of the League were woman-friendly, stipulating that "women will be admitted under the same conditions and with the same rights as men" (no. 88: 156).[32]

Given flourishing mobilization elsewhere, it may come as a shock, then, that a mere few weeks later Wood used her editorial to break the news of the imminent closure of her periodical at the end of 1869. For attentive readers, it had been clear for quite a while that there weren't enough subscriptions to cover the running costs of the enterprise. However, financial considerations were not among the reasons invoked, as Francisca lamented instead that, save a few exceptions, Portuguese women did not seem to be interested in emancipation and that the Catholic Church had stealthily campaigned against her (no. 94: 179). The issue was very cleverly laid out, since the next page featured, in the rubric "O que se faz lá fora," a rousing report of the third Congress of the League for Peace and Freedom in Lausanne. It highlighted the presence of a number of French luminaries, and cited the closing speech, in which Victor Hugo stressed that "Socialism is vast, it reaches all human problems, the whole of social conception […] It proclaims the *rights of woman – she who is equal to man*" (180; emphasis in the original).[33] In other words, the news of the imminent demise of the magazine in Portugal appeared significantly at odds with what was going on elsewhere in Europe. A subsequent number also followed a similar strategy, this time in reverse: Wood used editorial space to transcribe (in Portuguese translation) a speech by the president of the International Association of Women, Mme Goegg, delivered at the aforementioned Congress (no. 97: 191–92). This upbeat piece of news contrasted sharply, however, with a letter addressed to Mrs André Léo in which Wood, reiterating in French what she had already explained to her readers three weeks earlier, announced to her "Chère Soeur" (Dear Sister) the news of the imminent closure of the periodical at the end of 1869 (no. 97: 192).[34] One suspects that Wood was again consciously playing with the design of the periodical to foreground the extent to which the prevailing narrow-mindedness of the Portuguese milieu was at odds with the international mood of the time.

As is apparent from the above stark juxtapositions, even after the periodical's days became numbered, Wood maintained her fighting spirit and sense of humour. This can be equally seen in the last couple of issues, where she seemed determined to showcase the European-wide spread of women's progress. In no. 101, in "O que se faz lá fora," she cited a number of periodicals from a range of countries including Italy, Germany, the United States, and Switzerland, mentioning that even Russian women were opening their eyes (208).[35] Again, this can be read as a thinly veiled criticism of the short-sightedness of her fellow countrymen and women. She indicated, by way of conclusion, that she would tackle the British case in the following issue. Indeed, the last ever "O que se faz lá fora" spotlighted the progress achieved in England in more detail, although it briefly invoked several other countries too, including France and Germany (no. 102: 212–13). Of particular note are references to John Stuart Mill and his seminal work *The Subjection of Women*; to a speech delivered two years earlier by the politician Disraeli; and to Professor Newman and his stance in favour of women's vote. She concluded by asking her readers to subscribe to the French magazine *Le Droit des femmes*, with which she was familiar through Mme Goegg.[36] To facilitate this, immediately below Francisca's swansong, readers could find a description of *Le Droit des femmes*, complete with information about how to subscribe to it.

in the aftermath of the demise of *a voz feminina/o progresso*

There is no doubt that *A Voz Feminina* was a pioneer in the Portuguese context and not only on the subject of women's emancipation. In fact, the periodical encompassed a range of politically minded editorials on issues as diverse as the protection of animals or the ongoing revolution in neighbouring Spain. Nor did it shy away from controversial religious matters such as an editorial arguing against priests' celibacy (no. 99). Less than two years after the demise of *A Voz Feminina*, Lisbon – a city that had been described by *The Athenaeum* as "so little likely to be stirred by sentiment" – was shaken up with the lecture series that subsequently became widely regarded as an era-defining moment in Portuguese cultural history, synonymous with the start of modernity: the 1871 Casino Lectures. These lectures were forcibly closed down, but projected the all-male Geração de 70 (Generation of 70) into the limelight.

Among its leading members was Eça de Queirós. The 1870s saw him launch a satirical paper, *As Farpas*, jointly with Ramalho Ortigão, and publish two realist novels: *Cousin Basilio* (1878) and *The Crime of Father Amaro* (1880). The first examined female adultery, while the second tackled head-on the widespread abuse of power by the clergy. While Queirós' fiction chronicled stark asymmetries in the gendered distribution of power that resulted in the death of his female protagonists at the end of both novels, it failed to offer any concrete solutions to redress the balance. Ironically, even though the editorials in the Woods' periodical were considerably more radical than Queirós' articles in *As Farpas*, not least in respect of women's emancipation, the latter's cultural intervention nonetheless displaced from collective memory the earlier one by *A Voz Feminina*. The erasure from cultural history of a radical feminist thinker like Francisca Wood confirms what the critic Chatarina Edfeldt has identified as one of the mechanisms of exclusion of women from the Portuguese literary canon: the silencing of works that deal with gender inequality and feminist questions. Edfeldt's analysis concerns individual twentieth-century authors, but is equally applicable to collective enterprises such as that undertaken by *A Voz Feminina*.

One question that arises is what became of Francisca once her periodical folded. Since her husband was the proud owner of Tipografia Luso-Britânica, which continued to print and publish a number of publications, it seems natural for her to have played a part.[37] One of these warrants closer attention given that it is another periodical: *O Zoophilo*. This fortnightly magazine, launched nearly one decade after *A Voz Feminina* in January 1877, was sponsored by the newly created Portuguese Society for the Protection of Animals, but published by the Tipografia Luso-Britânica during the first year of its life, according to the information given at the bottom of the last page of each issue. It had a familiar format, being four pages like *A Voz Feminina*. Furthermore, the English influence seems obvious, given that one of the articles in the inaugural number referred to the fact that the Society for the Protection of Animals had been created in London fifty years earlier. More telling still, the motto of the newly founded magazine was a quotation by Wilkie Collins: "The misery of a weak, helpless, dumb creature is surely one of the saddest of all the mournful sights which this world can show."[38] This quotation may point to involvement by the Woods, all the more so because only a few years earlier, in 1873, Collins' novel *Armadale* (1866) had been translated into Portuguese and published by no other than Tipografia Luso-Britânica.

Of particular interest when trying to identify the possible involvement of Francisca Wood in *O Zoophilo* is an unsigned note concerning the forthcoming publication of a serialized "Folhetim" entitled *Jane Eyre* featured in the inaugural issue of 14 January 1877 (no. 1: 4). This short introductory note presupposed a fairly detailed knowledge of the contemporary reception of Brontë – which Francisca Wood would have had first-hand, since she was living in England in 1847. In particular, it mentioned that *Jane Eyre* was first published under the pseudonym Currer Bell; that the first edition sold out in two months; and that only then did it become known that the novel had been penned by a woman writer, Carlota (Charlotte) Brontë, "to the great pride of all women" (4). There is reason to suspect, therefore, that Francisca Wood may have been the anonymous translator of Brontë's famous novel, serialized under the title *Joanna Eyre* in the pages of *O Zoophilo*. The serialization, which began in the second issue, would carry on for nearly six years, with the last published instalment, numbered 81, on 28 September 1882 (1–2). Although it promised "continua" (to be continued), as usual, it appears to have been discontinued thereafter, without any word of explanation about why it failed to reach its proper conclusion. The rebellious Jane had initially shocked many readers in Britain; it was therefore actually quite daring to serialize Brontë in a Portuguese translation. But the point is that it showed that, against all odds, not unlike the eponymous Brontë heroine, Francisca Wood could be relied upon to continue having a mind of her own: *Jane Eyre* provided empowering models of womanhood for Portuguese readers, countering those presented in the aforementioned *Cousin Basilio* or *The Crime of Father Amaro* where, moreover, the culpable men identified in the novels' respective titles ultimately remained unpunished.

Wood alluded twice in the last few issues of *O Progresso* to the fact that she intended to join forces with her English and French counterparts, and therefore it is conceivable that she may have gone on to write articles for the press elsewhere. The fact that she was considered to be part of an emerging international network is certainly documented by an immediate display of solidarity in the pages of *Le Droit des femmes* (22 January 1870), where Goegg duly transcribed snippets of Francisca's open letter to André Léo (Anteghini 137–38). Further research may help to bring to light the existence of more material, but in the meantime it is worth noting that fifteen years later, when Theodore Stanton – with whom William Wood had corresponded back in 1869 – published *The Woman Question in Europe: A Series of Original Essays* (1884), the entry on Portugal stuck out like a sore thumb, for it was the only one to be wholly written by a man, the Republican Rodrigues de Freitas. Stanton provided an explanation of sorts in his Editor's Preface, stating that the authoress (*sic*) Maria Amália Vaz de Carvalho had been enlisted but had been unable to carry out the task, owing to illness (v). It is certainly fair to say that one might have expected Wood, rather than Vaz de Carvalho, to be approached. Assuming that Wood had been sidelined in favour of the latter, this seems especially ironic considering that she had made an enemy of the young Vaz de Carvalho when in 1868 she had chided her for refusing to contribute to *A Voz Feminina* (no. 25: 4). In the intervening period, Vaz de Carvalho – who was broadly in favour of female education but advocated that women should not seek political rights – had gradually built a reputation in literary circles as a journalist and writer. Since her ultimately conservative positions did not present a threat to the men of the Geração de 70, her salon, especially from the 1880s onwards, became a meeting-point for the leading intellectuals of the period.

The extent to which Wood was silenced during her own lifetime and subsequently overlooked is such that the present article is the first to confirm basic biographical information, including her dates (1802–1900). Equally extraordinary is the fact that the online catalogue WorldCat (http://www.worldcat.org/) registers the existence of only one copy in book form of her novel *Maria Severn*: the aforementioned one, held in the British Library, bearing a handwritten dedication to Charles Wentworth

Dilke. One explanation for this extreme cultural memory loss may be that Wood had no children (as far as we know), while her closest heir, her nephew Clarimundo, to whom she had dedicated her novel *Maria Severn*, was living far away in the Cape Verde Islands.[39] Moreover, the wave of anti-British feeling that spread across Portugal after the British ultimatum of 1890 no doubt further conspired to silence Francisca's legacy. A third factor in her neglect may be that her intellectual heir, the combative Guiomar Torresão, was busy fighting her own battles: Torresão was criticized, and indeed ridiculed, by several of the leading men of the Geração de 70, especially in the 1870s when she started the annual *Almanaque das Senhoras* [*Ladies' Almanac*], which she nevertheless managed to direct successfully until her death in 1898.[40] By the time that a new generation of women intellectuals and activists such as Adelaide Cabete (1867–1935), Ana de Castro Osório (1872–1935) and Carolina Beatriz Ângelo (1878–1911) – the latter one of the first women in Europe to vote, in the Portuguese national elections of 1911 (Silva) – embarked once more on the struggle to gain the vote in the very first years of the twentieth century, Francisca Wood's intervention more than thirty years earlier was but a distant memory. They were thus unable to claim her as a foremother.[41]

conclusion

In the last twenty-five years, research has convincingly stressed the pioneering role of *A Voz Feminina*.[42] Nonetheless, as this article has sought to demonstrate, Wood's extensive engagement with the "Woman Question" was quite unheard of in the Portuguese context and, for that reason, it must simultaneously be considered from a transnational perspective. Such an undertaking sheds fresh light on the infectious sense of excitement felt by an early Portuguese feminist on the European periphery, determined to act as cultural mediator during the early beginnings of the first international suffragette movements. In so doing, it furthermore showcases the practical role played by the press in the dissemination of radical ideas in the second half of the nineteenth century, as revolutionary women availed themselves of budding opportunities to create international networks and support each other across national boundaries. The present article has sought to do justice to the pioneer collective vision of a courageous woman and her cast of loyal contributors, in order to shed light on the extraordinary consciousness-raising role of *A Voz Feminina* and *O Progresso* and problematize male-centred accounts of nineteenth-century Portuguese cultural history. The inspirational Francisca Wood deserves to be remembered as part of a broader transnational movement, alongside her European sisters Lydia Becker, André Léo, and Marie Goegg, as well as mid-Victorian male advocates of the female cause, ranging from her own husband William Thorold Wood to younger supporters such as Charles Wentworth Dilke and, further afield, the American Theodore Stanton.

disclosure statement

No potential conflict of interest was reported by the author.

notes

1 Their neglect may have been compounded by the fact that the first full-length book to examine the relationship between women and the Portuguese press was published only subsequently (Lopes, *Imagens*) – even if it built on previous research showcasing the extent to which *A Voz Feminina* marked a significant moment in the public visibility of women as intellectuals in nineteenth-century Portugal (Leal; Ildefonso).

2 For further details, see Smith; Pugh.

3 Monday 8 June 1868: *Dundee Courier*, Angus, Scotland; *Birmingham Daily Post*, Birmingham. Tuesday 9 June 1868: *Western Daily Press*, Bristol. Wednesday 10 June 1868: *Liverpool Mercury*, Liverpool (repeated 12 June). Thursday 11 June 1868: *Hull and Eastern Counties Herald*, East Riding of Yorkshire. Friday 12 June 1868: *Newcastle*

Courant, Tyne and Wear; *Tipperary Vindicator*, Tipperary, Ireland. Saturday 13 June 1868: *Sheffield Daily Telegraph*, South Yorkshire; *Lancaster Gazette*, Lancashire; *Leicester Chronicle*, Leicestershire; *Kentish Mercury*, London; *Berkshire Chronicle*; *Birmingham Journal*, West Midlands; *Tower Hamlets Independent and East End Local Advertiser*, London; *Manchester Times*, Manchester. Saturday 11 July 1868: *Pall Mall Gazette*, London. Tuesday 14 July 1868: *Southern Reporter and Cork Commercial Courier*, Cork.

4 My breakthrough came with a visit to the British Cemetery in Lisbon. I wish to thank Andrew Swinnerton, Honorary Administrator of the Cemetery, for verifying Church records which register Francisca's death on 27 November 1900. She was buried with her "darling husband" William Thorold Wood (1816–88). His dates do not feature on their tombstone (though records indicate that he passed away on 22 April 1888), but hers are inscribed as 1802–1900. For the sake of completeness, her date of birth was checked in the Torre do Tombo Archives against baptism records, narrowing the search to the parish of Santos-o-Velho, according to *A Voz Feminina* (no. 35: 1), where she was born and christened. There were several Franciscas born in 1802, but only one had a father whose name matched that of Narciso Martinz (the name that appeared on the Woods' marriage records). The relevant entry stated that Francisca was born in October 1802 (day of the month illegible).

5 This information transpires from *A Voz Feminina* (editorial in no. 35: 1, and open letter penned by William Wood in no. 73: 4).

6 For further details about his maternal grandfather, see Purcell.

7 The words to "The Peoples' Anthem" were written by Ebenezer Elliott, an anti-Corn Law poet, and can be seen at <http://www.hymnary.org/text/when_wilt_thou_save_the_people>.

8 Their relocation may have been as part of the movement towards the creation of a Lusitanian church, according to Lopes ("Religião"). Their Protestant ethos is attested to by the fact that William Wood's publishing press published the Bible in Portuguese translation: *O Novo Testamento de Jesus Christo* (Lisbon: Typ. Luso-Britânica, 1870); and *O Novo testamento de Jesus Cristo* (Lisbon: Typ. Luso-Britânica de W.T. Wood, 1873).

9 "a acquisição do saber humano; a superioridade espiritual; a perfectibilidade enfim; essa utopia grandiosa." Portuguese spelling has been modernized. This and all subsequent translations from Portuguese and French into English are mine.

10

> homens sensatos, tais como Mr Stuart Mill, que creem dever a mulher exercer em toda a amplura da esfera pública, a influência a que as suas faculdades inatas são adaptadas; que desejam vê-la analisar os grandes tópicos do bem e do mal público; enfim, lançar o peso da sua influência moral e intelectual na balança da justiça.

11

> Num distrito ao noroeste de Inglaterra mil e cem senhoras, entre as quais se acham os nomes de Lady Elizabeth Drummond, da Sra. Berkley [*sic*] e de outras pessoas de distinção, requereram ser admitidas na lista de eleitores para Manchester, alegando que se achavam legalmente qualificadas, pois que como donas de casa e proprietárias contribuem para o estado. Noutros condados as senhoras hão reclamado os mesmos direitos, e nalguns já as autoridades civis das paróquias as têm admitido nas listas de eleitores.

The Mrs Berkley she alluded to may conceivably have been a typo for Miss Lydia Becker (see next note).

12 Becker was secretary of the Manchester Suffrage Committee founded in February 1867, now often cited as a landmark for the start of the suffragette movement. That very same year, Becker had published an article on "Female Suffrage" in *The Contemporary Review* (1867). For further details, see Walker.

13 The slogan was first used by Francisca on 22 November 1868, in an editorial that highlighted progress in various European countries, including England (with an allusion to the fifth annual meeting of the Women's Medical Society). Her article closed with a call for men to embrace "A mulher livre ao lado do homem livre" (Free women by the side of free men) (no. 45: 1). The motto had featured as an epigraph in an earlier editorial in favour of women's instruction penned by F.A. de Mattos (no. 24: 1). The sentence was ascribed to another male contributor, Ferreira

Farol, who wrote in defence of women's rights (see, for instance, no. 81: 127).

14 See Rappaport 259–61 for further details on Goegg.

15 "O Congresso reconhece, como princípio, que todos os direitos humanos, económicos, civis, sociais e políticos, pertencem à mulher, e decide estudar os meios mais apropriados a aproximar a época em que ela possa gozar pleno uso desses direitos." It is probable that Goegg had written to Francisca in French, and that the latter would have translated her letter and speech into Portuguese, although she doesn't say so specifically. Since most educated Portuguese women at the time would have been able to read French fluently, the decision to publish the article in Portuguese reflects the fact that Francisca thought it important enough to reach the widest possible audience.

16

> autorizando o marido a lançar uma corda ao pescoço da mulher e levá-la à venda no mercado. Duas foram assim ignominiosamente vendidas entre os anos de 1830 e 1850 em diferentes datas, estando eu então em Inglaterra.

17 For further details about this novel, see Pazos-Alonso.

18 For further details, see Morse; Webb; Creese.

19 According to Webb, in fact for fourteen years, between 1852 and 1866.

20

> A batalha poderá ser longa e renhida, mas por fim a causa da justiça há de triunfar assim como triunfou a causa do servo contra o poderoso senhor que se arrogava o direito de dispor até da sua vida e da honra de suas filhas.

21

> Talvez haja quem ria de me ouvir dizer que as mulheres devem ter direito a escolher os seus representantes; mas o que importa isso! Também o Velho Mundo riu, quando ouviu o brado de Washington pela independência do Novo Mundo, e contudo o Novo Mundo é independente.

22 For further details about Philippine Kyllmann (1834–1916), see Rappaport 329–30. The entry clarifies that she resigned from the committee soon after, over a disagreement with Lydia Becker.

23

> Quinze senhoras votaram em Finsbury [. . .] Em Manchester nove senhoras votaram e várias em Lancashire.

24 For further details about Léo (1824–1900), see Chauvaud.

25 This policy had been stated from the early numbers. In this issue, she seeks to provide a clarification about the cast of contributors, since there had been doubt about the authenticity of female contributors. Francisca acknowledged that at the outset there were two men writing under female pseudonyms, A.P. Carlota (who had written several of the early editorials) and A.P.G. Leonor, but she insisted that all other participants were female. This certainly seems to have been the case, since several of them continued to write, either for newspapers or in book form, after the demise of the magazine. The accusation shows how unusual the significant female make-up of the magazine was at the time.

26 For further information, see Kramarae.

27 Charles Wentworth Dilke (1843–1911) was elected Liberal MP for Chelsea in 1968 at the age of twenty-five and went on to become a major Victorian figure (Jenkins). According to Crawford, "Dilke, a Radical Liberal, closely associated with J.S. Mill [. . .] had in July 1869 spoken at the first public meeting of the London Society for [W]omen's [S]uffrage" (169).

28 The name of his younger sibling is not given but it is presumably Eliza Elliott, whose translation from English of the novel *Cecília* was serialized from no. 85.

29 Professor F.W. Newman (1805–97) was the younger sibling of Cardinal Newman. In 1868, he published *Old England – Women's Right of Suffrage*. See Crawford 449.

30 Girton College was established in 1869 by Barbara Bodichon and Emily Davies (already referenced as Mrs Davies in an earlier issue). See Rappaport 794. The creation of the college elicited

another mention in the periodical, this time as Hitchins (no. 92: 172).

31 The problems experienced by non-married women, in particular in securing honest gainful employment, are highlighted more than once in the periodical (for instance, when Francisca rejoiced about British printers employing women).

32 "[A]s mulheres serão admitidas sob as mesmas condições e com os mesmo direitos que os homens." Its aim, it was stated, would be the "formation of a federation of European states" (no. 88: 156). The pacifist newspaper *Les Etats-Unis d'Europe* had started publication in 1868.

33 "O socialismo é vasto, alcança todos os problemas humanos [. . .] proclama *o direito da mulher, – essa igual do homem.*" This is one of the few times that the word socialism appears in the periodical.

34 The imminent closure was reiterated in an open letter published in English addressed by Francisca to *The Printers' Register* (no. 95: 184).

35 Since some of the information overlaps with an article published in *Le Droit des femmes* a fortnight earlier, on 4 December 1869, there is a fair chance that the French periodical would have been one of the sources of information. See Anteghini 132–36 for a transcription of the relevant article.

36 In a letter addressed in English to Mme Goegg, Francisca thanked her for sending her a copy of *Le Droit des femmes* (no. 74: 4). The French periodical, co-edited by Léon Ritcher and Marie Desraimes, started in 1869. See Finch 247.

37 So far, I have been able to ascertain that the Biblioteca Nacional de Portugal holds more than forty titles published by Tipografia Luso-Britânica between 1868 and 1877 on a wide range of subjects. Unfortunately, a thematic search "by publisher" is rather hit and miss, so the list is still evolving.

38 "O padecer de uma criatura fraca, e indefesa na sua mudez, é certamente um dos espectáculos mais aflitivos para a alma compassiva." The citation can be traced back to Collins' famous sensation novel, *The Woman in White* (1860).

39 Clarimundo Martins (1835–95) was appointed to oversee the Banco Nacional Ultramarino in Cape Verde when it opened its first branch in Praia in 1865, according to information given on the website of the Banco de Cabo Verde (http://www.bcv.cv/vPT/O%20Banco/Historia/Paginas/Historia.aspx). After marrying Apolónia Ferreira Martins Burnay on 15 December 1871 in Lisbon, he returned to Cape Verde. See Burnay.

40 For further details about how she was criticized by both Oliveira Martins and Ramalho, see Lopes, *Imagens*, especially 511–31.

41 For a discussion of the extent to which Portuguese feminism remained anti-British, see Abranches.

42 During the Salazar dictatorship, Francisca Wood remained generally overlooked, save for some brief dictionary entries (see, for example, "Francisca Wood"). For increasingly in-depth attempts to reclaim the contribution of women to nineteenth-century print culture, see Leal; Ildefonso; Lopes, *Imagens*.

bibliography

Abranches, Graça. "Homens, mulheres e mestras inglesas." *Entre ser e estar: raízes, percursos e discursos da identidade*. Ed. Maria Irene Ramalho and António Sousa Ribeiro. Porto: Afrontamento, 2001. Print.

Anteghini, Alessandra. *Parità, pace, libertà: Marie Goegg e André Léo nell'associazionismo femminile del secondo Ottocento*. Genoa: Name, 1998. Print.

Burnay, J. "A Família Burnay e Cabo Verde." *Geneall* 20 Feb. 2008. Web. 26 Feb. 2016.

Chauvaud, Frédéric, et al., eds. *Les Vies d'André Leo. Romancière, féministe et communarde*. Rennes: PUR, 2015. Print.

Crawford, Elizabeth. *The Women's Suffrage Movement: A Reference Guide, 1866–1928*. London: Routledge, 2001. Print.

Creese, Mary R.S. "Somerville, Mary (1780–1872)." *Oxford Dictionary of National Biography*. Oxford: Oxford UP, May 2008. Web. 26 Feb. 2016.

Delafield, Catherine. *Serialization and the Novel in Mid-Victorian Magazines*. Farnham: Ashgate, 2015. Print.

Duby, Georges, and Michelle Perrot, eds. *Histoire des femmes en Occident*. Vol. 4. Paris: Perrin, 2002. Print.

Edfeldt, Chatarina. *Uma história na História*. Montijo: Câmara Municipal do Montijo, 2006. Print.

Fawcett, Millicent Garrett. "The Women's Suffrage Movement." *The Woman Question in Europe: A Series of Original Essays*. Ed. Theodore Stanton. New York: Putnam's Sons, 1884. 1–29. Print.

Finch, Alison. *Women's Writing in 19th-Century France*. Cambridge: Cambridge UP, 2000. Print.

"Folhetim." *O Zoophilo* 14 Jan. 1877: 4. Print.

"Francisca Wood." *Dicionário mundial de mulheres notáveis*. Ed. Lopes de Oliveira and Gonçalves Viana. Porto: Lello, 1967. Print.

Hippeau, C. "Educação nos Estados Unidos, Colégio Vassar." *O Progresso* Aug. 1869: 129–30. Print.

Ildefonso, Maria Isabel Moutinho Duarte. "As mulheres na imprensa periódica do séc. XIX." Diss. Universidade Aberta, 1998. Print.

Jenkins, Roy. "Dilke, Sir Charles Wentworth, second baronet (1843–1911)." *Oxford Dictionary of National Biography*. Oxford: Oxford UP, May 2008. Web. 26 Feb. 2016.

Joanna Eyre. *O Zoophilo* 14 Jan. 1877: 4. Print.

Kramarae, Cheris, and Lana F. Rakow, eds. *The Revolution in Words: Righting Women, 1868–1871*. London: Routledge, 1990. Print.

Leal, Maria Ivone. *Um século de periódicos femininos*. Lisbon: Comissão para a Igualdade e para os Direitos da Mulher, 1992. Print.

"Literature. Review of John Stuart Mill, The Subjection of Women." *The Athenaeum* 19 June 1869: 819–20. Print.

Lopes, Ana Maria Costa. *Imagens da mulher na imprensa feminina de oitocentos. Percursos de modernidade*. Lisbon: Quimera, 2005. Print.

Lopes, Ana Maria Costa. "Religião e género como formas de discriminação no século XIX: o casal Wood, um study case." *Gaudium Sciendi* 2 (Jul. 2012): 51–65. Web. 26 Feb. 2016.

Morse, Elizabeth J. "Marcet, Jane Haldimand (1769–1858)." *Oxford Dictionary of National Biography*. Oxford: Oxford UP, May 2008. Web. 26 Feb. 2016.

"Our Weekly Gossip." *The Athenaeum* 6 June 1868: 799. Print.

Pazos-Alonso, Cláudia. "A Newly Discovered Novel and its Transnational Author: *Maria Severn* by Francisca Wood." *Portuguese Studies* 32.1 (2016): 48–61. Print.

Pugh, Martin. *The March of the Women: A Revisionist Analysis of the Campaign for Women's Suffrage, 1866–1914*. Oxford: Oxford UP, 2000. Print.

Purcell, Mark. "Thorold, Sir John, ninth baronet (1734–1815)." *Oxford Dictionary of National Biography*. Oxford: Oxford UP, May 2008. Web. 26 Feb. 2016.

Rappaport, Helen. *Encyclopedia of Women Social Reformers*. Vol. 1. Santa Barbara and Oxford: ABC-CLIO, 2001. Print.

Silva, Maria Regina Tavares da. *Carolina Beatriz Ângelo*. Lisbon: CIDM, 2005. Print.

"Sir Henry Raeburn (1756–1823)." *Tennants Auctioneers*. Tennants, The Auction Centre. Web. 25 Feb. 2016.

Smith, Harold L. *The British Women's Suffrage Campaign, 1866–1928*. Rev. 2nd ed. Harlow: Longman, 2010. Print.

Stanton, Theodore, ed. *The Woman Question in Europe: A Series of Original Essays*. New York: Putnam's Sons, 1884. Print.

Torresão, Guiomar. "Uma Senhora Portuguesa Médico." *A Voz Feminina* 82 (1869): 134. Print.

Walker, Linda. "Becker, Lydia Ernestine (1827–1890)." *Oxford Dictionary of National Biography*. Oxford: Oxford UP, May 2008. Web. 26 Feb. 2016.

Webb, R.K. "Martineau, Harriet (1802–1876)." *Oxford Dictionary of National Biography*. Oxford: Oxford UP, May 2008. Web. 26 Feb. 2016.

Wood, Francisca d'Assis Martinz. *Maria Severn*. 2 vols. Lisbon: Tipografia da Voz Feminina, 1869. Print.

Wood, Francisca d'Assis Martinz, ed. *A Voz Feminina* (1868–69). All. Print.

Wood, Guilherme [William], and Francisca Wood, eds. *O Progresso* (1869). All. Print.

Cláudia Pazos-Alonso

natsumi ikoma

ENCOUNTER WITH THE MIRROR OF THE OTHER

angela carter and her personal connection with japan

the mystery of her japan days

Angela Carter is one author among many whose literary style changes drastically with exposure to other cultures. Scott A. Dimovitz, for instance, separates her career into "pre- and post-Japan" ("Cartesian Nuts" 15). However, little has been known to the public about what Carter personally experienced in Japan, even though her works have been the focus of extensive academic research around the world. She came to Japan in 1969 with the award money she received from the Somerset Maugham Literary Award, and after living in Japan for a while she returned to England in 1972. During her stay, she wrote a novel, *The Infernal Desire Machines of Doctor Hoffman* (hereinafter IDM), and an array of journalistic pieces on Japan, some of which touch upon a relationship she appears to have had with a Japanese man. Only that much has been known, and researchers have merely speculated on the possible Japanese influences in her works – speculation derived mainly from Carter's writings on Japan – while the rest has been regarded as "mysterious" (Gamble 106) up until this point.[1] For instance, *The Infernal Desire Machines* has been discussed not from the perspective of its Japanese influence but mainly through its relation to Western theories and literature. This paper attempts to fill that gap with original information drawn from interviews with Carter's former Japanese boyfriend, whose existence has been vaguely recognized but not officially documented, combined with analyses of her unpublished journal entries archived in the British Library. It seeks to bring to light the Japanese influences in Carter's work in general, and in *The Infernal Desire Machines* in particular – in order to supplement one of the underdeveloped areas of research in Angela Carter scholarship. With hope, this paper will also reveal the scale of impact that her romantic encounter had on her later literary career. It seemed, for her, to be an experience of losing one's subjectivity within masculinist discourse, and putting herself and her lover in a situation she described as "a philosophic assassination" (*Angela Carter Papers: Japan 1*, Add MS 88899/1/80 n. pag. (hereinafter *Japan 1*)). In the end, this experience might have helped Carter to obtain a very postmodern and positively feminist sensibility that enabled her to playfully upset masculinist narratives and their core motif of woman as the other.

the infernal desire machines and the japanese assassin

Although Dimovitz is among the few scholars who analyse the influence of Japanese culture on Carter's works, the main focus of his analysis is the way in which Carter develops/refutes the European psychoanalytic discourses of Freud and Lacan, or the philosophical discourses of Plato and Surrealism.[2] To be sure, *The Infernal Desire Machines* could be read as a subversive narrative that mockingly mimics European masculine/masculinist discourses of desire, such as psychoanalytic theories and Proust's famous narrative *À la recherche du temps perdu* (1913–27), as analysed by Maggie Tonkin and me.[3] Carter is known to refer to – and often parody – many literary, philosophical, and theoretical works and their authors; *The Bloody Chamber* (1979), for instance, is a collection of subversive retellings of fairy tales, and *Wise Children* (1991) is a parodic narrative on Shakespeare and his legacy. Her retellings offer new and alternative perspectives, at once feminist and postmodernist, to upset the masculine narratives prevalent in the literary world.

Subversion and disruption are two of Carter's favoured qualities in narratives, as she writes:

> To try to say something simple – do I situate myself politically as a writer? Well, yes; of course. I always hope it's obvious, although I try, when I write fiction, to think on my feet – to present a number of propositions in a variety of different ways, and to leave the reader to construct her own fiction for herself from the elements of my fictions. (Reading is just as creative an activity as writing and most intellectual development depends upon new readings of old texts. I am all for putting new wine in old bottles, especially if the pressure of the new wine makes the old bottles explode.) (*Shaking a Leg* 37 (hereinafter SL))

The Infernal Desire Machines features many such "old bottles" into which new wine has been poured, so as to make them burst. One big old bottle – psychoanalysis – is extensively utilized for explosive new wine in this novel. As Dimovitz puts it:

> *Doctor Hoffman*, therefore, systematically literalizes the stages of various psychoanalytic traditions in order to subvert those traditions. Psychoanalysis, the novel suggests, serves as a useful tool to describe our Western culture not because of its objective validity for interpreting our culture, but because that very structure, in fact, *causes* our culture. ("Angela Carter's Narrative Chiasmus" 99)

A number of feminists, including Betty Friedan and Kate Millet, criticize the male-centrality of psychoanalysis for the way it indiscriminately defines whatever is the opposite of reason and order, such as non-reason, illogicality, madness, etc., as "feminine." In *The Infernal Desire Machines*, as if to reflect these feminist sensibilities, the "feminine" defined by psychoanalysis, such as desire, non-reason, and madness, is represented by the male character, Doctor Hoffman, thus suggesting that the psychoanalytic "feminine" is in fact a male creation, and therefore "masculine." Similarly, fantastic images of Albertina in the work are presented as mere reflections of the desire of Desiderio, and have nothing to do with the real woman named Albertina, whose existence is ultimately terminated by Desiderio himself. Indeed, Carter "literalizes" criticisms of psychoanalysis, even preceding major feminist criticism.

In the quotation above, however, Dimovitz seems to extend the scope of this novel's criticism only to "*our* Western culture" (emphasis mine). Is this novel solely about Western culture, then? Are we supposed to read it only as a criticism of Western society and its narratives on desire? Though Carter might initially have written it for a Western readership, I would like to suggest the scope of its criticism is not confined to Britain, or even to Europe for that matter, but is in fact much wider, including Japan and other patriarchal societies. As will be explored in this paper, the journal entries that Carter wrote while living in Japan show that Carter wrote this novel while heavily under the influence of Japanese society and what she experienced there, both on cultural and personal levels.[4] The City in this story, though unspecified, greatly resembles the Japan that Carter describes in an unpublished manuscript fragment titled "Summer '70," as "a great country for appearances and it is often hard to tell what is real and what is not" (*Angela Carter Papers: Japan 2*, Add MS 88899/1/81 n. pag. (hereinafter *Japan 2*)). Some of the "old bottles" that Carter aims to explode in this novel, therefore, may very well reflect some aspects of Japanese society and culture.

However, we need to bear in mind that Desiderio, as his name suggests, is the personification of universal masculine desire. He is a typical hero-in-the-making. He pursues Albertina, his object of desire, yet his real objective is to assassinate Doctor Hoffman (and Albertina, in fact) to become a hero, a masculine subject. Desiderio is not primarily Albertina's lover but her assassin, though the romantic discourse serves as a façade to cover up the male homosocial arena in which Desiderio moves, similar to that described by Bakhtin:

> Truth's earthly adventures take place on highroads, in brothels, dens of thieves, taverns, market places, prisons, at secret cults' erotic orgies […] The man of an idea – the wise man – is confronted with the extreme expression of worldly evil, depravity, baseness and vulgarity. (94)

It is rather revealing that Bakhtin assumes the personified "Truth," who is to be challenged by various difficulties, as masculine here. The challenges he encounters are those suited to proving his manhood, his status as hero. This kind of unconscious gender assumption in the patriarchal and masculinist imagination is what Carter attacks, although Bakhtin's dialogism is in tune with Carter's intertextuality. Bakhtin's "Truth" is named "Desiderio" in Carter's work, and he is challenged by similar difficulties in the unspecified setting of *The Infernal Desire Machines*. The racial ambivalence of Desiderio is no coincidence, then; the novel is not a narrative targeting a specific society, culture or race. In my opinion, Carter deliberately creates Desiderio as a universal subject, almost an abstract notion, and his Albertina as nothing more than the reflection of his own desire, so that they serve to parody the male-centrality of literary narratives in patriarchal cultures. In such narratives, the hero and the heroine are totally dependent on each other to establish their status as hero and heroine. The heroine, if she wants to remain in his masculine discourse, needs to conform to the hero's desire, to reflect his desire for the other, and lose her own agency to the extent that she becomes the hero's mirror. She needs to conceal her true form, and personify the otherness the hero imagines her to possess. With a shred of suspicion, of her heterogeneity and of her self, independent of his desire, this harmonious unity between the hero and the heroine is shattered, and they become each other's assassins, as Desiderio and Albertina demonstrate. Interestingly, Desiderio and Albertina seem to be modelled after the same person, Sozo Araki, the Japanese man with whom Carter had an intense relationship when she was in Japan. She called Sozo "my assassin" in her journal, and she dubbed his native country "a country of beautiful assassins" (*Angela Carter Papers: Journal*, MS 88899/1/93 n. pag. (hereinafter *Journal 93*)).[5]

The Infernal Desire Machines is just one example among many stories written by Carter that suggest what a strong impact her personal encounters in Japan had on her creativity in her later career. By "encounters," I do not mean a mere brush with foreign culture as an outsider might enjoy, but much more personal and intimate experiences, so as to change who one is; Carter seemed to be so in love that she became almost an insider to Japan when she dated and lived with Sozo. She chose to immerse herself among Japanese people and within the Japanese family system to the extent that she communicated with Sozo's family members constantly.[6] As I suggest in this paper, this personal relationship with Sozo Araki affected Carter potentially more than any cultural observation she made during her stay in Japan or her studious research on Japanese society – so much so that it may have been one of the key factors in the transformation of her writing style from pre-Japan to post-Japan.

The basis of this speculation is derived from the insight made possible by my personal contact with Sozo Araki himself. Carter's journals, as well as her unpublished works-in-progress written during and after her stay and now archived in the British Library, contain numerous entries about Sozo and support what I have heard from him. Besides Desiderio and Albertina, there are several other characters apparently modelled after Sozo: for instance, Taro in "A Souvenir of Japan" is one of them. In one of her journal entries, Carter scribbles "A Memory of Skin" juxtaposed to "A Souvenir of Japan," under which is written the following:

> Short Story: ~~Sozo~~
> Simple style – the basis, the absolute impossibility of the relationship – the desperate attempt to get through male arrogance, the bed duty bit. (*Journal 93* n. pag.; strike-through in original)

It testifies to the fact that "A Souvenir of Japan," included in *Fireworks* – a collection of short stories – was initially inspired by Sozo and Carter's relationship with him (Carter also refers to him as "my friend S" in many pieces, including her essay on Mishima[7]).

Carter and Sozo met each other in 1969, seemingly not long after she arrived in Japan. They fell in love and, after an interval, spent about a year and a half together. At one point, Carter wrote in an undated journal entry:

> He is so beautiful, so variously beautiful [...] Sozo has the perfect languorous gracefulness of the man in the Hilliard miniature, whose legs, their musculature so exquisitely delineated by the close silken skin of his white stockings, have a superb gracefulness – an animal rather than human repose. In sleep, however, he becomes purely Polynesian, a Gauguin. (Ibid.)

Their relationship seems to have been intense, bittersweet, and the break-up painful. After a heated quarrel, Carter wrote in a journal entry:

> We came to no conclusions; but I, at least, came to a conclusion in my mind. That, unless he changes – which is unlikely in someone so profoundly neurotic – I shall leave him at, I think, the end of summer. Until then, I shall watch him, study him & learn all I can. On the other hand – to further confuse the issue – I discover I love him more than anything in the world. (Ibid.)

I interviewed Sozo Araki several times, and partly use the information I obtained from him in this paper to suggest the impact of the personal as well as cultural experiences Carter had in Japan on her writings, in the hope that Sozo's testimony fills the formerly uncharted gap between Carter's hands-on experience and final literary products.[8] I also attempt to compensate for the one-sidedness of Sozo's narrative with Carter's own, recorded in her journals and other unpublished works. Indeed, I believe what she experienced and learned in Japan during her romantic involvement with Sozo might have helped Carter to develop her theory of gender performativity, even before the term was coined by Judith Butler in the late 1980s. This paper, therefore, is an attempt at weaving a discursive tapestry that reveals the hitherto unexamined influence of the years Angela Carter spent in Japan.

life as the other: a woman in love

Many of Carter's journal entries archived in the British Library, as well as what Sozo relayed to me in our interviews, testify to the fact that Sozo and Carter experienced a very intense and turbulent romance. When they first met, they both were in their twenties, though Carter was five years older than Sozo. Carter had distanced herself from her husband, but was still technically married to him. After years of frustration, Carter was perhaps ready for a new adventure. Upon meeting Sozo – who seems to have possessed a melancholic, Asian handsomeness in his youth – Carter, it seems, promptly fell in love with him. According to Sozo, after a short period of dating and her brief return to England, she persuaded him to live with her in a corner of Tokyo, as though they were a married couple.

With Sozo, Carter was able to visit places where foreign tourists did not usually venture, and witness the lives of ordinary Japanese people behind the formal, polite façades they tend to wear in front of guests from overseas. Partly because of him, Carter was able to see the real Japan some forty-odd years ago, which must have been far more exotic than, and different from, today's globalized, uniformed, Westernized Japan. The stories contained in *Fireworks*, and many of her essays published in *New Society*, are described from this unusual standpoint that Carter had as both insider and outsider, or rather, as neither one nor the other.

Carter was very keen to know Japanese culture, its traditions and its way of life. According to Sozo, she was particularly interested in the sexual mores of Japanese people, her curiosity most probably stirred by her own relationship with a Japanese man. She frequently asked Sozo why Japanese men or women behaved in a certain way. For instance, she could not understand why Japanese women behaved childishly and demurely at first. For a person coming from Swinging London, Japanese women in those days must have seemed extremely backward and un-liberated.

However, according to Sozo, Carter had to completely rethink her view of Japanese women one night when she was infuriated by a Japanese woman who seemed neither particularly beautiful nor intelligent, but upon arrival managed to steal all the attention of the men, which previously had been focused on Carter. She did not understand why this unremarkable woman was capable of monopolizing male attention. Sozo explained that the very qualities that woman exhibited – such as immaturity, childishness, demureness and reserve – were the qualities appreciated by the Japanese men gathered there. On that day, Carter must have become aware of the cultural specificity of gender norms and of the Japanese definition of an "attractive woman," which was quite distinct from the European one. The Japanese woman she met that day may not have been innately childish or immature, but she certainly acted as such in accordance with the social norms in Japan.

This realization possibly led Carter to scrutinize her own popular status among Japanese men. In those days, when foreign tourists were not a common sight, Carter stood out as a Caucasian woman, an exotic object, a rarity in Japanese society. Though Japan today still exhibits what can be called a "foreigner complex" – a residual feeling from over two hundred years of closed-door policy by the Edo government, perhaps – the Japan of forty-odd years ago was extremely awe-stricken by Caucasians. Depending on the situation, Caucasians were feared, idolized or sexualized, but in all cases they were objectified. Women in general were "others" in Japanese society, but Caucasian women were doubly so. In "A Souvenir of Japan," Carter writes: "I had never been so absolutely the mysterious other. I had become a kind of phoenix, a fabulous beast; I was an outlandish jewel. He found me, I think, inexpressibly exotic. But I often felt like a female impersonator" (*Fireworks* 7).

It is noteworthy that she writes "a female impersonator" here, to signpost the narrating woman's awareness of the gendered expectations imposed upon her, and of the difference between what was desired and what she herself felt she was. Similarly, although on the surface Carter was adored and respected, she was able to penetrate that façade to see how Japanese society robbed her of her subjectivity and agency. Instead, she was turned into an object: a beast, a jewel, an automaton.

A similar conclusion was drawn when Carter worked as a part-time bar hostess in Ginza. This particular bar hired many foreign women to serve as hostesses as a kind of "special attraction" for male customers. After working for hours as a hostess, Carter visited a sex shop and listened to a male shopkeeper's description of a product: "[T]he salesman explained: 'a masturbatory device for gentlemen.' Which is, presumably, the same function Suzy and I had performed for the last two and a half hours" (SL 254).

Here, Carter seems to realize the extreme male-centrality of Japanese society, and how it renders women agency-less, whether they are Japanese or otherwise. Having found how women are excluded from society and how they are denied existence other than in relation to men, Carter then seems to have formed some kind of sympathy towards Japanese women, to whom she had felt hostility previously. Once, in a town famous for its hot springs, Carter witnessed a shooting game that displayed dolls of nude women as targets, and wrote: "This seemed to me a fitting parable of the battle of the sexes in Japan. True femininity is denied an expression and women, in general, have the choice of becoming either slaves or toys" (249).

In these essays, Carter found that Japanese women were objectified so as to become slaves or toys, and foreign women, including her, were objectified so as to become exotic jewels or beasts. In the end, the fact that both of them were objectified for the convenience and pleasure of men was the same. She also wrote: "[T]he hostess – the computerized playmate – may conceivably be an illustration of the fact that Japan is just the same as everywhere else, only more so; perhaps she is indeed the universal male notion of the perfect woman" (251).

In the quotation above, Carter recognizes that Japanese society is not fundamentally different from other patriarchal societies, and that universally, in male-dominant societies the notion of the perfect woman has nothing to do with the reality of those with female bodies. This increased awareness may have built the foundation of Albertina, the character who reflects universal male desire. The same awareness also might have led Carter to write: "In Japan, I learnt what it is to be a woman, and became radicalised" (*Nothing Sacred* 28). No longer hindered by personal antagonism and rivalry, Carter here seems to discover a commonality between herself and Japanese women.

the theatre of romance and the mirror of the other

According to Sozo's testimony, Angela Carter was in love for at least the first half of the period she was in Japan. And because of this, even though she was consciously a feminist and remained as such, she was nevertheless at risk of losing her subjectivity, affected by the power of male-centrism in Japanese society. What Judith Butler calls "a sedimentation of gender norms" ("Performative Acts" 524) possesses its greatest force in the framework of romantic love, as Carter demonstrates in a story titled "Flesh and the Mirror," a story that greatly resembles what Carter actually experienced in her relationship with Sozo.

In this story, the narrator is a foreign woman in love, who wanders around the city of Tokyo looking for her heartless Japanese male lover, whom Carter undoubtedly created out of Sozo. This narrator is aware that she is performing the role of a romantic heroine, and is confident that she is controlling her own script and performance. The story begins as follows: "It was midnight – I chose my times and set my scenes with the precision of the born artiste" (*Fireworks* 61). The protagonist is a Caucasian woman in a romantic script. With a touch of narcissism, the narrator seems confident in her own stage management skills. Even though her Japanese lover does not come to greet her as promised on her return to Japan, she still executes a romantic performance, as she wanders around Tokyo at midnight, crying, cutting an exotic and romantic figure – a perfect heroine in distress. Contradictorily, however, she also desires the genuine feelings of a romantic heroine, from which she is removed because of her self-conscious performance:

> It was as if there were glass between me and the world. But I could see myself perfectly well on the other side of the glass. There I was, walking up and down, eating meals, having conversations, in love, indifferent, and so on. But all the time I was pulling the strings of my own puppet; it was this puppet who was moving about on the other side of the glass. And I eyed the most marvellous adventures with the bored eye of the agent with the cigar watching another audition. I tapped out the ash and asked of events: "What else can you do?" (63)

In spite of, or rather because of, her longing to be a true heroine in a romantic discourse, the narrator becomes at once the impresario and the puppet, thus driven further away from truly feeling the emotion of love. She takes her own power for granted and this routine performance bores her. Up to this point, it is beyond her imagination that someone other than herself could have, in fact, been the puppet master. Gradually, however, she is consumed by her own show:

> On the night I came back to [the city], however hard I looked for the one I loved, she could not find him anywhere and the city delivered her into the hands of a perfect stranger who fell into step beside her and asked why she was crying. (Ibid.)

The subject of the sentence shifts from "I" to "she," indicating her loss of subjectivity and agency in the performance. The script she has written – a script about a great romance – no longer functions, and the narrator becomes a third-person character in a script written by someone else.

The mirror motif used in the story reminds the reader of the Lacanian mirror when the narrator is faced with the reality of finding herself in a hotel room with a stranger:

> The magic mirror presented me with a hitherto unconsidered notion of myself as I. Without any intention of mine, I had been defined by the action reflected in the mirror. I beset me. I was the subject of the sentence written on the mirror. (64–65)

In Lacanian theory, the mirror offers the infant a sense of self, with its capacity and limitation, formerly unknown to him/her. But Carter does not just utilize Lacanian theory here; again, she seems to criticize it. Unlike the Lacanian mirror, the sense of subjectivity or agency found within the mirror in Carter's story offers no consolation to the narrator. Rather, it makes her realize the deep chasm between her former sense of self and reality: the "real" condition of herself as an object. The former is within her control, the latter beyond it. This difference in the mirrors may be a reflection of Carter's critical reading of Lacan. Lacanian psychoanalysis is applicable to a "masculine subject" but not to its feminine counterpart, since the latter is imbued with perpetual otherness in his theory; in other words, there is no "feminine subject" in psychoanalysis.

The narrator of "Flesh and the Mirror" now realizes that, though she had believed she was the scriptwriter and puppet master of the theatre of romance, in fact she is just a character without any agency or control:

> The fancy-dress disguise I'd put on to suit the city had betrayed me to a room and a bed and a modification of myself that had no business at all in my life, not in the life I had watched myself performing. (65)

The loss of the narrator's agency could be a consequence of her own naïve performance as a "romantic heroine" in accordance with the gender norms imposed upon her. Although the narrator is self-conscious and does not really believe in essential femininity, the ideal discourse of a romantic heroine still makes her want to feel truly "in love" amidst her suffering. Thus, the "sedimentation of gender norms" as described by Butler has piled up to fix her as a woman in patriarchal discourse – in other words, as an object, which she herself does not recognize. When the narrator's romantic relationship with a man is what triggers her fall – she who has travelled the world alone of her own free will – the story demonstrates how gender norms exert their power with a vengeance in romantic ideology: "So, although I thought I was the most romantic spectacle imaginable as I wandered down the alleys, I was in reality at risk" (66–67). Blinded by love and intoxicated by her mental state as a romantic heroine, which is equal to narcissistic masochism in the masculinist definition, the narrator actually enjoys this objectification of herself, her sufferings, her pain, her devastation and her patience.

The heroine of the story is, at least in part, Carter herself, since this story is based partly on facts – Carter, too, was stood up by her lover when he was supposed to pick her up from the airport – and presumably reflects Carter's own feelings and mental state. Sozo was a bit of a player, and Carter sometimes had to compete with Japanese women. In one of her journal entries with the heading "Sozo, cont," she writes:

> When he is away from me, I believe he spends much of the time savouring the most exquisite ravages of guilt; yet out he goes the next night, or the night after, and even if he fully intends to return home early, he never quite contrives to do so, somehow inevitably forced by circumstance to always find himself, sodden with drink & self-disgust, moving as if in trance through the echoing vaults of a mysteriously deserted & unlike-itself Shinjuku station at 5 in the morning, tortured by the ghastly notion – which yet contains a savagely damped down spark of hope – that, this time, he may have gone too far. My rave fears he misinterprets; yet they excite him. (*Journal 93* n. pag.)

In the following entry, subtitled "Sozo, cont or completed," Carter continues:

> He says these things to me & they don't mean a thing. No; that's not fair; When he says them, he means them; when he kisses my thighs, & to excite himself, speaks of love, he means every word; every choked syllable. But it is impossible, when he is away from me, for him not to betray me or, at least, in word & thought, I constantly betray him, & far more grievously, did he but know it. So he will propose the old answer, the love suicide, to preserve the notion that our love is ultimate from that contact with the quotidian world which will inevitably destroy it. I have this desperate love & I do not know what to do with it. (Ibid.)

Although this entry may not be a totally truthful description of what had actually occurred between Carter and Sozo, there appear to be elements in their relationship that inspired this writing. Amidst the turbulent and somewhat co-dependent relationship described here, Carter may have found herself becoming someone she was not. Whether done consciously or unconsciously, she might have acted in a way that was in response to Sozo so as to please him in part, and also to perform the role of a heroine properly. Without really intending to, she might have conformed to certain gender norms imposed upon her by Japanese society. She seems to have found that shocking after a certain time, as she writes in a journal entry presumably some time after her return to England:

> Bradford, again; and here I am, in the grey, discomforting city, my new easy, strenuously disaffected self – how difficult, indeed, to retain calm. It doesn't matter, of course. Self-possession. To be in possession of one's self. That's the only thing, really […] My self & I – I & me, subject & object, the oscillation between the two when it should be a dialectic, I should be in control of my double, my most intimate other, myself as me, my own reflection […] I am not my self. Ego as subject, ego as object; experiencing one self as object – onanistic sexuality since I was the object on which they focused their frigidity at its fullest intensity, I perceived it as passion. (*Angela Carter Papers: Journal*, Add MS 88899/1/94 n. pag.; underlining in original)

Going beyond personal and culturally specific experiences, Carter further developed her ideas on the power of gender norms for general application. The protagonist of "Flesh and the Mirror," for instance, inquires into general objectifications at work in romantic relationships, and finds herself not only as a victim but also as a perpetrator of objectification:

> So I suppose I do not know how he really looked and, in fact, I suppose I shall never know, now, for he was plainly an object created in the mode of fantasy. His image was already present somewhere in my head and I was seeking to discover it in actuality, looking at every face I met in case it was the right face […] So his self, and, by his self, I mean the thing he was to himself, was quite unknown to me. I created him solely in relation to myself, like a work of romantic art, an object corresponding to the ghost inside me. (*Fireworks* 67–68)

Deeply embedded in gender norms working within heterosexual romantic ideology, the narrator objectifies herself and her partner without realizing. In fact, she starts to think she has invented her "romance" in order to satisfy social norms that require her to be in love, to have a heterosexual relationship:

> In order to create the loved object in this way and to issue it with its certificate of authentication, as beloved, I had also to labour at the idea of myself in love. I watched myself closely for all the signs and, precisely upon cue, here they were! Longing, desire, self-abnegation, etc. […] I no longer understood the logic of my own performance. My script had been scrambled behind my back. The cameraman was drunk. The director had a *crise de nerfs* and been taken away to a sanatorium. (68)

What is described here is how coercive romantic ideology, heterosexism and gender norms take away the agency of both parties in a romantic relationship. They feel they are falling in love willingly, believing love is by nature spontaneous and natural. But, in fact, they are ideologically led to "fall in love willingly," are persuaded, educated and coerced to plunge into heterosexual relationships. The script of romance they believe they have written themselves is in fact written by society and its ideology. Consequently, her subjectivity and his subjectivity are erased from the script. They are both puppets pursuing a goal set by society. No mutual respect can be attained in such a relationship, and the lovers end up becoming each other's assassins. Perhaps, after the turbulent relationship and bitter break-up with Sozo, Carter came to this conclusion about "love"; that is, it is an illusion created by the sheer force of imagination, and the ones involved inevitably act out parts for reasons unbeknownst to themselves, in order to fit the concept of what lovers "should be like."

The protagonist of "Flesh and the Mirror" comes to the conclusion that every act, not merely in romantic relationships, is a performance to fulfil some sort of expectation imposed upon us when she says: "The most difficult performance in the world is acting naturally, isn't it? Everything else is artful" (70).

This ultimate realization of performativity in human life seems to have resulted from Carter's experiences in Japan, to some extent. Being coerced into gender norms foreign to her and having every movement watched because of her otherness must have made her into a self-conscious actor, even leading her to pay attention to how she moved her own body.

In her journal, seemingly recorded during her return to England to sort out her marriage after the initial bout with Sozo, she writes:

> Home again, in that contented boredom which signifies "at home"; I remember my magic other, as again I grow aware of, or grow back into, my peculiar identity; and how much, not so much of self-deceit but of sleight of hand, went into the effortful creation of the idea of myself in love. And perhaps I should say: "I am not the thing I am" or "Cogito non ergo sum." (*Journal 93* n. pag.)

Even the most intimate feeling of being "in love" is a self-conscious, effortful performance here. Her "self" is her "magic other," and she categorically defines her "self" as "not the thing I am." This loss of her "self" and "essence" is characteristic of her post-Japan fiction, in which human performativity is explored in various ways.

woman as the other: the tanizaki connection

As mentioned above, *The Infernal Desire Machines*, the novel that Carter wrote in Japan, can be interpreted as a subversive narrative that mimics masculinist discourses. In the novel, the heroine, Albertina, is a reflection of the male protagonist, Desiderio. Just like the heroine in "Flesh and the Mirror," Albertina is, until the final part of the novel, merely a character within the male romantic discourse who has neither agency nor subjectivity, and the idea of performativity – especially of gender performativity – is most vividly expressed in Albertina. Gender performativity itself had been a recurring topic that Carter addressed from the very early stages of her writing career, although it was not as developed as in her post-Japan novels. This is striking, considering that most of her works were published before *Gender Trouble* (1990), Judith Butler's seminal work on gender performativity.[9] As early as 1964, using the motifs of theatre and performance, Carter theorized gender as part of a performance in *The Magic Toyshop*, for instance, in which Melanie, the protagonist, is forced to perform "femininity" according to a script of heterosexuality and violence.

However, nobody would disagree that after her years in Japan, Carter's work became more fantastic and positively feminist. As to the performativity aspect, for example, the essential femininity retained by Melanie in *The Magic Toyshop* evaporates in her post-Japan works. What contributed to this shift could be the coercive power of gender norms that Carter experienced in her romantic relationship as explored in the previous section, together with her cultural observations, including Kabuki theatre (all-male traditional theatre) and Joruri puppet theatre, which, according to Sozo, Carter visited with great interest. In those theatres, an extremely elegant and stylized femininity is put on show by a male actor in the former or by a puppet in the latter, further consolidating the fact that "femininity" is a performance. According to Sozo Araki, Carter also had an insatiable appetite for books on Japan; among them, Jun'ichiro Tanizaki and Akiyuki Nosaka were her favourite authors. With these experiences and observations combined, Carter seems to have come to question the general meaning of "being a woman" and the existence of a female "essence."

Carter's works contain much intertextuality, as I have argued previously, and in terms of *The Infernal Desire Machines*, specifically, Tanizaki and Nosaka seem to have influenced her research. The particular novels I would like to refer to in conjunction with *The Infernal Desire Machines* are Tanizaki's *Naomi* (1924–25) and Nosaka's *The Pornographers* (1966). The romantic love and sexual desire portrayed in these two novels could be seen as the basis of Carter's own novel, though Carter uses these works in order to subvert them.

Tanizaki is one of the literary authors that Carter adored and respected, and of whom Carter wrote: "Tanizaki Jun'ichiro is one of the greatest of twentieth-century novelists, of the rank of Thomas Mann" (SL 267). *Naomi*, one of Tanizaki's masterpieces, was her favourite, and she even wrote a book review on it. The story is set in the Taisho period (1912–26), when Japanese society was undergoing Westernization and the people were striving to act like Westerners. Kawai, the protagonist, is in his late twenties when he meets a girl of fifteen, Naomi, to whom he is strongly attracted. Kawai is a representation of Japanese society in those days; behind his attraction to Naomi are her outlandish, Westernized face and name. He basically purchases her from her family to raise her to be his ideal wife. Naomi, though at first a naïve girl, grows into a cunning, treacherous and voluptuous nymphet who toys with many lovers and retains Kawai as her financial source. Kawai repeatedly tries to cut her out of his life, but ultimately fails. In the end, he accepts his defeat, and caresses the knees of the evil Naomi, who is almost deified in his mind.

It is needless to mention that Carter sees through the façade of romantic love described in Tanizaki's story. In Carter's assessment, Naomi, including her evil nature, is Kawai's creation to fit his own desire. Carter writes: "Naomi is drawn entirely from the outside, the very type of the faithless female lover that haunts the universal male imagination, tacky, meretricious and irresistible" (269).

Carter sees Naomi entirely as a creation of this "male imagination." She analyses Naomi's imagined "otherness" as originating from Kawai:

> For Kawai, Naomi stands for all the allure of the exotic – but she only *stands for it*, she does not embody it. She is, in reality, just as Japanese as he is. His own sense of self is never at risk with her, as it would be with a real foreigner. (268; emphasis in original)

At the end of the story, Naomi completely transforms herself into a Western goddess and reappears in front of Kawai to make him succumb to her. But Carter feels that Naomi's exoticism does not arise from her inherent "otherness." Rather, it is exactly what Kawai created her for and what Kawai embedded in her. Kawai brings about this exoticism in Naomi so that he can safely succumb to it and worship it. In the end, Naomi is there for Kawai's pleasure. As Carter grasps, the real otherness that is too disturbing and threatening is tactfully avoided and replaced by an artificial replica, which is the exoticism of Naomi. Paradoxically, it suggests how dangerous and threatening real otherness can be, which Kawai experiences in the middle of the story when he compares Naomi with "real foreigners"; real foreigners are far more sophisticated than Naomi, and beside them, Kawai can only feel belittled, inferior and ashamed. Carter writes in one of her unpublished works titled "Tokyo":

> Nowhere in Tokyo has an authentically cosmopolitan atmosphere, for the Japanese outnumber everyone, but Shinjuku is a pastiche of cosmopolitanism because it is a playground and the foreign may be reproduced, for entertainment purposes only, in a series of lovingly executed tableaux made of plywood and papier mâché. Once reduced to a stereotype of itself, the foreign, disarmed of strangeness, ceases to be a menace. Foreigners who live in Japan long enough become affected by the benign refusal of their hosts to take them seriously and start to parody their national characteristics; they force us to behave as they have seen us on the movies. (*Japan 2* n. pag.)

In the style of Tanizaki, Carter here refers directly to the threat that the Japanese feel with the truly foreign. In much the same way, the truly foreign is too scary for Kawai to handle. On the other hand, he finds Naomi's shortcomings disgusting, yet contradictorily irresistible, because he feels superior to her. The story of Naomi – as Carter interprets it – is the story of a narcissistic male ego, in which the male raises his ideal goddess from scratch so that he can enjoy succumbing to her without any real threat to his ego. In this story, Naomi is a mere receptacle, a doll, a theatrical device of male desire. Even at her evilest and worst self, she is not a threatening figure; after all, she is a docile being acting to satisfy Kawai's masochistic desire. As Carter writes: "Naomi, as she matures into a tramp, does him the service of gratifying it" (SL 269). Only, this male-centric mechanism is carefully hidden in the name of love.

Carter was likely drawn towards *Naomi* because it deals with a sadomasochistic relationship between a Japanese man and a foreign-looking woman. Carter may have associated Kawai's attraction to, and simultaneous repulsion at, Naomi's foreignness and otherness with Sozo's. She writes in an unpublished paper: "He perceived me, not in terms of the senses, but as an intellectual idea – as a baleful threat to his own precarious autonomy, for he was too proud to subsume his self to mine & love & pride cannot live in the same house" (*Japan 1* n. pag.). In this entry, Sozo resembles Kawai, in that they both cling to their autonomy by turning their partners into fantastic objects.

The Infernal Desire Machines employs the same motif utilized in *Naomi*: the woman as a receptacle of narcissistic male desire. The novel pursues Carter's speculation on what would happen to "romantic love" if the real "otherness" of the woman appeared to threaten the male ego. What if the woman did not remain the hero's doll? Up until the denouement, the relationship of Desiderio and Albertina is, though more fantastic, quite similar to that of Kawai and Naomi. Desiderio in *The Infernal Desire Machines* is a character created out of the "universal male imagination," a representation of "male desire" that makes his love object change her shape and migrate her gender to suit his fantasy. The ecstatic words uttered by Desiderio when he dreams of reuniting with Albertina echo Kawai's voice: "I would fall on my knees and worship" (IDM 41).

However, Carter makes Albertina more resistant than Naomi, in that she does not remain Desiderio's doll, but gradually reveals her heterogeneous shape. Carter rips off the theatrical veil that conceals the mechanism of desire and thrusts it upon Desiderio, who laments:

> Here, nothing could possibly be fantastic. That was the source of my bitter disappointment [...] My disillusionment was profound. I was not in the domain of the marvellous at all. I had gone far beyond that and at last I had reached the powerhouse

> of the marvellous, where all its clanking, dull, stage machinery was kept [...] I was already wondering whether the fleshly possession of Albertina would not be the greatest disillusionment of all. (IDM 200–01)

It is revealed here that what Desiderio had imagined as exotic and fantastic is instead "stage machinery." Unlike in *Naomi*, the stage machinery in Carter's retelling is shattered and the love story of Albertina and Desiderio meets its fatal ending, in which Desiderio kills Albertina. If a love is this kind of narcissistic projection of the self onto the imagined otherness of the partner, then it is bound to end like Desiderio and Albertina, because Albertina's actual otherness has no place in this masculinist "love" story. Commenting on her own "love" story, Carter writes as follows:

> I came to define my own existence entirely in relation to him; he became the pole of my world, my sun, the core of my self. He – I. In a sense, it was a demonic possession. He was myself; I am Heathcliff. I abnegated my existence to his & in return, I demanded absolute submission. He, my magic other, my assassin. We reached a condition of absolute, grovelling, whining, total dependence on one another, so it was agony to be apart even if it was torture or ennui to be together [...] Then, at the end, [we were] like sharks, helplessly devouring one another; until there was no way in which we could speak the truth. (*Journal 93* n. pag.)

Unlike Tanizaki, Carter chose to tell the story of Desiderio and Albertina until its conclusion, with its bitter tragedy and impossibility of "love," and her hands-on experience with Sozo appears certainly to have contributed to the making of the story.

the ideal woman in homosocial discourse: the nosaka connection

Another novel Carter was likely influenced by is *The Pornographers*, written by Akiyuki Nosaka. This novel informed Carter more in terms of the male-centric sexual formation of contemporary Japanese society. According to Sozo Araki, Carter praised this novel and its author, remarking that Nosaka would be recognized in the future and valued more highly abroad. *The Pornographers* was translated into English in 1968 and reviewed in both the *New York Review of Books* and the *New York Times*, and it must have been this English version that Carter read.

The protagonist is Subuyan, a small-time trader and producer, making his living in a corner of the sex industry. He harbours an illicit desire for his step-daughter, Keiko, but finds himself impotent when the occasion arises. The majority of the novel describes what goes on behind the scenes in the sex industry; it reveals how "virgin" prostitutes fake their virginity, and how one pair of pornographic actors are in fact a father and a daughter, etc. The theatrical mechanism that creates erotic illusion, or what Carter calls "clanking, dull, stage machinery," is grotesquely laid bare here.

The highlight of the novel is the scene in which one of the members of Subuyan's team, Hack, who penned all the scripts of the pornographic films produced by Subuyan, dies of a heart attack after masturbation. Subuyan visits Hack's lodge and talks with the other members of the team:

> "The first time Hack sat down to write a pornographic book, that's what probably came to him and got him excited. And now here at the end, he went over it again so that he could get worked up and go to it [...]"
>
> "So it was just for himself he wrote all those books," said Subuyan, shaking his head sadly.
>
> "I don't know, but doesn't it sort of remind you of the human torpedoes during the war?"
>
> "Yeah, that's it! Grab yourself tight, go plunging ahead in a world all your own, and with a burst of semen you blow yourself up." (Nozaka 240)[10]

There is a certain irony in comparing death by masturbation to a suicide attack during the war. It shows how Subuyan feels about the team: they are brave soldiers, tragically fighting for some great cause. But it is not only homosocial camaraderie that Subuyan feels for Hack; Hack told Subuyan that he wrote pornographic stories as a requiem for his dead mother, who sacrificed her sexual pleasure, and eventually her life, by selling her body in order to raise her son. Subuyan and his team are touched by Hack's love for his mother, and the mother's dedication to her son.

As suggested in the episode with Hack, Subuyan, the impresario of this theatre of sexuality, regards his profession as an act of humanism:

> True, he had gotten into pornography for the sake of the money; but more recently he had begun to see his profession as a genuine means of alleviating human suffering. The chairman of the board, so pathetically eager for a girl untouched, had been taken in in more ways than one; but still he lived now with the sense that he was truly a conqueror of virgins, and, thanks to this illusion, whenever the fatal moment came, he would die happy [...] "Who would have brought them salvation if it wasn't for me, Oharu? Isn't that right? So you see, there's nothing at all to be ashamed of about this business." (63)

What is interesting about this novel, and what I believe was intriguing to Carter as well, is that it is thoroughly, defiantly male-centric. The "human suffering" that Subuyan mentions only applies to men, and it is only to the menfolk that Subuyan thinks of bringing salvation. When planning a large erotic enterprise, in which Subuyan aims to create the "ultimate woman," Subuyan's team does not pay attention to the concept of love at all. Moreover, this woman is nothing like the mythic goddess in Western narratives:

> Now as for the women, that'll be my department. And we don't want any of these old relics. I'm going to get hold of some young seventeen, eighteen-year-olds and train them properly in every detail right from the beginning. And we'll eventually have some call girls that are real paragons [...] We'll groom them right from the start, teach them how to please a man, keep an eye on them all the time, and turn them out first-class women in every respect. (191)

This may sound similar to what Kawai had in mind when he met Naomi. But what makes Subuyan different from Kawai is that Subuyan is aware that these women are not real. He tells a woman when he recruits her as a prostitute:

> "Now, every man's got a dream woman he's always looking for. The thing for you is to be that kind of ideal woman, to fulfill, in other words, the man's dream. Let's see ... another way of putting it in a simple way is to say that, above all, you've got to hide what you really are." (141)

What is important to Subuyan is the illusion she has to offer, and not the real woman herself. He is an illusionist, a peepshow proprietor; in a way, he is Doctor Hoffman or Mendoza, a minor version of Doctor Hoffman. They use male sexual desire to fill the world, just as Subuyan attempts to do. Subuyan's homosocial project of serving male sexuality does not go smoothly, however, as the women do not conform to his plan. Subuyan laments to his colleague at one point: "This business of grooming women [...] believe me, it's not easy. It's like making your own Frankenstein monsters" (236). Real women are beyond Subuyan's control; Keiko, his love interest, runs away, and the sex doll he obtains for masturbation is raped by his teammate. What is more, Hack's mother appears one day, alive and kicking, shattering the image fabricated by Hack. Hilariously enough, the women Subuyan thought he could mould into the shape he desired are so cunning that they subvert his plan. Finally, Subuyan dies in an accident, but the irony is that his dead body shows that his impotence has been cured. The story ends with Keiko's guffaw.

We can see why Carter liked this novel so much when we consider the ironic ending. This novel demonstrates how male desire is sustained by illusions, and how consummation, which is often described as the ultimate goal of a romantic relationship, becomes something to be dreaded; happy consummation can only occur in death. Subuyan's impotence, which occupies a central place in this novel, suggests the alienation of reality in male eroticism within a modern patriarchal society. Women and their bodies are important only as receptacles of male desire, as theatrical devices to create illusions. As this homosocial novel shows, real women only bring about fear and impotence.

A similar observation was made by Carter when she wrote a review of Oshima Nagisa's film *Ai No Corrida*, which was based on a real incident in 1936 in which a woman killed her lover and cut off his penis. Oshima's film is full of depictions of them having sexual intercourse, to which Carter objects: "what does he mean by all this screwing, what does he *mean*? […] About female sexuality it is not, although it exploits male fear" (SL 357).

What she grasped from Japanese literature is the sensibility that takes femininity not as an essential attribute of anyone with a female body but as an artificial concept created by a male-centric society and forced upon her, like theatrical costumes that actors must wear in order to keep their role in a theatrical project, however little importance that role may have. The actor analogy does not go any further, though, because while actors might be appreciated outside of the theatre in other capacities, women are appreciated only within the theatre. Women are treasured as long as they conform to the norm and stay within the illusory definition of themselves. However, when they overstep their boundaries, women become fearful monsters that bring about castration and death.

What Carter learned, read, heard and experienced in Japan seems to have helped her to construct a comprehensive thesis on desire in a male-dominant society, which suggests "love should end in the death of the object of the other's desire" (ibid.). Carter explains her thesis as "a refinement of a notion of sexual love as transgression, which is not unique to Judaeo-Christian culture" (ibid.). Here, she takes both the exclusion of women in Japanese culture and the mythologization of women in Western culture as rooted in the same ideology that alienates real women and their bodies. This "femininity," so dissociated from women's own identities, as Carter herself experienced in Japan, was combined with her study of "womanhood" in Tanizaki's and Nosaka's novels to create a fantastic tale that is also a theoretical speculation on desire and women as its object, brought to fruition in *The Infernal Desire Machines*.

kaleidoscope

The Infernal Desire Machines and other writing produced during Carter's stay in Japan are all kaleidoscopic: they have many facets, a mixture of creative imagination and descriptions of Carter's own experiences. I hope this paper shows some of those facets of her writing in this period that might have resulted from what Carter experienced and observed in Japan. In particular, Albertina's gender performativity and her tragic obliteration at the end of the novel mirror the place of women in Japan at the time Carter lived there, as well as her own romantic relationship with Sozo – the experience of double assassination. She writes in her unpublished manuscript:

> <u>Fiction Written in a Certain City</u>
> Victims of Circumstances
> He enslaved me in order to avoid his own enslavement; until, it seemed to me I had become him, by a process of transmigration of souls. ("I <u>am</u> Heathcliff.") Mirrors showed me his face where my own should be; so the city gave me an extraordinary experience of the exacerbated & self-lacerating nature of pre-revolutionary love, which is nothing but a form of philosophic assassination. He had an assassin's rage to annihilate the attributes of my self that perturbed him &, with this, necessitated a total annihilation – for the self (is it not) is nothing more than the sum of its attributes […] I found I no longer knew my self, who was a stranger with another's face, whose lineaments spelled out hypocrisy. (*Japan 1* n. pag.; underlining in original)

Having survived this assassination competition, it appears that Carter obtained a sensibility she had not previously possessed. After a series of entries about Sozo in *Journal 93* is this entry:

> A young man of 23, who follows the Stendhalian avocation of teaching English to women

> in coffee shops & has aspirations towards literature, picks up a girl in a coffee shop. She is English; he is Japanese. She is starkly beautiful, comic, clever, hysterical, passionate & polyneurotic. (Is that really how I saw myself? Never mind. I'm re-reading this in the autumn of 1973; & would add, maybe, that all experience is unique – that is the nature of experience. Two years later, two men later. Poor, darling Sozo, I never meant you harm.) (*Journal 93* n. pag.; underlining in original)

A few years after the relationship with Sozo ended, Carter here seems to observe it from a distance, and marvel at the effect it once had on herself, and how both of them had helplessly turned into devouring monsters, consumed by masculinist romantic ideology. As a writer, she was empowered by these personal experiences in Japan and also by her analyses of Japanese literature – as in the cases of Tanizaki's and Nosaka's works, as explored above – and became better equipped with the literary imagination and strategies to subvert the universal structure of masculine discourses. Using these techniques, Carter's stories came to positively show the feminist sensibility, humour and postmodernity peculiar to Angela Carter, and she began to create stories in which love does not necessarily mean double assassination. In the playfully heterogeneous voices of the characters in her later works, such as Fevvers in *Nights at the Circus* and Dora in *Wise Children*, the reader can detect the confidence and wisdom of one who has survived the peril of double assassination in the mirror of the other.

disclosure statement

No potential conflict of interest was reported by the author.

notes

This paper was supported by KAKENHI 24520307 (Grant-in-Aid for Scientific Research(C)) from the Japan Society for the Promotion of Science (JSPS).

1 After this paper was submitted, the official biography written by Edmund Gordon was published and it shed some light on Carter's life in Japan (see Gordon).

2 Dimovitz observes that "[i]t was in Japan that she experienced what she saw as a truly structured, patriarchal system, predicated on a massive cultural repression, which she then re-read back into English and American culture" ("Cartesian Nuts" 15). He also analyses the influence of Japanese comic books and Sade, both of which Carter picked up in Japan for the first time, and whose association, he argues, "seems to have helped to develop Carter's 1970s technique of making literal the unconscious and unspoken assumptions and symbolic forms that define a culture" (16).

3 See Tonkin; Ikoma.

4 In her journal, Carter records: "Dr Hoffman; Dec 24, 1970–May 20, 1971. (Actual writing finished, March 1971)" (*Journal 93* n. pag.).

5 In her journal, Carter contemplates calling a story on Sozo "The Assassin Sings" (*Journal 93* n. pag.).

6 Sozo told me how Carter talked with his father, and one of Carter's journal entries records her conversation with Sozo's sister-in-law in detail, showing that they frequently communicated with one another (*Journal 93* n. pag.).

7 See "Mishima's Toy Sword" in Carter's *Shaking a Leg* 241.

8 I also persuaded Sozo Araki to write a memoir about Carter. It was completed, translated into English by me, and – I am hoping – will be published in the near future.

9 Carter's concept of gender performativity and Butler's are not exactly the same, as Joanne Trevenna points out. Trevenna links Carter's gender formation more closely to the theories of Simone de Beauvoir, as Carter seems to presuppose the pre-gendered subject, than to Butler's. However, she also appreciates the contemporary resonance of Carter's theory, for it

> moves beyond the feminism of de Beauvoir and invites a more contemporary critical debate through its presentation of the pre-gendered subject as unstable and fragmented. Undermining the unity and integrity of the

"one" presented by de Beauvoir, this more postmodernist/poststructuralist treatment of identity, in turn, reopens a partial link to the work of Judith Butler. (275)

10 Nosaka's name is misspelled as Nozaka in this translation.

bibliography

Bakhtin, Mikhail. *Problems of Dostoevsky's Poetics*. Ed. and trans. Caryl Emerson. Ann Arbor, MI: Ardis, 1973. Print.

Butler, Judith. *Gender Trouble: Feminism and the Subversion of Identity*. New York: Routledge, 1990. Print.

Butler, Judith. "Performative Acts and Gender Constitution: An Essay in Phenomenology and Feminist Theory." *Theatre Journal* 40.4 (1988): 519–31. Print.

Carter, Angela. *Angela Carter Papers: Japan 1*. N.d. Add MS 88899/1/80. British Lib., London.

Carter, Angela. *Angela Carter Papers: Japan 2*. 1969–74. Add MS 88899/1/81. British Lib., London.

Carter, Angela. *Angela Carter Papers: Journal*. 1969–72? Add MS 88899/1/93. British Lib., London.

Carter, Angela. *Angela Carter Papers: Journal*. 1972. Add MS 88899/1/94. British Lib., London.

Carter, Angela. *Fireworks*. 1974, 1987, 1992. London: Virago, 1995. Print.

Carter, Angela. *The Infernal Desire Machines of Doctor Hoffman*. 1972. London: Penguin, 1982. Print.

Carter, Angela. *The Magic Toyshop*. 1967. London: Virago, 1981. Print.

Carter, Angela. *Nights at the Circus*. 1984. London: Vintage, 1994. Print.

Carter, Angela. *Nothing Sacred: Selected Writings*. London: Virago, 1982. Print.

Carter, Angela. *Shaking a Leg: Collected Writings*. London: Penguin, 1998. Print.

Carter, Angela. *Wise Children*. 1991. London: Vintage, 1992. Print.

Dimovitz, Scott A. "Angela Carter's Narrative Chiasmus: *The Infernal Desire Machines of Doctor Hoffman* and *The Passion of New Eve*." *Genre* 42 (Spring–Summer 2009): 83–112. Print.

Dimovitz, Scott A. "Cartesian Nuts: Rewriting the Platonic Androgyne in Angela Carter's Japanese Surrealism." *Femspec* 6.2 (2005): 15–31. Print.

Gamble, Sarah. *Angela Carter: A Literary Life*. Basingstoke: Palgrave, 2006. Print.

Gordon, Edmund. *The Invention of Angela Carter*. London: Chatto, 2016. Print.

Ikoma, Natsumi. "The Proustian Mystery of the Black Swan in Angela Carter's *The Infernal Desire Machines of Doctor Hoffman*." *Contemporary Women's Writing* 2.2 (2008): 155–73. Print.

Nozaka (sic), Akiyuki. *The Pornographers*. Trans. Michael Gallagher. London: Secker, 1969. Print.

Tanizaki, Jun'ichiro. *Naomi*. Trans. Anthony H. Chambers. New York: Vintage, 2001. Print.

Tonkin, Maggie. "Albertine/a the Ambigious: Angela Carter's Reconfiguration of Marcel Proust's Moderninst Muse." *Re-visiting Angela Carter: Texts, Contexts, Intertexts*. Ed. Rebecca Munford. Basingstoke: Palgrave, 2012. 64–86. Print.

Tonkin, Maggie. *Angela Carter and Decadence: Critical Fictions/Fictional Critiques*. Basingstoke: Palgrave, 2012. Print.

Trevenna, Joanne. "Gender as Performance: Questioning the 'Butlerification' of Angela Carter's Fiction." *Journal of Gender Studies* 11.3 (2002): 267–76. Print.

eriko hara

TRANSNATIONAL THEATRICAL REPRESENTATION OF THE AGING

velina hasu houston's calligraphy

Velina Hasu Houston has written her plays from her feminist perspective: in fact, it integrates into what she terms "the politics of life." Houston clearly explains the reason why her first anthology is entitled *The Politics of Life* (1993):

> It is not enough, then, simply to write about ordinary life in ordinary ways because life can never be ordinary for the female of color. Asian American women playwrights are faced with the task of creating meaningful theater and expressing themselves artistically while sustaining sensitivity toward culture and gender. These women are doing it with determination, as are a host of other Asian American women playwrights. The politics of living as women of color in this society and in the global village must continue to be examined. (29)

By focusing on "the politics of life" for the female of color, her anthology expressly features pioneering Asian American women playwrights such as Wakako Yamauchi, Genny Lim, and Velina Hasu Houston herself. These writers span two generations, two countries, and two cultures with their critical minds in their concern about women's spirit, intellect, and lives. With the continued and strong determination to write as, for and about the female of color, Houston's work has evolved further towards a future vision of women's issues and global matters.

In particular, Houston is a prolific transnational artist. She was born to an interracial and international couple of a Blackfoot Indian and African American father and a Japanese mother during the US occupation of Japan after World War II. Thus the terms used to identify for her community and cultural identity such as Amerasian, Hapa and multiracial Asian Pacific American have been important to her work. Since creating the trilogy about Japanese war brides in the 1980s, *Asa Ga Kimashita (Morning Has Broken)* (1980), *American Dreams* (1983), and *Tea* (1987), Houston has explored the issue of war and women from the perspectives of culture/gender and "the politics of life." In doing so, she has actively served to redefine and vitalize not only American theater but also women's writing.

In this context, Houston's theatrical representations seek to explore cultural collision and coalescence in transnational communities. By challenging the assumptions of ethnic theaters in the United States, she finds herself writing about her own unique identity and crucial role in American theater:

> As a multicultural, transnational person, I remain open to new ways of thinking about Japan and the US and the world in general. This approach deepens and enhances my existence. In the midst of this posture, however, I respectfully sustain the cultural practices and idiosyncrasies of my motherland. (Houston, "Investing" 3)

Calligraphy (2010) is quite challenging in that it looks at her mother's aging from transcultural perspectives. *Calligraphy* was first produced at Los Angeles Theatre Center in 2010 and it is about two female cousins – one is a Japanese/African American who lives in Los Angeles; the other is a Japanese who lives in Japan. The two women are finding it difficult to cope with life's many changes while dealing with their respective mother's aging. This paper examines how Houston's strong awareness of the transnational connection between identity and change inspires her to re-envision women's writing, which highlights the need for a re-examination of the power of love and beauty.

Calligraphy sheds new light on not only understanding the beauty in the aging process but also women's traumatic memories that have value beyond the personal. Since she wrote *Tea* based on her mother's life as a war bride, Houston has presented a pioneering, in-depth exploration of Asian women's memories that have been historically ignored in the United States. Similarly, "Asian American women artists each reclaim untold histories from their personal and communal pasts that have been silenced or erased within a national history mapped in visible 'differences' across boundaries of nationality, culture, gender, race, and ethnicity" (Hara 130). According to Asian American theater scholar Esther Kim Lee,

> Houston admits that while her plays deal with women's issues in general and minority women's issues in particular, she has had more interest in the Asian female perspective. She attributes this interest to the way she was raised: by a Japanese mother who taught her the Japanese language, customs, and folklores. (Lee 151)

Moreover, Houston asks us to hear the "double" voices and visions of war-affected people as they share traumatic memories. Concerning this sense of "doubleness" in Houston's second anthology, *But Still, Like Air, I'll Rise*, Robert Uno, the founding artistic director of the New WORLD Theater writes in the Foreword: "Velina's metaphor for her own multiracial, multicultural, and binational identity is that of 'double,' a concept that at once subverts and obliterates historical notions of fragmentation, impurity, and displacement" (Houston, *But Still* xi). What Uno finds in Houston's plays develops an embracing framework for culturally understanding both women's issues and global matters.

In fact, Houston remarks, "My approach is dualistic in many ways. I am transnational, looking at the world through pre-1960s Japanese female perspectives and through American perspectives" (Houston, Abstract 3). Houston's plays thus resist the monolithic categorization and description of Japanese women whose survival stories are different. In regard to trying to adjust to exile in a new community, Esther Kim Lee, in her book *A History of Asian American Theatre*, argues that:

> According to Houston, the play [*Tea*] tells a story that comes from the personal but that has the power to "resonate into the universal." And it has resonated with audiences of all backgrounds because it tells an immigrant story about "survival of the outsider in a new and strange environment." (150)

In fact, this theme of transnational survival for the female of color is central in Houston's plays.

Eventually the production of *Tea* came to be professionally performed at the Off-Broadway Manhattan Theatre Club in New York. Since then, Houston's work started to be accepted in so-called mainstream theaters and *Tea* has become a play that is quite often locally staged at regional theaters and performed globally, for instance, in China, Singapore, Malaysia, Indonesia, Japan and Australia. We can observe that in Houston's plays the personal is the political; at the same time, the personal links to the universal. With regard to her mission as a playwright, Houston offers a clear vision:

> the plays I write must give something to the world in which we live; they must recycle our emotions, spirit, and intellect to refuel and improve the world – not destroy it. They must reflect a social consciousness without losing a sense of the personal. (Houston, *Politics* 209)

At the outset of the twenty-first century, Houston's artistic mission and vision have become more transnational. In her new works such as *Calling Aphrodite* (2007), *The House of Chaos* (2008) and *Calligraphy* (2010), what evolves in Houston's theatrical innovation is the description of women's transnational survival in shaping community and cultural identity. In doing so, Houston rejects pre-conceived stereotypical ethnic representations, and instead aims to observe deep aspects of human reality from both Japanese and American perspectives. Houston thus focuses on their "differences" in a more complex reality in order to illustrate transcultural interconnectivity. It is my view that the interconnectivity between two different cultures makes her assert that her innovative challenge beyond tradition cannot fit simply into any one category and features Houston's work as women's writing across cultures.

In this regard, for Houston at the present time, looking back on past history is very significant. For instance, *Calling Aphrodite* is set in the years 1945–55 and deals with a historical fact, that is, "the Hiroshima Maiden Project that brought 25 female bomb victims to New York for free plastic surgery in 1955" (Houston, *Calling Aphrodite* 3–4). By representing the Ancient Greek goddess Aphrodite as a symbol of beauty, this historical play highlights the need to inquire afresh into the politics of beauty. Houston thus tells a sensational story of two Japanese sisters, Shizuko and Keiko, who are internally and externally different.

However, we can find in *Calling Aphrodite* that war changed equally the fate of the two sisters. They passed through strange vicissitudes of fortune. For instance, Shizuko was chosen to be the first member for the project as a symbol of peace, but died on the operating table due to an overdose of anesthesia. In every critical moment of the inevitable, Aphrodite appears and advises Keiko who survived the free plastic surgery in New York to understand the meaning of women's survival in a global and local community. Beyond Shizuko's death, Aphrodite urges Keiko to live: "You're still at war. With yourself" (57). Houston asks us to consider war not only on the battleground but also in real life. That means we are fighting with ourselves, not others. In this sense, *Calling Aphrodite* is a profoundly significant play for women who are living in a global and local community to understand both the way and the meaning of survival beyond the traumatic war memories.

After Shizuko's death in New York, as Keiko reflects, "I just want to go home," Aphrodite remarks, "There is no home until you stop fighting Fate. The war changed Hiroshima and it has changed you. It is up to you to accept change and carry on towards newfound wisdom" (ibid.). These words by Aphrodite are crucial for women to move on. Houston calls for a deeper understanding of how humanity, and in particular, love, faith, courage, and forgiveness, which are poles apart from war, violence, and the destruction caused by male-dominated history, encourage women to survive. Keiko, one of the Hiroshima bomb victims, is finally transformed into a strong and stupendous survivor, accepting her fate and appreciating both Japanese and American doctors. With Keiko's identity transformed, the play attempts to tell the women's story and its power to change the male-dominated world and history.

Furthermore, Aphrodite represents "all countries, all cultures, all of the power of love" (7). It is no doubt important to remember Aphrodite's words, "Because if love does not prevail, this world will cease to exist" (43). This configuration of love is a reflection of Houston's biographical and cultural truth.

Similarly, with the power of theatrical representation and dramatic effect as well, Houston has been calling into question the label of traditional community identity from multicultural perspectives. Most significantly, before the current times of blurring color-lines and new immigrant communities contributing to the mix that is the United States, Houston was already representing such racially mixed people as well as multiethnic/multicultural America on stage and has been re-articulating their aesthetics in her plays.

In *Tea*, in regard to trying to adjust to exile in a new community, Houston focuses on "the politics of war, love, culture, class, racism and nationalism" (Houston, *Politics* 209). Through the violent suicide of a woman in the Japanese war brides' community, four other women are forced to face their traumatic realities and secrets that have long been sealed in their minds. One of the reasons why Houston's plays have been produced and accepted across cultures is her strong feminist awareness. Esther Kim Lee argues that: "In fact, almost all of her plays feature women and their issues" by quoting Houston's words, "'I have remained very interested in exploring the way that women face challenges, special challenges that maneuvering in our society causes them to be confronted with'" (Lee 151). In other words, Houston's main concern can be considered as the politics of women's survival. Houston's new plays, including *Calligraphy*, examine this.

For instance, *The House of Chaos* deals with international marriage. Similar to *Tea*, the portrayal in *The House of Chaos* sheds new light not only on *transformative passing* beyond the fixed identity of race, ethnicity, culture and gender but also transforming the local community of Japanese women who are surviving in the United States into global issues of self–community definition. Yet, unlike *Tea*, in the situation of cultural displacement the female protagonist Mina tries to find strong bonds in the mother–daughter relationship in order to overcome the hardships she faces in a new immigrant community in the United States.

Accordingly, the issues of belonging and relationship in transnational studies reflect on Houston's feminist perspective as a politically, economically, and culturally autonomous/independent self in a national/transnational community. Mina also strongly suggests to her Amerasian daughter this idea that they must find strength in being both international and female. Similarly, in *Calligraphy*, Brades' theater review for the *Los Angeles Times* refers to this: "Although her play is not strictly autobiographical, the bicultural Houston writes with the authority of firsthand experience about the difficult choices facing Los Angeles-based Hiromi, the daughter of an African American WWII veteran and his Japanese war bride, Noriko."

Yet Houston emphasizes Hiromi's strength in the new potential of home for women to survive across cultures. While Noriko says to Hiromi, "You're always in the middle, no place to call home," Hiromi asserts, "Everywhere is home and that's even better. I'm okay, Mom. And so are you. And we've lived through a lot of crap, but it's only made us stronger, okay?" (364). According to Houston, the politics of belonging is the more fascinating aspect of reinventing the authentic self. It is not geographical, it is the inner self. Regarding this, Peggy Shannon, in the Introduction to Houston's first collection of selected plays, entitled *Green Tea Girl in Orange Pekoe Country*, points out:

> Her plays explore social fragmentation as a result of differences – in culture, age, class, ethnicity, gender, and personality – and the individual's struggle to find a place of belonging, to create "home" in the midst of the complexities of contemporary life. (Houston, *Green Tea Girl* 21)

It is, therefore, Houston's Japanese mother who has not only survived transnationally and transculturally as a war bride but also prompted her daughter's theatrical representations for developing this new potential of home. Houston comments on this:

> I adore the human being that she was. Her choice to marry a black man in 1950s Japan was a huge thing. I began to understand the impact that choice had to have on her life.

> She had to have courage. So I admire her pioneering spirit. (Donloe 2)

Houston clearly argues that there is no question that "the international community" (Houston, "Civil Good Will Ambassador" 201) of war brides and her immigrant mother were the driving forces behind the playwright's great interest in identity and change. This is also reflected in her writing about the power of love as well as beauty in *Calligraphy*.

In this regard, theater scholar S.E. Wilmer, in *Theatre, Society, and Nation: Staging American Identities*, contrasts Houston's more unique dimension of multiracial, multicultural identity in her innovative challenge with other American playwrights:

> Moreover, by focusing on multi-national and inter-ethnic family relations and multi-ethnic (and transnational) children, Houston highlights a different aspect of America's multicultural identity than Anna Deavere Smith and Tony Kushner. But like Anna Deavere Smith, Houston is not so much interested in the blending or melting of cultures but the clash of cultures and the individuated results of that disharmony. (188–89)

In writing about cultural displacement and disharmony, Houston's plays consistently put emphasis on women's survival in the male-dominated global power politics of war, violence and destruction. She admits that "our species, like most species, is motivated by the desire to survive, but we haven't always been successful at figuring out how to survive together once our differences become established and entrenched" (Houston, "Hiking" 43).

In this context, *Calligraphy* illustrates the differences in our aging process. As an aspect of Japanese traditional culture, Houston hints at the significance of the play's title,

> because when you draw with that dark black India ink, you make bold strokes. That's how we live life – with bold strokes. Then it begins to fade but it fades into different forms of beauty. We should be able to appreciate the aging. (Houston quoted in Donloe 2)

It should be noted that the writing of text with brush and ink in Chinese characters, used in China and other countries such as Japan, is an art form. In terms of Japanese art, "Because the movement of the brush occurs in an instant, with no room for second-guessing or fixing, *shodo* [in Japanese, emphasis added] is said to reveal the inner spirit of the practitioner" (Miura 193). Houston's commentary on the play's title shares this idea of revealing the inner spirit of the aged and gendered bodies across cultures.

Like her trilogy of war brides, *Calligraphy* also started with her personal experience of her mother's getting dementia. By doing her research for the play for five years in communities in both Japan and the United States, Houston comes to both recognize that "there was a large part of culture that didn't have patience for aging" and to understand "the beauty in the aging process" (Houston quoted in Donloe 2). Indeed, in the background of Asian American women and aging, it is significant to understand that there are ethnic variations, but they have not been completely explored. In addition, in "Issues and Trends Affecting Asian Americans, Women, and Aging," "it is important to recognize the diversity included in the demographic description of Asian Americans. Asian Americans are not a homogeneous group and are composed of people from diverse cultural and ethnic backgrounds" (Yee 317). In this sense, these facts are reflected in Houston's *Calligraphy* and women's issues of aging are addressed on both an individual and collective level.

Calligraphy consists of Act I and Act II including fourteen scenes. By rethinking the mythical and stereotypical representation of the aging, the play unfolds across American and Japanese cultures thereby invoking different spaces for traumatized memories and different times such as past and present as well. The play is

> Set in a season in the lives of the four Matsuda women at the turn of the 20th Century, the years 2000 and 2001. Los Angeles, Tokyo, Matsuyama; and the mind

> of Noriko. The home/garden of Noriko Matsuda Jameson is primary with other sites represented by light and sound. (Houston, *Calligraphy. Green Tea Girl* 317)

Geographically, *Calligraphy* is also a transnational theatrical representation. While Matsuyama might be an unknown city to people around the world, it comes to be a highly significant place for the survival of "the four Matsuda women" and Houston as well. Like Houston's mother, they come from Matsuyama, which can be the place of both reunion and cultural regeneration for them. It is one of the southern cities in Japan, and it can be said that Matsuyama is the starting point of Houston's writing career as a playwright.

As Houston notes, "The play is about identity – who we would like to be, who we are, what we might become" (*Calligraphy* (MS) 84). *Calligraphy* is one of the excellent plays in which Houston eloquently addresses the issues of gender, culture and aging and encourages us not only to reconsider problematic mythical and stereotypical representations of aging but also to find "a place of belonging" (Houston, *Green Tea Girl* 21) with the power of love and beauty as the art of aging. *Calligraphy*'s prologue thus introduces us to Noriko's girlhood and what the art of calligraphy means to her: "A Japanese girl in formal *kimono* kneels in front of her calligraphy with brush in hand and makes a bold stroke" (Houston, *Calligraphy. Green Tea Girl* 319). It is suggested that Houston wishes for this girl to represent both Noriko's beautiful memories of her native country and her longing for calligraphy, with which she is identified.

After the prologue, the play starts with the dialogue between Noriko and her daughter Hiromi in Kansas, USA. While they discuss Noriko's future after her husband Eamon's death, Noriko considers her migration back to Japan where her sister lives now. In order to take Noriko's mind off Eamon, Hiromi makes a proposal for a family reunion in Matsuyama. In fact, Noriko would love to revisit Japan after forty years, but she hesitates to do so, because she considers herself too old.

Thus Noriko tells Hiromi, "You don't know what old is: a seed stuck between your teeth. Sometimes young people look right through me. But you see me. I keep *Yamato Nadeshiko* spirit alive in you. Hold on to it. You're one of a kind. Even your scent, like cinnamon" (320). In examining the women's aging process, for Houston's transnational plays, the idea of the *Yamato Nadeshiko* spirit, that is a role model for the traditional Japanese female way of life, is both a critical and a theatrical innovation. While Houston explores the concept of aging from the perspective of growing old in gendered bodies, she demonstrates the importance of the inner spirit such as "the necessary virtues: filial piety, integrity" (ibid.) in *Calligraphy*. Such virtues, according to Houston, partly make up the transformative nature of shared identity between grandmother/mother and daughter. We can infer that Noriko was brought up by one of the "Meiji grandmothers" (ibid.) who would have survived in that era. "Meiji" refers to the period when Japan was ruled by the Emperor Meiji (1868–1912). At that time, while Japan involuntarily struggled with the changes of modernization and Westernization, it also tried to hold on to its national identity with the so-called Meiji spirit.

Much like her mother, Noriko tries to keep this inner spirit alive in her daughter, Hiromi, after immigrating to America. In her essay entitled "Matters of the Heart: To be a Dragon Slayer," Houston states that "A love abounds that assures me that all is well among my ancestral spirits, that I have done the right thing and that the only path to take leads forward with the wind at my back" (1). In this sense, Hiromi understands the power of love as "balancing two different ways of being" (Houston, *Calligraphy. Green Tea Girl* 320). Although Noriko's mother had never left Matsuyama, "She loved difference" (321) and Noriko's husband who was racially different. Interestingly, Hiromi, who was born and brought up in the United States, is very conscious of "Love, Japanese style" (320), for she understood this when she fell in love with Michael. Noriko refers to this kind of love in the relationship between Hiromi and Michael: "He thought you

[Hiromi] would love him as a Western woman, but you love him like a Meiji granddaughter" (321).

Calligraphy thus takes an inventive perspective on old age as a transcultural and transformative identity, foregrounding gender, aging and the power of love and beauty. Indeed, Houston assures us in her "The Note on the Play":

> The art of calligraphy in terms of lettering is a meticulous craft that grows refined with experience if discipline and determination are applied. Life is not dissimilar. We are born, smudge the lines, learn, grow, spill ink, mature, and so forth. Even in the most finely tuned and dedicated effort, ink fades. It is part of aging. What was created hopefully with love and vigor feels, looks different. But it is still art – sometimes even more valuable than at the time of its creation and vitality. (Houston, *Calligraphy* (MS) 84)

At the same time, her "Note" reminds us of the importance of Japanese calligraphy as an art form as well as a representation of the inner spirit of its practitioner. As Houston claims, the relationship between life and aging is like the art of calligraphy. Moreover, her plays, with their focus on women's transnational survival, infuse the transformation of cultural identities with changes. Thus, Houston highlights how there should be subtle variants in each life journey as a female survivor across cultures.

Accordingly, individual and collective memories are more valuable for the four Matsuda women in order to interrogate the politics of trauma. Noriko's dead husband Eamon "appears in World War II-era US military police uniform" (Houston, *Calligraphy. Green Tea Girl* 322) as a historical ghost on the stage. By enacting traumatic memories, he encounters Noriko in Kobe where she is studying *ikebana*, that is, Japanese flower arrangement. As Eamon emphasizes, they share something in common in that both are geographically southerners. Eamon was from the South of the United States and Noriko was from Matsuyama, southern Japan. Although Eamon's father was African American and Cuban, his mother was Native American, Noriko tries to find their commonality by seeing his color of skin as soy sauce. These memories associated with war, race, gender and culture remind us of Cathy Caruth's "idea of trauma as a means of connecting with the other, of 'a speaking and a listening *from the site of trauma*'" (Modlinger and Sonntag 7).

By drawing attention to the individual and collective trauma of both past history and aging, which provide the link between cultures, Houston attempts to create a scene of harmonious coexistence in the relationship between the mother–daughter bond and calligraphy. Even though Noriko is getting old, Hiromi strongly suggests that her mother can do her calligraphy again and travel, too. Doing calligraphy together with her daughter makes Noriko feel very peaceful and relaxed. Indeed, they used to do it together. Noriko inspires Hiromi with the power of love and beauty in this valuable memory that has deepened the mother–daughter bonds. Eventually Hiromi comes to recollect untold memories from one of Noriko's calligraphy pieces: "Love between mother and child / it never tires / Remember me please" (Houston, *Calligraphy. Green Tea Girl* 357). This work expresses the power of love and the act of remembering beautifully.

Nevertheless, Hiromi has to accept the reality that the neurologist's diagnosis for her mother is Alzheimer's. Noriko suggests that it is not her daughter's fault, but rather that her loss of memory should be blamed on her nursing her husband for years. But she doesn't forget important things, like the art form as well as the inner spirit of calligraphy. Hiromi also believes that Noriko's calligraphy is both her art and her life itself. Houston's position as a transnational artist, therefore, derives from her observation that Noriko's calligraphy is not just something that reminds her of Japanese culture. Importantly as well, Noriko's calligraphy transforms into a symbol of the power of love and beauty in order to survive her aging process across cultures.

Regarding Noriko's self-reliance in this aging process, she tells Hiromi, "At least I have my calligraphy and the courage to say to everybody, including you, leave me alone. You should never have stopped your calligraphy. Everybody needs something that's just for themselves" (330). For Noriko, staying alive must be calligraphy. Noriko's loss of memory, however, is getting worse. Because of American cultural myths and stereotypes of aging and also as a result of the lost relationship with her husband, her identity has to face changes. She starts to mix up past and present. Houston reclaims and redefines what it means to be old for women across cultures in identity and change.

Whenever Noriko's memories of the past fail her, the ghost of her dead husband appears on the stage like the Greek goddess in *Calling Aphrodite*. He advises Noriko that "Things change. We get older. Things don't seem to be what they were or we find them in an entirely new place" (335). His ghost character plays a prominent role in making Noriko and Hiromi learn to be old and then survive it across cultures for the process of rediscovery and re-empowerment of themselves. When asked by Noriko, "When will you come back?," he answers definitively, "Whenever you remember me" (336). Houston illustrates both the act and the art of remembering for the power of love and beauty. Without these memories for self-discovery and re-empowerment, women cannot survive, in particular, transnationally and transculturally.

Yet Noriko's memory problem becomes more serious. She doesn't remember her husband's death and Hiromi is no longer sure what her mother remembers. At last Los Angeles-based Hiromi and her cousin in Japan realize the revisit to Noriko's birthplace and reunion of their multicultural, transnational family. By comparing women's issues of aging in two different cultures and intersecting present with past, the sisters' memories of a feud have gradually become visible. As Brades' theater review in the *Los Angeles Times* puts it, "'Calligraphy' is not a play about huge events, but the emotional stakes are high as Hiromi and her cousin try to bring about a face to face reconciliation between their feuding mothers while there's still time."

Hiromi encourages her aging mother by saying "We want to help you so you can enjoy life" (Houston, *Calligraphy. Green Tea Girl* 348). Interestingly, Hiromi used exactly the same words as Noriko told her husband when he suffered from alcoholism because of the traumatic memories of war. He regretted taking Noriko away from her family and her country. He thought that war changed her, but Noriko believed that it was he who became both her dance and life partner. At least Noriko's love could survive across two different cultures. In reunion, Noriko's sister tries not to dwell on the past, but talks about the present by mentioning that "All the beautiful days are gone" (336). She also notices Noriko's dementia. Houston thus foregrounds the fact that there comes a time when everyone has to accept his/her growing old. The most moving moment of Houston's *Calligraphy* is portrayed: beyond their family feud, the transnational sisters share a persimmon as they did during childhood; Noriko also puts great emphasis in the revisit on sisterhood and deep love from their blood ties.

However, after Noriko is blamed by her sister, Noriko can't say any words and stops mid-sentence. Hiromi confesses to her cousin her mother's illness and her determination not to leave her mother. After her cousin exits, Hiromi picks up the calligraphy set gifted by Noriko to her sister and tries to remember the choreography of the stroke. In this way, Houston vividly makes it clear that the art of calligraphy is her mother's legacy of *transnationalism* in linking cultures and can produce a feeling of personal and cultural regeneration beyond traumatized memories of war, violence, and destruction. In *Calligraphy*, the issues of identity and change are fully explored "through the prism of five interconnected lives in a global transnational family" (Houston, *Calligraphy* (MS) 84).

In 2009 the edited collection *Crossing the Ocean: A New Look at the History of Japanese Picture Brides and War Brides* was published in Japan. Houston contributed an essay in which she describes Japanese war brides like her own mother as "civil good will ambassadors" (Houston, "Civil Good Will Ambassador" 184) in bridging two different cultures, and argues that they have created a rich legacy of transnationalism between Japan and the United States through their offspring. For Houston, thus with her feminist perspective, her theatrical presentation of aging can be said to be no more than claiming to move from national to transnational, sameness to difference in both contemporary American theater and women's writing.

As we have seen, *Calligraphy* takes an original perspective on old age as a transformative feature of cultural identity, foregrounding the dynamic interplay of nation, gender, race and ethnicity with aging. Houston brilliantly illuminates the concept of aging from the transnational and transcultural perspective of growing old in gendered bodies. As we can see in *Calligraphy*, Houston's theatrical innovation is thematically and formally evolving. At the same time, Houston's work has the great potential to demonstrate the power of love and beauty for critique, negotiation, and transformation in the still male-dominated world. To conclude, the critique for change, transformation of reality and negotiation of cultural identity in a global/local community continue to be salient topics for women's writing in the multiplicity, hybridity, and fluidity of the twenty-first century.

disclosure statement

No potential conflict of interest was reported by the author.

note

An earlier version of this paper was presented at the "Women Writing Across Cultures: Past, Present, and Future" international conference at the University of Oxford in 2014. I wish to thank Dr Pelagia Goulimari and other members of the committee for their feedback.

bibliography

Brades, Philip. "Theater Review: 'Calligraphy' at Los Angeles Theatre Center." *Los Angeles Times* 18 Nov. 2010. Web. 8 Feb. 2011.

Donloe, Darlene. "Velina Hasu Houston Gets it Write with Calligraphy." *LA Stage Times* 10 Nov. 2010. Web. 8 Feb. 2011.

Hara, Eriko. "An Untold History: The Challenges of Self-Representation in Asian American Women's Theatre." *Crucible of Cultures: Anglophone Drama at the Dawn of a New Millennium*. Ed. Marc Maufort and France Bellarsi. Brussels: Lang, 2002. 129–40. Print.

Houston, Velina Hasu. Abstract for "Matsuyama Daughter: Japanese War Brides in Kansas." Unpublished 2008 and forthcoming.

Houston, Velina Hasu. *Asa Ga Kimashita (Morning Has Broken). The Politics of Life: Four Plays by Asian American Women*. Philadelphia: Temple UP, 1993. 220–74. Print.

Houston, Velina Hasu. *But Still, Like Air, I'll Rise: New Asian American Plays*. Philadelphia: Temple UP, 1997. Print.

Houston, Velina Hasu. *Calligraphy*. 1 Jan. 2011. MS.

Houston, Velina Hasu. *Calligraphy. Green Tea Girl in Orange Pekoe Country: Selected Plays of Velina Hasu Houston*. South Gate: NoPassport, 2014. 315–77. Print.

Houston, Velina Hasu. *Calling Aphrodite*. 5 Sept. 2007. MS.

Houston, Velina Hasu. "Civil Good Will Ambassadors: Japanese War Brides in the United States of America." Shimada 184–215. Print.

Houston, Velina Hasu. *Green Tea Girl in Orange Pekoe Country: Selected Plays of Velina Hasu Houston*. South Gate: NoPassport, 2014. Print.

Houston, Velina Hasu. "Hiking the DNA Trail: 7 Playwrights Reckon with Science's Most Personal Relations." *American Theatre* 27.3 (2010): 40–43. Print.

Houston, Velina Hasu. *The House of Chaos*. 7 Jan. 2008. MS.

Houston, Velina Hasu. "Investing in the Future: Identity and Transformation." Japanese Chamber of Commerce of Southern California, 28 June

2007, Montebello, CA. Japanese American Treaty Centennial Scholarship Fund. Address.

Houston, Velina Hasu. "Matters of the Heart: To be a Dragon Slayer." 28 Nov. 2006. MS.

Houston, Velina Hasu, ed. *The Politics of Life: Four Plays by Asian American Women*. Philadelphia: Temple UP, 1993. Print.

Houston, Velina Hasu. *Tea. Unbroken Thread: An Anthology of Plays by Asian American Women*. Ed. Roberta Uno. Amherst: U of Massachusetts P, 1993. 155–200. Print.

Lee, Esther Kim. *A History of Asian American Theatre*. Cambridge: Cambridge UP, 2006. Print.

Miura, Fumiko. *The Japan Culture Book*. Tokyo: Japan Times, 2015. Print.

Modlinger, Martin, and Philipp Sonntag, eds. *Other People's Pain: Narratives of Trauma and the Question of Ethics*. Bern: Lang, 2011. Print.

Shimada, Noriko, ed. *Crossing the Ocean: A New Look at the History of Japanese Picture Brides and War Brides*. Tokyo: Akashi Shoten, 2009. Print.

Wilmer, S.E. *Theatre, Society, and Nation: Staging American Identities*. Cambridge: Cambridge UP, 2002. Print.

Yee, Darlene. "Issues and Trends Affecting Asian Americans, Women, and Aging." *Handbook on Women and Aging*. Ed. Jean M. Coyle. Westport, CT: Praeger, 1997. 316–34. Print.

claire williams

TRACING BACK TRAUMA

the legacy of slavery in contemporary afro-brazilian literature by women

During excavations at sites in central Rio de Janeiro, to develop the area in preparation for the 2016 Olympic and Paralympic Games, archaeologists unearthed the remains of the Valongo Wharf, where more than 600,000 African slaves entered Brazil.[1] The clash between these tangible reminders of the country's shameful past and its reinvention as the host of mega-events can be seen as a physical manifestation of the efforts to deny racism, prejudice and inequality in a country where over half the population is of African descent. Contemporary Brazilian literature tends to focus on the present too, although four recent novels, all by women, have tackled painful truths about the country's past with great energy, laying bare the roots of family trees and bringing together traumatic histories and uncomfortable realities.

In her study of personal and cultural memory *Family Secrets*, Annette Kuhn declares that "Telling stories about the past, our past, is a key moment in the making of our selves."[2] For writers from minority groups, who are often erased from official histories, this looking backwards and coming to terms with traumatic events in the past, even the distant past, is a necessary process in enabling them to reconfigure their identity in the present and move forward into the future with understanding and confidence. In this article I want to examine the way in which four contemporary Brazilian women writers have used genealogies to trace back traumatic problems for Brazilian women in the present to pre-abolition times: Adriana Lisboa's *Os Fios da Memória* [*The Threads of Memory*] (1999), Conceição Evaristo's *Ponciá Vicêncio* (2003), Ana Maria Gonçalves's *Um Defeito de Cor* [*A Defect in Colour*] (2006) and Tatiana Salem Levy's *Paraíso* [*Paradise*] (2014).[3] Lisboa and Levy identify as white, and Evaristo and Gonçalves as Afro-Brazilian. By creating a transgenerational or palimpsest[4] narrative structure in which a family tree is initiated by a nineteenth-century ancestor and ends with the narrator or protagonist in the present (late twentieth/early twenty-first century), the authors show how the individual members of their families are caught up in their nation's chequered history, in some cases becoming representative of particular periods.[5] Furthermore, they offer a counter-hegemonic version of "History" by foregrounding the voices of individuals marginalized by the mainstream: women, and, in particular, black women. Most importantly, the youngest members of the families, living in the present, are "forced to adopt a bitemporal perspective that shows the continuity and discontinuities from the period of slavery," manifesting clearly how "the institutions that first created the social meanings of blackness and whiteness continue to exert influence on the contemporary significance of those categories."[6]

By the very fact of asserting themselves as authors in a literary tradition that has excluded them and a society that has discriminated against them, these women can be seen to be making a political statement.[7] In the words of Chandra Talpade Mohanty:

> If the everyday world is not transparent and its relations of rule, its organizations and institutional frameworks, work to obscure and make invisible inherent hierarchies of power [...], it becomes imperative that we rethink, remember and utilize our lived relations as a basis of knowledge. Writing [...] is one site for the production of this knowledge and this consciousness.[8]

Following on from this notion, it is also useful to think of such strategies being used by specific groups of women to raise consciousness of cultural heritage as a way of bolstering self-esteem in the present. According to Dawn Duke, in her study of Afro-Cuban and Afro-Brazilian women poets:

> Literature connects with the woman-centred notion of female historical worth by glorifying historical initiative and confirming a contemporary awareness and appreciation of the cultural specificities of women of African ancestry in the Americas [...] Other forms of motivation include an inner pride in African heritage and outstanding female icons of the distant and recent past [...] Drawing attention to great female achievement is a strategic ideological move that facilitates the reversal of historical silencing and social hierarchical exclusion even as it simultaneously confirms the deep roots of female accomplishments today.[9]

The achievements of some of the female characters in these novels may not appear to be as glorious as those of others, but there is no doubt that the narratives do recognize women's heroic behaviour, sacrifices and subversive forms of resistance in a society in which they were the most powerless and vulnerable members.[10] People of all races were socialized to believe in a strict racial hierarchy which attributed the greatest power to white men. Through violent control, negative incentives, terrorization and constant humiliation enslaved black people were forcibly migrated, disempowered, dehumanized and de-gendered.[11] Woman-centred narratives, female narrators and maternal genealogies therefore function to counteract the myths and stereotypes about black (and white) women, and the psychological damage to identity engendered by slavery and lasting long after it was legally abolished.

four novels and an introduction

Before analysing the themes that these novels share, I will briefly introduce each one.

Os Fios da Memória was Adriana Lisboa's first novel, published in 1999. She has since become one of Brazil's most fêted contemporary writers, with six novels and several prizes under her belt.[12] Her debut novel narrates the story of the appropriately named Brasil family, which includes African, European and indigenous members, in the voice of the youngest member, Beatriz (whose generation identifies as white). Beatriz employs a verbose, ironic, digressive style that owes much to the narrators created by nineteenth-century master Machado de Assis. From self-imposed isolation in the house she has inherited from her aunt and uncle, she reconstructs her family tree with the use of diaries written by her great-great-aunt Antônia (born 1885). Of the four, this is closest to the magical realist sagas of the Latin American boom period, for it incorporates strange events that could be considered supernatural (a man who sleeps for three months, a spontaneous pregnancy, disappearing characters, characters with eccentric habits that could be called madness).

Conceição Evaristo's work deals clearly with the lives of black women in contemporary Brazil, particularly their family and love relationships.[13] *Ponciá Vicêncio*, her first published novel, tells the story of a girl growing to womanhood haunted by the accumulated suffering of her family and other Afro-descendants trying to survive in a society that considers them second-class citizens. Told in the third person, the narrative's frequent use of free indirect style provides access to several characters' thoughts: Ponciá, her brother Luandi and their mother Maria. Three generations of Ponciá's family are portrayed: each reacting in a different way to their abuse by the white Vicêncio landowning family from whom everyone on the plantation takes their surname. Ponciá, and later Luandi, moves to the city in search of a better standard of life, but soon discovers that the opportunities for an Afro-Brazilian woman, even a literate one, are few and far between. The characters come to realize the importance to their identity of the family unit, home and community, and do all they can to reunite.

In 2002 Ana Maria Gonçalves gave up her job in advertising in São Paulo, and moved to the north-eastern city of Salvador (through which the majority of slaves were imported into Brazil), where she researched and then wrote *Um Defeito de Cor*. Published in 2006, the novel won the Cuban "Casa de las Américas" prize for a work of Brazilian literature the following year. It is the fictionalized autobiography of Kehinde (aka Luísa Gama, aka Luísa Mahin), born in Benin in 1810, sold into slavery and sent to Brazil. She eventually buys her freedom, tries several lucrative business ventures, discovers all she can about different African religious practices and participates in a number of revolts. The search for her lost son (sold by his father to pay off gambling debts) takes her to Rio de Janeiro and São Paulo, but when the trail goes cold she returns to West Africa and once again prospers due to her business acumen, although she refuses to trade slaves. The novel ends as she is completing a final transatlantic voyage to Brazil to finally be reunited with her son. References make it clear that Kehinde is based on a real historical figure, whose son, Luiz Gama, was a mixed-race lawyer, journalist and poet who played a prominent role in the abolitionist struggle.

Tatiana Salem Levy's third novel, *Paraíso*, was published in 2014. In a newspaper interview she explained that she wrote it in part because "O Brasil tem dificuldade em escrever a própria história" (Brazil has trouble writing its own history).[14] Ana, the protagonist, takes refuge in the country house of a friend, ostensibly to write a novel, but also to keep occupied before she takes a test which will confirm whether or not she has contracted AIDS after a one-night stand.[15] Believing the legend that the female line in her family has been cursed, she hopes that writing a novel in the voice of the murdered slave woman who uttered the malediction will help to lift the spell. Ana's memories of moments of violence against her and her female family members (from a car crash to grooming by a paedophile) are interwoven with stories of domestic violence in the present, and of the struggles of her own narrator Júlia's foremothers to find love and peace during different eras in Brazil's history: the colonial era, the dictatorship, exile.[16]

There are many differences between these four novels, not least the disparity in length: the shortest, *Ponciá*, has 132 pages and *Defeito* 950. Each came out with different publishers, ranging from the prestigious and prolific Record (established in the 1940s) to newly founded Foz (2012), and Mazzá (1981), which exclusively publishes works by and about Afro-Brazilians.

However, these novels have much in common, their themes intertwining. They all place an emphasis on recovering the past in order to enable healing from trauma in the present. With the exception of *Defeito*, which narrates the seven decades of one woman's life in chronological order, with a few digressions and observations, they use a fragmentary structure, rebounding back and forth in time, for a number of reasons: to mimic the way memory works, through triggers leading the mind backwards; to withhold family secrets and create suspense; to encourage the reader to compare events distant in time and draw conclusions about historical and social development, or the lack of it. All four are concerned with gender and race issues, as well as claiming justice, rather than threatening revenge, and making sure that those whose lives were erased or forgotten by official historians are given faces, voices and names.

Most interestingly, perhaps because such material is less expected in works by female authors, these novels do not shy away from horrific episodes of violence against women in Brazil's history, nor from reproducing them graphically.[17] They highlight the ways in which slaves were reduced to disposable property for the use and abuse of their owners, their bodies no longer their own. Family histories unfold against the background of Brazilian history from the nineteenth century onwards: the most relevant references being to the laws which saw the abolition of slavery granted in slow and gradual steps, and significant historical events.[18] Over the seven decades chronicled in *Defeito*, the most historically significant event is the failed Malê Revolt of 1835, organized by a group of Muslim slaves, intended to free all the slaves in the north-eastern state of Bahia.[19] *Ponciá* references the laws leading up to abolition with great bitterness, since it concludes that a form of slavery and a racist mentality still exist in Brazil. Since it is a parody of historical discourse, *Fios* rushes through and mentions nationally important dates only in passing, including: the arrival in Brazil of the Portuguese Court (fleeing from Napoleon) in 1808, the proclamation of the Republic in 1889, the impeachment of Fernando Collor in 1992. Lisboa's novel punctures the pomposity of official history by warning the reader:

> Se esperais por grandes feitos, leitor, abandonai-me. Refrescai-vos com biografias de gente ilustre e famosa, porque Manoel Brasil foi um homem absolutamente comum, desses que vêm e vão como formigas operárias. (90)
>
> (If you are expecting great feats, reader, abandon me. Refresh yourself with the biographies of illustrious and famous people, because Manoel Brasil was a completely ordinary man, of the kind who come and go like worker ants.)

Brazilian novels set on *fazendas* (plantations) in the colonial era, depicting households and working farms, are no longer fashionable, nor politically necessary, in the way that abolitionist literature was. The typical slave-owning household is usually depicted in Brazilian literature as a patriarchal institution in which a white male controlled the white womenfolk, who produced legitimate heirs, and the black workforce, who were at his mercy: "Total domination by one group [the masters] over the other [the slaves] in a spirit of isolation from the wider world of urban life, had unleashed possibilities of perversion which had sedimented in the subconscious of many Brazilians."[20] Enslaved black women characters are objectified, sexualized and silenced:

> Disempowered even when central to events in the novel, she serves to complement literary action that emphasizes European cultural values and the prestigious life style of the dominant white class. She remains valuable only in so far as she remains powerless and upholds the status quo as the lowest, most afflicted creature. Victim of a literary silencing, she suffers from being totally absorbed into the slave masses, a situation that is evident in most writers of abolitionist prose and poetry.[21]

This is made explicit in *Fios*:

> a escrava Joaquina era somente um número, somente um par de pernas e um par de braços para a lavoura cafeeira [...], uma entre os dois milhões de escravos que ajudavam a povoar a vastidão do Brasil. (47)
>
> (the slave Joaquina was just a number, just a pair of legs and a pair of arms to work on the coffee plantation [...], one among the two million slaves who helped populate the vastness of Brazil.)

It is interesting, then, that this shameful period, and shockingly brutal events that seem to prove wrong the myths of gentle colonization and harmonious racial democracy, should be chosen as subject matter by four women writers. I cannot think of any contemporary Brazilian male writer who deals so frankly with slavery over the same period (1999–2014), although there are many whose narratives of urban violence and social inequality implicitly reflect the impact and legacy of slavery on contemporary society.[22]

ancestors and origins

All four novels feature at least one black female ancestor whose influence on their most recent descendant is significant.[23] In *Fios* and *Paraíso* she is a tragic figure, crucial to the plot, as I will explore shortly, but firstly I will consider the hugely important role of the wise African-born ancestors in *Ponciá* and *Defeito*. Dawn Duke states that

> Older women have tremendous status and gain substantial prominence as the revered bearers of the Yoruba legacy in the Americas. They are stately figures indelibly associated with the legacy of African spirituality and a deep-rooted historical wisdom passed on to them as the natural inheritors of ancient traditions and customs from the old continent.[24]

They provide a link to the past and to the country of origin, through language, religion and cultural heritage (stories, songs, recipes, herbal remedies). They are a strong female role model and figure of trust, in a world where blacks were so vulnerable. In *Ponciá*, the village elder Nêngua Kaínda is a wisewoman and a healer, who sees and knows all. She still speaks her native language. Her advanced age signifies knowledge and commands respect and all three protagonists of the novel ask for her advice and her blessings. She is a *guia* (guide),[25] instrumental in the family's eventual reunion, yet her life force ebbs away during the course of the narrative, as if her job is done. The effects of age on her body are always described in contrast to her perceptive gaze, which is very much alive:

> O som de sua boca era quase inaudível, enquanto seu olhar penetrante vazava todo e qualquer corpo que se apresentava diante dela. (95)

> (The sound from her mouth was almost inaudible, whereas her penetrating gaze emptied each and every body that appeared before her.)

> Continuava ereta, apesar da idade, como uma palmeira seca. A pele do rosto, das mãos, do pescoço e dos pés descalças era enrugada como a de um maracujá maduro. Tinha o olhar vivo, enxergador de tudo. (59–60)

> (Her bearing was still erect, despite her age, like a dry palm tree. The skin on her face, her hands, her neck and her bare feet was wrinkled like that of a ripe passion fruit. Her gaze was alive, noticing everything.)

In *Defeito*, Kehinde's mother and twin sister, but more often her grandmother Dúrójaiyé, return to her in dreams as *eguns* (spirits or souls of the dead), predicting imminent danger or joy and even, if we are to believe in the powers of African religion, acting from beyond the grave to protect her.[26] Kehinde finds mother substitutes wherever she goes, gravitating towards communities of women. Her grandmother was a respected priestess within the *Vodun* religion, her name known to others dispersed around Brazil by the slave trade, creating a network of allies who come to Kehinde's rescue in moments of need.[27]

Since each of these novels is purportedly historical, they all present an original couple from whose union the other characters are descended. All but one of these couples are composed of a white European man and a black African woman forced to submit to his lust; bringing together the most and least powerful members of society.[28] In all the novels but *Fios* there is a particularly traumatic moment of violence at the beginning of the narrative, followed by further acts of abuse. These atrocities make it clear to the reader that the texts are going to confront the full horrors of slavery and, as Toni Morrison puts it, "rip that veil drawn over [what most slave narratives avoid as] 'proceedings too terrible to relate'": rape, mutilation, and physical and mental torture.[29] This graphic material serves to open the readers' eyes to a brutality often hidden or glossed over in historical accounts, opening the door onto a shameful period of Brazilian history.

In all the texts but *Ponciá* the mixed-race child born from the union between enslaved black woman and white Portuguese man becomes the next branch on the family tree. This formulation echoes the "foundational fictions" written by nineteenth-century novelists in order to neutralize the violent first encounters between European settlers and indigenous women.[30] Tracing her origins well before her own conception, Beatriz Brasil claims, in *Fios*:

> Acredito que comecei efetivamente a existir quando uma negra natural de Angola foi metida, junto com outros quase trezentos cativos, dentro do navio *Arsênia*, no ano de 1828. (20)

> (I believe that in actual fact I began to exist when a black woman born in Angola was put, along with almost three hundred other captives, into the ship *Arsênia*, in the year 1828.)

Since all the information about the Angolan woman is second hand (told to the slave's daughter, who passed the information down the family line), it is potentially even more disturbing than it first appears: "Era possível que a escrava Joaquina não tivesse mais de quinze anos de vida e que fosse virgem" (Joaquina the slave could well have been no older than fifteen and still a virgin) (48).[31] This quasi-accusation that Baron Eustáquio Miranda (and other slave-owners) was a child rapist is meant to outrage the reader on Joaquina's behalf, making the figure herself appear even more helpless. Nor does Beatriz ever discover her ancestor's real name, because the baron calls his dark-skinned concubine after the milk-white prostitute who initiated him into the pleasures of the flesh, in his youth.

The narrator imagines Joaquina's body in lyrical terms, linking her closely to the natural world:

> Calhou, por sorte ou azar, de ser mercadoria boa, jovem e forte e além disso muito bonita, túrgida como um broto de planta, incisiva como o sol dos trópicos, a pele brilhante como fruta fresca. (24)

> (It so happened, through good luck or bad, that she was a good piece of merchandise, young and strong, and also very pretty, plump like a bud, direct like the sun in the tropics, her skin shining like fresh fruit.)

The metaphors emphasize her ripeness, vitality and youth, which should not be constrained, but will soon be stolen from her. Since resistance would lead to certain death, the only way she can protest against her situation ("tão poucas opções tinha" (so few options were available to her) (83)) is to refuse to speak:

> A escrava Joaquina perdeu a conta dos anos em que viveu presa de um silêncio cortante e impotente. Talvez não tenham sido muitos, mas foram suficientes para cauterizar as raízes de qualquer esperança disposta a brotar. (57)

> (Joaquina the slave lost count of the years she lived enclosed in a silence that was acute and impotent. They were not many, perhaps, but enough to cauterize the roots of any hope that may have tried to grow.)[32]

This nameless, voiceless, powerless woman dies in childbirth, and plays no further role in the novel, but her plight is recorded for the readers' pity, and as a point of contrast with the lives and rights of her descendants. As the novel is a parody of official history, the disappearance of the black ancestor is par for the course.

In *Paraíso*, a sense of justice, as well as a shared fear of imminent tragedy and death, drives Ana, the narrator, to imagine the life of her great-great-great-grandmother, another nameless African woman transported to Brazil. In this novel, however, there is more information provided about the slave's life before she was captured, sold and exported, in particular the fact that she was a princess and a Gelede sorceress in the kingdom of Ketu (Benin), making her enslavement even more tragic because of her loss of status.[33] In her own anxious state, Ana starts to believe that the slave woman is haunting her, to the extent that she feels that her ancestor is demanding that her story is finally told. This quasi-possession is reminiscent of the spirit possession common in some Afro-Brazilian religions, as well as a strategy which functions to give the slave-sorceress a voice that stretches across the centuries. A Faustian pact is agreed, in her mind, between the two women: if Ana tells the true story of how her foremother died, the latter's curse will be revoked and Ana will, unlike the four generations of women who have gone before her, be able to find happiness in love. Ana makes it clear who is in ultimate control, however, advising the slave-sorceress "escrevo a sua história, mas à minha maneira" (I'll write your story, but I'll do it my way) (144).

The circumstances of the nameless slave's death are outlined in the text as part of Ana's blueprint, before they are narrated in her own voice, indicated visually by the use of a smaller font.[34] The subsequent fragments of the slave's narrative give a much more fleshed-out backstory than traditional historical accounts: her family set-up, her apprenticeship with the Gelede sorceresses, her unlucky capture, the transatlantic crossing. Little, though, is told of her daily life on the coffee plantation in Vassouras (in the state of Rio de Janeiro). The plantation owner initially forces her to have sex with him, but, after the birth of her son, treats her kindly, and she admits to feeling a certain amount of affection towards him.[35]

This relationship with a slave woman enrages his wife, Mariana, whose jealousy takes a gruesome turn. Not only does she command that her rival be buried alive in front of her, but, when she discovers that the slave woman's dying scream was a Gelede curse, she is disinterred, still alive, and her tongue cut out. Although buried for good after that, her tongue outlives her, and her words have an impact felt for centuries to follow. This symbolic piece of flesh represents the slave's legacy: the words screamed in her native language performing a curse. The severed tongue is then used in a soup which Mariana arranges to be served to her husband upon his return to the *fazenda*, to show him, and the other slaves, the violent lengths she will go to in order to prevent his adultery. In symbolic terms, this slave's body is fragmented, but her words live on. Indeed, she gains access to expression, explanation and self-justification (even if Ana becomes her "mouthpiece") in the course of the novel.

In Levy's novel, the white woman is the villain of the peace in this traumatic episode from which the main plot originates. The plantation owner's wife, like the "angel in the house" of Victorian literature, is generally an ineffectual character in North American novels about plantation life.[36] As a character, she functions as a contrast to the enslaved black women: a self-sacrificing wife and mother, representing innocence and virtue, the slave seen as sexually incontinent and a breeder incapable of maternal instincts.[37] However, in Brazil, the literary figure of the *Sinhá* (a contraction of *Senhora*: "Mis'ess") was known for her

> sadistic behavior [...] towards their black companions in childhood and towards the [...] house-servants in later life, which [Gilberto] Freyre attributes to the stifling nature of the white female's existence within the four walls of the "casa-grande" (the planter's mansion).[38]

In three of the novels under analysis here, perhaps because they are authored by women, the plantation owner's wife plays a much more active role.

The authors of *Fios*, *Paraíso* and *Defeito* all portray the wives and daughters of plantation owners as more complex than conventional representations. The wives have to deal with their husbands' constant infidelities and the number of illegitimate children they manage to sire. Their duty is to manage domestic matters and, principally, produce heirs.[39] The daughters suffer the same fate as their mothers: being married off for business purposes. Like Dona Mariana (*Paraíso*), *Sinhá* Ana Felipa, who rules the household where Kehinde first works (*Defeito*), is bitter, jealous and sadistic, both of them taking out their own frustrations on vulnerable slave women who cannot react. Baroness Maria Miranda (*Fios*) is a much more sympathetic, rather pitiful figure, supplementing a loveless marriage with an interest in music and musicians, and treating her slaves kindly and respectfully. Ana Felipa is the most brutal of these *Sinhá* characters, on one occasion viciously gauging out the eyes of Verenciana, a slave pregnant with her husband *Senhor* José Carlos's child.[40] She then arranges for the eyes to be served up to her husband for dinner, signalling to him that she knows about his infidelity and reminding him of his conjugal duties towards her.[41] This torture of women by other women is extremely painful to read about, seldom written about, and yet diverts attention from the real issue: the injustice of slavery and the dehumanization it breeds in both slave and mistress. In other words, although there is no excuse for her brutality, mitigating circumstances are shown which explain Ana Felipa's behaviour: fury at her husband's serial adultery with slave women and her inability to conceive a child.

Although *Defeito* includes the harshest portrait of a *Sinhá*, it also presents a firm, if unexpected, friendship between the daughter of the house, *Sinhazinha* (Miss) Maria Clara, and Kehinde, who is originally bought by the plantation owner to be her playmate. Kehinde is at first overwhelmed by Maria Clara's doll-like pale blue eyes and blonde hair, then there is a certain rivalry between them, but they develop a true friendship and help each other in later life; indeed, Kehinde names her daughter after her friend.

In *Fios* and *Paraíso*, then, the black female ancestor dies tragically but begins the family line, their child conceived through violence. In *Ponciá* and *Defeito*, though, there are much more positive portrayals of foremothers who provide love, support and blessings even beyond the grave. In all four novels there are hard-hitting episodes of sexual violence and humiliation, which bring home the brutality of the slave experience, should the reader not be aware of its true horrors.[42]

names and nothings

The third line of *Defeito* asserts "O meu nome é Kehinde porque sou uma ibêji e nasci por ultimo" (My name is Kehinde because I'm a twin, the one born second) (19). The character is in part defined by this Yoruba name, for when her twin sister dies she loses a part of herself that she is constantly trying to find, in friends, lovers, her children. She knows that she must keep this name so that she will be recognized by the spirits, so she refuses to be baptized with a Portuguese Christian name. Nonetheless, in order to be purchased legally (and thus have a chance of survival), a name is needed for the accounts book and she chooses Luísa:

> Para os brancos fiquei sendo Luísa, Luísa Gama, mas sempre me considerei Kehinde [...] Mesmo quando adotei o nome de Luísa por ser conveniente, era como Kehinde que eu me apresentava ao sagrado e ao secreto. (73)
>
> (To the whites I became known as Luísa, Luísa Gama, but I've always considered myself Kehinde [...] Even when I adopted the name Luísa because it was convenient, it was as Kehinde that I made myself known in sacred, secret situations.)

She gives her children Yoruba and Portuguese Christian names so they can benefit from their multicultural heritage. Her surname is imposed on her and all the slaves owned by *Senhor* Gama. This was practical as a way of branding of a slave-owner's merchandise, but a cruelly paternalistic practice since the owner usurped parents' passing on names; another sign of the dehumanization of slaves through denying them a genealogical positioning beyond that of the slave "family" and severing links between true family members.

The association of name and identity becomes a serious issue in *Ponciá*, combining with many forms of resentment towards the white plantation-owning Vicêncio family.[43] When she calls to her reflection in the river, Ponciá felt

> como se estivesse chamando outra pessoa. Não ouvia o seu nome responder dentro de si. Inventava outros [...] Ela, inominada, tremendo de medo, temia a brincadeira, mas

insistia. A cabeça rodava no vazio, ela vazia se sentia sem nome. Sentia-se ninguém. (16)

(as though she was calling someone else. She couldn't hear her name reply inside her. She invented others [...] Nameless, trembling with fear, the game scared her, but she kept going. Her head spun in the emptiness, feeling empty herself it was as if she had no name. She felt she was no one.)

This emptying out of Ponciá's sense of self represents the prejudice and oppression imposed on Afro-Brazilian women until they believe themselves to be worthless. Overwhelmed by the centuries-old forces of prejudice that block her development and progress, through constant humiliation and negation, she tells her husband not to call her Ponciá Vicêncio again: instead, he should call her "nada" (nothing) (17).[44]

Ponciá's name, because it seems to her so divorced from her own sense of self, actually starts to hurt her. When she writes it down:

era tão doloroso quando grafava o acento. Era como se estivesse lançando sobre si mesma uma lâmina afiada a torturar-lhe o corpo. (27)

(it was so painful when she wrote on the accent. It was as if she was thrusting a sharp blade at herself and torturing her own body.)

It turns out that this pain and torture are linked to her false ancestry, which she rejects:

sabia que o sobrenome dela tinha vindo desde antes do avô do seu avô [...] O pai, a mãe, todos continuavam Vicêncio. Na assinatura dela, a reminiscência do poderio do senhor, de um tal coronel Vicêncio. O tempo passou deixando a marca daqueles que se fizeram donos das terras e dos homens [...] Ponciá Vicêncio era para ela um nome que não tinha dono. (27)

(she knew that her surname had come from before her grandfather's grandfather [...] Her father, her mother, they were all still Vicêncios. In her own signature was the reminder of the power of the master, a certain "Colonel" Vicêncio.[45] Time passed leaving the mark of those who had appointed themselves owners of the land and the men [...] Ponciá Vicêncio was to her a name with no master.)

Nevertheless, the name appears on almost every page of the book, taunting her and constantly reminding her (and the reader) that she is a divided self.

As I have already mentioned, the narrators of *Fios* and *Defeito* do not know the real names of their ancestors, whose namelessness emphasizes their dislocation from their African roots. It could also reflect their extreme distance from their descendants not only in time and space but also culturally, since neither Beatriz nor Ana identify as Afro-descendants in any way and, after generations of miscegenation, their skin is more white than black.

Kehinde is undoubtedly the most vocal female slave protagonist in these four novels. The whole narrative, bar the short prologue by author Ana Maria Gonçalves, chronicles the life and opinions of a slave woman in her own words. The book itself, 950 pages long, with a distinctive matt gold cover, is an impressive testament to the life story of an individual, valuable particularly because of the surprising lack of slave narratives in existence in Brazil.

Many of the documents relating to slavery held or produced by the Ministry of the Treasury, across the country, were burned in 1890 following the orders of Minister and Secretary of State for Business and Finance Rui Barbosa. The consensus among historians is that this act of wilful destruction was carried out in order to prevent any claims for payment of indemnities not only to former slaves but also to former slaveowners. There was also, it is believed, an urge "to 'cremate' the idea of humans as objects on fiscal balance sheets, even when the indemnities proposed were nominal and symbolic."[46] Nonetheless, since personal documents (such as letters or diaries) are extremely scarce, scholars have made recourse to religious and legal documents transcribing the words of slaves in order to reconstruct details of their lives.[47]

Robert Krueger contends that the reasons for this comparative paucity "must at the very least take into account such factors as the illiterate nature of Luso-Brazilian Catholicism, Brazil's pre-industrial stage of development, a late and bourgeois abolitionist movement, and the racist suppression of the slavocratic culture."[48] Exceptions are the papers, journalism and poetry of mixed-race abolitionist lawyer Luis Gama[49] (1860s–80s) and Mahommah Gardo Baquaqua's *Biography* (1854).[50] This is in complete contrast to the United States, where large numbers of documents and testimonies have been preserved, dating from before abolition to statements collected in the mid-twentieth century.[51] As Toni Morrison puts it: "no slave society in the history of the world wrote more – or more thoughtfully – about its own enslavement."[52]

In a 1987 speech later published as "The Site of Memory," Morrison reflects on the content of slave narratives, which she reads as having particular missions: firstly as the story of an individual life, that at the same time represents the race, and secondly to prove that slaves were human beings (their literacy acting as proof to that end), and that readers should support abolition. The political motives behind their publication, she argues, constrained the authors somewhat, because they could not afford to offend their readers; something that she, as a twentieth- (and twenty-first) century writer whose work faces historical and contemporary racism head on, feels the need to do:

> The narratives are instructive, moral and obviously representative. Some of them are patterned after the sentimental novel that was in vogue at the time. But whatever the level of eloquence or the form, popular taste discouraged the writers from dwelling too long or too carefully on the more sordid details of their experience. Whenever there was an unusually violent incident, or a scatological one, or something "excessive," one finds the writer taking refuge in the literary conventions of the day. But most importantly – at least for me – *there was no mention of their interior life*. For me [...] the exercise is very different. My job becomes how to rip that veil drawn over "proceedings too terrible to relate."[53] (Emphasis mine)

The four Brazilian writers discussed in the present essay make a point of foregrounding slaves' interior lives, and are not afraid to dwell on sordid, violent, scatological or "excessive" incidents. Ana Maria Gonçalves's novel is an extreme example, not just because it narrates a whole life story, but because it is almost completely composed of the purported author's "interior life," opinions, thought processes, motivations and desires. Late in the novel Kehinde explains that her thoroughness has a motive: since she doubts she will ever see her son again, it is a cautionary tale providing all the advice, warnings, recommendations drawn from her own experience that he could ever need:

> tento me lembrar de cada detalhe importante da minha vida, para responder a todas as dúvidas que você pode nem saber que tem. (662)
>
> (I'm trying to remember every important detail of my life story, to answer all the questions you might not even know you want to ask.)

Above all, it is a relieving of her conscience, for having lost him and not done more to find him: it is "meu pedido de desculpas" (my request for forgiveness)," and "um grande mea-culpa" (a great *mea culpa*) (954).

genealogy and generations

The four novels being studied create clear family trees originating with the slave ancestor and progressing through the generations.[54] This format enables the reader to observe one family line in relief against the backdrop of official, national history, but also the ways in which that backdrop of historical circumstance impacts upon the characters, as well as the effects on them of genetic traits, and destiny, or serendipity.

Kehinde's curiosity and close observance of others leads her to describe in great detail the minutiae of everyday life, some chapters reading more like historical, anthropological and even theological research. There is no doubt that readers will learn something about 1800s Brazil that they did not know, and this consciousness raising and dispelling of myths is an important motive driving the text. Unlike the stereotype of the submissive, trapped, promiscuous, pitiful slave woman, Kehinde is strong, self-aware, proud, upwardly (and geographically) mobile and extremely enterprising. Her voice is strong and assertive: she immediately recognizes injustice and questions the status quo which relegates her to beast and chattel. As omniscient narrator of her life story she looks forward and back, nostalgic for what she has lost, but optimistic for future successes and reunions. The author realizes that sentences like "I should have paid more attention" will have repercussions later in the text. Also noteworthy in Kehinde's narrative is her determination to report information correctly and faithfully, for example when she combines data she has learned from different sources at different times in order to draw conclusions or make a point retrospectively.

Her motivation is also to share the knowledge she has accumulated, whether wanting to pass on advice and warnings to her son, describe the impressive architecture and size of (São) Salvador to friends back in Ouidah or conspire with plotting rebels. Kehinde always feels the support of her ancestors and benefits from becoming part of the anti-establishment networks pulsing beneath the surface of the slavocratic society. Her survival instinct is strong and even though she sometimes makes hasty decisions resulting in tragedy (the worst leading to the loss of her son), she experiences great joy in her life too.

In *Ponciá*, the "terrible proceedings" involve Ponciá's male forebears. Her grandfather, Vô Vicêncio, suffering under the weight of the constant and unrelenting degradations of slavery, is driven mad by his owner's shameless sale of his children, despite the Law of the Free Womb making such an act illegal. In despair, Vô Vicêncio kills his wife and chops off his own hand with a sickle. This act of self-mutilation, with the tool he uses to work the cane fields, has symbolic meaning. It is at once a form of castration, in anger at his impotence against the powerful white landowner, making him, as a result, useless as a labourer, but also alludes to his despair at the complete lack of control he has over the fate of his offspring, his descendants (50).[55]

Although he achieves a form of happiness with his own family, Ponciá's father, who is never named, and rarely speaks, succumbs to his repressed anger and sense of injustice. When he was a child, despite being forced to obey the *sinhô-moço* (young massa), he was able to express his feelings openly and emphatically: "revelava as suas tristezas com imensas lágrimas, assim como gritava alto os seus risos" (he revealed his sorrows with copious tears, just as he laughed his happiness out loud) (29). For self-preservation, he gradually learned to control his emotions: "Entretanto, foi crescendo e aprendendo a disfarçar o que lá dentro vinha" (In the meantime, he grew up and learned to disguise what came from within) (ibid.). His death, which takes place while he is working in the landowner's fields, is presented as a kind of surrender:

> foi se curvando, se curvando ao ritmo da música, mas não colheu o fruto da terra, apenas à terra se deu. (29–30)
>
> (he bent further forward, further, to the rhythm of the music, but he did not reap the fruit of the land, he simply gave himself to the land.)

It is the shock of her father's death, and the fact he "left" without saying goodbye, which felt like a betrayal, that prompts Ponciá to reject life in the country, where nothing ever changed, and seek her fortune in the big city:

> Estava cansada de tudo ali [...] Cansada da luta insana, sem glória, a que todos se entregavam para amanhecer cada dia mais pobres, enquanto alguns conseguiam enriquecer-se a todo o dia. Ela acreditava que poderia traçar outros caminhos, inventar uma vida nova. (32)
>
> (She was tired of everything there [...] Tired of the insane struggle, without reward, to which everyone surrendered themselves, waking up poorer every day, whereas some people managed to get richer over the

course of each day. She believed she could follow other paths, invent a new life.)

However, in the city, all attempts to build a better life and fulfil her potential are thwarted when she realizes that there are no possibilities there for a black woman except menial jobs or prostitution. "A vida escrava continuava até os dias de hoje" (Slavery continued even today) (83), and she too is a slave in all but name: "Escrava de uma condição de vida que se repetia" (Slave to a condition of life that kept repeating itself) (84).

Ana also determines to break the cycle that holds her trapped in misery, although hers is not as all-encompassing as Ponciá's. The source of her misfortune is traced back to the novel's primal scene, *Sinhá* Mariana's brutal punishment of the slave-sorceress, who retaliates with a curse on her female descendants:

> Ana acreditava que a violência da sua antepassada era o motor que explicava a fúria da sacerdotisa. De nada adiantaria repetir a história e continuar falando do mesmo lugar. Queria que a literatura salvasse não apenas a si e às mulheres da sua família, mas também àquela princesa que tivera a vida interrompida pelo capricho de uma senhora rica e mal-amada. (20–21)
>
> (Ana believed that the violence of her foremother was the motivating factor which explained the sorceress's fury. There was no point in repeating the story and continuing to speak from the same place. She wanted literature to save not only herself and the women in her own family, but also that princess whose life had been interrupted on the impulse of a rich lady, unlucky in love.)

In the course of Levy's novel, Ana revisits traumatic moments from her own past which, rather than being seen as effects of the curse, are instead blamed on the inequalities of a patriarchal society that so often leaves women vulnerable to the violence of men. She reveals family secrets, grieves for loved ones, punishes (with words) men who have hurt women, and keeps back one secret to prevent the novel having a conventional happy ending. Relationships between the sexes are reconciled in Ana's narrative, when the fourth generation, Lúcia, confides to her daughter Julia (representing Ana) that the curse can be reinterpreted. Instead, the message seems to be that happiness is within one's own grasp: "Julia lhe prometeu, em silêncio, que não seria infeliz. Já não era" (Julia promised her silently that she would not be unhappy. She wasn't any more) (166). Love and happiness are uncoupled from the notion of a long-lasting heterosexual relationship and recast as a woman's freedom, independence and power to influence her own fate. *Paraíso* advocates resistance against patriarchy and the strengthening of bonds between women. At the same time as it realigns Ana's thinking about male–female relationships, it also brings race into the equation: in Ana's narrative, she/Julia is the descendant of both the evil white *Sinhá and* the murdered black slave-sorceress.

legacy and literacy

Family novels involve not only the passing on of names and stories but can also describe the bequeathing of money, heirlooms, property and land, not to mention traits and behaviour. Since slaves had no belongings and no rights over their children, they could not pass on any tangible goods, but they could do their best to ensure their children learned about their African heritage by oral means. Oral transmission of stories and lessons remains important, but access to literacy provides access to power. Reading, writing and teaching become significant symbols in the four novels.

Ponciá refers frequently to Grandpa Vicêncio's mysterious "herança" (legacy), which turns out not to be in the form of goods but another form of curse. Grandpa Vicêncio passes on to his son, and then his granddaughter, the psychological and emotional effects of living through slavery: constant abuse and dehumanizing treatment, erasing confidence and self-awareness. Ponciá becomes more and more depressed, described with metaphors of emptiness and hollowness, as she seems to be increasingly possessed by the spirit of her grandfather, mumbling like him and imitating his walk. From active, joyful, hardworking, optimistic girl she becomes a lethargic, depressed woman, absorbing, it seems, his impotence and uselessness. Her mental and correspondent physical suffering is a constant reminder to other characters, and to the reader, of the suffering her people have undergone but, in the end, it does act also as an encouragement to her brother to join with others and persist in the fight for equal rights.

If the male line bequeaths Ponciá a legacy of pain, the female line brings her healing and a sense of heritage. Nêngua Kaínda, the village elder, passes down songs, stories and healing potions, as well as wise words of advice when they are needed. Ponciá's mother Maria teaches her the craft of pottery, which can enable her to earn an independent living as a skilful artisan. Their clay artefacts, made for domestic use, also appear in the text on display in an exhibition of Folk Art. The label on the display case records the "Autor" (author/potter) who made each piece, as well as the "Proprietário" (owner), showing how they are now merchandise absorbed into a capitalist economy: what was a kitchen utensil intended for use is now an art work. The pots are evocative of home, but can also be seen as "trabalhos que contavam partes de uma história. A história dos negros talvez" (works that told different parts of a story. The history of the blacks, maybe) (130). Like the families dispersed by slavery, too, the Vicêncios dream of being reunited.

Ponciá's story also raises the question of the role of literacy and education in transforming Afro-Brazilian lives. Her grandfather loses his faculties of speech, communicating only in a mixture of laughter and tears. Her father learned the alphabet with his young master, but no more. Her mother's distinctive pots are a form of self-expression. Ponciá discovers that her own literacy cannot help her improve her life in the city, although handwritten notes with addresses on do help to reunite her family. Nonetheless, in the last pages of the novel, her brother Luandi's realization of the importance of education and knowledge, the next step, becomes clear:

> não bastava saber ler e assinar o nome. Da leitura era preciso tirar outra sabedoria. Era preciso autorizar o texto da própria vida, assim como era preciso ajudar a construir a história dos seus. E que era preciso continuar decifrando nos vestígios do tempo os sentidos de tudo que ficara para trás. E perceber que, por baixo da assinatura do próprio punho, outras letras e marcas havia. (131)
>
> (it wasn't enough to know how to read and sign his name. He had to extract another kind of knowledge from reading. He had to be the author of the text of his own life, just as he had to help to construct the history of his people. And he had to continue deciphering in the traces left through time the meanings of everything that had been left behind. And realise that there were other letters and marks beneath the signature written by his own hand.)

Luandi recognizes the palimpsest of history. The potential for empowerment travels down the generations from the grandfather's stump to Luandi's determination to engage with, respect and learn from his people's history, using his fist to write, not fight. Although there are no outright accusations of racism in this novel, none are needed. It clearly presents the limits imposed on Afro-Brazilians and the discrimination they face. But it does not advocate violent revolt. Instead it emphasizes the importance of family, home and community, a strong sense of identity and tradition that can be combined in peaceful but determined resistance against oppression.

Kehinde goes through *Defeito* accumulating skills and knowledge, from the recipe for cookies at the origin of her first business venture, to mastering several languages and forms of worship, to the fact that the whole narrative is actually a letter.[56] By the end of the novel, she is able to send her daughter to the Sorbonne, where she gains a university degree from a European university representing the apex of education, returning to Lagos to be a teacher.

In a way, these four works comply with Law 10.639 passed by the Brazilian government in January 2003 to ensure that Afro-Brazilian history and culture is taught in schools.[57] The African ancestors in *Fios* and *Paraíso* are silenced, but the narrators are determined to tell their stories and enable them to speak at last. The very existence of *Ponciá*, a novel published by an Afro-Brazilian woman, can be seen as a triumph and a political act in response to the *sinhô-moço*'s question, after realizing that blacks (in this case Ponciá's father) can learn to read: "Mas o que o negro ia fazer com o saber do branco?" (What would a black do with the white man's knowledge?) (15).

At least slave literacy was not illegal in Brazil, as it was for some time in the United States.[58] In the last few years, debates on access to higher education finally led to the passing of Law 12.711 in 2012 reserving 50 per cent of university places at federal institutions for students from low-income families and/or state schools. Places must also be set aside for students of African or indigenous Brazilian descent, in proportion to their numbers in the local state.[59] It will take some time to see the effects of this law, and the law introducing material about Afro-Brazilian history and culture into the school curriculum.

conclusion: my history, my voice

Paraíso is told in fragments that cross three time frames, intertwining Ana's present with her past and her memories of the women in her family, and the slave's narrative (written in a smaller font to distinguish it from the body of the text). In Ana's novel, the unnamed slave-sorceress continues to describe the lives of her descendants from beyond the grave and into the twentieth century. It is suggested that she is in some kind of limbo, waiting to see her curse inflicted upon five generations of women:

> Hoje faz 147 anos que assisto à repetitiva infelicidade da família Albuquerque Junqueira. Em breve, Julia, a última descendente da sinhá, vai descobrir o segredo escondido pela mãe e, finalmente, poderei retornar ao Ayé e me entregar aos prazeres. (24)
>
> [I've been observing the repeated unhappiness of the Albuquerque Junqueira family for 147 years, now. Soon Julia, the last descendant of the *Sinhá*, will discover the secret her mother is keeping and, at last, I will be able to return to the Eternal Heaven and surrender myself to its pleasures.

Secrets emerge in the course of Ana's novel, which lead her to reflect on her life. The biggest bombshell is that the legitimate, white daughter of the baron and baroness falls in love with the illegitimate, mixed-race son of the baron and the slave-sorceress – her half-brother. Like the family tree in *Fios*, this one is made up of legitimate and illegitimate children, the product of miscegenation between descendants of Africans and Europeans, and even an indigenous Brazilian, replicating the multiracial, multicultural nature of Brazilian society. Rather than illegitimacy or mixed-race parentage being seen as shameful and needing to be hidden or forgotten, however, these novels embrace it. In *Fios*, the mysterious Antônia has black skin and emerald-green eyes; her brother's liaison with an indigenous girl produces the next link in the generational chain leading to Beatriz.

Fios, the story of the Brasil family, appears to be an alternative history of Brazil, in which most of the members are "comum" (ordinary), but also includes plenty who do not reproduce (through choice, sexual preference, infertility) and some who actually disappear. The family tree, then, shows a family that incorporates spouses/partners, who help it multiply, but then it shrinks. The successive tiers of the family cannot really be said to have evolved, or become more successful, however, and, with Beatriz, it reaches a kind of stasis. Independently wealthy, she chooses to remain in her aunt's library, writing the family's story with the aid of her great-great-aunt's diaries, occasionally visited by her boyfriend, but with no intention of having children, nor following a paid profession. The family seems to have reached a standstill, which, if the novel is an allusion to national history, does not bode well. In fact, this novel represents more of a metafictional exercise and a parody of conventional historical discourse than a political statement.

What do we learn from the representation of enslaved women in these novels? *Fios* tells the story of a multicultural Brazil through the generations of one family which ends rather inconclusively at an impasse (literally, in an enclosed garden at the end of a cul-de-sac). There is some sense of development over the years: whereas the slave known as Joaquina was forcefully removed from her homeland, Beatriz is an independent heiress, with a room of her own, where she writes her family's story. Joaquina's only form of protest is silence, but the sorceress in *Paraíso* takes revenge on her mistress and murderer in the only way she can, by asserting her existence and her background: using her native language and supernatural skills to curse the *Sinhá* and her female offspring. If the novel Ana is writing is indeed the story of her own family, and the sorceress her own ancestor, this suggests the contradictory conclusion that the sorceress cursed her own descendants, but also that maybe Ana has inherited some of her powers. The anger of the enslaved at the injustices and violations they have endured is channelled by Ana, someone at a crossroads between life and death, although someone who, had she not made a mistake, would be living a comfortable life as a writer and independent woman.

In Conceição Evaristo's novel, successive generations of the Vicêncio family make small gains (each generation is more literate, more optimistic about the future) but by the end Ponciá realizes that she is still the victim of a racist, sexist society: she concludes that slavery lives on, well past abolition. It falls to her brother Luandi to reunite his family and community and make a stand against injustice.

Defeito is a masterpiece of assertiveness: a huge, gold brick of a book based on facts and historical research. Based on one remarkable woman's life, it dispels myths and tells history from a highly individual point of view. Kehinde forms family units, only for them to separate, making reunion of the different members the quest that pushes her forward. In the preface to the novel, the author describes it as "fruto da serendipidade" (the result of serendipity) and "a consequência de uma outra história" (the consequence of another story) (9), linking the text inextricably to events which took place in her own life. Despite the disclaimer of ambiguity ("pode não ser" (it might not be)), Ana Maria Gonçalves's words emphasize the vital importance of engaging with the facts of slavery in Brazil in order to understand its devastating impact on all those who experienced it, and the knock-on effects on their descendants:

> Esta pode não ser uma simples história, pode não ser a história de uma anônima, mas sim de uma escrava muito especial, alguém de cuja existência não se tem confirmação [...] Especula-se que ela pode ser apenas uma lenda, inventada pela necessidade que os escravos tinham de acreditar em heróis, ou, no caso, em heroínas, que apareciam para salvá-los da condição desumana em que viviam. (16)

> (This might not be a simple story, it might not be the story of an anonymous woman, but actually that of a very special slave, someone whose existence still has not been confirmed [...] There is speculation that she may have been just a legend, invented out of slaves' need to believe in heroes or, in this case, heroines, who came along to save them from the inhuman condition in which they lived.)

This quotation encapsulates the issues I have tried to highlight above in analysing four remarkable novels which trace back trauma: women's history, visibility, individuality, legacy and heroism.

disclosure statement

No potential conflict of interest was reported by the author.

notes

1 Nicolas Bourcier, "Brazil Comes to Terms with its Slave Trading Past," *Guardian Weekly* 23 Oct. 2012, available <https://www.theguardian.com/

world/2012/oct/23/brazil-struggle-ethnic-racial-identity> (accessed 5 Sept. 2016). The remains have been integrated into an African Culture and Heritage Route around Rio.

2 Annette Kuhn, *Family Secrets: Acts of Memory and Imagination* [1995] (London: Verso, 2002) 2.

3 For ease of reference, I shall refer to the first three novels in abbreviated form as: *Fios*, *Ponciá* and *Defeito*. Note: all translations from Portuguese are my own.

4 "Palimpsest narratives," in the words of Ashraf H.A. Rushdy, are texts that

> ask questions about cultural and family secrets, explore the idea of a memory repetitively haunted by a historical event [in this case, slavery], and meditate on what the past means, can mean, should mean, for a present [...] subject tortured by a recollection of the past in an ahistorical society. (*Remembering Generations: Race and Family in Contemporary African American Fiction* (Chapel Hill and London: U of South Carolina P, 2001) 5)

Rushdy is looking particularly at 1970s African American fiction from the United States. Although there are many differences between both the histories of slavery and the literary histories of the United States and Brazil, there are also many overlaps; therefore I will use some critical theories about African American literature and writing by African American women in my analysis of Brazilian women's writing, taking care to explain any Brazilian specificities.

5 Rushdy argues that what palimpsest narratives insistently suggest "is that the family secret of an individual family is symptomatic of the family secret of the nation – slavery itself" (ibid. 10).

6 Ibid. 5, 27.

7 According to a research project conducted by the University of Brasília between 2003 and 2005, which analysed all the novels (258) published by Brazil's three largest publishing houses between 1990 and 2004, 23.8 per cent of the authors were women, 37.8 per cent of the characters were female, and only 7.9 per cent of characters were Afro-Brazilian, 5.8 per cent protagonists and 2.7 per cent narrators. And there were only three Afro-Brazilian female protagonists and one Afro-Brazilian female narrator. See Regina Dalcastagnè, "A personagem do romance brasileiro contemporâneo, 1990–2004," *Estudos de Literatura Brasileira Contemporânea* 26 (2005): 13–71, 45, 46; Regina Dalcastagnè, "Quando o preconceito se faz silêncio: relações raciais na literatura brasileira contemporânea," *Gragoatá* 24 (2008): 203–19.

8 Chandra Talpade Mohanty, "Cartographies of Struggle: Third World Women and the Politics of Feminism" in *Third World Women and the Politics of Feminism*, eds. Chandra Talpade Mohanty, Ann Russo, and Lourdes Torres (Bloomington and Indiana: Indiana UP, 1991) 34–35.

9 Dawn Duke, *Literary Passion, Ideological Commitment: Toward a Legacy of Afro-Cuban and Afro-Brazilian Women Writers* (Lewisburg, PA: Bucknell UP, 2008) 17.

10 Leila Lehnen notes that the story of Kehinde, the protagonist of *Defeito*, is "composed of many smaller acts of bravery, rather than grand gestures – though these are also present" ("Growing Up to Human Rights: The *Bildungsroman* and the Discourse of Human Rights in *Um Defeito de Cor*" in *Literature and Ethics in Contemporary Brazil*, eds. Vinícius de Carvalho and Nicola Gavioli (Abingdon: Routledge, in press) 88–105.

11 See Herbert S. Klein and Francisco Vidal Luna, *Slavery in Brazil* (Cambridge: Cambridge UP, 2010) 121; bell hooks, "Sexism and the Black Female Slave Experience" in *Ain't I a Woman: Black Women and Feminism* [1982] (London: Pluto, 1990) chapter 1.

12 <http://www.adrianalisboa.com>. The homepage of the author's website includes a quotation by the Nobel Prize winning Portuguese author José Saramago that "Adriana Lisboa é uma autora para o presente e para o futuro" (Adriana Lisboa is an author for the present and the future).

13 <http://nossaescrevivencia.blogspot.co.uk>. The publication of *Ponciá Vicêncio* was part funded by the author herself and despite being on several university syllabi, part of the Vestibular (university entrance exam), and translated into English (by Paloma Martínez-Cruz (Austin: Host, 2007)) and French (by Paula Anacaona (Paris: Anacaona, 2015)), it is poorly distributed in Brazil and very difficult to find in bookshops there.

14 José Riço Direitinho, interview with Tatiana Salem Levy, "O Brasil tem dificuldade em escrever

a própria história" [Brazil finds it hard to write its own history], *Público* online 7 May 2016, available <https://www.publico.pt/culturaipsilon/noticia/o-brasil-tem-dificuldade-em-escrever-a-propria-historia-1730288> (accessed 9 Aug. 2016).

15 Since her race is not mentioned (and that of some other characters is), the reader assumes that Ana and her family are white because of the lifestyle that is described, as well as physiological features. However, her racial heritage becomes more complicated as the novel progresses, perhaps in order to make a comment about the mixed-race past of those who identify as white – in other words, many Brazilians.

16 See Paula Queiroz Dutra, "O paraíso não é aqui: a violência contra a mulher em Tatiana Salem Levy," *Estudos de Literatura Brasileira Contemporânea* 48 (2016): 209–28.

17 In 1989 Deborah McDowell noted that whereas the majority of slave narratives in the United States were authored by black men, black women had written most of the contemporary novels about slavery. The same appears to be the case in twenty-first-century Brazil. See "Negotiating Between Tenses: Witnessing Slavery After Freedom – *Dessa Rose*" in *Slavery and the Literary Imagination*, eds. Deborah McDowell and Arnold Rampersad (Baltimore and London: Johns Hopkins UP, 1989) 144–63, 150.

18 In 1850 the Maritime Slave Trade was abolished in Brazil. In 1871, the Rio Branco Law (also known as the Law of the Free Womb) was passed, freeing all children born to slave women. In 1885 the government passed the Saraiva-Cotegipe Law (also known as the Sexagenarian Law), which freed all slaves over the age of sixty and created a state-administered Manumissions Fund. Finally, in 1888, abolition was proclaimed with the passing of the "Golden Law."

19 It was in this state that the Portuguese fleet first touched Brazilian soil, in 1500. The first settlement was built there shortly after, and Salvador, the state capital, became the port through which the greatest numbers of slaves were imported into the country. Today it is seen as the state where Afro-Brazilian culture is most visible.

20 David Brookshaw, *Race and Color in Brazilian Literature* (Metuchen and London: Scarecrow, 1986) 122.

21 Duke, *Literary Passion* 19.

22 For example, Luiz Ruffato, Paulo Lins, Ferréz, Marcelino Freire, and Fernando Molica.

23 In *Defeito* I consider the author, Ana Maria Gonçalves, who signs the introduction of the novel, to be the spiritual, if not biological, descendant of Kehinde. Over the course of the text there are several female elders (living and dead) who influence Kehinde herself, but the impact of her narrative (no matter whether it is true or fiction) on the author and readers is just as important.

24 Duke, *Literary Passion* 18.

25 In Afro-Brazilian religions, *guia* also refers to the spirits who visit mediums in order to do good works, such as give advice.

26 The night after Kehinde is brutally raped by her owner, she dreams of her grandmother weaving a carpet featuring the symbol of a snake biting its tail. The next day, in the sub-chapter entitled "Vinganças" [Revenge], a poisonous serpent hiding in his bed bites *Senhor* Gama's genitals, which become infected, leading to a humiliating, malodorous and painful death.

27 Voodoo is still practised in Benin where it was acknowledged as a national religion in 1989 and is now followed by 17 per cent of the population. See "Benin Voodoo Festival," *The Guardian* online 15 June 2012, available <https://www.theguardian.com/world/gallery/2012/jun/15/benin-voodoo-festival-in-pictures> (accessed 9 Aug. 2016).

28 The originary couple in *Ponciá Vicêncio* are both slaves, referred to as Vó and Vô (Grandma and Grandpa) Vicêncio. We learn nothing about their forebears.

29 Toni Morrison, "The Site of Memory" in *What Moves at the Margin: Selected Nonfiction*, ed. and introduction Carolyn C. Denard (Jackson: U of Mississippi P, 2008) 65–80, 70.

30 See Doris Sommer's well-known study *Foundational Fictions: The National Romances of Latin America* (Berkeley: U of California P, 1991).

31 The narrator almost always refers to her ancestor as "a escrava Joaquina" (Joaquina the slave), perhaps in allusion to the well-known abolitionist novel *A Escrava Isaura* (1875) by Bernardo Guimarães, later made into an internationally

successful soap opera in 1976, about the fortunes of a beautiful and virtuous slave so pale she can pass for white, trying to escape the lecherous clutches of her owner.

32 There is not even a chapter named after her in the novel, although chapter 2 is entitled "Eustáquio Miranda," after the Baron. This could be a conscious effort to replicate in subversive mimicry the lack of attention paid to the history of slavery from the female slave's point of view.

33 In the Yoruba belief system, Gelede was a secret religious sect which involved the worship of mother goddesses.

34 Literacy was "a way of assuming and proving the 'humanity' that the Constitution denied [North American slaves]. That is why [slave] narratives carry the subtitle 'written by himself,' or 'herself'" (Morrison, "Site of Memory" 68).

35 This is sensitive territory. The extent to which master–slave sexual relationships were consensual is almost impossible to confirm. In *Fios*, *Defeito* and *Paraíso* there are a majority of slave women characters who submit rather than struggle but others who manage to benefit from their masters' desire for them.

36 There are, of course, exceptions, in novels such as Willa Cather's *Sapphira and the Slave Girl* (1940) and Sherley Anne Williams's *Dessa Rose* (1986).

37 See hooks, *Ain't I a Woman* chapter 1; Venetria Patton, *Women in Chains: The Legacy of Slavery in Black Women's Fiction* (Albany: State U of New York P, 2000) chapter 2.

38 Brookshaw, *Race and Color* 122.

39 Maria Miranda (*Fios*) does give the baron a son and heir but, perhaps to subvert traditional history, his story goes untold, and the narrative follows the adventures of his illegitimate daughter instead. Mariana (*Paraíso*) has two daughters. Ana Felipa (*Defeito*) suffers a series of miscarriages and stillbirths caused, it is suggested, by herbs put in her food by the slave women.

40 In a combination of jealousy, fury and grief, having recently miscarried herself, the mistress explains that it is a very sad affair when a mother cannot see her own child, and that Verenciana is going to find out what that feels like (*Defeito* 106–07).

41 Ana Felipa gets her comeuppance: the kitchen slaves put herbs in her food to make her sterile (*Defeito* 114), then, years later, she is publicly humiliated when Kehinde arranges for her mistress to be discovered in bed with a male slave, by a priest.

42 *Defeito* begins with a horrific scene in which Kehinde and her sister and grandmother witness the gang rape of their mother by a group of warriors from a different tribe, and the murders of their mother and brother by the same men who force the five-year-old girls to perform sex acts on them. This shocking opening has recently been translated into English by Eric M.B. Becker as "Fateful Hour" and published in "Women Writing Brazil," *Glossolalia* 2 (2016): 41–51. Ten years later, Kehinde is raped by her owner, and her lover raped and castrated before her eyes, in yet another example of the terrorization of slaves and exercise of power over their bodies and minds. *Ponciá* also opens with a distressing scene, but in this case between men. Ponciá's unnamed father is forced to be his young master's companion and follow his every command. The spoilt white boy rides him like a horse, and, in a form of violation, urinates in the black boy's mouth: "Sinhô-moço ria, ria. Ele chorava e não sabia o que mais lhe salgava, se o gosto da urina ou se o sabor de suas lágrimas" (Young Massa laughed and laughed. He cried and he didn't know what was saltier, the tang of the urine or the taste of his tears) (14).

43 Evaristo admitted in an interview in 2007 that she chooses her characters' names almost instinctively:

> Sim, eu não sei por exemplo, de onde veio o nome Ponciá. O nome Nêngua foi intuitivo, sonoro [...] Gosto também de inventar nomes. Fico procurando aqueles que me lembram a sonoridade das línguas africanas, como Ponciá, Nêngua e Luandi. O prazer que o som da palavra me dá, me ajuda na escolha dos nomes. (101)
>
> (Yes, I don't know, for example, where the name Ponciá came from. The name Nêngua I chose intuitively for its musicality [...] I also like inventing names. I try to find ones that remind me of the music of African languages, like Ponciá, Nêngua and Luandi. The pleasure the word gives me helps me choose the names.) (Interview with Aline

Alves Arruda included as an Appendix (101–04) in her Master's dissertation "*Ponciá Vicêncio*, de Conceição Evaristo: um *Bildungsroman* feminino e negro," presented to the Universidade Federal de Minas Gerais in 2007, available <http://www.bibliotecadigital.ufmg.br/dspace /bitstream/handle/1843/ECAP-76RF2H/aline _alves_arruda_texto.pdf?sequence=1> (accessed 30 Aug. 2016))

44 Her despair echoes that of the colonized, as described by Albert Memmi:

> He has been torn away from his past and cut off from his future, his traditions are dying and he loses the hope of acquiring a new culture. He has neither language, nor flag, nor technical knowledge, nor national or international existence, nor rights, nor duties. He possesses nothing, is no longer anything and no longer hopes for anything. (In *The Colonizer and the Colonized* [1957], trans. Howard Greenfeld (London: Earthscan, 2003) 172)

45 The term "coronel" (colonel) came to be used generically to refer to landowners and men of power.

46 Amy Chazkel, "History Out of the Ashes: Remembering Brazilian Slavery After Rui Barbosa's Burning of the Documents" in *From the Ashes of History: Loss and Recovery of Archives and Libraries in Modern Latin America*, eds. Carlos Aguirre and Javier Villa-Flores (e-publication: A Contracorriente, 2015) n. pag.

47 See Jane Marie Collins, "Intimacy and Inequality: Manumission and Miscegenation in Nineteenth-Century Bahia (1830–1888)," Ph.D. thesis submitted to University of Nottingham (2010), available <http://eprints.nottingham.ac.uk/11801/1/JMC_THESIS_APRIL_2010.pdf> (accessed 9 Aug. 2016). See also Robert Krueger, "Brazilian Slaves Represented in their Own Words," *Slavery and Abolition* 23.2 (2010): 169–86; Sandra Lauderdale Graham, *Caetana Says No: Women's Stories from a Brazilian Slave Society* (Cambridge: Cambridge UP, 2002).

48 Krueger, "Brazilian Slaves" 172.

49 The reader is encouraged to think that Luis Gama is the lost son to whom Kehinde's narrative is addressed. A remarkable figure, he managed to achieve free status through legal means, having discovered he had been enslaved illegally.

50 Born in West Africa, Baquaqua worked as a slave in Brazil and Haiti, and travelled to Canada, the United States, where his narrative was dictated and published, and the United Kingdom, where he appears to have settled. I have not been able to consult Francisco Marques's *Ilê Aiê: Um Diário Imaginário* (Belo Horizonte: Formato, 1994), the fictional diary of an Angolan slave transported to Brazil, covering the years 1845–1938. It is categorized as children's/young adult fiction, like much of the writing by Afro-Brazilians (e.g., recent editions of *Quarto de Despejo* [*The Junk Room*], published in English translation as *Child of the Dark* (1962), the diary of rubbish picker Carolina Maria de Jesus, which was a bestseller in 1960) and indigenous authors (like Daniel Munduruku, for example).

51 Some 6,000 accounts survive, according to Krueger, in comparison to 170 slave narratives in Brazil.

52 Morrison, "Site of Memory" 69.

53 Ibid. 69–70.

54 There is a family tree at the beginning of *Fios* to aid the reader in working out the relationships of the characters to one another.

55 Ponciá's "legacy" from her grandfather means in practice that she inherits many of his traits and could be the reason none of her seven pregnancies produces a healthy child. His act of murderous mercy, attempting to save his wife and children from further suffering, is somewhat reminiscent of Sethe's behaviour in Toni Morrison's 1987 novel *Beloved*, inspired by a true story.

56 By the end of the novel, Kehinde is elderly and blind, so she dictates, rather than actually writes, the letter herself.

57 The Law decrees that the curriculum must include

> o estudo da História da África e dos Africanos, a luta dos negros no Brasil, a cultura negra brasileira e o negro na formação da sociedade nacional, resgatando a contribuição do povo negro nas áreas social, econômica e política pertinentes à História do Brasil.
>
> (study of the history of Africa and the Africans, the blacks' struggle in Brazil, black Brazilian culture and the role of blacks in the formation of Brazilian society, thus

rescuing the contribution of the black peoples towards the areas of society, economics and politics relevant to Brazilian history.) (<http://www.planalto.gov.br/ccivil_03/leis/2003/L10.639.htm> (accessed 24 Aug. 2016))

58

No law in Brazil made slave literacy illegal or threatened punishment for others – whites or blacks – who taught slaves to read or write, and so far I have found no instance of violent retribution against any Brazilian slave for knowing how to read or write. (Sandra Lauderdale Graham, "Writing from the Margins: Brazilian Slaves and Written Culture," *Comparative Studies in Society and History* 49.3 (2007): 611–36, 615)

59 The law was passed by President Dilma Rousseff on 29 August 2012. See <http://www.planalto.gov.br/ccivil_03/_ato2011-2014/2012/lei/l12711.htm> (accessed 24 Aug. 2016). See also H.J., "Affirmative Action in Brazil: Slavery's Legacy," *The Economist* (online) 26 Apr. 2013, available <http://www.economist.com/blogs/americasview/2013/04/affirmative-action-brazil> (accessed 24 Aug. 2016).

mona el khoury

TO BE OR NOT TO BE *MÉTIS*

nina bouraoui's embodied memory of the colonial fracture

In the context of Franco-Algerian history, using the term *métis*, which means in French "mixed-race individual," may initially seem inappropriate. Indeed, Algeria was the only colony in the French Empire where there was officially no "*métis* question," as historian and sociologist Emmanuelle Saada reminds us in her book *Les Enfants de la colonie. Les Métis de l'Empire français entre sujétion et citoyenneté* (15). She demonstrates that from Indochina to French West Africa, and with the exception of Algeria, the *métis* constituted if not a collective common identity at least a legal and administrative criterion inscribed into colonial law. Philanthropists, administrators, and jurists created a *métis* category that progressively allowed these children who were most often illegitimate, not recognized, and then abandoned by their father, to be included in the domain of French citizenship. The inclusion into citizenship of these transitional people, born in the majority of cases to a European man and an indigenous woman, had several motivations, ranging from demographic considerations based on populationist theories to arguments related to colonial political strategies, in which the *métis* allowed for the forging of a bond between the colonists and colonized people (229–35). After independence, these *métis*, most of whom came from Indochina, were repatriated to France – with their father's homeland often unknown to them – a displacement that created a brutal rupture with their emotional and socio-cultural environment: namely their mother, their language and their customs (17, 235–40).

At a glance, this history does not have much in common with Nina Bouraoui's story, as narrated in *Garçon manqué* (2000) and *Mes mauvaises pensées* (2005): daughter of a French woman and an Algerian man, she was born in 1967 in Rennes and grew up in Algiers up until the 1980s.[1] Not only is the gender relationship reversed (compared to the stereotypical *métis* situation) and the parents' union legal and recognized, but also the temporal referent is no longer the colonial period. Nonetheless, Bouraoui's stories, which recount being torn between two lands, two cultures and two parents, clearly pertain to this history of *métis* identity, "une identité de fracture" (fractured identity) (*Garçon manqué*, hereinafter GM, 19) induced by colonialism or its memory.[2] For if there was no "métis question" in French Algeria from the point of view of politics and law, because the criterion that differentiated French and indigenous populations in Algeria pertained to religion rather than race (Saada 40), demographically speaking mixed individuals did exist, although certainly less numerous than in other French colonies.[3]

The invisibility of racialized Franco-Algerian *métis* in official discursive practices during and after colonization is, however, in tension with socio-cultural representations and discourses that have constructed a racialized Algerian other.[4] This lasting contradiction betrays a French discursive hesitation over the first criterion used to categorize Algerians, whose ethnic difference was less obvious to French people than Indochinese or sub-Saharan people. Religious and racial criteria often merged together, and still today "Arab" and "Muslim" are often, in public discourses, interchangeable terms. This confusion echoes the colonial legal category of "Français Musulmans d'Algérie" (French Muslim of Algeria) (in effect after the revolt of 1947) which was based on the idea that these people were not of "European" descent, and had "a Muslim status originally from Algeria" (National Archive) – a status that, as Jim House notes, "introduced an ethnically-inspired sub-category of citizens that Algerians resented."[5]

These questions of ethnicity and religion haunt Bouraoui's narratives, which evoke the persistence of these colonial-based criteria after independence. Notably, she mentions that her parents – when they were living in France, where they met before moving to Algiers – were referred to as "la Blanche avec l'Algérien. La femme du Français musulman" (the White woman with the Algerian, the French Muslim's wife) (GM 148). In Algeria, the political processes of "Arabization" and Islamization of the country in the 1970s and 1980s, foreshadowing the downward spiral of the Civil War, threatened diversity, especially the French way of living, and in particular that of mixed families. About this period in her childhood, Bouraoui writes:

> Nous sommes déjà dans la guerre [...] Leurs regards sur la plage. Nos corps trop nus. Leurs yeux derrière les buissons. Leurs mots. Leurs insultes. Tout se presse soudain. La haine revient. La haine vient. Ils nous accusent. Ils disent: Vous êtes des pieds-noirs de la deuxième génération. Vous êtes des colons. Vous êtes encore français.
>
> (We are already at war [...] Their glances at us lying on the beach. Our naked bodies. Their eyes from behind the bushes. Their words. Their insults. All of a sudden there is a rush. Hatred is back. Hatred heats up. They accuse us. They say: You are the second generation of settlers. You are colonists. You are still French.) (GM 72)

These sentences show a brutal opposition, highlighted by the choppy style, between a visible ("nos corps trop nus") and European ("pieds-noirs") "us" ("nous") and a violent "them" ("ils") in the background ("derrière les buissons"). The misperception of the *métis* families, inaccurately perceived as "pieds-noirs" (European settlers) by Algerians, brings back the antagonism of the colonial period and shows a certain spectrality of historical roles – the "them" being portrayed as the aggressive ones, a myth of colonial times which Bouraoui revives.

Reviving colonial paradigms, Bouraoui's texts echo some contemporary French political discourses which tend to "ethnicize" identities, proving the point of scholars who contend that since the late 1990s in France there has been a "return of the colonial mindset" in contemporary debates.[6] No later than September 2015, French politician Nadine Morano, a former minister of Nicolas Sarkozy, publicly declared that France is a "white race" country.[7] This growing socio-political context in which identities are "racialized" and difference presented as radically other and antagonistic to a fantasized "us" is key to understanding Bouraoui's textual struggle with claiming a Franco-Algerian identity. I will thus explore a tension in Bouraoui's work: while giving visibility to her hybrid identity, Bouraoui represents the *métis* as the embodied perpetuation of the historical tensions that have opposed France and

Algeria. In other words, Bouraoui's narratives construct and deconstruct at the same time her Franco-Algerian *métis* identity and reflect a national identity crisis, in both countries.

I will first show how Bouraoui paradoxically reappropriates her Algerian body through the French language (her writing). Then I will analyze metaphors of rejections of her French legacy. Finally, I will examine how Bouraoui succeeds, or not, in producing a *métis* textual self.

reclaiming "her" algerian skin

Despite independence in 1962, the lines of colonial divide and confrontation persist, an idea expressed through the sentence: "la guerre d'Algérie ne s'est jamais arrêtée. Elle s'est transformée. Elle s'est déplacée. Et elle continue" (the Algerian War has never stopped. It has been transformed. It has shifted. And it still goes on) (GM 101). Pointing at this continuous asymmetrical relation, Bouraoui writes: "Je viens de la guerre. Je viens d'un mariage contesté. Je porte la souffrance de ma famille algérienne. Je porte le refus de ma famille française [...] La violence ne me quitte plus. Elle m'habite" (I come from the war. I come from a contested marriage. I carry my Algerian family's suffering. I carry the refusal of my French family [...] Violence does not leave me. It dwells in me) (GM 32). Her maternal family never accepted being bound to an Algerian. Throughout her narratives, Bouraoui merges her familial story with collective history, playing on the ambiguous French term "histoire" (story and history): "c'est toujours cette histoire, au fond de moi, de venir de deux familles que tout oppose, les Français et les Algériens" (It has always been about this hi/story, deep down in me, of coming from two families who are in total opposition, the French and the Algerians) (*Mes mauvaises pensées*, hereinafter MP, 53).

By means of hyperbole and dramatization, Bouraoui constructs a total antagonism and places herself on its fold, claiming that she embodies the colonial split, and thus attaching to the image of the postcolonial Franco-Algerian *métis* this idea of an impossible harmonious sense of self through the image of a dual body: "mon corps français et mon corps algérien" (my French body and my Algerian one) (MP 213). In *Garçon manqué*, she highlights the singularity of the mixed-race children, like her and her friend Amine, through a geographical image: "Nous sommes entre la France et l'Algérie [...] Nous ne serons jamais comme les autres [...] Deux bâtards sur la plage. Deux métis" (We are in-between France and Algeria [...] We will never be like the others [...] Two bastards on the beach. Two mixed-race children) (GM 21, 23, 29). This hesitation over the nature of her *métis* identity is striking at the opening of *Garçon manqué*, where she writes, as a prescription, "Ne pas être algérienne. Ne pas être française" (Not to be Algerian. Not to be French) (GM 33). Later, speaking of her *métis* friend Amine, she alternates between "sa peau blanche" (his white skin) and "sa peau brune" (his dark skin) (GM 35). She claims not being able to be Algerian because of her inability to speak Arabic. Yet immediately after, she adds: "Mais je suis algérienne. Par mon visage. Par mes yeux. Par ma peau" (But I'm Algerian. It's my face. My eyes. My skin) (GM 12).

As the narrative progresses, Bouraoui reclaims her "Algerianness" through what she elaborates as a "corporeal" legacy. Representing her Algerian genealogical connection as an embodied inheritance, she repeats that she is "traversée" (GM 92), inhabited, haunted by the bodies of her paternal family:

> Par mon corps traversé du corps de mes grands-parents. Je porte l'odeur de leur maison. Je porte [...] [verb repeated seven times] Je porte la main de Rabiâ [her Algerian grandmother] sur mon visage fiévreux. Je porte la voix de Bachir [her Algerian grandfather] [...] Elle me rattache aux autres. Elle m'inclut à la terre algérienne.
>
> (Through my body inhabited by the body of my grandparents. I bear within me the smell of their house. I bear [...] [repeated seven times] I bear Rabiâ's [her grandmother's] hand on my feverish face. I carry Bachir's [her grandfather's] voice [...] It links me to

others. It unites me with the land, connecting me to Algeria.) (GM 12)

The insistence on the ambiguous verbal expression "je porte" (to carry, to bear, to convey, to remember), defining both a physical gesture and an intellectual one, indicates the psychosomatic nature of the legacy conveyed in Bouraoui's discourse. The transmission of an Algerian identity is further mentioned throughout the novel through expressions highlighting the intergenerational transfer of what constitutes identity: "[par] mon père [...] par ses parents dans son corps, une invasion" (through my father [...] his parents inhabiting his body like occupiers) (GM 23, 24). Bouraoui seeks to represent processes of identification taking place through that which is beyond or below discourse; in other words, through the body. Such a paradigm can be understood through the socio-historical context in which Bouraoui lives, that is, a familial and societal environment dominated by silence over the past. While, on the one hand, it became difficult and dangerous to show off "Frenchness" in Algeria after independence, on the other, in France where Bouraoui reconstructs herself after exile, everything related to Algeria was suppressed from the public scene and absent from representation.

In this particular situation of double concealment, history and memory are not articulated through speech. Instead, in Bouraoui's narratives, the body appropriates a familial heritage expressed physically. She says: "Chaque corps est la contamination d'un autre corps. Chacun forme la strate de l'autre" (Each body gets contaminated by another. Everyone shares a common heritage, forming a single body in the end) (GM 40). In a context of silenced history, her parents' and grandparents' psychological wounds alone (and not an articulated memory) are transmitted to Bouraoui – "leur blessures transmises" (their transmitted wounds) (GM 130) – through a sort of psychosomatic transfer, suggesting that flesh contains memory. Hence when Bouraoui claims "Je porte la guerre d'Algérie" (I carry the Algerian War) (GM 30), we should read it as if the trauma of the war suffered by her grandparents was her own.

Thus, speaking about her anger provoked by a racist comment on Arabs made by her maternal (French) grandfather, Bouraoui says: "quand ma colère vient, je crois qu'elle passe par ce lien [between herself and her father], je crois qu'il y a une information familiale, on ne transmet pas seulement la chair à ses enfants mais aussi les conflits" (when anger invades me, I believe that it goes through this link [between herself and her father], I believe that [like genetic information] familial information exists, one does not only give her flesh to her children but one also passes on conflicts to them) (MP 157).[8] In addition to suggesting a transgenerational transmission of a wound, Bouraoui presents through the metaphor of the "link" what Teresa Brennan calls a "transmission of affect," accompanying the "projection or introjection of a judgment" (Brennan 5). For instance, in this scene where Bouraoui alludes to her anger, the grandfather makes a judgment about Arabs, implicitly attacking Bouraoui's father. Rachid does not answer anything, but his affect, this "physiological shift" (Brennan 5) – which consists probably of a mix of anger and pain – is transmitted to his daughter who gets angry for her father.

In the later narrative, *Mes mauvaises pensées*, Bouraoui elaborates a paradigm, that is, a framework of images representing a transmission of affects based on the motif of the skin. The word "skin" is already omnipresent in *Garçon manqué*, but it really becomes an obsessive theme in *Mes mauvaises pensées*.[9] This contact zone between self and other represents the location where transmission of affects occurs. Hence, Bouraoui provides images of her skin in contact with her paternal relatives' skins, a contact that becomes an embodiment or an inclusion: "mon grand-père algérien [...] Il y a sa peau sous la mienne" (my Algerian grandfather [...] Under my skin, there is his skin") (MP 45), "Je suis la peau de ma grand-mère" (I am my [Algerian] grandmother's skin) (MP 83), "au travers de ma peau [...] mon père" (across my skin [...] my father) (MP 36), "J'ai le visage de Rabiâ. J'ai la peau de Bachir" (I have Rabiâ's face. I have Bachir's skin) (GM 92), adding "Rien de Rennes. Rien. Qu'un extrait de naissance. Que ma nationalité française" (Nothing from Rennes. Nothing. Only my birth certificate. Only my French nationality) (ibid.).[10]

Her *métis* identity is composed of a French official person (her ID papers, her language) and an Algerian body: Bouraoui indeed textually constructs her body as a skin palimpsest whose layers are made of her paternal family's skin, conceived as a legacy of affects regarding history. The affects "contained" within a body can circulate from one individual to another thanks to the porosity of the skin. That is what Bouraoui means by her phrase "peau buvard" (MP 66): literally a "blotting skin," absorbing like blotting paper. She writes: "Je lis dans un livre qu'il y a un sujet buvard dans une famille, que c'est dans le système même de la famille, une peau qui prendrait tout" (In a book I read that in each family there is a blotting subject, that the family system functions through this sensitive skin that absorbs everything) (MP 28). What does this "everything" signify? How can circulating affects bond someone to the history of someone else?

Through her metaphorical "peau buvard" Bouraoui receives affects that are correlated to her family members' representations of the past – in other words, to their personal memory. In her book *The Generation of Postmemory*, Holocaust scholar Marianne Hirsch calls this inheritance of "something" that resembles memory but is not memory a "postmemory," which she characterizes as:

> the relationship that the "generation after" bears to the personal, collective, and cultural trauma of those who came before – to experiences they "remember" only by means of the stories, images, and behaviors among which they grew up. But these experiences were transmitted to them so deeply and affectively as to *seem* to constitute memories in their own right. (5)

The generation "before," who experienced trauma, does not speak out its memory to the generation after, as the rupture defining traumatic events cannot be apprehended through conscious or direct representations.[11] Thus, the traumatic memory is still somehow communicated through the convoluted ways of stories, images, and behaviors (including silence) that still induce affects linked to the trauma. In *Garçon manqué*, a picture of Rachid's brother, Amar, killed during the War of Independence, catalyzes such a relation of postmemory for Bouraoui:

> Je garde la photographie d'Amar. Mon secret. Sa dernière photographie. Prise au maquis. Il porte une chemise militaire. Il braque un fusil. Il vise le photographe. Pour rire. Il vise l'objectif. Pour se souvenir. De la douleur. Du combat. De l'Algérie française [...] Il vise toute ma famille française. Amar est le fils aîné disparu. Amar est le frère perdu. Amar est le silence de mon père. Sa séparation. Amar vient la nuit par sa dernière image, mon obsession [...] Je suis dans la guerre d'Algérie. Je porte le conflit.
>
> (I keep Amar's photograph. My secret. It's his last photograph. Shot on the battlefield. He is dressed in military uniform. He is cocking a gun. He is aiming at the photographer. As a joke. He aims at the camera lens. As a reminder. A reminder of the pain. Of the battle. Of French Algeria [...] He is aiming at my entire French family. Amar is the dead eldest son. Amar is the lost brother. Amar is my father's silence. His separation. Amar appears at night through the last photograph of him, my obsession [...] I am in the midst of the Algerian War of Independence. I bear the conflict.) (GM 30–31)

Bouraoui affectively invests the picture as if this image of Amar, who died before her birth, belonged to her own memory. The relationship she bears to Amar's story is intensively emotionally charged, as if she had known her uncle. She probably saw her father's or grandparents' pain while looking at the picture, and this affect was transmitted to her like an "obsession" (Bouraoui), "so deeply," as Hirsch writes, that she made the painful memory her own – "je porte," as she repeats. Bouraoui's narrative appropriation of her Algerian family's memories and histories, at the root of her claiming of an Algerian "skin," pairs up with a detachment from her French legacy.[12]

distancing her french legacy

Both *Garçon manqué* and *Mes mauvaises pensées* refer extensively to stories of asphyxiation. First, there is a series of episodes of near-drowning experiences involving, each time, a white woman. Two of them, one in *Garçon manqué* and the other in *Mes mauvaises pensées*, are particularly revealing of the metaphoric connection that Bouraoui creates between drowning and her apprehension of her French identity. At the beginning of *Garçon manqué*, Bouraoui recounts that during her childhood in Algeria she almost drowned during an outing to Zeralda's beach (in the suburbs of Algiers) with her friend Amine and his (French) mother. She writes, through short, sharp sentences characteristic of the style of this indicting, brutal text:

> Le soleil est une folie. Le soleil est un homme qui dévore l'Algérie. On fuit la plage [...] On va vers l'hôtel de Zeralda [...] Le soleil vient jusqu'à l'hôtel de Zeralda. Je saute du plongeoir [...] Je reste au fond longtemps. Le soleil incendie. Le feu contre mon souffle. Le feu contre ma volonté [...] Le soleil révèle. Je ne suis pas algérienne [...] Le soleil est une vengeance. Je ne suis pas d'ici. Je ne remonte pas.
>
> (The sun is madness. The sun is a man who devours Algeria. We run away from the beach [...] We are headed to Zeralda's hotel [...] The sun reaches Zeralda's hotel. I jump off the diving board [...] I stay at the bottom for a long time. The sun is burning. Fire against my breath. Fire against my will [...] The sun uncovers the truth. I am not Algerian [...] The sun is a kind of vengeance. I am not from here. I won't resurface.) (GM 28–29)

The passage reads as an opposition between Bouraoui and the omnipresent sun, a fight between Algeria's natural conditions and Bouraoui's body. The scene symbolizes the ordeal that the *métis* confronts: proving that she belonged to that country; and the truth is ("le soleil *révèle*" (the sun *uncovers* the truth)) that she failed ("Je ne suis pas algérienne [...] Je ne suis pas d'ici" (I am not Algerian [...] I am not from here)).

Moreover, the swimming pool drama happened at the same time as another scene, whose parallel narration casts light on the meaning of Bouraoui's representation of her near-drowning. While Bouraoui and her friend were venturing away in Zeralda, Amine's mother, who stayed at the beach, was also fighting against the sun:

> La mère d'Amine. Sa peau blanche. Son visage contre le soleil, une guerre. Elle est démunie, là, sur la plage algérienne [...] Elle est écrasée par l'Algérie. Elle est plus qu'une étrangère. C'est une femme française [...] Le soleil brûle la peau blanche de la femme française. Il tombe sur les corps. Il étouffe les voix.
>
> (Amine's mother, with her white skin. Her face against the sun, a war. She is powerless, here, on the Algerian beach [...] She is crushed by Algeria. More than a foreigner. She is a French woman [...] The sun burns the white skin of the French woman. It falls on bodies. It muffles voices.) (GM 27)

Both women (young Bouraoui and Amine's mother) are devoured by the sun, against which they are fighting ("contre" (against), "guerre" (war)). Both are asphyxiated: "Noyer le visage de la mère d'Amine [...] Noyer ma vie algérienne" (To drown Amine's mother's face [...] To drown my Algerian life) (GM 29). Beyond the sexual metaphor of a masculine domination (both French and Algerian) over women, the two passages, which are textually intertwined, establish a web of equivalences that is to be found throughout the two novels: first, white skin is clearly defined as a synonym of stranger to Algeria – the *métis* skin defines a form of strangeness, while the all-French skin, like Amine's mother, is "plus qu'une étrangère," more than a foreigner and a stranger combined: it is the enemy. The second and important imagery that the passage sets up is the link between "white" people and suffocation or asphyxiation.

These two paradigmatic connections are fleshed out in *Mes mauvaises pensées*, in which allusions to near-drowning events recur throughout the narrative. The second near-drowning I would like to point out is one noticeable past event which returns to Bouraoui's mind during her therapy. *Mes mauvaises pensées* indeed is composed of the narrator's monologue to her doctor, and the run-on sentences connote the flow of repressed memories backlash. This near-drowning episode is articulated right in the middle of the text (MP 138–39), suggesting how central this event is in the "drowning" semiotic chain. It is about the near-death of a young girl at the friend's house of Bouraoui's sister, where Bouraoui was staying while her mother was running some errands:

> Il y a ces yeux sur moi, qui arrivent, ce sont les yeux d'une fille de mon âge, elle longe la piscine, puis vient vers moi, elle cherche madame B. [the friend's mother], elle doit lui remettre quelque chose [...] il y a un bruit d'eau dans ma tête, ce sont les filtres de la piscine qui se vident, c'est l'orage au loin [...] il y a le corps de cette fille debout, devant moi, cette fille qui commence à rire, à tourner autour de moi, c'est comme une danse au début, puis c'est comme une folie dans ma tête, je me relève, je me tiens au bord de la piscine, elle dit: "Attention, tu pourras tomber", et c'est elle qui tombe [...] je ne sais pas ce que j'ai fait mais elle se noie, devant moi, et je ne l'aide pas, je la regarde, parce que je sais que c'est ma main qui l'a poussée, au début, pour rire, vite, parce que je ne supporte plus son corps et sa peau blanche [...]
>
> (There are these eyes looking at me, getting closer, they are the eyes of a girl of my age, she walks along the swimming pool, then comes to me, she is looking for Mrs B. [the friend's mother], she has to deliver something to her [...], there is a water noise in my head, it comes from the pool's filters that empty, it may be the storm in the distance [...] there is the body of this girl standing in front of me, this girl who starts to laugh, turning around me, at the beginning it looks like a dance, but then it makes me dizzy, I get back up, I am standing by the pool, she says: "Be careful you could fall into the water!" But she is the one who falls [...] I don't know what I did but she is drowning, right in front of me, and I am not helping her, I am looking at her, because I know that my hand pushed the girl, at first, for a laugh, quickly, because I cannot stand her body and white skin anymore [...]) (MP 138–39)

Bouraoui eventually ended up rescuing the girl. But the point is Bouraoui sees herself in that girl, and the reason why she felt the urge to commit this almost-crime is the white-skinned body of the girl ("parce que je ne supporte plus son corps et sa peau blanche" (because I cannot stand her body and white skin anymore)). A few pages later, the color of the skin is confirmed as being the apparent motivation of Bouraoui's violent and aggressive act: "Après ce jour, toutes les nuits se font écho, des nuits à penser à madame B., des nuits à revivre le jour de février, l'orage, mes mains, *la peau blanche de la fille*" (After that day, I spend night after night thinking of Mrs B., nights reliving that day in February, the storm, my hands, *the white skin of the girl*) (MP 143; emphasis added).

These two repressed drowning memories trace back to the very first "near-drowning" experience in life: the baby in the mother's waters. "Mère" (mother) and "mer" (sea) symbolically become a unique motif connected to Bouraoui's unease with her French identity (symbolized by the white skin), which she inherited from her mother. These obscured near-drowning memories function like what Abraham and Torok call a "phantom," that is, an unconscious "concern" caused by a shameful secret inherited from a family member:

> The phantom is a formation of the unconscious that has never been conscious – for a good reason. It passes [...] from the parent's unconscious to the child's [ ] The phantom is what works in the unconscious from an unspeakable shameful secret belonging to another [...] Its manifestation, the

> haunting, is the phantom's return in the form of bizarre words and actions [...] (173, 189)

Abraham and Torok demonstrate that the child does not consciously understand the secret that the parents bear in silence, but that s/he acts it out, driven by a "thing" wedged in his or her unconscious. So a question arises: what shameful secret of asphyxiation does Bouraoui's mother carry and how does Bouraoui textually present it?

This question brings me to the second type of asphyxiation I announced above, a suffocation not caused by water but by lack of air. Bouraoui's mother, Maryvonne, suffers from asthma, a metaphorical drowning which Bouraoui does not miss highlighting: "l'asthme, c'est comme la noyade, l'asthme c'est sa propre noyade" (Asthma, it's like drowning, asthma is her own way of drowning) (MP 60). She often mentions her mother's "maladie" (illness) (MP 28, 30, 37, etc.): "ma mère qui étouffe, sa peau bleue" (my mother suffocating, her blue skin) (MP 24), "son asthme" (her asthma) (MP 55), "œdème" (edema) (MP 56), "trachéotomie" (tracheotomy) (MP 59), "l'asphyxie de ma mère" (my mother's asphyxiation) (MP 178), "ses asphyxies" (her asphyxiations) (MP 197). But asphyxiation, literally referring to the pathological condition of lack of normal breathing, has a figurative sense: "étouffement de facultés intellectuelles ou morales du a la contrainte ou au milieu de vie" (stifling of intellectual or moral faculties caused by pressure or intimidation or constraint) (*Le Petit Robert*). Maryvonne's shameful secret lies precisely in this shift from literal to figurative. The portrayal of Bouraoui's ill mother in *Mes mauvaises pensées* functions as a literal and somatic representation of a mental, psychic condition: precisely, the mother's anxiety created by her own parents' anti-Arab racism.

In the narrator's recollections, the maternal grandfather is described as nostalgic for French Algeria, as a racist man who refers to Arabs with insulting names (*bicots, bougnoules*), and who threatened his daughter with a "tu n'épouseras pas un Algérien" (you will not marry an Algerian man) (GM 31) when she met Rachid, Bouraoui's father. The grandfather later admonished his daughter through violent statements, such as "tu vas mal finir" (It's going to turn out badly for you) (MP 97), and "Tu es la honte de la famille" (You're the shame of the family) (MP 232). Bouraoui often highlights her maternal family's abjection of her Arab identity, an abjection which informed her public identity, in her very name. Indeed, Bouraoui's desire to change her first name from Yasmina to Nina is presented as a reaction to her grandparents' decision to name their black poodle "Jasmine" (MP 137) as if Arabic names were only good for dogs; a comparison often made by the grandmother, as narrated in *Garçon manqué* (e.g., GM 127, 130–32, 153). Ironically, this change of name satisfied the grandparents who once mentioned, during a family vacation in their native Brittany, "On préfère t'appeler Nina plutôt que Yasmina. Nina ça arrange. Ça fait espagnol ou italien. Comme ça on n'a pas à expliquer nos fréquentations" (We prefer to call you Nina rather than Yasmina. It is more convenient. It sounds Spanish or Italian. This way, we don't have to explain our company) (GM 123).

All these childhood memories returning to Bouraoui provoked behavioral troubles, as the title *Mes mauvaises pensées* announces, which prompted the narrator to go and see a professional.

(im)possible *métis*?

Significantly, one of the obsessive "bad/evil thoughts" that Bouraoui confesses to her doctor directly relates to her French grandfather and symbolically deals with her mixed identity. She narrates a memory about a family dinner with her maternal relatives. Despite the grandfather's warning, young Bouraoui orders a "pied de cochon" (pig's trotter) – a big piece of pork that, according to the grandfather, a little girl can hardly eat by herself. The threat and anger of the old man: "Tu as intérêt à le manger!" (You'd better eat the whole thing!) (MP 210), terrorizes Nina, who is then unable to eat the dish: "le pied arrive [...] et je ne peux pas le manger [...] et bien sûr mon grand-père est en colère, et il m'en veut et il me punit, et je me couche sans dîner" (the pig's trotter is on the table [...] and I cannot eat it [...] and of course my grandfather is upset, he is angry at me, and punishes me, and I go to bed without having eaten dinner) (MP 210). Well, incidentally, Bouraoui's inability to ingest the pork – an animal whose consumption is forbidden under Islamic dietary laws, and associated with French cuisine – represents a symbolic resistance: she cannot swallow a certain France's imperialism which rejects difference and is embodied by her grandfather.

But my point is about her subsequent evil thought. She writes: "tout se lie, puisque dans mes mauvaises pensées il y a l'idée fixe d'un ongle géant qui gratterait ma peau jusqu'au sang" (it all makes sense, since, in my bad thoughts, there is an obsession of a giant nail that would scratch my skin until it bleeds) (ibid.). The pig hoof's scratching her skin is a literalization of a metaphor associated with the grandfather who wishes to "Frenchify" Nina: that is, to remove the melanin of her mixed skin, to scratch off the Algerian layer of her skin as it were. The physical skin is linked to the psychological one in an anaphoric relation. This is what psychoanalyst Didier Anzieu calls the "ego-skin" (*Moi-peau*): it is a fantasized reality, a representation that the child uses in early phases of her development to represent herself as a "me" based on the experience of her body surface. In his book *Le Moi-peau*, Anzieu explains how the defining interface ego/skin in child psychology is based on a similarity of structures and functions between the ego and the skin that he summarizes with the concepts of limitation, capacity or composure, and organization. Hence the scratching of the skin is analyzed as an attempt to feel the limits of one's ego-skin: "Les mutilations de la peau – parfois réelles, le plus souvent imaginaires – sont des tentatives dramatiques de maintenir les limites du corps et du Moi, de rétablir le sentiment d'être intact et cohésif" (Mutilations of the skin – sometimes real, most often imaginary – are dramatic attempts to hold the limits of the body and the ego, to re-establish the feeling of being intact and cohesive) (Anzieu 42). The narrator's fantasized scratching should be understood as her attempt to hold her identity as differing from that of her French family, as a virtual inscription of her Algerian difference on her ego-skin. Through the narration of this fantasized psychosomatic inscription of Franco-Algerian identity, Bouraoui imprints textually a sense of hybridity in her written self.

The scratching of the skin is not only a fantasy; the narrator claims rubbing her skin for real, because she wants "to get rid of [her] shame" (Je frotte ma peau pour [...] me défaire de ma honte) (MP 85). Expressions of shame and guilt come back recurrently in the novels, and especially in *Mes mauvaises pensées* (75, 85, 99, 171, 220, etc.), and they manifest the idea of intergenerational guilt, that Bouraoui's mother (ashamed of her own father) is shown to have physically manifested through her illness. Indeed, speaking of the confinement ("claustra" MP 43) and "porosity" between her mother and herself, Bouraoui says: "la tristesse de ma mère que je reprends comme une maladie, que je revis comme un devoir" (my mother's sadness that I appropriate like an illness, that I live myself like a duty) (MP 28), "c'est comme si mon corps avait la mémoire du corps de ma mère" (it is as if my body bore the memory of my mother's body) (MP 218).

And what's interesting is that most of Bouraoui's evil thoughts, which are diagnosed as "phobies d'impulsion" (impulse phobias) (MP 12) by her doctor, are about her mother's body, and specifically her white skin. She indeed repeatedly claims such ideas: "ma mère [...] sa peau [...] la beauté de sa peau que j'ai peur d'ouvrir avec une petite paire de ciseaux qu'elle a laissé près du téléphone" (my mother [...] her skin [...] her beautiful skin that I dread to cut with a pair of scissors that she left near the telephone) (MP 24). And further in the text: "Dans mes mauvaises pensées, il y a la vision de cette peau que j'ouvre au couteau et de ces viscères que je déchire comme du tissu fin [...] entailler, dépecer, saigner" (In my bad thoughts, I have this vision of this skin that I open with a knife and these viscera that I rip off like a fine fabric

[...] cutting, ripping apart, bleeding her dry) (MP 123). How to interpret such images?

In the chapter "Chosen Trauma: Unresolved Mourning" of his book *Bloodlines*, psychiatrist Vamik Volkan examines a case of transgenerational transmission of trauma, which he defines as "when an older person unconsciously externalizes his traumatized self onto a developing child's personality. The child becomes a reservoir for the unwanted, troublesome parts of an older generation" (Volkan 43). He explains that, whether or not what is transmitted changes, the mechanism of transmission is the same: "The person in the first generation of this family [...] may be said to have had a traumatized (imprisoned) self-representation that he enveloped and externalized onto a member of the second generation in an attempt to repair it. The person in the second generation, who has absorbed the wish of his elder, in turn externalized his and his [parent's or trauma transmitter's] aspects onto [the object associated with trauma]" and takes action upon it "in an effort to erase the bad feelings" it "represented" (44). Using Volkan's terminology – which actually coincides with Bouraoui's own vocabulary – the child becomes a "reservoir" for the parent, who "envelop[s] and externalize[s] the unacceptable aspect of [herself] onto others who fit [her] perception of [her] traumatized self" (42). In this way, in Bouraoui's text, the narrator's fantasy of cutting off and getting rid of her mother's white skin is the repairing externalization of her mother's transmitted traumatic self-representation.

Finally, the attempt to repair, so to speak, the ruptured, broken *métis* identity is performed, or at least made visible, through the writing of the text. Writing in French and from France about Algeria and her childhood memories conveys, for Bouraoui, a sense of completed reappropriation of her several identities. She writes: "L'écriture c'est la terre, c'est l'Algérie retrouvée [...] je couvre la terre quittée" (Writing is the land, it's Algeria regained [...] I cover the land I left) (MP 201). Yet there is a notable evolution between *Garçon manqué* and *Mes mauvaises pensées*. The first book is divided into four parts: "Alger," "Rennes," "Tivoli," and "Amine." The first two parts, roughly equal in length, compose most of the narrative: on the one hand, the memories from Algeria, on the other, the memories from France. This division reflects her schismatic sense of self. Following this, the four pages entitled "Tivoli" recount how a trip to Italy modified Bouraoui's struggle with her identity. She indeed writes: "Je n'étais plus française. Je n'étais plus algérienne. Je n'étais même plus la fille de ma mère. J'étais moi. Avec mon corps [...] Je suis devenue heureuse à Rome. [...] Je venais de moi et moi seule" (I was not French anymore. I was not Algerian anymore. I was not even my mother's daughter. I was just me. My body [...] I had become happy in Rome [...] I came from myself, and myself alone) (GM 184–85). So there is a sort of radical resolution of her problems: distance (geographical, since she is not in France nor in Algeria, and affective: she is not with any family members) and desire ("le désir" GM 184) allowed Bouraoui to regain a sense of self and agency but without an emotional (and textual) integration of her dual legacy ("Je venais de moi et moi seule" (I came from myself, and myself alone)).

This idea is confirmed through the very last three pages entitled "Amine" and composed of a letter to her friend; a letter of disappointment following a reunion after Bouraoui's trip to Rome. She says that Amine looked at her differently, sensing a new body full of desire. What is interesting about this letter is that Amine can be conceived as a symbolic "location," just like the three other chapter titles. Amine would symbolize the *métis* place, which Bouraoui leaves behind after Tivoli, the place of her brand new self. So despite her recognizing an indelible trace of Amine on her identity ("Il restera toujours une trace de toi, Amine. Sur ma peau. Un petit tatouage bleu, comme le ciel d'Alger" (There will always be a trace of you, Amine. On my skin. A small blue tattoo, like the sky in Algiers)) (GM 188–89), she says goodbye to her double, a mirror-*métis* friend. The *metis* compromise has failed, as it were.

Yet, five years later, the question is back in *Mes mauvaises pensées*. With comparison with *Garçon manqué*, the very textual form is striking: the 277-page narrative is written as one paragraph devoid of chapter divisions. As critic Adrienne Angelo notes, "this structure reproduces the narrator's self-identifying metaphor 'ma vie est d'un trait' [my life is in one go] [MP 245]" (88). Angelo remarks that the polysemic possibilities of the word "trait" suggest both rupture and forgetting, and incorporation: on the one hand, "trait" recalls the expression "tirer un trait sur quelque chose" (literally: to draw lines; to forget about something); but, on the other, it connotes the phrase "boire à grands/à longs traits" (to drink in one gulp, in one go). So, between integration of a traumatic past in the self and separation from it through writing, the text eventually reads as "trait-d'union" (hyphen) between Bouraoui's different selves and always-changing identities.

Within the narrative, the story ends with a significant image: Bouraoui mentions Charles de Foucauld (1858–1916), who was an officer in the French Army but who, after a revelation in the Algerian desert, became a Catholic priest. He then decided to go and settle in the Hoggar region in the Sahara and live with the Tuaregs. Ending a series of sentences beginning with "Je garde" (I keep/I remember), Bouraoui says: "Je garde l'image du couvent du père de Foucauld, dans le désert" (I keep (remember) the image of Father de Foucauld's monastery, in the desert) (MP 286). This reference to a Frenchman who became an Algerian offers a vision of hybridity as a potential place of peacefulness, but at the cost of loneliness.

Bouraoui's work reminds us that Ella Shohat's thoughts in her "Notes on the 'Post-Colonial'" are just as topical as ever:

> Since most of the world is now living after the period of colonialism, the "post-colonial" can easily become a universalizing category which neutralizes significant geopolitical differences between France and Algeria [...] A celebration of syncretism and hybridity per se, if not articulated in conjunction with questions of hegemony and neo-colonial power relations, runs the risk of appearing to sanctify the *fait accompli* of colonial violence. (103, 109)

Hence, when she asks herself the question "Qui suis-je?" (Who am I?) (GM 135), Bouraoui cannot answer other than saying "une peau déchirée" (a ruptured skin) (GM 60).

disclosure statement

No potential conflict of interest was reported by the author.

notes

1 *Garçon manqué* [*Tomboy*] and the Renaudot Prize-winning *Mes mauvaises pensées* [*My Bad/Evil Thoughts*] are considered autobiographical by Trudy Agar-Mendousse, in her *Violence et créativité de l'écriture algérienne au féminin*.

2 The translations throughout are mine.

3 On the reasons for such a relative quantitative difference, see Saada 37. Essentially, Algeria being a colony of settlement, with therefore a relatively proportionate male–female ratio, and the structure of feminine sexuality in the Maghreb region would explain the low frequency of sexual relations between colonists and the colonized people.

4 Unlike Saada, Olivier Le Cour Grandmaison, in *Coloniser, exterminer. Sur la guerre et l'Etat colonial* (2005), and Patricia Lorcin, in *Imperial Identities: Stereotyping, Prejudice and Race in Colonial Algeria* (1995), contend that "race" was, in fact, invoked in colonial political discourses regarding Algeria and that the motif was used precisely to exclude the indigenous population from the nation.

5 House n. pag. In his *The Invention of Decolonization*, Todd Shepard shows that between 1956 and 1962 the French Republic relied on this category to establish quotas to redress the effects of discrimination on its Muslim Algerian minority – a sort of affirmative action that, according to Shepard, goes against the idea that France's practice has always been "color-blind."

6 See, for example, Coquio's *Retours du colonial?*; Blanchard and Veyrat-Masson's *Les Guerres de*

mémoires; and Bancel, Blanchard, and Boubeker's *Le Grand Repli*.

7 *Le Monde*, "Nadine Morano évoque la race blanche de la France"; *Le Point*, "ONPC: Nadine Morano, La France un pays de race blanche."

8 The idea of an intergenerational transmission of a wound in a context of silenced history is expressed by Nadine Fresco in her article "La Diaspora des cendres" about families of Holocaust's victims. She draws from Michel Schneider's notion of "blessures de mémoire" (wounds of memory), defining parents who suffered and who would not communicate their traumatic memory. Fresco argues that this interruption of transmission of memory makes the wound become the idea standing for memory ("blessures *pour* mémoire" (wounds *as* memory)): "Aux enfants, à qui la mémoire était refusée, on transmettait seulement la blessure [...] Du deuil inachevé des parents les enfants héritent" (Only the wound was transmitted to the children, to whom memory has been refused [...] The children inherit their parents' unfinished mourning) (217).

9 Just to mention some occurrences of "skin" (*peau*) in *Mes mauvaises pensées*, see 24, 45, 54, 62, 69, 70, 76, 81, 82, 85, 88, 90, 102, 117, 121, 123, 125, 127, 130, 139, 143, 145, 193, 196, 197, 202, 203, 204, 210, 254, 283.

10 Rennes, in Brittany, is where Bouraoui was born. Her mother is from this region, and her maternal grandparents live there.

11 As psychiatrist Judith Herman says:

> Traumatic memories [...] are not encoded like the ordinary memories of adults in a verbal, linear narrative that is assimilated into an ongoing life story [...] [They] lack verbal narrative and context; rather, they are encoded in the form of vivid sensation and images. (37–38)

12 Bouraoui's emphasis on her Algerian skin also entails a deconstruction of her gender, and progressively leads to her claim of lesbianism. The theme of "Algerianness" is linked to that of gender in the two novels. However, I do not develop the gender question here, as a discussion of Bouraoui's lesbian identity is not relevant to my general argument.

bibliography

Abraham, Nicolas, and Maria Torok. *The Shell and the Kernel: Renewals of Psychoanalysis*. Trans. Nicolas T. Rand. Chicago: U of Chicago P, 1994. Print.

Agar-Mendouse, Trudy. *Violence et créativité de l'écriture algérienne au féminin*. Paris: L'Harmattan, 2006. Print.

Angelo, Adrienne. "*Sujet buvard, sujet bavard*: Nina Bouraoui's Words to Say It." *Women's Self-Narrative Across the Francophone World*. Spec. issue of *Women in French Studies* (2011): 79–90. Print.

Anzieu, Didier. *Le Moi-peau*. Paris: Dunoz, 1985. Print.

Bancel, Nicolas, Pascal Blanchard, and Ahmed Boubeker. *Le Grand Repli*. Paris: La Découverte, 2015. Print.

Blanchard, Pascal, and Isabelle Veyrat-Masson, eds. *Les Guerres de mémoires. La France et son histoire*. Paris: La Découverte, 2008. Print.

Bouraoui, Nina. *Garçon manqué*. Paris: Livre de Poche, 2000. Print.

Bouraoui, Nina. *Mes mauvaises pensées*. Paris: Stock, 2005. Print.

Brennan, Teresa. *The Transmission of Affect*. Ithaca, NY: Cornell UP, 2004. Print.

Coquio, Catherine, ed. *Retours du colonial? Disculpation et réhabilitation de l'histoire coloniale*. Nantes: L'Atalante, 2008. Print.

Fresco, Nadine. "La Diaspora des cendres." *L'Emprise* 24 (1981): 203–20. Print.

Herman, Judith. *Trauma and Recovery*. London: Pandora, 2001. Print.

Hirsch, Marianne. *The Generation of Postmemory: Writing and Visual Culture after the Holocaust*. New York: Columbia UP, 2012. Print.

House, Jim. "The Colonial and Post-Colonial Dimensions of Algerian Migration to France." *History in Focus*. Institute of Historical Research, 2006. Web. 10 Mar. 2014.

Le Cour Grandmaison, Olivier. *Coloniser, exterminer. Sur la guerre et l'Etat colonial*. Paris: Fayard, 2005. Print.

Le Monde. "Nadine Morano évoque la race blanche de la France." *Le Monde* 27 Sept. 2015. Web. 22 Nov. 2015.

Le Point. "ONPC: Nadine Morano, La France un pays de race blanche." *Le Point* 27 Sept. 2015 (modified 28 Sept.). Web. 22 Nov. 2015.

Lorcin, Patricia. *Imperial Identities: Stereotyping, Prejudice and Race in Colonial Algeria*. London: Tauris, 1995. Print.

Saada, Emmanuelle. *Les Enfants de la colonie. Les Métis de l'Empire français, entre sujétion et citoyenneté*. Paris: La Découverte, 2007. Print.

Shepard, Todd. *The Invention of Decolonization: The Algerian War and the Remaking of France*. Ithaca, NY: Cornell UP, 2006. Print.

Shohat, Ella. "Notes on the 'Post-Colonial.'" *Social Text* 31–32 (1992): 99–113. Print.

Volkan, Vamik. *Bloodlines: From Ethnic Pride to Ethnic Terrorism*. New York: Farrar, 1997. Print.

tessa roynon

CONSTRUCTING SELFHOOD THROUGH RE-VOICING THE CLASSICAL PAST

bernardine evaristo, marlene nourbese philip, and robin coste lewis

introduction

"I know I can't change the future," Toni Morrison once said, "but I can change the past […] Our past was appropriated. I am one of the people who has to reappropriate it" (Taylor-Guthrie xiii). This essay examines three works by three women writers whose strategies for rewriting the past include a revisionary engagement with the cultural legacies of Ancient Greece and Rome. The first text discussed here is the verse novel *The Emperor's Babe*, published in 2001 by the British-based writer of mixed Nigerian and British parentage Bernardine Evaristo. The second is a hybridized poetry and prose work, *Looking for Livingstone: An Odyssey of Silence*, published in 1991 by the poet and lawyer Marlene NourbeSe Philip, who was born in Tobago and now lives in Canada. The third is the recently published long poem *Voyage of the Sable Venus* – the central work in a collection of the same title – published in 2015 by Robin Coste Lewis. Lewis is an American woman of colour who was born and lives in Los Angeles, and whose family were from New Orleans.

While each of these works is one of a kind, and is strikingly different from the others in terms of setting, technique, mood and effect, there are also significant commonalities between them. Most obviously, each embodies a mode of resistance that both protests the historic oppression of women of colour and asserts a black female agency, insisting (to a greater or lesser degree) on an empowered present and future. In achieving this, all three transgress or subvert conventional generic distinctions between verse and prose, and, in Lewis's case, between the cultural forms and academic disciplines of art, art history and literature. Each work insists on a transnational conception of black identity, implicitly tracing black diasporic experience through Africa, Europe and the Americas, and asserting the continued interconnections between these three. And, in their confrontations with the histories of colonialism, empire and slavery, each invokes not just the history of the seventeenth to twenty-first centuries CE but also the cultures of Ancient Greece and Rome, the legacies of which underpinned these modern European processes of domination. Crucially, Evaristo and Lewis also engage with the traditions of Ancient Egypt, Nubia and Sudan, strategically insisting on their inseparability from the

European traditions that are conventionally conceived as "classical." Evaristo and Lewis thereby position themselves in a genealogy of black intellectuals and artists who, as scholarship such as Daniel Orrells, Gurminder Bhambra, and Tessa Roynon's 2011 work *African Athena* has demonstrated, reclaim to subversive, resistant ends the key role played by Nubia, Libya, Ethiopia and Egypt in so-called European civilization.

Evaristo's *The Emperor's Babe* is set in London of the third century CE. As many critics have discussed, in her brilliant depiction of the city as a colonial backwater, a dank and watery peripheral town ruled by the glamorous metropolis of Rome, the author explores a range of contemporaneous postcolonial preoccupations.[1] The protagonist is Zuleika, a young woman of Sudanese descent (she was born in London but her parents emigrated there from Sudan), and the narrative (told in the first person by Zuleika) relates her compelled marriage as a child bride to a distinguished but unattractive Roman statesman named Felix. The protagonist describes her uncomfortable transformation from shopkeeper's daughter, one of a group of rebellious female friends, to aristocratic lady of a villa of distinction; her education in classical poetry and her own ambitions to be a poet; her passionate love affair with the Emperor Severus (himself of Libyan descent), and her imminent death by poisoning at the hands of her jealous husband. A hilarious and provocative take on both the classical epic and the *Bildungsroman*, it is an alternative or speculative history which foregrounds female oppression and subjection to sexual violence, as well as fulfilled female emotional and intellectual ambition and sexual desire. The writing is a romping, energized pastiche of verse forms and ingenious twenty-first-century "neo-Latinisms." Zuleika's prologue, for example, describing her forced acculturation to her refined and lonely life as Felix's wife, includes the following:

Zuleika accepta est.
Zuleika delicata est.
Zuleika bloody goody-two shoes est.

But I dreamt of creating mosaics,
Of remaking my town with bright stones and glass.

But no! Numquam! It's not allowed.

[...]

Solitudoh, solitudee, solitudargh! (5)

Evaristo's ironic, comic tone is key to the power of her piece but, as I shall demonstrate, her political concerns are profoundly serious.

Philip's *Looking for Livingstone: An Odyssey of Silence* is completely different from Evaristo's piece in tone and method, but no less serious in its political intervention. Through a combination of prose and verse, told from the first-person perspective of "the Traveller" – "an allegorical narrative repeatedly interrupted by a continuing lyric poem" (Miller 140) – it relates a quest, a journey through unidentified Africa in search of "silence" and "surrender" (Philip 11, 38). Seeking to counteract the predominant narrative of Livingstone and Stanley's explorations in East Africa, it depicts the Traveller's proto-Odyssean encounters with seven tribes or ethnic groups, each named in a different anagram or near-anagram of "silence": the ECNELIS (10), the SINCEEL (11), the LENSECI (14), the SCENILE (19), the CESLIENS (35), the CLEENIS (41) and the NEECLIS (48), before culminating in a surreal and parodic encounter between the Traveller and Livingstone himself. Philip's commitment to the power of silence continues her concern in the earlier long poem *She Tries Her Tongue, Her Silence Softly Breaks* (1988), wherein she calls the English language, "a foreign anguish" (148), a compromised medium that cannot articulate the postcolonial condition. Eschewing realism, the 1991 work is every bit as speculative or alternative a history as Evaristo's, but it focuses more overtly on anger, pain and suffering. Loosely applying the Homeric version of the thematic of homecoming to her narrative, Philip's work can usefully be understood in relation to a range of African diasporic texts that stage troubled quests for origins or for "home" through a highly invested return to Africa, including, for example, Saidiya Hartman's 2008 memoir *Lose Your Mother.*[2] The Traveller ultimately realizes the truth of the prediction by the ECNELIS, made early on in her journey: the "thing" she is seeking, while impossible to articulate, is "not a thing to be discovered as much as recovered" (*Looking* 10).

Similarly concerned with "recovery," but also with the simultaneous continuity and resurgence of black female empowerment, Robin Coste Lewis's *Voyage of the Sable Venus* constitutes an eighty-page central section in her National Book Award-winning collection *Voyage of the Sable Venus and Other Poems.* Its title invokes the 1765 poem "The Voyage of the Sable Venus," a text by Isaac Teale implicitly celebrating the opportunities for white male sexual violence against black women that slavery provided. The original poem, accompanied by an engraving by Thomas Stothard which is a racist and lascivious parody of Botticelli's "The Birth of Venus" (1486), was published in a significant publication that defended slavery, namely Bryan Edwards's *History Civil and Commercial, of the British Colonies in the West Indies* of 1793 (Hall 9). Lewis's stunning creation writes back not just to this particular cultural moment but to centuries of the objectification, fetishization, enslavement, oppression and sexual exploitation of the black female as it is reflected and created in both the visual arts and written text. As she explains in the work's Prologue, her text consists "solely and entirely of the titles, catalog entries, or exhibit descriptions of Western art objects in which a black female figure is present, dating from 38,000 BCE to the present" (35). In this it significantly develops the engagement with canonical European painting by Claudia Rankine in her deployment of the F.M.W. Turner paintings in *Citizen* (2015; 160–61), or by Toni Morrison in her analysis of Géricault in *Etranger chez soi* (2–6; 13ff.).[3] Lewis refocuses our attention onto the discourses surrounding the works of art – onto text that may attempt to diminish or erase any radical potential within the art itself. Her poem ends with, instead of a bibliography, a list of around 150 museums located all over the world – from Khartoum to Copenhagen – which are the truly transnational sources for her text (111–14).

By definition, Lewis's poem writes "across cultures": it consists of eight "catalogs" that include "ANCIENT GREECE AND ROME," "ANCIENT EGYPT," "THE WOMB OF CHRISTIANITY" and others focused on more recent times such as "MODERN, CIVIL, RIGHT" (in which a great deal is neither modern, nor civil, nor right) (ix–x). The poet creates a transnational or even pre-national non-white female perspective through allying descriptions of West African, North African, Middle Eastern, African American, black Caribbean and Native American female figures. Her artistry is in the selection and in the ordering of the words and phrases of that selection; she erases all existing punctuation, she groups and juxtaposes like and unlike descriptions, and she puns on the new meanings that new contexts bring to words. The result is, among other things, a feminist re-voicing of prior hybridized masterpieces such as fusion of Robert Hayden's *Middle Passage* (1966) or Paul Metcalf's *Apalache* (1976). Lewis effects a comprehensive exposure of a violent and often-silenced history, accompanied by a comprehensive dismantling of the discourses and the institutions that shape and legitimate that history. The process and the effect have much in common with that achieved by Toni Morrison's *The Bluest Eye* (1970), with which Lewis enacts a significant intertextual dialogue. Like Morrison, Lewis exposes the perverse violence that at once underpins and is intensified by "Western" conceptions of the beautiful and the not beautiful. Perhaps unlike Morrison in that first, bleak novel, Lewis also creates an alternative voice, a reclamation of beauty and agency, and the potential not just for survival but for triumph.

The discussion that follows is comprised of three parts, treating *The Emperor's Babe, Looking for Livingstone* and *Voyage of the Sable Venus* in turn. In Part I, I build on existing scholarship on Evaristo's text by illuminating the central but hitherto insufficiently analysed engagement with a range of works by the Roman poet Ovid (43 BCE–17 CE), in this work's explorations of both sexual violence against women and female sexual desire. In Part II, I seek to explain the causes of the relative critical silence on Philip's *Looking for Livingstone*, suggesting that the work does not quite deliver on the promise of its title's classical allusiveness. It is arguably less successful than either Evaristo's or Lewis's work in constructing a viable female agency or selfhood. In Part III, in the current absence of scholarly precedent on Lewis's very new poem, I briefly outline the nature of the work before focusing on the brilliance of two of its sections, "ANCIENT GREECE AND ANCIENT ROME," and "ANCIENT EGYPT." Lewis creates an intertextual relationship with a range of cultural discourses, simultaneously critiquing the violent distortions of history while recovering and re-presenting a dynamic, indisputable, creative and empowered black female personhood.

part I – bernardine evaristo, *the emperor's babe* (2001)

In the fifteen years since its publication, several critics have analysed the subversive power of Evaristo's engagement with Ancient Greek and Roman culture. Katharine Burkitt and Justine McConnell, for example, have separately explored the ways in which the relationship between *The Emperor's Babe* and the epics of Homer and Virgil is key to its crossing of temporal, spatial and generic borders (McConnell, "Crossing" 103–04). The focus of my discussion here is on the importance of the intertextual relationship with the Roman poet Ovid in this verse novel – not just with the most well-known epic poem the *Metamorphoses* but also the earlier *Amores* and the *Heroides*, and the later *Fasti*. Evaristo deploys the mythical rapes that punctuate Ovid's works to protest sexual violence against women and the sexual subordination of women. She also alludes to and revises Ovid's preoccupation with passion and with the transformative effects of desire. In this duality her resistance constitutes both protest and the potential for a better, alternative reality. In her writing of Zuleika's love scenes with the Emperor Severus, she represents female agency through simultaneous fulfilled female erotic pleasure, female power and agency, and articulated female identity and experience. All of these representations depend on an ambivalent, revisionary relationship with Ovid's work.

Among her allusions to the Roman poets Catullus, Horace, and Virgil in the work, Evaristo directly mentions Ovid only once. This is at the start of her "Book IX," which she titles "EVERY LOVER IS A SOLDIER / [Militat Omnis Amans] / – Ovid" (217). Unlike many of the fabricated, satirical "quotations" from Roman literature in the text, this is a genuine quotation, from the first book of Ovid's erotic elegies, the *Amores*, "Every lover is a soldier, and Cupid has a camp of his own" (*Amores* I.ix.1ff.). As I shall go on to discuss, through Zuleika's discovery and achievement of sexual pleasure and power in her relationship with Severus, Evaristo revises the patriarchal perspective of Ovid's poem. Yet while this overt invocation of Ovid is a direct signal from the contemporary writer about the importance of this intertextual relationship, indirect but significant resonances of Ovidian themes pervade the work as a whole. These range from the thematic interest in the various changes and transformations that Zuleika undergoes (indeed, the first section of Part II is in fact called "Metamorphosis" (33)), to *ekphrases* that recall the Roman poet in their allusions to mythical figures who are the victim of rape in his work.

The novel is a kind of *Bildungsroman* in which Zuleika depicts herself as variously transformed. First, through her parents' immigration and assimilation, she becomes "Romanissimus"; like Jeffrey Eugenides's Cal in *Middlesex* (2002), she represents this as an Ovidian process. Next is the erosion of her childhood innocence. At first this is gradual: through her coming of age with Alba, she encounters the often-undignified ubiquity of adult desire and sexuality; this is a unifying prevalent theme in the *Metamorphoses*. Prowling around Londinium as *flâneurs* or voyeurs, Evaristo's young female protagonists:

> […] were amazed at the adult need to strip
> off
> and stick things in each other
>
> Men and women, women and women,
> Men and men, multiples of all sorts
>
> Groaning in pain. Absolutely fascinatio! (11)

Zuleika's friend Venus ("née Rufus") (46), meanwhile, who runs the drinking club named Mount Venus at which men like to dress as women, is a transgender person whose process of self-transformation recalls that of Tiresias, and of Hermaphroditus, in Ovid's epic poem (46–48; *Metamorphoses* Books III and IV). Zuleika's own comparable transformation is the process of being "elevated" (13), made fit for Felix, being sent off "for decorum classes" and being taught how to "talk, eat and fart" (4).

Zuleika makes frequent mention of the interior décor of the villa where she lives with Felix. Its murals – "vast mosaic walls full of the scenes on Olympus" (3) – recall both the myths made famous by Ovid and prior artwork that tells the story of mythical rapes, such as the tapestry that Philomel weaves (in *Metamorphoses* Book VI) to tell the story of her own rape at the hands of Tereus. Her bathroom boasts a Titian-like "mural on three walls: […] a brown swan; weather-nymphs bathe / under a weeping willow" (63), and "pastel painting / of scantily clad maidens by the lake / at Parnassus" (74). This is resonant of *ekphrasis* in the *Metamorphoses* such as the gates of the palace of the Sun (at the start of Book II). In Zuleika's atrium, when the "Medusa" fountain freezes, "her flying dreadlocks […] had grown icicle extensions," which, when she sucks them, results in Felix's rage "metamorphosing strangely into desire" (65). More overtly allusive, the triclinium walls depict "*The Rape of Persephone* in four gory stages – / all flailing limbs, flowing locks, a torn frock" (76). This explicit representation of an archetypal scene of sexual violence is a distillation of the frequent and recurring indirect references to the raped women of myth throughout the poem: to Ariadne (raped by Bacchus in the *Metamorphoses*; Evaristo 99); to Europa (raped by Zeus as a bull in the *Metamorphoses*; Evaristo 240); to Venus forced to "marry" Vulcan; and the repeated reference to a swan, which recalls Zeus raping Leda in the guise of a swan (also in the *Metamorphoses*; Evaristo 140, 107, 131).

It is surely significant that while watching the horrific eating of five pregnant women by lions, as part of the "entertainment" at the amphitheatre, when Zuleika recalls the custom of such women being raped by bulls, she feels "a trickle of moisture / crawl over each vertebra / like a spider" (178). This brings to mind her earlier observation, when she meets Felix for the first time, of his "utter imperium" and his "awful desire" (19), and of the "spiders" that "crawl up his forearm" (22). Both of these spider images bring to mind the "Arachne" section of Book VI of the *Metamorphoses*, wherein Arachne depicts the rapes of Europa, Leda and Proserpina (or Persephone) in her tapestry, and is then turned into a spider by the envious Pallas. Indeed, in describing the sexual coercion, rape and domination that her own marriage to Felix involved, Zuleika resorts to myth instead of a direct account to convey her experience. Describing her wedding night, after recounting how her husband injures and then silences her by putting his hand over her mouth, she states that she lost consciousness, and then simply:

> Pluto came for me that night,
>
> And each time I woke up, it was my first
> night
> In the Kingdom of the Dead. (29)

Watching the lion-eating carnage, she has a flashback to the trauma of the rape:

> Again and again and again and again
> And each time I woke up,
>
> It was my first night
> In the Kingdom of the Dad, Dead, Father?
>
> […]
>
> Why did you forsake me? (178)

The allusions, of course, invoke the abduction by Pluto of the playing girl, Proserpina, in the *Metamorphoses*, Book V.

When she decides she wants to seek a lover and her own sexual fulfilment, Zuleika's friend Alba offers a dazzling choice, as if reading from an Ovidian "catalogue" all the choices that the *Metamorphoses* encapsulates: "Male, female, hermaphrodite, eunuch or beast?" (100). Evaristo continues the dialogue with Ovid during the two scenes of intense erotic pleasure between the Emperor Severus and herself. Severus is the first to quote Ovid's *Amores*, pronouncing: "Candida me capiet; capiet me flava puella. / I'm a sucker for a blonde – and a brunette" (Evaristo 157; *Amores* II.4.39–40). Yet throughout these sex scenes, and the second time *Amores* is quoted, "Militat omnis amans" (217), Evaristo implies that Zuleika is referring to herself. Through the protagonist's sexual awakening the author depicts her increasing authority, agency, articulacy and power.

Erotic pleasure and autonomy are represented as inextricable in several key ways. First, during or after each consensual and mutually fulfilling sexual experience, Zuleika has the opportunity to speak, to describe herself and her life experience. Severus asks her a series of questions: "who are you?" (151); "what does life offer you, strange creature?" (154); "Always you ask who I am," and "what do you dream, carissima" (159). Evaristo revises Ovid's descriptions of rape that operate as metaphors for political conquest, excessive domination and colonialism, for example in his *Fasti* (which was the source for Shakespeare's 1594 poem *The Rape of Lucrece*). In her account of the pleasurable experience, Zuleika (and Evaristo) reappropriate the Ovidian language of male rape/military violence to express her own desire and pleasure: "besiege me / battery-ram my forted gateway" (134); "stab me to death, again and again, / stab me to death, soldier" (ibid.). In the second long sex scene Zuleika takes control, playing the dominatrix and demanding that Severus acknowledge "who's the boss now?" (224). While there is humour in these scenes it is not at Zuleika's expense, and it is important to note that Evaristo dispenses with Ovid's often-disturbing levity in her descriptions both of sexual violence and of Zuleika's sexual fulfilment. Zuleika's long, detailed erotic descriptions are both interspersed with her own poems and, crucially for this postcolonial context and its two immigrant African lovers, often expressed in the imagery of "homecoming." They have more in common with Ovid's *Heroides* than his *Metamorphoses* in that they constitute a woman character speaking in her own voice. Unlike in the *Heroides*, however, no act of gender-crossing ventriloquism is required of Evaristo, and there is no lament; the mood is rather a celebration of pleasure. In combining a compressed, indirect description of sexual violence (one which alludes to myth in order to avoid reinscribing the act) with detailed descriptions of autonomous female erotic pleasure, Evaristo anticipates the similar subversive strategy of Toni Morrison in her novels *Love* (2003) and *A Mercy* (2008).[4]

part II – marlene nourbese philip, *looking for livingstone: an odyssey of silence*

It is something of an irony that Philip's work *Looking for Livingstone* has itself met with a critical near-silence that contrasts strikingly with the accolades and intense critical discussion to which both the earlier *She Tries Her Tongue* and the later *Zong!* (2008) have given rise. The MLA International Bibliography testifies to the existence of around ninety published scholarly articles and chapters on Philip, but only five or six of these address the *Looking for Livingstone* piece, and among these only Miller's essay discusses the work in detail. It is noticeable that several assessments of her complete oeuvre pay this particular work little heed: Kristen Mahlis's 2005 article on the broad themes of "Language, Place, and Exile" in this poet does not even mention *Looking for Livingstone*, while a second critical response is epitomized by Curdella Forbes, whose discussion (also published in 2005) of "three Caribbean women's travel narratives" includes this piece, but who devotes only two paragraphs in her twenty-six-page article to its analysis.[5] My own critique to a large extent concurs with the suggestion in this prior scholarly disinterest – a suggestion implied rather than voiced – that *Looking for Livingstone* is by no means the most powerful or successful of Philip's works. Rather than ignoring or obscuring it, however, I illuminate, at times through contrast with Evaristo's and Lewis's texts, what in my opinion are some of the most problematic aspects of this work. Above all, comparison with *The Emperor's Babe* and *Voyage of the Sable Venus* highlights the extent to which Philip's piece creates only a partially identifiable discourse of flourishing, continuing black agency to complement its protest about the past.

As do both Evaristo's and Lewis's works, *Looking for Livingstone* takes issue with and takes apart key elements of the infrastructure of the Enlightenment worldview. Philip's targets in this work are the conventional, Eurocentric and linear measurement of time; the published word/purportedly "historical" narrative (in this case the autobiographical writings by and biographical writings about David Livingstone); the travelogue; the validity and authority of a sole third-person narrative voice; conventional Eurocentric means of communication such as the written letter; Eurocentric maps and the process of mapping; institutions such as museums and libraries; and the English language itself, revealed here (as in all of Philip's works) to be nothing but a debased currency. The journey of the Traveller takes a fantastical "eighteen billion years" (61); conventional time is mocked through the satirical log-book-style entries of the first-person prose narrative sections, for example recording her time with the "CLEENIS" on "THE SIXTH DAY OF THE HUNDREDTH MONTH / IN THE SIX BILLIONTH YEAR OF OUR WORD" at "5001 HOURS" (41). The non-grammatical, non-standard format, elliptical poetry sections that are interspersed with the prose, "– a universe of silence / within body / cell / atom" (39), aspire to be a voice that is more authentic and powerful than the prose that they undermine by their presence (ibid.). Similarly, the Traveller's map, consisting of scratching "on animal skin" (7), contrasts with the range of guides, compasses, and "the good book" available to David Livingstone (62).

Most critics would agree, however, that the relationship with classical precedent in *Looking for Livingstone* is not nearly as powerful as that which Philip constructs with Ovid's *Metamorphoses* and its myths of rapes and silencing in her earlier masterpiece *She Tries Her Tongue*. One aspect of the Enlightenment worldview that Philip's poem does not significantly challenge, as a result, is the centrality of the classical (Greek and Roman) tradition in dominant Euro-American culture. Unlike *The Emperor's Babe* and *Voyage of the Sable Venus*, *Looking for Livingstone* does not convincingly take issue with the insidious symbiosis between classicism and the colonial project that works such as Gilroy's *Black Atlantic* (1997) and Orrells, Bhambra, and Roynon's *African Athena* have illuminated. While both the Homeric *Odyssey* and Philip's account are homecomings of different sorts, Philip's is not really Odyssean in feel; it is much more explicitly in the quest narrative genre. The tribes that the Traveller encounters – the ECNELIS, the SINCEEL and so on – are arguably more like Jonathan Swift's Lilliputians or Houyhnhnms in his 1726 work *Gulliver's Travels* than like the Cyclops or Circe in the Ancient Greek epic. Given that Swift's work can itself be read as a satire of the travelogue and of early colonial exploits, it is arguable that this intertextual relationship is somewhat lacking in political force. Moreover, while Philip does not push the *Odyssey* analogy beyond her title, she also avoids the potential for empowerment or resurgence that Evaristo and Lewis separately explore in the interrelationships (strategically obscured during the Enlightenment and afterwards) between Africa, Greece and Rome. To read *Looking for Livingstone* alongside the Evaristo and Lewis texts is to realize that Philip perhaps missed an opportunity, in her attack on Livingstone's status as "discoverer" of the "source of the Nile" (7), to illuminate the connections between the cultures of the Nile and Europe's classical inheritances.

In terms of protest, moreover (and again the contrast with the humour of Evaristo and the indirect, hybridizing technique of Lewis illuminates this point), it is arguable that Philip's articulations in this work are not as powerful as they might be because they are so obvious or so direct. From the first page of the piece, the sarcastic quotation marks around the verb "discovered" (7) and the description of Stanley and Livingstone as "white fathers of the continent" (ibid.) express an anger which, while fully justified, is somewhat glaring or deafening in its indisputability. Similarly, in the last section, when the Traveller encounters Livingstone in person, she observes: "How cocky he was – Livingstone – and proud of his discoveries" (62). When she tells him that she doesn't have any facts to prove that she discovered her "very own Silence," she says: "a fact is whatever anyone, having the power to enforce it, says is a fact. Power – that is the distinguishing mark of a fact" (67). Although Philip states in a 2005 interview that she hopes that through writing essays separate from her poetry she then "faces no temptation to make an argument" in the poetry itself, it is hard to read lines such as these without detecting the very didacticism that she hopes to eschew (Saunders, "Trying" 216).

Looking for Livingstone arguably displays a tendency to say things that are, certainly by 2017 but probably also by its publication in 1991, already understood, or a "given," about colonialism. For example, the Traveller describes Livingstone as one "riding on the adventure in the word that hacks and cuts and thrusts its way through the wet and moist climate of Silence, plunging ever deeper into the heart of a continent" (61–62). In lines such as these, or as "the dried dugs of my silence that haunt your turgid phallused word" (27), the author applies her postcolonial critique and her feminist theory perhaps too directly, too heavily, for aesthetic success or emotive power. Miller reads such lines as consciously "classically overdetermined" (142). Yet in my own opinion, Philip's analysis here of the inseparable nature of colonialism, language and sexual violence suffers from the absence of the paradoxically devastating lightness of touch and radical humour with which Evaristo advances the same theme. And Philip also omits here the sophisticated "showing not telling" technique of Lewis, who enables the colonizers to indict themselves through their own language.

As I have already argued, one means by which Evaristo undermines the power of the colonialism–language–sexual violence interrelationship that she satirizes is by creating an alternative picture of a fulfilled female erotic desire and pleasure that reappropriates such idiom to its own ends. There are two not dissimilar moments of autonomous, fulfilled female eroticism and desire in *Looking for Livingstone* – one when the Traveller is washed and massaged by the CLEENIS women and "surrendered completely" (42), and one of days of sexual pleasure with Arwhal, needlewoman of the NEECLIS (53). In contrast with Evaristo's strategy, the language of lesbian sexuality here eschews rather than reappropriates the conventionally male idiom of penetration and conquest. It is to some extent an effective means of envisioning resurgence or an alternative reality, although as these passages are both few and brief they are perhaps overwhelmed or overshadowed by the familiar, patriarchal domination that the descriptions of Livingstone constitute.

Looking for Livingstone closes with a surreal encounter between the Traveller and the eponymous white explorer. There are both strengths and weaknesses in this scene. It is possibly the most humorous moment of the text, and the Traveller's greeting to Livingstone, "You're new here, aren't you?," is fabulous in its irony (67). The meeting takes a bizarre twist when the pair sit down to converse over coffee and cognac, ending when the Traveller inexplicably demands a kiss from the man (it is refused), and then reaches out and takes his hand. In the 2005 interview with Saunders, Philip reflects on this moment: "I remember looking at that three years after I finished and thinking, my God, that is not politically correct, but at the time that was what the work demanded" (216). This is perhaps her own expression of a sense that the denouement of her work is not what it might have been. More successful, however, is the postmodern, undetermined epilogue, in the form of an "author's note" (76). The note documents the existence of the Traveller's diary in two bound volumes, stored at "the Bodleian Library, Oxford University," along with three Polaroid photographs, one of Livingstone, one of the Traveller and Livingstone, and one that is "entirely black, rendering nothing visible" (77). A note from the Traveller is apparently pinned to the volumes, saying it is only a facsimile and that the original is buried with the CESLIENS; this claim is refuted by the "Chief Archivist and Librarian" of the Bodleian, a man who asserts that the Bodleian text is the "only and original" one (78). This conscious confusion, this ending that refuses closure, is the most successful challenge to the conventional male, Enlightenment-style voice of authority in the work.

part III – robin coste lewis, *voyage of the sable venus*

Robin Coste Lewis conceives of her poem as itself a kind of voyage – one that at once recalls the full horrors of the Middle Passage and that constitutes an escape to new territory or existence where self-definition and fulfilment are possible. As this is a work that demands and rewards painstaking close reading, my focus here will be on its two preliminary parts, "The Ship's Inventory" (38) and the "Invocation" (41), followed by its first two "catalogs," "ANCIENT GREECE AND ANCIENT ROME" (43), and "ANCIENT EGYPT" (55). My analysis demonstrates first the protest in the poem: the way Lewis exposes the violence and subjugation – physical, institutional, intellectual – to which European colonialism and slavery in the Americas have subjected women of colour, and which the dominant culture perpetuates. Second, it illuminates the resurgent voice or voices that her hybridizing, re-combining and re-ordering techniques enable. I demonstrate that through her dense palimpsest she positions herself within the genealogy of writers and artists (one that includes Evaristo as well) who reclaim and exploit the strategically obscured interconnectedness of Africa, Greece and Rome to brilliant and emancipatory effect. She also resists closure and definition – the kinds of closure and definition that her work continually undermines – through compelling strategies that demand a black female agency in lived experience, visual art and text.

The work's extensive paratexts, consisting of the Prologue, which explains the poem's method, and the epigraphs (excerpts from an advertisement for a minstrel show in 1936 and from a letter requesting the purchase of a "small healthy negro girl" (37)), both parody and exploit the conventions of the Western European literary tradition. The subsequent "Ship's Inventory" begins as follows:

> Four-Breasted Vessel, Three Women
> In Front of a Steamy Pit, Two-Faced
> Head Fish Trying on Earrings, Unidentified.
>
> Young Woman with Shawl
> And Painted Backdrop, Pearl
> Of the Forest, Two Girls
>
> With Braids People
> On a Ship with Some Dancing
> Girls. Our Lady of Mercy, Blue. (38)

The subsequent invocation begins:

> Untitled
> Anonymous
> Clay
>
> Prehistoric
> Cow
> Bone […] (40)

These brief extracts give some indication of the nature and impact of the work. The "Four-Breasted Vessel," presumably in a museum a description of some kind of bowl or jug, constitutes in this new context a pun in which "vessel" suggests a ship. The conflation of the slave trade and unlicensed sexual exploitation enjoyed by the enslavers is suggested in this very first stanza, while the contrasting second stanza, bringing to mind dignified and beautiful people, epitomizes the constant juxtaposition of the hellish and the transcendent that characterizes the work as a whole. In the "Invocation," the simple, non-defining descriptions ("Untitled / Anonymous / Clay") which invoke West African myths about the creation of the first humans from clay, go on to contrast with the beguiling-sounding but also implicitly violent definitions of Greek and Latin aesthetic discourse on the same page: "*Obverse anthropomorphic sarcophagus. / Alabastron eulogia ampulla*" (40; original italics).

One of the most repeated words in the poem is "fragment," and another is "damaged." In their new de-institutionalized contexts, away from the museum, these words speak to the history of dislocation and both literal and cultural dismemberment to which colonialism and slavery gave rise. Towards the end of the "Invocation," Lewis writes:

> Heads and Busts
> Headless – Footless – Armless
>
> But with a Strongly
> Incised Vaginal
>
> Opening: (41)

In a similar vein, "Catalog I: ANCIENT GREECE AND ROME" opens as follows:

> Statuette of a Woman Reduced
> To the Shape of a Flat Paddle
>
> Statuette of a Black Slave Girl
> Right Half of Body and Head Missing
>
> Head of a Young Black Woman Fragment
> From a Statuette of a Black Dancing Girl (43)

As *New Yorker* reviewer Dan Chiasson observes, this process of defamiliarization and recontextualization is profoundly disturbing:

> Lewis's technique returns the humanity to these anonymous women, which, in turn, makes the objects depicting them feel like examples of, and even instruments of, real historical violence. In a gallery, it seems perfectly natural to see a woman missing her head and half of her body. Here, in a list that feels like a catalogue of atrocities, it's nearly unbearable. (92)

Lewis's listing here captures the purportedly objective voice of authority that characterizes conventional art historical discourse, as well as something like the tone of newspaper headlines reporting racial violence. She thereby collapses the distant and recent past into a chilling continuous present. It is a profound protest against discourses of the original "Voyage of the Sable Venus" poem/engraving combination and of the histories and processes to which it speaks.[6] At the same time, Lewis intervenes in the ongoing nature of this kind of oppression.

There is a second kind of distortion or violence which the poem captures and protests. In her Prologue, Lewis observes that "because black female figures were also used in ways that [she] could never have anticipated" she was "forced to include […] combs, spoons, buckles, pans, knives, table legs" in her re-created catalogues (35). The "ANCIENT GREECE AND ANCIENT ROME" section, in particular, draws attention to this phenomenon; its Part II is an energetic accumulation of objects in which a black figure is either decorative or integrated into the object's use, or both. These range from the strange but possibly beautiful:

> necklace
> with two heads
> of black women forming
> a clasp (50)

to the bizarre, grotesque and ironic:

> shovel
> with a Negro head attached
> to handle
>
> a girl
> with long corkscrew curls
> round face wide
> flat nose and mouth
>
> open
> and jutting forward
> to form
>
> a spout

inkwell
in the form of a crouching
Negro Negro
seated writing on
a scroll (Ibid.)

This extract exemplifies Lewis's technique of simultaneous protest against subordination and celebration of resurgence. She illuminates the way in which slavery – a system of treating humans as objects or property – is translated or literalized in the fusion of the black figure with tools of labour such as the "shovel" (ibid.). The pouring vessel in which the girl's mouth is distorted and manipulated to compel its usefulness as a "spout" becomes symbolic of the distortions and manipulations of black bodies that slavery involves. The painstaking observational detail of her curls, face and mouth reflects and becomes a parody of the "natural scientist" approach to defining the features of black people that characterized writing by Enlightenment philosophers such as Hume and Kant, and that informed pseudo-scientific racial hierarchies such as those of Linnaeus. It recalls the exercises favoured by Schoolteacher in Toni Morrison's *Beloved* (1987), for whom Sethe has to make the ink with which her "animal" and "human" characteristics will be described in two columns (228). In including an inkwell here, however, Lewis reclaims the power to define and articulate the black figure, transforming that figure from object to subject. The "crouching Negro" – conventionally perceived as cowering from physical violence, confined into a small space such as the hold of a slave ship, or kneeling in supplication – becomes a "Negro / seated writing on / a scroll" (50). The ending of the section with this description, and without punctuation, attests to the power of black knowledge, expression and communication.

Towards the end of the "ANCIENT GREECE AND ANCIENT ROME" section, the representations and mood of the poem become increasingly energetic, positive and beautiful in themselves. Representations of black female figures as actors rather than as distorted into objects ("Young Nubian Girl Carrying an Ointment Vase" (52)) build up to a litany of eleven lines on the "female figure" in dignified positions such as "rhythm pounder," and with an emphasis not on fragmentedness or damage but on the repeated word "standing" (53). In section V (and throughout the poem) Lewis puns wonderfully on the word "relief"; the aesthetic term becomes the emotional concept of the ending of anguish or pain:

Vase with painted
Decoration relief

Site relief
Relief fragment

From the tomb (Isis
Receiving the Sacrifice)

Relief
Relief

Relief
Relief (54)

The transcendent, near-euphoric tone of lines such as "God of joy / and of the Dance" are developed more fully in the "ANCIENT EGYPT" section, "Catalog 2." While some broken and damaged figures are included in this section, the emphasis here is on lyrical beauty, visual richness and celebration. The figures depicted are often wealthy, physically beautiful in ways not expressed through the male, sexualized gaze, and highly skilled: a "Woman with a Jeweled Garland Shroud Bracelet" is present, for example (56), while "a little girl sings / with musicians playing" (57). One piece of *ekphrasis* comprises "lotus leaves / buds and cornflowers / poppies and grapes" (ibid.), while in another scene, in some kind of religious ceremony,

the curve

of the sandaled feet
vividly conveys

the excitement
of the event (Ibid.)

And the very shape of the words as they are arranged on pages 60–61 suggests two standing, active, female figures.

It is surely no accident that moments of transformation from oppression to joyful agency in "Catalog 1" and "Catalog 2" often occur at a nexus of Greek, Roman and Egyptian traditions. For example, the "Young Nubian Girl" whom I have just quoted, who appears towards the end of the "ANCIENT GREECE AND ANCIENT ROME" section, is "Wearing a necklace / of the God Bes"; Bes is an Egyptian god who is associated here with "joy" and "the dance" (52). The description of the "relief" (quoted above) which closes the Greek/Roman section depicts the Egyptian goddess "Isis / Receiving the sacrifice" (54). In this insistence on the place of Egyptian culture in the Greek and Roman catalogue, and the focus on triumph in the "ANCIENT EGYPT" section, Lewis deploys the strategy of invoking or performing a radical, triumphant and liberating Egypt – one (through Nubia) also merging with Ethiopia – which has long been central to the African American tradition of resistance. As Martin Bernal illuminated in his 1987 work *Black Athena*, from the eighteenth century onwards the interconnectedness of North African and Greek and Roman cultures was strategically obscured, along with theories that Egypt wasn't really "African" (or that Egyptians were not really people of colour), as part of the Eurocentric Enlightenment narratives that bolstered colonialism and imperialism. A reclamation of the key role played by Nubia/Lybia/Ethiopia/Egypt in so-called "Western" or European culture is a central feature of a long line of black thinkers that includes (but is not restricted to) Phillis Wheatley, Pauline Hopkins, W. E. B. Du Bois, Marcus Garvey, Frank Snowden, Paul Gilroy, Derek Walcott, Toni Morrison and, as this article demonstrates, Bernardine Evaristo.[7] In "ANCIENT EGYPT," Lewis plays brilliantly with what I term "the Africanness of classicism" (Roynon, "Africanness" 381), when she splits the name "Aphrodite" into "Aphro / Dite," and "Isis" into "I Sis." Her punning on the sound of "Aphro" as "Afro" – hence "Aphro / Dite rising from the bath. I Sis Aphro […]" – positions herself as a "Sis" or African "sister" to this Greek/Egyptian symbiosis (Lewis 56).

Such a genealogy gives huge intertextual resonance to the allusions in Lewis's *Voyage*. When she includes mention of "Libyan Sybil" in the "Inventory," for example (38), she invokes not just the captured Libyan slave in Herodotus but also the fascinating history of Harriet Beecher Stowe's essay on Sojourner Truth which, as Sarah Meer has documented, then inspired the white American sculptor William Wetmore Story, whose statue "The Libyan Sibyl" (based on Stowe's account of Truth) was to become "an antislavery sermon in stone" (Meer 37). In a similar vein, Lewis's inclusion of the title "The Queen of Meroë Spearing / Captives" (52) recalls Pauline Hopkins's novel *Of One Blood* (1902–03), in which the African American archaeologist Reuel discovers and then inhabits the city of Telessar, descended from the lost kingdom of Meroë (Hopkins 546–47). (It also recalls Zuleika's father's claim to be descended from the "King of Meroe" in *The Emperor's Babe* (*sic* 24).) As Hazel Carby attests, Pauline Hopkins's work charts the progress of "the light of civilization from Ethiopia to Egypt, to Greece to Rome" (Carby 183). Lewis, in positioning her "ANCIENT GREECE AND ANCIENT ROME" catalogue as both separate from and prior to her "ANCIENT EGYPT" catalogue, on first glance appears to comply with the dominant historiographical narrative of a pure, non-African origin of civilization in Greece and Rome. The presence of Isis, Bes and Meroë in this first catalogue, however, and the overwhelming celebratory beauty of the second combine to disrupt and overturn this received order of things, even as they draw attention to its fabricatedness.

As I discuss in my 2013 work *Toni Morrison and the Classical Tradition*, Hazel Carby attributes to Pauline Hopkins an anonymous article in *Colored American Magazine* of 1903, "Venus and Apollo Modelled from

Ethiopians" (Roynon, *Toni Morrison* 183). That article argues that "the most famous examples of classic beauty in sculpture […] were chiselled from Ethiopian slave models" (Carby 159). Lewis's *Voyage of the Sable Venus* clearly engages with such theory in its challenge to Western ideas of beauty. It thereby echoes Morrison, who, in *The Bluest Eye*, refers to "beauty" and "romantic love" as "probably the most destructive ideas in the history of human thought" (95). Implicit throughout Lewis's poem is a dialogue with Morrison's deconstruction of white beauty in that novel (embodied in Claudia's disassembling of the white doll), and with Morrison's illumination of "pigmentocracy," intra-racial racism and the utter self-destruction to which racialized self-contempt and self-hatred give rise. This dialogue becomes explicit in "Catalog 7" of *Voyage*, entitled "MODERN POST" (101), which includes the phrase, "Dick-and-Jane-with-Me Page Spread." This line replicates in the first instance the title of a 1989 "artist's book" by the artist Clarissa Sligh, entitled *Reading Dick and Jane with Me*.[8] Both Sligh's and Lewis's invocations of the American "Dick and Jane" primers, however, are of course indebted to *The Bluest Eye*, in which Morrison famously quotes from and then reduces to crazed nonsense this primer that conveyed white middle-class life as the desirable norm during the 1940s and 1950s. While Morrison's challenge to dominant culture implicit in the change from "Here is the house […] Here is the family. Mother, Father, Dick and Jane live in the green-and-white-house […]" to the psychotic "LOOKLOOKHERECOMESAFRIEND […]" (1, 152) echoes in Lewis's poem, Lewis's inclusion of the Mirror that tells the "Black Bitch" that "Snow White" is the "finest of them all" (102–03) speaks to the series of rejections, including self-rejection, to which Pecola is subject in Morrison's novel.

Lewis continues the dialogue with *The Bluest Eye* in her final, very brief catalogue, "Catalog 8," which is entitled "THE PRESENT/OUR TOWN" (110). Morrison's novel famously ends with a bitter revision of the affirmative mood of Thornton Wilder's 1938 play *Our Town*, which focuses on "ordinary" white lives in an early twentieth-century New Hampshire community. Claudia, surviving witness to the destruction of Pecola, tells us that, "on the edge of my town, among the garbage and sunflowers of my town, it's much, much, much too late" (165). Ultimately, however, Lewis rejects the unrelieved bleakness and finality of Morrison's vision in *The Bluest Eye*. *Voyage of the Sable Venus* does not follow a progression from injustice to triumph or from suffering to joy, but it does move cyclically, round and round or back and forth between these. In another allusion to Sligh's work, Lewis tells us "Enough / reframing the past" (101).[9] This is surely one indication that the positive and the future are as important as the negative and protests about the past in her poem. For while she does illuminate and destroy the power of the multiple framings of the black female figure through history, she not only clears a new space but also begins to inscribe it by her focus on autonomous black aesthetics and expression, reclaiming a black agency as a physical and intellectual beauty to be celebrated.

Lewis's list of the figure "Venus" in a range of allusive guises – "Tinted Venus / African Venus / […] / Venus of Willendorf / […]" (108; this last an allusion to Rita Dove's poem of that title) and so on – enacts, but then goes beyond, the protest against Western art historical discourse. It also critiques the contemporary fashion industry, satirized by Morrison when it labels Jadine "the Copper Venus" in *Tar Baby* (115). And it ultimately transcends Claudia Rankine's angered punning on the names of Serena and Venus Williams in *Citizen* (25). As Chiasson observes, the final name in Lewis's list here, "Venus of Compton," is presumably a reference to herself, in that Compton, L.A. is her home (Lewis 109). The effect of her presence in the list's finale, followed by the positive compound "Young Woman and Hope" (ibid.), is to transform the old, abusive "voyage" that the work's title invokes into a completely new voyage, replete with possibility.

conclusion

The strategic omission by Lewis of either a definite or indefinite article in her title, *Voyage of the Sable Venus*, imbues it with a non-specificity that makes it infinitely flexible, applicable to a range of situations. She similarly creates potential, or clears out space for the future, through her attention to the unlabelled, the unnamed, and the undefined. The title "Untitled" is repeated throughout the work, as is "anonymous," and she also includes the word "unidentified" (40, 38). These correspond with the wonderfully indeterminate final entry in her list of museums, "LOCATION UNKNOWN" (114). Through the resolute "both [...] and" stance of her work – negative and positive, historically specific and universal – Lewis creates an ethical, politicized poetics that changes the past while maintaining the generative possibilities of the present. Key words and phrases in her poem, moreover, speak to the significance of all three of the works discussed in this essay – *The Emperor's Babe* and *Looking for Livingstone* as well as *Voyage*. Lewis begins the final section of her poem with the all-important word "Still," by breaking up "still life" into "Still: life [...]" (110). She thereby exploits the two opposing meanings that the word "still" involves: "without movement" and "ongoing" or "continuous." In their own innovative rewritings of the past, to a greater and lesser extent revising the cultures of Ancient Greece and Rome as they do so, Evaristo and Philip likewise show that history is not after all fixed or without movement, and they too thereby create (Evaristo perhaps more forcefully than Philip) a dynamic and generative present. Each work ultimately attests to the ongoing power and subversiveness of that all-important figure represented in Lewis's poem:

> Negro Woman Seated
> At a table, facing
>
> Left, writing
> with a quill (77)

disclosure statement

No potential conflict of interest was reported by the author.

notes

1 Much scholarship on Evaristo is in the form of interviews, such as those with Hooper; Niven; or Collins. Key essays on *The Emperor's Babe* include Barchiesi; Burkitt; and McConnell, "Crossing."

2 See McConnell, *Black Odysseys*, for a study of African diasporic literary engagements with Homer's *Odyssey*.

3 Claudia Rankine includes reproductions of Turner's "The Slave Ship" (*c.*1840) and "Detail of Fish Attacking Slave" from "The Slave Ship" in *Citizen* 160–61. During her guest curatorship at the Louvre in 2005–06, Morrison wrote a lecture and essay inspired by Géricault's "The Raft of the Medusa" (1819), later published in her thematic collection *Etranger chez soi.*

4 I discuss Morrison's strategic juxtaposition of sexual violence against women with autonomous female erotic pleasure in these two novels in my 2010 article "Sabotaging the Language of Pride."

5 As with Evaristo, significant scholarly responses to Philip take the form of interviews; see, for example, Saunders, "Trying"; idem, "Defending."

6 As Hall writes, the Teale/Stothard poem/engraving constitutes an "obscene travesty of what Africans really experienced on the Middle Passage," one that also serves "to illustrate and legitimize white female fantasies about the black women in their possession," in a way that "effaces all anxiety, violence and coercion from the relationship" (10).

7 On "black classicism" see, for example, Greenwood; Rankine, *Ulysses*; and Cook and Tatum, besides McConnell, *Black Odysseys*; and Orrells, Bhambra, and Roynon.

8 See <http://clarissasligh.com/themes/identity/reading-dick-jane/> (accessed 22 Mar. 2016).

9 See <http://clarissasligh.com/themes/identity/reframing-past/> (accessed 22 Mar. 2016).

bibliography

Barchiesi, Alessandro. "Lane-Switching and Jughandles in Contemporary Interpretations of Roman Poetry." *Transactions of the American Philological Association* 135.1 (2005): 135–62. Print.

Burkitt, Katharine. "Imperial Reflections: The Post-Colonial Verse-Novel as Post-Epic." *Classics in Post-Colonial Worlds*. Ed. Lorna Hardwick and Carol Gillespie. Oxford and New York: Oxford UP, 2007. 159–69. Print.

Carby, Hazel. *Reconstructing Womanhood: The Emergence of the Afro-American Woman Novelist*. New York and Oxford: Oxford UP, 1987. Print.

Chiasson, Dan. "Rebirth of Venus: Robin Coste Lewis's Historical Art." *New Yorker* 19 Oct. 2015: 91–92. Print.

Collins, Michael. "'My Preoccupations are in my DNA': An Interview with Bernardine Evaristo." *Callaloo* 31.4 (2008): 1199–203. Print.

Cook, William W., and James Tatum. *African American Writers and Classical Tradition*. Chicago: U of Chicago P, 2010. Print.

Evaristo, Bernardine. *The Emperor's Babe: A Novel*. London: Penguin, 2001. Print.

Forbes, Curdella. "Selling that Caribbean Woman Down the River: Diasporic Travel Narratives and the Global Economy." *Journal of West Indian Literature* 13.1–2 (2005): 1–27. Print.

Greenwood, Emily. *Afro-Greeks: Dialogues Between Anglophone Caribbean Literature and the Classics*. Oxford: Oxford UP, 2010. Print.

Hall, Edith. "Introduction: A Valuable Lesson." *Ancient Slavery and Abolition: From Hobbes to Hollywood*. Ed. Edith Hall, Richard Alston, and Justine McConnell. Oxford: Oxford UP, 2011. 1–40. Print.

Hooper, Karen. "On the Road: Bernardine Evaristo Interviewed." *Journal of Commonwealth Literature* 41.1 (2006): 3–16. Print.

Hopkins, Pauline. *Of One Blood, or, The Hidden Self. The Magazine Novels of Pauline Hopkins*. Ed. Hazel Carby. New York and Oxford: Oxford UP, 1988. 440–621. Print.

Lewis, Robin Coste. *Voyage of the Sable Venus and Other Poems*. New York: Knopf, 2015. Print.

Mahlis, Kristen. "M. NourbeSe Philip: Language, Place, Exile." *Journal of West Indian Literature* 14.1–2 (2005): 166–201. Print.

McConnell, Justine. *Black Odysseys: The Homeric Odyssey in the African Diaspora, since 1939*. Oxford: Oxford UP, 2013. Print.

McConnell, Justine. "Crossing Borders: Bernardine Evaristo's *The Emperor's Babe*." *Callaloo* 39.1 (2016): 103–14. Print.

Meer, Sarah. "The Libyan Sibyl: Slavery, Neoclassical Images, and a Non-Atlantic Africa." *Complexions of Race: The African Atlantic*. Ed. Fritz Gysin and Cynthia S. Hamilton. Münster: Lit, 2005. 23–42. Print.

Miller, Cristanne. "M. Nourbese Philip and the Poetics/Politics of Silence." *Semantics of Silences in Linguistics and Literature*. Ed. Gudrun M. Grabher and Ulrike Jessner. Heidelberg: Winter, 1996. 139–60. Print.

Morrison, Toni. *Beloved*. New York: Vintage, 2005. Print.

Morrison, Toni. *The Bluest Eye*. New York: Vintage, 2005. Print.

Morrison, Toni. *Etranger chez soi*. Paris: Musée du Louvre, 2006. Print.

Morrison, Toni. *Tar Baby*. New York: Vintage, 2004. Print.

Niven, Alastair. "Bernardine Evaristo." *Writing Across Worlds: Contemporary Writers Talk*. Ed. Susheila Nasta. New York and London: Routledge, 2004. 279–91. Print.

Orrells, Daniel, Gurminder K. Bhambra, and Tessa Roynon, eds. *African Athena: New Agendas*. Oxford: Oxford UP, 2011. Print.

Ovid. *Amores. Heroides, Amores*. Trans. Grant Showerman. Cambridge, MA: Harvard UP, 1977. 323–512. Print.

Ovid. *Metamorphoses*. Trans. A.D. Melville. Oxford: Oxford UP, 1986. Print.

Philip, Marlene NourbeSe. *Looking for Livingstone: An Odyssey of Silence*. Toronto: Mercury, 1991. Print.

Philip, Marlene NourbeSe. *She Tries Her Tongue, Her Silence Softly Breaks*. Charlottetown: Ragweed, 1988. Print.

Rankine, Claudia. *Citizen: An American Lyric.* London: Penguin, 2015. Print.

Rankine, Patrice. *Ulysses in Black: Ralph Ellison, Classicism and African American Literature*. Madison: U of Wisconsin P, 2006. Print.

Roynon, Tessa. "The Africanness of Classicism in the work of Toni Morrison." Orrells, Bhambra, and Roynon 381–97. Print.

Roynon, Tessa. "Sabotaging the Language of Pride: Toni Morrison's Representations of Rape." *Feminism, Literature and Rape Narratives: Violence and Violation*. Ed. Sorcha Gunne and Zoe Brigley Thompson. New York and London: Routledge, 2010. 38–53. Print.

Roynon, Tessa. *Toni Morrison and the Classical Tradition: Transforming American Culture*. Oxford: Oxford UP, 2013. Print.

Saunders, Patricia. "Defending the Dead, Confronting the Archive: A Conversation with M. NourbeSe Philip." *Small Axe* 26 (June 2008): 63–79. Print.

Saunders, Patricia. "Trying Tongues, E-raced Identities, and the Possibilities of Be/longing: Conversations with NourbeSe Philip." *Journal of West Indian Literature* 14.1–2 (2005): 202–19. Print.

Taylor-Guthrie, Danille. *Conversations with Toni Morrison*. Jackson: UP of Mississippi, 1994. Print.

cynthia aalders

FAITH, FAMILY, AND MEMORY IN THE DIARIES OF JANE ATTWATER, 1766–1834

Jane Attwater was just twelve years old when she first wrote in her diary. It was June 1766 and she had just travelled from her home near Salisbury in England to visit her friend and cousin Mary Steele, who lived in the nearby village of Broughton. Attwater was eighty-one years old when she made her final extant entry in 1834. In nearly seven decades, she amassed a vast and complex diary record that speaks eloquently of the meaning of faith, family, and memory in her life. Why did she do it? Her diary was a religious practice. She was a member of a family that had been Baptist for generations and, alongside chapel meetings, her diary was one of the chief means by which she practised her faith. It was also a family practice. What was begun alongside Mary in 1766 was continued amongst her family – past, present, and future, near and far. In this essay I use Attwater's diary to explore the boundaries between, on the one hand, individual faith and writing and, on the other, communal faith and writing. How did her diary hold together personal, "private" meaning and communal, familial meaning? And how did religious women's diaries preserve community history and contribute to the production of religious culture?

Jane Attwater (1753–1844) was the youngest of four children born to Thomas and Anna Attwater of Bodenham, a village just outside of Salisbury. By the time Attwater was twenty she was living alone with and caring for her mother, a widow since 1767, and when her mother died in 1784 Attwater remained at home alone. In 1790 she agreed at last to marry Joseph Blatch, who had pursued her for fourteen years, and together they had one much-loved daughter, Anna. Attwater's extended family was well known for their religious and literary activities. Nonconformist for at least five generations before her, Attwater's relatives included well-known Baptist preachers such as Richard Gay, who had been imprisoned with John Bunyan in the previous century, when nonconformity to the Established Church was punishable by law.[1] In the eighteenth century her extended family became increasingly preoccupied with writing poetry and hymns, some of which was published, including the popular hymns of her older cousin Anne Steele.[2] An extensive and multi-generational family archive, rich with letters and diaries, grew throughout the eighteenth century, and it is in this archive that Attwater's substantial diary was preserved. The most extensive diary written by a nonconformist woman in either the eighteenth or nineteenth century, Marjorie Reeves considers it a "pile of breathless notebooks."[3] While this description suggests something impulsive and impassioned, Attwater was actually an incredibly disciplined and purposeful diarist and she carefully tended her diary, regularly turning back through it to reread, annotate, and carefully preserve it for her own use and that of her family.

In some respects Attwater's diary is the kind of "spiritual diary" that scholars often depict as inherently personal and private, a "stimulus to pious resolve, self-examination, and praise," a highly individualized and confidential text sometimes compared to a Protestant "confessional."[4] In this sense, Attwater conceived of her diary as a personal aid to faith: she made notes on the sermons she heard, described the religious meetings she attended, and she reflected on her inner state of mind and her spiritual aspirations. Such qualities have led Reeves to conclude that Attwater's diary is "intensely private."[5] Attwater had certain verbal and poetic codes to evoke the sense in which her diary was a spiritual aide-mémoire. When she filled a notebook and opened a new one, she would often inscribe a few lines of verse on the theme of memory. Often these lines were from the nonconformist writers Isaac Watts or Philip Doddridge. In 1769 she opened a new booklet and transcribed Watts's verse on its inside cover: "Oft I frequent thy holy place / And hear almost in vain / How small a portion of thy grace / My memory can retain."[6] At other times she inserted her own verse, as in 1786 when she transcribed into her diary her poem, which began: "Sacred to memory and religion pure, / Let these mementoes, and these lines endure."[7] Her diary was a store of personal memory, and she continued to remind herself of this purpose throughout the years. In 1781 she wrote, "My diary is a kind of repository which reminds me of past experience and in the various dispensations of Providence."[8] It was a material artefact to which she could, and did, return for spiritual comfort in times of trouble. In 1805 she reflected on how it had long been a "faithful repository" into which she could pour the "Effusions of [her] heart" and where she found peace and comfort in conversing with God and herself.[9] She wrote in a very personal way to give shape and meaning to her own emotional and religious experience.

So, on the one hand, Attwater's diary was a tool for self-examination and self-discipline, but on the other it was, quite literally, a layered account of her family's life and faith. When she became a mother in 1793 her diary took on an added educational function. While continuing to use it to record her own religious experience, she now also began to write it for her daughter Anna, whom she often addressed directly in its pages. She was creating and preserving a book of religious instruction, which she intended to give to Anna someday. When her daughter was just six years old, Attwater heard a sermon for young people and made notes in her diary for Anna's future perusal, adding, "if it should please God to spare her to years of understanding."[10] Attwater pinned into her diary notes to her daughter, such as, "My dear Anna, remember your dear Father's remark at breakfast this morning," and transferred to the written page religious instruction given at the dining table.[11] Framed as question and answer, the note is catechetical: "What is it constitutes our usefulness and comfort in life? Proper thoughts, proper words, and proper actions. Proper thoughts are the buds, proper words the flowers, and proper actions the fruit."[12] She reviewed her record regularly, sometimes adding notes to Anna, as she did in 1805 when she reread her diary for 1795 and wrote, "My beloved Anna, I am not willing to destroy these papers for your sake."[13] She hoped that Anna would one day find pleasure in reading her mother's words, but more than this she hoped that by passing on her diary she would pass on her faith. As her daughter grew, Attwater was pleased to observe her increasing spiritual seriousness and her hopes for Anna's future enlarged. She tucked a prayer into her diary, and while elsewhere she addressed Anna in her diary, here she addressed God:

> I trust thou hast made my dear child a partaker of rich and saving grace [...] Thou hast inclined her heart to attend *constantly* to the duty of prayer and reading thy word. O shine on her soul, enlighten her mind, draw her by the cords of love, establish her heart in the truth.[14]

Perceiving Anna's increasing spiritual sensitivity, Attwater now taught her to narrate her own life and faith by training her to keep a diary of her own. Evidence of her instruction is embedded in Attwater's own diary.[15] Here we find a notebook once given to Anna by her mother, with a note instructing her to "write down the texts" she heard.[16] Also tucked into Attwater's diary is a sheet written in a childish hand, a fragmentary record of Anna's first diary-writing efforts.[17] Anna must have been quite young when she first took up her pen to write in her diary: her handwriting is large and uncertain, her spelling difficult, and she interrupted herself often to write her name in large script, "Anna Blatch," and once to draw a little horse. But, supervised by her mother, her religious instruction proceeded in step with her literary education as she carefully recorded preacher and text and her thoughts on what she heard and experienced.

This method of recording preacher and text, along with sermon notes, was passed from generation to generation within Attwater's extended family, and in particular is found in the diaries of women in the family. Such attention to the sermons they heard located them within religious cultures while also functioning as a form of education, both of self and others. Kenneth Charlton observes women's religious agency as "gadders to sermons" (a pejorative term applied to especially devout women in the period), noting how women's memorization of sermon heads and note-taking during or after sermons were directed towards both their own spiritual edification and that of their households.[18] Attwater's mother kept a diary in the familiar format: she drew a line down the edge of each page and in this margin she recorded date, preacher, and biblical text for each sermon she heard; the rest of the page she used for sermon notes and more personal reflections. Attwater's great-aunt, Anne Cator Steele, employed a similar format throughout the seventeen years for which her diary is extant. She noted Bible texts as marginalia, marked Sundays as such in the margin, and added an "X" to signify those days on which she received communion (the "X" marking the place from which she would review her diary in preparation for receiving her next communion). Some of Attwater's own earliest diary entries likewise use the margin in this way. In later years her style became more her own, though she never stopped recording her participation in the formal rounds of religion (a practice that led Reeves to describe Attwater as an "addicted sermoniser").[19] Still, when the time came to teach her own daughter to keep a diary, the form she taught mimicked that which she had been taught: a systematic recording of date, biblical text, preacher, notes. Perhaps it was this practice that caused Anna to refer to her diary as her "text-book."[20] It was a textbook in a double sense: Anna knew it as the book in which she recorded the texts she heard; but it was also a book of religious instruction, a textbook, and Attwater was her instructor.

Anna's writing and religious education proceeded more broadly by example, for she must have observed her mother performing the same task she described to her, as she filled notebook after notebook, year after year. Indeed, Anna had access to her mother's diary and sometimes wrote in it herself. When she was eleven years old, perhaps having been assigned "lines" to write as a punishment, she repeated in large script "very very bad bad [...] sin and sorrow [...] Anna Jane Blatch" around the edges of her mother's more measured diary entries.[21] When she was fourteen she carefully labelled Attwater's diary, "Mrs Joseph Blatch's Book."[22] Perhaps it was this dual function – self-reflection and spiritual exemplum – that introduced Attwater's practice of censoring her diary, for even as she wrote for her present and future daughter, she withdrew into secrecy and encryption. Helen Wilcox considers this tension between public and private to be an essential quality of life writings, which are "poised at the borderline between hiddenness and expressiveness."[23] Attwater experimented with a cipher for a few years, using John Byrom's system of shorthand, published as *The Universal English Shorthand* (1767), to conceal especially personal details or private thoughts. She censored other entries by carefully excising whole lines from the text, while other lines she heavily blacked out.[24] Codes and ciphers, present in diaries expressly written for Anna, confirm the complexity of the genre and demonstrate how the individual and "private" purposes of religious diaries could coexist with pedagogical purposes. Clearly diaries – even so-called spiritual diaries – do not provide unmediated access to the interior life, but rather they were carefully crafted as authors considered intended and loved, or future and unknown, audiences.

In 1809, when Anna was sixteen years old, she became seriously ill with consumption, and Attwater documented her declining health and eventual death in poignant detail in a separate diary kept solely for the purpose of remembering those heartbreaking months and memorializing her daughter. Patricia Jalland observes how Victorian families kept special diaries to memorialize the death of loved ones, but the practice can be traced further back.[25] Attwater frequently re-examined Anna's death narrative – rereading her accounts, but also revising and rewriting them, again and again. She was, in a sense, curating her daughter's life and death, preparing it for future readers. To one account she pinned a correction beginning, "I was mistaken in the hymn she wished to repeat," and included a transcription of the hymn by Philip Doddridge that Anna had wanted those gathered at her deathbed to sing.[26] Another poignant account reveals Attwater and her husband's profound grief, even as they attempted to work through to the expected submission to God's good will:

> For only sixteen hasty years did we enjoy this inestimable bloom, when God the giver saw fit to resume the gift and left us bereft of our dearest earthly treasure [...] In silent awe we adored the goodness of God in manifesting his grace so evidently to our dear Anna and endeavored to comfort each other with the shortness of that period which might separate us from her.[27]

Another record elides her facility for "sermonizing" with her desire to memorialize her daughter: in a booklet especially for this purpose, Attwater made extensive notes on the sermon preached at Anna's funeral. Here we read that Anna engaged wholeheartedly in "devotional exercises" like self-examination (which must have included diary-writing) from the age of eight or nine.[28] Attwater's successive accounts of her daughter's death demonstrate her attempts to infuse Anna's life and death with meaning and then to embed that meaning, that perfected narrative, within the larger family record.

Anna's death reveals another way in which this layered, longer religious and familial history can be traced. Rather than straightforwardly expressive of a sole, interior voice, Attwater's diary became a place of conversation. Attwater's own mother kept a diary that survives only in fragments tucked inside Attwater's diary, and these insertions tend to occur at times of particular personal meaning. As Anna lay dying, Attwater tipped into her diary a page from her mother's diary, adding one more layer of textual complexity to the diary.[29] The entry records her mother's loss of her own child (Attwater's brother) over fifty years earlier. She wrote, "The death of my dear little babe was a sharper affliction than anyone can think it was."[30] In conversation with this, on the facing page, we have Attwater's entry: "My beloved Anna departed this life about half after twelve. O solemn day ever to be remembered [...] with the keenest anguish."[31] As Attwater grieved her daughter's death, she turned to her own mother's diary for comfort. Her mother had suffered a similar loss, and her earlier efforts to practise pious resignation now guided Attwater's response to her own loss. Her diary-conversation with her mother had its parallel in a diary-conversation with

Anna. After her daughter's death, Attwater picked up one of the notebooks that she had given Anna to record thoughts and texts in, and addressed her daughter one more time:

> Alas, my beloved Anna, little did I think when I desired you to make this text book for you to write down the texts you heard [that] I should survive you and fill it up – at least begin to fill it. Dear happy spirit, you are now arrived where the instructions from mortals are no more needed. You now know as you are known – you excel the most favored preacher.[32]

Attwater also engaged in a diary-conversation with her mother over the theme of baptism and commitment to God. Attwater sometimes attended the Baptist church at Salisbury where John Saffery was minister, and one Sunday he conducted a service in which four young people were baptized. Baptism was an important milestone in the Baptist denomination, a matter of confessional and personal identity, and Attwater took the moment to remember her own baptism, identifying with the young people who were joining the church that day. At this point she again slipped a page from her mother's diary. This page included an entry for the day on which her mother had been baptized in 1740:

> This day I was baptized. I hope I went away truly rejoicing that I was counted worthy to fulfill this ordinance [...] At all times may I be more than a conqueror through him that I trust has loved me and gave himself for me.[33]

Attwater had been experiencing a period of spiritual dryness, one in which she recorded feeling "lethargic" and regretted being "remiss in many duties"; she wrote with frustration and feeling, "my heart seems hard or stupid."[34] In such a period, she found encouragement in the confidence of those who were newly baptized, including her mother, decades earlier. "I feel my frailty," Attwater wrote:

> and desire to be freed from all weakness of every kind. And when, O when shall my mind rise superior to every trial and disappointment [...] I am led to see many things which are causes of uneasiness to me, are temptations and injections of Satan in order to disturb my peace and hinder my progress in the divine life.[35]

And then she quoted her mother (and Romans 8.37): "O my God, be thou my helper. Enable me to rise superior to every false rebuke [of] my grand adversary and enable me to come off more than conqueror over all my temporal and spiritual foes."[36] Attwater's diary-conversation with her mother enabled her to recommit herself to God, as she had first committed herself at her own baptism in 1776: "I commit my soul to thee. O guard the sacred trust, my constant guide and saviour."[37]

Attwater's diary represents a layering of religious experience and family connections. It contains pages from her mother's diary, providing posthumous guidance, and fragments of her daughter's diary, lovingly preserved as a memorial to Anna – more poignant and personal than the black-edged undertaker's card "in memory of the late Miss Blatch" that is likewise preserved.[38] Other written records also are tucked, pinned, and stitched into Attwater's diary. These include original poetry (sometimes written by or for friends and family), letters both written and received, and transcriptions from others' diaries. Also inserted is an epitaph in memory of her daughter, beginning:

> In Memory of Anna Jane Theodosia Blatch
> Who finally resigned her spirit to God her saviour
> July 28th 1809 aged 16
> From a Child she knew and loved the holy scripture
> Young Reader attend to her solemn admonition
> Enforced by her own serious example
> Remember your Creator in the days of youth.[39]

Earlier we observed Attwater's practice of rewriting and perfecting her daughter's life, and here a reader is introduced: of the epitaph, but also of the most extensive curated records of Anna's life. The reader is a "young reader," and the goal in writing was to inspire spiritual seriousness. Attwater wrote solemnly, "Prepare to meet your God."[40] If this seems to exploit her daughter's life and death to teach a hard lesson, there also is preserved more heartfelt verse, including a poem written two years after Anna's death: "Ah! how poor is language to impart / The feelings of my grief-worn heart ... / My much-loved Anna whilst in thought I trace / Thy dignity of mien, thy well-known face."[41] Elsewhere is found a poem written by her niece, in love and gratitude for the "counsel" she received from Attwater:

> The counsel you gave of beginning each day
> I remember, admire, and *wish* to obey,
> Yet slothfully waste many hours in bed.
> When called to consider – the way God has led,
> Ah! here let me ponder on what you now say.
> Ere a drone or gay butterfly crosses my way.[42]

In the inclusion and preservation of documents in this way we can see the diary as a collage of her family's collective religious identity – a document able to be consulted by later generations, who encountered in it not an individualistic and solely internal spiritual account book but an intimate and richly layered portrayal of interwoven family and religious life.

One further generation can be traced in Attwater's diary. In 1786 she again travelled to Broughton to visit her friend and cousin Mary, who had been with her when she began her diary twenty years earlier. While there she read her late great-aunt Anne Cator Steele's diary. Her mother had only recently died, and Attwater was interested in her mother's representation in the diary, particularly as an earnestly religious young woman. She transcribed these sections into her own diary:

> The past week I have been reading in my honored Aunt Steele's diary. May it tend to quicken me in religious duties wherein she was so diligent speaking of my honored parent in May 1739. She says, "Cousin Waters came. Had a good deal of sweet agreeable talk with my niece – she designing, God willing, to offer herself to the church the ensuing day in order to be baptized [...]" Thus far my Aunt's recital of what concerned my dear mama at that time. There is through the book very frequent mention made of my dearest friends.[43]

On another occasion Attwater read her great-aunt's diary as she was considering marriage to Joseph Blatch, and then she turned to the sections of Anne Cator Steele's diary in which she reflected on her upcoming marriage to William Steele. Attwater then wrote in her own diary, "It gives me pleasure to find her thoughts in some respects so similar to my own," adding, "though I confess I should never like to enter into a united state if I felt so much reluctance at the time as she expressed."[44] Still, after fourteen years of refusing Blatch, Attwater soon married him. In reading her great-aunt's diary Attwater learned something more about her position in her family's generational faith – she found herself in her great-aunt's diary – and in transcribing it into her diary she made it part of her own book of memory.

This sense of her diary as a book of memory is evoked by her habit of writing (on the inside covers of her diary booklets) the word "Ebenezer" – a biblical reference to the stone Samuel raised as a physical reminder of God's help, beside which Samuel said, "Hitherto hath the Lord helped us."[45] With one word she captured her understanding of the diary as a memorial of God's comfort and support. She began this habit in the earliest years of her diary keeping, and if as a young woman her statement was untested by trials, in later years it acquired a greater poignancy and articulated a deeper faith. At the beginning of 1833, the year she turned eighty, she began another booklet and again headed the first page "Ebenezer," and then she wrote with gratitude that she had been able to attend church that day after being "long absent" owing either to her husband's or her own declining health.[46] More than six decades had passed since she began to raise her paper Ebenezer, and in that time she had experienced much sorrow and loss – in the deaths of her daughter and many dear friends and family members, and more recently in her loss of mobility and health. Yet she persisted in this habit of faith, continuing to claim that God had helped her this far and would continue to care for her, even through the darkest days.

Attwater's Ebenezer was constructed from paper, fragile and changeable, yet its significance imbued it with a permanence akin to Samuel's stone. The diary survives still in manuscript and was cherished by her family and carefully preserved in family homes until it entered public archives in the last years of the twentieth century. This was not wholly the result of later family members' intercession. Rather, Attwater was the first conserver of her diary. She had access to women's manuscripts that had been preserved within the family and consulted by later generations, including the hymns and poetry of Anne Steele and the diary of Anne Cator Steele, and these served as her model. Attwater carefully constructed the record she left, intending to leave a document that would have lasting effect. In 1805, she reviewed the diary she had been keeping for nearly forty years, and wrote, "Looked over some of these papers so as to put them in a little more regularity."[47] In the same year she wrote a note to her daughter Anna, then eleven years old:

> My beloved Anna, I am not willing to destroy these papers for your sake. Not that I think them worthy your or anyone's perusal, as it would be a task too great to read them through. But should there be any sentence in the whole or similar circumstance which may give you pleasure and profit in reading it, my end in saving them is answered. I commit them into your care and keeping. There is great weakness discoverable. Forgive all defects and let no one see them but serious and affectionate friends who will not criticize, but read with a simple desire to improve by the simplest means. I was never fond of convening much, nor had I opportunity, being the most part of my life bred up in retirement. This [diary] was my faithful repository and my ever-fond companion.[48]

She demurred carefully. The diary was likely unworthy of Anna's reading, she wrote, and was the "fond companion" of a woman who lived quietly, in domestic seclusion. Yet alongside this conventional feminine modesty we see that Attwater was planning to entrust the diary to her daughter and was preparing it for "anyone's perusal," and that she believed it capable of improving and profiting others.

Attwater had a sense of herself as an archivist. Indeed, her efforts to conserve personal papers extended beyond her own, and it was through her intervention that many family papers were preserved into the nineteenth century.[49] Women were frequently involved in preserving manuscripts and, thus, in assembling and shaping a community's memory. In her study of eighteenth-century American women and memory, Susan Stabile argues that women's efforts to preserve memories were uniquely associated with the local and particular, including family homes, and she understands such efforts to be part of the process of building national memory in the early American Republic.[50] In her study of eighteenth- and nineteenth-century Quaker women, Sandra Stanley Holton observes that it was frequently women who preserved the letters and diaries of previous generations. She describes this as a typically feminine "work of kin," consistent with women's greater likelihood to seek out family connections, exchange family news, ensure that family bonds were not broken, and serve as family chroniclers.[51] This more domestic, relational approach to archives reveals women's historical activity in ways that are often missing from or hidden in the "official" archives of Church and state.[52]

The material nature of Attwater's and other women's writings constituted religious and family memory in a candid, personal, and particular way. Manuscripts themselves might be said to be "lieux de mémoire": what Pierre Nora considers "sites for anchoring" a group's memory, the "embodiment of memory in certain sites where a sense of historical continuity persists," places "where memory crystallizes."[53] Attwater's use of her great-aunt's diary is suggestive of the memorial meaning instilled in it. Women were particularly active in constructing such memory. Melanie Bigold and others have shown that while men had greater access to print in the period, women nonetheless actively engaged in the circulation of ideas and making of meaning through manuscript.[54] Attwater's diary was a memorial act for future generations; it interwove the meaning of faith and family and preserved this meaning for later Attwaters, Blatches, Whitakers, and others. At the same time the diary was a memorial act of past generations; embedded in it were the writings and memories of women who had guided her own life.

Attwater's diary-writing practice had both individual and communal meaning. Her diary is a narrative of life and faith – not only her own but that of her family, for diary entries of four generations are contained within it. Unlike prayer or other religious practices, writing diaries led to the creation of material, permanent objects that could serve as a commemoration of God's help and as a memorial of family life. Yet rather than a passive memorial, diaries were used actively to teach faith and build bonds across generations. For sixty-eighty years Attwater wrote her diary, not in confessional isolation but in the very midst of – even with and for – her family.

disclosure statement

No potential conflict of interest was reported by the author.

notes

1 On Richard Gay, see Kerry J. Birch, "Richard Gay of Haycombe: An Exploration of a Story and its Influence on Local Baptist Family and Community History," *Baptist Quarterly* 37.8 (1998): 367–85.

2 On Anne Steele, see Cynthia Aalders, *To Express the Ineffable: The Hymns and Spirituality of Anne Steele* (Milton Keynes: Paternoster, 2008).

3 Marjorie Reeves, *Sheep Bell and Ploughshare: The Story of Two Village Families* (Bradford-on-Avon: Moonraker, 1978) 44; Timothy Whelan, ed., *Non-Conformist Women Writers, 1720–1840*, 8 vols. (London: Pickering, 2011–12) 4: 191–92. For more detailed introductions to Attwater, see Timothy Whelan, *Other British Voices: Women, Poetry, and Religion, 1766–1840* (New York: Palgrave, 2015) 126–53; Whelan, ed., *Nonconformist Women Writers* 4: 191–200; 8: 105–16; Marjorie Reeves, *Pursuing the Muses: Female Education and Non-Conformist Culture, 1700–1900* (London: Leicester UP, 1997) 95–139. The diary itself is preserved in the Attwater Papers at the Angus Library, Regent's Park College, University of Oxford (hereinafter Attwater Papers); the Reeves Collection at the Bodleian Library (hereinafter Reeves Collection); and the Whitaker Collection at Trowbridge Museum (hereinafter Whitaker Collection).

4 D. Bruce Hindmarsh, *John Newton and the English Evangelical Tradition: Between the Conversions of Wesley and Wilberforce* (Oxford: Oxford UP, 1996) 30; William Haller, *The Rise of Puritanism* (New York: Columbia UP, 1938) 38.

5 Marjorie Reeves, "Jane Attwater's Diaries" in *Pilgrim Pathways: Essays in Baptist History in Honour of B.R. White*, eds. William H. Brackney, Paul Fiddes, and John H.Y. Briggs (Macon: Mercer UP, 1999) 207. See further Effie Botonaki, "Seventeenth-Century Englishwomen's Spiritual Diaries: Self-Examination, Covenanting, and Account Keeping," *The Sixteenth Century Journal* 30.1 (1999): 3–21; Tom Webster, "Writing to Redundancy: Approaches to Spiritual Journals and Early Modern Spirituality," *Historical Journal* 39 (1996): 33–56; Margo Todd, "Puritan Self-Fashioning: The Diary of Samuel Ward," *Journal of British Studies* 31 (1992): 236–54.

6 Isaac Watts, "Unfruitfulness, Ignorance, and Unsanctify'd Affections" in *Hymns and Spiritual Songs*, 2nd ed. (London: Printed by J.H. for John Lawrence, 1709) 274. Jane Attwater diary, 14 August 1769. Attwater Papers. To ease reading, when quoting manuscript sources I have made small changes to spelling and punctuation to correspond to modern usage.

7 On a copy of the poem kept for herself, Attwater wrote: "Some lines I wrote to cousin Philip to be inserted in his book designed for texts and particular events, January 1786." Attwater

Papers. See also Reeves, *Sheep Bell and Ploughshare* 44.

8 Jane Attwater diary, 17 May 1781. Attwater Papers.

9 Jane Attwater diary, note dated 13 July 1805. Attwater Papers.

10 Jane Attwater diary, 27 October 1799. Attwater Papers.

11 Jane Attwater diary, 2 February 1804. Attwater Papers.

12 Ibid.

13 Jane Attwater diary, note dated 13 July 1805. Attwater Papers.

14 Jane Attwater diary, n.d. Attwater Papers.

15 Margaret Ezell considers such fragments, as well as manuscript references to life writings that have not survived, to be significant "fossil" remains. Margaret J.M. Ezell, "Domestic Papers: Manuscript Culture and Early Modern Women's Life Writing" in *Genre and Women's Life Writing in Early Modern England*, eds. Michelle M. Dowd and Julie A. Eckerle (Aldershot: Ashgate, 2007) 45.

16 Jane Attwater diary, n.d. Attwater Papers.

17 Anna Blatch diary, preserved in Jane Attwater diary, July 1804. Attwater Papers.

18 Kenneth Charlton, *Women, Religion, and Education in Early Modern England* (London: Routledge, 1999) 154–61.

19 Reeves, "Jane Attwater's Diaries," 208.

20 Anna Blatch diary, n.d. Attwater Papers.

21 Jane Attwater diary, 1804. Attwater Papers.

22 Jane Attwater diary, 1807. Attwater Papers.

23 Helen Wilcox, "Private Writing and Public Function: Autobiographical Texts by Renaissance Englishwomen" in *Gloriana's Face: Women, Public and Private, in the English Renaissance*, eds. S.P. Cerasano and Marion Wynne-Davies (Detroit: Wayne State UP, 1992) 60. See further Dan Doll and Jessica Munns, eds., *Recording and Reordering: Essays on the Seventeenth- and Eighteenth-Century Diary and Journal* (Lewisburg, PA: Bucknell UP, 2006) 20; Ezell, "Domestic Papers."

24 Jane Attwater diary, 1780–82. Attwater Papers. On codes in diaries, see Ezell, "Domestic Papers," 40–41; Sara Heller Mendelson, "Stuart Women's Diaries and Occasional Memoirs" in *Women in English Society, 1500–1800*, ed. Mary Prior (London: Methuen, 1985) 183.

25 William Gladstone, for example, kept a daily diary, but when his young daughter Jessy was gravely ill he began to keep a separate detailed account of her last days, which he marked "most private." Patricia Jalland, *Death in the Victorian Family* (Oxford: Oxford UP, 1996) 168–69. See also Ralph A. Houlbrooke, *Death, Religion and the Family in England 1480–1750* (Oxford: Oxford UP, 1998).

26 Jane Attwater diary, note pinned at 28 July 1809. Attwater Papers.

27 Jane Attwater diary, n.d. Whitaker Collection.

28 Jane Attwater diary, 6 August 1809. Whitaker Collection.

29 Anna Attwater diary, n.d., and Jane Attwater diary, 28 July 1809. Attwater Papers. For a methodology for reading inclusions in manuscript diaries, see Cynthia Huff, "Reading as Re-Vision: Approaches to Reading Manuscript Diaries," *Biography* 23.3 (2000): 504–23.

30 Anna Attwater diary, n.d., found in Jane Attwater diary for 1809. Attwater Papers.

31 Jane Attwater diary, 28 July 1809. Attwater Papers.

32 Jane Attwater diary. Attwater Papers. Cf. 1 Corinthians 13.12: "For now we see through a glass, darkly; but then face to face: now I know in part; but then shall I know even as also I am known."

33 Anna Attwater diary, 17 May 1740. Found in Jane Attwater's diary. Attwater Papers. Cf. Romans 8.37: "Nay, in all these things we are more than conquerors through him that loved us."

34 Jane Attwater diary, 2 October [unknown year]. Attwater Papers.

35 Ibid.

36 Ibid.

37 Ibid.

38 Whitaker Collection.

39 Whelan, *Nonconformist Women Writers* 4: 208. Anna was named after her hymn-writing aunt

Anne Steele, who published under the penname Theodosia. Cf. Ecclesiastes 12.1: "Remember now thy Creator in the days of thy youth, while the evil days come not, nor the years draw nigh."

40 Whelan, *Nonconformist Women Writers* 4: 208.

41 Ibid. 4: 209.

42 Reeves Collection. The identity of this niece is uncertain.

43 Jane Attwater diary, 26 March 1786. Attwater Papers.

44 Quoted in Whelan, *Nonconformist Women Writers* 4: 199 n. 4.

45 Cf. I Samuel 7.12: "Then Samuel took a stone, and set it between Mizpeh and Shen, and called the name of it Ebenezer, saying, Hitherto hath the Lord helped us."

46 Jane Attwater diary, 20 January 1833. Attwater Papers.

47 Jane Attwater diary. Attwater Papers.

48 Jane Attwater diary, note dated 13 July 1805. Attwater Papers.

49 Cynthia Aalders, "Writing Religious Communities: The Spiritual Lives and Manuscript Culture of English Women, c.1740–90," D.Phil. diss., U of Oxford, 2014, 261–63.

50 Susan M. Stabile, *Memory's Daughters: The Material Culture of Remembrance in Eighteenth-Century America* (Ithaca, NY: Cornell UP, 2004). Tanya Fitzgerald also explores the connection between archives and family homes in her efforts to explore women's missionary activity in nineteenth-century New Zealand. Tanya Fitzgerald, "Archives of Memory and Memories of Archive: CMS Women's Letters and Diaries, 1823–35," *History of Education* 34.6 (2005): 657–74.

51 Sandra Stanley Holton, *Quaker Women: Personal Life, Memory and Radicalism in the Lives of Women Friends, 1780–1930* (London: Routledge, 2007) 24–28. See also Sandra Stanley Holton, "Family Memory, Religion and Radicalism: The Priestman, Clark and Bright Kinship Circle of Women Friends and Quaker History," *Quaker Studies* 9.2 (2005): 156–75; Amanda Vickery, *The Gentleman's Daughter: Women's Lives in Georgian England* (New Haven: Yale UP, 2003); David Warren Sabean, *Kinship in Neckarhausen, 1700–1870* (Cambridge: Cambridge UP, 1998); Margaret Benefiel, "'Weaving the Web of Community': Letters and Epistles" in *Hidden in Plain Sight: Quaker Women's Writings, 1650–1700*, eds. Mary Garman et al. (Wallingford: Pendle Hill, 1996) 443–52.

52 Helen M. Buss and Marlene Kadar, eds., *Working in Women's Archives: Researching Women's Private Literature and Archival Documents* (North York: Wilfrid Laurier UP, 2001).

53 Pierre Nora, "Between Memory and History: Les Lieux de Mémoire" in *Memory and Counter-Memory*, spec. issue of *Representations* 26 (1989) 9, 7.

54 Melanie Bigold, *Women of Letters, Manuscript Circulation, and Print Afterlives in the Eighteenth Century* (Basingstoke: Palgrave, 2013); George L. Justice and Nathan Tinker, eds., *Women's Writing and the Circulation of Ideas: Manuscript Publication in England, 1550–1800* (Cambridge: Cambridge UP, 2002).

Cynthia Aalders

kim treiger-bar-am

WOMEN'S VOICES OF RENEWAL WITHIN TRADITION

the women of the wall of jerusalem

Israel today is witnessing a renewal of women's voices in prayer, song and dress, all of which are protected forms of expressive behaviour under the law's freedom of expression doctrine.[1] Women's voices are expressed in the current revival of Jewish traditions, known in Israel as *hithadshut*.[2] These moves raise tensions within the religious world and the civil legal realm. In addition to the women's rights to expression, discussion here highlights the need to recognize duties of respect for the women's voices. The analysis is both moral and legal.

The movements of rejuvenation incorporate a multiplicity of voices.[3] In focus here is a much-debated instance: the nearly thirty-year effort by women to pray in a group in song, and to read from the Bible (Torah), at the Jewish holy site of the Western Wall in Jerusalem. The group, known as Women of the Wall (WoW), has met with resistance and confrontation from some sectors, and praise and support by others.

Israel is defined constitutionally as a Jewish and democratic state. Judaism has a strong tradition of embracing a multiplicity of voices: while Jewish law upholds the majority view, also minority views are held in esteem. As a democracy, pluralism in speech is to be protected. Indeed, the Israeli judicial system has maintained a strong protection of speech. The speech of WoW is among the multiplicity of voices due respect.

The women's voices are to be respected because of the dignity of the speakers and their freedoms of speech in the Jewish and democratic traditions, and also because of the duties of respect that the traditions embody. The Jewish and democratic traditions recognize central positions for both freedoms and duties. Jewish thought and Kantian theory, both of which constitute the basis of liberal democratic thought, are in view. At the theoretical foundation of both traditions, rights are not only correlative with duties but also embody duties intrinsically. Those duties are of respect. Hence, according to the values of the traditions, intrinsic to the rights of prayer of other worshippers – as well as to the right to control prayer at the Wall held by rabbinic authorities – are duties to respect WoW's speakers and speech.

This essay begins by setting forth recent Jewish renewal developments in Israel, and in particular WoW's efforts and legal battles. The nature of the rights and duties derived from the character of Israel as a Jewish and democratic state is then explored. Jewish thought and tradition, as well as democratic theory and US and Israeli legal doctrine, are examined. Concluding remarks reflect upon the duties to respect women's voices in Israel's Jewish rejuvenation.

I *hithadshut*: renewal and revival

Initiatives of renewal of Judaism in recent years in Israel have come from many quarters, and have taken on various forms. Secular and religious Jewish sectors have seen increased activity taking numerous directions. The diverse efforts have been called *hithadshut*, although any one effort may not identify with other activities. *Hithadshut* does not refer to a unified movement but describes a phenomenon.[4] It is about revival and renewal – rather than rebellion or revolution.

Secular Jews in Israel commonly practise Judaism through celebrations of Jewish festivals and life-cycle ceremonies. Alongside the Jewish nature of Israeli society and ways of life of its majority, Jewish identity has been complicated for many years by the tensions of the religious–secular divide. A feeling abounds that the Jewish religion in Israel has come to be defined exclusively by one religious Jewish sector, the Orthodox. Israeli Jews often distinguish themselves from the religious, and hence from the religion. While many remain alienated from Jewish identity, however, recent years have seen a change. There has been a rise in activities reflecting interest in Israeli Jews' redefinitions of their Jewish identity – and not necessarily in its religious form.

Examples range from programmes for post-high-schoolers with instruction in Jewish history and Jewish thought. Also for young adults, secular institutes of Jewish learning have taken form. People meet on the beach and at popular spots such as the Port in Tel Aviv for readings of ancient texts, prayers in song to bring in the Sabbath, and gatherings for Sabbath meals.[5]

Religious affiliations of varied forms have also been on the rise. Movements originating in the eighteenth and nineteenth centuries including the Reform (as well as Progressive or Liberal) and Conservative (or Masorti) are still small in number in Israel, but are growing. While the Orthodox control the Israeli rabbinical authority (and hence family matters including marriage and divorce, pursuant to a compromise at the time of Israel's founding), challenges to this control have been prevalent and profound.

Within Orthodoxy in Israel, there are groups of women who have taken active roles in religious life. Orthodox women in some very religious areas have formed women's gatherings for prayer and study. Women have gained recognition for their learning, and recently a handful of women have been qualified as rabbis by an orthodox institute. A small but growing number of religious communities offer women close to equal participation in prayer services, including reading from the Torah,[6] which more conservative communities reject. More and more women say the prayer for bereavement – the recital of which was traditionally for men only. (Recently a bereaved mother, a learned teacher of Torah, made headlines when she read out the prayer in front of a large crowd, including the current Chief Rabbi – who himself made history when he affirmed her recital of the prayer, in saying "amen."[7])

These moves are religious. While the religious and the political cannot easily be divided – as authority and control play a role in both – other moves which are clearly political can be seen as well. Some ultra-orthodox (*haredi*) women attempted to form a political party in the recent elections to Israel's parliament (*Knesset*), although they did not receive enough votes to enter the *Knesset*. Years ago Leah Shakdiel broke the glass ceiling that kept women from towns' religious councils, and today there are a number of women holding these municipal posts.

Women's voices in *hithadshut* must be heard. Support must be extended to these women advancing the voice of women *from within* the tradition. They are not acting against it but remain loyal to it, and help it grow. As Saba Mahmood has written, "it is important to take into consideration the desires, motivations, commitment and aspirations of the people to whom these practices are important."[8] Mahmood praises the agentival capacity not only for change but also to continue tradition.

Frances Raday has taken a similar position, in particular with regard to WoW's case, which she litigated at the Supreme Court. The religious women of WoW are not claiming a right of exit.[9] What these brave women are doing is within the existing structure of religion and within the bounds of the religious law (an interpretation of Jewish law acknowledged by Israel's Supreme Court). Women of the Wall's challenge is a dissenting voice from within the patriarchal, authoritative voice in Judaism's traditional religious establishment in Israel.[10]

2 women of the wall

Women of the Wall does not refer to itself as women *at* a *wall of separation*, but as women *of* the Wall, which they embrace – namely of the religious tradition, including the separation it entails. As strong, independent women, they are forging their own space. Discussion here will trace the history of the group, the motives of WoW and of the opposition, and the law. In the series of legal cases reviewed it shall be seen that discussion has focused on *authorization* and *authority*: who is authorized to pray and who is authorized to decide how others pray. Rather, it is suggested that the focus should instead be on right and duty – rights of dignity and speech, and duties of respect. Israel as a Jewish and democratic state must support both right and duty.

2.1 history

Beginning in 1988, women began to hold prayer services celebrating the monthly new moon,[11] at the Western Wall in Jerusalem. Women from all parts of the religious Jewish spectrum – including orthodox women, in focus in much of the discussion here – and from all over the world, joined together for the group prayers.[12] The Wall was erected in the first century BCE as the outer wall of the Second Temple in Jerusalem, on the site of the First Temple built by King Solomon in the tenth century BCE. The Second Temple was destroyed in the year 70 CE by the Romans, and the Western Wall is the only part left standing. It is perhaps the most central location for religious worship and non-religious cultural identification in Judaism.[13] Men and women pray in separate spaces designated in the plaza in front of the Wall.[14]

The group that came to be known as WoW met on the women's side of the partitioned space, and recited the prayers marking the monthly festival. *Haredi* men and women continually objected to the women's prayers in song, to their holding a Torah, and to the donning by some of a prayer shawl (*tallit*), traditionally worn by men alone. Protests ensued, including verbal harassment and violent outbreaks against WoW.[15] Women of the Wall filed a lawsuit seeking protection, and their case was considered a number of times by the Israeli Supreme Court. Despite the strong civil rights perspective in certain areas for which the Supreme Court is well known, the Court recognized but declined to uphold WoW's rights, and passed the issue on to committees established to consider the conflict and to find a compromise. In the intervening years, the women ascended from the plaza adjacent to the Wall to an enclosed area in which they read from the Torah and sing their prayers.

A partial legal resolution finally came with a 2013 District Court decision, as described below. In practice, however, the saga continues. For instance, the women are not allowed to bring their own Torah scroll to the Wall, and are not allowed to use one that is present at the Wall. In 2015 men in support attempted to pass a Torah scroll from the men's side to WoW but were prevented from doing so, again upon physical outbreaks of violence. In January 2016, the government voted to build a new space on the southern edge of the Wall, near an archaeological site. The decision has met with strong opposition.

2.2 women of the wall's motives

Why are the women doing what they are doing? To speak. Their voices sing out. Perhaps some of the women are intent on being heard outside of their communal gathering, whether by the men across the partition or in the outside world. Yet for many it is an effort to sing their prayers within their group. They wish to be heard by others in the prayer gathering, and by other religious women throughout Israel.

Women of the Wall is not seeking an exit from the religious tradition and community, nor to change that tradition or community. The women are not storming the men's section and seeking to break down the partition separating the space at the Wall for men and women. They are embracing the Wall for its sanctity. The women are riding on changes in an evolving tradition – and are effecting those changes. Theirs is a voice of renewal from within, rather than from without.[16]

Why are they making that choice? Perhaps the women want to stay within the religious tradition because they crave legitimacy, and do not want to disturb the status quo and the controlling powers. Raday also suggests that "beyond theological religious identity, there is a question of community and family identity."[17] Yet I see them (and can speak for myself and others I encountered in the group when I took part in it) as motivated by belief in the religious tradition. I would tend to avoid what I see as a patronizing questioning of whether their motives are genuine or a constructed reflection of a patriarchal society that gives rise to false consciousness.[18] It is who the women are – and have chosen to be, at whatever level of choice. I do not doubt the veracity of their choice. Interestingly, the Supreme Court remarked again and again in its opinions that WoW had a right to ritual prayer in good faith. I do not see any reason to question it, as the Supreme Court likewise noted.[19] I see the motives of WoW as embracing the tradition and moving it ahead.

The bravery of these women entails risks. As Raday writes, the women risk being rejected by both the Orthodox and by feminists, in the group's attempt to be both.[20] Yet the women are progressing in an effort to change things from within, and centrally so. The struggle is at the heart of the public ritual of orthodox Judaism, as well as a space around which Israel's national and cultural symbolism spins.

2.3 objections

Objections under Jewish law to WoW's form of prayer have been refuted by religious thinkers and the Supreme Court. Yet non- or a-religious considerations surround the conflict, as well.

Over the years, a number of grounds have been raised by the ultra-Orthodox in opposition to WoW's practice of praying aloud and in song in a group, carrying and reading from the Torah, wearing religious articles known as phylacteries (*tefillin*, small leather boxes with scrolls containing Torah verses) and the *tallit* prayer shawl. *Haredi* men and women were and remain opposed to collective audible women's prayer, as *haredi* women pray silently and individually. Women are not to touch a Torah scroll, as they may be religiously impure. Wearing the *tallit* and *tefillin* are commandments upon men, and the Torah instructs that women and men should not wear the other's garb.

Most closely touching upon our subject here is the restriction on a woman's voice. The restriction is taken from a passage in the biblical *Song of Songs* denoting the beauty of a woman's voice, and a passage in the Talmud[21] discussing whether a woman's voice distracts men's prayer. The per se restriction on women's voice in song did not come into play until the eighteenth to nineteenth centuries, by a rabbi whose views have been disputed by many others. Discussion of the basis in Jewish law for the restriction is extensive, and includes the position rejecting such a restriction.

In the first decision of the Israeli Supreme Court, former Deputy Chief Justice Menachem Elon, a practising orthodox Jew well versed in Jewish law, reviewed Jewish law and concluded that the women's prayer in a group with ritual objects does not violate Jewish law. The objection was said to be based on custom, namely, on things not traditionally done.[22]

What is behind it all? Raday writes that the opposition is for patriarchal religious control over the public sphere of social and religious life.[23] Indeed, WoW wants not a side show but to pray at the Wall, and hence for the women to become active participants in public life. The effort noted above of the *haredi* women who ran for the *Knesset* in the recent national election may be compared. Moreover, the refusal of the secular judges to engage the issue of equality can be attributed to a presumption of the autonomy of religion: sub-groups who belong to the religious community are taken to have consented to its entire set of mores, including their own inequality.[24]

Challenges are also presented by religious thinkers not to WoW but to the symbolism represented by the Wall itself. Objecting to making a geographical space sacred, Professor Yeshayahu Leibowitz considered the attitude of veneration towards the Wall as idolatrous. Others, including radical feminists, challenge valuing the Wall as a symbol of national sovereignty.[25]

I would call the opposition political in the sense of power. It comes down to the question of who has control over custom at the Wall, and generally, over religious custom in Israel. The sensitivity to politics of power can be seen in the law's protection of religious sentiments of the men in control of the area so central to Israel's society religiously, culturally, historically and politically. For many years the Court avoided making changes as to who holds control, and upheld the status quo.

2.4 *law*

Women of the Wall has faced a complex history of legal consideration of the issue by courts, the Attorney General, and governmental committees. In some of the Supreme Court rulings the women's rights of ritual worship were pitted against sensitivities of the *haredi* male authorities and the custom of the religious place. It is put forward that duties of respect for the women as speakers and for their speech may ease some of the tensions that are still current and wrought. The discussion returns to the law on freedom of speech later in the essay.

2.4.1 *supreme court rulings*[26]

Upon WoW's seeking of protection in 1989, the first ruling of the Supreme Court sitting as the High Court of Justice was given in 1994. The Court ruled that in principle WoW's activities were to be upheld, but it was for the government to find an administrative solution to safeguard the women's rights and protect sensitivities and traditions – namely the "customs of the place." After a year in which the government provided no solution, WoW again filed suit. Following years of deliberation, in 2000 the Supreme Court ruled unanimously that WoW had an absolute right to pray at the Wall, to wear *tallit* and *tefillin* and read from the Torah. The Court ruled that the government had erred in seeking to balance the rights and interests of both parties, as the rights of WoW took precedence over the sensitivities that opposed them.[27] The government was given a fixed period of time (six months) to devise a solution.

Furious opposition to the Court's decision erupted. A bill (which was not passed into law) setting a prison term for women praying at the Wall in the manner of WoW was even introduced in the *Knesset*. The Attorney General asked the Court for a rehearing of the case before the full Court, in which all nine Justices heard the case. In 2003, the Supreme Court reversed its 2000 ruling. The majority recognized the right of WoW to pray in their way at the Western Wall plaza but not as an absolute right, and held that the best way to implement it in a manner that would reduce offence to the sensitivities of other worshippers would be to provide WoW with an alternative location for their prayers.[28] The government was required to provide such a solution. An area known as Robinson's Arch was proposed, adjacent to the central area for prayer at the Wall and surrounded by archaeological activity. Women of the Wall rejected this as a permanent compromise.

2.4.2 *reasons for the outcomes*

Arguably, the Supreme Court was hesitant to open up an issue which was under intense debate, and to face the critique that it knew would come from the rabbinical authority. The Court maintained the status quo – the "custom of the place," protected by statute, and held by a powerful monopoly. Also, the Court was bound by law to consider possible "offense to religious sentiments."[29] The sentiments that were seen to be at issue were those of the *haredi* worshippers who objected to the women's prayers. Women of the Wall was not deemed to have "religious sentiments" that required protection.

Israeli law provides that religious sentiments may justify the restriction of expression.[30] The sentiments of religious groups were at issue, for instance, in a case where *haredi* members of a residential community wanted to block entry of vehicles on the Sabbath. Certain traffic restrictions on the Sabbath were upheld and others disallowed (*Kvish Bar-Ilan*),[31] to respect the *haredi* sentiments and also the right of movement. A number of cases have surrounded films said to threaten injury to feelings, both religious and national. The case of *Universal Studios* involved the film board's censure of a film whose depiction of the life of Christ was considered objectionable to Christians, and the case of *Laor* involved a film which addressed the Israeli army in a confrontational mode. The Supreme Court reversed the censorship of both films.[32] In *Bakri*,[33] the Court rejected a ban on the screening of a film despite its arousal of emotions of distress on the part of soldiers and their families, as well as of the nation as a whole. It was found that restrictions on freedom of expression will occur where offences "shake the very foundations of mutual tolerance" that touch upon "the deepest foundations of our existence [...] [and] may harm the nation."[34]

In the conflict over WoW's prayer, the rabbinical authority of the Wall thus holds a double monopoly. It controls how the Jewish religion is practised at this central location for religious worship and identification. The ultra-Orthodox also hold a monopoly over the definition of religious sentiments. Even while "sentiment" has often been characterized as a female phenomenon, here the possibility of offence to the *haredi* emotions defined by the male rabbinical authority took a paramount position, while those of the women of WoW were not considered.

2.4.3 current legal status

Finally, in 2013 a District Court ruling made legal headway for WoW's case. Arrests and detentions of women in prayer had continued throughout the period since WoW began prayer sessions, with WoW members succumbing in acts of civil disobedience. In 2013 the District Court rejected the state's request that the defendants – women arrested during prayers – be released on bail only upon the condition that they not celebrate the new month in prayer at the Wall for three months. The Court found that there was no reason to suspect the women's causing public disorder which would justify restricting their right.[35]

It is interesting that the move forward came from a District Court ruling. Perhaps the local court felt more able than the Supreme Court to shake off the burden posed by the national spotlight. Local courts also play a different national role from the Supreme Court, which is pressured by political powers of control. Interestingly, the US Justice Department has recently been seen to advance civil rights through local courts.[36]

Further with regard to pressures and litigation strategy, WoW may be considered a good test case for demanding support of women's voices. The case involves upholding the voice of prayer for orthodox women who may not be considered threatening (at least by some). Such strategic thinking may recall the famous Montgomery bus boycott that triggered the civil rights movement in the United States in the 1960s: Rosa Parks, an upstanding citizen on her way to work, set the ball rolling.

Recently, other Israeli court rulings have supported women's voices. A local court ruled in favour of women petitioning the municipality of Beit Shemesh to remove signs that *haredi* men had placed, demanding that women dress in modest attire.[37] A District Court required a *haredi* newspaper to publish announcements of the *haredi* women running for office in *Knesset* elections.[38] The Supreme Court ruled that a *haredi* radio station must include broadcasts of women's voices, noting the importance of a plurality of voices.[39]

The governmental decision in 2016, which has not yet received support from its coalition, would establish a platform at the southern Wall. Currently an archaeological site, it would serve as an alternative forum for prayer by non-orthodox groups (including reform and conservative) and mixed-gender prayer. Ministerial regulations would establish a committee to govern the site based on principles of gender equality and pluralism.[40] Women of the Wall would find a place there, with a further compromise allowing its members to place a barrier separating men from women's orthodox prayer. While the majority of WoW's members have accepted the government's decision, a very few women have objected to it, as they want to pray at the main site. The *haredi* parties in the *Knesset* have mounted fierce opposition.

2.4.4 rights and duties

The Supreme Court's opinions referred to certain rights, and arguably affirmed them in principle even while the Court did not rule for their enforcement. Raday critiques the scarcity of discussion of the right to equality, and others fault the Court's failure to uphold the freedom of religion.[41] I highlight the paucity of consideration of the rights to speech and dignity. My main concern in this analysis is the absence of addressing duties of respect, both for the women as speakers and for their speech.

Rights: the right to access and right to prayer were articulated in the second Supreme Court ruling *Hoffman II*. The right to movement was strongly affirmed in the 2013 District Court decision regarding detention conditions.

Dignity: dignity was present in the first Supreme Court ruling *Hoffman I*. Justice Elon cited the *Shakdiel* opinion, noting that it would be an insult to Leah Shakdiel not to be able to serve on the religious council,[42] and noting religious law on the honour of women.[43] He discussed the dignity of holy places, as well. Dignity was also referred to by Justice Shamgar, the Chief Justice at the time of the ruling, in *Hoffman I*.[44] Implicitly, the dignity of both sides was referenced. Shamgar wrote of the necessity in a free society to honour dignity in balancing between the right to access, the sentiments of the other worshippers, and the sanctity of the place.[45]

Duties: the state was said to have a duty to protect history, public order, and sentiments – namely, those of the *haredi* worshippers – in *Hoffman I*. Respect for the "custom of the place" was also required.[46] Significantly, Shamgar implied duty when he wrote that tolerance must be mutual, also in *Hoffman I*.[47]

Rights and duties regarding speech were recognized only in Justice Shlomo Levin's opinion in *Hoffman I*, in dissent from the Court's decision not to enforce an operative order. Levin noted the freedom of expression of both sides. The rights of speech were referred to in a very brief statement. Yet Levin also referred to a pluralism of voices, which, in fact, freedom of expression envisions. Further, Levin's reference to tolerance – like Shamgar's referral to tolerance also in *Hoffman I* – approaches a duty of respect. Levin wrote:

> As I see it, the phrase "local custom" should not necessarily be interpreted according to Jewish law or according to the *status quo*. The nature of a custom is that it changes according to the changing times, and [the phrase] should express a pluralistic and tolerant approach to the opinions and customs of others, subject to those reservations which I have already mentioned above.[48]

This phrase was cited in *Hoffman II* and *Hoffman III*. It was also recalled in the 2013 District Court ruling.[49]

Hence freedom of speech and the duty to respect speech were little discussed by the Court, but were present. Repeated again and again were the phrases regarding the pluralism of speech (or views and practices) and tolerance of that speech (or of those views and practices). It is those points which must be further developed and advanced.

How should the conflict play out? It is put forward that the legal case and cultural debate surrounding WoW and situations like it should be approached from the perspective of duties, in addition to rights. Women of the Wall's rights of speech are to be protected, but in addition to their rights the women are owed respect. Both the dignity of the speaker and the plurality of speech are to be respected. Duties are inextricably linked with rights in both the Jewish and democratic values of the State of Israel, as seen below.

The ethical duty of respect must be present in culture as well as law. Duties to respect the voices of the women are to be borne by the ultra-Orthodox, the authorities governing affairs at the Wall, the state, and the Court. The horizontal application of duties between and among individuals and the vertical application of duties between citizens and the state are set forth below.

3 multiplicity of voices in the jewish and democratic state of israel

Israel is defined constitutionally as a "Jewish and democratic state."[50] Both Jewish and democratic theory and practice affirm rights and duties, and in particular rights and duties of respect in speech. Jewish thought as well as Kantian theory, at the base of the Western democratic tradition, are seen here to be analogous in considering freedom together with duties of respect for speech and speaker. I believe that these values can be seen to ease conflicts such as those faced by WoW. The rights of WoW, as well as the duties of respect for the women's voices, are to be upheld.

Jewish and democratic values are often perceived as in conflict. Whether the values can live side by side has been a subject of debate for decades, and in recent times the debate has sharpened. I propose that the presumed conflict between Judaism and democracy, which has been characterized in a number of ways, can be seen as one between duty and right: it is often presumed that duty is central in Judaism, and rights in democratic theory. Yet the two must be seen to coincide, as both traditions understand the essence of freedom as obligation, and the essence of right as duty.[51]

While the theoretical resolution proposed here points to ethical guidelines, it may be effected in law, as well. The rhetoric of duty must complement the rhetoric of rights, both in culture and in law, as Mary Ann Glendon has written.[52] The critiques of liberal theory for focusing too heavily on the isolated individual in her rights may be eased by the understanding that, at its base, democratic theory envisions both right and duty to others.[53]

3.1 *jewish values*

The Jewish tradition is rich with voices. Speech is free; biblical narrative is suffused with accounts of arguments of humans with each other and with God, such as by Abraham, Moses, and the prophets. Abraham negotiates with God against the destruction of Sodom (Genesis 18), Moses persuades God not to destroy Israel (Exodus 32.9–14; Numbers 14.11–20, 16.19–23), and verbal disputes between God and humanity are shown in narratives surrounding King David, Isaiah, Jeremiah, Ezekiel, Habakkuk, Jonah, and Job.[54]

Women's voices also abound in the biblical narrative. Exodus tells us that "all of the women" of the Sinai generation followed Miriam in singing and drumming. Deborah sang from the very seat of government. Hannah delivered a poetic thanksgiving to God. The first book of Samuel relates that women from all the towns of Israel sang after David slayed Goliath. In post-biblical times as well, talmudic sages include (albeit rare) female voices, such as that of Bruria.[55]

The plurality of voices in Judaism's age-old tradition of interpretation is shown below. It is further shown that in Jewish tradition, freedom is closely tied with the obligation of respect. The necessary application of these principles to WoW is apparent: women's voices are to be respected in interpretation and in prayer.

3.1.1 freedom of interpretation

Interpretation of the Bible and Jewish law is not based only on the monopoly of authoritative rulings. Minority voices are included. Change in Jewish rulings and reasoning is a revered tradition in Jewish legal discourse.[56] Such changes take a view of practice.[57] Practices indeed can be expected to change on the basis of the changing status of women.[58]

3.1.1.1 bible. The biblical tradition teaches that all of the Jewish people stood at Mount Sinai when the Torah was given (Exodus 19.8; Exodus 20.14; Deut. 29.13–14). Every Jew, including the souls of future generations of the Jewish people, are said to have been present. Each of those receiving the Torah lent his or her interpretation of the words of the law. All heard the words – in Hebrew, *shema* – and each gave his or her interpretation to its meaning – *mashmaut*, from the same linguistic root. It is said that there are seventy faces to the Torah, namely a myriad of interpretations of the Torah.[59]

Interpretation continued with the canonization of the Bible by Ezra at the time of the rebuilding of Jerusalem in the fifth to fourth centuries BCE, according to the biblical account. After canonization of the Divine word, the tradition moved from revelation to exegesis.[60]

3.1.1.2 jewish law. The law continued to progress through legal commentary known as the Oral Law, where opinions build upon each other.[61] The interpretations are subjective views, and hence reflect human freedom (which Rabbi Joseph Soloveitchik calls autonomy, recalling the Kantian concept).[62] While nearly 2000-year-old talmudic discussions are still accepted today as its basis, Jewish law continues to develop.

The multi-voiced, dynamic nature of rabbinic discourse can be seen even from the structure of the Talmud, where on each page a text is set in the middle of the page and is surrounded by commentary from different periods. Throughout the ages, the rabbis perceived the discourse of Jewish law as a "process of constant confrontation between contesting views, each one in its own time and place."[63] Israel's former Chief Rabbi Avraham Kook wrote that "the multiplicity of opinions [...] is the very thing which enriches wisdom and causes it to expand."[64]

Contradictory rulings under Jewish law coexist side by side. God is said to have appointed as a successor to Moses a leader "who tolerates every single person according to his opinion."[65] In talmudic times, two schools often in disagreement were those of Rabbis Hillel and Shamai (*Bet Hillel*, *Bet Shamai*). While the position adopted upon was generally that of *Bet Hillel*, the position of *Bet Shamai* was also valued. It is written in the Talmud that a heavenly voice proclaimed: "these and these are the words of the living God but the law follows *Bet Hillel*." Further to this principle, known as "these and these," the arguments between the two schools are termed in the name of Heaven.[66] It is even said that the views of *Bet Hillel* won precedence for acknowledging the opposing views of *Bet Shamai* before its own.[67] Women of the Wall's prayers should be accepted on the principle of "these and these," even without the *haredi* Jews accepting WoW's views as the legal ruling. Women of the Wall's prayers, which were seen by the Supreme Court to be undertaken in good faith, can also be deemed as in the name of Heaven.

Differing views on a point of Jewish law are to be respected – even if mistaken.[68] The views of one great talmudic rabbi labelled "the Other," whose path led him to depart from the rabbinic community, were still recorded even after his rejection. In the well-known talmudic story of the Akhnai oven,[69] the majority view was accepted even while the minority view was accompanied by a series of miracles to underscore its correctness; yet the Talmud critiques the subsequent demeaning of the minority voice and its proponent.[70] Like other minority views and voices which are to be preserved and honoured, so too are those of WoW.

3.1.1.3 ongoing study of bible and law. The interpretation of the Bible and Jewish law continues to evolve. The continuing interpretation is not only by rabbis, and certainly not only by rabbis from the talmudic generations. Readers lend meaning. Female voices are among them.

Interpretative biblical commentaries have developed throughout the ages by rabbis and educators and in communal dialogue.[71] New meaning is constantly found in *drash*, the interpretative commentary on the Torah and the Talmud, which is considered part of the oral tradition of the Bible.[72] *Midrashim*, or the singular *midrash*, are interpretations of the biblical text by the use of illustrative stories, explanations, commentaries, and other forms of exegesis. Spanning geography and generations, Jews responded to biblical text with questions, challenges, and ideals of their time and place. Their insights enrich the Oral tradition, and have taken on the power of the Bible itself.[73]

It may be asked who is authorized to give interpretative *drash* or develop a *midrash*. This "never-ending discussion of the Bible" is not exclusive.[74] The medieval commentator Ibn Ezra wrote that "anyone with a little bit of intelligence and certainly one who has knowledge of the Torah can create his own *midrashim*."[75]

A postmodern-like role of readers may be seen in the development of *drash* and *midrash*.[76] In the postmodern world of literature it has become widely accepted that the meaning of a text evolves through its readers' interpretations. A multiplicity of voices – those of readers, rather than of authors with a single voice – is seen to develop meaning. Roland Barthes is an early thinker who put forward this view,[77] and many have followed in his path.[78] The liberty of the audience engaged in its own ascription of meaning is underscored. Similarly to the multiplicity of readers in postmodern theory, where interpretative voices function collectively, the learning of the Talmud is not done on one's own but upon interaction with learning partners.

The multiple voices of WoW offer an interpretation of tradition and continue the tradition of interpretation. Women of the Wall may be seen as readers lending meaning to the Torah and Jewish law.

3.1.2 duties of respect

Judaism links freedom and the multiplicity of voices with obligation, which gives rise to duties of respect. Judaism's affirmation of rights and duties sets forth an ethic of communication. It is submitted that ethics require respect for the voices of WoW.

3.1.2.1 freedom and obligation. Humanity is able to take upon itself legal obligation only once people are free, according to Jewish teaching. The giving of the law ensued after the Jews' exodus from slavery in Egypt.[79] Indeed, it is said that there is no law without freedom.[80] While freedom precedes duty in time, the Talmud teaches that freedom is inherent in the commandments that proclaim duties. According to the Talmud, we are to read the biblical description of the "engraving" (*harut*) of God's writing on the Tablets of Stone (Exodus 32.16) as "freedom" (*herut*) – a term with the same linguistic root.[81]

The obligation at the heart of freedom is the duty of respect for another's dignity. In Hebrew, both dignity and respect are termed *kavod*. *Kavod* has held a central place in biblical narrative and rabbinic commentary throughout the ages.[82] In ancient Israel the biblical revolution was in seeing honour belonging not only to kings but also generalized to all humans.[83] As biblically recorded and developed under Jewish law, all humans are created in the image of God, and hence are both due respect and obligated to show respect.

Dignity and respect play a central role in the public sphere in Israel – in the culture, intellectual history, and self-image of the state. The Basic Law: Human Dignity and Liberty (1992) provides strong protection to human dignity. Jewish law and modern Israeli law uphold freedom and rights, and also duties of respect.[84]

3.1.2.2 duties in speech. Speech is central in Judaism. Freedom, dignity and duties of respect abound with regard to speech. The ethics of communication guiding speech between individuals are well developed in

Jewish law and thought, and require that respect be shown to and among speakers.

The profound nature of communication may be seen from the biblical narrative of creation of the world by God in speech ("Let there be light," Genesis 1.1). The ancient Book of Creation (*Sefer Hayezira*) forges a mystical link between the letters of the Hebrew alphabet and the creation of the world. The Decalogue, labelled in English the Ten Commandments, is referred to in the Bible as the Ten Sayings. God's directive to Moses to speak to the rock in order to bring forth water can be taken as a command to recognize the power and beauty of speech.[85]

The ethics of speech are detailed in the freedoms of the speaker seen above, and duties regarding speech. The Bible (Leviticus 25.17) instructs against short-changing one's neighbours, and sages state that speech alone can constitute cheating. The talmudic discourse *Ethics of the Fathers* includes numerous warnings regarding speech.[86] The Talmud lists five items for payment in the case of injury to a human being independent of criminal liability, including assault through speech.[87] The expansion of the biblical injunction against gossip by Rabbi Chofetz Chaim is well known.[88] In modern writings, ethics of communication are apparent, for example, in Martin Buber's dialogic theory,[89] and in Emmanuel Levinas's view that language is responsibility.[90]

Israeli law gives strong protection to the freedom of speech, and to the duty to protect it. Principles from the Jewish tradition in this regard were affirmed in the Declaration of Independence[91] and the Basic Law of Dignity.[92] In addition to the vertical requirement that the state not restrict the freedom of speech, a horizontal application of rights between private parties may be seen in Israeli law.[93] While the duty of respect for speech and speakers is correlative to rights of free speech in a Hohfeldian sense,[94] it also must be understood as intrinsically a part of freedom. The law ought to embrace Judaism's emphasis on duties.[95]

It is put forward that the duty of respect intrinsic to the right of speech requires respect of WoW by the *haredi* worshippers and the administrators of the Wall, as well as vertically by the state. While freedom is to be accorded to WoW, also the freedom of the *haredi* men who define Judaism and prayer according to their ultra-orthodox views, and the freedom that adjoins the authority of the rabbi overseeing the Wall, must be accompanied by duties of respect for a plurality of voices. The Court bears a duty to ensure that these duties by others are ascribed to.

3.2 democratic values

Israel's support for a multiplicity of voices arises from its values as both a Jewish and democratic state, which cohere in requiring the freedom of and duty to respect such voices. Here the discussion moves from Jewish tradition to the upholding of both freedom of speech and duties of respect for speech in democratic theory and legal practice. Israeli law is in view, as well as US case law, to which Israeli courts often refer.

3.2.1 free speech

Three main rationales justify the freedom of speech: Autonomy, Democracy, and Truth.[96] Israeli legal doctrine has reinforced these rationales.[97] The rationales support WoW's voices.

Free speech is necessary for the realization of every individual's autonomy. The right to speech must be protected in respect of the nature of humans as speaking beings.[98] In addition to its deontological justification, autonomy is said instrumentally to enable human self-flourishing.[99] The autonomy of WoW justifies the protection of the women's speech.

Democracy further justifies speech being free. Members of society need to speak and hear others in order to participate in democracy. Free speech enables citizens to present and consider policies, and to run and vote in elections. On Alexander Meiklejohn's town-meeting model for free speech in a democracy, "what is essential is not that everyone shall speak, but that everything worth saying shall be said."[100]

On the truth rationale, free speech is said to allow competition in the marketplace of ideas leading towards truth. On this view, the more voices that are heard, the closer society will be brought to attaining the truth.[101] The three rationales underscore the importance of protecting the speaker as well as the speech itself – and hence WoW's speech in Judaism's renewal (*hithadshut*).

3.2.2 duties of respect

3.2.2.1 theory. The concept of an individual's autonomy, at the centre of free-speech theory and doctrine, brings us to Immanuel Kant. The Kantian concept of autonomy lies at the base of democratic theory and its understanding of freedom. Kantian roots are apparent in the modern concept of autonomy,[102] and indeed the legal concept of autonomy of speech.[103] On a Kantian view, as we saw with Judaism as well, freedom and obligation – and rights and duties – are inextricably tied. The mandatory duty is one of respect.

Kantian autonomy is positive freedom, namely the freedom to legislate the moral law, and hence consists in obligation to moral law. Autonomy consists in the categorical imperative, which requires that one consider others before devising maxims for one's own behaviour.[104] Autonomy both grounds dignity[105] and also entails the rational being's obligation to respect the autonomy and dignity of others. I have labelled this obligation an ethic of care.[106]

A conception of autonomy of expression has taken hold. In contrast with analyses that reject this view,[107] I believe the autonomy of expression is to be seen in Kant's own writings.[108] For Kant, expression and communication are a person's natural ends, and an innate right.[109] Moreover, Kantian thought influenced later thinkers who developed the evolving concept of autonomy.[110] As Kant taught regarding autonomy, so too the autonomy of expression must be understood to entail both freedom and obligation: the freedom of speech as well as the obligation to respect speakers.

Democracy supports both WoW and the ultra-Orthodox in their autonomy and dignity as speakers. With their freedom comes obligation – the duty to respect the autonomy and dignity of the other. The duties of respect that the *haredi* worshippers owe to the WoW are correlative to the women's rights in a Hohfeldian sense. Yet, in addition, obligation is intrinsically a part of autonomy, and duty an intrinsic element of right. The *haredi* worshippers have duties of respect intrinsic to their own free-speech rights of prayer. Also, the right to control prayer that the *haredi* authorities at the Wall maintain is a freedom that entails a right of respect for the prayer of WoW.

3.2.2.2 doctrine. When is speech present? Women of the Wall's voices in prayer and reading from the Torah scroll would clearly be considered speech under law. Also the women's wearing *tallit* and *tefillin* would be protected as speech. Conduct and dress which are expressively communicative are protected as speech, as the US Supreme Court wrote in *Clark* v. *Community for Nonviolence*: "a message may be delivered by conduct that is intended to be communicative and that, in context, would reasonably be understood by the viewer to be communicative."[111]

We have seen that Israel's free-speech case law is strong.[112] Recent court rulings discussed above have required that women's voices be heard on radio and in print, and protected women's choice of clothing – all three in response to ultra-orthodox restrictions placed on women.[113] The US Supreme Court saw the donning of a shawl by a Muslim woman as protected speech.[114]

Together with this freedom appears a duty. The duty to respect the readers' interpretations and the pluralism of voices abounds. The readers' role in interpreting text and developing meaning, seen above, is also accorded by free-speech doctrine. The call present in contemporary hermeneutics and literary criticism for the recognition of a plurality of voices giving meaning to works may be seen in law as well. For instance, the US Supreme Court's decision in *Pleasant Grove City* v. *Summum*[115] included a lengthy analysis of how "different observers, in a variety of ways" over time afford meaning to speech, in that instance monuments. First

Amendment free-speech doctrine follows the hermeneutic shift from the author's intention to the reader's understanding.[116] The multiplicity of readers' voices – rather than the singular, monopoly-control of the author's voice – has been protected.[117] A plurality of voices must be protected. Women of the Wall too must be recognized for developing the meaning of the Jewish tradition.

Thus both the Jewish and democratic values of the State of Israel call for the freedom of and duties of respect for speech, and for a multiplicity of speakers' voices. Israeli law and society must recognize freedom and obligation, and hence rights and duties. Rights must be accorded to all of the *hithadshut* voices in renewal, including those of WoW. Also, duties of respect must be acknowledged, requiring the respect of those voices. The Jewish and democratic state must uphold WoW's enriching and renewing of Jewish tradition, and their autonomous speech in a democracy.

4 closing remarks

Discussion here has surrounded women's voices in prayer, song and dress. The voices in view are those of Israel's Women of the Wall. They are women *of* the Wall, accepting tradition and wanting to take hold of their part in it. These women do not seek to deny but to renew the tradition, by expanding the views and visions – and voices – it encompasses.

The current debate over WoW involves positions taken in sharp opposition to each other. The women claim rights, and the *haredi* authorities opposing them claim control. I have attempted to put forward that in addition to WoW's rights the women are also owed duties of respect.

While Israeli law has a strong free-speech doctrine, Israeli courts have expressed scant recognition of WoW's rights of speech. Moreover, while concern for dignity and respect is very strong in Israeli society and Israeli law, duties of respect are all too often not taken into consideration. The duty to respect the dignity and the speech of the other ought to take a central place in popular culture and legal discussion generally, as well as with regard to WoW.

Both Jewish and democratic values infuse Israel. Constitutionally, as well as in practice, Israel is a Jewish and democratic state. In Israeli society, culture, ethics and law, the values of those systems are to be upheld. The values support the freedom of a multiplicity of voices, as well as duties of respect. The voices of the women of WoW are to be respected.

disclosure statement

No potential conflict of interest was reported by the author.

notes

1 See note 114 below.

2 Progressive trends can be witnessed in Jewish communities outside of Israel as well. See *Tikkun* magazine, available <http://www.tikkun.org/nextgen/what-is-jewish-renewal> (accessed 1 Jan. 2017).

3 For an extensive report, see <http://www.avichai.org.il/en/node/79> (accessed 1 Jan. 2017). Yair Ettinger writes a series of articles in the *Ha'aretz* newspaper, including on women's efforts at renewal within Orthodoxy.

4 *Hithadshut* is the most widespread name, but not the only one. See Guy Ravid, Guy Beigel, and Moran Berman et al., "Executive Summary of a Study by Joint Organizations and Funds" in *Hithadshut Yehudit – Jewish Renewal in Israel: An Analysis of the Field* (Tel Aviv: Midot, 2013) 6 ff.

5 See, for example, <http://www.tabletmag.com/jewish-life-and-religion/152871/tel-aviv-religious-revival> (accessed 1 Jan. 2017).

6 For instance, congregations following Rabbi Carlebach, and those modelled on Jerusalem's Shira Hadasha synagogue, meet throughout Israel. On this latter model, see the account by its founder, Tova Hartman, *Feminism Encounters Traditional Judaism* (Waltham, MA: Brandeis UP, 2007).

7 See the article by Yair Ettinger in *Ha'aretz* newspaper 24 July 2015 (magazine, 25).

8 Saba Mahmood, "Feminist Theory, Embodiment, and the Docile Agent: Reflections on the Egyptian Islamic Revival," *Cultural Anthropology* 16.2 (2001): 202–36, 225. Yet the shyness ("passivity and docility" 212) cultivated for piety that Mahmood describes does not characterize the *hithadshut* movement. I also would distinguish a goal of Mahmood's analysis from my own. While I agree with her effort at "uncoupling the notion of agency from the progressive goal of emancipatory politics" (208), and see "agency not simply as a synonym for resistance to relations of domination, but as a capacity for action," I distance the instance of WoW from her claim that a capacity for action may be created and enabled by "specific relations of *subordination*" (210).

9 Frances Raday, "Claiming Equal Religious Personhood: Women of the Wall's Constitutional Saga" in *Religion in the Public Sphere: A Comparative Analysis of German, Israeli, American, and International Law*, eds. Winfried Brugger and Michael Karayanni (Heidelberg: Max Planck Institute, 2007) 255–99, 283. Hartman also writes of her position within the traditional structure. Hartman, *Feminism Encounters Traditional Judaism*.

10 Raday writes that WoW is seeking to "transform the patriarchal public space" (298). Yet WoW does not seek to change the religion. I extend my thanks to Frances Raday for her comments on this point.

11 The marking of the new month has been associated with the monthly celebration of womanhood.

12 On the relationship between US and Israeli women involved with WoW, see Pnina Lahav, "The Woes of WoW: The Women of the Wall as a Religious Social Movement and as a Metaphor" in *Women's Rights and Religious Law: Domestic and International Perspectives*, eds. Fareda Banda and Lisa Fishbayn Joffe (Abingdon: Routledge, 2016) 123–51.

13 Raday notes that it is also of historical and national significance (265). Likewise, the Supreme Court (see n. 26) wrote that the Wall is "a symbol of the sadness of generations and the desire to return to Zion [. . .] an expression of the strength and survival of the nation and of its ancient roots and eternality" (*Hoffman I*, Justice Shamgar, par. 2).

14 The partitioning at the Wall between men and women began only in 1929. See Patricia J. Woods, *Courts and Gender in the Religious–Secular Conflict in Israel* (New York: State U of New York P, 2008).

15 For a monthly recording of events and incidents of attacks, see WoW's website. The women were accused by opponents of creating disruption and interfering with public order, even though the violence was by *haredi* men and women against them. For personal accounts of the occurrences, see *Women of the Wall: Claiming Sacred Ground at Judaism's Holy Site*, eds. Phyllis Chesler and Rivka Haut (New York: Jewish Lights, 2002).

16 Raday cites the perspective of female insiders in world religions (283). See *Feminism and World Religions*, eds. A. Sharma and K.K. Young (Albany: State U of New York P, 1999) 18–22. See also Mahmood (viewing the situated subject).

Yet WoW's opponents view the efforts as a revolution. See Susan Sered, "Women and Religious Change in Israel: Rebellion or Revolution?," *Sociology of Religion* 58.1 (1997): 1–24. Women of the Wall's status as outsiders, in the eyes of their opponents, can be seen in the invectives used against them, including "pigs" and "Nazis" (18).

17 Raday 259.

18 Mahmood writes that Islamic women's piety efforts may have been accounted for in the 1960s in terms of "false consciousness, or the internalization of patriarchal norms through socialization" (205).

19 *Hoffman III*, Justice Englard, par. 1. See note 26.

20 Raday 258.

21 The Talmud comprises rabbinic discourse interpreting the Torah and Jewish law from the third and fourth centuries, and is still accepted today as the basis of Jewish law.

22 Justice Shamgar conjectured that the opposition may be to the identity of the singers themselves (*Hoffman I*, Shamgar, par. 3). See note 26.

23 Raday 260.

24 Ibid. 280. Analyses of the case also regard relations of state and religion; see Yuval Jobani and Nahshon Perez, "Women of the Wall: A

Normative Analysis of the Place of Religion in the Public Sphere," *Oxford Journal of Law and Religion* 3.3 (2014): 484–505.

25 Leah Shakdiel, "Women of the Wall: Radical Feminism as an Opportunity for a New Discourse in Israel," *Journal of Israeli History* 21.1 (2002): 126–63. Raday also names Ran Hirschl's account of the conflict as a contest for cultural hegemony between a secularist-libertarian elite and traditionally peripheral groups, in this case the ultra-orthodox community (271). See Ran Hirschl, *Towards Juristocracy: The Origins and the Consequences of the New Constitutionalism* (Cambridge, MA: Harvard UP, 2004) 67–68.

26 The rulings are designated as *Hoffman I* (High Court of Justice (H.C.J.) 257/89, 2410/90 *Hoffman* v. *Western Wall Commissioner*, 48(2) P.D. 265 (1994)); *Hoffman II* (H.C.J. 3358/95 *Hoffman* v. *Prime Minister Office* (22 May 2000)); and *Hoffman III* (Additional Hearing H.C.J. 4128/00 *Director of Prime Minister's Office* v. *Hoffman* (6 Apr. 2003)). It is noted that varying interpretations of the Court's rulings have been offered.

27 In its first decision, the Court had recommended that the government find a solution which "would allow the petitioners to enjoy freedom of access to the Wall, while minimising the injury to the sensitivities of other worshippers" (*Hoffman I*, Justice Shamgar, par. 3).

28 Four Justices in a minority opinion advocated full and immediate acceptance of WoW's petition to pray at the Wall plaza. The two religious members of the Court opposed any recognition of WoW's rights of prayer there.

29 The Western Wall is governed by the Protection of Holy Places Law – 1967, which seeks to prevent desecration of holy places as well as behaviour which is likely to offend the sensitivities of the members of the religious communities to whom the places are holy.

30 See Daniel Statman, "Hurting Religious Feelings," *Democratic Culture* 3 (2000): 199–214; Meital Pinto, "Offenses to Feelings in Israel: A Theoretical Explication of an Exceptional Legal Doctrine," *Ethnicities* 12.2 (2012): 233–48.

31 H.C.J. 96/5016 *Horev* v. *Minister of Transportation*, P.D. 51(4)1.

32 H.C.J. 14/86 *Laor* v. *Films and Plays Censorship Board*, 41(1) P.D. 121; H.C.J. 806/88 *Universal City Studios Inc.* v. *Films and Plays Censorship Board*, 43 (2) P.D. 22.

33 H.C.J. 316/03 *Bakri* v. *Israel Film Council*, 58(1) P.D. 49 (2003). The specific sentiments to be protected by law are not clearly defined. The Israeli Court in *Bakri* (2003) (par. 7) referred interchangeably to "pain" and "harm" without identifying the emotion at issue more specifically. See also H.C.J. 14/86 *Laor*, 41(1) P.D. 121; H.C.J. 6126/94 *Senesh* v. *Broadcasting Authority*, 53(3) P.D. 817.

34 *Bakri* (Justice Procaccia concurring, par. 9) (citations omitted); see also ibid. par. 12 ("Protecting the sensitivities of the public is part of the concept of public safety and public order").

35 Appeal by the State 23834-04-13 *State of Israel* v. *Ras* (District Court Jerusalem, 24 Apr. 2013).

36 Matt Apuzo, "Department of Justice Presses Civil Rights Agenda at Local Levels," *New York Times* 20 Aug. 2015: A1.

37 41269-02-13 *Phillip* v. *Abutbul* (Magistrate's Court Beit Shemesh, 25 June 2015).

38 25435-03-15 *Koliach* v. *Yatadot Tashmar Publishing Ltd* (District Court Lod, 13 Mar. 2015); Request for Appeal 1868/15 *Yatadot Tashmar Tashmar* v. *Koliach*.

39 Request for Appeal 6897/14 *Radio Kol BeRama Ltd.* v. *Kolech* (Supreme Court, 2015) par. 9.

40 *Recommendations of the Advisory Team for the Issue of Prayer Arrangements at the Western Wall*, Appendix C – Draft of Proposed Amendments to the Regulations 4B(D)(Jerusalem 2016):

> With regard to the southern section –
>
> Local custom will be based on the principles of pluralism and gender equality […]

41 WoW has been seen to emphasize the right to pray, rather than women's rights. See Sered 12.

42 Justice Elon (par. 29), citing *Shakdiel* v. *Minister of Religions*, H.C.J. 153/87 42(2) P.D. 221, 268.

43 Justice Elon (pars. 22, 34).

44 Justice Shamgar (par. 2).

45 *Hoffman II* (par. 7) recalls this discussion of dignity in *Hoffman I*.

46 Justice Shamgar (par. 2).

47 Ibid. (par. 2).

48 Justice Shlomo Levin in dissent (par. 6).

49 *State of Israel* v. *Ras* (par. 8).

50 Israel's Basic Law: Knesset (as amended in 1985); Basic Law: Human Dignity and Liberty.

51 The discussion here moves from obligation to the duties to which they give rise. Kant wrote that the objective necessity of an action from *obligation* is called *duty*. Immanuel Kant, *Groundwork of The Metaphysics of Morals* in *Practical Philosophy*, ed. and trans. Mary J. Gregor (Cambridge: Cambridge UP, 1996) (GMM) 4: 439. See also Immanuel Kant, *The Metaphysics of Morals* in *Practical Philosophy* (MM) 6: 222.

52 Mary Ann Glendon, *Rights Talk: The Impoverishment of Political Discourse* (New York: Free, 1991). See also Robert M. Cover, "Obligation: A Jewish Jurisprudence of the Social Order" in *Law, Politics, and Morality in Judaism*, ed. Michael Walzer (Princeton: Princeton UP, 2006) (rpt. from *Catholic U. Law Review*).

53 Kim Treiger-Bar-Am, *Freedom as Respect: Freedom, Duty and Expression in Kantian Theory and Jewish Thought* (forthcoming).

54 Yoram Hazony, *The Philosophy of Hebrew Scriptures* (Cambridge: Cambridge UP, 2012) 104, 138–39.

55 See Amos Oz and Fania Oz-Salzberger, *Jews and Words* (New Haven: Yale UP, 2012) 61, and generally 57–105.

56 Jonathan Sacks, "Creativity and Innovation in Halakhah" in *Rabbinic Authority and Personal Autonomy*, ed. Moshe Sokol (Northvale, NJ: Aronson, 1992) 147. See Joseph B. Soloveitchik, *Halakhic Man* (Philadelphia: Jewish Publication Society, 1983) 99: Jewish legal discourse affords the power of creative interpretation.

57 Torah refers to an evolving body of laws and customs. Kenneth Seeskin, *Autonomy in Jewish Philosophy* (Cambridge: Cambridge UP, 2001) 69. With regard to Jewish law reflecting women's changing roles, see Roberta Rosenthal Kwall, "The Cultural Analysis Paradigm: Women and Synagogue Ritual as a Case Study," *Cardozo Law Review* 34 (2012): 609–65, 623.

58 *Hoffman I*, Justice Elon, par. 81.

59 Babylonian Talmud (BT) – *Bamidbar Rabbah* 13.15. The Jerusalem Talmud: *Sanhedrin* 4.2 states that the Torah must be capable of forty-nine interpretations affirming an opinion, and forty-nine opposing it. See Eliezer Berkovits, *Not in Heaven* (Jerusalem: Shalem, 1983) 78; Michael Rosensweig, "*Eilu ve-Eilu Divrei Elohim Hayyim*: Halakhic Pluralism and Theories of Controversy" in Sokol, *Rabbinic Authority* (the Maharal and Maharsal wrote of forty-nine conduits to the Torah); *Midrash Pesikta Derav Kahana* (millions of interpretations arise, one for each person standing at Mount Sinai), cited by Rabbi Professor David Golinkin, "Is Judaism Really in Favor of Pluralism and Tolerance?," *Responsa in a Moment* 9.6 (June 2015). See also David Golinkin, *The Status of Women in Jewish Law: Responsa* (Jerusalem: Schechter Institute, 2012) 117–18.

60 David Weiss Halivny, *Revelation Restored: Divine Writ and Critical Responses* (Boulder, CO: Westview, 1997) 83; David Novak, *The Jewish Social Contract: An Essay in Political Theology* (Princeton: Princeton UP, 2005) 79. See the biblical books Ezra 7 and Nehemia 8.

61 Menachem Elon, *Jewish Law: History, Sources, and Principles*, vol. 1 (Philadelphia: Jewish Publication Society, 1994) 115–16, 232; David Novak, *Covenantal Rights: A Study in Jewish Political Theory* (Princeton: Princeton UP, 2009).

62 Soloveitchik compared and yet distinguishes the two, in *Halakhic Man* 66 n. 80. See Aaron Kirschenbaum, "Subjectivity in Rabbinic Decision-Making" in Sokol, *Rabbinic Authority*; Berkovits 28 (subjectivity is present in equitable interpretation).

63 Avi Sagi, *The Open Canon* (London: Continuum, 2007) 188; Berkovits 174. Interpretation throughout the generations is underscored by the Talmud tale that portrays Moses ascending to heaven and seeing first- to second-century Rabbi Akiva stating with respect to an interpretative ruling: "This is a law given to Moses on Mount Sinai" (BT – *Menahoth* 29b).

64 Golinkin, "Is Judaism Really in Favor of Pluralism and Tolerance?," citing *Olat R'iyah* vol. I: 330. See also BT – *Chagigah* 3b (the wise sit in manifold assemblies and offer different rulings of law, and all are given by God).

65 *Midrash Tanhuma* (*Pinhas*, par. 10), cited by Golinkin, "Is Judaism Really in Favor of Pluralism and Tolerance?"

66 BT – *Eruvin* 13b ("these and these"); BT – *Pirkei Avot* 5.17 ("in the name of Heaven"). I refer to these sources to underscore principles of pluralism and respect, rather than to render an argument under Jewish law.

67 Rosensweig. Another explanation of the preference for *Bet Hillel* points to his school's acknowledgement that Divine Truth is complex, and may include what humans consider contradictory. Reuven Kimmelman, "Judaism and Pluralism," *Modern Judaism* 7.2 (1987): 131–50, esp. 137. See also Joseph B. Soloveitchik, *The Halakhic Mind* (New York: Seth, 1986): "absolute reality [...] reveals itself in manifold ways to the subject," such that a "pluralistic cognitive approach" is necessary (16); the white light of divinity is always refracted through reality's "dome of many coloured glass" (46).

68 One must say that God gave the Torah as taught by the Sages, "*even if they were to err*," according to thirteenth-century biblical commentator Nahmanides' commentary to Deuteronomy 17.11 (trans. C.B. Chavel); BT – *Baba Batra* 130b (even a rejected ruling may represent a valid approach).

69 BT – *Baba Metzia* 59. The tale of the Akhnai oven is more fully recorded in Kim Treiger-Bar-Am, "The Transformative Authorial Self in Jewish Thought," *The World Intellectual Property Organization Journal* 6.2 (2015): 149.

70 Zachary Braiterman, "The Patient Political Gesture: Law, Liberalism, and Talmud" in *Judaism, Liberalism, and Political Theology*, eds. Randi Rashkover and Martin Kavka (Bloomington: Indiana UP, 2013) 251.

71 Joel Roth, "Midrash and the Legal Process" in *Etz Hayim: Torah and Commentary*, eds. David L. Lieber et al. (New York: Rabbinical Assembly, 2001) 1470–74.

72 David L. Leiber, "Introduction" in *Etz Hayim* xx.

73 I thank Rabbi Susan Silverman for insights on *midrash.* For more on *midrash*, see Daniel Boyarin, *Intertextuality and the Reading of the Midrash* (Bloomington: Indiana UP, 1990).

74 Alan M. Dershowitz, *The Genesis of Justice* (New York: Warner, 2000).

75 Ibid.

76 On readers and the Talmud, see Leon Wiener Dow, "Opposition to the 'Shulhan Aruch': Articulating a Common Law Conception of the Halacha," *Hebraic Political Studies* 3.4 (2008): 352–76, 360.

77 Roland Barthes, *Image, Music, Text*, trans. Stephen Heath (London: Fontana, 1977); idem, "From Work to Text" in *Textual Strategies: Perspectives in Post-Structuralist Criticism*, ed. Josué V. Harari (London: Methuen, 1979).

78 See Pelagia Goulimari, *Literary Criticism and Theory: From Plato to Postcolonialism* (London: Routledge, 2015). Regarding the influence of this hermeneutic shift in law, see notes 115–17 below.

79 Exodus: *Yitro* 20.2–14, *Mishpatim* 21.

80 Nahmanides' commentary on Exodus: *Mishpatim* 21.2.

81 BT – *Eruvin* 54.1, *Pirkei Avot* 6.2.

82 Yitzhak Englard, "Human Dignity: From Antiquity to Modern Israel's Constitutional Framework," *Cardozo Law Review* 21 (2000): 1903–28.

83 Yair Lorberbaum, "Blood and the Image of God: On the Sanctity of Life in Biblical and Early Rabbinic Law, Myth, and Ritual" in *The Concept of Human Dignity in Human Rights Discourse*, eds. David Kretzmer and Eckart Klein (The Hague: Kluwer, 2002) 55, 58.

84 See, for example, Haim Cohn, *Human Rights in Jewish Law* (Jerusalem: Ktav, 1984); Yehuda Brandes, *Judaism and Human Rights* (Jerusalem: Israel Democracy Institute, 2013) (Hebrew).

85 I thank Rabbi Elisha Wolfin for this insightful interpretation of Numbers 20.8.

86 See Yeshayahu Leibowitz, *Discussions on Pirkei Avot* (Jerusalem: Schocken, 1979) 91.

87 BT – *Baba Kama* 8.86.

88 Rabbi Israel Meir Kagan (*Chofetz Chaim*), *Desirer of Life* (1873), expounding upon, for example, Leviticus 19.16 (against spreading slander); Jeremiah 23.30 (false prophets steal words); Numbers 12.1, 12.10 (Miriam's punishment for speaking about Moses).

89 Martin Buber, *I and Thou* [1923], trans. Ronald Gregor Smith (Edinburgh: Clark, 1937, 1958); idem, *Between Man and Man*, trans. Ronald Gregor Smith (London: Routledge, 1947).

90 Edith Wyschogrod, *Emmanuel Levinas: The Problem of Ethical Metaphysics* (New York: Fordham UP, 2000) 128, 152.

91 H.C.J. 73/53 *Kol Ha'am* v. *Minister of Interior*, P.D. (7) 871. See below, note 97.

92 See Aharon Barak, *Human Dignity* (Cambridge: Cambridge UP, 2015).

93 Cf. Aharon Barak, "Constitutional Rights in Private Law" in *Israeli Constitutional Law in the Making*, eds. Gideon Sapir, Daphne Barak-Erez, and Aharon Barak (Oxford: Hart, 2013) 379–401.

94 Hohfeldian correlativity indicates that X's right means that Y has a duty to respect that right. Wesley N. Hohfeld, "Fundamental Legal Conceptions as Applied in Judicial Reasoning," *Yale Law Journal* 23 (1913): 16–59.

95 See above, notes 52 (Cover), 81 and 84.

96 See Eric Barendt, *Freedom of Speech*, 2nd ed. (Oxford: Clarendon, 2005); Frederick Schauer, *Free Speech: A Philosophical Inquiry* (Cambridge: Cambridge UP, 1982). Speech and expression are used here interchangeably. For a view as to their difference, see Barendt.

97 *Kol Ha'am,* P.D. (7) 871.

98 *West Virginia State Board of Education* v. *Barnette*, 319 U.S. 624, Supreme Court, 1943.

99 Joel Feinberg, *Freedom and Fulfillment* (Princeton: Princeton UP, 1992) 91, 92–97, 316.

100 Alexander Meiklejohn, *Free Speech and its Relation to Government* (New York: Harper, 1948) 25.

101 *Abrams* v. *U.S.*, 250 U.S. 616, 630, Supreme Court, 1919 (Holmes J, dissenting). On different views comprising the truth in Jewish thought, see note 67 above.

102 See John Christman, "Introduction" in *The Inner Citadel: Essays on Individual Autonomy*, ed. John Philip Christman (New York: Oxford UP, 1989) 3–26.

103 Christina E. Wells, "Reinvigorating Autonomy: Freedom and Responsibility in the Supreme Court's First Amendment Jurisprudence," *Harvard Civil Rights–Civil Liberties Law Review* 32 (1997): 159–96.

104 GMM 4.440.

105 GMM 4.436.

106 Kim Treiger-Bar-Am, "In Defence of Autonomy: An Ethic of Care," *N.Y.U. Journal of Law and Liberty* 3.2 (2008): 548–98.

107 Onora O'Neill, *Autonomy and Trust in Bioethics* (Cambridge: Cambridge UP) 83. I thank Professor O'Neill for discussion of Kant's concept of autonomy.

108 Autonomy entails self-determination (Immanuel Kant, *Critique of Pure Reason* in *The Cambridge Edition of the Works of Immanuel Kant*, ed. Paul Guyer, ed. and trans. Allen W. Wood (Cambridge: Cambridge UP, 1998) A534/B562), and self-development of one's capacities (GMM 4.423), including of expression. Kant further connects artistic expression to the autonomy of a reasoning will. With aesthetic cognition the imagination is free, giving itself its own rules (Immanuel Kant, *Critique of the Power of Judgment*, ed. and trans. Paul Guyer, trans. Eric Matthews (Cambridge: Cambridge UP, 2000) 5: 306–17).

109 The human being has a "natural purposiveness," an "inner end," to fulfil the speaker's capacity to "communicate his thoughts" (MM 6.429–30). As it is his end, so then is "communicating his thoughts" a man's innate right (MM 6.238).

110 In Hegel's theory of self-development, for example, expression is a necessary element. Charles Taylor, *Hegel and Modern Society* (Cambridge: Cambridge UP, 1979) 11, 16. See Treiger-Bar-Am, "In Defence of Autonomy."

111 468 U.S. 288, Supreme Court, 1984. With this definition the Court recognized the hermeneutic elements of intent, readers' meaning and text, as discussed in notes 78 and 115–16.

112 See notes 32, 91 and 97 above.

113 6897/14 Radio Kol BeRama; 41269-02-13 *Phillip* v. *Abutbul*; 1868/15 *Yahadot Tashmar* v. *Koliach*, note 38 above.

114 *EEOC* v. *Abercrombie and Fitch*, 575 U.S. – (Slip Op No 14-86) (Supreme Court, 1 June 2015). Conservative former US Justice Scalia called it an easy case. The US Supreme Court also protected

as speech the donning of a jacket with an anti-war slogan, in *Cohen* v. *California*, 403 U.S. 15, Supreme Court, 1971.

The donning of a Moslem headscarf was the subject of a number of ECHR cases, for example *Sahin* v. *Turkey*, ECHR 44774/98, 2005. The regulation of the donning of a Moslem headscarf in a Christian school was discussed in 9022-06-10 *Nimri* v. *Lebanot* (Schmidt Girls' School) (Jerusalem Labour Court, 2010).

115 555 U.S. 460, 464, 474–7, Supreme Court, 2009.

116 See, for example, *Hurley and S. Boston Allied War Veterans Council* v. *Irish American Gay, Lesbian and Bisexual Group of Boston*, 515 U.S. 557, Supreme Court, 1995; *Falwell* v. *Hustler Magazine*, 485 U.S. 46, Supreme Court, 1988; *Virginia* v. *Black*, 538 U.S. 343, Supreme Court, 2003.

117 On the recognition of the pluralism of meanings and use of hermeneutics in US free-speech doctrine and in copyright doctrine, see Kim Treiger-Bar-Am, "Copyright, Creativity, and Transformative Use" in *Copyrighting Creativity: Creative Values, Cultural Heritage Institutions and Systems of Intellectual Property*, ed. Helle Porsdam (Farnham: Ashgate, 2015); Leslie Kim Treiger-Bar-Am, "Christo's Gates and the Meaning of Art: Lessons for the Law," *European Intellectual Property Review* 27.11 (2005): 389–90.

emily spiers

ATTITUDES TO FUTURITY IN NEW GERMAN FEMINISMS AND CONTEMPORARY WOMEN'S FICTION

In her 2011 monograph *Why Stories Matter: The Political Grammar of Feminist Theory*, Clare Hemmings analyses the narratives recounted by feminists about Western feminism's recent past. She identifies three types of story, each matching the ideological viewpoint of its narrator. The "narrative of progress" is linear and future-oriented; it characterizes second-wave feminism as an essentialist, universalizing discourse located firmly in the past, which has been corrected by poststructuralist accounts of fluid identity and by theories of intersectionality, so that diverse life experiences and multiple differences between women are now consistently taken into account. Hemmings glosses this story of progress in the following manner:

> We used to think of "woman" or feminism as a unified category, but through the subsequent efforts of black and lesbian feminist theorists [...] the field has diversified and feminism itself has become the object of detailed critical and political scrutiny. Far from being a problem, difference within the category "woman," and within feminisms, should be a cause for celebration [...] Since "woman" is no longer the ground of feminism [...] an intellectual focus on gender or feminism alone may indicate an anachronistic attachment to false unity or essentialism. (Hemmings 3–4)

The "narrative of loss," on the other hand, characterizes recent feminist history in terms of the perceived undoing of unified political engagement in the face of "progressive fragmentation of categories," whilst the "narrative of return" celebrates the long-awaited recuperation of earlier feminist theories after a period of perceived postmodern distraction. Those earlier theories – so the narrative goes – might in fact still have something to offer despite the "valuable critiques of essentialism" they were exposed to (4).

Hemmings argues that these stories should not be taken at face value and should instead be exposed to careful scrutiny, due to the ways in which they "intersect with wider institutionalizations of gendered meanings" that depict feminism as generally anachronistic and irrelevant (1). Indeed, the narrative of progress, the focus of the first section of this article, emerges not only in Anglo-American accounts of feminist history but also in European discussions of the recent Western feminist past, where feminist texts often endorse, reproduce and augment this logic.

In this paper, I begin by analysing how a corpus of essayistic feminist texts published in Germany around the mid-2000s invokes a narrative of progress, and I go on to think through the implications of relying on its logic. The volumes under discussion include the pop-theoretical text, *Wir Alpha-Mädchen: Warum Feminismus das Leben schöner macht* [*We Alpha-Girls: Why Feminism Makes Life More Beautiful*] (2008), by Meredith Haaf, Susanne Klingner and Barbara Streidl; the essayistic, autobiographical work, *Neue deutsche Mädchen* [*New German Girls*] (2008), by Jana Hensel and Elisabeth Raether; Mirja Stöcker's edited work *Das F-Wort: Feminismus ist Sexy* [*The F-Word: Feminism is Sexy*] (2007); and Thea Dorn's *Die F-Klasse: Wie die Zukunft von Frauen gemacht wird* [*The F-Class: How Women are Making the Future*] (2006). These contemporary texts, which purport to mark a new departure in feminism for a generation of young women, tend to legitimize their own future-oriented position by (to a greater or lesser degree) disparaging prominent second-wave feminists and repudiating second-wave strategies, which they often deem to be dogmatic and hopelessly anachronistic. In their place, the new feminisms emphasize the importance of individual choice, with the result that the target of the new feminism often becomes (their notion of) second-wave feminism itself.

After analysing the ways in which these new German feminists deploy the narrative of progress, I turn to a discussion of two German first-person novels which were published around the same time as the feminist volumes and which engage with many of the same issues. The novels can be compared fruitfully with the feminist texts due to their shared themes, on the one hand, and their contrasting temporal schema, on the other. The distinction lies in the disparate approaches to questions of futurity in the novels and in the essayistic texts, a divergence generated in part by the novels' narrative strategies and the use of rhetoric in the feminist volumes. In stark contrast to the new feminist texts, the literary narratives under discussion, Helene Hegemann's *Axolotl Roadkill* (2010) and Antonia Baum's *Vollkommen leblos, bestenfalls tot* [*Completely Lifeless, Preferably Dead*] (2011), disrupt notions of linear progress and problematize future-facing orientations.

They also resist the logic of loss or return narratives, by which I mean a sense of nostalgia for a more politically progressive time, or hope for its return. I will demonstrate how these novels, in fact, invoke a sense of disorientation and asynchronous temporality that is productively queer. Their queer disruptions of time and space, of language and form, combine with decentred central protagonists to throw doubt on the figure of the coherent sovereign subject who lurks persistently behind the new German feminists' configuration of the self-empowered "individual." It is my contention that the queer temporality and disorientation generated by the novels in fact allow the opportunity of imagining alternative modes of being which are potentially politically transformative. By focusing on the stalled and troubled transitions from adolescence to young adulthood of two disruptive female protagonists, the novels pose important questions about the political implications of subscribing to the available "substantializations of identity," in Lee Edelman's terms, within contemporary neoliberalism and the notion of "history as a linear narrative [...] in which meaning succeeds as revealing itself – as itself – through time" (4). By refusing to partake in this "narrative movement toward a viable political future" the protagonists and their textual vehicles enact a queer resistance to the socio-political status quo (ibid.). They also critically illuminate the, in fact, normative trajectories invoked by the feminist narratives of progress under discussion. In contrast, the novels' young, disoriented protagonists and the fragmented form of the novels themselves embody what Judith Halberstam has called a postmodern rupture in the "stability of form and meaning," which, according to Halberstam, constitutes both a "crisis and an opportunity" (*In a Queer Time* 6).

Haaf, Klingner and Streidl's *We Alpha-Girls*, Hensel and Raether's *New German Girls*, Stöcker's *The F-Word* and Thea Dorn's *The F-Class* construct a temporal model of recent feminist history arranged to position their work in the vanguard of relevant, popular feminist thought. A visual depiction might illustrate this strategy in the form of a unidirectional arrow pointing from left to right, where the tip of the arrowhead represents both the present and the implied future of feminism. The arrow's point of origin and the base of the arrow shaft connote a homogenized notion of 1970s second-wave feminism situated firmly in a discrete and completed past. The length of the arrow represents a linear process moving through the 1980s, during which time the ground is prepared for 1970s feminism to be overhauled, in the first place through the influence of poststructuralism and 1990s Anglo-American feminist theorists who explode the category "woman," and now, finally, by these young writers in Germany located at the very tip of the arrowhead. Thematic progress becomes artificially mapped on to the temporal model: the arrow functions at different times to connote a move from sameness to difference, from anti- to pro-sex, from anti- to pro-men, from homo- to heterosexual, from proscription to permission, and, finally, from victimhood and anger to agency and fun.

The reinvigoration of published popular feminist discourse arising in the 2000s with the emergence of these volumes was all the more striking as a result of the prolonged dominance of Germany's equivalent to second-wave feminism in the German public sphere. I say "equivalent" as the wave metaphor does not constitute a part of feminist terminology in the German-language context. In fact, the post-1968 feminist resurgence in Germany, Austria and Switzerland became known as *Neufeminismus* (new feminism), leading me to use the Anglo-American terminology "second-wave" here to avoid confusion with the most recent volumes under discussion. The absence of the wave metaphor in the German context, however, which symbolically links stages in Anglo-American feminist discourse while simultaneously distinguishing between them, also contributed to the sense of abrupt caesura upon publication of the latest texts. In those recent volumes, the authors employ rhetorical strategies and a narrative structure in order to consign the, in their opinion, anachronistic tenets of second-wave feminism to the past and situate their own works firmly in the present. Techniques employed to achieve this include creating and sustaining a lexical dichotomy between "new" and "old" feminisms (they rename the (second-wave) "new feminists" "old feminists" and appropriate the moniker "new" for themselves), the use of comparative syntactical structures, the reconfiguration of the word "feminism" (it becomes the F-Word, the F-Class, and feminists become Alpha-Girls or New German Girls) and the employment of a linear structure within the physical texts, which invariably includes a simplistic account of 1970s and 1980s Western feminism, from which their "new" feminism emerges as a seemingly inevitable development.

The second-wave feminists in Germany become proponents, therefore, of an anachronistic "Altfeminismus" (old feminism), which is frequently conflated with the person of the prominent feminist journalist and media figurehead Alice Schwarzer, a strategy which tends to homogenize an in fact rich and varied period of German-language feminist history. The new feminists, on the other hand, align themselves in their volumes linguistically with the here and now, and "die Probleme junger Frauen von heute" (the problems of young women today) (Haaf, Klingner, and Streidl 14). And, in the case of the title to Thea Dorn's volume (*The F-Class: How Women are Making the Future*), the present stretches into a future already being constructed by women – and that future reaches back into and inflects the present. The Alpha-Girls justify their work by claiming that the "old feminism" has lost its relevance for young women, proposing, "dass der Feminismus einfach nur mal auf den neuesten Stand gebracht werden muss" (feminism has just got to be brought up to date) (Haaf, Klingner, and Streidl 14). Their volume, they claim, marks the beginning of this process of making a new feminist future (ibid.).

New German Girls Jana Hensel and Elisabeth Raether also focus on Alice Schwarzer as the embodiment of "old feminism." Despite dedicating a large amount of print to her, they assert that Schwarzer's generation – implying the second wave – has become anachronistic. In unequivocal language, the New German Girls place Schwarzer firmly in the past: "mehr als das, was sie bis jetzt erreicht hat, wird diese [Schwarzer's] Generation nicht erreichen. Die Zeit hat sie eingeholt, ihre Rhetorik ist oll, Alice Schwarzer und ihre Frauen sind Historie geworden" (this generation won't achieve any more than what they've already achieved. Time's caught up with them, their rhetoric is old-hat. Alice Schwarzer and her women are history) (Hensel and Raether 14). The non-standard term "oll" in German functions something like the English "of yore," in order to "other" the second wave linguistically. Following Hemmings, their generational logic constructs others, in this case Alice Schwarzer and her "women," as "less invested in feminism by privileging time over context" (Hemmings 150). In this excerpt, what matters is that time has caught up with them, rather than the matter of contextually based distinctions.

The Alpha-Girls deploy their own rhetorical figures strategically and, in the process, oversimplify feminism's recent past. This ensures that the new feminism may be viewed favourably by comparison. For example, one of the opening chapters concludes with the following anaphoric call and response:

> Der alte Feminismus hat keine Lösung für das Dilemma "Beruf oder Familie"? Dann muss der neue Feminismus eine finden! Der alte Feminismus will die Frauen stärken, indem er die Männer ausschließt? Dann muss ein neuer Feminismus den Männern erklären, warum es auch für sie super ist, wenn wir uns weiterentwickeln.
>
> (So the old feminism has no solution for the dilemma "career or family"? Then the new feminism has to find one! So the old feminism wants to empower women by shutting out men? Then the new feminism has to explain to men how our further development is also great for them!) (Haaf, Klingner, and Streidl 14–15)

Thematically, the progress narrative in these texts configures second-wave feminism as a movement based around the notion of "woman" as a unified category; the universalizing tendency of 1970s feminists, they claim, resulted in hierarchies and exclusions which led to internal conflicts and schisms. In *We Alpha-Girls*, the 1970s and 1980s connote almost exclusively a time of "Grabenkämpfe und Rechthaberei" (sectarianism and self-righteousness) (194), during which the women's movement disintegrated in the face of conflicts between heterosexual and lesbian feminists, pro- and anti-sex feminists and pro- and anti-pornography feminists (194–96). The Alpha-Girls fall back on the generalization that this infighting and feminism's consequential downfall resulted from certain second-wave feminists' "Kontrollzwang und ideologischer Totalanspruch" (control issues and exhaustive ideological demands) (195). Their central target for accusations of such tendencies in Germany is, once again, Schwarzer, who is accused of proselytizing, condescension and of disparaging women who have contrasting ideas or lifestyles. As a direct textual contrast, their subsequent chapter is entitled "Und Jetzt?" [And Now?], and begins with an aspirational reference to 1990s American third-wave feminism, with its more permissive attitude towards sex, sexuality and pop-cultural playfulness.

In order to construct a persuasive and comprehensively relevant progress narrative, the Alpha-Girls must perform an anti-universalizing gesture in order to signal a move from the universalist identity politics they associate with Schwarzer to a poststructurally inflected politics of difference and intersectionality that they associate with American third-wave feminism. Yet in their introduction the Alpha-Girls admit that some readers "werden vielleicht die spezifischen Perspektiven lesbischer Frauen oder etwa Migrantinnen vermissen" (will perhaps miss the particular perspectives of lesbian or migrant women) (8), for these are not included in their allegedly all-inclusive feminism. This is why the Alpha-Girls offer the disclaimer that their book does not intend to unite all viewpoints because they are aware that not all women in Germany live their lives in the same way (ibid.). This disclaimer has a useful if pernicious rhetorical function: a professed understanding of difference and intersectionality as progressive turns in Western feminism relieves the narrators of the burden of engaging fully with their details or their implications within their texts.

The Alpha-Girls also stress the importance of the theoretical insights provided by "die Genderforschung" (gender studies) for their own work (30). These include an awareness of the importance of differentiating between "biologischem und sozialen Geschlecht sowie zwischen Geschlecht und Geschlechtsidentität" (biological and social sex, as well as between gender and gender identity) (ibid.). Referring to "gender studies" functions as shorthand for describing the intervention of poststructuralist, queer, and postcolonial feminist critiques, which are portrayed as interrupting the self-absorbed universalism and essentialism of the second wave. In her work, which does not draw on German feminism, Clare Hemmings notes that Judith Butler's *Gender Trouble* (1990), in particular, functions as a threshold text in anglophone feminist texts, in particular, providing the same kind of shorthand for this shift as does the choice of naming gender studies rather than women's studies. These strategies are also visible in the new feminist German texts under discussion. For example, in her contribution to the multi-authored volume *Das F-Wort: Feminismus ist sexy*, Jenny Warnecke credits Butler with the single-handed dismantling of the category "woman," indeed of the subject itself. Warnecke locates the origins of twenty-first-century feminist thinking in Butler's account of the incoherent subject and glosses the latter's impact:

> Mitten hinein in dieses Wir-Gefühl hat Judith Butler die Frau als Handlungssubjekt in Frage gestellt und philosophisch kurzerhand aufgelöst, stattdessen hat sie Bündnispolitik und Netzwerke empfohlen. Aktionen nehmen ihren Ausgangspunkt in einem gemeinsamen Problem und nicht in einer vermeintlichen Geschlechtsidentität.
>
> (Judith Butler interrupted this sense of a feminist "we" by scrutinizing the acting subject category "woman" and, without further ado, philosophically dismantling it. In its place, she proposed a politics predicated on alliances and networks. Action originates in mutual problems and not in an alleged gender identity.) (Warnecke 36)

At another point, Warnecke claims that "[d]ie Frau im Plural gibt es nicht mehr. Das ist seit Judith Butlers Buch *Gender Trouble* klar" (woman in the plural doesn't exist anymore. That's been clear ever since Judith Butler's *Gender Trouble*) (25).[1] Butler's deployment as a textual grenade in the new German texts achieves several complex goals at once. Firstly, Butler constitutes a shorthand for the seismic shift in feminist theory which the young authors claim as their inheritance. Secondly, it distances these authors from their second-wave feminist forebears theoretically (difference over universalism) *and* spatially (US over German influence); the mention of Judith Butler, along with other aspects of Anglo-American and French theory, signals a turn away from a domestic tradition of feminist thought. Thirdly, it provides the appearance of a dalliance with queer theory without actually requiring full engagement with its finer details. This is because these volumes are generally entirely heteronormative and draw on Butler almost exclusively for her insights into sex and gender as social constructs and the deconstruction of the category "woman," as the above passage demonstrates.

The progress narrative as it appears in the German texts is problematic for several reasons. Firstly, it reduces complex historical developments to oversimplified summaries. Secondly, as Hemmings has noted, it "coincide[s] unnervingly with those [narratives] that place Western feminism firmly in the past in order to 'neutralize' gender equality in its global circuits" (11). The intention to reinvigorate feminist discourse in the face of malignant mainstream representations of feminism that consign second-wave feminism to history requires the construction of a linear narrative of progress distancing the new feminists – and their intended audience – from the perceived negativity of "Altfeminismus" (old feminism). This strategy ultimately results in an all-pervasive textual preoccupation with the process of disentanglement from the past, to the extent that feminism itself appears to become the sole object of critique. The new feminisms thus collude with post- and anti-feminist narratives which themselves place feminism in the past, and reinscribe precisely those malignant popular representations of second-wave feminism. "Altfeminismus" becomes the problem instead of the social constellations which gave rise to feminist intervention in the first place. Thirdly, the texts' vision of the future is somewhat ephemeral, as almost every thorny issue is dealt with by insisting that women must make their own individual choice.

As a result, concrete strategies for specific issues are lacking, as are suggestions for the interventions that the community of Alpha-Girls could make. The notion of a better future for women is rhetorically invoked but ultimately appears to be confined within the paradigm of the neoliberal status quo. In the place of a coherent political agenda for the future, the Alpha-Girls in fact appear to propose a withdrawal from radical feminist politics to that which Jana Hensel calls "normality." She observes that "in den letzten Jahren wurde immer deutlicher: Längst ist es die Normalität, die zu unserer größten Sehnsucht geworden ist" (in the last few years it's become increasingly apparent that what we really desire is normality) (Hensel and Raether 15). This brand of feminism thus aligns itself with normative mainstream culture and circumvents the radicalism – and the concomitant exposure to censure – linked with Schwarzer's generation. The Alpha-Girls have been exposed to, and in turn impose, what in Michel Foucault's terms might be called the disciplinary function of patriarchal institutions enacted by the power of the norm (Foucault 92–108; Caputo and Yount 6). Normalization monitors and disciplines those who stray beyond the limits of the norm, which, as Hensel's comment implies, makes the norm an object of aspiration.

I move now to an analysis of futurity in Helene Hegemann's *Axolotl Roadkill* and Antonia Baum's *Vollkommen leblos, bestenfalls tot*. Both debut novels, they present the reader with two young female protagonists, Mifti and Rosa, whose aggressive self-awareness, acerbic commentaries and ironic attitudes place both themselves and the reader at one remove from their otherwise palpable existential distress. Baum and Hegemann disturb representation at the formal level. Their complex, self-reflexive novels question the terms in which the experience of consciousness is represented and examine the possibility of coherent subjectivity, eschewing mimetic representation and disturbing linearity. Emily Jeremiah has noted that the dramatic circumstances surrounding the publication of Hegemann's debut, when the author was seventeen, produced a particularly "instructive controversy," which revealed a "great deal about contemporary German literary and cultural ideals, especially as far as girls and young women are concerned" (Jeremiah 400). (Hegemann was at first embraced as a "Wunderkind," then, as the extent and variety of her intertextual approach became known, was publicly derided by the male literary establishment as derivative and/or deceitful.)

Nevertheless, the authors distance their protagonists from the feminist *grand récit* as a solution to crises in female subjectivity and agency. Instead, the novels hurtle towards their protagonists' seemingly inevitable psychological and physical breakdown, offering them no system of belief or ideology on which to gain a purchase. Thus, Baum and Hegemann express ambivalence towards feminism – an ambivalence that Hegemann herself publicly identifies with – even while they draw in part on a tradition of feminist aesthetics and tackle the issue of female agency thematically.[2]

The relentless inner monologue from which *Vollkommen leblos, bestenfalls tot* is constructed captures the complex thought processes of its psychologically unstable protagonist, Rosa Sperrlich. Scattered amongst the many fantastical sequences that could be dreams or hallucinations, there are conversations, at times in e-mail or text message form. Baum's protagonist moves to the city after her final school exams. She looks forward to escaping the toxic influence of her family, but instead she finds a controlling boyfriend, a tedious job in new media, and drug and alcohol excess. Thwarted in her attempts to find a foothold on her life, she rails against what she calls the "Werde-Pflicht" (compulsory-becoming) (Baum 237) of her generation. After two damaging relationships, Rosa becomes pregnant but aborts. She withdraws into a cocoon of lethargy, first starving herself then beginning to cut herself. The novel's conclusion finds her about to commit suicide by jumping from a tall building, and ends with a moment of insight on Rosa's part into her parents' messy lives and past mistakes. In the first edition (published by Hoffmann and Campe, 2011), the last line is the postscript "Rosa Sperrlich, Marcialla im Sommer 2011," which suggests that the novel is, in fact, the narrative that Rosa attempts to write during the period of her illness, completed at a later date in Italy. The 2013 Suhrkamp edition omits this postscript, effectively sustaining the gesture of refusal to think the future enacted by the novel as a whole.

In *Axolotl Roadkill* the streams of consciousness are interspersed with flashbacks to the protagonist, Mifti's, troubled childhood. As in Baum's novel, it becomes clear that the novel we are reading is Mifti's diary. Meanwhile, Mifti takes drugs, has sex, steals money from her father, goes to parties in Berlin and yearns after her older ex-girlfriend, Alice. When her family finally expresses concern about her behaviour, Mifti allows herself to get caught whilst shoplifting in order to force an encounter with Alice. The novel ends with a hallucinatory reunion of sorts between the lovers and a replication of a hate-filled letter of maternal rejection signed in the name of Mifti's mother.

It may seem counterintuitive to select two novels for comparison which appear to withdraw from feminist engagement, indeed from the viability of socio-cultural critique per se, moving, as they do, between critical ambivalence and ironic observation. At one and the same time, the novels both express and thwart the yearning for an alternative mode of being, countering the contemplation of a better future with cynical posturing, self-harm, and the rejection of the future in the form of adulthood. But this rejection, or refusal, can be understood to constitute a productive queer intervention by offering an alternative to compulsory future-oriented positivity of the type displayed by the new feminists, which is based on a binary mode of thinking that privileges linear time over context. As Halberstam notes, "[w]hile liberal histories build triumphant political narratives with progressive stories of improvement and success, radical histories must contend with a less tidy past, one that passes on legacies of failure and loneliness" (*In a Queer Time* 98).

Both characters must contend with "untidy" pasts in the form of their experience of traumatic childhood events: Mifti was physically and psychologically abused by her mother, who died two years before the novel begins, and she lives with her siblings, away from her emotionally distant father. Rosa grew up with a depressed, alcoholic mother, whose unhappy marriage led her to leave her husband and child in order to return to her studies, which she had broken off when pregnant with Rosa. Both characters' families are materially wealthy, but dysfunctional. Rosa describes her family as "ein asozialer Familienrest mit Geld" (the anti-social remnants of a family with money) (Baum 7). In fact, families connote for them the most dangerous thing in the world (see, for example, ibid. 17), engendering a fear of adulthood, which expresses itself in Mifti's desire never to grow up (Hegemann 15) and in Rosa's rejection of what she calls the "Zukunfts-Krankheit" (the scourge of the prospective) (Baum 13).

The fear of growing up can be understood as part of the protagonists' awareness of the normative trajectories they have been and will be exposed to. Rosa's initial celibacy and, later, her anorexia can be seen as attempts to return to a less complex state of being in the form of prepubescence, and the only wish that Mifti expresses explicitly (and arguably without irony) is "nicht erwachsen werden" (not to grow up) (Hegemann 15), a desire which explains her sense of kinship with the axolotl of the title. This type of salamander, renowned for its regenerative qualities, reaches adulthood without metamorphosis, entailing that it remains – in human terms – prepubescent. Like the axolotl, both Mifti and Rosa appear to be suspended in stasis, stuck in a present determined by the past and unable to find any productive way of moving into the future: they spend hours sleeping, drifting in and out of consciousness or seeking escape in drug-induced altered states of consciousness. As Mifti writes: "ich traue mich nicht, an morgen zu denken, ich traue mich eigentlich überhaupt nicht, zu denken" (I don't trust myself to think about tomorrow. I don't even trust myself to think at all) (135).

The novels' narrative structure reflects the characters' sense of stasis, of refusing, or being unable, to move on; it also functions to render textually the overwhelming simultaneity of consciousness, i.e., the debilitating presence of the past and the (fear of the) future in the present. Thus, the linearity of traditional narrative form is perpetually disrupted, impeding forward propulsion, and disorientating the reader, who becomes as wrong-footed as the protagonists themselves. As Jeremiah notes:

> The disorienting effect of Hegemann's own novel can be seen as queerly instructive. The novel's failure to offer orientation, or to orient itself according to literary conventions, provokes a consideration of what those norms actually constitute, just as Mifti's failure to fit in prompts a challenge to the very idea of fitting in. (Jeremiah 404)

Axolotl Roadkill is constructed from a patchwork of non sequiturs and provocatively self-contradictory statements; indeed, Mifti's brother suggests at one point that her writing (in the form of her diary) resembles roadkill. It is also often difficult to distinguish between past and present events and real or imagined scenes. In *Vollkommen leblos*, Rosa's inner monologue is relentless and repetitive. This evokes the cyclical nature of Rosa's jammed thought patterns. Sentences spread over pages, pinned down by an "I think" at each end, whilst her thoughts range across time, and space, and her narrated movements are punctuated by events, often sudden and violent, which are never identified as real or imagined.

When the reader first encounters Rosa, she is criticizing her teachers' "Zukunfts-Besessenheit" (obsession with the future) (Baum 13), which she feels focuses only on the conventional markers of neoliberal success: wealth, career, and heteronormative nuclear family. She observes:

> In den Klassenzimmern haben sie uns jahrelang terrorisiert mit ihren Einschüchterungs-Parolen über die Zukunft und über Berufe mit bzw. ohne Zukunft und wenig Zeit, das haben sie immer wieder gesagt, dass wir keine Zeit haben und uns beeilen müssen.
>
> (In the classrooms they terrorized us for years with their threatening speeches about the future and about careers with – and careers without – a future and so little time, that's what they said over and over again, that we had no time and had to hurry up.) (12)

This pressure can be understood in terms of the narrative of neoliberal self-optimization which, as I have argued elsewhere, exposes young women to relentless pressure to aspire and succeed (Spiers, "Long March"; "'Mädchen'"). Alongside school, the protagonists' families constitute another source of this pressure. As a result, the unhappy and dysfunctional biographies of the parental generation in Baum's and Hegemann's novels function as a mode of queer critique of the heteronormative nuclear family, which aligns with the characters' initial avowals that they will not cooperate with the imperative to procreate.

Rosa rails against what she calls "nationalsozialistisch[e] Popkultur" (national-socialist pop-culture) (Baum 207), a homogeneous postmodern culture, in which identity has become a lifestyle commodity, the pivotal consumer product concept driving neoliberal economics, or as Rosa puts it "I.C.H. inc." (M.E. Inc.) (104). Rosa satirizes a culture in which individual self-responsibility has become the dominant narrative and citizens exist in solitary units, protecting themselves from intersubjective encounters with headphones (206). The consequence of freedom of individual choice and self-empowerment is that "[l]etzlich ist jeder für sich selbst verantwortlich" (ultimately everybody is responsible for themselves) (62), a line which echoes the Alpha-Girl rhetoric discussed above. Such a climate has no patience for those who are relentlessly exposed, buffeted and subsumed by the weight of social expectations. Instead, Rosa and Mifti are each reminded constantly: "Du sollst das einfach durchziehen" (you've just got to see it through) (Hegemann 77), an imperative they push against.

At the beginning of *Vollkommen leblos*, Rosa views her imminent move to the city as an opportunity to shape her own life: "Man kann alles machen. Ich will was werden" (Anything is possible. I want to become something) (Baum 16). However, once in the city, Rosa experiences difficulty in establishing relationships, theorizing that, due to her traumatic childhood, something has been "ripped out" of her and never replaced (42). Like Mifti, she begins to perceive herself as fatally determined, a product of social construction which prevents her from truly autonomous action. These reflective passages constitute the interrogatory dimension inherent in these works of fiction, which remains lacking in the pop-feminist non-fiction. For example, in her relationship with her boyfriend Patrick she feels unable to be anything but "ferngesteuert" (remote-controlled) (Baum 30), a victim of the "seit Jahrhunderten überlieferten Schlamm" (legacy of centuries'-old sludge) of social convention and fixed gender roles (37). Convention and passive constructions of femininity clash with more recent postfeminist propaganda that demands that women become "total befreit. Sei weiblich und sei dabei wie ein Mann. Sei auch sexuell befreit […] lass' dich krass überall rein ficken und wirke dabei möglichst selbstbewusst" (totally liberated. Be feminine and, at the same time, be like a man. Be sexually liberated, too […] let yourself be fucked like crazy in every conceivable hole, but make sure you look as self-confident as you can while you do) (ibid.). This passage aligns strikingly with my critique of Alpha-Girl pop-feminism, which often foregrounds confident sexuality as one of the only viable sites of agency.

Having attempted and failed to gain a purchase on life Rosa becomes pregnant. After taking her mother's advice to abort, Rosa realizes she has undertaken that which her mother wishes she had done when she was pregnant with Rosa, increasing Rosa's sense of being socially alienated. She isolates herself still further, experiencing herself as trapped in a "Kopfgefängnis" (head prison) (233), eventually developing an eating disorder. Rosa describes her illness as a "Leistungssport" (competitive sport), satirically inverting the social demands placed upon her to succeed (209). Success in this case constitutes the complete destruction of self.

Rosa even views her disorder with ironic detachment: "Ich fand es nicht sehr originell essgestört zu werden, das störte mich tatsächlich, aber man braucht irgendein Geländer, irgendetwas was einem sagt, was man ist" (I didn't find it very original to develop a disturbed eating disorder. In fact, that really disturbed me. But you need some kind of handhold, something that tells you what you are) (ibid.). When her subsequent attempt to find this point of purchase at university fails, viewing the education offered there as an extension of her intellectual cage, Rosa begins to "open herself up" in other ways (232). She cuts herself because "[r]ot zeigt dir an, wo du im Raum stehst, Rot zeigt dir, dass du dich nicht irrst, Rot macht dich sichtbar, Rot schafft Ordnung, Einheit, Unterschied, ein Oben, ein Unten, einen Anfang und ein Ende" (red shows you where you are in space, red shows you that you're not mistaken, red makes you visible, red creates order, coherence, difference, an above, a below, a beginning and an end) (ibid.).

These passages are striking for their representation of Rosa's grappling with her sense of being socially determined not just in temporal but also in spatial terms. Stuck in the "prison" of her brain, Rosa rejects the imperative to pull herself together and in fact pursues an alternative path of self-orientation. Following Sara Ahmed, what Rosa has uncovered are the invisible lines of orientation that have determined the path her life would take. As Ahmed notes, "[w]e follow the line that is followed by others: the repetition of the act of following makes the line disappear from view as the point from which 'we' emerge" (21). Rosa's process of enquiry into the normative processes of orientation involves exploring alternative models of orientation. These include the eating disorder, which functions as one kind of "handhold," "something that tells you what you are," or indeed orientates you. Cutting, too, becomes described in spatial terms that imply the processes of orientation: the red blood becomes the "line" that "shows you where you are in space." Rosa's non-normative spatial orientation makes visible the usually invisible normative lines and orientations directing individuals' progression through life by her very deviation from the path. Yet as Ahmed notes, "risking departure from the straight and narrow makes new futures possible, which might involve going astray [or] getting lost" (ibid.).

The novels, however, do not seek to portray this refusal to toe the line as necessarily liberating or pleasurable. The disorientation experienced by the protagonists, which becomes the reader's disorientation, is painful and, as Emily Jeremiah notes, frightening (405). Mifti and Rosa withdraw from a social world they view as culturally and politically bankrupt, seeking even to escape the body and the psyche, which proves impossible. They are portrayed as symbolically fragmented individuals, experiencing themselves as alienated from their own bodies and disconnected from any sense of personal agency. Mifti often dreams of her mutilated body, where only "[d]as Gesicht ist übrig geblieben, ein paar Fetzen an den Fingerknöcheln auch. Hände und Füße baumeln, weil sie im Gelenk getrennt wurden" (my face is left, also a few shreds hanging off my knuckles. Hands and feet are flopping around because they've been severed at the joint) (Hegemann 40). Mirrors, which feature heavily in *Axolotl Roadkill*, function as a tool for Mifti's attempts to overcome the association of her body with abuse and weakness:

> Nur noch die grenzenlose Schwäche ist sichtbar und diese daraus entstandene Unschuld. Ohne den Blick von mir selbst abzuwenden, versuche ich mir in Erinnerung zu rufen, dass die Haut oberhalb meine Kniekehle, das Narbengewebe zwischen den Schultern und das Sommersprossenfeld auf meinem Oberschenkel zu mir gehören.
>
> (I can only see limitless weakness and the innocence it generated. Without taking my eyes off my reflection I try to call to mind that the skin above the back of my knee, the scar tissue between my shoulders and the sprinkle of freckles on my thigh belong to me.) (110)

Her body has become a cipher for those abstract qualities of weakness, but also innocence, a vehicle onto which can be projected intolerable experience. As long as the body remains something "[d]er eigentlich nichts mit dir zu tun hat" (which has nothing to do with you) (96), that is, remains disconnected from consciousness per se, Mifti is able to retain a sense of at least mental resilience: "weil mein Körper im Gegensatz zu mir selbst ein auf körperliche Schmerzen reagierendes Reflexbündel ist" (because in contrast to my self, my body is just a bundle of reflexes reacting to physical pain) (84).

But Mifti despises the way in which her body continues to experience sensations despite being "disconnected" from her consciousness. For example, she becomes disgusted with her body's ability to experience orgasm during sex with a stranger despite the sensation that her consciousness remains disconnected from the event (113). The world of sex, which becomes connected with corporeality and abuse, entails the loss of language (ibid.), a capacity Mifti at times appears to align with her "self." While this sense of self is fragmented, it is divided rigidly into binaries: the body is associated with victimhood, and language at first appears to equate with consciousness or "self." For example, after being attacked by her sister, Mifti observes that "[s]elbst das Schreien hat nichts mit mir selbst zu tun, sondern mit der unvermittelten Reaktion eines Organismus auf einen bestimmten Reiz. Ich bin nicht meine Schreie, ich bin nicht mein physisches Schmerzempfinden, ich bin kein Tier" (even the screaming has nothing to do with my self, only with an organism's sudden response to a certain stimulus. I am not my screams. I am not my physical experience of pain. I am not an animal) (84). Yet, with a gesture that aligns with a Lacanian perspective, Mifti ultimately resists the equation of language with consciousness, or self. Acknowledging that even the language she uses is a result of her socialization, she asserts that "[m]ir wurde eine Sprache einverleibt, die nicht meine eigene ist" (I've assimilated a language that is not my own) (47).[3]

Mifti's sense of alienation from the world, her body, and her language does not result in resignation but in fact a stubborn refusal to participate in life as it has been offered to her. She claims, furthermore:

> Ich wollte aufhören zu denken, weil Wörter bedeutungslos waren, weil Bedeutungslosigkeit bedeutungslos war, weil das Leben nichts wert war, weil meine komplette Physiognomie Teil des in sich stimmigen Organismus eines belebten Himmelskörper ist, von dem ICH mich abgrenze.
>
> (I wanted to stop thinking because words were meaningless, because meaninglessness was meaningless, because life was worth nothing, because my entire physiognomy is part of the inherently consistent organism of a populated celestial body from which I distance myself.) (166)

This refusal of body–mind and self–social integration is part of the novel's broader emphasis on the fragmented and disorientating nature of subjective consciousness. But it also connotes a radical act of refusal in the face of the normative options available to a young woman like Mifti. Turning again to Halberstam, Mifti's "refusal of self" can be understood as "an antiliberal act, a revolutionary statement of pure opposition that does not rely upon the liberal gesture of defiance but accesses another lexicon of power and speaks another language of refusal" (*Queer Art* 139).

As both texts move towards crisis, not progress, and their conclusions deny the conventional happy ending, they enact a subversion of the *Bildungsroman*, or the "Coming of Age Dramolette," as Mifti puts it (Hegemann 199). Indeed, they subvert the narrative of progress that I have argued defines the essayistic feminist texts discussed above. On the one hand, the new feminist texts appear at first glance to offer a liberating narrative of progress: from a politics of "freedom from" to one of "freedom to."[4] However, their focus on rescuing feminism from what are anyway fallacious representations of second-wave feminism and their empty rhetoric, which conjures the smooth transcendence of social contingency and bright futures, undermines their own agenda.

But is the radical refusal of the future performed by the novels preferable to the naïve, unreflecting optimism of the essayistic texts? Does the bleakness of the future, or refusal to imagine one, "access another lexicon of power"? And what might that look like? In the novels under discussion, the answer to these questions perhaps lies with their emphasis on the generative act of writing, and on the capacity of narrative to hold a fragmenting subject within constantly shifting imaginary paradigms. For the ability to make and re-make the self with narrative is what finally allows the characters in the novels to test their capacity for generative action. As an alternative to cutting, Rosa attempts to write down her experiences in order to find the structure and coherence she desires. This is perhaps why she states: "Erst versuchen wir was Ganzes, eine Erzählung" (First, let's try something whole: a story) (Baum 234). For Rosa, a story represents something necessarily coherent due to the conventions of narrative structure and the telos propelling it. However, the procedure initially produces only distress:

> Denke ich, fällt mir sofort das Gegenteil dazu ein, denke ich, sehe ich immer die eine und die andere Seite, gibt es niemals etwas ganzes, gültiges […] Aber so denkt man heute, dachte ich, als sich Alles in mir zerlegte, alles falsch war und nichts stimmte. Unverschämt, anmaßend, überheblich fand ich es von mir zu denken, es könne überhaupt einen ganzen Satz oder gar eine ganze Geschichte geben.
>
> (I think and then the opposite thought occurs to me immediately, I think and I always see both sides, there's never anything whole and valid […] But that's how people think today, I thought, as everything in me fragmented, everything was wrong and nothing added up. I found it shameless, presumptuous, arrogant of me to think that there could ever be a whole sentence let alone a whole story.) (235)

Although Rosa claims towards the novel's conclusion that she never succeeded in writing (235–36), the inscription included in the first edition of the novel suggests that writing did in fact present one reason for her stepping back from the edge of the building she is about to jump off when the novel ends. Suhrkamp's editorial decision to remove the inscription, however, undermines that reading and prolongs the sense of radical refusal sustained throughout the text.

For Mifti, writing does provide a sense of coherence where it is subjectively lacking and represents an externalized connection of sorts. It becomes clear that the novel the reader is reading "is" Mifti's diary, which she views as "die Ausdruckswaffe gegen meine Angst" (the weapon of expression against my fear) (Hegemann 38) and as an attempt to make whole and long-lasting – even temporarily – that which might otherwise disappear (67).

It is worthwhile recalling here the arguments made by Lois McNay and Adriana Cavarero concerning the role played by the narrative medium in the "active process of configuration whereby individuals attempt to make sense of the temporality of existence" (McNay 27). Through their explorations of two characters struggling against the effects of social circumstance and psychological damage, Hegemann and Baum foreground the "retentive dimension of the sedimented effects of power on the body" (McNay 4–5). Yet the authors also develop a generative logic which imagines a more creative and imaginative stratum to action. As McNay contends, it is "crucial to conceptualize these creative or productive aspects immanent to agency in order to explain how, when faced with complexity and difference, individuals may respond in unanticipated and innovative ways which may hinder, reinforce or catalyse social change" (5). In this case, the narrative impulse experienced by Mifti and Rosa can be understood as what Cavarero calls the subject's desire for unity of the self in the form of a story. The subjects who emerge coincide with the "uncontrollable narrative impulse of memory" that produces the story the reader has before her, and are also "captured in the very text itself" (Cavarero 35).

For this reason, the novels appear to possess a self-awareness lacking in the essayistic texts; in short, they understand their own fictitious nature, and, consequently, the role of narrative in identity construction. Whilst the essayistic feminist works also construct a narrative, a fiction of recent feminist history to create their own identity and to serve their agenda, they do not acknowledge the constructed nature of their own story, but offer it up as the "truth." In the final analysis, however, linear narratives of progress and "truth" are unable to fully express – as the novels attempt to – the simultaneous temporality of consciousness, where agency may stem from a reconciliation of past and future in the present, and not from linear narratives of progress which disavow the past.

disclosure statement

No potential conflict of interest was reported by the author.

notes

1 It is troubling that the new feminists all focus on Butler and not on any feminists of colour, such as

Kimberlé Crenshaw or bell hooks, who intervened in debates concerning the universal female subject before Butler.

2 Helene Hegemann has publicly distanced herself from feminist debate, claiming: "[i]ch habe mich mit so etwas nie beschäftigt, weil ich in einer Generation – naja, verankert bin ich eigentlich in keiner Generation – aber in einem Jahrzehnt groß geworden bin, in dem sich Fragen nach Geschlechterrollen kaum mehr stellten" (I've never really thought about stuff like that because I'm of a generation – well, actually, I'm not really rooted in any generation – but I grew up in a decade when questions about gender roles were no longer relevant). Nevertheless, she acknowledges that members of the literary industry "sind mit anderen Standards sozialisiert worden, da wird mir dann ab und zu dieses Biologie-Intuitions-Monster-Ding angehängt und jede Form von Rationalität aberkannt, mit der ich an meine Arbeit herangehe" (were socialized with different standards and so occasionally I get lumbered with this biology-intuition-monster-thing and denied the rationality with which I go about my work). Furthermore, she is able to identify continuing gender bias inherent in literary institutions, acknowledging: "Trotzdem, wenn Hamlet auf die Bühne kommt, vertritt der ein Menschheitsproblem, und wenn Medea auf die Bühne kommt, ist sie eine Frau, die schwerstneurotisch ist" (Nevertheless, when Hamlet comes on stage he embodies the human condition, whereas when Medea comes on stage, she's a crazy neurotic woman). She nevertheless refuses to be drawn on the issue, claiming: "ich rede da total ungern drüber, weil ich denke, je mehr darüber gesprochen wird, desto mehr bestätigt es einen darin, sich weiter in solchen Mustern wohlzufühlen" (I don't like talking about it because I think the more it gets talked about, the more you feel justified in staying in those kinds of roles). See Hegemann in Cosima Lutz, "Helene Hegemann beraubt ihre Freunde schonungslos," *Welt Online* 10 Feb. 2010, available <http://www.welt.de/News/article6329626/Helene-Hegemann-beraubt-ihre-Freunde-schonungslos.html> (accessed 5 Sept. 2016).

3 This statement can also be read, of course, as an ironic authorial aside regarding Hegemann's intertextual strategies.

4 For a full discussion of the paradigms of "freedom from" and "freedom to," see Grosz.

bibliography

Ahmed, Sara. *Queer Phenomenology: Orientations, Objects, Others*. Durham, NC: Duke UP, 2006. Print.

Baum, Antonia. *Vollkommen leblos, bestenfalls tot*. 2011. Berlin: Suhrkamp, 2013. Print.

Butler, Judith. *Gender Trouble: Feminism and the Subversion of Identity*. 3rd ed. New York and London: Routledge, 2006. Print.

Caputo, John D., and Mark Yount. *Foucault and the Critique of Institutions: Studies of the Greater Philadelphia Philosophy Consortium*. University Park: Pennsylvania State UP, 1993. Print.

Cavarero, Adriana. *Relating Narratives: Storytelling and Selfhood*. Trans. Paul A. Kottman. London: Routledge, 2000. Print.

Dorn, Thea. *Die neue F-Klasse: Wie die Zukunft von Frauen gemacht wird*. Munich: Piper, 2006. Print.

Edelman, Lee. *No Future: Queer Theory and the Death Drive*. Durham, NC: Duke UP, 2004. Print.

Foucault, Michel. "Two Lectures [Lecture 2]." 1976. *Power/Knowledge: Selected Interviews and Other Writings, 1972–1977*. Ed. Colin Gordon. Hemel Hempstead: Harvester, 1980. 92–98. Print.

Grosz, Elizabeth. "Feminism, Materialism, and Freedom." *New Materialisms: Ontology, Agency, and Politics*. Ed. Diana Coole and Samantha Frost. Durham, NC: Duke UP, 2010. 139–57. Print.

Haaf, Meredith, Susanne Klingner, and Barbara Streidl. *Wir Alpha-Mädchen: Warum Feminismus das Leben schöner macht*. Hamburg: Hoffmann, 2008. Print.

Halberstam, Judith. *In a Queer Time and Place: Transgender Bodies, Subcultural Lives*. New York: New York UP, 2005. Print.

Halberstam, Judith. *The Queer Art of Failure*. Durham, NC: Duke UP, 2011. Print.

Hegemann, Helene. *Axolotl Roadkill*. Berlin: Ullstein, 2010. Print.

Hensel, Jana, and Elisabeth Raether. *Neue deutsche Mädchen*. Reinbek bei Hamburg: Rowohlt, 2008. Print.

Hemmings, Clare. *Why Stories Matter: The Political Grammar of Feminist Theory*. Durham, NC: Duke UP, 2011. Print.

Jeremiah, Emily. "The Case of Helene Hegemann: Queerness, Failure, and the German Girl." *Seminar: A Journal of Germanic Studies* 49.4 (2013): 400–13. Print.

McNay, Lois. *Gender and Agency: Reconfiguring the Subject in Feminist and Social Theory*. Cambridge: Polity; Malden, MA: Blackwell, 2000. Print.

Spiers, Emily. "The Long March through the Institutions: From Alice Schwarzer to Pop Feminism and the New German Girls." *Post-War Literature and Institutions*. Spec. issue of *Oxford German Studies* 43.1 (2014): 69–88. Print.

Spiers, Emily. "'Mädchen haben keine Lobby im Pop': Writing the Performative Popfeminist Subject." *German Pop Literature: A Companion*. Ed. Margaret McCarthy. Berlin: de Gruyter, 2015. 143–65. Print.

Stöcker, Mirja, ed. *Das F-Wort: Feminismus ist sexy*. Königstein: Helmer, 2007. Print.

Warnecke, Jenny. "'Das ist mir zu extrem!' Eine Generationen-Studie." Stöcker 23–40. Print.

mariela e. méndez

"AULINHAS DE SEDUÇÃO" [SMALL LESSONS IN SEDUCTION]

clarice lispector on how (not) to be a woman

Clarice Lispector (1920–77) has been praised, together with João Guimarães Rosa, as the best Brazilian fiction writer of the twentieth century. Since the publication in 1943 of *Perto do Coração Selvagem* [*Near to the Wild Heart*], a book unlike anything ever written hitherto in Brazil, her fiction has garnered the attention of critics who have hailed her work as a breakthrough within the prevailing narrative patterns of the twentieth century. What often tends to be overlooked, however, is that even before the publication of this first novel, Lispector initiated a relationship with the press in 1940 with the publication of the story "Triunfo" [Triumph] in the magazine *Pan*. This relationship lasted until the very end of her life in the form of chronicles, short stories, translations, interviews, and, last but not least, women's pages. In particular, the chronicles she wrote for the *Jornal do Brasil* between 1967 and 1973 made her popular among a more heterogeneous audience that read her regularly every Saturday, bringing about a readership that conversed with her via letters and even phone calls and casual street conversations. In 1970, in one of these contributions to the *Jornal*, an influential newspaper that had led the way during the modernization of the Brazilian press a decade earlier, Lispector engages in a very brief discussion about the peculiar genre of the women's page, that section typically authored by a woman or a female persona addressing topics of interest for its explicitly assumed female readership. She speculates upon a letter received from a reader in these terms: "Li duas vêzes o meu nome para me certificar de que a carta era para mim mesma dirigida, e não para as ótimas redatoras de assuntos femininos do *Caderno B*. Era para mim mesma. Por que fui escolhida? Nunca saberei" (I read my name twice to make sure that the letter was indeed addressed to me, and not to the excellent writers on feminine issues of *Caderno B*. It was indeed for me. Why was I chosen? I'll never know") ("Só para Mulheres" [Just for Women] 2). Lispector's surprise at being asked by a young female reader for advice on going out for lunch or dinner with a young man is, at the very least, intriguing, since she did in fact fill the women's page with this sort of advice on three separate occasions. In 1952, temporarily in Brazil before leaving for the United States with her husband, she was the Tereza Quadros signing the section "Entre Mulheres" [Between Women] of the tabloid *Comício*. Evidence found in Lispector's personal archive suggests that Lispector was also, from August 1959 to February 1961, the Helen Palmer behind "Correio Feminino-Feira de Utilidades" [Ladies' Mail] in the newspaper *Correio da Manhã*. For part of this time, from April 1960 until March 1961, she also agreed to be the ghostwriter for the actress and fashion model Ilka Soares for the column "Just for Women" of the tabloid *Diário da Noite*.

In this essay, I analyze an understudied area of Clarice Lispector's work (her women's pages for *Correio da Manhã* and *Diário da Noite*) to provoke a series of questions about the writer's motivations for producing these pieces and the likely impact these had on the writer's readership. While there has been a slight displacement of criticism on Lispector's work towards those areas of her production considered to be more marginal or distanced from the texts that have entered the literary canon, criticism of her journalistic prose has been at best sparse.[1] Cristina Ferreira-Pinto Bailey points to this critical gap in the Introduction to the volume *Clarice Lispector: Novos Aportes Críticos* [*Clarice Lispector: New Critical Approaches*] published by Instituto Internacional de Literatura Iberoamericana in 2007, where the contributions of Debra Castillo, Maria Aparecida Ribeiro, Claire Williams, and Regina Zilberman all highlight the importance of studying Lispector's journalism for a reappraisal of her entire oeuvre (16–17). This essay aims to broaden existing scholarship by approaching Lispector's pages for *Correio da Manhã* and *Diário da Noite* – the object of study of Aparecida Maria Nunes's book *Clarice Lispector Jornalista* – as discursive gestures that destabilize normative models of femininity and denaturalize gender binarisms. According to Nunes, Lispector's reasons for refusing to sign with her own name seem to have stemmed from fear that the "lighter" and "less polished" nature of the journalistic medium could compromise her reputation and even "confuse" faithful readers of her novels and stories (112–13).[2] As her above-mentioned testimony from *Jornal do Brasil* reveals, Lispector also seems skeptical about her ability to craft a column structured, according to Dulcília Buitoni in her study *Imprensa Feminina*, around the triad of fashion/home/heart. Is it false modesty, that trope so often favored by women writers throughout Latin America? Is she indeed wary of alienating her readers? Is she truly dismissive of a genre that perpetuates normative models of "femininity," models she herself sometimes evokes in her private correspondence? Does she only agree to comply with this ideological operation for the income she needs to support herself and her two children once divorced from her diplomat husband? Whatever the case might be, Lispector's reluctance to publish under her own name points to an equally covert gesture in the construction of the women's page itself, a subtle reappropriation of this rigidly codified space that encourages an interrogation into what it is, exactly, to write (as) a woman.

It is relevant here to focus on the columns the Brazilian writer produced for *Correio da Manhã* and *Diário da Noite* between 1959 and 1961 in order to examine Lispector's transgressive reappropriation against a common set of social, historical, and cultural operations traversing Brazilian society as the new decade rolled on. In 1960, the new capital of Brasília was inaugurated, one of President Juscelino Kubitschek's major accomplishments. Brasília was a city that, like Kubitschek's government, promised a modern, egalitarian and democratic future for a country that felt a need to move past its backward history. JK, as Kubitschek is best known, based his entire presidency on striving to empower Brazil to catch up on the past fifty years via a clearly laid-out plan for his five-year presidency (1956–61). His so-called Programa de Metas (Program of Goals) would achieve this, according to Joel Wolfe, "through an expanded economy that would produce advanced consumer goods (e.g., automobiles and domestic appliances), and by reshaping the physical spaces of Brazil and, in the case of his new, modernist capital city, Brasília, even transform residential patterns"

(100). The transition from the populist government of Getúlio Vargas (1951–54) to JK's presidency, centered on development, also signaled a shift in the place that women occupied within each president's political discourse "from women as workers to women as housewives" (93). The automotive industry – the centerpiece of Kubitschek's plan – created a large number of well-paying jobs with extremely good benefits for men, enabling most women to stay at home as mothers and wives. Additionally, while women were included in the new training programs launched by Kubitschek's presidency, these programs were still traversed by a rigid sexual division of labor: "men operated huge stamping equipment, women sewed seat cushions" (102), which was likely a strategy that was intended to counteract the leadership women had exercised during the strikes of the 1940s and 1950s under Vargas.

In sum, despite the fact that women were entering the workforce in larger numbers than before, as Carla Bassanezi points out,

> There coexisted, then, oftentimes in conflict, the traditional visions about feminine roles with the new reality that attracted women to the labor market, the achievement of a greater independence and the possibility of satisfying increasing needs of personal and familial consumption. (625)[3]

The readership of "Ladies' Mail" and "Just for Women" was assuredly comprised of women who were heirs to the ideal of domesticity still prevalent in Brazilian society and at the same time transforming themselves into the "garota moderna" (modern woman) who avidly consumed the goods that the new modern society had to offer. A burgeoning cultural industry and a newly empowered mass media targeted these "garotas modernas" as some of their most coveted consumers. "Ladies' Mail," in particular, plays into this dynamic since this column is published under the sponsorship of the cosmetics company Pond's, as evidenced by a contract where Helen Palmer agrees to persuade her reader subliminally, without mentioning specific names, to buy Pond's products. Ninety percent of the advertising campaigns flooding the media at the time, according to Palmer herself, targeted women. In her column, she summarizes it thus: "Agradar à mulher! Eis, condensada em três palavras, a razão de ser, não sò da quase totalidade do comércio, mas da maior parte dos empreendimentos humanos, quer estejam ou não, interessados em vender mercadorias às mulheres" (To please women! Here is the *raison d'être*, condensed down to three words, not only for practically all commerce, but for most human undertakings, whether or not they are interested in selling goods to women) ("A Grande Compradora" [The Great Buyer]). As is to be expected, the narrative constructed by these advertising campaigns was aimed at normalizing women's behavior, molding their consuming habits, shaping their tastes, visualizing certain types of bodies while obliterating others, in short, anchoring women firmly within strictly preconceived notions of an "ideal femininity."

Clarice Lispector is deeply aware of this narrative aimed at commodifying female subjectivity. The numerous letters she sent to her sisters during her stay abroad reveal through comments on fashion, beauty tips, and discussion of domestic issues that the writer herself knew how to perform this "ideal femininity."[4] In *Diário da Noite*, a paper that reinvents itself along the parameters of American journalism, becoming the first tabloid to be published in Rio de Janeiro, as the ghostwriter for Ilka Soares, Lispector introduces a section called "Você e Eu nas Compras" [You and I Shopping]. Resorting to a certain complicity with the reader, a typical discursive strategy of all women's pages, Lispector/Soares devotes herself to window-shopping in the reader's company, or rather as her proxy, and dedicates the entire section to highlighting the advantages and disadvantages of various products: tights, perfumes, creams, hair curlers, etc. In passing, she remarks: "Foi quando, de repente, me lembrei … quase tudo o que interessa a uma mulher, interessa a outra também" (That was when, suddenly, I remembered … practically everything that interests one woman, also interests another). Such acknowledgment, even if made underhandedly, of the standardization of the reader's profile and her consuming tendencies becomes all the more suspicious as one notices that, at times, Lispector's language for her columns unmistakably adopts pseudo-advertising overtones, as if echoing that discourse. As will become evident later in this essay, however, an alternative narrative subtly persists throughout her pages against the grain of the advertising discourse aimed at commodifying female subjectivity.

In Lispector's column for *Diário da Noite*, the subliminal message underlying its counterpart in *Correio da Manhã* is disclosed when a sales promotion by the Hair Salon Salão Dir, in Centro Comercial de Copacabana, store 215, offers a free oil massage to those customers bringing one of the "Aulinhas de Sedução" included in "Just for Women." The "Small Lessons" were sections meant to be cut out and collected by the reader, as suggested by the drawing of a pair of scissors accompanying them. These "Small Lessons" cover essential components of the "art of seduction," methodically explained to the reader: perfumes, jewelry, hair care, colors, etc. Like the rest of Lispector's column for *Diário da Noite*, the "Small Lessons in Seduction" overemphasize the meticulous and obsessive performance of normative femininity, and the same can be said of "Ladies' Mail" in *Correio da Manhã*. The women's pages crafted by the Brazilian writer are consistently traversed by the same underlying message: there is indeed a clear and precise set of steps to be followed, relentlessly, to achieve the ideal of elegance and beauty. The small box frequently appearing in "Just for Women" under the number 3 and the word "Três" (Three) is in fact a gesture in this direction: three pieces of advice pronounced with the pseudo-scientific tone of a physics law: from a home-made recipe to obtain smooth skin, to the secret for removing tenacious stains, to a list of foods rich in iron. The three short recipes regularly featured under "Three" epitomize the reading patterns staked out for readers who are persuaded to see the entire column itself as a recipe. "Ladies' Mail" in *Correio da Manhã* fits into the same pattern. The "Decálogo da Beleza" [Beauty Decalogue] appearing on 11 September 1959, for instance, presents readers with a tidy set of precepts for skin care, physical exercise, hair treatments, and so on, and this gesture is reiterated ad infinitum in both publications under titles such as "Voz Irresistível" [Irresistible Voice], "Limpe A Sua Pele Diariamente" [Clean Your Skin Daily], and "Seu Andar" [Your Gait].

In fact a woman's gait becomes the subject of an entire text published without a title in the section "Nossa Conversa" [Our Conversation] of "Just for Women." In this particular issue of 23 May 1960, Lispector/Soares painstakingly describes the sequence of motions to be followed to beautify one's legs. Having argued that the secret of beauty is in the pose, the narrator enumerates various pieces of advice on how exactly the reader should stand, sit down, and even walk:

> E eis algumas sugestões para a pose de suas pernas …
>
> 1 – Quando você estiver de pé, mantenha os joelhos juntos, mas não rápidos. O calcanhar de um pé deve tocar ou estar à frente dos dedos do outro pé.
>
> 2 – Ao sentar-se, ponha os pés para a direita ou esquerda, a ponta de um dos pés "dando a volta" atrás do calcanhar do outro.
>
> 3 – Ao caminhar, os dedos devem apontar para a frente.
>
> 4 – Ao caminhar, mova os pés ao longo de duas linhas paralelas imaginárias, com um pequeno espaço entre ambas.
>
> 5 – E, ainda ao caminhar, limite seu passo ao comprimento de seu pé. (Em outras palavras, o passo não deve exceder, em tamanho, o tamanho do pé – está mais claro?)
>
> (Here are some suggestions for your legs' pose …
>
> 1 – When you are standing, bring your knees together, but not for long. The heel of one foot should touch or be at the front of the toes of the other foot.
>
> 2 – As you sit down, place your feet towards the right or the left, the point of one of your feet "going around" behind your other heel.
>
> 3 – As you walk, toes have to point to the front.
>
> 4 – As you walk, move your feet along two

imaginary parallel lines, with a little space between them.

5 – And, as you walk, limit your step to the length of your foot. (In other words, your step should not exceed, in size, your foot's size – is this clear?))

Such strict adherence to a specific manner of walking, composed as it is of fixed and rigid actions, underlines the artificiality of the advice itself and also mocks the belief that there is indeed a recipe for everything. Through the use of parody, the endless recipes provided by Lispector via her "proxies" in the various pages she authored hyperbolize the performance of those gender-coded attributes deemed to be ideal within such spaces of enunciation. After all, "When it comes to legs, it's just a question of pose," the writer summarizes ironically. Lispector's pages enact a discursive transvestism understood, on the one hand, as parody of the discursive space of the women's page featured in all magazines and newspapers of the period, and, on the other, as an excessive, over-the-top performance of "femininity." As if mirroring the sartorial inventory informing the transvestite's performance, Lispector's column ratifies the inclusion of all the necessary components underlying the prescribed script for her female readership. The transvestite subject displays a rhetoric of wearing, naming, and acting a specific gender. Likewise, "Ladies' Mail" and "Just for Women" enact a ritualistic performance of actions, gestures, and behaviors associated with "femininity."

Lispector's pages for *Correio da Manhã* and *Diário da Noite* not only adhere in their design and layout to the characteristic sections full of tips, instructions, and recommendations, they also extensively foreground the presence of lists, decalogues, and checklists. The writer also resorts to a subtle use of irony, the characteristic trope of parody, to mimic these numberless catalogs and inventories. In the piece titled "O que Os Homens não Gostam" [What Men Don't Like] for *Correio da Manhã*, for instance, Helen/Clarice describes everything men dislike about women and ends her piece by seeking the reader's confirmation: "Chamar a atenção não é a finalidade de uma mulher elegante e inteligente. Mas sim ser atraente e ... agradar aos homens. Estou certa?" (Drawing attention is not the goal of an elegant and intelligent woman. It is instead to be attractive and ... to please men. Am I right?). Immediately below, the section "Nova Maneira de Prender Marido" [New Way of Securing a Husband] unsettles her affirmation that being physically attractive is what comes first in the list of qualities that might help women land a good match. In response to some of her readers' anxiety over this issue, the writer dismisses the decalogue just outlined above to suggest instead that it is indeed intellect that can guarantee success: "Muitas vezes, uma mulher dona de casa restringe sua vida a probleminhas domésticos, que de forma alguma agradam ao seu marido. Tentem ler um pouco" (Many times, a housewife limits her life to domestic problems that are in no way attractive to her husband. Try reading a little) (5). "What Men Don't Like" underlined the exact opposite; the only occasion when intellect actually appeared, it did so disparagingly, through the term "sabichona" (know-it-all). In this piece, Lispector resorts to a discursive transvestism – a pronounced accentuation of what is culturally constructed as "feminine" – even as she warns the reader against the dangers of exaggeration. Excess, "that which overflows a boundary," constitutes the privileged space for the transvestite, according to Marjorie Garber (28), that which exceeds binary distinctions via overstatement, superimposition, and overlayering. The boundary thus becomes permeable, allowing "border crossings from one (apparently distinct) category to another," staking out a conflicting area of overdetermination which foreshadows a crisis of all binary categories, indeed, according to Garber, a category crisis (16–17).

"What Men Don't Like" warns against overdone makeup, exaggerated lipstick, excess of jewelry, pronounced neckline, excessively tight clothes, everything that the column, paradoxically, revolves around. These phrases could actually appear inside quotes; so could the various sections that make up "Ladies' Mail" and "Just for Women," as they expose their own artifice and underline the ensuing irony.

In their own construction, the columns designed by Lispector draw attention to themselves, to the arrangement of signifiers on the page as a self-referential message, on the one hand, and, on the other, as a self-enclosed universe centered on the triad described by Buitoni. Alberto Dines recalls how Clarice would send the column "Just for Women" for *Diário da Noite* practically ready to be published. She would put it all together at home, including pictures cut out from foreign magazines such as *Vogue* or *Elle*, and would turn it in edited and dated, without any need to add or remove anything. This "editora caprichosa" (willful editor), as Dines referred to her, would nevertheless make a point of following his guidelines (*Correio Feminino* 5). Inspired by the *Daily Express* and *Daily Mirror*, Dines launched a paper dominated by big photographs, sensationalist language, and short, colloquial pieces, in an unusual time slot – the evening – in the hope that *Diário da Noite* would manage to compete with the morning papers *Ultima Hora* and *O Globo* then dominating the press. In the same year in which Brasília was inaugurated, Dines's paper hit the newsstands displaying the names of celebrities such as Ilka Soares who agreed to lend their names to different sections and columns.

Not only did Lispector make all the decisions pertaining to the texts included, but she also meticulously thought through the layout of the entire page. The pictures she selected typically displayed the latest designs on the bodies of famous models, including Soares herself, and generally looked towards the interior of the column or else faced the reader. The emphasis placed on the composition of the column evokes, in turn, the "adornment," the careful act of choosing and donning all the accessories and accoutrements necessary for the ideal performance of femininity. It is possible, therefore, to think of the column itself as performance, enclosing it in quotes. Several decades after Lispector, Marjorie Garber would stress the similarity between the advice characterizing magazines targeting a transvestite audience and that appearing in magazines such as *Cosmopolitan* with the following words:

> Gender is commodified and constructed in the pages of these journals, so that the article's title begs for double quotation marks: "'Woman' to 'Woman'." But so, we might say, have the woman's magazines. The anxiety of artifice that marks such a check list emphasizes the degree to which the "'woman'" speaking, and the "'woman'" listening, are unsure about the legibility of their desired social identities. But – and this is the key point here – so are the "women" who read "women's magazines" – or, for that matter, feminist journals [...] The social critique performed by these transvestite magazines for readers who are not cross-dressers is to point out the degree to which *all* women cross-dress as women when they produce themselves as artifacts. (49)

However hard Lispector's columns strive to give the impression that there is a unified, coherent, and stable identity that readers can relate to and aspire to replicate, the columns' performance is constantly dislodged, unsettled. Identities are mere fabrications, women themselves are mere artifacts, like the models cut out, pasted and laid out on the page, like the pages themselves, like Helen Palmer or Ilka Soares, like the reader. Palmer herself suggests this in so many words when she proclaims that everything is possible "com um pouco de trabalho, muito de perseverança e alguma inteligência" (with a little bit of work, a lot of perseverance, and some intelligence) ("Ser Feia" [Being Ugly] 5). About a month later, the columnist revisits the same idea to articulate a more explicit connection between the assemblage of female subjectivity and the commodification shaping consuming patterns through the new mass media: "A beleza é hoje produto de laboratório, que se compra, se estuda, e se controla" [Beauty is today a laboratory product, which is bought, studied, and controlled] ("Beleza é Cuidado e Perseverança" [Beauty is Care and Perseverance] 5). Palmer's declarations undermine the reliability of sections such as "Sempre Mulher através dos Tempos" [Always a Woman Throughout Time] or "O Que é uma Mulher Bonita?" [What is a Pretty Woman?], foregrounding instead the absolute contingency and artificiality behind the construction and marketing of gender norms.

The mini-series based on a selection of the women's pages studied here, aired by Brazilian TV Globo in 2013, provides a relevant counterpoint. Directed by Luiz Fernando Carvalho, "Correio Feminino" [Ladies' Mail], a segment of the popular Sunday program *Fantástico*, consists of eight episodes highlighting moments in the life of a reader at three distinct stages in life – youth, adulthood, and maturity. What is revealing in most of the episodes, which are about twenty or thirty minutes long, is the emphasis on the artificiality of a setting where the scarce props point to the material conditions of the lives of the emerging Brazilian middle class of the 1950s and 1960s. Modern cars, washing machines, television sets, and other gadgets intended to modernize domestic life fill the space inhabited by a middle-class housewife, who was the target of messages explicitly intended to help her save time while simultaneously dictating exactly how she was supposed to use that time. Carvalho's re-creation of Lispector's columns underlines in its anachronism the artificiality of a narrative that responded to "bourgeois rules of respectability," as Jack J. Halberstam calls it (5), a linear temporal sequence punctuated by birth, marriage, and reproduction. In fact, we see the characters going through life-changing crises associated with these three landmarks. It is no coincidence that the women's pages of the period insist on fostering virtues such as caution and moderation in their female readership, advocating controlled behaviors and admonishing against excess or overreaction. Notions of respectability for the readers of these pages are predicated on a normative performance of gender that is in turn sustained by a "middle-class logic of reproductive temporality" (4). These technologies of gender make themselves ever more powerful through advertising and marketing strategies. Helen Palmer, whose voice is the only one we hear throughout the TV episodes, also delivers advice through the Internet website specifically created for the program, where viewers/readers can leave questions, concerns, comments, and opinions. Now, as previously, technologies mold women's lives in accordance with strictly heteronormative patterns.

"Just for Women" in *Diário da Noite* is itself built upon a marketing dynamic; the picture of iconic Ilka Soares evokes beauty standards imported into Brazil through Hollywood movies in the 1940s and is used to foster copycat tendencies in the audience. Nevertheless, the column is once again slightly destabilized as Lispector/Soares warns the reader in the following terms: "Cuidado com a moda. Ela é uma generalidade, e você é um individuo, isto é alguem muito particular" (Be careful with fashion. It is a generalization, and you are an individual, that is, someone special) ("Nossa Conversa" [Our Conversation] 22). As if gesturing intertextually to this statement, "Ladies' Mail" in *Correio da Manhã* pronounces similar words of caution, but takes the warning further to address explicitly readers' tendencies to aspire to become carbon copies of Brigitte Bardot, Gina Lollobrigida, Marilyn Monroe, or Ilka Soares ("Cultive A Sua Personalidade" [Cultivate Your Personality]). It is possible to argue that both "Ladies' Mail" and "Just for Women" are parodying themselves. The two sections are also carbon copies of other comparable columns and pages in similar publications; their content is apparently the same. Nevertheless, it is precisely the ways in which this content is performed within Lispector's columns, put into action and mobilized, that reveal the imposture. Irony, as the characteristic trope of parody, is, paraphrasing Linda Hutcheon, what allows for the simultaneous interiorization of a norm and its deviation ("Ironía, sátira, parodia" [Irony, Satire, Parody] 177).[5] This duplicity is seen also in the dynamic that parody sets in motion via irony as it demands the presence of a reader who is at once complicit enough to recognize herself in the situations enacted by the column but distant enough to engage in critical reflection (Hutcheon, *Theory of Parody* 32). Subtle rhetorical displacements triggered by the tension between conflicting and contradictory meanings punctuate the discursive spaces assembled by Lispector for the women's page between 1959 and 1961. As these spaces are dislocated, the heteronormative ideology underlying them is also disrupted, even if temporarily, to hint at a potential queer temporality, a potential deviation or rebellion for the middle-class readers prone to identify with Lispector and her doubles. The women's pages fashioned by the famous Brazilian writer thus manage to circumvent the normalization and systematization typically governing this discursive space.

While it is true that exaggeration as the characteristic trope of all transvestism runs the risk of becoming mere parody, a meaning that is in fact present in its own etymological origin, Lispector's gesture does not remain caught up in pure imitation for its own sake. Rather, there is in her writing for these spaces a surreptitious disruption of the imitative sequence, an unsettling disturbance of the motions repeated ad infinitum. I want to argue, then, that her imitative act can be seen as strategic and deliberate, a pointed, opportune transgression that has political potential insofar as it is the result of a specific tactical operation, and not just direct corollary of mere reiteration. The resulting tension reveals that heteronormative representations of gender have not gained their full inscription. In his study of transvestism and Latin American literature, Ben Sifuentes-Jáuregui argues that "transvestism does not always necessarily mean 'crossing the divide' of gender difference. In some cases, [it] is about 'affirming' gender by performing one's own" (196). Like the transvestite's act that exposes what is culturally constructed as feminine or masculine, Lispector's pages designed "just for women" overemphasize what is fabricated as "feminine" and, in so doing, expose the artificiality not merely of the copy but also of the original. The writer's habit of recycling the content of her stories and chronicles, a habit that she carried into her writing for the women's pages, confirms the impossibility of distinction between the two terms of the binary. Recipes migrate from one column to another, evoking the transvestite skills of recycling and reinterpreting, while pointing to the repetition at the core of every performative act. We find in these pages "the complex interplay, slippage and parodic recontextualization of gender markers" that Marjorie Garber perceives in the ritualized repetition of the transvestite fantasy (134). The columns' potential to insinuate a transvestite narrative, to offer a glimmer of an alternative queer temporality, is dependent upon the existence of a reader capable of decoding Lispector's apparently innocent discursive and rhetorical maneuvers, a reader not unlike that of her short stories of the 1940s and 1950s who was also made aware of the gender ideologies shaping their behavior. Lispector's performing columns betray a conscious act of thinking through what it means to read and write as a woman, helping destabilize mainstream conceptions of womanhood and becoming, against all odds, unpredictable spaces of potential cultural and political intervention.

disclosure statement

No potential conflict of interest was reported by the author.

notes

1 Among these more recent, innovative approaches to Lispector's work, it is worth mentioning Vilma Arêas's *Clarice Lispector com A Ponta dos Dedos* (2005), in which she describes these "marginal" texts of Lispector's as written "with the tips of the fingers," as the title indicates, rushed, as it were, and, in Arêas's opinion, simultaneously avant-garde and under-developed. *A Doméstica Imaginária*, published by Sônia Roncador in 2008, also offers an original interpretation of Lispector's work as it devotes an entire chapter to an analysis of the figure of the maid in part of the writer's literary and journalistic production.

2 In an interview with Editora Rocco, the publishing house responsible for bringing out the two collections *Correio Feminino* and *Só para Mulheres* mentioned above, Aparecida Maria Nunes explains Lispector's consistent use of pseudonyms as a columnist with these words:

> [Clarice] was afraid of compromising her literary production with the less elaborate texts for the newspapers. According to her family, Clarice even wanted to keep her activity as a writer parallel to or separate from her activity as a journalist, even fearing she would confuse her readers. Because of that, she would sign her journalistic texts with a pseudonym. ("Entrevista com Aparecida Nunes, organizadora de Só para mulheres," *Editora Rocco Online* (accessed 1 Apr. 2012))

All translations from Portuguese into English are my own.

3 In this respect, it is important to remember that it was not until 1943 that Brazilian legislation granted women permission to work outside the home without the husband's express authorization (Scott 23).

4 See *Minhas Queridas*, a collection of 120 letters exchanged between Clarice Lispector and her sisters Tania Kaufmann and Elisa Lispector between 1940 and 1957, edited by Teresa Montero.

5 This article was originally published in number 45 of *Poétique*, Ed. du Seuil. The translation quoted here is by Pilar Hernández Cobos from the book *De la ironía a lo grotesco*.

bibliography

Arêas, Vilma. *Clarice com a Ponta dos Dedos*. São Paulo: Companhia das Letras, 2005. Print.

Bassanezi, Carla. "Mulheres dos Anos Dourados." *História das Mulheres no Brasil*. Ed. Mary del Priore and Carla Bassanezi. São Paulo: UNESP–Contexto, 1997. 607–39. Print.

Buitoni, Dulcília H. Schroeder. *Imprensa Feminina*. São Paulo: Ática, 1986. Print.

Buitoni, Dulcília H. Schroeder. *Mulher de Papel: A Representação da Mulher pela Imprensa Feminina Brasileira*. São Paulo: Loyola, 1981. Print.

Ferreira-Pinto Bailey, Cristina. "Clarice Lispector e a Crítica." *Clarice Lispector: Novos Aportes Críticos*. Ed. Cristina Ferreira-Pinto Bailey and Regina Zilberman. Serio Antonio Cornejo Polar 4. Pittsburgh: Instituto Internacional de Literatura Iberoamericana, 2007. 7–23. Print.

Garber, Marjorie. *Vested Interests: Cross-Dressing and Cultural Anxiety*. 3rd ed. New York: Routledge, 2011. Print.

Halberstam, J. Jack. *In a Queer Time and Place: Transgender Bodies, Subcultural Lives*. New York: New York UP, 2005. Print.

Hutcheon, Linda. "Ironía, sátira, parodia: Una aproximación pragmática a la ironía." *De la ironía a lo grotesco (en algunos textos literarios hispanoamericanos)*. Iztapalapa, Mexico: U Autónoma Metropolitana, 1992. 173–93. Print.

Hutcheon, Linda. *A Theory of Parody*. New York: Methuen, 1985. Print.

Lispector, Clarice. "Beleza é Cuidado e Perseverança." *Correio da Manhã* 23 Nov. 1959, 2° Caderno: 5. Print.

Lispector, Clarice. *Correio Feminino*. Ed. Aparecida Maria Nunes. Rio de Janeiro: Rocco, 2006. Print.

Lispector, Clarice. "Cultive A Sua Personalidade." *Correio da Manhã* 18 Nov. 1959, 2° Caderno: 5. Print.

Lispector, Clarice. *A Descoberta do Mundo*. Rio de Janeiro: Rocco, 1984. Print.

Lispector, Clarice. "A Grande Compradora." *Correio da Manhã* 8 July 1960, 2° Caderno: 5. Print.

Lispector, Clarice. "Limpe A Sua Pele Diariamente." *Correio da Manhã* 16 Sept. 1959, 2° Caderno: 5. Print.

Lispector, Clarice. *Minhas Queridas*. Ed. Teresa Montero. Rio de Janeiro: Rocco, 2007. Print.

Lispector, Clarice. "Nossa Conversa." *Diário da Noite* 4 May 1960: 22. Print.

Lispector, Clarice. "Nova Maneira de Prender Marido." *Correio da Manhã* 7 Oct. 1959, 2° Caderno: 5. Print.

Lispector, Clarice. "O que Os Homens Não Gostam." *Correio da Manhã* 7 Oct. 1959, 2° Caderno: 5. Print.

Lispector, Clarice. "Ser Feia." *Correio da Manhã* 23 Oct. 1959, 2° Caderno: 5. Print.

Lispector, Clarice. "Seu Andar." *Correio da Manhã* 16 Sept. 1959, 2° Caderno: 5. Print.

Lispector, Clarice. "Só para Mulheres." *Jornal do Brasil* 30 May 1970: 2. Print.

Lispector, Clarice. *Só para Mulheres – Conselhos, Receitas e Segredos*. Ed. Aparecida Maria Nunes. Rio de Janeiro: Rocco, 2008. Print.

Lispector, Clarice. "Você e Eu nas Compras." *Diário da Noite* 25 June 1960: 13. Print.

Lispector, Clarice. "Voz Irresistível." *Correio da Manhã* 23 Oct. 1959, 2° Caderno: 5. Print.

Nunes, Aparecida Maria. *Clarice Lispector Jornalista: Páginas Femininas e Outras Páginas*. São Paulo: SENAC, 2006. Print.

Roncador, Sônia. *A Doméstica Imaginária: Literatura, Testemunhos e a Invenção da Empregada Doméstica no Brasil (1888–1999)*. Brasília: Editora U de Brasília, 2008. Print.

Scott, Ana Silvia. "O Caleidoscópio dos Arranjos Familiares." *Nova História das Mulheres no Brasil*. Ed. Carla Bassanezi Pinsky and Joana Maria Pedro. São Paulo: Contexto, 2012. 15–42. Print.

Sifuentes-Jáuregui, Ben. *Transvestism, Masculinity, and Latin American Literature: Genders Share Flesh*. New York: Palgrave, 2002. Print.

Wolfe, Joel. "From Working Mothers to Housewives: Gender and Brazilian Populism from Getúlio Vargas to Juscelino Kubitschek." *Gender and Populism in Latin America: Passionate Politics*. Ed. Karen Kampwirth. University Park: Pennsylvania State UP, 2010. 91–109. Print.

alison winch

"DOES FEMINISM HAVE A GENERATION GAP?"

blogging, millennials and the hip hop generation

This article explores a number of instances when generation is invoked and discussed in three feminist blogs: the UK *The Vagenda* (2012–), the US-based *Crunk Feminist Collective* (2010), and the UK *Feminist Times* (2013–14).[1] More specifically, it examines how generation is discussed in terms of a feminist identity, especially in relation to intergenerational conflict. I contextualize a textual analysis of these blogs within a conjunctural and intersectional understanding of generation. That is, I look at how these narratives of intergenerational feminism are produced or emerge from specific UK and US historical conditions, and the organization of social forces within them. I also look at how they map on to popular media discourses about generation. In addition, this article explores the ways in which generational identity intersects with categories of race, gender, class, sexuality and place.

I have chosen these three blogs because they usefully intervene in and illustrate key concerns around generation, intersectionality, and coming of age in the neoliberal conjuncture. Significantly, none of these sites are funded through advertising or brand sponsorship, and in this way their online practice is coterminous with their feminist politics. However, the obstacles that online feminist writers and editors face in corporate-run digital spaces are part of the subject of this article. *The Vagenda* blog is pertinent because the editors are white, heterosexual "millennials" who articulate a new brand of feminism that is distinct from what they characterize as a privileged (and implicitly white) previous wave. Located in London, UK (although not originally from there), they partly speak to and against a popular feminine metropolitan culture. In contrast, *Crunk Feminist Collective* are US based and define themselves as belonging to the "Hip Hop generation." They are part of a growing network of feminists of colour who advocate for and develop intersectional theory by blogging, including *Colorlines*, *The Feminist Wire*, *Racialicious*, *Black Girl Dangerous* and *Janet Mock's Blog* (see Collins and Bilge 106). *Crunk Feminist Collective* situate their feminist politics within the context of a white supremacist neoliberal landscape, and the representation of their generational identities explicitly intersects with other axes of oppression. For these reasons, this blog is a productive case study in relation to *The Vagenda*, whose generational identities are articulated quite differently. Finally, *Feminist Times*, which I focus on to a lesser extent than the other two blogs, presents itself more as an online magazine. It ran for less than a year but is worthy of analysis because, as a feminist enterprise which pays its contributors, it could not compete financially within branded and corporate-run digital spaces.

why generation?

Generation is a slippery concept. It is used by politicians and policy makers, as well as the mainstream media, to decentre issues such as class and race. For example, the characters of the millennial and the baby-boomer circulate in the mainstream media, particularly in the United States and the United Kingdom, in order to personify certain ideologically driven anxieties about contemporary culture (Little). Those who were born on or before 1980 and are coming of age in the neoliberal era are conventionally known as Generation Y, or the millennials. They are often constructed as narcissists who are pathologically obsessed with social media and high-end brands. Simultaneously they are represented as suffering from the selfishness of the post-war baby-boomer generation who have apparently contributed to rising house prices, job scarcity, and other socio-economic obstacles that hamper young people's trajectory into adulthood. This is evident in such inflammatory book titles as David Willetts' *The Pinch: How the Baby Boomers Took Their Children's Future – And Why They Should Give it Back* (2010) and Neil Boorman's *It's All Their Fault* (2010). Generation is also employed to scaffold inaccurate and often politically charged historical narratives. This is evident, for example, in the framing of feminist history as an evolutionary series of waves (Hemmings). Furthermore, within feminist contexts, it can invoke sameness. In other words, a blanket theory of generation assumes that feminists born around the same date have similar experiences of gendered oppression, regardless of race, class, sexuality, place or disability.

Despite these critiques, this article also argues for the productivity of thinking through and with the category of generation. In other words, it is useful to examine the various ways in which generation is talked about and deployed, particularly in the media. Furthermore, I want to suggest that generation can be a powerful analytical and intersectional tool. This is especially the case when we use the concept of generation alongside the framework of the conjuncture. Thinking about generation within what Doreen Massey – following Antonio Gramsci – calls a "conjunctural analysis" is fruitful, because it locates generational identities within the context of wider, and often contradictory, social and historical forces. In Massey's words, "A conjunctural approach leads us to examine the movements of the different instances in a social formation" (Massey 102). The conjuncture is partly about periodization, but it also understands historical change as contingent, conflicting and partial. Because of this, a conjunctural analysis does not frame history as evolutionary or predetermined. This renders the framework useful when applied to narratives about feminist generations as it understands history as being open to political actors, thus offering opportunities for intervention.

This conjunctural analysis of feminist generations is located within an intersectional understanding of identity. In other words, the concept of generation has explanatory force when making sense of identity categories, but it only does so when read alongside other vectors of oppression such as race, class, sexuality, place, and disability. For example, much of the mainstream media discourse about baby-boomers and millennials focuses on white middle-class generational identities which are located primarily in the United States and the United Kingdom. This has the effect of erasing experiences of, for example, working-class young people or young people of colour who do not fit in to the mainstream media characterization of the millennial. Simultaneously, generational location can intensify someone's experience of other intersecting forms of oppression: *when* you're born does matter. As Patricia Hill Collins and Sirma Bilge argue, "Race, class, gender, and citizenship categories disadvantage many groups under neoliberal policies, yet, because age straddles all of these categories, young people's experiences of social problems are more intensified" (Collins and Bilge 117). Collins and Bilge focus on age rather than generation because they are discussing the contemporary neoliberal moment. As I discuss towards the end of this article, age and generation can be thought of as different but related categories.

In addition, I locate the textual analysis of these blogs within the discipline of women's writing, and note the affordances as well as the misunderstandings that can occur when writing feminism online. Digital feminisms are sometimes framed as radically different from previous generational articulations of feminism. However, as Jessalynn Keller argues in the context of girl blogging in the United States, online activist blogging is part of a lengthy tradition of feminist media production (Keller 2). Even though the networked site of the blog, as well as the fact that it is in constant process, forges a distinct type of feminist conversation and politics, there are still continuities as well as conversations with earlier feminist writing; although this might depend on how the bloggers forge and represent their generational identities. In addition, the writers and editors of these online sites practise their feminisms in online and offline spaces so I am keen not to offer a reductive analysis which celebrates a new kind of online feminism, one which is ontologically distinct from what can only be an imagined narrative of a coherent feminist past.

Rosi Braidotti's description of feminist timelines as "zigzagging" is pertinent here as I am also critical of using linearity as conceptual tool to define intergenerational feminisms (Braidotti 4). Nevertheless, this article argues that the relative newness of these media platforms for feminist activism and consciousness-raising raises fascinating questions. How does participating within what critics call the networked society enable, transform, inflect or circumscribe the ways in which feminists can write to and about each other? How does the platform of the blog or online magazine affect the kinds of dialogues that feminists can have? How do feminists write in tension with pervasive branded cultures? This article explores conversations that these feminists hold around generation, it locates digital feminist writing as both a continuation of and as distinct from other modes of writing feminism, and it examines the productivity of looking at how historical periods shape one's feminist politics and what effect this might have on intergenerational dialogue.

feminist generations

Feminism is frequently talked about in terms of generation, both by feminists and the mainstream media. It is often framed as intergenerational conflict by deploying the familial metaphors of mothers and daughters – or more recently grandmothers (Walker; Henry). The wave metaphor is sometimes invoked in order to distinguish different generations of feminists: from the suffragettes, through the "second-wave" Women's Liberation movement in the 1970s, to the "third wave" in the 1990s, culminating in the contemporary resurgence in feminist activism, which has been called by some commentators the "fourth wave" (Cochrane). However, the use of waves to describe the multiplicity of feminist activism through history has been critiqued. Erin Sanders McDonagh and Elena Vacchelli argue that the "concept of temporal 'waves' of feminism serves to create a version of feminist activity that is presented as monolithic, and neatly ensconced in a clearly defined and delineated period of time." They maintain that temporal metaphors should be replaced by "a more geographic understanding of feminist activism" (Sanders McDonagh and Vacchelli).

The wave metaphor is also viewed problematically by Kimberly Springer ("Third Wave") who asserts that the wave analogy is untenable when thinking about black feminist activism; it obscures the historical role of race in women's organizing during the antebellum and abolitionist periods, as well as in the civil rights movement. Springer suggests that for black feminists, "The recuperation of the self in a racist and sexist society is a political enterprise and a Black feminist one that deprioritizes generational differences in the interest of historical, activist continuity" (Springer, "Third Wave" 1061). Moreover, the narrative of waves has functioned to whitewash feminist histories. Within a queer feminist context, Jack Halberstam argues that casting conflict "in the mother–daughter bond" is "transhistorical, transcultural, universal," and that it ignores "the instability of gender norms, the precarious condition of the family itself" as well as "the many challenges made to generational logics within a recent wave of queer theory on temporality" (Halberstam). In her interviews with self-defined radical feminists, Finn McKay argues that because women of different ages identify with radical feminism so conflicts between feminists should be discussed in terms of political differences rather than generational ones, and Rosalind Gill argues that framing feminism in generational terms seems "to risk pulling us back into polarized positions characterized by mistrust and suspicion on both sides (and why are there always only two sides, rather than three or four generations?)" (Gill 612).

When feminists criticize each other using generation, these instances are often picked up in the mainstream media and exploited. For example, the media report and foreground moments when feminists disparage each other, homing in on instances of generational hostility in order to amplify them. Using the trope of the catfight between women of different ages is a key way in which feminism is depicted as it is effective in locating feminism in the past, as no longer relevant, while simultaneously framing differences between activists as insurmountable (McRobbie). This has the function of personalizing feminist politics, locating it in the private sphere. Moreover, domesticating feminism in this way means that political difference is recast as a bicker or a row, rather than the performance of adversarial politics; adversarial politics being (still) a legitimate male performance. This is not to say that feminists themselves do not use generation as a call to arms. Indeed, generation is debated in different ways in all three blogs that I am looking at here.

the vagenda and millennial feminism

The UK blog *The Vagenda* (hereafter referenced as TV) is run by two friends in their twenties, Holly Baxter and Rhiannon Lucy Coslett, who work out of their kitchens. *The Vagenda* is a satirical take on women's magazines, an industry where both Baxter and Coslett have interned. The tagline for their blog is "King Lear for girls" and in their editorial they state that

> It is not, as the tagline says, like King Lear for girls (that is just a quote we nicked from Grazia that was so CRINGE – as they'd put it – that we totes had to use it, tbh). What the Vagenda is is a big "we call bullshit" on the mainstream women's press. (TV, "A Letter from the Editor")

They appropriate the hyperbolic language of postfeminism as circulated in women's magazines in order to critique and disrupt the power of the magazines themselves, as well as the branded landscape of the neoliberal girl and its feminine constructions (Negra; Winch). But what they call their "sweary" feminism is also part of a counter-discursive "loud, proud, sarcastic" feminist sensibility used by young online feminists (see Keller 76). *The Vagenda* writes about issues as diverse as female Shakespeare characters, through to marriage and abortion, but its main source of material is popular culture, and more specifically magazines targeting a female demographic.

Internships, working out of the kitchen, feminist blogging and the postfeminist media landscape are typical of what the mainstream media represent as the millennial experience, and this precarity is key to *The Vagenda*'s articulation of a new kind of feminism that is distinct from that practised by "our elders" (TV, "Girl Trouble"). The period that partly enabled the conditions of UK and US feminism in the 1960s onwards was defined by the welfare state, public ownership and wealth distribution through taxes. Those born in the United

Kingdom and the United States after the Second World War – particularly if they were white and middle class – had more political representation in mainstream politics, partly because of the demographic bulge at this time but also because of the influence of the 1960s countercultural movement, as well as the supportive framework of the social democratic conjuncture. In contrast to this, young people forming their political consciousness under neoliberalism are alienated from the political process and tend not to vote, with the result being that the government can ignore them in terms of state aid, thus alienating them still further. The terrain where the so-called millennial generation forges their feminism is influenced by these contradictions. For example, in the United Kingdom these young people are witnessing the breakdown of the NHS, dwindling and insecure pensions, the withdrawal of state aid in the form of higher tuition fees, the imposition of bedroom tax, decreased levels of housing benefit and the withdrawal of Education Maintenance Allowances. At the same time they are caught up in circuits of debt and what David Graeber calls "bullshit jobs." *The Vagenda*'s depiction of precarious working lives, as well as its resentment towards older feminists, is partly a result of being young in this neoliberal conjuncture.

The Vagenda asks: "Does feminism have a generation gap? And is that a problem?" (TV, "Girl Trouble"). It explicitly locates itself as a "new wave" and it pits this against a more austere one:

> One of the things I love (and I mean LOVE) about this new wave of feminism, is that it features a range of women campaigning on different, varied issues. A war on many fronts, if you will. I see it as progress, as the feminist movement moving on from a time where you were essentially supposed to sign up to some kind of bullshit feminist charter in order to join the club. (TV, "I am Sexy")

Feminism is cast here teleologically, moving from a "bullshit feminist charter" and exclusive "club" to a freer, wittier and more plural feminism. The editors note that as young women they experience generational hostility from older feminists: "As writers of *The Vagenda* book, we (and from what our friends/colleagues say, young feminists in particular) have come to see being criticised by our elders as an occupational hazard when writing about women's issues" (TV, "Girl Trouble"). One contributor to *The Vagenda* with the initials "VH" (*The Vagenda* does not credit its authors with full names) writes in another post:

> Here's a manifesto I can get on board with: feminism isn't a sliding scale. You don't get rated out of 10 or have to sit an oral exam at the end of it. So just do whatever the fuck in your noble quest for gender equality, and don't attack other ~~women~~ people for doing the same. (TV, "How to Tell")

In *The Vagenda* blog we can see how wider historical shifts, which are personified in the mainstream media by the characters of the baby-boomer and the millennial, are mapped on to feminist generations. More specifically, the so-called second-wave feminist is framed as coterminous with the apparently privileged and selfish post-war baby-boomer. Significantly, *The Vagenda* pits its "new" feminism against one that is imbued with class privilege and as benefiting from a more robust public sector:

> Much of this criticism (well, what which [*sic*] didn't come from journalists who completely coincidentally ALSO WRITE FOR WOMEN'S MAGAZINES) came from middle class women in their late middle age who were lucky enough to have benefited from much feminist consciousness-raising when they were attending their progressive Russell Group Universities – talk to a state school educated girl who grew up in the feminist vacuum of the nineties (hiya!) and it is, of course, a different story. (TV, "On Bikini Body Bullshit")

Second-wave feminism is located in a distinctly different and more fortunate era and is being produced and performed in the spaces of elite universities. These opportunities are framed as being denied to young feminists today.

Significantly, a conjunctural analysis can productively excavate the antagonism that is being enacted here. It can widen the field of vision so that the conflict does not have to be between older and younger feminists but can be seen as part of a larger shift in social and historical forces. Indeed, this characterization of the old and young feminist in conflict dovetails with popular media discourses about the selfish baby-boomer generation, the prudish second-wave feminist, and the betrayal of one generation by another. It glosses over specific and often contradictory historical conditions, and how they impact differently on different people, thus deflecting from an effective critique of patriarchal power structures.

blogging poetics

Random House published *The Vagenda: A Zero Tolerance Guide to the Media* in 2014, and it received unfavourable reviews in the mainstream press. (The front cover sports a supportive tagline from Jeanette Winterson which demonstrates that not all "elders" turned against Baxter and Coslett.) In fact, the book's reviewers – typically it was women who were tasked with doing the write-ups – were of different ages. However, and significantly, Germaine Greer condemned the book in the *New Statesman*, casting its writers as "two young experts" who "yelp" their hyperbole but who reveal "a level of ignorance that is positively medieval" (Greer). Asking Greer to review the book could have been a tactical manoeuvre by the magazine's online editors as she is frequently used to invoke a nostalgic feminism. Moreover, she can be relied upon to critique other feminists, thereby depicting both herself and those under attack as ridiculous. Because she has come to stand in for second-wave feminism – a clearly ahistorical positioning – she is symbolically harnessed as a divisive means to mock the feminist movement.

Part of the problem that *The Vagenda* faced when its book was reviewed, and which was not foregrounded, was that its writing originated in the blogosphere and its popularity sprang from a connection with this digital genre. Despite this, its publication was put under the journalistic scrutiny usually given to a traditional book, and which did not pay attention to the ways in which a blog – unlike the relatively static medium of the book – can become untethered from its host website and flow through social media networks. *The Vagenda*, like all blogs, is networked; it is in constant process. Its content is frequently updated, amended, commented upon, reworked. Furthermore, the design, layout, embedded links, and comments are intrinsic to the ways in which digital feminisms are read, as well as influencing how they are written. A blog can function as a hub and in this way can facilitate dialogue between multiple sites. Indeed, *The Vagenda*'s writing is specific to a "networked counterpublic" of feminist activists, and this is quite a different form of communication from journalism, essay-writing, non-fiction or even a feminist newsletter (Keller).

Hosted by the free platform Wordpress, the editors upload posts which are later archived and still accessible. Simultaneously they microblog on feminist issues using Twitter. They have a comment function which is open to all so that there are loops of feedback which in turn affect the activism they practise; their writing is part of a larger digital feminist conversation. Their language is the brash, sarcastic and "sweary" language of some digital feminisms that talk back to postfeminist popular culture by using and amplifying its tone, partly to render the object of their critique absurd. It also creates affective links between feminists who are both beguiled but also oppressed by the power of women's magazines. Their blog needs to be understood as part of the online feminist "phatic economy" (Miller). That is, a networked feminist consciousness is performed online through such contentless activity as the "like" button and pokes, as well as retweeting, links, memes, giffs; the objective is to be social as well as to share information. Furthermore, as women in their twenties, Baxter and Coslett are also operating in a precarious labour market where they must continuously promote themselves to garner attention and receive freelance paid work. In a creative economy, labour is largely dependent upon using strategies of self-branding, and blogging is a way to cultivate recognition from potential employers. Indeed, *The Vagenda* attributes its subsequent work for the mainstream press, television and other media outlets directly to its blog.

These are all partly generational issues as younger feminists are more likely to develop their feminist consciousness online through blogs and social media. This is not to say that older feminists do not converse or strategize digitally, but they are more likely to have forged their feminist consciousness in a considerably different media environment. Significantly, coming of age in a new conjuncture – including its mediated landscape – does impact upon one's political identity, but in uneven and heterogeneous ways. Andra Siibak and Nicoletta Vittadini, following the sociologist Karl Mannheim, theorize the process of "generationing." They argue that generationing is

> founded on historical events and the socio-techno-cultural milieu experienced in the formative years, as well as the development of the narrative of collective memories and frames of interpretation of "times"; and rituals and habits developed during the following stages of life. (Siibak and Vittadini 3)

It is important to note that this process of generationing is not homogeneous. That is, not all young people coming of age in the neoliberal conjuncture harness the same collective memories or even have the same access to media. Because of this, understanding feminist identities in terms of generation has its limitations; that is unless we intersect the category of generation with other vectors of oppression. In addition, using digital media is often overemphasized in discussions of feminist generations. It is important to keep in mind that there are continuities in modes of feminist media production through different conjunctures; that feminist activism takes place in both online and offline contexts; and that there are differences in contemporary online participation among generational peers. The discussion of Hip Hop generation feminism below is an attempt to illuminate these synchronic generational differences.

crunk feminist collective and hip hop generation feminism

Crunk Feminist Collective (hereafter referenced as CFC) is a resource "for hip hop generation feminists of color, queer and straight, in the academy and without." Its members aim to create

> a community of scholars–activists from varied professions, who share our intellectual work in online blog communities, at conferences, through activist organizations, and in print publications and who share our commitment to nurturing and sustaining one another through progressive feminist visions. (CFC, "Mission Statement")

A hub for social justice organizing, *Crunk Feminist Collective*'s members explicitly define themselves generationally, rather than in waves. This is in order to ally themselves with the Hip Hop generation of social justice activists, as well as being an implicit rejection of the narrative of feminist waves. Situated within the Hip Hop generation, *Crunk Feminist Collective*'s members assert their intersectional politics and identities as feminists of colour, as well as noting how they have "come of age" in the neoliberal era: "our connection to Hip Hop links us to a set of generational concerns, and a community of women, locally, nationally, and globally" (CFC, "Hip Hop Generation Feminism").

In her discussion of youth of colour and activism, Adreana Clay explores the various ways in which Hip Hop is a key component in the development of young people's political consciousness, noting that it is an organizing tool and an important cultural art form. Moreover, Clay identifies some of the crises and contradictions that young people coming of age in the Hip Hop era face, and distinguishes these from those shaping the historical and political terrain inhabited by a previous generation of activists. These contemporary contradictions include the fact that the legislative gains of the civil rights movement are set against the persistence of racial segregation and discrimination. White supremacist power structures are evident, for example, in the extreme violence of police surveillance as well as the prison industrial complex, not to speak of the vast discrepancies in wages and employment opportunities between youth of colour and white young people. Another generational issue facing Hip Hop generation activists is that they must mobilize "*in the shadow* of previous social movement activists" (Clay 7; author's emphasis), and that this "shadow" includes the mass commodification of the representations of these activists, such as T-shirts embossed with the face of Angela Davis. This "shadow" is evident in one of the discussions of intergenerational feminism in the *Crunk Feminist Collective* blog which I discuss below.

In contrast to *The Vagenda*, *Crunk Feminist Collective*'s writers define themselves most succinctly in relation to a feminist history. In their manifesto, they invoke their "feminist big sister Joan Morgan" who invited us to "'fill in the breaks, provide the remixes, and rework the chorus,'" but maintain:

> While our declaration of feminism pays homage to our feminist foremothers and big sisters, Hip Hop generation feminism is not just a remix but also a remake that builds on the beats and rhythms from the tracks already laid down, but with a decidedly new sound, for a new era. This, in other words, ain't ya mama's feminism. This is next generation feminism, standing up, standing tall, and proclaiming like Celie, that we are indeed Here. We are the ones we have been waiting for. (CFC, "Hip Hop Generation Feminism")

Significantly, the time in which they were born – which signifies their feminist identity by generation rather than wave – is crucial to the political thrust of *Crunk Feminist Collective*. Their concerns are specific to their generation and being women of colour in America:

> We are members of the Hip Hop Generation because we came of age in one of the decades, the 1990s, that can be considered post-Soul and post-Civil Rights. Our political realities have been profoundly shaped by a systematic rollback of the gains of the Civil Rights era with regard to affirmative action policies, reproductive justice policies, the massive deindustrialization of urban areas, the rise and ravages of the drug economy within urban, semi-urban, and rural communities of color, and the full-scale assault on women's lives through the AIDS epidemic. We have come of age in the era that has witnessed a past-in-present assault on our identities as women of color, one that harkens back to earlier assaults on our virtue and value during enslavement and imperialism. (Ibid.)

The members of *Crunk Feminist Collective* define themselves and their politics as part of a specific historical moment. Their feminism is exhilaratingly marked against the neoliberal white supremacist and patriarchal "past-in-present."

Crunk Feminist Collective's articulation of feminist generational difference can be understood in relation to the larger shifts taking place in some social justice activism among people of colour in the United States, particularly in relation to Black Lives Matter. In her article "Black Lives on Campuses Matter: The Rise of the New Black Student Movement" Khadija White discusses the ways in which Black Lives Matter is distinct "from previous iterations of Black activist periods, most notably the modern civil rights movement" (White 88). One of these differences is that Black Lives Matter is a network rather than a movement. This is key when thinking about blogging as feminist activism; the blog is always connected and in process rather than being a static entity. White argues that there are continuities with previous black activist movements but that Black Lives Matter is defined by a radical self-care as well as "strong female leadership, an insistence on inclusion, and, among some parts of the network, a repulsion of the 'respectability' politics that had been a core feature of civil rights organising" (89). In their ethnographic work on social justice work, generation and black women, Carolyn D. Love, Lize A.E. Booysen and Philomena

Essed note how younger women whom they interviewed in Colorado, whom they term "Millennials," were much more open to working with LGBTQ communities than the "Gen-Xers and Baby Boomers" (Love, Booysen, and Essed 12). This is also something that is key to *Crunk Feminist Collective*'s political organizing. As one blogpost maintains: "Heterosexism is a structural impediment. Patriarchy is a structural impediment. Cissexism is a structural impediment" (CFC, "Say No to Noteps").

The writers for *Crunk Feminist Collective* practise their feminism offline and online; they give talks, participate in protests, teach in universities, speak in churches, make films, among other political activities. Significantly, and unusually, there are no advertisements, pop-ups or brands sponsoring the site. This is a blog devoted to feminist activism without the compromises that inevitably come from having to refrain from talking about certain topics – sex, race and politics – in order to conform to the dictates of advertising companies. *Crunk Feminist Collective*'s site is maintained by donations (there is a click button for potential donors) and it is sponsored by Media Equity Collaborative. It is also crucial to locate the blog within a wider context of feminists of colour working towards social justice. *Crunk Feminist Collective*'s website has embedded links to Hip Hop artists, locating its feminist project within a broader generational culture that is not necessarily feminist but which shapes and reshapes feminist practice. By integrating links to Hip Hop artists, *Crunk Feminist Collective*'s members forge direct connections between the cultural forms that define their generational identity, as well as their writing. In addition, their content is inflected with Hip Hop – in its rhythms, lyrics, frequent intertextual allusions, and the socio-economic and generational terrain that is held in common. In their "Mission Statement" they define "crunk": "As part of a larger women-of-color feminist politic, crunkness, in its insistence on the primacy of the beat, contains a notion of movement, timing, and of meaning making through sound, that is especially productive for our work together" (CFC, "Mission Statement").

Participating in the online discussion around bell hooks calling Beyoncé a "terrorist," the black feminist theorist Brittney Cooper, writing for *Crunk Feminist Collective* as "Crunktastic," invokes the complexities of generational difference to explain her mixed response:

> [bell hooks and Cornel West] both make our work possible. But if the rhetoric continues, the two of them may also become a cautionary tale in what it means for revolutionaries not to age well. (Yeah, I said it.) And with regard to their speaker's fees, "I ain't sayin they golddiggers, but ... " (And check it: I think they should make their paper, because I don't believe revolutionaries should live in poverty.) Anyway, we are all just trying to find our way here. My generation of intellectuals definitely could benefit from a more radical edge to our critique. But if the argument is that we have to violently mow down our icons, leaving a trail of their blood on the way to this new "radicalism," then you can keep it. Because something about that sounds alarmingly like the patriarchal, black male-centered, radical Black radicalism of old. (CFC, "On bell, Beyoncé and Bullshit")

The writing delineates its contradictory responses: it is a homage to bell hooks; an allegiance to Beyoncé as black female cultural icon; a critique of the hierarchy of black academics indicated through their fees, gender and age; anxiety over "my generation's" radical politics; a treatise against neoliberalism, among other insights. Cooper reveals the structures of her intellectual and emotional working through of a painful intergenerational moment. The invoking of Black Southern culture, Hip Hop references, brackets, asides, interwoven with the language of academia, layer the palimpsest of this particular online black feminist rhetoric. Feminist generations are positioned as contradictory, shaped through miscommunication and difference, but also in process and open to conversation – both because they are networked and also because Cooper's response, which exposes its own paradoxes, is not closed.

Blogs are usually intensely personal and written in the first person. This mode of writing is amenable to black feminist autobiographical poetics as well as an intellectual politics that is grounded in experience. As Patricia Hill Collins argues, black feminist writing is less about mastering white male epistemologies than about "resisting the hegemonic nature of these patterns of thought in order to see, value, and use existing alternative Afrocentric feminist ways of knowing" (Collins 267–68). Cooper, writing for and with *Crunk Feminist Collective*, forges her own feminist writing located within the Hip Hop generation. Denied a consistent and prominent voice in the mainstream media, this is an example of radically networked media production.

digital feminist burnout

The founder of *Feminist Times* (hereafter referenced as FemT), Charlotte Raven, was born in 1969 and therefore would be understood in the mainstream media's framing of generation as a "Gen-Xer." This term was coined by Douglas Coupland in his book *Generation X: Tales for an Accelerated Culture* (1991). This generation is demographically smaller than the millennials and the baby-boomers – the two generations it is represented as being sandwiched between – and consequently attracts less coverage in the media. However, as with the categories of baby-boomer and millennial this particular generational grouping is problematic, not least because the dating of generational cohorts is inconsistent. Moreover, *Feminist Times* does not define itself generationally as its writers are of diverse ages and from different generational categories. *Feminist Times* offers a "pluralist platform for the stories and women often sidelined by the major magazines and newspapers" (FemT, "About Us"). The online magazine has an art director and the website is professionally and colourfully designed. Like *Crunk Feminist Collective* and *The Vagenda*, it is a brand-free space; its tagline is "life not lifestyle." It aims to address issues of age, generation, race, disability, sexuality, trans identity, among others, while seeking (and paying) feminists with a multiplicity of identity formations to write for them.

Pertinent to this article, and in particular to the intergenerational antagonisms invoked by Greer and *The Vagenda*, is a piece by Lynne Segal on ageing feminists. Segal notes how feminist movements have always alienated older women:

> In this country the Older Feminist Network was founded in 1982 by feminists, who felt that the women's liberation movement took little notice of them or the challenges they faced as women in an ageist culture (including, so it seemed, the women's movement itself). (Segal, "Who's Afraid of Old Age?")

Age can be a structure of oppression in a different way from generation. In other words, whereas being born in the United Kingdom or United States after 1980 means that – dependent on social class and other intersecting factors – one has less state support than those born before, women born post-war must contend with ageism in the workplace and the fetishization of youth as beauty. Even if some of them might hold a relatively fortunate position in relation to pensions or home ownership, they still face public erasure. Segal argues, in relation to ageing women, that these "frightening figures are not incidentally female, but quintessentially so, seen as monstrous because of the combination of age and gender" (ibid.).

Feminist Times was embroiled in what might seem like an intergenerational conflict. Raven wanted to revitalize the feminist magazine *Spare Rib* (1972–93) by appropriating its name. However, this resulted in a legal dispute with *Spare Rib*'s founders, Marsha Rowe and Rosie Boycott. Reading Rowe's and Boycott's position in *The Guardian* and in their blog, alongside Raven's narrative of the case, it seems that the conflict was not so much about generation as about misunderstandings, missed communications and miscommunication. It is pertinent to note, however, the different ways in which *Spare Rib* and *Feminist Times* were funded, and how this links to a conjunctural analysis of generation. *Spare Rib* (which is now available through the British Library's digital archives) was partly funded by the Greater London Council. It also had a price tag for each issue. That is, it was not free or expected to be free because it was a print magazine, competing in the print magazine market. Furthermore, it was able to exist because of the counter-hegemonic project of municipal socialism. *Feminist Times*, however, exists in the corporate spaces of digital culture where the assumption is that things are free. Of course, like much offline writing, online content is not free. Google's and Facebook's shareholders must be paid with users' content and users' data which are sold on to third-party organizations.

Branded spaces benefit from the unpaid labour of users who participate in the creation of content, as well as offering up lucrative data (Taylor). This inevitably feeds into issues of funding and ethical dilemmas about how to sustain a website and forge feminist connections while being dependent on business and advertisers. Feminists campaign against the ways in which corporations exploit people and land for profit, so how can they rely on these companies to fund their projects? *Feminist Times* (which, like *The Vagenda*, was kitchen based) funded itself through crowdfunding and a membership policy which was generated through direct debits. Importantly, it was committed to paying contributors. However, because it refused to compromise its politics, it was forced to "put the project on ice." It was not able to continue the project while being "both ethical and sustainable" (FemT, "Feminist Times: My Feminist Times 'Journey'").

Similarly, in July 2015 *The Vagenda* posted that it was having a "summer hiatus," and there have been no blogs since then, although the website is still live. It is noteworthy that *The Vagenda* is open to contributors but, partly because it is not funded by public- or third-sector bodies or by advertising, does not offer money or employment. *The Vagenda*'s editors cite the fact that "it's a lot of work. It's a full time job, actually, and one that we're not actually paid for. And that is part of the problem – the amount of time this blog needs is not time that either of the two of us can afford." Situating themselves within a community of "feminist labour" they state that "you're in it for love, not for money":

> And we are tired. We are ever so, ever so tired, and in order to prevent the burnout that afflicts so many feminist writers and to quote our mothers: we need a lie down. (TV, "We Need a Lie Down")

Inevitably feminist writing takes place online and offline and there needs to be a funding infrastructure so that feminists can be paid to write, as well as do the inevitable administration involved in sustaining a website. These case studies are evidence that sustainable and ethical models of online publishing that do not rely on corporate sponsorship, PR, or advertising revenue, and where work is remunerated, are essential. In the neoliberal conjuncture there is an ideological belief that not-for-profit political organizations and collectives should give away their labour without a fee, while corporations' bottom line is to make profit, in this case from the networked society's participatory culture. Nevertheless, the writers of the blogs discussed here are not remunerated for their blogging labour. This is clearly an untenable situation leading to frequent online feminist burnout (Martin and Valenti; Loza). Interestingly, both *Feminist Times* and *The Vagenda* participated in *Elle* magazine's feminist rebranding exercise for *Elle*'s November 2013 issue. Working with advertising companies as well as *Elle*, both blogs created brief campaign logos designed to flow through social media. For Baxter and Coslett this was a positive experience. However, Raven found this a deeply uncomfortable exercise that revealed how far magazines like *Elle* were circumscribed and held to account by commercial enterprises. For Raven it demonstrated how far brand domination inevitably stifles politics and creativity.

Another crucial issue facing digital feminisms is archival. Feminist writing is part of the creation of feminism; it constructs, in Kimberly Springer's words, "*our* reality" (Springer, "Radical Archives"; author's emphasis).

Springer argues, in relation to her worries about leaving the preservation of activist material to corporations like Facebook: "This shaping and documenting of *our* reality means that activists are building a foundation *today* that will allow future organizers to not have to reinvent the wheel" (ibid.; author's emphasis). Working towards a more ethical way of hosting and enabling online feminist writing is also a means to preserve memory for future activists. Protecting feminist archives is fundamental because they have the valuable potential to run counter to the mainstream media's one-dimensional and divisive feminist narrative. They would allow for the plurality of feminist collective writing to be accessible. Claire Colebrook maintains that "any feminist claim in our present is in harmony and dissonance with a choir of past voices" and we read a feminist text "not according to the time within which it occurred but to a time it might enable" (Colebrook 14, 13). It is for this reason, and not because we should reify an imagined past feminist history that we are indebted to, that paying attention to and discovering ways of archiving online feminist writing is vital.

conclusion

The term "generation" can fit neatly into pervasive discourses of nostalgia or fear of the new. In other words, anxieties over a neoliberal networked society and the commodification of women by brands can be easily projected on to younger feminists who practise their politics online and who operate within (and against) the discourses of popular culture. Similarly, worries about the authenticity of one's feminism or one's authority as a feminist might be glossed over by blaming those who formed their feminism in a conjuncture with more resources and more political optimism. In other words, behind antagonistic narratives about "older" and "younger" feminists could lie tensions engendered by shifts in historical and social forces. Moving the focus away from the age differences of the feminists involved and looking at the broader political contradictions at work allows for a more nuanced understanding of patriarchy and the way it functions, particularly within online branded spaces.

Generational categories – personified by the baby-boomer, Gen-Xer and the millennial – are not homogeneous. The socio-economic and cultural location of today's young people is dependent on vectors of gender, race, ethnicity, disability, sexuality, religion, place. Ken Roberts argues that working-class young people in the United Kingdom experienced the devastating impact of neoliberal policies before those protected by their middle-class status. Diane Negra and Yvonne Tasker maintain that although the recession has been branded a "mancession" it has disproportionately affected women. In their manifesto – and throughout their content – *Crunk Feminist Collective*'s members articulate how the present neoliberal moment in the United States is experienced differently by women of colour because the socio-economic, cultural and legislative forms of white supremacist patriarchy intersect to impact disproportionately on them. Thinking about generation within the context of contradictory and specific historical conditions, as well as thinking about it in relation to other vectors of identity such as race and place, can be useful in understanding bloggers' experiences and political motivations. It is through this understanding that intergenerational dialogue – including antagonistic dialogue – can progress.

disclosure statement

No potential conflict of interest was reported by the author.

note

1 In November 2016, after this article was accepted, *Feminist Times* was relaunched as an online monthly magazine via the digital publishing site "issuu." Significantly, it has rejected some of the affordances of the blog format. There are no comment functions and the magazine will be issued on a monthly basis rather than being

continually updated. Raven frames this as an intergenerational feminist strategy by stating:

> Our new incarnation is tethered to the past because we want to receive something from feminism's golden age. We owe it to those who came before us to get this right so instead of being updated daily, like a blog, we will be producing monthly issues. This will give us plenty of time to reflect on the content and work constructively with our writers rather than hit them with idea-sapping deadlines. (FEM 001 5)

In addition, Raven aims to counteract the burnout experienced by feminist bloggers, as discussed above. We can see a deep concern around connecting to previous feminist publishing incarnations in *Feminist Times*' attempt to connect with "our foremothers": "Tethered proudly to the past, we are walking in the footsteps of our foremothers, respectful of their legacy" (FEM 001 3). Raven points out that there are no comment boards on the site as "I want to encourage a different kind of debate where there is time to reflect rather than fire off responses a mile a minute." Instead, she offers an e-mail address and promises to reply "and, who knows, you could even become one of our contributors" (FEM 001 5).

bibliography

Baxter, Holly, and Rhiannon Coslett. *The Vagenda: A Zero Tolerance Guide to the Media*. London: Random, 2014. Print.

Boorman, Neil. *It's All Their Fault*. London: HarperCollins, 2010. Print.

Braidotti, Rosi. "Introduction." *Australian Feminist Studies* 24.59 (2009): 3–9. Print.

Clay, Adreana. *The Hip-Hop Generation Fights Back: Youth, Activism, and Post-Civil Rights Politics*. New York: New York UP, 2012. Print.

Cochrane, Kira. "The Fourth Wave of Feminism: Meet the Rebel Women." *The Guardian* 10 Dec. 2013. Web. 4 Apr. 2016. <www.theguardian.com/world/2013/dec/10/fourth-wave-feminism-rebel-women>.

Colebrook, Claire. "Stratigraphic Time, Women's Time." *Australian Feminist Studies* 24.59 (2009): 11–16. Print.

Collins, Patricia Hill. *Black Feminist Thought: Knowledge, Consciousness and the Politics of Empowerment*. London and New York: Routledge, 1990. Print.

Collins, Patricia Hill, and Sirma Bilge. *Intersectionality*. Cambridge: Polity, 2016. Print.

Coupland, Douglas. *Generation X: Tales for an Accelerated Culture*. New York: St. Martin's, 1991. Print.

Crunk Feminist Collective. "Hip Hop Generation Feminism: A Manifesto." 1 Mar. 2010. Web blog post. 14 Feb. 2016. <www.crunkfeministcollective.com/2010/03/01/hip-hop-generation-feminism-a-manifesto/>.

Crunk Feminist Collective. "Mission Statement." N.d. Web blog post. 14 Feb. 2016. <www.crunkfeministcollective.com/about/>.

Crunk Feminist Collective. "On bell, Beyoncé and Bullshit." 20 May 2014. Web blog post. 14 Feb. 2016. <www.crunkfeministcollective.com/2014/05/20/on-bell-beyonce-and-bullshit/>.

Crunk Feminist Collective. "Say No to Noteps and Straight Black Pride." 15 Jul. 2015. Web blog post. 14 Feb. 2016. <http://www.crunkfeministcollective.com/2015/07/15/say-no-to-noteps-and-straight-black-pride/>.

Feminist Times. "About Us." Web blog post. 14 Aug. 2014. Web. 4 Apr. 2016. <www.feministtimes.com/about/>. [Note that this URL is no longer active. Material will be available shortly via the *Feminist Times* archive at <http://www.feministtimes.com>.]

Gill, Rosalind. "Post-Postfeminism? New Feminist Visibilities in Postfeminist Times." *Feminist Media Studies* 16.4 (2016): 610–30. Print.

Graeber, David. "On the Phenomenon of Bullshit Jobs." *STRIKE! Magazine* 17 Aug. 2013. Web. 4 Apr. 2016. <strikemag.org/bullshit-jobs/>.

Greer, Germaine. "The Failures of New Feminism." *New Statesman* 14 May 2014. Web. 4 Apr. 2016. <www.newstatesman.com/culture/2014/05/germaine-greer-failures-new-feminism>.

Halberstam, Jack. "Justifiable Matricide: Backlashing Faludi." *Bullybloggers*. 19 Oct. 2010. Web blog post. 30 Sept. 2014. <https://bullybloggers.wordpress.com/2010/10/19/justifiable-matricide-backlashing-faludi-by-jack-halberstam/>.

Hemmings, Clare. *Why Stories Matter: The Political Grammar of Feminist Theory*. Durham, NC: Duke UP, 2011. Print.

Henry, Astrid. *Not My Mother's Sister: Generational Conflict and Third-Wave Feminism*. Bloomington: Indiana UP, 2004. Print.

Keller, Jessalynn. *Girls' Feminist Blogging in a Postfeminist Age*. London and New York: Routledge, 2015. Print.

Little, Ben. "A Growing Discontent: Class and Generation under Neoliberalism." *Soundings* 56 (2014): 27–40. Print.

Love, Carolyn D., Lize A.E. Booysen, and Philomena Essed. "An Exploration of the Intersection of Race, Gender and Generation in African American Women Doing Social Justice Work." *Gender, Work and Organization* (2015). Web. 16 Aug. 2016. doi:10.1111/gwao.12095.

Loza, S. "Hashtag Feminism, #SolidarityIsForWhiteWomen, and the other #FemFuture." *Ada: A Journal of Gender, New Media, and Technology* 5 (2014). doi:10.7264/N337770V.

Martin, Courtney E., and Vanessa Valenti. "#Femfuture: Online Revolution." Barnard Center for Research on Women. Vol. 8 (2012). Web. 16 Feb. 2016. <bcrw.barnard.edu/publications/femfuture-online-revolution/>.

Massey, Doreen. "Ideology and Economics in the Present Moment." *The Neoliberal Crisis*. Ed. Sally Davison and Katherine Harris. London: Lawrence, 2015. 102–12. Print.

McKay, Finn. "Political Not Generational: Getting Real About Contemporary UK Radical Feminism." *Social Movement Studies* 14.4 (2015): 427–42. Print.

McRobbie, Angela. *The Aftermath of Feminism: Gender, Culture and Social Change*. London: Sage, 2009. Print.

Miller, Vincent. *Understanding Digital Culture*. London: Sage, 2011. Print.

Negra, Diane. *What a Girl Wants? Fantasizing the Reclamation of Self in Postfeminism*. London and New York: Routledge, 2009. Print.

Negra, Diane, and Yvonne Tasker. *Gendering the Recession: Media and Culture in an Age of Austerity*. Durham, NC: Duke UP, 2014. Print.

Raven, Charlotte. "Feminist Times: My Feminist Times 'Journey.'" Web blog post. 16 July 2014. Web. 4 Apr. 2016. <http://www.feministtimes.com/category/charlottes-editorial/>. [Note that this URL is no longer active. Material will be available shortly via the *Feminist Times* archive at <http://www.feministtimes.com>.]

Roberts, Ken. "The End of the Long Baby-Boomer Generation." *Journal of Youth Studies* 15.4 (2012): 479–97. Print.

Sanders McDonagh, Erin, and Elena Vacchelli. "The Rebirth of Feminism? Situating Feminism in the Popular Imaginary." Part of "The Rebirth of Feminism?" symposium at Middlesex University. 30 Oct. 2013.

Segal, Lynne. "Who's Afraid of Old Age?" *Feminist Times* 6 Nov. 2013. Web blog post. 30 Sept. 2014. Web. 4 Apr. 2016. <www.feministtimes.com/whos-afraid-of-oldage/>. [Note that this URL is no longer active. Material will be available shortly via the *Feminist Times* archive at <http://www.feministtimes.com>.]

Siibak, Andra, and Nicoletta Vittadini. "Introducing Four Empirical Examples of the 'Generationing' Process." *Cyberpsychology: Journal of Psychosocial Research on Cyberspace* 6.2 (2012): 1–10. Print.

Springer, Kimberly. "Radical Archives and the New Cycles of Contention." *Viewpoint Magazine* 5 (2015). Web. 16 Feb. 2016. <viewpointmag.com/2015/11/02/issue-5-social-reproduction/>.

Springer, Kimberly. "Third Wave Black Feminism?" *Signs* 27.4 (2002): 1059–82. Print.

Taylor, Astra. *The People's Platform: Taking Back Power and Culture in the Digital Age*. New York: Fourth Estate, 2014. Print.

The Vagenda. "Girl Trouble: What is Everyone's Deal with Young Women?" 11 June 2014. Web blog post. 14 July 2015. <vagendamagazine.com/2014/06/girl-trouble-what-is-everyones-deal-with-young-women/>.

The Vagenda. "How to Tell if You're Feminist Enough." 11 Sept. 2014. Web blog post. 14 July 2015. <vagendamagazine.com/2014/09/how-to-tell-if-youre-feminist-enough/>.

The Vagenda. "I am Sexy, I am Funny, I am a Fucking Feminist." 28 Feb. 2013. Web blog post. 14 July

2015. <vagendamagazine.com/2013/02/i-am-sexy-i-am-funny-i-am-a-fucking-feminist/>.

The Vagenda. "A Letter from the Editor." 19 Jan. 2012. Web blog post. 14 July 2015. <vagendamagazine.com/2012/01/a-letter-from-the-editor/>.

The Vagenda. "On Bikini Body Bullshit." 24 June 2014. Web blog post. 14 July 2015. <vagendamagazine.com/2014/06/on-bikini-body-bullshit/>.

The Vagenda. "We Need a Lie Down." 3 July 2015. Web blog post. 14 July 2016. <vagendamagazine.com/2015/07/we-need-a-lie-down-2/>.

Walker, Rebecca. *Baby Love: Choosing Motherhood After a Lifetime of Ambivalence*. London: Souvenir, 2008. Print.

White, Khadijah. "Black Lives on Campuses Matter: The Rise of the New Black Student Movement." *Soundings* 63 (2016): 86–97. Print.

Willetts, David. *The Pinch: How the Baby Boomers Took Their Children's Future – And Why They Should Give it Back*. London: Atlantic, 2010. Print.

Winch, Alison. *Girlfriends and Postfeminist Sisterhood*. Basingstoke: Palgrave, 2013. Print.

OPEN ACCESS

julia novak

FEMINIST TO POSTFEMINIST

contemporary biofictions by and about women artists

Biographical novels about women artists have been experiencing a veritable boom in recent years. Since the turn of the millennium, the lives of Frida Kahlo, Sylvia Plath, Murasaki Shikibu, Artemisia Gentileschi, Marilyn Monroe, Jane Austen, Gwen John – to name just a few – have been made subjects of imaginative re-tellings, some of them in multiple versions. These biofictions are the product of both biographical scholarship and authorial imagination. As most of them are written by women, they also mark women authors' attempts to reach out across time (and often, space) to other "artistic" women whose lives "speak to us" today. Thus, while for Martin Middeke (3) self-reflexivity constitutes a chief characteristic of postmodern biofictions in general, novels by and about women artists are self-reflexive in two ways: as narratives of artistry and femininity. This paper compares two novels – Janice Galloway's *Clara* (2002) about nineteenth-century German pianist Clara Wieck-Schumann and Priya Parmar's *Exit the Actress* (2011) about Restoration actress Nell Gwyn – in view of the particular images of women artists they present.

While contemporary biofictions about historical women artists must be situated in the context of a general boom in biofiction since the 1980s,[1] the origins of this trend can also be traced to the mid-twentieth-century surge in biographies about "notable" women of the past, as part of the so-called second wave of feminism. Reacting against Thomas Carlyle's famous dictum that "the history of the world is but the biography of great men" (Carlyle 26), feminist biographers aimed to "restore" women to the historical record. Many biographers aimed specifically at making women's achievements visible, and this strand of exemplary feminist biography still continues today – in individual women's biographies as well as in inspirational collective biographies such as Caroline Criado-Perez's recent *Do It Like a Woman ... and Change the World*. Their purpose is to offer readers stories about exceptional women "reinventing what it means to be female" ("Do It Like a Woman" n. pag.).

Like these exemplary feminist biographies, the overwhelming majority of women artist biofictions centres on canonical artists and, hence, on famous, "exceptional" women, whose lives can teach us something about "reinventing what it means to be female." And as in biography, the image of the woman artist emerging from a novel depends on the particular life narrative the writer constructs on the basis of the available material. It has long been a key insight of historical fiction research that a historical novel reveals more about the time in which it was written than the time in which it is set. As such, it can be assumed that contemporary biofictions about women speak as much to twenty-first-century conceptions of femininity as to particular historical moments of female subjectivity. And again, similar arguments have been put forward about "factual" biography.[2]

However, unlike the biographer, the novelist is not bound by historical fact and biographical convention. As products of the postmodern disregard for generic boundaries, biofictions can thus participate in biographical as well as in fictional subgenres and align their structure, narrative mode and character properties with the requirements of these subgenres. Given the function of genre as a power discourse that contributes to the "social structuring of meaning" (Frow 1), female subjectivities in biofictions can be related to the specific subgenres that come into play in the texts. In the following, Janice Galloway's novel *Clara* and Priya Parmar's *Exit the Actress* will be examined with regard to the relation between their generic layering and their gender politics. Both novels are conspicuous for their formal experiments: they employ shifts in the narrative perspective, unusual typography, and graphic elements. The primary impulse for this paper came from my curiosity to find out how these formal experiments relate to the two novels' generic make-up – to the genres in which they participate – and to particular visions of femininity which these entail.

re-writing clara wieck-schumann

Janice Galloway's fictional account of the life of German pianist Clara Wieck-Schumann covers the artist's early childhood and the musical training she received from her father Friedrich Wieck, the legendary legal battle between Friedrich Wieck and composer Robert Schumann who was to be her husband, the years of the Schumanns' marriage, and ends on Robert Schumann's death in 1856.

When Clara is eighteen, she has her international breakthrough in Vienna. The following quotation illustrates the tone of Galloway's narrative:

> Poor Herr Wieck! He bawls like a baby and blasts his capacious nose into his handkerchief, has to sit for support. A foreigner, a Protestant, a *girl* – he had thought every fibre of Austrian tradition worked against it; yet there she is, Royal and Imperial Chamber Virtuosa to the Austrian Court, glittering with medals, and his own, entirely, wholly, legally and morally his own. (Galloway 154–55)

Friedrich Wieck's claim to ownership over his daughter is emphasized and clearly ironized in the novel, which functions as a feminist comment. Galloway's approach to her heroine is generally marked by a focus on gender norms, which is a chief characteristic of feminist biography. "When the subject is female, gender moves to the center of the analysis" (7), Sara Alpern notes in her introduction to *The Challenge of Feminist Biography*. And, indeed, Galloway's Clara Wieck is continuously positioned within the sex/gender-system of her day by the narrator; her actions are explicitly assessed with regard to prevailing gender norms, which are then implicitly or explicitly critiqued.

Clara emerges as a talented and ambitious artist who enjoys performing, who initially finds herself controlled by her father, for whom her talent has become a major source of income, and then constrained by her overbearing, mentally unstable husband: "Not that he will stop her playing," he notes, "not at all! She will play endlessly, he hopes, but suitably, appropriately, at home" (Galloway 156). The following scene occurs after one of the Schumanns' house parties:

> He returned some hours later when she was already in bed, and had sex with her as immoderately and repeatedly as he had earlier praised her. Do not play so much, he said abruptly when it was done. The soul sickens of too much. If it had not been for my eyes willing it to stop, you should have driven me from the house. (200)

Consequently, Galloway's heroine enacts what has been identified as a classic trope of feminist biography: the overcoming of obstacles in her path to self-actualization and artistic independence (Ní Dhúill 116). At one point the narrator asks:

> And was it worth it? All the anguish and isolation of selling her playing abroad, of leaving her spouse and child, of braving storms and ships and the ghastly business of organisation all alone? Was it? No one would have asked Liszt such a question. Or Thalberg or Henselt or Mendelssohn. No matter. No one passed up the opportunity to ask Clara Schumann. (Galloway 236)

This passage serves, on the one hand, to drive home to the reader the cultural significance of Clara Wieck-Schumann's achievement – her name is up there with all the musical greats of her day – and simultaneously, to highlight the different standards to which women were held in terms of their domestic responsibilities.[3] Some of the numerous lists that constitute one of the novel's conspicuous graphic features perform a similar function. Clara returns from a concert tour which she has undertaken without her husband:

> HERS The chopping of cabbage. First teeth.
> Hire of new housemaid, interviews, checking of references.
> Listing of all household stock.
> Local concert for Hamburg fire victims.
> Accounts. And silence. Much silence.
>
> HIS A minor. F major. A major.
> Three quartets in as many weeks.
> Three children barely born, yet beautiful.
>
> She was home.
>
> (Galloway 237)

However, a feminist biography not only addresses "woman's condition in history" (Gutiérrez 54) – as Galloway's narrative clearly does – but, according to Liz Stanley, it also adopts a metabiographical stance: it "textually recognizes that its facts and arguments are contingent" and that "biographical as any other writing is produced from a particular viewpoint" (250). Galloway's *Clara* contains an interesting example – a letter – in which the typography enacts a self-reflexive gesture towards biography's limitations:

> **Dear Mother**
> **You have as yet heard Nothing from me but now I can write a little** a little is it modest to say a little **I will send you** Herr Bargiel is it impolite not to mention Herr **a Letter which will please you** will be proud of my spelling I am trying my handwriting
>
> […]
>
> Scales a ruler under my wrist passing the thumb beneath **I was not at all frightened but the Clapping troubled me** my bow is not good I am ungainly and embarrassed to bow so close in our own parlour **Emilie Reichold and M Kupfer played too** Emilie looks like an angel she is blonde where I am **The day before my Birthday I went to Malger with father** father is reading this **Please give my Love to Grandmama and my Brothers.** (Galloway 62–63)

The words in bold are what the child Clara actually writes down. As in other instances where Galloway includes lines from letters, the way these are set off from the rest of the text – italicized or indented – points to the novel's intertextuality, to the fact that it is based on, and quotes from, historical documents. In this sense, typography communicates authenticity: it stages the text's reference to real-world characters and events.[4] Besides lists and letters, *Clara* also contains samples of musical notation and concert programmes that are visually set off from the text and have a similar function: as markers of authenticity they evoke the historical artist's experiences and achievements.

In the example of the above letter, however, the small print in between the larger words imagines the thoughts and constraints Clara experiences in the act of writing ("father is reading this"). Clara's inability to translate her feelings and experience into words is, in fact, a recurrent motif in Galloway's novel. This letter equally points to the selective and refracted nature of what *is* written down as to what is omitted. Its typographical variation thus visualizes the unreliability of the available records on which any biographical endeavour must depend. The novel can be conceived as a "fictional metabiography," to use Ansgar Nünning's term (202): it draws attention to the epistemological challenges of life-writing and, ultimately, questions the possibility of distinguishing fact from fiction. In this example, then, the postmodernist variant of the biographical novel converges with feminist biography, as Clara's deliberate or imposed silences reflect a central feminist concern: the inaccessibility of female experience as a subject of biography (Ní Dhúill 113).

The novel already hints at its metabiographical framework in the fictive concert programme at its very beginning, which announces a performance of Robert Schumann's opus 42 *Frauenliebe und -Leben* – Woman's Life and Love – as a "*revised edition of eight songs with piano accompaniment*," and whose end reads:

> *Finale*
> Concerto for lone piano
> Work in progress
>
> (Galloway 3)

The qualifier "revised" can be read in two ways: it can point to the fact that Clara Wieck-Schumann's life as such departed markedly from the story Schumann's song cycle tells about "woman's life"; more likely, though, it can be read as a programmatic statement on Galloway's own narrative about that life, which places Clara centre stage. While Galloway's creative paratext thus points to the ways in which representations of the pianist have traditionally been circumscribed by her husband's work, it ends on a "concerto for lone piano" and "work in progress" (3), also suggesting a provisional quality, a fundamental unfinishedness, of biographies about women.

nell gwyn: mad about the king

Priya Parmar's *Exit the Actress* opens with an adolescent Nell Gwyn who is beginning to write a diary in 1662. It follows the years in which she is discovered by the King's Company at Theatre Royal, Drury Lane, where she becomes one of the very early star actresses on the Restoration stage, and closes on her retreat from the stage once she has established herself as mistress to King Charles II.

The visual appearance of Parmar's text is similarly fragmented as Galloway's. Nell's diary entries alternate with articles from the *London Gazette*, "London's Best and Brilliant Broadsheet" (16), echoing the tone of contemporary gossip columns, with notes from the Secretary of State, Lord Arlington (underlain in grey), theatre programmes, and letters to and from other characters, such as Queen Henrietta Maria, King Charles II, and his sister Minette, which have ornamental frames drawn around them. As in Galloway's novel, Parmar's inclusion and visual separation of life-writing formats such as letters and diary entries gesture towards the factual basis of her narrative. However, while the visual fragmentation of Galloway's *Clara* coincides with its deconstruction of traditional gender norms, *Exit the Actress* cannot as easily be subsumed under the label of feminist biography, as I will demonstrate.

Like Galloway's *Clara*, Parmar's novel opens with a metafictional gesture: it presents a playbill listing the narrative's "cast," and, subsequently, a "Prologue spoken by the actress Mrs. Nelly Gwyn upon her Farewell Performance" (5–7), which closes as follows:

> Young girls ask how did you do it? Your cheeks are so pink? Your hair is so *red*? True, you are a stage delight, your waist is

> slim, your tread is light – but is that *all*? After all, you are so *small*. You are so like us. So here. So wicked. And yet, he loves you so. Why?
> (*Quietly*.) And the answer is always the same: I really do not know. (7)

"How did you do it?" How did she manage to capture the heart of the king? This passage anticipates what can be identified – despite its narrative fragmentation – as the novel's overall trajectory: the heroine's successful quest for true love. Superficially, *Exit the Actress* could therefore be aligned with the historical romance novel: its beautiful, spirited young heroine enacts the Cinderella-like ascent typical of the genre, winning the love and devotion of an aristocratic, saturnine hero (as well as his economic support) – in a period that is historically removed and therefore suitably "romantic" as a setting for the central love plot. In fact, *Exit the Actress* is the most "romantic" in a series of recent Gwyn novels.[5] Without bending biographical facts too much, Parmar even manages to approximate the romance novel's required Happily Ever After ending – its promise of a lasting, monogamous love relationship – by cutting her narrative off at the precise point when, historically, King Charles's earlier mistress Barbara Palmer falls out of favour and shortly before Gwyn's great rival (or co-mistress) Louise de Keroualle is about to enter the scene.

However, with its bustling urban setting, its contemporary diction, its quirky humour, and its heroine's serial dating efforts, *Exit the Actress* is, in fact, more reminiscent of another popular genre that Stephanie Harzewski has termed "Postmodernism's Last Romance" (24): the chick lit novel.

> This morning (after lengthy debate) I wore my new white muslin gown (Rochester's choice) with the cream *pointe*, blue sash, and my delicate little silver mules – lovely! (Teddy's choice). But nothing! No response. The king does not seem to notice me at all. Grumble. (Parmar 287)

Its episodic form and informal first-person diary voice in fact associate *Exit the Actress* closely with Helen Fielding's *Bridget Jones's Diary* – one of the *ur*-texts of postfeminist chick lit:

> Ugh. Cannot face thought of going to work. Only thing which makes it tolerable is thought of seeing Daniel again [...] Love his wicked dissolute air, while being v. successful and clever [...] Think might wear short black skirt tomorrow. (Fielding 17–19)

> Nightmare day in office. Watched the door for Daniel all morning: nothing. (28)

The resemblance between the two novels is reinforced by the trope of the gay best friend (in *Exit the Actress* it is Edward "Teddy" Kynaston) and a meddling, judgmental mother figure, here in the guise of Queen Henrietta Maria, whose letters to and about the king provide much of the novel's humour: "*For heaven's sake, Charles, stop frolicking through the countryside like a milkmaid and get a tighter rein on your government*" (Parmar 250). On Queen Catherine's infertility, for instance, she writes: "*We certainly know the problem does not lie with Charles – at least he has shown himself capable of this much*" (92).

Similarly, King Charles's letters to his sister Minette in *Exit the Actress* serve to reveal aspects of the king's private life, which is again done primarily in a light-hearted, humorous tone:

> *Yes, I have attempted conjugal duties – no, it did not go well, although I do hope to entertain her better than the Monsieur did you. Your nightmarish account of that encounter haunts me still; I cannot imagine being unattracted to women – one or two perhaps, but* all? *Mystifying.* (33)

Parmar's Nell also repeatedly goes on shopping sprees with her girl-friends (280, 316, 345), thus playing to another trope of postfeminist popular culture: that of the female consumer, which, according to Yvonne Tasker and Diane Negra, envisions "consumption itself as both therapeutic and transformative" (10). Parmar's novel fits Munford and Waters' description of postfeminist TV shows set in the past as typically marked by the "glorification of old-style femininities and masculinities" (28) and tending to "present affluent worlds in which women have limited power, but fabulous clothes" (ibid.).

Despite the heroine's preoccupation with finding Mr Right, *Exit the Actress* is, like other postfeminist texts, repeatedly haunted by the "breaking through of a feminist consciousness" (Whelehan xi), which it projects onto its historical protagonist. Star actor Charles Hart, Nell's first "date," initially forbids Nell to exercise her talent as a comedienne on the grounds that he "will not have her laughed at" (147) but finally relents, on the condition that he play opposite her. "I know I should not but I resent his intrusion," Nell writes. "Can I not stand alone as an actress, unclaimed and unsupervised?" (148). Parmar also has Nell protest again and again how much her profession means to her: "They [...] cheer for me as the curtain comes down. It is an intoxicating thing to feel their love. It keeps me strong. It keeps me safe. No man can take this from me" (215). When King Charles does "take it from her" at the end of the novel, asking her to leave the stage when she is expecting his child, she first resents his attempt at controlling her but then agrees after joyfully realizing that it is his great love and concern for her health that is making him anxious. In this way, Parmar presents her seventeenth-century protagonist as a distinctly modern career woman but ultimately retains the conservative notion, familiar from historical romance novels, of woman's development as geared towards finding their ultimate fulfilment in a monogamous love relationship.

conclusion

Like many other biographical novels about women artists published these days, Galloway's and Parmar's biofictions both constitute attempts at telling stories about women that resonate across the centuries. As has been demonstrated, their interpretations of what it meant to be a woman artist in a period long gone are shaped considerably by the novelists' freedom to draw on biographical as well as fictional modes of writing, and to deliberately cross the lines between fact and fiction in their work.

Although *Clara* and *Exit the Actress* resemble each other in the way they experiment with typography and layout, they differ markedly as regards the biographical and fictional subgenres in which they participate and, hence, in their gender politics. This difference, I suggest, is symptomatic of a time when feminist narratives of progress co-exist with a postfeminist nostalgia for "a lost, uncomplicated past" (Whelehan 11) and the "glorification of old-style femininities" (Munford and Waters 28). *Clara* focuses on its heroine's struggle for her musical career in the spirit of feminist biography and points to the inaccessibility of female experience and hence the difficulty of writing a woman's life, which also turns Galloway's novel into an example of fictional metabiography. The fragmentation of Parmar's novel, by contrast, serves mostly to add some historical colour to her narrative and break the first-person solipsism of the diary to introduce other voices, chiefly for the purpose of humour. While *Exit the Actress* is occasionally haunted by feminist ideas, it can be understood more readily in terms of both the historical romance novel and its postfeminist offspring the chick lit novel. Together, the two novels analysed demonstrate that biographical fictions about historical women, although concerned ostensibly with past lives, can serve as a barometer of shifting gender discourses of the twenty-first century.

disclosure statement

No potential conflict of interest was reported by the author.

notes

Supported by the Austrian Science Fund (FWF): T 589-G23.

1 On the rise of biographical fiction in the twentieth century, see Middeke; Lackey.

2 Feminist critics' preoccupation with "situated knowledge" can also be read in this light and is often discussed in the work of feminist biographers; cf., for example, Stanley 250.

3 For a more detailed analysis of the way in which Galloway projects contemporary feminist ideas onto historical characters and events, see Novak, "Father and Daughter Across Europe."

4 In an interview, Janice Galloway points out that while her novel is based on six years of biographical research and thus contains a wealth of factual material, she occasionally took liberties with her sources and made up some of the lines in the letters the novel purports to cite in translation (Galloway Interview). The reader has no way of telling whether or not her lines are faithful to the source material (unless s/he compares them with an edition of the Schumanns' letters). Notwithstanding the uncertain status of the letters in *Clara*, I suggest that the very fact that some passages in the novel are narrated in the form of letters points to the biographer's practice of piecing a life together from the available life-writing records and thus serves as a reminder that Galloway's novel narrates the life of a historical person and is based on biographical research.

5 For an analysis of Diane Haeger's *The Perfect Royal Mistress* (2007), Susan Holloway Scott's *The King's Favorite* (2008) and Gillian Bagwell's *The Darling Strumpet* (2011), see Novak, "Nell Gwyn in Contemporary Romance Novels."

bibliography

Alpern, Sara, ed. *The Challenge of Feminist Biography: Writing the Lives of Modern American Women*. Urbana: U of Illinois P, 1992. Print.

Carlyle, Thomas. *On Heroes, Hero-Worship, & the Heroic in History*. 1840. *The Norman and Charlotte Strouse Edition of the Writings of Thomas Carlyle*. Ed. Michael K. Goldberg. Berkeley: U of California P, 1993. Print.

Criado-Perez, Caroline. *Do It Like a Woman … and Change the World*. London: Portobello, 2015. Print.

"Do It Like a Woman." *Portobellobooks.com*. 7 May 2015. Web. 31 Mar. 2016.

Fielding, Helen. *Bridget Jones's Diary: A Novel*. 1996. London: Picador, 2001. Print.

Frow, John. *Genre: The New Critical Idiom*. London: Routledge, 2006. Print.

Galloway, Janice. *Clara*. London: Cape, 2002. Print.

Galloway, Janice. Interview with Julia Novak. 22 Dec. 2015.

Gutiérrez, Rachel. "What Is a Feminist Biography?" *All Sides of the Subject: Women and Biography*. Ed. Teresa Iles. New York: Teachers College P, 1992. 48–55. Print.

Harzewski, Stephanie. *Chick Lit and Postfeminism*. Charlottesville: U of Virginia P, 2011. Print.

Lackey, Michael. *The American Biographical Novel*. London: Bloomsbury, 2016. Print.

Middeke, Martin. "Introduction." *Biofictions: The Rewriting of Romantic Lives in Contemporary Fiction and Drama*. Ed. Martin Middeke and Werner Huber. Rochester, NY: Camden, 1999. 1–25. Print.

Munford, Rebecca, and Melanie Waters. *Feminism & Popular Culture: Investigating the Postfeminist Mystique*. Foreword by Imelda Whelehan. London: Tauris, 2014. Print.

Ní Dhúill, Caitríona. "Am Beispiel der Brontës. Gender-Erzählungen im biographischen Kontext." *Spiegel und Maske. Konstruktionen biographischer Wahrheit*. Ed. Bernhard Fetz and Hannes Schweiger. Vienna: Zsolnay, 2006. 113–27. Print.

Novak, Julia. "Father and Daughter Across Europe: The Journeys of Clara Wieck Schumann and Artemisia Gentileschi in Fictionalised Biographies." *European Journal of Life Writing* 1 (2012): 41–57. Web. 21 Dec. 2016.

Novak, Julia. "Nell Gwyn in Contemporary Romance Novels: Biography and the Dictates of 'Genre Literature.'" *Contemporary Women's Writing* 8.3 (2014): 373–90. Print.

Nünning, Ansgar. "Fictional Metabiographies and Metautobiographies: Towards a Definition, Typology and Analysis of Self-Reflexive Hybrid Metagenres." *Self-Reflexivity in Literature*. Ed. Werner Huber, Martin Middeke, and Hubert Zapf. Würzburg: Königshausen, 2005. 195–209. Print.

Parmar, Priya. *Exit the Actress: A Novel.* New York: Touchstone, 2011. Print.

Stanley, Liz. *The Auto/Biographical I: The Theory and Practice of Feminist Auto/Biography.* Manchester: Manchester UP, 1992. Print.

Tasker, Yvonne, and Diane Negra. "Introduction: Feminist Politics and Postfeminist Culture." Ed. Yvonne Tasker and Diane Negra. *Interrogating Postfeminism: Gender and the Politics of Popular Culture.* Durham, NC: Duke UP, 2007. 1–25. Print.

Whelehan, Imelda. "Foreword." Munford and Waters vii–xiv. Print.

fei-wen liu

PRACTICE AND CULTURAL POLITICS OF "WOMEN'S SCRIPT"

nüshu *as an endangered heritage in contemporary china*

Sitting alone in an empty room, I'm thinking of nothing,
But writing a piece to lament my misery.
I was born a female of withered fate,
Who had no father to take care of me from the age of three …
When I turned twenty,
It was my two brothers who presided over my marriage.
Five or six years after I married,
I had borne neither a daughter nor a son, a constant worry.
My parents-in-law worked out bringing in a second woman [i.e., a concubine].
Having her company to rely on, I was happy …
For four years, our lives went well …
But someone must have said something to change her heart
And she ran away,
Which made us, husband and wife, angry and dismayed.

In 1982 a piece of blue cloth on which was written an unknown script was found in a rural community in Jiangyong County of Hunan Province in southern China. Could this be an ancient ethnic minority's writing system? Considering that Jiangyong has been a borderland where Han Chinese and Yao ethnic people had lived for more than a millennium, this was a real possibility. But further investigation revealed that this is the world's only "women's script," called *nüshu* (women's writing), a script that men could not read. The writing on the blue cloth relates a Jiangyong peasant woman's life story, as shown in the excerpt above. With the escape of the concubine who had been brought in to produce an heir, this woman named He Xijing ended up a childless widow in her late thirties. She laments this in her *nüshu* text: "Others who have a lowly fate can still find some outlet. But I have nothing, inside or out" (see Fig. 1).[1]

The discovery of *nüshu* opened a new window onto women's lifeworlds, especially the experiences of peasant women. In China, writing history has long been the exclusive preserve of men. In this male-controlled historiography, women often go unmentioned, whether as subjects to be recorded or subjects who write. In the histories, women were documented only when they demonstrated exceptional moral achievements, such as a heroic act of martyrdom or the virtue of being a chaste widow for decades (Carlitz, "Social Uses"; "Shrines"; Liu, "Confrontation"). Needless to say, women only

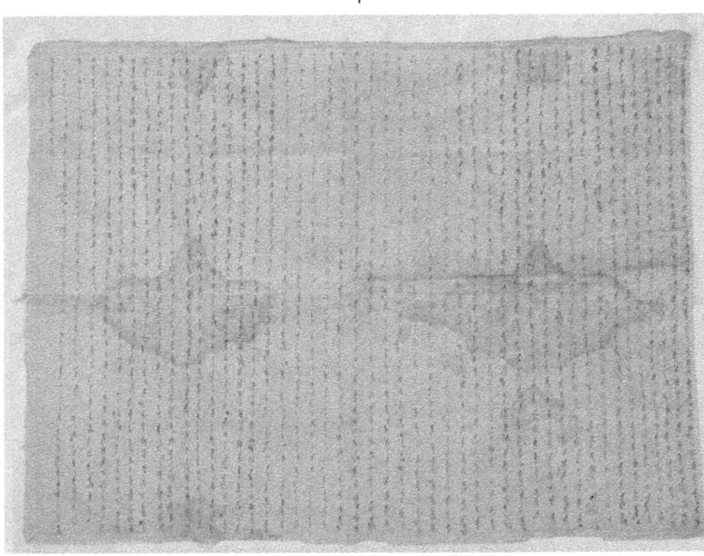

Fig. 1. The world's only "women's script," discovered in 1982. Courtesy of Women's Culture Museum of Shaanxi Normal University.

rarely took on the role of the writing subject, partly because in androcentric China the women's "inner quarter," which included their writing, was deemed inappropriate for the public gaze,[2] and partly because women had only limited access to literacy education.[3] Jiangyong women's invention of *nüshu*, however, enabled them to establish their own historiography and document a history of their own, from their own perspectives. What is recorded in *nüshu* is not confined to women's moral pursuits but more broadly reveals women's "self-reflective metacommentaries" (Seremetakis 2) on society and their personal feelings, in particular their lamentations about life's hardships, called *su kelian* (lamenting one's miseries), as is plain from the verse cited above. *Nüshu* fills in the blanks in Chinese history regarding women's perceptions and lived experience in rural settings, and how they adjusted to changes in their social milieu.[4]

Given its distinctive gender positionality, in both historiographical and epistemological senses, *nüshu* soon attracted scholars at home and abroad who were eager to explore its social and cultural implications. The task of exploration, however, was challenging, mainly because *nüshu* as a local practice had largely faded away. When it was discovered in the early 1980s, only two women still able to compose in the tradition had been identified. They were Gao Yinxian (1902–90; hereafter Gao) and Yi Nianhua (1907–91; hereafter Nianhua). With a sense of urgency about salvaging this endangered heritage, scholars made great efforts to collect *nüshu* texts, and within ten years three major anthologies comprising more than 500 pieces had been published (i.e., Gong, *Nüshu*; Xie; Zhao, *Anthology*; see also Zhao, *Compilation*).[5] In the 1990s a few more *nüshu* writers were located – the most important being Yang Huanyi (1909–2004), He Yanxin (b. 1939), and He Jinghua (b. 1939) – whose identification made further *nüshu* research possible.[6]

In contrast to scholars' endeavors and enthusiasm, the Jiangyong local authorities paid little attention to this disappearing cultural heritage. As one local cadre, Yang Renli recalled: "We thought the scholars could do a better job than we cadres, so we didn't make much effort to collect or preserve *nüshu* materials."[7] Back then, local resources were devoted largely to improving the region's economy and developing Jiangyong into a Yao autonomous county. It was twenty years after *nüshu* became an academic hit that the Jiangyong government first took account of *nüshu*. To promote it as a UNESCO intangible cultural heritage, two measures were implemented: first was the establishment of a *nüshu* museum in 2002, and second, the official qualification of "*nüshu* transmitters" (*nüshu chuanren*) was institutionalized in 2003.

Scholarly investigations and governmental involvement have shaped *nüshu*'s cultural politics, and both have exerted great influence on how *nüshu* is represented and even practiced in contemporary society. Based on fieldwork conducted since 1992, this article traces the trajectory of *nüshu*'s development in changing rural China, in particular its evolving function and social meanings. *Nüshu* in the past gave women a vehicle by which to recount and release their perturbations and transformed their vulnerable being into a resilient and strengthened becoming; it brought them self-worth, preserved their dignity, and won for them social respect (Liu, "From Being"). This power to transform, however, has become a liability now that *nüshu* is an academic property and writing *nüshu* has become a government-supervised profession. All this calls for a rethinking of where *nüshu*, a rural women's endangered expressive tradition, might be heading.

In the following analysis, after briefly introducing the Jiangyong cultural context wherein *nüshu* was nurtured for its utility in local society, I will describe its practice by three women born between 1900 and 1970: Bamboo (*c.*1910–72), a typical Jiangyong peasant woman; Nianhua, one of the two major informants that *nüshu* scholars counted on when "women's script" was first identified; and Meiyue (b. 1963), the granddaughter of the first *nüshu* informant Gao and representative of the younger generations of the officially approved *nüshu* transmitters. These three women's stories demonstrate different aspects of *nüshu*: how it functioned as a communication platform and social forum in the traditional setting, how *nüshu*'s becoming a scholarly subject has affected its practitioners' autonomy and control of the pieces they write, and how *nüshu*'s emotionally charged character, i.e., its capacity for *su kelian*, exerts a psychological effect on the practitioner who writes not for the sake of lamenting her own misery but to fulfill her obligation as an officially appointed transmitter.

Before moving on, allow me to clarify that Bamboo – the woman I use to lend insight into how *nüshu* functioned in traditional Jiangyong – was not a *nüshu* literate herself. She is, nonetheless, included here for methodological and ethnographical reasons. Methodologically, if she had been able to read or write *nüshu*, she would have been subject to interviews or pulled into research projects, which would make it difficult for me to discern the effects of academic influence from *nüshu*'s "original" social effects. Despite her *nüshu* illiteracy, Bamboo is without doubt an invaluable source of inspiration, thanks to her knowledge of Jiangyong women's singing tradition, called *nüge* (women's song) – a tradition that was largely interchangeable with *nüshu* in the sense that the written *nüshu* must be performed by singing. The shared sung character of written *nüshu* and oral *nüge* means that women unversed in the "women's script" could still get access to its texts by listening and participant observation. As many elderly women in Jiangyong reported to me, almost every woman born prior to China's 1949 Liberation could sing the *nüshu* songs. Some had even participated in producing *nüshu* texts, even if they did not personally commit their stories to paper. A Jiangyong woman named Tang Baozhen (*c.*1912–99) is perhaps the best example of this. Tang herself never learned the *nüshu* script, but she could "read" *nüshu* letters written by her sworn sister Hu Cizhu (*c.*1905–76; hereafter Cizhu) with the help of another sworn sister, Gao. Gao had also transcribed Tang's biographical lament into *nüshu* (see Liu, *Gendered Words* ch. 3). Like Tang, Bamboo had composed self-laments in the *nüge* form. Her experiences illuminate how women could find relief from their misery by composing *nüshu*/*nüge*, and by their performance receive sympathy and moral support from the local community. And this provides an intertextual reference to how scholarly investigation and official administration insert themselves into the practice of *nüshu* in contemporary society.

linguistic characteristics and social settings

Jiangyong, located in Hunan's borderland with Guangdong Province and Guangxi Autonomous Region, is populated with Han and Yao Chinese. While the Yao people lived in the mountains and in lower Jiangyong, the Han Chinese, together with the sinicized Yao groups, settled in upper Jiangyong. Upper Jiangyong, including Shangjiangxu and Chengguan townships, is where *nüshu* circulated and is the geographic locus of this research.

Before the communist takeover in 1949, the upper Jiangyong was characterized by the Confucian androcentric practices of patrilineality and a village-based agrarian economy, with women defined by the ideology of *sancong* (thrice-following) – that is, female status was derived from relationships with one's father, husband, and sons. Subject to strict gender-based labor divisions, women were viewed as "inner personae" whose duties focused on household chores and needlework rather than fieldwork, especially once footbinding became widespread. Unmarried women were referred to as "upstairs girls," since they spent most of their time in groups doing embroidery and weaving in second-story rooms. These upstairs gatherings also provided occasions when they could learn singing as well as "women's script."

The significance of singing while doing needlework was picked up by local scholar-gentry elites. As described in one local gazetteer, "By singing, they rid themselves of physical fatigue and maintain high spirits" (*Yongming Gazetteer* 3: 8b–10b). In contrast, and interestingly enough, the existence of a "women's script" remained completely obscure. The fact is, not a single historical document on Jiangyong makes any mention of *nüshu*.

Due to the lack of historical records, it is still a mystery when, why, and by whom the *nüshu* script was created. But according to local legend, *nüshu* was started by a Jiangyong girl named Yuxiu. At age eighteen she was sent to the Imperial Palace as a concubine of an emperor of the Song dynasty in the twelfth century, not because of her beauty but because of her literary talent. In the palace, failing to win the emperor's favor, she is said to have created the *nüshu* script to record the dialect of her hometown, and with which she wrote a letter to her family expressing her loneliness and distress:

> I have been in the Palace these seven years;
> Yet only three nights did I accompany his majesty.
> Other than that, I do nothing.
> In the Palace, my mind has never been settled.
> I would rather stay in my embroidering chamber at home,
> Where I could see my family every day ...
> You may say that the house at home is as cold as snow,
> But the Palace is ten times colder.[8]

In great despair, Yuxiu grieved, "When will this life be over? / When will such distress come to an end?"

This legend perfectly captures the key generic effect of *nüshu*: expressing lamentation. But like many folktales, this story cannot be confirmed since no documents have been found to verify it. The earliest historical account of *nüshu* found so far was written in 1931; in it, *nüshu* was described as "fly-head-like tiny script that no man can read" (Zeng 99). Reconstructing the origin of this tradition has been made even more difficult by the local custom of burning *nüshu* texts upon their owners' deaths, or burying them with the deceased. On the basis of my fieldwork, I can only trace the use of *nüshu* back 150–200 years – many of the elderly women I spoke with recalled *nüshu*'s popularity among their grandmothers' and great-grandmothers' generations. The last traditionally nurtured *nüshu* practitioner, He Yanxin, reported that her grandmother Yang Canxian (hereafter Canxian), who was born about 1875, was quite famous for her *nüshu* expertise in those days. From this, we can imagine that it should have already been popular in the mid-1850s or even earlier.

Traditionally, learning *nüshu* started with singing or chanting *nüshu/nüge* stories before practicing the written script. Unlike standard Chinese *hanzi*, which is ideographic in nature, the *nüshu* script is pegged principally to sound. Words that sound the same can be written the same way. For instance, in Yuxiu's *nüshu* letter discussed above, the words "Palace" (*gong*), "amid" (*zhong*), and "end" (*zhong*) are all written as [illegible], for they are all pronounced the same in the local dialect. This phonetic nature makes *nüshu* much easier to master for native dialect speakers. According to Orie Endō's survey, the grasp of about 400 graphs will suffice for basic expression.

The *nüshu* and *nüge* traditions began to fade as a result of social changes brought about by the Communist Liberation of 1949.[9] On the one hand, the introduction of formal female education replaced the social function of *nüshu* – after all, official *hanzi* is not dialect- or gender-circumscribed and therefore can do a better job at communication nationally. On the other hand, the collectivization of production practiced from the mid-1950s to the early 1980s, which required women to work in the fields and outside the home, deprived them of the free time in which they had been able to learn *nüshu* and *nüge* in the upstairs chamber. Nowadays, only women over sixty years of age have knowledge of traditional *nüge* and only a very few know how to write and compose *nüshu*. Among them, He Yanxin, who learned *nüshu* from her grandma Canxian, is the most prolific (see Endō; Kuo; Liu, *Gendered Words* ch. 4).

The *nüshu* and *nüge* collected so far include various types. Before marriage, young girls wrote *nüshu* letters to ritually form sworn-sisterhood pacts (Chiang, *We Two*; Liu, "Literacy"; Silber, "From Daughter"). Brides performed *nüge* laments at their weddings, and their peers or female relatives prepared and presented them with bridal *nüshu* literature called *sanzhaoshu* (third-day book), which would be performed in the grooms' villages (Liu, "Literacy"; "Text"; Zhao, "From *Sanzhaoshu*"). Married women relied on *nüshu* and *nüge* as sources of strength over the course of their difficult lives. Mothers wrote *nüshu* prayers to local female deities in supplication for bearing sons, and widows composed biographical laments to assuage their frustrations (Liu, "Confrontation"; "Biographical Writing"). Some women may also have composed narratives as commentary on extraordinary events they witnessed, such as women courageously saving men's lives, or stories of notorious extramarital affairs (Liu, "From Being"; "Elaborating"). In addition to creating original compositions, *nüshu* was also used to transcribe favorite ballads originally written in the standard Chinese (Idema, "*Changben* Texts"; *Heroines*; Liu, "Righteousness"; "Narrative"; McLaren). Written in seven-syllable lines, these long ballads (the so-called *changben*, "sung book") were challenging to memorize and recite. *Nüshu* as a writing tool enabled women to record the ballads verbatim so they could enjoy the stories whenever they wished. These different types of *nüshu* – sisterhood correspondence, *sanzhaoshu* for weddings, worship verses, and long ballads – used the script as a memory aid, in ritual presentations, or for crossing social, sacred, and spatial boundaries. The biographical laments and story narratives, however, could be either written or orally composed. Bamboo, whom I discuss in the following section, composed her self-laments in the *nüge* form.

bamboo: *nüge* as communication platform and social forum

Born in the early twentieth century, Bamboo was a typical Chinese peasant woman: bound feet, illiterate, and promised in childhood in an arranged extra-village marriage. She married at age fifteen. On the wedding day, she was taken to her new home not by the groom but by his family – the local custom mandated that the groom had to stay at home and wait for the bride's arrival. But when Bamboo arrived, she saw no groom; he had just been taken away to enlist in the army. Conscription was not uncommon in the first half of the twentieth century when China struggled to survive a series of conflicts, including civil war and foreign invasions. One *nüge* that describes how people suffered from conscription during the Sino-Japanese War (1937–45) grew so popular that even men could sing it:

> I sit alone in my room thinking of nothing
> But how the world suffers.
> In China we have Chiang Kai-shek,
> Who fights the Japanese without mercy.
> The Japanese devils have big plans.
> They ride in airplanes, flying all over the sky.
> These planes are really something;
> They bomb the provinces, prefectures, and counties.
> The superiors thus send out the order
> That every county and township must carry out conscription.
> They recruit new soldiers,
> Who turn into veterans three years later.
> The young men of 25 or 26 are the best qualified;
> Those 33 years old are also conscripted.
> Those who fit the qualifications are all taken away,
> Making the civilians uneasy …
> From 18 to 45 years old,
> How many are left at home?[10]

Faced with her husband's conscription, Bamboo had no power to resist but could only accept the situation. Without ever meeting her husband, she lived as a quasi-widow in her affinal village. Five years later both of her in-laws passed away. With no one to count on there, Bamboo decided to return to her natal home for refuge. But on her way home her sedan chair was "intercepted" by three brothers from a neighboring village called Zixitang. These brothers, knowing of Bamboo's plan beforehand, had waited by the road to grab her. In Jiangyong such abductions were not unusual, for a widow outside her affinal and natal domains was like an untitled object, seen as available to be claimed or possessed. Bamboo became the wife of one of her abductors and bore a son with him. She spent the remainder of her life in Zixitang.

When I first visited Jiangyong in 1992, Bamboo had been dead for many years, so I did not meet her in person. I learned about her from a schoolteacher named Juan. Juan knew Bamboo's story because she had composed her lived experience into songs and sang them out. Juan recalled:

> It was probably during the early Cultural Revolution (1966–76). In the early evening when the peasants were finished with their farm work or after super, they sat around the village pavilion to chat and relax. On such occasions, some elderly women would be asked to sing *nüshu* or *nüge*. Bamboo was one of those versed singers.[11]

As Juan described her:

> She could sing for hours, even the whole night … She sang and paused if explanation was needed before moving on … Her audiences varied, young and old, male and female. Bamboo would sing popular *nüge*; she would also sing her self-laments, songs describing how she was harassed during her quasi-widowed years, how she was badly treated by her daughter-in-law when she got sick, how her son changed his heart after marriage, etc. … Bamboo was very nice looking and dressed herself well, always neat and clean, so you can imagine that some men must have tried to take advantage when she lived alone in her first husband's village – there were so many juicy stories.

At that time Juan was only a child, too young to remember verbatim what Bamboo had sung, but she got a rough idea of what had happened. She added, "Bamboo shed tears while singing her own stories, and the audience members would weep along with her."

Her having composed a *nüge* to "accuse" her daughter-in-law certainly made the protagonist unhappy, so Bamboo never sang it in front of her. "But if it was about her son, that was fine, for he never minded what she sang. After all, singing was women's stuff, and men were in no position to interfere," said Juan.

For Bamboo, *nüge* not only allowed her to articulate what she had suffered and what she had to complain about – a quasi-widowed life, a marriage to her kidnapper, a malicious daughter-in-law, and an unfilial son – it served also as a medium through which she, a woman abducted from elsewhere, could be known to other villagers. Even a young girl like Juan was able to understand something about Bamboo from her self-laments and developed a sympathetic tie with her. So strong was the impression she left that some twenty years later Juan would share her memories of that long-suffering woman with an anthropologist. Bamboo's case demonstrates that in traditional rural Jiangyong *nüge* was not only a vehicle for discharging personal misery but also a social field whereby one built connections with the community – a function that could be extended to *nüshu* thanks to their shared sung character. But once scholars and officials stepped into the women's community, *nüshu* would become a liability for its writers, as we'll see in the cases of Nianhua and Meiyue.

nianhua: scholarly inspiration and intervention

Nianhua was born in 1907 in Tangxia Village. She lost her father at age four and then followed her twenty-eight-year-old widowed mother to live in her mother's natal home in Baishui Village, where she learned the official *hanzi*, referred to as "men's script" by local women. At age fourteen, Nianhua moved back to her father's, where she learned "women's script" from her *shu'niang* (father's younger brother's wife). In the 1960s, she became a sworn sister with Cizhu of Getang Village and they exchanged *nüshu* letters (Silber, "*Nüshu*"). She wrote more pieces in the 1980s when she became the *nüshu* scholars' major informant. Some local women also approached Nianhua, asking her to compose biographical *nüshu* on their behalf after learning about the presence of this *nüshu* scribe from local TV broadcasts. Requests for composing *nüshu* were not uncommon in traditional Jiangyong, especially on the occasion of a wedding when a *sanzhaoshu* was needed. Canxian, for example, wrote many *sanzhaoshu* on request. As He Yanxin describes in the *nüshu* she wrote in memory of her grandma Canxian: "People from all over came to present invitations / Because of [her] good reputation for doing needlework and writing *nüshu*" (Liu, *Gendered Words* 126).

Of nearly seventy biographical *nüshu* collected by scholars so far, about twenty pieces were written by Nianhua. She explained: "Only the stories of women who asked for them were written" – these requests usually came with a payment of four eggs and four RMB dollars (Silber, "*Nüshu*" 147). Whether the subject came to Nianhua with the stories fully versified in her mind or simply recounted her story, leaving Nianhua to do the versifying, is difficult to determine. But according to He Yanxin, those who came to her grandma for *sanzhaoshu* provided only basic information and her grandma then "composed the [provided] facts into a sensible narrative" (Liu, *Gendered Words* 89).

In addition to writing on behalf of others, Nianhua had also composed a 3,000-word *nüshu* biography for herself in about 1988. It begins with the stock phrases often seen in narrative ballads: "I will not sing of former kings or the latter Han / I will sing only of the woman called Nianhua surnamed Yi" (Zhao, *Anthology* 277–92). And then she introduces her mother and father:

> My mother was named He Guangci;
> My father, called Yi Xijun,
> Died at age 27,
> Leaving my mother to inhabit an empty room ...
> Since my mother was widowed at a young age,
> My maternal grandparents grew worried,
> They sent my junior uncle to bring her home.
> We three – mother and two daughters – spent most of our time with my uncles.

When Nianhua grew up, she moved back to her father's village. Three years later, at age seventeen, she was married to a man in Tongkou Village, where she was faced with a harsh mother-in-law:

> Three and four years [after I married],
> I gave birth to a daughter.
> One day when my husband went to the academy,
> Mother accused me of doing something I didn't:
> She accused me of cooking eggs for myself on the sly.
> Which god could prove my innocence? ...
> I had been serving my parents with all my heart;
> How could I possibly do such a thing?
> But that day my mother-in-law demanded that I kneel down;
> She spat curses at me.
> I was sleepless for several nights, crying throughout ...
> I thought of ending my life but then the truth could not be made clear.
> What could I do?
> I could only await my husband's homecoming and explain it all to him.

When Nianhua's only son died, her mother-in-law showed no mercy but again condemned Nianhua for this misfortune:

> When my boy was three years old,
> He was afflicted with a mouth infection – I was worried sick.
> We spent hundreds and hundreds of dollars to treat his illness,
> But in vain – both my child and the money were gone.
> And then I was reminded how vicious my mother-in-law was.
> She spat curses at me,
> Cursing me for being no good, and
> That was why my son died at age three.

Even worse, a year after her son died, when her second daughter was a year old, she lost her husband. Like her mother, Nianhua had become a widow in her late twenties with two young daughters to raise. But unlike her mother, Nianhua had no brothers to count on and therefore no natal home to support her. She had to face life's ordeals all by herself. During the Japanese invasion of Jiangyong in 1944, for example, she wrote:

> I took my daughters to flee the Japanese; ...
> But I had no husband to build us a shelter.
> Other male kin and villagers took pity on us;
> They invited us to take refuge in their places ...
> Living in the mountains for several months,
> We suffered from cold and frost, like the plum covered with snow.

A few years later came the Communist Liberation, which meant that many traditional practices were also "liberated." To plan for her future, Nianhua decided to marry in a son-in-law for her second daughter, an option that had just become available after Liberation. But the second daughter had a different idea. Probably because matrilocal marriage was not widely accepted at the time – and the idea of not marrying out made the second daughter feel demeaned and ashamed – she insisted on moving to her husband's place:

> Who knew that my younger daughter had a malicious heart ...
> She did not wish to stay home to serve her mother.
> She let her mother stay alone, like a solitary bird,
> Let her mother lead a life as cold as frost on the snow.

The unpleasant interactions with her second daughter forced Nianhua to remarry in her fifties, after she had preserved her widowhood for more than two decades. The second marriage, however, did not survive into a second year. Her stepsons could not accept the death of their father and blamed Nianhua for bringing bad luck on the family. Unable to bear such criticism, Nianhua remarried once again, a marriage that fortunately lasted for twenty years or so.

It was in the 1980s when Nianhua was widowed for the third time. At that time she had already been identified as a *nüshu* writer. Coveting the profits associated with Nianhua's *nüshu* status, her second daughter, the one who abandoned her in the 1950s, brought her back to Tongkou Village. But soon her daughter and son-in-law began to complain. They eventually expelled Nianhua from their family:

They wished I would just hang myself or throw myself in the river …
She and her children also discussed how to throw me out.
She scolded that I had returned home just to enjoy a fun life,
That I should know what kind of person I was.

In conclusion, Nianhua cried out for help:

I'm like a bird in a cage,
A bird with wings but no feathers – how can I fly? …
I wish to go to the hospital to see a doctor,
But my daughter refuses to give me any money …,
I can only go to the periodic market to seek help from a friend,
To borrow enough money to get some shots …
Now my own daughter has thrown me out,
What place can I call home?

The second daughter not only refused to take care of Nianhua but also would not allow Nianhua to visit her eldest daughter. Nianhua indeed led a very difficult life. "She dwelt in a house that was small and dirty" and "suffered from asthma," *nüshu* scholar Gong Zhebing wrote (*Women's Script* 214). Fortunately, the academic interest in *nüshu* was timely and partially relieved her destitution. Many scholars visited Nianhua and asked her for *nüshu* pieces. To better support herself, "When she wrote *nüshu*, she would use carbon paper to make extra copies, and sold those for twenty bucks a piece," *nüshu* scholar Zhao Liming recalled.[12] In one *nüshu* written in 1990, Nianhua also made this clear: "If you don't deem my writing useless, I'll write the *nüshu* you ask for. In my mind, each piece is worth 20 dollars, and I won't sell it for less" (Zhao, *Anthology* 864–65). *Nüshu* gave Nianhua not only emotional relief but also a means of economic survival.

But note, of the dozens of *nüshu* she wrote, there was one she never sold – that is, her own *nüshu* biography.[13] On the one hand, she expanded and edited this work from time to time, and on the other, she was concerned with possible "side effects" if her biographical *nüshu* were published. As Cathy Silber ("*Nüshu*" 160–61), who worked with Nianhua for several months during 1988–89, reported, Nianhua would not lend this *nüshu* to her because "She was afraid I would publish it in the newspaper and her daughter would see it and punish her for it."

Scholarly investigation of *nüshu* enabled Nianhua to earn a living in her aging years after she had been abandoned by her daughter; it also inspired her to write many *nüshu* on behalf of other Jiangyong women, helping them to vent their frustration over the misery in their lives. As author, she might have found relief from writing *nüshu* but, ironically, she might also have been victimized, since the publication of these pieces in scholarly research deprived her of control over the *nüshu* she authored. She had no way to limit their readership or respond to the reception of her work, a situation quite different from Bamboo's. By writing *nüshu* for academic ends, was Nianhua empowered or disempowered?

meiyue: a *nüshu* transmitter's emotional burden

Besides Nianhua, Gao was the other major informant of the 1980s, and Meiyue was Gao's granddaughter. In 2003, with the *nüshu* knowledge learned from her grandmother, Meiyue was appointed a "*nüshu* transmitter" by the Jiangyong Propaganda Office, the local authority in charge of promoting *nüshu* as a UNESCO intangible cultural heritage since the early 2000s.

Although born after Liberation when many traditions were considered "feudal poisons" and targeted for eradication, Meiyue still had an opportunity to learn women's "traditional" script thanks to her grandma Gao's *nüshu* practice. Gao had been sworn into a sisterhood composed of seven members – they called themselves "the Seven Sisters." On occasions when these seven sisters gathered, they would sing *nüshu* songs to entertain themselves. And if one of them encountered some difficulty, they would compose a *nüshu* piece to console her and pay her a visit. The *nüshu* cited at the opening of this article, for instance, was written by one of the sisterhood, Cizhu.

By observing how much her grandma's sworn sisters enjoyed *nüshu*, Meiyue developed a special admiration for the practice and began to learn the script from her grandma. But Meiyue's *nüshu* knowledge went unnoticed by the scholars in the 1980s when most attention was paid to her grandmother. And then she married and went to live in her husband's village in the mid-1980s, which drove her out of her grandma's *nüshu* spotlight.

Meiyue's ties with *nüshu* were reinvigorated some ten years later. In early 2001 when she returned to her natal village for the Chinese New Year festival, she came across several teenage girls who developed an interest in *nüshu*. This was when the *nüshu* museum was under construction in their village, Puwei, where the first scholar-identified *nüshu* practitioner Gao had lived for over seventy years. When these young girls saw Meiyue, they grew excited, as if they had found the answer to their curiosity: "Sister, we would like to learn *nüshu*. Would you please teach us?"

These young girls' curiosity about *nüshu* triggered Meiyue's sense of mission to celebrate the *nüshu* heritage her grandma once represented. With the help of her brother, she immediately organized a *nüshu* class in Puwei, which was also her own natal village. For two years, she traveled from her affinal village to Puwei to give a *nüshu* lesson almost every week. With Meiyue's contribution to transmitting *nüshu* knowledge, in 2003, at age forty, she was appointed a "*nüshu* transmitter," alongside He Yanxin, He Jinghua, and Yang Huanyi, who were in their sixties and nineties.[14]

Being a *nüshu* transmitter comes with rights and obligations. The transmitter is entitled to a monthly stipend, which went from 20 RMB dollars in 2003 to 100 dollars in 2010. In return, she is obliged to create *nüshu* at the government's request and provide, free of charge, reproduction copies of all her *nüshu* works at the pleasure of the local authorities. But for Meiyue, "*nüshu* transmitter" is more than an official title; it is also a point of family pride. To honor her grandma, she expects herself to be versed not only in singing and writing but also in versifying, especially with regard to biographical *nüshu* – after all, *nüshu* is a genre for lamenting one's misery. To undertake this task, she began to observe the life experiences of people around her. In 2004 Meiyue completed her first biographical lament for a woman called Fang.

Fang gave birth to her first baby three years after she had married. To build a better future, she and her husband took their newborn to Guangdong to earn a living as "floating labor," a rite of passage for youths in contemporary rural China. But sadly, this new family soon fell apart. The husband died in a car accident eighteen days before their second child was born, as shown in Meiyue's *nüshu* about Fang:[15]

> In spring, a warming season,
> The swallows leave the nest and fly south …
> In winter, the season of cold, snow, and frost,
> All the leaves fall because of the chill, …
> And you returned to the nether world,
> Leaving your wife and daughters behind.

Meiyue felt driven to write a *nüshu* about Fang not just because of Fang's own misfortune but also because of the miseries faced by Fang's mother-in-law, a widow. This widow lost her husband when her son was only three years old. She was in poor health and depended on her little son who went begging for food to maintain the family's subsistence. And just when they finally seemed about to enjoy a better life, she lost her son:

> All my family were pushed from me …, and
> All my complaints can never be fully expressed …
> I don't blame Heaven or Earth;
> I can only blame my destiny for not being lucky enough …
> I called to Heaven but Heaven didn't respond;

I called on Earth and Earth didn't answer.
It's all because I didn't cultivate a good fate in past lifetimes, and so ...
This old white head has to see off the young black one.

When I collected this lament from Meiyue in 2004, I was also introduced to Fang. And from my interview with her I learned that some crucial incidents were left out of Meiyue's *nüshu*. I then encouraged Meiyue to further develop the storyline of this piece. But she never did. Whenever I visited her in subsequent years and asked about her progress on it, she always said to me, "I'm too busy to work on it." It was not until 2009 that she finally confessed:

> I no longer write *nüshu* lament ... I used to be an optimistic person. But when I wrote *nüshu*, I had to express sorrow and melancholy. Pouring my emotions into it left me in a state of misery. So I asked myself, "Why write about this? It only causes me more pain."[16]

Meiyue's answer was puzzling, considering that her grandma Gao had not shied away from writing laments on others' behalf, and we had never heard her say that writing *nüshu* made her feel more bitter. Meiyue then explained:

> Grandma's heart had gone through all that suffering in the first place. She had two daughters and they all died before her – experiences like that were certainly depressing. It occurred when the Japanese army invaded Yongming [i.e., Jiangyong]. My aunts [Gao's daughters] had already fled, but then they returned home for some things and got caught.[17]

Meiyue did not elaborate, but according to local villagers' reports, those women who got caught by Japanese soldiers were often raped before being killed. For Gao, this was truly an unbearable tragedy. And perhaps, because she had suffered such severe hardship, she had developed certain "antibodies," thus making her immune to any further emotional attack. But Meiyue was different. She was like a fresh recruit with no defense mechanism, and as such she found herself caught up in *nüshu*'s web of misfortune from which there was no way out.

"No way out" means not only the absence of an outlet for negative emotions but also a lack of feedback from the subject that would have made Meiyue feel worthy to undertake this difficult emotion-charged versifying task. She expanded on this:

> In 2004 when you asked me to ... write more about Fang, I did try. I went to interview Fang further, as you scholars did. But she responded, "What's the use? It won't change anything" ... After I had pursued it several times, she finally revealed her true concern, "Spreading my life story around won't do any good for my reputation."[18]

Fang's answer got Meiyue thinking: what does writing one's suffering in *nüshu* mean to the subject in contemporary society?

Of course, Meiyue understands that as a *nüshu* transmitter on the government payroll she is obliged to write and compose, and she readily provides her works to her superiors. After all, to sustain *nüshu* as a living heritage, composing new texts, rather than merely reciting old ones, is key. As a compromise, she now chooses to work on pleasant or aphoristic texts, such as "Wish you good luck and propitiousness" (*jixiang ruyi*). At the very least she wishes to versify on something that will not engage too much of her emotions. The following *nüshu* is one she wrote on a fan for sale in the *nüshu* museum, where she has also worked as a full-time guide since 2004:

This is a novel, exceptional, and unique script,
A script of women, composed for women, and read by women.
It enables women to express their heartfelt sentiments;
It carries women's history of thousands of years.
Who says that women are inferior to men?
Women hold up half of the sky.
Women of Xinhua [i.e., Shangjiangxu Township] are talented and learned;
They have written *nüshu* that will be transmitted all over the world.

Despite the fact that *su kelian* is *nüshu*'s traditional generic affect, Meiyue as an official *nüshu* transmitter has no intention of being trapped by the emotional burdens of *nüshu*'s lamenting nature.

conclusions

"Writing a piece to lament my misery" is a stock phrase often heard in *nüshu* and *nüge*. *Nüshu* together with *nüge* in fact show us a lot about common miseries of women's lives, whether they have lost their family (especially their male relations – fathers, husbands, or sons), lack natal backup (i.e., having no brothers), or must deal with unsupportive affinal kin (especially mothers-in-law), unfilial sons, daughters, or daughters-in-law. These miseries might result from irresistible macro-socio-political chaos, such as warfare and its corollary, conscription, or from women's structural vulnerability within the Chinese patriarchal agrarian context, where they lacked resources, knowledge, or skills to sustain themselves, or were deemed an "untitled object" to be claimed when outside their affinal and natal domains. Perhaps their suffering was simply a matter of destiny, of not having cultivated enough merit in their previous lives. Whatever the situation, the misery they faced was a lived reality that could never be undone. Then what was the point of lamentation?

Lamentation obviously had considerable power, so much so that an entire genre, *nüshu*, developed primarily to express it, to *su kelian*. On the psychological level, it helped "liberate one's heart," as Meiyue eloquently put it when she tried to understand the *nüshu* practice of her grandma's Seven Sisters in retrospect.

> When we encounter certain misfortunes, if we didn't have *nüshu* to write them down, we would become sadder and sadder. With *nüshu*, we don't have to dwell on the sadness. Whenever we need to remember what we've gone through, we just read the *nüshu* and get the feeling of it back from that. Our mind is thereby set free.[19]

In other words, *nüshu* helped them discharge negative emotions and restore psychological balance; it also helped them preserve the memory without being burdened by it.

On the social level, *su kelian* as performance served two purposes. On the one hand, it opened up a communication platform for the protagonist and others, mostly women but not necessarily limited to them, of the *nüshu/nüge*'s circulation community. This helped empower the miserable protagonist by building connections between her and her fellow villagers. That connectedness was a form of moral support that diluted the lamenter's sense of helplessness and solitude; furthermore, it recognized her fortitude and perseverance in facing life's ordeals, which in turn motivated her to stand strong. Perhaps that is why some women would come to Nianhua and ask her to write biographical *nüshu* on their behalf. On the other hand, *su kelian* functioned as a social forum where one expressed criticisms on certain subjects (e.g., Bamboo's unfilial son and daughter-in-law), commented on certain events (e.g., conscription and warfare), and called for justice (e.g., Nianhua's cry "What place can I call home?").

As a communication platform and social forum, *nüshu* together with *nüge* gave voice to rural women's silenced existence in traditional Jiangyong. And *nüshu* scholars' main responsibility is to channel these women's muted voices to the outside world at both historiographical and epistemological levels. But Nianhua's example shows another side of the issue. The problem is that any academic research (or news coverage) inevitably results in publication; it may thus assume the authority that used to rest in the *nüshu* practitioners' hands. This may put them in an even more vulnerable situation. In the past, as Bamboo's case shows, when a critique was issued about a certain target, the *nüshu/nüge* performer enjoyed the autonomy to decide whether to sing or how to rephrase her verses during performance so as to avoid unnecessary confrontations. But as the traditional circulation mode has been replaced by publication networks – in some sense an "imagined community" for the *nüshu* practitioner – the *nüshu* writer's direct and immediate link with her audience is lost. Losing control of who receives her *nüshu* and how means that the *nüshu* writer has to think twice when she shapes a criticism. In this sense *nüshu*'s function as a communication platform collapses, and so does the *nüshu* writer's power to critique, comment, and assert claims for justice.

While Nianhua's example highlights the paradox of academic research, Meiyue's illustrates the dilemma of being an institutional *nüshu* transmitter. Meiyue writes not out of her spontaneous revelation of heartfelt sentiments, nor upon others' request, but to fulfill her job description. In the process of writing *su kelian*, she immersed herself in others' misery, and as she developed empathy with her subjects and translated that understanding into verse, she found herself devoured by the sentiments of misery. Even more discouraging, her endeavor was not appreciated by the subject of her text. This was partly because her subject, Fang, could neither read nor sing the *nüshu*/*nüge*, and partly because Fang was uncomfortable with the "exotic gaze" cast by readers of the "imagined community" created through the enterprise of publication.

In contrast to Meiyue's practice in the modern setting, her *nüshu* predecessors, such as Nianhua, Gao, Cizhu, or Canxian, might have been emotional or even have shed tears when writing on commission or upon request, but they felt comforted in the knowledge that their subject could always get relief from the *nüshu* they wrote. "Emotion" for these scribes was not a psychological burden but an act of altruism that had the merit of benefiting the vulnerable. If the scribe could relate the subject's misery to her own experience, writing for others was even curative, for that writing was like writing for oneself, helping to discharge pent-up sadness. This emotional transference could also take place among the audience when *nüshu* was performed. In this way, the *nüshu* scribe, subject, and audience all together constituted a "community of sentiment" (Appadurai) wherein they shared one another's lifeworlds and found consolation in one another's empathetic understanding. And this is how *su kelian* developed into *nüshu*'s generic affect.

Nüshu research has certainly filled what used to be a "blank page" in Chinese history: it has uncovered women's hidden and unheard voices, and recovered and valued their subjectivity. But ironically, its corollary – publication – has also threatened to overwrite women's authority. Similarly, the institutionalization of transmission was originally aimed at preserving this endangered heritage, but if preservation comes at the cost of imposing emotional burdens or psychological discomfort on the subjects or agents of these works, is this effort still meaningful and worthwhile?

At this crossroads between tradition and modernity, between the old community of sentiment and the imagined community of publication, which way should *nüshu* go? The story of this tradition, surviving to give voice precisely because it was ignored, has arrived at a point where it is now also largely dispossessed from its community of practice. Is it time for *nüshu* to pass into history? Or should we preserve it as an icon of rural women's insistence that their lives matter, whatever the cost?

disclosure statement

No potential conflict of interest was reported by the author.

notes

1 According to Cathy Silber ("*Nüshu*" 141–42), this piece was written in 1972 in condolence to He Xijing over the death of her husband in 1969. In addition to lamenting her miserable life, it also includes a description of He Xijing's sworn sisterhood pact. For the whole text, see Xie (506–45); and Zhao (*Anthology* 358–66).

2 A woman of the Qing era named Zhong Yun, for example, had tried to burn her poems; fortunately her son Cha Shenxing (1650–1727) had stopped it and later published those works (Sun 138–39).

3 It was not until after the Ming-Qing era (1368–1911) that female literacy gained social recognition

as "cultural capital" (Bourdieu), but even so it was confined mainly to the scholar-gentry class or new urban elites. For most Chinese women, who were peasants, literacy remained an unattainable luxury. For pioneering work on Chinese gentry women's writing world, see, for example, Hu; Ko; and Mann.

4 These "blanks" have only recently been addressed by way of oral life histories in Bossen; Hershatter; and Li and Chen.

5 Zhao revised her 1992 edition into a five-volume set in 2005.

6 For Yang Huanyi, see Zhao (*Collection*). For He Yanxin, see Endō; Kuo; and Liu (*Gendered Words* ch. 4). For He Jinghua, see Liu ("Biographical Writing"); and Luo.

7 Interview conducted in August 2015.

8 Sung by He Yanxin and recorded in November 2004. See also Gong (*Nüshu* 60–65) for the whole text.

9 For how these social changes influenced women's lives, see Bossen; Hershatter; and Li and Chen.

10 Sung by Mo Yuexing (b.1918) and recorded in October 2000. See also Gong (*Nüshu* 252–53); Xie (679–83); Zhao (*Anthology* 473–75); and Zhao (*Compilation* 2531–40) for slightly different versions.

11 The quotes in this section are based on interviews with Juan conducted in October 1993 and August 2015.

12 Interview conducted in August 2013.

13 However, according to William Chiang (*Women's Mysterious Codes* 90), who conducted *nüshu* fieldwork in the late 1980s, he had spent ten dollars to borrow this *nüshu* and made a transcript.

14 The year 2003 was the first point at which the title of "*nüshu* transmitter" was offered. This status was based on one's reputation in *nüshu* writing. To ensure the selection of qualified *nüshu* transmitters, Interim Measures for the Administration of Nüshu Chuanren were promulgated in 2004. According to the Measures, a transmitter has to qualify in four areas: proficiency at singing and writing *nüshu*, skill in "female needlework" (embroidering and weaving) and knowledge of the local dialect and local customs, demonstration of one's civic virtue (e.g., observing national laws and village protocols), and loyalty to the Center for Nüshu Cultural and Research Administration, which is supervised under the Jiangyong Propaganda Office.

15 Fang's biographical *nüshu* was provided by Meiyue in November 2004.

16 Interview conducted in July 2009.

17 Interview conducted in July 2009.

18 Interview conducted in August 2010.

19 Interview conducted in July 2009.

bibliography

Appadurai, Arjun. "Topographies of the Self: Praise and Emotion in Hindu India." *Language and Politics of Emotion*. Ed. Catherine A. Lutz and Lila Abu-Lughod. Cambridge: Cambridge UP, 1990. 92–112. Print.

Bossen, Laurel. *Chinese Women and Rural Development: Sixty Years of Change in Lu Village, Yunan*. Lanham, MD: Rowman, 2002. Print.

Bourdieu, Pierre. "The Forms of Capital." *Handbook of Theory and Research for the Sociology of Education*. Ed. J.G. Richardson. New York: Greenwood, 1986. 241–58. Print.

Carlitz, Katherine. "Shrines, Governing-Class Identity, and the Cult of Widow Fidelity in Mid-Ming Jiangnan." *Journal of Asian Studies* 56.3 (1997): 612–40. Print.

Carlitz, Katherine. "The Social Uses of Female Virtue in Late Ming Editions of *Lienü Zhuan*." *Late Imperial China* 12.1 (1991): 117–48. Print.

Chiang, William W. *We Two Know the Script: We Have Become Good Friends*. Lanham, MD: UP of America, 1995. Print.

Chiang, William W. 女性密碼:女書田野調查筆記 [*Women's Mysterious Codes:* Nüshu *Field Notes*]. Taipei: Sanmin shuju, 2002. Print.

Endō, Orie. 中国女文字 [*Research on Chinese Women's Script*]. Tokyo: Meijishoyin, 2002. Print.

Gong Zhebing, ed. 女書:世界唯一的女性文字 [Nüshu: *The World's Only Women's Script*]. Taipei: Funü xinzhi, 1991. Print.

Gong Zhebing. 女性文字與女性社會 [*Women's Script and Women's Society*]. Wulumuqi: Xinjiang renmin chubanshe, 1995. Print.

Hershatter, Gail. *The Gender of Memory: Rural Women and China's Collective Past*. Berkeley: U of California P, 2011. Print.

Hu Siao-chen. 才女徹夜未眠 [*Talented Women Sleepless the Whole Night*]. Taipei: Maitian renwen, 2003. Print.

Idema, Wilt L. "*Changben* Texts in the *Nüshu* Repertoire of Southern Hunan." *The Eternal Storyteller: Oral Literature in Modern China*. Ed. Vibeke Bordahl. Richmond: Curzon, 1999. 95–114. Print.

Idema, Wilt L. *Heroines of Jiangyong: Chinese Narrative Ballads in Women's Script*. Seattle: U of Washington P, 2009. Print.

Ko, Dorothy. *Teachers of the Inner Chambers: Women and Culture in Seventeenth-Century China*. Stanford: Stanford UP, 1994. Print.

Kuo Yu-i, dir. *Calling and Recalling: The Sentiments of Women's Script* (Nüshu). Prod. Liu Fei-wen and Hsieh Chia-kuen. 74 mins. Turnbox Production Studio, Taiwan, 2013. Documentary.

Li Qiaoning, and Chen Hairu. 陕西農村婦女的日常生活 *(1949–1965)* [*Peasant Women's Daily Life in Shaanxi Province, 1949–1965*]. Beijing: Zhongguo shehui kexue chubanshe, 2014. Print.

Liu Fei-wen. "女書傳記書寫的歷史意涵與當代困境" [The Biographical Writing of Nüshu: Its Historical Implications and Cultural Practice in Changing Rural China]. *Research on Women in Modern Chinese History* 23 (2014): 65–125. Print.

Liu Fei-wen. "The Confrontation between Fidelity and Fertility: *Nüshu*, *Nüge* and Peasant Women's Conceptions of Widowhood in Jiangyong County, Hunan Province, China." *Journal of Asian Studies* 60.4 (2001): 1051–84. Print.

Liu Fei-wen. "開顯Geertz的深描闡幽:女書文本的述說、閱讀與展演" [Elaborating on Geertz's "Thick Description": From Text to Reading, Narration, and Performance]. *Taiwan Journal of Anthropology* 5.1 (2007): 63–107. Print.

Liu Fei-wen. "From Being to Becoming: *Nüshu* and Sentiments in a Chinese Rural Community." *American Ethnologist* 31.3 (2004): 422–39. Print.

Liu Fei-wen. *Gendered Words: Sentiments and Expression in Changing Rural China*. New York: Oxford UP, 2015. Print.

Liu Fei-wen. "Literacy, Gender, and Class: *Nüshu* and Sisterhood Communities in Southern Rural Hunan." *Nan Nü: Men, Women, and Gender in Early and Imperial China* 6.2 (2004): 241–82. Print.

Liu Fei-wen. "Narrative, Genre, and Contextuality: The *Nüshu*-Transcribed Liang-Zhu Ballad in Rural South China." *Asian Ethnology* 69.2 (2010): 241–64. Print.

Liu Fei-wen. "情意:性別與階級的再現與超越:梁祝敘說與文體之音" [Righteousness, Romance, and Transcendence: Gender, Class, and Generic Expressive Niches of Liang-Zhu Narratives]. *Journal of Theater Studies* 5 (2010): 27–68. Print.

Liu Fei-wen. "文本與文境的對話:女書三朝書與婦女的情意音聲" [Text, Context, and Women's Voices in *Nüshu* Wedding Literature (*Sanzhaoshu*)]. *Taiwan Journal of Anthropology* 3.1 (2005): 87–142. Print.

Luo Wanyi. 一冊女書筆記 [*A Volume of* Nüshu *Notes*]. Hongkong: Xin funü xiejin hui, 2002. Print.

Mann, Susan. *Precious Records: Women in China's Long Eighteenth Century*. Stanford: Stanford UP, 1997. Print.

McLaren, Anne. "Women's Voices and Textuality: Chastity and Abduction in Chinese *Nüshu* Writing." *Modern China* 22.4 (1996): 382–416. Print.

Seremetakis, C. Nadia. *The Lost Word: Women, Death, and Divination in Inner Mani*. Chicago: U of Chicago P, 1991. Print.

Silber, Cathy. "From Daughter to Daughter-in-Law in the Women's Script of Southern Hunan." *Engendering China: Women, Culture, and the State*. Ed. Christina Gilmartin, Gail Hershatter, Lisa Rofel, and Tyrene White. Cambridge, MA: Harvard UP, 1994. 47–69. Print.

Silber, Cathy. "*Nüshu* (Chinese Women's Script) Literacy and Literature." Ph.D. Diss. U of Michigan, 1995. Print.

Sun Kangyi (Kang-i Sun Chang). 古典與現代的女性詮釋 [*Classical and Modern Interpretations on Women*]. Taipei: Lianhe wenxue, 1998. Print.

Xie Zhimin, ed. 江永女書之謎 [*The Myth of Jiangyong* Nüshu]. 3 vols. Zhengzhou: Henan renmin chubanshe, 1991. Print.

永明縣志 [*Yongming Gazetteer*]. Comp. Wang Chunzao et al. Rpt. in 1933. N.p.: n.p., 1846. Print.

Zeng Jiwu, ed. 湖南各縣調查筆記 [*Notes on the Investigation of Each Hunan County*]. Hunan: Heji yinshuasuo, 1931. Print.

Zhao Liming, ed. 中國女書集成 [*Anthology of Chinese* Nüshu]. Trans. Zhou Shuoyi. Beijing: Qinghua daxue chubanshe, 1992. Print.

Zhao Liming, ed. 陽煥宜女書作品集 [*Collection of Yang Huanyi's* Nüshu *Works*]. Beijing: Guoji wenhua chuban gongsi, 2004. Print.

Zhao Liming. 中國女書合集 [*Compilation of Chinese* Nüshu]. 5 vols. Beijing: Zhonghua shuju, 2005. Print.

Zhao Liming. "從三朝書看女書的社會學意義" [From *Sanzhaoshu* to Examination of *Nüshu*'s Sociological Meanings]. 奇特的女書 [*The Peculiar* Nüshu]. Ed. Shi Jinbo, Bai Bin, and Zhao Liming. Beijing: Beijing yuyan xueyuan chubanshe, 1995. 14–28. Print.

jane dowson

"MY MAIN JOB IS TO TRANSLATE / PAIN INTO TALES THEY CAN TOLERATE // IN ANOTHER LANGUAGE"

women's poetry and the health humanities

This article considers the exchanges between medicine and literature in some poems written by British and American women over the last fifty years. The poems selected examine the interface of pain and poetic language in such contexts as: the communications between patient and doctor; a depressed person's sensed effect on their loved ones; and a cancer sufferer's altered subjectivity. Medical Humanities, an established field of enquiry, depends upon an identifiable concept of humankind, a collective noun that implies some unity of the species. Thus, the fundamental idea of "Medical Humanities" poses a challenge to a feminist politics of difference. However, women have a vital part to play in its scope, approach and developments. In *Feminism as Radical Humanism* (1994), Pauline Johnson argues that although feminism never found a home in such historical projects as the Enlightenment, Liberalism, or Marxism, it can have a stake in recent discourses around New Humanism. Furthermore, it is crucial to present feminism as one articulation of humanism in order not to relegate women, yet again, to "[feminism's] own oppositional consciousness in an autonomous sphere of aestheticized images of non-subordinated femininity" (Johnson xv). By pluralizing these modern humanisms, we avoid the discredited universals of the earlier projects and can profess interconnecting commitments both to humankind and to the uniqueness of each human personality. Importantly, however, Johnson insists:

> While modern feminism is both a manifestation and an interpretation of modern humanism, it is also, at the same time, a critic of all those constructions of an image of human subjectivity which presuppose the normativity of a particular socialized gender identity. (ix)

In emphasizing poems that both expose and disturb supposedly normative accounts of illness and its treatments, I illustrate how the woman poet operates "as both interpreter and critic" (ibid.) of the Medical Humanities. For example, we can find a feminist politics in poems that challenge the esoteric language and patriarchal assumptions of certain medical practices. Such counter-discursiveness is a necessary phase and means for the purpose of social equality but it can also reinforce the centrality of male power and subjectivity. Therefore, the woman writer speaking in non-gender-specific pronouns and contexts on behalf of humanity is arguably more radical. Irish poet Eavan Boland (b. 1944), who spelled out her own specifically female negotiation with national and poetic traditions in *Object Lessons: The Life of the Woman and the Poet in Our Time* (1995), evokes an ideal of feminizing humanity that goes further than "humanizing femininity" (254). Accordingly, some poems specify female subjectivity, some express agency as autonomous individuals, while others presume to speak of common human experience. Collectively, the poems document and effect shifts in knowledge about, and the associated stigmas concerning, illnesses that carry secrecy and shame, notably depression and cancer. Cancer notoriously affects the most private bodily parts, such as male prostates and female breasts. In poetry, women find a language for female perspectives on how this disease raids their bodies and contingently their self-identification. Crucially, poetry defines itself against discourses that assume a full apprehension and disclosure of experience. It thus both contributes to and checks the ways in which literature is appropriated by the biomedical sciences.

"Medical Humanities" is a recent but established interdisciplinary field that restores a lost understanding of how humanity – rather than the laboratory, performance indicators, or profit – is at the heart of medical education and practice. In bridging conceptual binary oppositions between science and the arts, it also queries other conceptual polarities, such as the mind and feelings, the personal and the social, and the sick and the well. According to one definition,

> The disciplines actually involved in it are familiar humanities and social sciences disciplines, having in common both an interest in individual experience (which in this context means individuals' experiences of health, illness, disability, diagnosis, treatment and care), and recognition that *subjective experience* can be a legitimate source of knowledge. (Evans n. pag.)

Evans also implies that the role of the Humanities is to hold medical practice to account, for the field involves the "humanities looking at medicine, looking at patients, and – crucially – *looking at medicine looking at patients.* The way medicine conceives and represents patients shows up in the way that it treats patients" (n. pag.). Crawford et al. propose "Health Humanities" as a more appropriate title in that it accommodates the contribution to knowledge by a broader spectrum of participants in the diagnosis and treatment of illness. They argue that "Health Humanities" thus takes the emphasis off the scientific realm of medicine, stressing:

> One of the key concerns linking the healthcare disciplines and the humanities is the notion of meaning [...] A consideration of meaning is central to both the humanities and healthcare because people ascribe specific values and purpose to their experiences, conduct and relationships. Matters are made meaningful when people understand and make sense of their actions, feelings and thoughts. (Crawford et al. 4)

Furthermore, illness propels the sufferers into more intense versions of what humans innately do: "human beings [are] continually seeking meaning, interpreting their environment, other individuals, and themselves in a process of dynamic interaction with the world around them" (5). Crawford et al. believe that this quest for meaning is grounded "in interactions and dialogue" and tends to function through symbols (ibid.). Referring to the work on physical suffering by Elaine Scarry (1985), they explain how symbols are necessary because pain "is at once the most irreducible of subjective experiences and the most incommunicable [...] rarely rendered in detail in most novels, yet [it] haunts the warp and weft of human cultures" (Crawford et al. 5).

This remarkable absence of illness in literature was noted by Virginia Woolf (1882–1941) almost a century earlier in her provocative essay "On Being Ill" (1930). No stranger to physical and mental afflictions, she ponders why writers have avoided the subject when it is as common as love, war, and jealousy, the staple foods of novelists. She concludes that literature tends to elevate the mind over the body and thereby maintains "that the body is a sheet of plain glass through which the soul looks straight and clear, and, save for one or two passions such as desire and greed, is null, and negligible and non existent" (193). Another reason, Woolf suggests, is the difficulty of finding words for pain:

> Finally, to hinder the description of illness in literature, there is the poverty of the language. English, which can express the thoughts of Hamlet and the tragedy of Lear, has no words for the shiver and the headache. It has all grown one way. The merest schoolgirl, when she falls in love, has Shakespeare or Keats to speak her mind for her; but let the sufferer try to describe a pain in his head to a doctor and language at once runs dry. There is nothing ready made for him. He is forced to coin words himself, and, taking his pain in one hand, and a lump of pure sound in the other (as perhaps the people of Babel did in the beginning), so to crush them together that a brand new word in the end drops out. Probably it will be something laughable. (194)

The very elusiveness of understanding the self, let alone communicating it, is both the essence and method of Woolf's thesis. While acknowledging that illness "is the great confessional" (196) and thus potentially liberates the expression of common human thoughts and feelings that normally we hide from one another, her startling point is that a fully sympathetic understanding is both an illusion and undesirable:

> We do not know our own souls, let alone the souls of others. Human beings do not go hand in hand the whole stretch of the way. There is a virgin force in each; a snowfield where even the print of birds' feet is unknown. Here we go alone, and like it better so. Always to have sympathy, always to be accompanied, always to be understood would be intolerable. (Ibid.)

Woolf thus both endorses but also criticizes the assumptions of Medical or Health Humanities that would elicit personal narratives about a condition and interpret them as authentic knowledge about a particular disease. She also indirectly questions the viability of Freudian concepts of a cure based on the premise that the unknowable unconscious can be made knowable through talk. Additionally, the above extracts illustrate how Woolf's essay mediates its argument through metaphors that transpose the personal realm into something common to its readers. At the same time, these metaphors conceal the full sense of Woolf's unique inner "snowfield."

In *Literature after Feminism* (2003), Rita Felski points out that feminists have a hard time with the notion of universality due to its equation with normative maleness yet believes that "it is also obvious that art does speak across social boundaries" (15). She sees analogy as the means to negotiate between similarity and difference, the particular and the general. Correspondingly, Woolf's densely metaphoric and poetic prose models how women can pioneer in writing about health and illness and in formulating a concept of a human condition that is no longer premised on a particular kind of male. Woolf concludes: "We need the poets to imagine for us [...] Indeed, it is to the poets that we turn. Illness makes us disinclined for the large campaigns that prose exacts" (199). In other words, the solitude of illness is matched by the solipsism of lyrical poetry. In her treatise on the relationship between authenticity and authority in poetic accounts of illness, Fiona Sampson echoes Woolf: "poetry challenges the authority of self grounding discourses, such as clinical diagnosis, which rely on the possibility of stability in the ways in which their language functions" (Sampson 262). Sampson asserts that poetry exclusively can afford "the chance for nonsense and obliquity," "to mix up discourses," and to "don the liberating mask of metaphor" (262–63). Furthermore, since poetry defines itself against any kind of linguistic stability, it can offer individuals who find themselves in the position of "discursive weakness," specifically the ill and women, a voice to undermine the hegemonic discourses that put them there:

> As an unstable and destabilizing discourse, poetry presences the inauthenticity of many of language's other claims to authenticity.

> Moreover, and at this final margin, poetry may perhaps after all offer its writers and readers, through its very discursive obliquity, some soundings of what we might almost be tempted to call authentic experience. (264)

Paradoxically, then, the authenticity lies in the "discursive obliquity" of poetry's non-verbal signs.

The remainder of this essay looks at how poems are often counter-discursive to the specialized jargon that is still rife in medical hegemony. Furthermore, they keep check on the disciplines of Medical and Health Humanities by maintaining the element of incommunicability about each unique virgin "snowfield" that is, as Woolf points out, fundamental to the experience of being human and that is accentuated by being ill. In recognizing "subjective experience as a legitimate source of knowledge" (Evans n. pag.), Medical or Health Humanities looks to literature, whether by established writers or therapeutically by sufferers, as documentary. However, poets can stand as critics of how academic disciplines or medical professionals might make assumptions about the capacity of words to fully relate experience. In her introduction to *Signs and Humours: The Poetry of Medicine*, a product of her residency at the Royal Society of Medicine in 2005, poet Lavinia Greenlaw writes: "Medicine is a science, but it also belongs to a general field of human enquiry which encompasses poetry. Both begin with the self and neither escapes it" (14). She notes the breakage in language that illness brings, cites the Czech poet Miroslav Holub, "'pain [...] is a pretence of silence,'" and comments: "It's not saying nothing, but it is saying something in a way that withholds itself [...] Poetry activates all that is liminal and residual in language" (17–18).

The work of poet Elizabeth Jennings (1926–2001) illustrates how reading subjective experience as a source of knowledge has to take account of what the subject leaves out as much as what they say. In the 1960s, Jennings spent many months in Oxford's Warneford mental hospital due to depression and suicide attempts. Her private papers incorporate records of that period, including notes about the pills and other treatments she was given. Her journals and correspondence also refer to the plights of her fellow patients, some of whom received the controversial electroconvulsive therapy. These papers reveal her qualms about the drugs that seemed to exacerbate her anxieties; they register the depths of her despair and her terror of the Freudian doctor who intimidated her.[1] She bravely reworked these bleak experiences into poetry published in two particular volumes, *Recoveries* (1964) and *The Mind Has Mountains* (1966), which, interestingly, damaged her reputation as a literary poet. In "The Interrogator," she writes back against the godlike stature of the psychiatrist who is "always right," "always has an answer," "always knows best" and "can always find words": "And if you covered his mouth with your hand, / Pinned him down to his smooth desk chair, / You would be doing just what he wishes. / His silence would prove that he was right" (Jennings 73–74). The poem's fantasy repudiates the unequal process of the medical confessional while also forming a conspiratorial bond between poet and reader. Nevertheless, Jennings's poems withhold much of her inward drama and she privately acknowledged that some pain was always unfathomable and inexpressible: "There are some unhappinesses which can never be transformed into art. They are deep, dark, cold places – utterly infertile. Nothing grows there."[2] Jennings's imagery shares the coldness of Woolf's snowfield but is less inviting. However, snow does, of course, simply cover up the mud.

Some of the poems by Jennings's near contemporary, U.A. Fanthorpe (1929–2009), are similarly counter-discursive but more direct. They stem from her post as a medical receptionist in a hospital's neurological department where she observed the interactions between patients and doctors:

> From my glass dugout I could feel that I was doing something to redress the way patients are spoken of in case notes, and also to

> celebrate the tremendous energy and resourcefulness of their ways with words [...] The important thing was to make what I wrote as unlike the official, the authoritative, the rational, as I could. (Fanthorpe, "Hospital Speak" 32)

In the poem "Job Description: Medical Records," she parodies the voice of the institutional "we" to satirize its hierarchal structures and impersonal ethos: "We prefer you / not to think of patients as people, but / Digits. That makes it much easier. Our system / Is terminal digit filing" (*New and Collected Poems* n. pag.). Fanthorpe explains how she "tipped over into poetry": "I could think of no other way of responding to this babel of voices, this jumble of codes, everyone wanting something and most of them held back, by illness or etiquette, from achieving the effective spark of communication" ("Hospital Speak" 33). In "Casehistory: Julie (Encephalitis)," Fanthorpe intersperses the girl's voice with italicized fragments from Shakespeare's Ophelia: "I must be mental. / I'll do meself in. // *There is a willow*" (*New and Collected Poems* n. pag.). The dialogism of the vernacular and the literary contrasts the impoverished speech of Julie with the poetic beauty of Ophelia's lines. However, this linguistic hybridization also conflates their situations, for both young women are distraught about their losses and have the same inaccessible inner "snowfield." Discussing the poem, Elizabeth Sandie comments on the final lines, "What about me dad? / Me dad's not gone is he?": "We see simultaneously the patient's pain in constantly having to meet these griefs afresh, as well as experiencing the uncomfortable, painful immediacy of the listener. The space at the end of the poem implicates us in its silence" (Sandie 154). In such pieces by Jennings and Fanthorpe, poetry puts centre stage the voices of characters and experience that might be overlooked or misrepresented. It can also contain several linguistic registers and perspectives at once – here, that of the speaker, the professional listener, the reader, and public notions of social responsibility. Furthermore, it draws attention to silence: what Julie flounders to say and the impossibility of any consoling response. Thus, Fanthorpe's poem unsettles the assumptions about what health means, for illness can bring its own clarity. As Woolf put it:

> But in health the genial pretence must be kept up and the effort renewed – to communicate, to civilize, to share, to cultivate the desert, educate the native, to work together by day and by night to sport. In illness this make-believe ceases. (196)

In her poetry collection *Off Colour* (1998), Jackie Kay (b. 1961) accords with the aforementioned task of Medical Humanities in "looking at medicine, looking at patients, and – crucially – *looking at medicine looking at patients*. The way medicine conceives and represents patients shows up in the way that it treats patients" (Evans n. pag.). "Crown and Country" exposes economic differences when it comes to dental treatments that in turn symbolize "the entire population grinding its teeth" in disaffection and dysfunction (Kay 14). In "Where it Hurts" her speakers log and investigate "The weary wabbit world of the worried unwell" (12), marking the distance between patient and doctor in the health services. "Where it Hurts" is in the voice of a woman frustrated with the doctor's misuse of power that shuts down any meaningful dialogue. She confides in the reader: "I go to the Doctor but what does the Doctor say? / He looks at me as if I were a germ, a sudden outbreak. / When did you start feeling this way? He mumbles, / already scribbling my sentence, my fate?" (10). Similarly, in her volume, provocatively titled *Keeping Mum* (2003) – playing on the idiom meaning to be quiet – Gwyneth Lewis has a sequence of dramatic monologues, "Memoirs of a Psychiatrist," that offer the pleasures of collusion and empowerment to the reader through an irony that punctures the doctor's vanity. In "What They Don't Teach You in Medical School," the doctor condemns himself: "Beware / of omniscience, it makes a fool / of every psychiatrist. Play Virgil / to Dante as he walks through hell / then let him decide if he wants to be well" (*Chaotic Angels* 178). The appropriation of Dante's inferno, to allegorize the private hell of illness, threads through the sequence:

> I am the one who makes the statues move,
> who teaches the dead to rise and love
>
> again, more wisely. I help the damned
> explore what happened, who condemned
>
> them each to their particular hell.
> Yes, I'm in favour of using pills,
>
> but my main job is to translate
> pain into tales they can tolerate
>
> in another language. We've pleasant grounds.
> Care to come with me on my rounds?
>
> ("Consultant," *Chaotic Angels* 160)

Whereas Jennings's Freudian doctor was explicitly male, Lewis's pronoun is not gender specific but the reader is likely to assume a masculine bravado in the unashamed hubris. In the lines that I took as my title, "my main job is to translate / pain into tales they can tolerate // in another language," the word "tales" indicates how the consultant's version of suffering will be a fiction that the patients must swallow, like his pills. They also make a parallel between the doctor and the poet in that both seek a language for pain. However, as stressed previously, the poet is distinctively the interpreter and critic of the doctor/patient situation. Lewis states:

> Therapy's based on the premise that an accurate description of a situation releases the patient from being neurotically bound to it. Psychoanalysts have even more faith in language than do poets. In the face of experience our explanations always break down. Far from being a failure, however, this wordlessness is usually a clue that something more truthful than our own account of the world is being approached. (*Chaotic Angels* 144)

Nevertheless, the monologues illustrate how poetry can include more than one voice and perspective. It can be critical of clinical discourse for what it stifles or omits and for belittling patients but it can also point to a partnership between doctor and patient in the business of recovery – "then let him decide if he wants to be well" ("What They Don't Teach You in Medical School," *Chaotic Angels* 178).

We see, then, how poems accommodate some of the insoluble mysteries of being human that are magnified by being ill, as Woolf mooted:

> In illness words seem to possess a mystic quality. We grasp what is beyond their surface meaning, gather instinctively this, that, and the other – a sound, a colour, here a stress, there a pause, – which the poet, knowing words to be meager in comparison with ideas, has strewn about his page to evoke, when collected, a state of mind which neither words can express nor the reason explain. Incomprehensibility has an enormous power over us in illness, more legitimately perhaps than the upright will allow. (200)

So, through its mix of verbal and non-verbal signs, poetry can mark the inadequacy of available language to access and express "the snowfield of the mind." It thus unsettles the assumptions about an all-knowing all-powerful medical discipline. In *Acquainted with the Night: Psychoanalysis and the Poetic Imagination* (2003), Margot Waddell draws on her work as a psychoanalyst and therapist to emphasize the wordless incomprehensibility of being human that is exacerbated in suffering. Introducing the book, Hamish Canham and Carole Satyamurti point out the similarities between poetry and psychoanalysis that can be put in helpful dialogue:

> Both depend on paying unusual attention to nuances of language [...] Both operate in the realm of the symbolic. Both are concerned with condensation, with the way meaning is compressed – in the poem and in the dream. Both invite us to look differently at the world by challenging our taken-for-granted perceptions and assumptions. (Canham and Satyamurti 2)

In his Foreword, however, Al Alvarez argues for the distinction between the activities: "The business of poetry is not just to express thoughts and feelings in the purest, most concentrated form, but also to think about them or even, as Bion put it, to make them thinkable" (xiv).

Indeed, poetry allows patients and others involved in suffering and health care to individuate and authenticate their experience and thus to resist, challenge or negotiate with medical and other social discourses about them. In *Illness as Metaphor: Aids and its Metaphors* (2009), Susan Sontag illuminates how social metaphors become a currency with which people travel through an illness, particularly embarrassing conditions that carry conversational taboos and euphemisms. Metaphors of a cancer "victim" or of "succumbing" to depression conceive the diseases as overpowering enemies. With reference to mental health, Sontag comments: "unromantic depression has supplanted the romantic notion of melancholy [...] Depression is melancholy minus its charms" (51). American poet Jane Kenyon's (1947–95) nine-part sequence "Having it Out with Melancholy" is, however, decidedly unromantic. She personifies the disease as an unwelcome opponent who stalks her from cradle to grave when it finally pushes her over the edge to death (Kenyon 21–26). Part One, "In the Nursery," opens with, "When I was born, you waited / behind a pile of linen in the nursery, / and when we were alone, you lay down / on top of me, pressing / the bile of desolation into every pore" (21–22). The intimations of sexual abuse are necessarily shocking to communicate the sense of powerlessness in the face of a sickness that has no visible symptoms to tell of its presence or nature. In the title's epigraph from Chekhov, depression is announced as incurable: "'If many remedies are prescribed for an illness, you may be certain that the illness has no cure'" (21). Added to this implied hopelessness is the unutterable burden of guilt. One section of Kenyon's poem is simply the voice of a friend telling her that she should have faith in God. Another section conveys the temporary relief that the right drugs gave her. As Charles Simic wrote:

> The drama of being unable to say what we feel most deeply is the subject of lyric poems. At the heart of the lyric, as Jane Kenyon knew very well, language fails us. The experience of the naked moment is incommunicable except in the finest lyric poems [...] This work, of course, can only be done in solitude and in silence. That's the voice of the poems. A voice shadowed by solitude and silence. (173)

Simic, like Woolf, puts his finger on the pulse of poetic expression:

> It's like coming upon someone we know and love lost in reverie. When we touch them and ask them what they're thinking of, they're unable to tell us. We assume they can, but won't, but this is not the case. Jane's poems measure the gap between language and what it presumes to name. That distance to her at times appears infinite, and that is the cause of her melancholy. She is the poet who opens her being toward everything that is unnameable and unknowable. (Ibid.)

It is poetry's intrinsically figurative language, along with its non-linearity and sound – rhythm, alliteration or assonance – that can depict what is hard to apprehend or say and that can animate or transform the dominant social metaphors and labels. In "Characteristics of Sadness," Jackie Kay uses the friendlier term "Sadness" for depression, while a series of images depict how the sufferer feels alienated from what seems to them a bright world outside. The metaphor for misery, "But right now inside this house, it stinks" (Kay 50), indicates how only an allusion to a nasty smell can relay what it feels like to be so cut off. The speaker attempts to alleviate the darkness with the tentative suggestion of redemption: "It could be made into something else. / recycled?" (ibid.). However, the internal monologue ends with self-blame that might echo the misunderstanding of others, "Cut the sniveling you sap" (ibid.), but that invites the reader to sympathize.

More recently, Gwyneth Lewis contributed towards the outing and understanding of depression through her creative journal *Sunbathing in the Rain: A Cheerful Book about Depression* (2006). Her poems on the subject take the personal account to a more universal realm through their metaphors. The sonnet "Angel Of Depression" masterfully condenses the prose narrative into fourteen lines and the symbolism opens the experience up to any reader. Again, the core misery of self-blame and affecting others is presentable only through analogy: "Don't say it's an honour to have fought / with depression's angel," for it "always wears the face of my loved ones as it tears / the breath from my solar plexus, grinds / my face in the ever-resilient dirt" (Lewis, *Chaotic Angels* 185). An angel is an appropriately ambivalent symbol of both disaster and good tidings. In biblical narratives, an angel comes to warn, protect or guide but in Greek tragedy it is usually a messenger of catastrophic news that cannot be represented onstage. In similarly ambivalent vein, the metaphoric logic of the sonnet "my limp is the best part of me" jostles with "and the way I hurt" (ibid.). Thus, Lewis questions common platitudes about finding new life through pain when it comes to the unrelenting psychological agony and the humdrum tedium of a condition that does not, like the common cold, just clear up.

While metaphors of angels or limps are gender free, analogies of illness as warfare can perpetuate medicine as a masculine territory and reinforce the socially prescribed discursive weakness of both women and the ill. In their section on "Applied Literature," Crawford et al. observe the role that literature can play in challenging sexual politics:

> Gendered exchanges that occur in the text may inform us about wider cultural issues relating to men, women and illnesses – the way in which a feminist analysis may look at how women are expected to respond passively to illness whereas men may be expected to be brave and battle, for example, or how exclusively female diseases like gynaecological cancers can be shrouded in mystery or shame. (42–43)

Siân Ede, Arts director of the Calouste Gulbenkian Foundation, notes how women artists have challenged the objectification of their bodies and now

> An engagement with new medical technologies is causing this [objectification] to change, for men and women, for the general public as well as artists [...] Knowledge is power, allowing us to combat fear, as if we can collude with the physicians to see ourselves as fascinating physical specimens rather than helpless sufferers. (Preface, Greenlaw 11–12)

In 1978, Sontag observed that for cancer, like tuberculosis before it, the dominant vocabulary was of invasion and losing the fight so that its spread seemed unstoppable. When little was understood about the disease, it was easy to fill the gaps in knowledge with myths about causes, such as diet or repression, and for the ill person to feel responsible. Furthermore, the metaphor "like a cancer" came to stand for what is socially or morally wrong: "Because of countless metaphoric flourishes that have made cancer synonymous with evil, having cancer has been experienced by many as shameful, therefore something to conceal, and also unjust, a betrayal by one's body" (Sontag 110).

Looking at poems on breast cancer published between 1986 and 2010 we see how metaphors move from depicting the sufferer as either passive or culpabilized for being morally weak to being empowered and even privileged. In "Mastectomy," first published in 1980, Boland recourses to extended symbolism in order to expose the sense of being ravaged when male surgeons remove a breast: "I flatten / to their looting, / to the sleight // of their plunder. / I am a brute site. / Theirs is the true booty" (*New Collected Poems* 77–78). These are the concluding lines to a poem in which the speaker has noted with irony how in their private lives the doctors would feast on a woman's breast in suckling and sex. The emphatic first-person voice and the changes of tempo – from the swift "looting" to the monosyllabic "I am a brute site" or "it has gone" (in an earlier line) – illustrate an equation between the semiotic coding in poetic and feminine languages that Julia Kristeva outlined in *Revolution in Poetic Language*. Kristeva explicates how the semiotic pushes through symbolic discursive registers to makes itself known: "Indifferent to language, enigmatic and feminine, this space underlying the written is rhythmic, unfettered, irreducible to its intelligible verbal translation, it is musical, anterior to judgement, but restrained by a single guarantee: syntax" (Kristeva 29). Thus, she proposes that the semiotic and the symbolic must be understood as being in dialogue with each other.

Writing of how poetry uniquely can authenticate the experience of being ill, Fiona Sampson refers to how Kristeva

> situates poetry at the border of language, where it breaks down into involuntary aporia, the gaps caused by complete lack of connection. Poetry may gasp exclamation, fail to make it across the page's dangerous width. Involuntary connections may bubble up in pun and allusion. (Sampson 262)

Illustrating Sampson's thesis and Kristeva's theory, Carol Satyamurti's (b. 1939) fourteen-part sequence on breast cancer, "Changing the Subject," registers a dialogue between symbolic and semiotic modes of expression when feeling at the "border of language." The title refers to how people avoided "the unsayable word": cancer (Satyamurti 23); it also signals how the patient feels diminished due to an altered subjectivity. The poet as speaker reconstructs the fumbling for some language with which to access and express this unfamiliar state:

> Since I have known this,
> language has cracked,
> meanings have re-arranged;
> dream, risk and fact
>
> changed places. Tenses tip,
> word-roots are suddenly
> important, some grip
> on the slippery.
>
> We're on thin linguistic ice
> lifelong, but I see through;
> I read the sentence
> we are all subject to
>
> in the stopped mouths of those
> who once were "I,"
> full-fleshed, confident
> using the verb "to die"
>
> of plants and pets and parents
> until the immense
> contingency of things
> deleted sense.
>
> They are his future
> as well as mine,
> but I won't make him look.
> I say, "I'm fine."
>
> ("How are You?," Satyamurti 29)

Although the metre and colloquial idiom seem lightweight in literary terms, they enact the gap between verbalized expression and what it withholds, as the metaphors and typography testify. The full stop and the white space after "slippery" indicate the subject's reticence to say "slope" and thus to face an inexorable decline towards death. The images of slippery slopes and thin ice thus signify how words alone are never fully reliable and how illness intensifies the sense of mortality that haunts each human. Elsewhere in the poem, the speaker confronts the metaphysical questions of "why me?" and "what have I done?" that are involved in the search for meaning that Crawford et al., like Woolf, foreground. In these ways, the poem moves the female patient from a position of discursive weakness to a person with a greater comprehension and vision than someone who is purportedly normal.

Into the twenty-first century, we find poets more consistently in a place of discursive strength as they write of their cancers not only on behalf of women but also on behalf of anyone who lives with a debilitating disease. Julia Darling (1956–2005) recorded her journey with breast cancer in several forms, from journals and blogs to drama scripts, but asserted: "'Poetry gave me a voice to express the comedy and tragedy of my illness'" (quoted in Crown n. pag.). In her well-circulated sonnet "Chemotherapy," Darling's narrative is more accepting than Satyamurti's although the word "cancer" is still absent. The speaker is ungendered but confronts the loss of hair that perhaps women particularly dread: "I did not imagine being bald / at forty four" (*Sudden Collapses* 50). This symbol – hair-loss – of a reduced self is offset by her vivid and serene awareness of being in the moment, mediated through chiming assonance and rhyme:

> I never thought that life could get this small,
> that I would care so much about a cup,
> the taste of tea, the texture of a shawl,
> and whether or not I should get up.
>
> I'm not unhappy. I have learnt to drift
> and sip. The smallest things are gifts.
>
> (Ibid.)

Greenlaw comments, using her own metaphors:

> Darling's "Chemotherapy" employs its submission to the sonnet form to reflect that "I never thought that life could get this small," the regulation iambic pentameter of the line bringing to mind a ticking clock but also a caged animal rocking or a trapped thought. (18)

Darling herself testified: "Poetry is the pioneer of language, and we can express things in new ways. One of the things I have found most interesting is developing new vocabularies for pain" ("My Joints" n. pag.). She concurred that poetry releases a new sense of agency:

> We can use this new [poetic] vocabulary to communicate to others what our pain is like. For doctors this can be incredibly helpful. So much can be lost or misunderstood in a medical consultation, and often doctors and patients cannot find a language to communicate effectively with one another. (Ibid.)

Echoing Kristeva, she stresses the effectiveness of the non-verbal: "poetry is all about music and rhythm, and music comforts and lulls us" (ibid.). Darling further explains: "I chose to imagine my body as a house, and wrote many poems during my treatment about 'living in the new extension' or about my fears" (ibid.). The image of a house occurs in poems by several poets as an unconscious representation of the physical and mental confinement accompanying chronic illness. Pertinently, too, the analogy of a house makes the previously feminine domain an ungendered one. Thus, we can argue for how these poems contribute to a feminizing of humanity, as Boland anticipated.

We have come a long way since Sontag recorded: "Cancer is a rare and still scandalous subject for poetry; and it seems unimaginable to aestheticize the disease" (20). Darling's poems are on the websites of men as well as of women who share their experiences of cancer. For example, Anthony Wilson, a poet who created a digital space in which to air his condition, included "Chemotherapy" in his commentary, proving how poetry does a job that the proliferation of confessional blogs or newspaper columns does not. Wilson also applauds Jo Shapcott's prize-winning *Of Mutability*, stating, "The book's achievement is to transform the vocabulary of discussions of cancer without ever using the word itself, whilst paying scrupulous attention to its effects on both mind and body" (Wilson n. pag.). Published in 2010, *Of Mutability* consists in a poetry sequence on Shapcott's breast cancer although the pronouns are gender neutral and the cancer is not specified. It uses terminology that records a more widespread scientific understanding of the disease and that could apply to any part of the body. The speaker is a person living with a cellular condition, rather than a victim in its grip or a changed subject. However, as in several of the previously discussed poems, the voice in Shapcott's title poem, "Of Mutability," revisits the expression on the doctor's face with her mind's eye: "Look down these days to see your feet / mistrust the pavement and your blood tests / turn the doctor's expression grave" (3). The poet re-creates the patient trying to decipher the doctor's reading of the signs. Shapcott's final line, "Don't trouble, though, to head anywhere but the sky" (ibid.), resonates with Woolf in her essay "On Being Ill" where she argues that confinement to bed can liberate us from the general march of mankind whereby we can

> float with the sticks on the stream; helter-skelter with the dead leaves on the lawn, irresponsible and disinterested and able, perhaps for the first time for years, to look round, to look up – to look, for example at the sky. (196)

Woolf pauses on this productive side-effect of being ill in typically figurative terms: "One should not let this gigantic cinema play perpetually to an empty house" (ibid.). She avers that humans find in nature and the poets the truly sympathetic companions that they may not find in one another:

> That snowfield of the mind, where man has not trodden, is visited by the cloud, kissed by the falling petal, as in another sphere, it is the great artists, the Miltons and the Popes, who console not only by their thought of us but by their forgetfulness. (197–98)

Woolf cites the evocations of Milton and Pope, Shakespeare and Keats, because she did not have the works of major female poets imprinted in her consciousness. In the twenty-first century, however, we can and must summon poems by women, for they not only explore and express the specifically female mental snowfields but also illuminate those of a feminized humanity. To some extent and for a period, women wrote back against a highly scientific male-dominated medical discipline. They exposed the unequal power dynamics in doctor–patient dialogues and explored female-specific conditions. More recently, they sometimes target the specialized jargon of the health industries and sometimes they express what is hard to put into words. We might detect a female aesthetic in offering a regenerative side to suffering or in drawing in the reader as confidant/e. The way in which poetry takes the individual into community, whereby not feeling alone is a kind of healing in itself, also demonstrates how it can feminize humanity. Referring to the appetite for poetry following the attack on New York's Twin Towers, September 2011, Ruth Padel asserts the place of poetry in the process of making meaning out of trauma: "Poetry helps us 'not feel so lonely.' The patterning of words, and the structure of thought, somehow echoes (and if it doesn't heal, it validates and sets in a world context) your own feelings" (49). In poetry, especially, writers develop symbols that express the psychological and emotional aspects of disease and pain and that retain the element of the incomprehensible and incommunicable. Symbols intensify the search for meaning that the Humanities especially add to the remit of biomedical sciences. These symbols also negotiate between preserving the highly solitary aspect of illness and making the experience more generally available. Thus, we can return to Johnson's claim:

> The double-sided character of feminism's relations with modern humanism, as both its interpreter and critic, does not, however, suggest any preferential discrimination between the above mentioned two faces of humanism's own value commitments [to humankind and to the individual]. Contemporary feminism is as much a specific articulation of the universalizing dimension of modern humanism as it is the inheritor and interpreter of the idea of self-determining individuality. (ix)

Ultimately, however, while recognizing the social implications of health and the health services, poetry maintains the pleasure of our unique inwardness on which Woolf insists and that must remain sacred in any concept of "Health Humanities."

disclosure statement

No potential conflict of interest was reported by the author.

notes

Gwyneth Lewis's poem "Consultant," from *Chaotic Angels: Poems in English* (Bloodaxe, 2005), and Julia Darling's sonnet "Chemotherapy," from *Sudden Collapses in Public Places* (Arc, 2003), are reproduced here by kind permission of the respective publishers. *Angelaki*'s publisher also wishes to thank Carol Satyamurti for permission to feature her poem "How are You?" in this special issue of the journal.

1 Information on Jennings's papers can be found at the Elizabeth Jennings Project, available <http://elizabethjennings.dmu.ac.uk/home2.html>

(accessed 19 Dec. 2016). See also "Poetry and Personality: The Private Papers and Public Image of Elizabeth Jennings" in *The Boundaries of the Literary Archive: Reclamation and Representation*, eds. Carrie Smith and Lisa Stead (Farnham: Ashgate, 2013) 105–20.

2 Reflection 23, Notebook C, Box 8 (1957–65), Elizabeth Jennings Papers, Washington University Library, St. Louis.

bibliography

Boland, Eavan. *New Collected Poems*. Manchester: Carcanet, 2005. Print.

Boland, Eavan. *Object Lessons: The Life of the Woman and the Poet in Our Time*. Manchester: Carcanet, 1995. Print.

Canham, Hamish, and Carole Satyamurti, eds. *Acquainted with the Night: Psychoanalysis and the Poetic Imagination*. London: Karnac, 2003. Print.

Crawford, Paul, Brian Brown, Charlie Baker, and Victoria Tischler. *Health Humanities*. Basingstoke: Palgrave Macmillan, 2015. Print.

Crown, Sarah. "Poet Julia Darling Dies of Cancer." *Guardian* 14 Apr. 2005. Web. 19 Dec. 2016. <https://www.theguardian.com/books/2005/apr/14/news.sarahcrown>

Darling, Julia. "My Joints are Rusty Cranes." *Guardian* 5 Aug. 2004. Web. 19 Dec. 2016. <https://www.theguardian.com/books/2004/aug/05/health.poetry>

Darling, Julia. *Sudden Collapses in Public Places*. Todmorden: Arc, 2003. Print.

Evans, Martyn. "Medical Humanities." Centre for Medical Humanities, U of Durham, 2009. Web. 5 Sept. 2014. <https://www.dur.ac.uk/cmh/medicalhumanities/>.

Fanthorpe, U.A. "Hospital Speak: The Neuropsychiatric Unit." *Contemporary Women's Poetry: Reading, Writing, Practice*. Ed. Alison Mark and Deryn Rees-Jones. Basingstoke: Macmillan, 2000. 31–34. Print.

Fanthorpe, U.A. *New and Collected Poems*. Preface by Carol Ann Duffy. London: Enitharmon, 2010. Print.

Felski, Rita. *Literature after Feminism*. Chicago: U of Chicago P, 2003. Print.

Greenlaw, Lavinia. *Signs and Humours: The Poetry of Medicine*. London: Calouste Gulbenkian Foundation, 2007. Print.

Jennings, Elizabeth. *New Collected Poems*. Manchester: Carcanet, 2002. Print.

Johnson, Pauline. *Feminism as Radical Humanism*. Boulder, CO: Westview, 1994. Print.

Kay, Jackie. *Off Colour*. Tarset: Bloodaxe, 1998. Print.

Kenyon, Jane. *Constance: Poems by Jane Kenyon*. Minneapolis: Graywolf, 1993. Print.

Kristeva, Julia. *Revolution in Poetic Language*. Trans. Margaret Waller. New York: Columbia UP, 1984. Print.

Lewis, Gwyneth. *Chaotic Angels: Poems in English*. Tarset: Bloodaxe, 2005. Print.

Lewis, Gwyneth. *Keeping Mum: Voices from Therapy*. Tarset: Bloodaxe, 2003. Print.

Lewis, Gwyneth. *Sunbathing in the Rain: A Cheerful Book about Depression*. London: Harper, 2006. Print.

Padel, Ruth. *52 Ways of Looking at a Poem*. London: Chatto, 2002. Print.

Sampson, Fiona. "Poetry and the Position of Weakness: Some Challenges of Writing in Health-Care." *Kicking Daffodils*. Ed. Vicki Bertram. Edinburgh: Edinburgh UP, 1997. 253–66. Print.

Sandie, Elizabeth. "Acts of Attention: The Poetry of U.A. Fanthorpe." *Contemporary Poems: Some Critical Approaches*. Ed. Lesley Jeffries and Peter Samson. Sheffield: Smith/Doorstop, 2001. 146–68. Print.

Satyamurti, Carol. *Changing the Subject*. Oxford: Oxford UP, 1990. Print.

Scarry, Elaine. *The Body in Pain: The Making and Unmaking of the World*. Oxford: Oxford UP, 1985. Print.

Shapcott, Jo. *Of Mutability*. London: Faber, 2010. Print.

Simic, Charles. "Jane Kenyon." *Columbia Review* 26 (1996): 172–73. Print.

Sontag, Susan. *Illness as Metaphor: Aids and its Metaphors*. Harmondsworth: Penguin, 2009.

Waddell, Margot. “The Vale of Soul-Making.” Canham and Satyamurti 9–30. Print.

Wilson, Anthony. “Lifesaving Poems.” Web. 19 Dec. 2016. <http://anthonywilsonpoetry.com>.

Woolf, Virginia. “On Being Ill” [1930]. *Collected Essays*. Vol. IV. Ed. Leonard Woolf. London: Chatto, 1967. 193–203. Print.

Jane Dowson

jean wyatt

LOVE IN THE NOVELS OF TONI MORRISON

In interviews, Toni Morrison often comments on her fiction's preoccupation with love:

> Actually, I think, all the time that I write, I'm writing about love or its absence. I think that I still write about the same thing, which is how people relate to one another and miss it or hang on to it [...] or are tenacious about love. About love and how to survive. (Bakerman 40)

Each of Morrison's novels offers a different model of love; and each form of love surprises conventional expectation, challenging a reader's preconceptions about what love is, how it is expressed, and who qualifies as a lover. As Morrison herself claims, her work is "sublimely didactic" (Koenen 74), teaching the reader something about love, as well as about race and gender. Whereas the early novels teach lessons in a straightforward fashion, through plot and character as well as an occasional authorial pronouncement, the later novels, beginning with *Beloved*, teach through an ethical dialogue between text and reader. That is, through various subtle techniques the text engages the reader's firmly held beliefs about love and then calls them into question, prompting the reader to rethink her or his convictions.

The novel *Love* (2003) is exemplary in this regard. The text is structured by a surprise ending which, like any surprise ending, causes us to reconfigure our interpretation of all that has come before. We realize that it is not after all Bill Cosey's wandering desire that the title *Love* refers to, as the body of the novel makes us think, but rather the deep love between two eleven-year-old girls that we see enacted in the final nineteen pages. The retrospective shift in our understanding can cause a reader to question the lens of assumptions about love through which she has been reading the novel. What kinds of preconceptions about love have made her complicit with the earlier text's subtle tilt toward a patriarchal perspective? What preconceived ideas have made her accept without question the implicit assumptions in the text that it is a man who gives meaning to a woman's story and that male desire is the only desire that counts? The narrative structure gives this love story an ethical dimension, as readers are prompted to confront, revalue, revise, and expand their notions of love.[1]

If the early novels are most beloved among Morrison's works – *The Bluest Eye*, *Sula*, and

Song of Solomon (as well as *Beloved*) are the Morrison novels most frequently taught in college classes and discussed in the scholarship – the later novels are distinguished by their intricate craftsmanship, by the various intriguing ways in which narrative style and structure reflect the novels' content and invite the reader to contribute her own politics to the reading. This essay begins with an overview of love as it functions in the early Morrison novels (*The Bluest Eye*, *Sula*, *Song of Solomon*, and *Tar Baby*) and then moves to a close reading of three later novels, *Beloved*, *Home*, and *Jazz*.

love in the early novels

Already in her first novel, *The Bluest Eye* (1970), Morrison distinguishes among different kinds of loving: "Love is never any better than the lover. Wicked people love wickedly, violent people love violently, weak people love weakly, stupid people love stupidly" (206). Writing against the prevalent cultural assumption that loving is by definition a good thing, Morrison de-idealizes love. The statement on love quoted above follows the sentence "Cholly loved Pecola." Since Cholly's repeated incestuous rapes of his daughter have destroyed her sanity, it may surprise a reader that Cholly's form of attention to Pecola receives the accolade of "love." In Morrison's storyworlds – quite provocatively – even incest and rape are not to be judged out of hand, but to be understood in the context of all the character's life events and historical circumstances. Thus, in this first novel, a US culture characterized by white supremacy, the mockery of black masculinity, and the denigration of black sexuality have shaped Cholly's chaotic and destructive form of loving. In each of Morrison's novels, both early and late, a character's way of loving is embedded in historical context. Not only the character's personal past but also the collective past of African Americans shape, or more likely warp, a character's form of loving.

The next three novels – *Sula* (1973), *Song of Solomon* (1977), and *Tar Baby* (1981) – are consistent in providing one overriding message on love: possessiveness destroys love. This is perhaps most obviously true of Hagar's obsessive "anaconda love" for Milkman in *Song of Solomon* (137). In *Tar Baby*, the intense reciprocal passion between Son and Jadine is strangled when each turns to controlling the other, trying to mold the beloved into the shape of the lover's ideal. In *Sula*, Ajax and Sula are lovers who enjoy each other freely and creatively. The relationship thrives, until one day Sula has a new feeling: "possession" (131). She anticipates Ajax's visit by tying a green ribbon into her hair and cleaning the house. Noting the green ribbon and the spotless bathroom, Ajax detects "the scent of the nest," and he is out of there – for good (133). One small step over the line from love to possessive love – all Sula did, after all, was put on a green ribbon – and Sula is punished by losing the one man who could interest and please her. Likewise, when Nel, assuming that marriage gives her exclusive rights to her husband Jude's body, rages at her best friend Sula for having sex with Jude, she is punished excessively for her possessiveness. It is not just that she loses both Jude and Sula, but that without Sula, whose companionship has been the source of Nel's vitality, Nel lives out a barren and colorless existence.

Thus the slightest taint of possessiveness is punished harshly in Morrison's early novels. Yet it is also clear that the isolated self cannot make it, that to be a self at all one needs to be in relationship. Sula strives to be the consummate self-created individualist: she says "I don't want to make somebody else. I want to make myself" (*Sula* 92). And Sula does not survive. Halfway through the novel she dies, leaving us to miss her presence through the remainder of the novel named for her. It is as if Sula is able to be physically as well as emotionally healthy only when she is developing and growing through her deep friendship with Nel. Solitary, she cannot even sustain a life. In the early novels, then, Morrison's idea of love is rigorous: one needs to be in relationship with an other, but the narrative severely punishes the slightest all-too-human slippage from love into possessive love.

I have said that in Morrison's fiction love is always embedded in historical context, both in the personal history of the protagonist and in his or her ancestral history. This may be true for Morrison's abhorrence of possessiveness, too, as we can see if we take a step away from the first four novels to consider the complications of possession in *Beloved*, Morrison's fifth novel. When Sethe says to her daughters "You are mine" and each responds "You are mine" (216), they are expressing reciprocal love for one another, to be sure, but also possession. *Beloved*'s tale of slavery reminds us that "You are mine" is also what the slaveholders said – and in the latter case the violence immanent in any claim to possess a human being is manifest. The profession of love, "You are mine," is a reminder that property relations can creep into family relations of love supposedly outside the realm of buying and selling, and lead to violence (see Peterson). As her characters experience love in forms inflected by collective history, so Morrison's strong aversion to possessive love may be informed by the collective African American memory of people literally owning people.

The one entirely positive vision of love in the four early novels is in *Song of Solomon*. Guitar, a friend of the protagonist Milkman, is talking to Hagar after Milkman has broken off his relationship with her:

> You think he belongs to you because you want to belong to him. Hagar, don't. It's a bad word, "belong." Especially when you put it with somebody you love. Love shouldn't be like that. Did you ever see the way the clouds love a mountain? They circle all around it; sometimes you can't even see the mountain for the clouds [...] [But they] never cover the head. His head pokes through, because the clouds let him; they don't wrap him up. They let him keep his head up high, free, with nothing to hide him or bind him. Hear me, Hagar? (306)

I claim that Morrison is drawing her inspiration for this model of love from Zen Buddhist philosophy, namely from the following passage in *Zen Mind, Beginner's Mind* by Shunryu Suzuki:

> The blue mountain is the father of the white cloud. The white cloud is the son of the blue mountain. All day long they depend on each other, without being dependent on each other. The white cloud is always the white cloud. The blue mountain is always the blue mountain [...] There may be many things like the white cloud and the blue mountain: man and woman, teacher and disciple [...] They are quite independent, but yet dependent. (Suzuki 13–14)

The parallel with Suzuki clarifies the terms of Guitar's harangue. The cloud hovers close to the mountain, but it does not impinge on the mountain's space, leaving it free to be what it is. Likewise, the mountain does not interfere with the cloud's autonomy. Each demands nothing of the other, yet each depends on the other being there. Guitar's sketch of a love that is non-possessive and non-intrusive is inspiring, but it remains in the abstract form of a lecture; there is no relationship in *Song of Solomon* that puts it into practice. Indeed, the idea of a non-possessive love hovers over Morrison's first four novels, but it never takes concrete shape: it is known only through its negation. "Belong is a bad word," as Guitar says: novel after novel portrays characters who wreck their love relationships through possessiveness.

As in the case of *The Bluest Eye*'s concluding aphorism on love, quoted above – "Wicked people love wickedly, violent people love violently, weak people love weakly, stupid people love stupidly" – Guitar's lesson on love is delivered as a lecture, a lecture that appears to come straight from implied author to reader, although in the case of *Song of Solomon* Guitar acts as its mouthpiece. Morrison's form of pedagogy in the later novels depends on more subtle – and, I would argue, more effective – literary techniques. Through Guitar's speech, the reader is certainly given a lesson in the right way to love, but the exhortation calls for no response. A reader need take no responsibility for this wisdom, nor need she contribute her own ideas on the subject, for the hortatory text is complete in itself. The later novels engage the reader in a dialogue between his or her ethical convictions and the structures of the text which call them into question. The subtle literary techniques Morrison employs to draw out and expose the reader's values and beliefs and then provoke a re-evaluation of them constitute Morrison's personal variation on the call-and-response method of African American art forms.

love in the later novels

Beloved (1987) marks a turning point in Morrison's oeuvre – not only a shift toward more complex, oblique language and discontinuous narrative structures but also a move toward more subtle inducements to readers to rethink ethical issues. Consider, for example, how narrative structure interacts with the subject of Sethe's mother-love to challenge and complicate a reader's habitual moral judgments on motherhood. For example, we do not know until well beyond the midpoint of the novel that Sethe killed her baby girl. That means that we read through multiple accounts of Sethe's devotion to her children – how, spurred on by her love for her children, Sethe manages to save all four of them from slavery, how she dedicates herself to her daughter Denver – before we encounter the fact that Sethe killed the baby she saved from slavery. (She tried to kill all four children and herself in order to escape the slave-hunters who would re-enslave them all.) The belated narrative disclosure of infanticide prevents a reader's too quick knee-jerk reaction to the fact that a mother killed her own child. Reading *Beloved* trains a reader to do something difficult – to suspend judgment until we take into account every facet of a perpetrator's life situation. A reader is forced by the delayed disclosure to consider the whole context of slavery in which the infanticide took place before she judges Sethe's act. By the time she learns about the murder she can understand it in context, as a result of Sethe's impossible maternal choice between her child's physical death and her child's soul-death, were she to be sent back into slavery. What George Eliot tries to do through direct moral exhortation – telling her reader that "moral judgments must remain false and hollow unless they are checked and enlightened by a perpetual reference to the special circumstances that mark the individual lot" (521) – Morrison accomplishes through the workings of the narrative structure on the reader. Encountering the news that Sethe killed her child belatedly, and within the context of Sethe's unquestionable love for her children, might even enlarge a reader's range of empathy and her understanding of maternal love enough to encompass the idea that killing one's child could be an act of love.

In more local instances, too, the text's discourse reflects the specific qualities of love in *Beloved*. When the dead baby returns to Sethe in the body of the eighteen-year-old Beloved, Sethe, overjoyed at getting a second chance to mother the well-loved baby she was forced to kill, withdraws from the world to devote herself to her living daughter Denver and her ghost daughter Beloved; she declares, "Nobody will never get my milk no more except my children" (200). The metaphor of breastfeeding governs Sethe's relation to her children, expressing her sense of a connection to her children so close that it is difficult to distinguish the boundary between self and other. The image of milk-provider gives body to the ideal of the mother who gives of herself to her children, without stint.[2]

Morrison does not, however, idealize this model of selfless maternal love. While affirming the courage and strength that this slave mother draws from her love for her children, Morrison also criticizes the absolutist, self-sacrificing qualities of maternal love. In an interview shortly after the publication of *Beloved*, she says: "The precious [...] loved self [...] is suppressed or displaced and put someplace else – in the children, in the lover, in the man. It's always something that is more valuable, more beautiful, more wonderful than the self – that's too bad [...] That's what maternity is" (Rothstein C17).

Adding to this explicit criticism, the narrative form of *Beloved* itself conveys to a reader something troubling in Sethe's kind of loving. In a dialogue between the mother and her two daughters, Morrison represents linguistically the erasure of boundaries that characterizes Sethe's love for her children, and their love for her. At first, the subject positions of mother and daughter are separate:

You are my sister
You are my daughter [...]
You are my Beloved

But references to breastfeeding blur boundaries:

I have your milk [...]
I brought your milk (216)

Who is speaking? It is not easy to determine. Does the "I" in "I have your milk" refer to Sethe, who might be saying that she "has" (is carrying) Beloved's milk, or to Beloved, who could just as well be the "I" who speaks, saying that she "has" Sethe's milk inside her? The de-differentiation of pronouns dramatizes the impossibility of separating what belongs to the one body from what belongs to the other when the two are joined by the milk that flows between them.

It is as if Sethe and her children are living in the belated time of trauma, repeating a moment before the infanticide traumatically interrupted their relationship, a moment of closeness that would have been appropriate to the mother and two nursing babies that they then were but is out of synchronicity with the current reality that the girls are eighteen and nineteen. The metaphor of mother's milk overrunning boundaries between self and other, conflating identities, implies the too-muchness of mother love, the inappropriate over-proximity of mother and daughters.

In this closed maternal circle, each completes the other. Mother and daughters experience a unity of mind and body so complete that each finds fulfillment in the other. The result is stasis:

I will never leave you again
Don't ever leave me again
You will never leave me again (ibid.)

The promise is: no change.

Dialogue among speaking subjects (ideally) moves toward the discovery of something new, as the exchange of ideas gives each speaker the opportunity to shift toward the position of the other. Here, repetition – each speaker using the same phrase as the others – annuls difference. There can be no movement when words enact inter-reflecting mirrors. Instead of moving toward the emergence of something new, dialogue reiterates stasis, reassuring each speaker that the other is there and the other is the same.

The narrative form implies a critique of selfless maternal love. Where the loving mother gives herself so completely to the child that the child feels no lack, there is also no desire, no impetus for the child to move outside the maternal circle in search of an object that might complete her.[3] In the interview quoted above, Morrison critiques excessive mother-love for logical reasons; here, a reader has the opportunity to experience, through the formal repetitions, the feeling of dead-end stasis that comes from an all-encompassing maternal love. As in many of her later works, the gaps and enigmas in the dialogue call on the reader to participate actively in making meaning and thus open the way for a reader to contribute his own views – admiring or critical – on Sethe's love and on the cultural ideal of selfless, dedicated, all-giving mother.

In contrast to the over-close mode of love in *Beloved*, Morrison's penultimate novel *Home* (2012) depicts love as difference – or, more precisely, love as change: when the beloved becomes different, undergoing a radical shift in self-image and identity, the lover can use this destabilizing turn of events to redirect his or her own energies toward new ways of desiring and being. Or, as Mari Ruti, building on Lacan's notion of love, says: "allow[ing] ourselves to be touched by the unknowable otherness of the other [enables us] to transform the basic parameters of our being" (177). In *Home*'s picture of sibling love, the change in his beloved sister is transformative for Frank, shocking him into facing what both the text and Frank's consciousness have until now repressed – his murder of an innocent young Korean girl.

Frank has always been an exemplary brother to his younger sister, Cee. In a world where there is no protection for black people, Frank, from the time that he was four years old and Cee was a baby, has taken it upon himself to protect and nurture her. Their love for each other is intersubjective in a specific sense: it rests on an interchange between what is inside – deep down – in the one and what is inside, deep down, in the other. Thus, for example, Frank locates his self-image in Cee: "She was the first person I ever took responsibility for. Down deep inside her lived my secret picture of myself – a strong good me" (104). One expects "down deep inside" to refer to Frank's own depths, where one would think to find his most cherished self-image, but the phrase refers instead to Cee's inner world: the intermingling of self and other depicts a depth of intimacy and interdependence unusual in Morrison's novels.

The steadiness of Frank's protective love for Cee is admirable. However, he admits that he is dependent for his positive self-image on her dependency: "Who am I without her?" he says (103). His manliness is premised on her helplessness: "Guarding her, finding a way out, not being afraid of anything [...] I felt heroic" (104). In embracing Cee, Frank is also embracing the cherished ideal self as heroic protector of innocent young girlhood.

But Cee changes. At the end of the novel Frank and Cee move back to the town, Lotus Georgia, where they were raised. Cee is almost dead as a result of a white doctor's experiments on her body. The community of women in Lotus heal her, not only in body but in spirit. The women's example of how to live strengthens her resolve to stand on her own as a responsible actor in the world. However, they cannot remedy the damage done to Cee's womb: as a result of the doctor's medical experiments on her uterus, she will never be able to have children.[4]

When Cee openly mourns the baby she will never have, Frank responds with his usual effort to comfort her and prevent her suffering. "'I'm sorry, Cee. Really sorry.' Frank moved toward her. 'Don't,' she said, pushing his hand away." Frank tries to shield Cee from sadness, to offer her the hand that has always reached out to comfort her; but she pushes it away. "'Don't [...] I'm not going to hide from what's true just because it hurts,' she says. 'I can feel miserable if I want to'" (131).

Something goes awry here in the dynamics of Frank's and Cee's reciprocal love. Jacques Lacan's notion of the strangeness of the other's desire can be helpful in understanding the effect of Cee's new-found autonomy on her relationship with Frank. In Seminar VIII (on transference) Lacan gives the following definition of love:

> l'amour, c'est ce qui se passe dans cet objet vers lequel nous tendons la main par notre propre désir, et qui, au moment où notre désir fait éclater son incendie, nous laisse apparaître un instant cette réponse, cette autre main qui se tend vers nous comme son désir. (216)

> (love is what occurs in this object toward which we hold out our hand through our own desire, and which, at the moment when our desire flames out, allows for an instant this response to appear to us, this other hand that is held out toward us as the other's desire.) (Lacan 216; my trans.)

Where the lover expects to see a reflection of his own desire, what he sees instead is a glimpse of the beloved's desire. What reaches back toward the lover is not the expected mirror image of his own hand (metaphor for his desire) but a hand (a desire) that is quite different. This different desire delivers a surprise, or shock. The sudden glimpse of what the beloved truly desires is so alien that it has the potential to shatter the lover's understanding of himself and of his relationship to the beloved.

By coincidence, Frank has also reached out his hand to Cee, to shield her from sorrow, as always. She pushes his hand away with her own hand. That gesture signals a huge transformation in the beloved sister. She has decided, as a result of the healing women's teachings, that "it was just herself [...] she wished to be the person who would never again need rescue [...] She wanted to be the one who rescued her own self" (129). One might expect that Cee's transformation would end their relationship. For Frank has to give up not only the sister he has loved all his life – the clueless, helpless young girl – but also his most cherished image of himself as heroic rescuer.

Instead of dissolving the relationship, however, Cee's change triggers a change in Frank. Cee mourns the child she will never have: "'It's like there's a baby girl down here waiting to be born [...] she picked me to be born to [...] You know that toothless smile babies have? [...] I keep seeing it [...] all around the house'" (131–32). The image of the little girl stranded outside life belongs to Cee's inner life, but it works on what is buried deep in Frank's inner world. Throughout the novel, he has repressed the image of the little Asian girl he killed while he was a soldier in the Korean War. That image, and that deed, have been the hidden core of his traumatic memory – hidden even, or most urgently, from himself. Now, he thinks, "Maybe that little girl wasn't waiting around to be born to her. Maybe it was already dead" – retrieving at that moment the repressed memory of the dead Korean child (133). It is a mark of their closeness that Cee's deeply felt image can travel to Frank's own psychic depths, where it becomes part of Frank's network of associations, bringing him face to face with repressed memory: "Now the hook was deep inside his chest" (135).

In giving back to the lover the unexpected, love jolts Frank into a deeper dimension of himself. He is brought to confront the buried trauma of the perpetrator and to begin the long labor of working through his guilt and shame (ibid.).

I return to Lacan's brief reference to the different, indeed alien, desire of the beloved to expand the conception of love as difference to a more general, and perhaps more useable, model of a love dynamic. For Lacan and for Jean Laplanche, whose philosophy was influenced by Lacan, there is at the heart of every human subject some twisted thing, an unconscious nonsensical fragment absorbed from early childhood relations with the parent. This "object a" (Lacan) or "enigmatic signifier" (Laplanche) that founds the subject "gives a particular torsion, or swerve" to the drives and to the subject's orientation toward the world (Santner 39). As Eric Santner puts it:

> What makes the Other other is not his or her spatial exteriority [...] but the fact that he or she is *strange*, is a *stranger*, and not only to me but also to him- or herself, is the bearer of an internal alterity, an enigmatic density desire calling for response beyond any rule-governed reciprocity. (9)

Thus the perilous aspect of intimacy: as Mari Ruti writes, true intimacy would involve exposing oneself to this strangeness at the core of the beloved – exposing oneself to the discomfort its oddness or even grotesqueness evokes (Ruti 176–77). It is this particularity or strangeness that Lacan is referring to when he says that the lover afire with desire expects to encounter in the beloved a desire that is the mirror image of his own, yet for a fleeting moment encounters instead the wholly other desire of the beloved – a desire that shocks through its strangeness. In that moment, the lover has the choice of running the other way in horror or using the shock of difference to abandon his hold on his old way of relating to the beloved and to himself, and to find a new direction through some accommodation to the true idiosyncrasy of the other's desire.

It is this second path that Frank takes in response to Cee's change. He lets go his old self-image as heroic rescuer, together with his image of Cee as vulnerable victim. He allows the blow of Cee's difference to shift not only the dynamic of their relationship but also the basic parameters of his identity. At the opposite pole from *Beloved*'s presentation of love as comfort, as a reciprocal mirroring that reassures the lover that the beloved is always there and always the same, the love modeled in *Home* is love as radical discomfort and change.

Jazz (1992) enacts in multiple ways the message that love demands creativity, a constant infusion of the lover's imaginative capacity to give love new and different shapes. *Jazz* plays with many different visions of love, and ultimately invites the reader to play, too – to contribute her own variation on the idea of love.

Some kinds of love in *Jazz* are stultifying in their persistence, like the love for their lost mothers that keeps both protagonists Violet and Joe bound to the past and distorts all their present-day loving. However, a model of love as a creative process, a process of innovation, ultimately replaces this static form of love bound to an absent beloved.

This new idea of love is most clearly articulated in a conversation that Alice is having with Violet. To Violet's query about what she is supposed to do with a flagrantly unfaithful husband, Alice answers, "'You got anything left to you to love, anything at all, do it.'" Violet responds, "'You saying take it? Don't fight?'" And Alice says, "'Nobody's asking you to take it. I'm sayin make it, make it!'" (112–13).

Alice suggests that love is creative, something you "make," or "make up," out of the materials available to you. Morrison seems to be signifying on Virginia Woolf's *Mrs Dalloway* here. For Clarissa Dalloway's way of loving is to throw her imagination into the world around her: "what she loved [was] life, London, this moment of June" (4); this loving, she thinks, is a continual process of "making it up, building it round one, tumbling it, creating it every moment afresh" (ibid.).

I think that Morrison is using the allusion to *Mrs Dalloway* to suggest that love is something you improvise – like jazz itself. You pour your imaginative resources into making something new of your love for another person, giving the love relationship a new shape, again and again. Or, in Woolf's words, you create love "every moment afresh."

This idea is enacted at the level of the characters, who make up unlikely love relationships. Thus, for example, Alice, the surrogate mother and protector of Dorcas, and Violet, the woman who slashed Dorcas's corpse in a final indignity inflicted on the murdered girl, establish a deep friendship based on openness and trust; their bond is resilient and nurturing for both. Joe and Violet come to love each other in ways that one would never have predicted from their former mutual alienation and anger. Felice, Joe and Violet "make up" their own unique and unexpected version of family love.

And the narrator, learning from her characters' creativity with love relations, becomes creative too, addressing a love song to the reader:

> I have loved only you, surrendered my whole self reckless to you and nobody else [...] I want you to love me back and show it to me [...] I love the way you hold me, how close you let me be to you. I like your fingers on and on, lifting, turning. I have watched your face for a long time now, and missed your eyes when you went away from me. (229)

This love song is a triumph of innovation, for it reaches across the impassable barrier between a narrator who is part of a disembodied text, made up of abstract marks on a page, and a flesh-and-blood reader; the narrator addresses the body of the reader directly and demands a physical communion.

Then, in another improvisational turn, the narrator ends the novel by inviting the reader to "Make me, remake me" (ibid.) – that is, to pick up the story the narrator has just finished telling and make her own version of it. Alice's sermon on how to love – "I'm sayin make it, make it" (113) – becomes in the mouth of the narrator a directive to love her in the way a reader *can* love a storyteller – by making up her own version of the story just told.

The invitation to the reader to improvise her own variation on the narrator's theme resonates not only with this novel's structuring idea of jazz improvisation but also with all the later novels' demands on the reader to complete the text with her own ideas – her own "politics" on love, gender and race ("Home" 7). And the idea of replacing the old love story with something new reflects an impulse that energizes all the later novels: the impulse to overthrow established, static models of love to make way for the creation of new and innovative forms of loving.

disclosure statement

No potential conflict of interest was reported by the author.

notes

Some of the ideas in this essay are also in my book *Love and Narrative Form in Toni Morrison's Later Novels* (2017). I thank the University of Georgia Press and its editor, Walter Biggins, for giving me permission to use materials from the book here.

1 For a full analysis of *Love*, see chapter 4 of my book *Love and Narrative Form in Toni Morrison's Later Novels* (2017), and "*Love*'s Time and the Reader: Ethical Effects of *Nachtraglichkeit* in Toni Morrison's *Love*."

2 Scholars have written from a number of perspectives on Sethe's connection to her children. Among them are Stephanie Demetrakopoulos, Rebecca Ferguson, Jennifer FitzGerald, Pelagia Goulimari, Mae Henderson, La Vinia Delois Jennings, Linda Koolish, Linda Krumholz, Lorraine Liscio, Jill Matus, Naomi Morgenstern, Andrea O'Reilly, Barbara Schapiro, Evelyn Schreiber, Valerie Smith, Molly Abel Travis, Laurie Vickroy, Teresa Washington, Philip Weinstein, and Jean Wyatt ("Giving Body").

3 Reading *Beloved* through a Lacanian lens, Sheldon George identifies Beloved as the "object a," the source-object of Sethe's desire. Once Sethe "embrac[es] Beloved as the objet a that fills her lack [...] Sethe becomes a *full*, desireless subject." That is, possessing the object a makes her feel whole and thus "eliminates the dimension of desire and all subjective aspirations" ("Approaching" 119). Cynthia Dobbs writes perceptively about Beloved's monologues (570–73).

4 In a series of historical allusions that draw parallels between Dr Beau Scott, whose "scientific experiments" on Cee's uterus destroy her capacity to conceive a child and the nineteenth-century figure of Dr J. Marion Sims, Morrison calls up a repressed US history of eugenics, forced sterilization of women of color, and "scientific" experimentation on unconsenting black bodies. For an account of how elements of Cee's story line up with Dr Sims's experiments on black slave women, see my *Love and Narrative Form in Toni Morrison's Later Novels*.

bibliography

Bakerman, Jane. "The Seams Can't Show: An Interview with Toni Morrison." Taylor-Guthrie 30–42. Print.

Demetrakopoulos, Stephanie. "Maternal Bonds as Devourers of Women's Individuation in Toni Morrison's *Beloved*." *African American Review* 26.1 (1992): 51–60. Print.

Dobbs, Cynthia. "Toni Morrison's *Beloved*: Bodies Returned, Modernism Revisited." *African American Review* 32.4 (1998): 563–78. Print.

Eliot, George. *The Mill on the Floss*. New York: New American Library, 1965. Print.

Ferguson, Rebecca. "History, Memory and Language in Toni Morrison's *Beloved*." *Feminist Criticism: Theory and Practice*. Toronto: U of Toronto P, 1991. 109–27. Print.

FitzGerald, Jennifer. "Selfhood and Community: Psychoanalysis and Discourse in *Beloved*." *Modern Fiction Studies* 39.3–4 (1993): 669–87. Print.

George, Sheldon. "Approaching the Thing of Slavery: A Lacanian Analysis of Toni Morrison's *Beloved*." *African American Review* 45.1–2 (2012): 115–30. Print.

Goulimari, Pelagia. *Toni Morrison*. London: Routledge, 2011. Print.

Henderson, Mae. "Toni Morrison's *Beloved*: Re-membering the Body as Historical Text." *Comparative American Identities: Race, Sex, and Nationality in the Modern Text*. Ed. Hortense Spillers. London: Routledge, 1991. 62–86. Print.

Jennings, La Vinia Delois. *Toni Morrison and the Idea of Africa*. Cambridge: Cambridge UP, 2008. Print.

Koenen, Anne. "The One Out of Sequence." Taylor-Guthrie 67–83. Print.

Koolish, Linda. "'To Be Loved and Cry Shame': A Psychological Reading of Toni Morrison's *Beloved*." *MELUS* 26.4 (2001): 169–95. Print.

Krumholz, Linda. "The Ghosts of Slavery: Historical Recovery in Toni Morrison's *Beloved*." *African American Review* 26.3 (1992): 395–408. Print.

Lacan, Jacques. *Le Séminaire, livre VIII: Le Transfert*. 1960–61. Ed. Jacques-Alain Miller. Paris: Seuil, 2001. Print.

Laplanche, Jean. *New Foundations for Psychoanalysis.* Trans. David Macey. London: Blackwell, 1989. Print.

Matus, Jill. *Toni Morrison.* Manchester: Manchester UP, 1998. Print.

Morgenstern, Naomi. "Mother's Milk and Sister's Blood: Trauma and the Neoslave Narrative." *Differences: A Journal of Feminist Cultural Studies* 8.2 (1997): 101–26. Print.

Morrison, Toni. *Beloved.* New York: Knopf, 1987. Print.

Morrison, Toni. *The Bluest Eye.* 1970. New York: Penguin (Plume), 1994. Print.

Morrison, Toni. "Home." *The House That Race Built: Original Essays by Toni Morrison, Angela Y. Davis, Cornel West, and Others on Black Americans and Politics in America Today.* Ed. Wahneema Lubiano. New York: Random, 1998. 3–12. Print.

Morrison, Toni. *Home.* New York and Toronto: Knopf, 2012. Print.

Morrison, Toni. *Jazz.* New York: Knopf, 1992. Print.

Morrison, Toni. *Love.* New York: Knopf, 2003. Print.

Morrison, Toni. *Song of Solomon.* 1977. New York: Penguin (Plume), 1987. Print.

Morrison, Toni. *Sula.* 1973. New York: Random, 2004. Print.

Morrison, Toni. *Tar Baby.* New York: Penguin, 1982. Print.

O'Reilly, Andrea. *Toni Morrison and Motherhood: A Politics of the Heart.* Albany: State U of New York P, 2004. Print.

Peterson, Christopher. "*Beloved*'s Claim." *Modern Fiction Studies* 52.3 (2006): 548–69. Print.

Rothstein, Mervyn. "Toni Morrison, In Her New Novel, Defends Women." *New York Times* 26 Aug. 1987: C17. Print.

Ruti, Mari. *The Singularity of Being: Lacan and the Immortal Within.* New York: Fordham UP, 2012. Print.

Santner, Eric. *On the Psychotheology of Everyday Life: Reflections on Freud and Rosenzweig.* Chicago: U of Chicago P, 2001. Print.

Schapiro, Barbara. "The Bonds of Love and the Boundaries of Self in Toni Morrison's *Beloved.*" *Contemporary Literature* 32.2 (1991): 194–210. Print.

Schreiber, Evelyn. *Race, Trauma, and Home in the Novels of Toni Morrison.* Baton Rouge: Louisiana State UP, 2010. Print.

Smith, Valerie. *Writing the Moral Imagination.* Chichester: Wiley-Blackwell, 2012. Print.

Suzuki, Shunryu. *Zen Mind, Beginner's Mind.* Boston: Shambhala, 2010. Print.

Taylor-Guthrie, Danille, ed. *Conversations with Toni Morrison.* Jackson: UP of Mississippi, 1994. Print.

Travis, Molly Abel. "Beyond Empathy: Narrative Distancing and Ethics in Toni Morrison's *Beloved* and J.M. Coetzee's *Disgrace.*" *Journal of Narrative Theory* 40.2 (2010): 231–50. Print.

Vickroy, Laurie. *Trauma and Survival in Contemporary Fiction.* Charlottesville: U of Virginia P, 2002. Print.

Washington, Teresa. "The Mother–Daughter *Àjé* Relationship in Toni Morrison's *Beloved.*" *African American Review* 39.1–2 (2005): 171–88. Print.

Weinstein, Philip. *What Else But Love? The Ordeal of Race in Faulkner and Morrison.* New York: Columbia UP, 1996. Print.

Wyatt, Jean. "Giving Body to the Word: The Maternal Symbolic in Toni Morrison's *Beloved.*" *PMLA* 108.3 (1993): 474–88. Print.

Wyatt, Jean. *Love and Narrative Form in Toni Morrison's Later Novels.* Athens, GA: U of Georgia P, 2017. Print.

Wyatt, Jean. "*Love*'s Time and the Reader: Ethical Effects of *Nachtraglichkeit* in Toni Morrison's *Love.*" *Narrative* 16.2 (2008): 193–221. Print.

Jean Wyatt

maría donapetry

ETHICAL WAYS OF SEEING THE FEMALE NUDE IN SPANISH CINEMA

It seems as if mentioning ethics is the same as proposing and joining what Sophie Ratcliffe has called "a vogue for empathy," "a fuzzy but general assumption that expressing sympathy or empathy, and engaging in purportedly 'empathetic literary encounters', may encourage civic virtue and humanitarianism" (5). Nothing could be further from my interest in ethics and ethical approaches to cinema. The encouragement of civic virtue and humanitarianism is admirable but it has little to do with good cinema. I am all for the questions, ambiguities and challenges that a work of art provokes. As the Spanish philosopher Fernando Savater says: "En el terreno de la ética, todo aquello que no es ambiguo, todo aquello cuya lectura pretende ser unívoca es dogma eclesiástico o código penal" (In the field of ethics, everything that is not ambiguous, everything whose reading tries to be univocal/unambiguous is ecclesiastic dogma or penal code) (*Pensamientos arriesgados* 101; my trans.). This does not mean that emotions can be left out of the cinematic experience, since they are not divorced from reflection. Both – emotions and the cinematic experience – are subjective and make us aware, if we pause to think, of our own subjectivity, perhaps moving us to further reflections. Most narrative cinema manipulates our perception both aesthetically (formally) and in terms of knowledge about and understanding of the story narrated. It also appeals to our emotions but, in the cinema I am interested in, the affects are not an end in themselves but the means to engage us in the stories and in the way they are told. In any case, these manipulations do not mean the film-maker can control our responses regardless of his or her intentions. In fact, the point is to let the spectators react and become aware and responsible for their own reactions, choices, pleasures or displeasures.

Let me give you an example of visual art: Bernini's sculpture *Ecstasy of Saint Teresa* (Teresa of Avila) having the vision of the angel. Given that this sculpture is found in a church (Cornaro's chapel in Santa Maria della Vittoria, Rome), the intention of the sculpture may have been edifying and promoting or encouraging mystical visions or, at least, it would have served to illustrate what Teresa of Avila describes as her experience of the divine. Bernini, though, could not and cannot control the reaction of the viewer. This particular sculpture has been interpreted widely in Freudian terms as an image of the female orgasm.

Something similar can be said of the many paintings of Saint Sebastian as one of the oldest gay icons. The image that Botticelli painted was definitely meant as an illustration of Saint Sebastian suffering martyrdom for his faith; however, the saint's gaze is absolutely ambiguous. Contemporary imitations such as those one can find in gay popular magazines (see *reFresh*, for instance) are just as definitely far from religious considerations and count on the understanding that the suffering (if any) is univocally linked to sexual pleasure.

Seeing the images (which I am not allowed to include here) will make clear what I mean. Ambiguous allures pose questions. It is completely up to us to indulge or not in the pleasures offered, to get involved in what we see and what we understand, to engage with the conflicts presented on screen and in ourselves in spite of our tendency to follow the demands of desire and gratification, no questions asked. Those pleasures can be simply enjoyed or they also can lead us to question them. In any case, we choose and are responsible for our reactions. According to Rosi Braidotti (who in turn follows Deleuze), "the proper object of ethical enquiry is not the subject's moral intentionality, or rational consciousness, as much as the effects of truth and power that his or her actions are likely to have upon others in the world" (14). And later on she adds, "The point about collective responsibility is that it calls for recognition, acknowledgement and understanding: this is the only ethical freedom we have" (151).

Let's now go into the area where aesthetics and ethics overlap in regard to the representation of naked women in film, and how some ideas of women's liberation through nudity are challenged, particularly those that traditionally in this context have confused "sexual liberation" with "availability."

In order to evaluate what is good and/or just, Paul Ricoeur suggests, we have no choice but to identify and distinguish, and to go from the moment "where the thinking subject claims to master meaning, to mutual recognition, where the subject places him or herself under the tutelage of a relationship of reciprocity" (25). This idea is linked to those of Jean-Paul Sartre about the individual's identity (in Cavallaro 116), and to those of Fernando Savater in regard to the humanity of the subject (*Invitación* 27), apart from many other philosophers who write about the consciousness of the individual as such. Here I want to show and analyse images of female nudes that appear in films made in the first decade of the twenty-first century directed by Spanish women directors, and explore from a feminist perspective how we can identify, acknowledge and distinguish the individuals we see on screen, and some of the ethical questions those images may pose.

What compels me to make an incursion into such a wide and convoluted area, in which ethics and aesthetics meet (and sometimes miss each other completely), is my will to recognize, identify, or identify with the representations of naked women on screen, and look for a meaning, if at all possible, I may relate to as a woman, not only in the sense of understanding what I see on the screen but also in the sense of finding what I see acceptable and not degrading. In other words: I would like to discern the politics of the discourse and the images of female nudity in certain cinema (and I invite you to do the same).

The female nude has been one of the most consistent themes in the art of all periods, most often as a spectacle which produces aesthetic pleasure in the observer. Both the technical competence and the sensitivity of the artist as well as the capacity for judgement of the observer legitimize these representations. Nudity here is controlled and contained by the artist, the medium and the observers. Theoretically at least, painting a naked woman and observing the painting are not furtive acts or series of acts. However, as John Berger has explained in *Ways of Seeing*, the legitimacy of this practice involves the objectification of the naked body: "The sight of it as an object stimulates the use of it as an object" (48). Cinema partakes of this kind of control and legitimacy. And yet the realism with movement, sound, and actresses (live bodies) in cinema transforms the female nude into something different from that of a painting, a sculpture or a photograph. The relationship between spectators and a female nude on screen is socially and culturally contextualized in a different way, among other things, because the film theatre (although it is a public space) fosters an illusion of intimacy impossible to replicate in a museum or in any open and illuminated space. Since nowadays films are widely watched in DVD format or on a computer screen, the degree of intimacy is not so much an illusion as a reality. When the nude that appears on screen is or is supposed to be erotic, we enter into the murky area of unclear borders between what is artistic and what is pornographic (or pseudo-pornographic) or, as Lynda Nead puts it, "[between] pure and impure desire" (104). That is, moral aspects are considered to be what determines whether or not a specific work is art. The fact that the intention of certain images is simply to sexually arouse the observer – to awaken impure desires in him or her – Nead seems to be saying, automatically disqualifies those images as art.

I do not agree, or not completely anyway, with this binary as a method of distinguishing and recognizing a work of art; even less in regards to the sexual arousal of the observer/ spectator, be it a woman or a man. The spectator's reaction, no matter how pure or impure his or her desires may be, does not determine the artistic quality of a work. No artist can predict or control the reaction of the observer (as I have already argued above).

The films I have chosen here are all directed by women. The female nude in each of them is treated with particular care as an answer or comment on the female nudes in most of mainstream cinema. The three of them also address diegetically the representation of the female nude, be it in films, in paintings or in photography. That is, they are all permeated by a reflection on the treatment of a woman's body in art vis-à-vis social experiences of women in reality.

Los años desnudos. Clasificada S [*The Naked Years. X Rated*] (2008), directed and scripted by Dunia Ayaso and Félix Sabroso, is a re-creation of the so-called "Undressing" period of Spanish cinema, just at the beginning of the Transition between the dictatorship and democracy in the late 1970s. Female nudity in cinema and the press at the time was considered a sign of liberation, of democracy. Of course, Ayaso and Sabroso literally review the circumstances and the price many women had to pay in order to promote that kind of "liberation."

The first scene of *Los años desnudos* shows starkly the crudeness with which an actress – Sandra, played by Candela Peña (and by extension any actress in those circumstances) – is told to undress in a casting session, how utterly dehumanized her body becomes, but also how the individual struggles to be recognized and acknowledged as such (see http://www.ecartelera.com/erotica/candela-pena-desnuda-escena-anos-desnudos-2008/original/). Sandra, while completely naked and obviously uncomfortable, asks the casting crew if they would like to hear her deliver part of a monologue from García Lorca's *Doña Rosita la soltera*; she wants to show them she is capable of acting and not just showing her body. The members of the crew, whom we hardly see, although obviously not interested, accept the offer and she starts reciting her monologue:

> ¿Y qué os voy a decir? Hay cosas que no se pueden decir porque no hay palabras para decirlas; y si las hubiera, nadie entendería su significado. Me entendéis si pido pan y agua y hasta un beso, pero nunca me podríais ni entender ni quitar esta mano oscura que no sé si me hiela o me abrasa el corazón cada vez que me quedo sola. Sería el cuento de nunca acabar. Yo sé que los ojos los tendré siempre jóvenes, y sé que la espalda se me irá curvando cada día. Después de todo, lo que me ha pasado le ha pasado a mil mujeres. (No sé por qué estoy hablando de todo esto.) No me agrada que me miréis así. Me molestan esas miradas de perros fieles. Esas miradas de lástima que me perturban y me indignan. (From Act III)

> (And what can I tell you? There are things that can't be said because there are no words to say them. You can understand me when I ask for bread or water, even for a kiss but you could never understand or take away this dark

> hand which I don't know whether it is freezing or burning my heart every time I am alone. It would be the never ending story. I know I will always have young eyes, and I know that my back will become arched more each day. After all, what has happened to me has happened to a thousand other women. (I don't know why I am talking about all this.) I don't like the way you look at me. Those faithful dogs' looks bother me. That way of looking and pitying me that disturbs and outrages me.)

As she speaks, the camera goes from a general view from the crew's perspective to a close up of Sandra's face. When she finishes, the camera goes back to the crew's point of view. The delivery of the soliloquy in such adverse setting, with the group of men as diegetic spectators, could easily stand as a manifesto for the actresses who have been undressed in film for no other purpose but the erotic titillation of some male spectators. Since this titillation depends on the imaginary availability of the naked female body, the imaginary control of the spectator and his power to degrade her, Doña Rosita's (and Sandra's) complaint "No me agrada que me miréis así" (I don't like the way you look at me) expresses the anger and the strength of the subject who has been literally divested of her humanity, of her individuality, but who states that the relationship between her and the crew is of equals at work. If any kind of identification could take place between the extra-diegetic audience (us) and the crew as a result of visual alignment, the statement would become an indictment difficult to ignore. Just before this "I don't like the way you look at me," Sandra has introduced a sentence of her own: "I don't know why I am talking about all this" as if it were part of the monologue. This sort of aside, while she looks at an indefinite point away from the casting crew as if she were talking to herself, seems to express her consciousness of the absurdity of the situation: to try to keep a relationship with art when the only prevailing interest is in the physical quality of her naked and silent body. Her artistic and ontological will is at complete odds with the situation.

The last words in the scene, already out of Doña Rosita's character, are unambiguously Sandra's. While she picks up her clothes from the chair where she has left them, she asks the crew who is going to pay for her taxi fare since "esto está en a tomar po'l culo" (this [place] is in bumfuck). We understand she means that the studio, or wherever they are doing the casting test, is really far from the city centre; we also understand, though, the whole situation for her lacks any personal or vital reference. The location and the experience have little to do with "the factory of dreams" that cinema is supposed to be for her.

Icíar Bollaín in *Te doy mis ojos* [*Take My Eyes*] (2003) and Isabel Coixet in *Elegy* (2008) are but two examples of the kind of awareness film directors can have about what showing a female nude (undressing a woman) on screen may mean aesthetically and ethically. Bollaín's film specially, because of its direct concern with domestic violence ("gender violence" or "violence against women" *tout court*), offers a scene which can be extrapolated to the general scope of this study. In it Pilar (Laia Marull), the battered wife, is getting ready to go to Madrid for a job interview. When her friends come to pick her up, her husband – Antonio (Luis Tosar) – gets upset because she is occupying her time in something unrelated to him, and starts tearing her art books apart. (The scene referred to here can be seen at <http://www.youtube.com/watch?v=eyWwvlMuNAY>.)

As his anger grows, he directs all sorts of abuse at her and proceeds to tear her clothes off until she is practically naked. While she tries to defend herself and keep her clothes on, Antonio pushes her to the balcony of the house so anybody in the street can see her naked. He eventually drags her back to the room and Pilar, paralysed by the horror of it all and by fear of him, wets herself.

Antonio does not undress Pilar in order to get sexual satisfaction but in order to degrade her even further. He undresses her or, more accurately, tears her clothes off as an act of personal violence (equated in his mind with forms of control and power) and magnifies this act by dragging her to the balcony and exposing her nakedness in public. As spectators we understand that Antonio's intention to humiliate and dehumanize Pilar actually dehumanizes him. In principle, and given the narrative of the film, there should not be room at all in this scene for erotic titillation. It is perfectly plausible that Bollaín may have taken this scene from some real testimony, since she conducted a lot of research on the topic of gender violence in Spain for this film; it is just as credible that she created the scene in order to say something about the female nude from a feminine and a feminist perspective. Pilar has recently started to work in a museum and her job, among other things, involves explaining well-known paintings with female nudes: Titian's *Danae*, Ruben's *Orpheus and Eurydice* and *The Three Graces*. Pilar's understanding of these nudes is definitely different from that of her husband's. For Antonio the feminine nude is degrading and "degradable." Pilar sees them as an acknowledgement of women's beauty, the kind of acknowledgement she would like to receive. Bollaín, through the inclusion of Pilar's descriptions of the nudes, brings to the screen the theme we are interested in here, the female nude, also in a dramatic way – that is, in a double ekphrasis (to speak of a work of art in a work of art) – and opts for a woman's position facing that female nude: a position which takes into account a woman's perspective when she knows she is being observed naked. This position, therefore, qualifies the politics of her filmic discourse as something in which the subject is interested and has an investment. As Arthur Danto puts it, "as far as showing the subject naked, the morality of that is altogether how the subject feels about [her]self as seen that way" (cited in Levinson 22).

There is a single scene in *Elegy*, directed by Isabel Coixet, in which the protagonist bares her breasts to the camera. Consuela Castillo (Penélope Cruz) has had an intense affair with David Kepesh (Ben Kingsley) but, after he has shown his inability to be part of her society, she disappears for a while. One day she calls him and goes to see him. She explains that her estrangement had also to do with the fact that she has breast cancer and that she will soon have a mastectomy. Consuela wants David to photograph her with her breasts bare, that part of her body that stands for all the sexual pleasure and the emotional bond they had while being lovers.

In this sequence,[1] Coixet's camera focuses on Consuela's expression, and then on David's reaction at the news. Although her body has not been mutilated yet, the sense of loss and threat for both is what dominates the scene. In an essay about Coixet's film, "La vida secreta de las palabras" [The Secret Life of Words] (2005), John Berger explains the kind of feeling I am referring to when talking about a scene in which the female protagonist also bares her breasts:

> Tampoco se rinde en ella culto alguno al dolor. Sencillamente se ofrece una visión de cómo a veces el sufrimiento conduce a una salvación compartida, que nunca es simple, que nunca es mera palabrería. Antigua. Algo que suelen descubrir quienes no tienen poder.
>
> (This film does not pay homage to pain. The film simply offers a vision of how sometimes suffering is the means to a shared redemption, which is never simple, which is never just empty words. Ancient. Something that is usually discovered by the powerless.) (Berger, "La vida secreta de las palabras" 95–96; my trans.)

After the explanations, David gets a camera and Consuela poses for him, removing her top very slowly until her breasts are bare; then she looks at David looking at her. The film camera follows both characters' gazes, forcing the spectator to align him- or herself alternately with David and with Consuela, and eventually with both. They are sharing the pain as they shared the pleasure because in that sharing the humanity of both characters is at stake. This particular scene diverges crucially from the text on which it is based, Philip Roth's novel *The Dying Animal*. In the source text, David cannot help being aroused at the sight of Consuela's breasts. Coixet makes a strong point regarding this female nude: the naked body of a woman is not on screen simply there to give necessarily voyeuristic pleasure either to a diegetic male character or to the male audience. There are other interpretative possibilities. Ignacio Vidal-Folch declares that

> Coixet es director de cine, no juez sentado en el trono de la moral; y en vez de dictar sentencias condenatorias o absolutorias, lo que hace es representar con elocuencia magistral la pavorosa carnalidad de Kingsley: esa calva con sus arrugas y ese labio superior fino como hoja de afeitar, por debajo de la cual salen las palabras "Estoy aquí ... " o "Ecce homo."
>
> (Coixet is a film director, not a judge sitting on the moral throne; instead of pronouncing sentences of approval or condemnation, what she does is to represent with magnificent eloquence the terrifying carnality of Kingsley's: that bald head with wrinkles and that upper lip as thin as a razor blade, through which the words "I am here ... " or "Ecce homo" come out.) (12; my trans.)

I would add that Kingsley's (David's) carnality/vulnerability is paralleled by Consuela's. David's vulnerability has to do with old age; Consuela's with the threat of cancer, and both face the proximity of death. In general, I agree with Vidal-Folch: Coixet is definitely not a moral judge; but she is interested in the moral plight of her characters and lets the audience observe, understand, recognize and find (or not) the ethical value of the story she is telling and how she is telling it. David's holding a camera and taking a picture of Consuela at her behest reminds us that the decision to undress and to be looked at is all hers, and that she expects recognition, not objectification. Like in Cavafy's poem "Body, Remember ... "[2] Consuela wants to revisit the sight of her naked body in the eyes of her former lover, to fix the memory in a photograph so as not to lose it completely. She wants art to rescue her body from the ravages about to happen. Once that memory is materialized, she will be ready for the operation and the changes. Of course, there may be spectators whose reaction to this scene would not be very different from the one they would have watching a semi- or pseudo-porno film. That, as I pointed out above, is not controllable by the director no matter how clear and careful her intentions are.

In his *Invitación a la ética*, Fernando Savater explains that

> Para la voluntad moral, no todo vale. En la vida – como en cualquier juego o cualquier arte – hay cosas que no vale hacer, mientras que otras jugadas son excepcionalmente valiosas. Lo que no vale es lo que no *nos* vale; aquello que nos hace perder, lo que debilita nuestro juego o nos excluye de él.
>
> (For the moral will, not everything is allowed. In life – like in any game or any art – there are things that are not allowed, while other ways of playing are exceptionally valuable. What is not allowed is what is not good for *us*; what makes us lose, what weakens our game or excludes us.) (*Invitación* 63)

As I am sure we all have seen in mainstream cinema, there are many female nudes that cheat us, that are on screen with the sole purpose of corroborating that a woman's image exists as the object of pleasure for heterosexual men. Those who make films of this kind count on the complicity of an audience who either are fully satisfied with what they see and consider it good and/or they perceive the images as "natural" and, therefore, consider them absolutely legitimate. Of course, such audiences do not question either the process by which the images are considered natural or the implications of this naturalization. On the other hand, as is the case in the scenes of the films discussed here, there are films which treat the female nude with the kind of realism in characters and situations that, as Gregory Currie suggests, "enabl[es] the sort of imaginative exercise that broadens rather than constricts our understanding of human possibilities of thought, feeling, and action" (cited in Levinson 13). Dunia Ayaso, Félix Sabroso, Icíar Bollaín and Isabel Coixet have made films precisely about the relationship between art and the living woman, between the creative exercises of film, painting and photography and their ethical engagement with the individual.

The most basic principle of humanity according to Savater is that "el yo necesita, para ser plenamente yo, verse confirmado – esto es, reconocido – por otro yo" (the I needs, in order to be I fully, to see itself confirmed – that is, recognized – by another I) (*Invitación* 27). Feminism in its broadest sense works so that this principle is considered as valid for men as for women. The treatment of the female nude in cinema is one of the many fields in which aesthetical reasons can function as "artistic" alibis in order to deny women that recognition. Ethics and aesthetics do not necessarily have to go hand in hand, no matter how much Wittgenstein insists on identifying one with the other (6.421). The conjunction of formal beauty with moral degradation is a possibility in art, but not at its best. In any case, we should be aware of that conjunction when it happens. There is arguably no point in even considering the possibility of imposing a certain "moral" code on the artist or the work of art since ethics has to do with what we want to be, what we aspire to be in order to become more human. "Art," says Schellekens, "is a means of expression – be it of emotions, political ideas or moral belief systems – and not a means of coercion" (90). However, every work of art, every film, has rules of engagement with its subject and with the audience. In the case of the female nude, because it affects women in the way we are recognized and identified as subjects through our naked bodies, those rules establish certain "*condiciones de humanidad* sin las cuales no ser[emos] admitid[as] como objeto[s] infinito[s] o se [nos] otorgará solo el reconocimiento cruel de la violencia" (*conditions of humanity* without which I will not be accepted as an infinite object or I will be given only the cruel recognition of violence) (Savater, *Invitación* 31).

disclosure statement

No potential conflict of interest was reported by the author.

notes

1 The scene referred to here can be seen at <http://www.youtube.com/watch?v=fWGpYmctEq4> (accessed 2 Oct. 2015).

2 Constantine P. Cavafy: "Body, remember not only how much you were loved, / not only the beds on which you lay, / but also those desires for you / that glowed plainly in the eyes, / and trembled in the voice – and some / chance obstacle made futile. / Now that all of them belong to the past, / it almost seems as if you had yielded / to those desires – how they glowed, / remember, in the eyes gazing at you; / how they trembled in the voice, for you, remember, body." Trans. Aliki Barnstone, available <http://bodyremember.com/cavafy-who-said-it-better/> (accessed 28 Sept. 2015).

films

Ayaso, Dunia, and Félix Sabroso, dir. *Los años desnudos. Clasificada S.* 2008. Universal Pictures Iberia, 2009. DVD.

Bollaín, Icíar, dir. *Te doy mis ojos*. 2003. Cameo Media, 2011. DVD.

Coixet, Isabel, dir. *Elegy*. 2008. Divisa Home Video, 2013. DVD.

bibliography

Andreu, Cristina, ed. *Una mujer bajo la influencia. Isabel Coixet.* Madrid: Iberautor, 2008. Print.

Berger, John. "Cuatro apuntes sobre *La vida secreta de las palabras*." Andreu 93–96. Print.

Berger, John. *Ways of Seeing*. London: Penguin, 2008. Print.

Bernini, Gianlorenzo. *Ecstasy of Saint Teresa*. Web. 22 Sept. 2015. <https://www.google.co.uk/search?q=Bernini+Teresa+of+Avila&espv=2&biw=1366&bih=620&tbm=isch&tbo=u&source=univ&sa=X&ved=0CCIQsARqFQoTCN2d262ii8gCFcZaPgod50MNtg#imgrc=0Z-whYV7R8SipM%3A>.

Botticelli, Sandro. *St. Sebastian*. Web. 22 Sept. 2015. <www.jdiezamal.com>.

Braidotti, Rosi. *Transpositions: On Nomadic Ethics*. Cambridge: Polity, 2006. Print.

Cavafy, Constantine P. "Body, Remember ..." Trans. Aliki Barnstone. Web. 28 Sept. 2015. <http://bodyremember.com/cavafy-who-said-it-better/>.

Cavallaro, Dani. *The Body for Beginners*. New York: Writers & Readers, 1998. Print.

Levinson, Jerrold, ed. *Aesthetics and Ethics: Essays at the Intersection*. Cambridge: Cambridge UP, 1998. Print.

Nead, Lynda. *The Female Nude: Art, Obscenity and Sexuality*. London and New York: Routledge, 1992. Print.

Ratcliffe, Sophie. *On Sympathy*. Oxford: Oxford UP, 2008. Print.

reFresh. Web. 22 Sept. 2015. <www.pinterest.com>.

Ricoeur, Paul. *The Course of Recognition*. Cambridge, MA: Harvard UP, 2005. Print.

Savater, Fernando. *Invitación a la ética*. Barcelona: Anagrama, 1982. Print.

Savater, Fernando. *Pensamientos arriesgados*. Ed. José Sánchez Tortosa. Madrid: La esfera de los libros, 2002. Print.

Schellekens, Elisabeth. *Aesthetics and Morality*. London: Continuum, 2007. Print.

Vidal-Folch, Ignacio. "Brindis por Isabel Coixet." Andreu 9–12. Print.

Wittgenstein, Ludwig. *Tractatus Logico-Philosophicus*. London: Routledge, 1961. Print.

morag shiach

ON OR ABOUT DECEMBER 1930

gender and the writing of lives in virginia woolf

Virginia Woolf wrote a striking number of texts around the year 1930 that engage in important and original ways with the nature of biography, autobiography, subjectivity, and (fictional) character. Her writings thus offer a complex set of responses to the possible relations between gender, identity and life-writing, which resonate productively with other articles in this volume. Throughout her writing career, Woolf deployed a wide range of modes of life-writing, and reflected explicitly on the literary, aesthetic, and theoretical questions these modes of writing raised both for a writer and for her readers. She was a novelist, a biographer, an essayist, a diarist, and a letter writer, and in all these genres she was intrigued by the possibilities for representing a life in words. In addition to such substantive engagement with issues of life-writing, Woolf's modernist literary style also opened up new possibilities for representing women, their lives, and their writing. The key aspects of this style on which this article concentrates include innovative approaches to the representation of subjectivity, productive and frequently surprising juxtapositions of ideas, formal innovations in relation to narrative temporalities, and the rich deployment of "imagist" ways of seeing and representing the world. These formal literary innovations created a space for Woolf to conceive and represent both gender and subjectivity as multiple, complex, and contested.

The decision to focus on the period "on or about December 1930" in this article is driven partly by the richness and diversity of Woolf's reflections on life-writing around this specific year. But it also reflects a broader commitment to the importance of critical and historical studies focused on a single year as a productive method within the overall field of cultural history. Focusing on a single year facilitates certain kinds of interdisciplinary work in cultural history that address a diverse range of texts and contexts. For example, George Cotkin's *Feast of Excess: A Cultural History of the New Sensibility* (Oxford UP, 2016) argues that in order to enable "interplay" between individual artists and their historical moment it is important that "each chapter deals with a single year" (13). The same approach can be found in Hugh MacDonald's *Music in 1853: The Biography of a Year*

(Boydell, 2012), and perhaps even more pertinently for this discussion of Woolf, in the highly original and influential study by Michael North, *Reading 1922: A Return to the Scene of the Modern* (Oxford UP, 1999). Each of these studies draws on the potential for such tightly temporally focused historical inquiry to enable productive comparison and contrast between diverse texts and events. This is not, of course, to deny the analytical and critical importance of engaging also with questions of geography and space within cultural history, as this volume as a whole so clearly illustrates. But the focus of this particular chapter is shaped by the rich possibilities generated by the study of a single year.

Reference to the cultural history of a single year is by no means an anachronistic or random imposition on Woolf's texts, of course. Indeed, many readers may well already have recognized that the title of this article is an allusion to an argument that Woolf developed in the 1920s about the nature of human character and its link to historical change, which focused particularly on the transformative potential of a single year. Woolf was thinking hard about literature, history and the representation of individual character in 1923 and 1924 when she published both an essay entitled "Character in Fiction" and a related essay focused on the representation of female character, "Mr Bennett and Mrs Brown." In these essays she argued that:

> On or about December 1910 human character changed. I am not saying that one went out, as one might into a garden, and there saw that a rose had flowered or a hen had laid an egg. The change was not sudden and definite like that. But a change there was, nevertheless; and since one must be arbitrary, let us date it about the year 1910.[1]

Although many readers have found Woolf's claim here excessive and unpersuasive, this is, I suggest, a serious attempt to articulate the various factors that can lead to the emergence of a significantly new cultural moment. Class mobility, changes in education, and the intensification of commerce are all factors that Woolf alludes to when she claims that there was a radical shift in 1910 that could be observed in human relations, both at work and within the family. These shifts led, necessarily she suggests, to transformations in religion, conduct, politics and literature, "on or about 1910."

I have used elements of this way of thinking about cultural change in shaping my overall argument in this article, but have picked a different moment (1930) that seems more significant to Woolf personally, and also to her experiments in the relations between gender, subjectivity and writing than does the year 1910, when she had not yet published her first novel. The second half of the 1920s had seen Woolf developing her thinking about writing, character, subjectivity and history in very productive ways. In late 1929 she published *A Room of One's Own*, an essay that explored both the history of women's writing and the creative possibilities of future literary engagements with gender and culture. The previous year had seen the publication of her fictional biography *Orlando*, which, as discussed below, stages radical experiments in the representation both of gender and of history, while in 1931 she was to publish one of her most radically experimental texts, *The Waves*. The years just before and after 1930 were thus a particularly fruitful moment in Woolf's life as a writer, which produced a range of texts that have a much broader significance for the analysis of life-writing as well as of women's writing more broadly.

orlando: a biography (1928)[2]

Woolf's *Orlando* is a fictional text that is presented in the guise of a biography. But this is no circumscribed "life" set in a precise historical period. Its central character begins life in the Elizabethan period as a man, and is last encountered in the early twentieth century as a woman. The text has a rich array of allusions to recognizable historical and literary figures, which creates a dense and humorous intertext, constantly troubling the reader's sense of the central character's identity and also of the novel's temporal framing. The character of Orlando is modelled closely on aspects of the life and history of Vita Sackville-West, Virginia Woolf's lover at the time the novel was written. As Woolf wrote in her diary, "instantly the usual exciting devices enter my mind: a biography beginning in the year 1500 & continuing to the present day, called Orlando: Vita; only with a change about from one sex to another."[3] The representation of character and of history in the novel are both imagined in terms of exciting fictional devices that make the writing of the novel seem to Woolf like "a treat."

The opening sentence of *Orlando* is: "He – for there could be no doubt about his sex, though the fashion of his time did something to disguise it – was in the act of slicing at the Head of a Moor" (11). Doubt about sexuality is thus there at the very beginning of the novel, even as it is disavowed – there could be "no doubt," but yet the style of Elizabethan dress "disguises" such apparent certainty. The masculine identity asserted with that opening "He" is rendered unstable before the end of the novel's first sentence. This opening sentence also introduces a clear association between masculinity and violence, which will continue to permeate the novel. The "head" that Orlando is caught in the act of slicing actually transforms into a skull in the next paragraph, and turns out to have been taken home as a trophy from Africa by one of Orlando's ancestors. This diminishes to some extent the shock of finding the novel's central character apparently in the middle of an act of murder, but only by displacing this violence into a much longer and larger history of colonial violence. Orlando carries the weight of his ancestry, and his masculine identity is a collective as well as an individual one.

By paragraph two of the novel Orlando moves swiftly from slicing at the Moor's head to writing poetry:

> Orlando [...] sat down at the table, and, with the half-conscious air of one doing what they do every day of their lives at this hour, took out a writing book [...] and dipped an old stained goose quill in the ink. (12)

Important intersections between gender, violence and writing are already being established at this early stage of the novel, as also is the question of the limitations of established literary form. Orlando's attempt at writing at this point in the novel fails because he becomes aware of the chasm between the literary forms at his disposal and his sense of their inadequacy to render the life he observes outside his window: "nature and letters seem to have a natural antipathy; bring them together and they tear each other to pieces" (13). Orlando's literary frustration here echoes arguments made by Woolf herself, for example in the essay "Modern Fiction" which she published in 1925. Here she argued that the naturalist modes of representation that dominated fictional writing in the period could never adequately capture the richness of "life" and indeed that "the form of fiction most in vogue more often misses than secures the thing we seek."[4] The parallel between Woolf's exploration of the writing of lives and Orlando's own literary endeavours is thus established at an early stage of the novel.

In the second chapter of *Orlando* Woolf goes on to develop some explicit reflections on the nature of biography:

> The biographer is now faced with a difficulty which it is better perhaps to confess than to gloss over. Up to this point in telling the story of Orlando's life, documents, both private and historical, have made it possible to fulfil the first duty of a biographer, which is to plod, without looking to right or left, in the indelible footprints of truth [...] But now we come to an episode which lies right across our path, so that there is no ignoring it. Yet it is dark, mysterious and undocumented; so that there is no explaining it. (41)

The incident that lies right across the biographer's plodding path is the moment when Orlando sleeps for seven days, and wakes up radically transformed (41–42). This fairy-tale metamorphosis sits perhaps oddly within the genre of biography, reaching out as it does to both fantasy and myth. But Woolf's literary text allows for such a hybrid generic approach, drawing on the links between life-writing and fantasy.

Such fictional exploration of the limits of biography in *Orlando* is part of a broader discussion of the art of biography in Woolf's work. Woolf had been closely connected to the genre of biography from her childhood, as her father, Leslie Stephen, was the founding editor of *The Dictionary of National Biography* between 1885 and 1891. She was also to address the genre of biography in a number of essays, reflect on it in her diary ("have a plan already to get historical manuscripts and write Lives of the Obscure"[5]), and test it through a range of texts including both *Orlando* and *Flush* (1933), an imaginative biography of Elizabeth Barrett Browning's dog. In her essay "The New Biography" (1927), Woolf suggested that the conflict between "truth" and "personality" was the central dilemma for the genre of biography, which had to steer a path between the "granite-like solidity" of the former and the "rainbow-like intangibility" of the latter.[6] She concludes this essay by suggesting that fictional character is in important ways more "real to us" than the objective representation of any historical individual, however clearly anchored in historical facts (100). She suggests that this insight signals the end of the Victorian style of biography, and shows the importance of a style of biography that can deploy imagination, psychological insight, and at least some of the devices of literary representation to produce a more persuasive and complete biographical portrait.

Her exemplar in "The New Biography" is Harold Nicolson, and in particular his biographies of nine individuals, published as *Some People* in 1927, of which the essay was initially a review. In her later essay "The Art of Biography," published in 1939, however, she turns to Lytton Strachey as the writer whose corpus illustrates the key theoretical and literary problems confronting the genre of biography. Woolf argues in this essay that biography is a relatively young genre, which achieved significant literary and cultural prominence only in the nineteenth century. She sees Strachey's (and her own) generation as developing important new freedoms within the genre, deploying more complex models of human subjectivity and a broader range of tone and style to render the "reality" that biography requires of its represented characters. In relation to *Orlando*, the most interesting part of this essay is its discussion of Strachey's *Elizabeth and Essex*, which was published in 1928 just after Woolf had completed *Orlando* with its opening sections set in the Elizabethan period. In her diary, Woolf makes it clear that she sees Strachey's biography as a failed experiment: "that lively superficial meretricious book [...] secretly pleased to find Lytton's book a bad one."[7] But in the essay her argument is more nuanced, stressing the importance as well as the limitations of Strachey's navigation of fact and fiction within his biography of Elizabeth and Essex. Woolf suggests that Strachey's experiment was relevant to her own writing of *Orlando* as she asserts that Elizabethan society is particularly alien and unfamiliar to the modern reader: "By what art are we to worm our way into those strange spirits? Those even stranger bodies?"[8] The strangeness of the period, as well as the need for literary devices to "worm one's way" into the embodied experience of character in the period, clearly inform both *Orlando*'s narrative and its style.

Some forty pages after Orlando's first transformative sleep, he wakes again from a long and deep sleep: "He stretched himself. He rose. He stood upright in complete nakedness before us [...] Truth! Truth! Truth! we have no choice left but confess – he was a woman" (83). The revelation is unexpected, and challenges one of the key gendered frameworks in which individual identity is typically lived and represented. The phrase "he was a woman" is an interesting one. The "was" is not here a past tense, and there is no suggestion that Orlando was and had always been a woman. Rather, the assertion is that he is now a woman, a transformation has taken place: "Orlando had become a woman – there is no denying it [...] Orlando was a man till the age of thirty; when he became a woman and has remained so ever since" (83–84).

The linguistic "strain" this change of sex causes within the novel is initially significant. Immediately after the transformation the narrator says rather emphatically, "the change of sex, though it altered their future, did nothing whatever to alter their identity" (83). This move from "his" or "her" to "their" is a way of addressing the constraints of gender within language, and in particular the difficulty of finding a gender-neutral pronoun in English, but it also can be understood as a way of rendering Orlando as an individual character confusingly plural. Such a linguistic choice by the narrator seems to undermine the claim that no aspect of Orlando's identity has been affected by becoming a woman. A few sentences later, however, the linguistic tension and ambiguity generated by the use of "their" is erased, with a clear statement of Orlando's new sex through a different use of pronouns: "the change seemed to have been accomplished painlessly [...] and in such a way that Orlando herself showed no surprise at it" (ibid.).

After this transformation into a woman, Orlando reflects on what such a change of sex means for her social identity, for her sexuality, and for her habits of living. The narrator suggests that Orlando may be discovering something of the androgyny that haunts all sexual identities:

> In every human being a vacillation from one sex to the other takes place, and often it is only the clothes that keep the male or female likeness [...] Of the complications and confusions which thus result everyone has had experience; but here we leave the general question and note only the odd effect it had in the particular case of Orlando herself. For it was this mixture in her of man and woman, one being uppermost and then the other, that often gave her conduct an unexpected turn.[9] (111)

Such an "unexpected turn" is experienced by Orlando through and in her literary writing, when she finds herself and her writing taken over in a way that is physical and corporeal by an obsession with the need for a husband. Her poetic writing style is transformed, "nothing more repulsive could be imagined than to feel the ink flowing thus in cascades of involuntary inspiration" (138). Orlando becomes "conscious of an extraordinary tingling and vibration all over her" (ibid.), and her writing is literally subsumed by the pressure of the domestic as blots of ink appear and erase her writing. She is at first rendered incapable of writing at all, but then is driven by forces she cannot control to create a completely different style of poetry. The narrator presents this episode as conclusive proof of the fact that writing is a physical act, intimately connected to the fibre and the fabric of the body, and therefore presumably that it has a sex:

> For it would seem – her case proved it – that we write not with the fingers, but with the whole person. The nerve which controls the pen winds itself about every fibre of our being, threads the heart, pierces the liver. (141)

The final image lends to the assertion a certain mythic quality, evoking as it does Prometheus' punishment for his theft of fire from Zeus, which was to be tied to a rock and to have his liver eaten daily by an eagle. The claiming of an embodied female form of writing is, it would seem, a risky transgression.

the waves (1931)[10]

The Waves is a formally experimental novel, centrally concerned with the question of how to write a life. As one of the six characters, Bernard, says in his final summary, discussing the factors that generate a sense of personal completeness: "'Muscles, nerves, intestines, blood vessels, all that makes the coil and spring of our being, the unconscious hum of the engine, as well as the dart and flicker of the tongue'" (156). *The Waves* is a structurally innovative text, punctuated by interludes describing the progress of the sun over a single day and across the globe (engaging with both the temporal and the spatial frameworks of selfhood), and organized around a series of episodes involving six characters whose perspectives, voices and lives unfurl across the text (though not all survive to the end as this is also a novel about death).

The Waves posed for Woolf, over a period of around four years, a series of technical writing problems about the representation of human character, and the impact of these complex problems is recorded at various points within her diary. For example, on 23 April 1930 she wrote:

> This is a very important morning in the history of The Waves, because I think I have turned the corner & see the last lap straight ahead. I think I have got Bernard into the final stride. He will go straight on now [...] We are at Rodmell & I daresay I shall stay on a day or two [...] & finish it. O Lord & then a rest. (301)

While on 20 August that year she wrote: "The Waves is I think resolving itself (I am at page 100) into a series of dramatic soliloquies. The thing is to keep them running homogeneously in & out, in the rhythm of the waves" (312). Despite this optimism, and the sense that she had found viable approaches to the representation of individual characters and their narrative interactions, it was to be another year before she was finally finished with the text.

So what are the literary and stylistic innovations of *The Waves*, with which Woolf was wrestling, and how do these relate to questions of gender and writing? In order to suggest how questions of life-writing and literary style are addressed in the novel I concentrate here on the representation of just one of the six narrators, Rhoda, and analyse some of the images and techniques that are deployed to represent her subjectivity, and to construct something like a first-person voice. We first encounter Rhoda reflecting on the aesthetic and personal meanings of the petals she is floating in a basin, the "ships" she is floating on the waves:

> "All my ships are white," said Rhoda. "I do not want red petals of hollyhocks or geraniums. I want white petals that float when I tip the basin up [...] And I will now rock the brown basin from side to side so that my ships may ride the waves [...] I hate dangling things. I hate dampish things. I hate wandering and mixing things together." (9)

The passage is striking in its insistent repetition of the first-person singular "I" while simultaneously describing a very tentative and fragile kind of subjectivity. Rhoda hates dangling, damp, wandering things, and yet occupies herself by looking into a basin of water with floating leaves that are presumably both damp and wandering as they "ride the waves." The waves of Rhoda's imagination seem to offer little consolation, but rather to be part of an impossible search for the fulfilment of what Rhoda "wants." The semantic range of such "wanting" stretches between desiring (what Rhoda would like) and lacking (what she does not have), creating a particularly unstable and precarious subjectivity.

Very quickly Rhoda's fascination with the leaves floating in a basin, and the associated impossibility of escaping from the things she "hates," moves towards a psychological state of terror, which is closely associated with the act of writing, or rather with the failure to write:

> Now the terror is beginning [...] Louis writes; Susan writes; Neville writes; Jinny writes; even Bernard has now begun to write. But I cannot write [...] Look, the loop of the figure is beginning to fill with time [...] I myself am outside the loop; which I now join – so – and seal up, and make entire. The world is entire and I am outside of it, crying "Oh save me, from being blown for ever outside the loop of time!" (11)

The scene is the classroom of her childhood, and the "writing" is the response required to what appears to be an arithmetic problem. The other children hand in their answers, but Rhoda "has no answer." The description of herself as "outside the loop" oscillates in its meanings between a literal failure to find meaning in the loops on the blackboard and the more metaphorical sense of Rhoda's isolation and exclusion from social relationships. Rhoda's isolated and alienated subjectivity leads her to quote herself in an effort to reassert some first-person reality as her sense of time spirals out of control. She imagines herself calling for help, asking to be saved, but fears that her subjectivity is already being blown beyond any secure narrative temporality. This narrative voice that is reduced to quoting only itself creates a powerful literary representation of a subjectivity that can ultimately be grounded neither in time nor in space.

The sense of disembodied, fractured and fragile subjectivity is built further as the novel progresses. Rhoda says:

> "Now I cannot sink; cannot altogether fall through the thin sheet. Now I spread my body on this frail mattress and hang suspended. I am above the earth now. I am no longer upright, to be knocked against and damaged [...] Out of me now my mind can pour. I can think of my Armadas sailing on the hard waves. I am relieved of hard contacts and collisions." (14–15)

She can survive only by being effectively disembodied, spread thin, suspended above the earth, relieved of hard contacts. A little later in the novel Rhoda's de-materialization becomes even more striking: "'That is my face,' said Rhoda, 'in the looking-glass behind Susan's shoulder – that face is my face. But I will duck behind her to hide it, for I am not here. I have no face'" (24). And ultimately identity fails her completely, in a strange contradictory passage where she simultaneously speaks and announces her own erasure, "'I came to the puddle, I could not cross it. Identity failed me. We are nothing, I said, and fell'" (37).

The potential for literature to inhabit this contradictory space, where identity is asserted through the very act of representation that negates it, is an important preoccupation of *The Waves*. The novel seeks to imagine ways of being that can be represented as partial, incomplete, and contradictory, and to avoid doing violence to the complexity and precariousness of human subjectivity. To do this requires new modes of narrative and new formal structures for the novel. Rhoda says:

> "If I could believe," [...] "that I should grow old in pursuit and change, I should be rid of my fear; nothing persists. One moment does not lead to another. The door opens and the tiger leaps. You did not see me come." (76)

In terms of novelistic form the key insight given to Rhoda here is that "one moment does not lead to another." The narrative structure of fiction cannot be shaped, Woolf is suggesting, by narrative causality, by one thing following another. Rather, the structural associations within the novel have to be driven by metaphor, by image, by the deeper meanings that can resonate through memory, and through the material relationships between signifiers deployed across the novel as a whole: the waves, the leaves, the water, the windows and the doors.

But the connections generated in this way remain both tentative and fragile. Subjectivity lived through the temporality and metaphoric complexity of modernist fiction does not prove viable for all of the characters in *The Waves*. Rhoda does not survive to the end of the novel, and the circumstances of and reasons for her death remain cruelly under-described:

> "Now to sum up," said Bernard [...] "I went into the Strand, and evoked to serve as opposite to myself the figure of Rhoda, always so furtive, always with fear in her eyes, always seeking some pillar in the desert, to find which she had gone; she had killed herself. 'Wait,' I said putting my arm in imagination (thus we consort with our friends) through her arm [...] For this is not one life; nor do I always know if I am man or woman, Bernard or Neville, Louis, Susan, Jinny, or Rhoda – so strange is the contact of one with another." (142, 168)

The conclusion is powerfully challenging for any notion of life-writing. If this, as Bernard concludes, is "not one life" then how can it be narrated or represented? And what kind of damage is necessarily done to any individual in the very act of writing a life?

virginia woolf's introductory letter to *life as we have known it; by co-operative working women* (1930)

The final experiment in life-writing that this article will discuss can be found in a letter written by Virginia Woolf in 1930. This letter formed the Introduction to a collection of letters written by members of the Women's Co-operative Guild, *Life As We Have Known It.* The Women's Co-operative Guild had been formed in the 1880s to work for improvements in the status of women and also to promote the principles and practices of the broader Co-operative Movement. *Life As We Have Known It,* a volume of letters exploring various aspects of working women's lives, was edited by Margaret Llewelyn Davies, who had been Secretary of the Guild from 1889 to 1921. Davies was born in 1861, educated at Queen's College, London and Girton College, Cambridge, and in the 1880s had been employed as a social worker in London. Under her leadership, the Women's Co-operative Guild became increasingly concerned with a range of campaigns addressing social issues that were key both for feminism and for socialism. By the 1890s the Guild not only promoted the principles of the Co-operative Movement but also involved itself in a number of political campaigns designed to improve the political, legal and social conditions of women, especially of working-class women. It encouraged women to join trade unions and lobbied for a minimum wage for women and for equal pay, and also campaigned on issues related to women's health. For example, *Maternity: Letters from Working Women* (G. Bell and Sons, 1915), also edited by Davies, documented through a series of letters the poor medical care received by women in pregnancy, and the economic vulnerability of women who had large families. Woolf had been an enthusiastic proponent of the publications of these letters on women's health, writing to Davies in December 1914: "Do publish those letters. I wish they could all be in full," and then again in February 2015, "I do hope they will be printed – with lots of photographs. They are so amazing."[11] The Women's Co-operative Guild was ultimately successful in forcing an amendment to the National Health Insurance Bill that meant maternity benefit would be paid to the mother and not the father of a child, a clear legislative response to issues raised in *Maternity: Letters from Working Women.*

Life As We Have Known It was published by the Hogarth Press some fifteen years after *Maternity*, in 1931. By the early 1930s the Guild had grown considerably in scale and influence, with over 70,000 members and more than 1,500 branches nationally. The publication of *Life As We Have Known It* thus took place at a time when the Guild had considerable public prominence. The volume consists of six reasonably substantial memoirs, augmented by a series of extracts from letters from members of the Guild, detailing specific aspects of their lives. Woolf had been invited by Davies to provide a preface to the volume, and she chose to do this in the form of a letter addressed to Davies herself:

> Turning the pages, I began to ask myself what is this book then, if it is not a book? What quality has it? What ideas does it suggest? What old arguments and memories does it rouse in me? And as all this had nothing to do with an introduction or a preface, but brought you to mind and certain pictures from the past, I stretched my hand for a sheet of notepaper and wrote the following letter addressed not to the public but to you.[12]

Woolf's letter here raises questions of identity and identification, of the nature of first-person narrative, and of the genre of the letter. First of all, Woolf's introductory letter avows itself personal: it is described as being written in response to the ways in which reading the volume brought Davies "to Woolf's mind," along with some unspecified, but presumably powerful, "pictures from the past." Woolf's letter is addressed directly to Davies, and "not to the public," but it also appears prominently in a published text from her own press.

Woolf's letter deploys a very complex temporality. It begins with a description of a past moment in which Woolf was invited by Davies to write a preface to *Life As We Have Known It.* The assumption is that Woolf's temporal reference point is the present (1930) in which she is writing to Davies, which is why she needs to explain the decisions in the past that got her to the point of writing. But in the next paragraph Woolf writes: "You have forgotten (I wrote) a hot June morning in Newcastle in the year 1913" (xviii). So we now encounter a different temporal framing, a past tense of writing – but what can this writing be if it is not the actual letter we are reading? Was there another version of this letter that preceded this one? Is Woolf quoting herself here? Is the current letter thus a subsequent construction based on a text to which we as the public have no access? Alongside the simultaneous invoking of a memory from Newcastle in 1913, the temporal complexity is disorientating and further undermines the stability of the letter writer's subjectivity.

Woolf goes on to describe her memories of the Co-operative Guild conference she attended in 1913, casting herself very much as an external, and somewhat alien, observer. Then she writes:

> Meanwhile – let me try after seventeen years to sum up the thoughts that passed through the minds of your guests, who had come from London and elsewhere, not to take part, but to listen – meanwhile what was it all about? What was the meaning of it? (xx)

What is the force of those adverbial "meanwhiles," and what are the temporalities that are being juxtaposed? "Meanwhile" is a wonderfully productive adverb, signifying both "during the intervening period" and "at the same time," and Woolf deploys this semantic ambiguity productively to set up questions about the temporal and the broader social relations between the moment of Woolf's writing the letter in 1930 and the experience of a conference in 1913.

A little later in the letter, Woolf poses the question of identification and identity more starkly:

> "Let's pretend," one said to oneself, looking at the speaker, "that I am Mrs. Giles of Durham City." A woman of that name had just turned to address us. "I am the wife of a miner" […] But after all the imagination is largely the child of the flesh. One could not be Mrs. Giles of Durham because one had never stood at the wash-tub; one's hands had never wrung and scrubbed. (xxii–xxiii)

The experiment in identification fails, but so too do Woolf's pronouns. She oscillates between the gender-neutral and class-specific indefinite pronoun "one," and what seems to be a very tentative first-person "I." The "I" ("I am Mrs. Giles […] I am the wife of a miner") would commit Woolf much more explicitly to an identification with the woman she is describing and performing, and she pulls back from this imagined subjectivity very clearly.

The pressure on the first-person singular pronoun (which one might think sat easily within the genre of the letter) continues as the letter progresses. Thus we find Woolf writing:

> Therefore, however much we had sympathized our sympathy was largely fictitious. It was aesthetic sympathy, the sympathy of the eye and of the imagination, not of the heart and of the nerves […] Let us explain what we mean, we said. (xxviii)

The collective "we" seems to allow Woolf some distance, in recognition of the very "failure" of the kind of sympathetic identification with another she describes, and perhaps even aspires to.

Woolf's very particular letter then finally hands the formal and technical challenges of life-writing back to the working-class women whose writings constitute the substance of the volume. But it does so with a strong warning that these memoirs and letters are limited by their genre, and cannot offer the kind of broader vision, or forms of intersubjective identification, that one might hope to find within a literary text:

> The writing, a literary critic might say, lacks detachment and imaginative breadth, even as the women themselves lacked variety and play of feature. Here are no reflections, he might object, no view of life as a whole, and no attempt to enter into the lives of other people […] These pages are only fragments. These voices are beginning only now to emerge from silence into half articulate speech. These lives are still half hidden in profound obscurity. To express even what is expressed here has been a work of labour and difficulty […] But hush! You will not

let me finish that sentence and therefore, with the old messages of friendship and admiration, I will make an end. (xxxix, xli)

The conclusion to Woolf's letter is surely uncomfortable, though it is important to note that Woolf appears to be setting a distance between the voice of the first-person letter writer and the harsh judgements of the (male) literary critic, noting that "he might object." Woolf "makes an end" of her letter certainly, but in doing so she also makes space for the "fragments," the "half articulate speech" and the "obscure" lives that are written through and in the rest of *Life As We Have Known It*.

disclosure statement

No potential conflict of interest was reported by the author.

notes

1 Virginia Woolf, "Character in Fiction" in *Virginia Woolf: Selected Essays*, ed. David Bradshaw (Oxford: Oxford UP, 2008) 37–54 (38). The significance of the changes associated with the year 1910 for Woolf is further considered in Morag Shiach, "Periodizing Modernism" in *The Oxford Handbook of Modernisms*, eds. Peter Brooker et al. (Oxford: Oxford UP, 2010) 5–6.

2 Virginia Woolf, *Orlando*, ed. Michael H. Whitworth (Oxford: Oxford UP, 2015).

3 Virginia Woolf, *The Diary of Virginia Woolf: Volume 3, 1925–30*, ed. Anne Olivier Bell, assisted by Andrew McNeillie (Harmondsworth: Penguin, 1980), 5 Oct. 1927, 161.

4 Virginia Woolf, "Modern Fiction" in Bradshaw, *Virginia Woolf* 6–12 (8).

5 Virginia Woolf, *Diary: Volume 3, 1925–30*, 28 Feb. 1927, 129.

6 Virginia Woolf, "The New Biography" in Bradshaw, *Virginia Woolf* 95–100 (95).

7 Virginia Woolf, *Diary: Volume 3, 1925–30*, 28 Nov. 1928, 208–09.

8 Virginia Woolf, "The Art of Biography" in Bradshaw, *Virginia Woolf* 116–23 (119).

9 This passage can be compared interestingly to Woolf's discussion of androgyny in the final chapter of *A Room of One's Own* (1929).

10 Virginia Woolf, *The Waves*, ed. David Bradshaw (Oxford: Oxford UP, 2015).

11 *The Letters of Virginia Woolf, Volume II: 1912–1922*, ed. Nigel Nicolson, assisted by Joanne Trautmann (London: Harcourt, 1976) 54, 59.

12 Virginia Woolf, "Introductory Letter" in *Life As We Have Known It; by Co-operative Working Women*, ed. Margaret Llewelyn Davies (London: Virago, 1977) xvii.

Morag Shiach

georgina paul

WRITING AS A "SIE"

reflections on barbara köhler's odyssey cycle niemands frau

In 2007 the German poet Barbara Köhler published a poem-cycle entitled *Niemands Frau* [*Nobody's Wife*], a response to and reworking of elements from Homer's *Odyssey*.[1] The cycle consists of twenty-one densely woven, highly complex poems, followed by three afterwords which can only partially be formally distinguished from the poetic speech of the poems: twenty-four texts in all, corresponding to the twenty-four books of Homer's epic poem. The aim of this paper is to engage with some of the implications for thinking about what women's writing is and might be that emerge from this challenging and utopian work.

Köhler's title refers to the episode in Book 9 of the *Odyssey* in which Odysseus, threatened by the Cyclops Polyphemus, says that his name is "Οὖτις" or Nobody.[2] This turns out to be to his advantage since it forms the basis of a misunderstanding that enables him ultimately to escape death at the hands of the Cyclops. However, Köhler's interest is directed not so much towards the male hero as towards the female figures who populate Homer's poem: Nausicaa, Circe, the Sirens, Helen, Ino Leucothea, the shades of the dead women whom Odysseus meets in Hades, and Penelope, the eponymous wife of Odysseus/Nobody. Opening as it does with an invocation of the Muse that addresses the puzzling change of dynamics when the sex of the poet is the same as that of the Muse, the cycle self-consciously broadcasts from the start the difference set in play when a *female* author takes up the Homeric theme, even as it alludes to the different theories concerning the authorship of Homer, among which are those suggesting that Homer was a woman or not a singular historical person at all:[3]

[…] Mir sage muse wer sagt dass er sei
Homer sei gewesen ein sie sei nicht einer sei ein
e mehrzahl wenn er ist bin ich dann muse

[…] Me tell muse
who says that HomER was ER was a SIE was THEY not
a one was a plural if HE is am I then muse

("01 MUSE : POLYTROP," *Niemands Frau* 10)

As this short extract (with its characteristic polysemy) displays, Köhler's poems establish a tension of difference between what it means to be an "er" – the German word for "he" – and what it means to be a "sie" – the German word for "she." Since the lyric persona identifies herself as a "she" (for example through the feminine adjective endings relating to her), at one level the poem-cycle enacts a reversal of the historically predominant reception of Homer's epic as a male author's account of the escapades of a male hero, instead instigating a female poet's identification with the female figures of the poem. This might suggest first and foremost a thematic interest in female experience as opposed to male experience, and indeed there are instances of such a thematic interest in the cycle: the recurring topos of weaving as a female labour with which the poet's task is also associated, for example, as in the poem "06 GEWEBEPROBE : PENELOPE" ("WEAVING SAMPLE : PENELOPE"), or the monologue "19 NACHTSTÜCK : ARRYTHMIE" ("NIGHT PIECE : ARRYTHMIA") where an "I" lying beside the sleeping Nobody reflects upon mutual touch as opposed to objectifying sight as the means of creating relationship. This gesture recalls Luce Irigaray's objection to the "age-old oculocentrism," or dominance of the gaze, in male-generated philosophy (in this particular instance in Freud) in *Speculum of the Other Woman* and her identification of touch instead as the sense from which woman derives pleasure in *This Sex Which Is Not One*.[4]

Yet Köhler's poetry is not as simple an assertion of a feminist project as this description suggests. The key to its complexity is to be found in the polysemy of the pronoun "sie," which grammatically not only denotes the feminine singular but also the gender-unmarked plural "they" and the gender-unmarked second-person formal "you" (which, as in English, can be either singular or plural). Furthermore, while the masculine singular pronoun "er" can only ever be understood as the nominative subject of a sentence – as the agent, so to speak, in the conventional "subject–predicate–object firing line / *one-liners*," as Köhler calls them in one of the three afterwords (*Niemands Frau* 74) – "sie" is grammatically ambivalent, since in all its forms, as "she," as "they," and as "you," it can be either the subject *or* the object of the verb, either nominative *or* accusative. (This is the reason why my translation retains the pronouns in the German at least some of the time, in order to preserve and to highlight the ambiguities.) In this cycle, in which frequent references to quantum mechanics are woven into the verbal texture, the pronoun "sie" acts as what Rebecca May Johnson has called the "quantum linguistic particle," transporting the reader from a world analogous to that conceived by Newtonian physics, where the action of one object on another is easily mathematically calculable, into a quantum universe of plural probabilities, a different order of rationality.[5] This means that writing as a "sie" is not about simply asserting a female perspective on reality and experience in contrast to a male one; in fact, it is not *simply* about anything. Rather, the "er" and the "sie" become associated with different ways of existing in and interacting with the data of reality, and *writing* as a "sie" might start to give readers an inkling of what the implications might be of *living* as a "sie."

Since the univocal pronoun "er" can only be the nominative subject of a grammatical sentence, the "er" as the hERo of HomER's work becomes in Köhler's poems a keyword in relationships of mastery and domination which go hand in hand with the establishment of the historical patriarchy. In this, Köhler's interpretation follows that of Theodor W. Adorno, whose essay on Homer's *Odyssey* in the *Dialectic of Enlightenment* reads Odysseus as the prototype Enlightenment subject, emerging from his multifarious encounters with a threatening mythologized natural world as a self-assertive individual who learns self-discipline and cunning in order to survive, and at the same time binds the many different stories that went into the making of the *Odyssey* into the epic tale of a singular hero:[6]

Mächtig & rede
begabt nennt er sie, sängerin
wissende vom Großen Gewebe in
dem er sich an den faden hält
an das schiffchen das hin&her
geworfne lässt sich erzählen:
ein weg ein bewegtes geschick
tes durchkommen sich nicht zu
verheddern verstricken lassen
in widersprüche etwa verlangt
glatte lügen und geschliffene
monologe die geschichte einen
der sie & der mein sagt MEINE
GESCHICHTE

Powerful and gifted
in speech he calls HER the singer
the adept of the Great Web while
he holds on to the thread the
shuttle that goes to & fro makes
a good yarn: a moving story of
pulling through skilfully not to
get caught up entangled in contra
dictions demands a smooth tongue &
polished monologues and history
a man who says THEM says HER says
MINE: MY STORY

("05 NAUSIKAA : RAPPORT," *Niemands Frau* 22–23)

As we can see in the emergence of the possessive pronoun at the end of this extract, the assertion of mastery is also related to ownership, a laying claim to what is "MINE," including "MY STORY," the story of the individual through which the individual comes into being. Once posited, the individual who lays claim to what is his own becomes opposed to others whom his grammar turns into (his) objects: hence the emergence of "sie" as an accusative object in the phrase "der sie & der mein sagt" (who says them/her/you & mine). Furthermore, the cultural history of this "er" is linked to the emergence of writing and of the written text, which as Walter J. Ong argued in his seminal 1982 study, *Orality and Literacy*, "separates the knower from the known and thus sets up conditions for 'objectivity', in the sense of personal disengagement and distancing."[7] In other words, writing creates the preconditions for the emergence of the kind of scientific observer that Köhler's poems identify with the masculine singular pronoun "er" and its mediated self, the *written* "ich." This written "ich" in turn becomes the cipher for the divinely endorsed, immortal self, for it is writing that enables the individual to transcend temporal embodiedness:

die wahrheit des Odysseus
HE'S NO BODY er hat das Wort er sagt er ist
DIE SCHRIFT Ich ist sein text entleibt & ab
geschrieben
the truth of Odysseus
HE'S NO BODY he has the Word he says HE is
HOLY WRIT: the "I" is his text disembodied
& written down

("03 POLYMORPHEM," *Niemands Frau* 16)[8]

By contrast, the pronoun "sie," indeterminately signifying a singular and a plural being, a "she," a "they" and a "you," which can all be both subject and object, invites the reader to reimagine not just grammatical but also intersubjective and even cultural relationships in terms of a plurality of possibilities. This is indicated by the interlinked relations between the female figures in the *Odyssey*, the way they (as Köhler's poems show us) form a complex network through Homer's text. In the poem "11 HADES : LEKTÜRE : HADES" ("HADES : READING : HADES"), which reflects on Odysseus' encounter with the shades of his dead female relatives in the so-called *nekyia*, or journey to the underworld, in Book 11 of the *Odyssey*, Köhler contrasts the line of inheritance from father to son that characterizes patriarchy with the web of female relatives, "alle ungenannt versippt verknüpft verbunden sind sie / DAS NETZ" (all of them / unnamed related by marriage linked and connected form / THE NET; *Niemands Frau* 41), wittily deploying the language of telephony to counter the patriarchal "PLEASE HOLD THE LINE" with the activity of the women figures: "WHILE WE TRY TO CONNECT YOU WHILE WE TRY TO CONNECT … " (ibid.). The idea of connection and linkage is associated throughout the cycle with the female characters, above all through the fact that not only Penelope but many of the other women are identified in Homer as gifted weavers. Christos C. Tsagalis has argued that the female figures in Homeric epic are nodal points in the poems' *poikilia*, defined as "the interweaving of various fabrics which interact, answer, contradict, or rival other fabrics, resulting in a thick web of associations metaphorically epitomized in the word *intertext*, a system or set of interwoven fabrics whose constituent parts are interrelated"[9] – as reminders, therefore, of the Homeric epic's complex relationships to other poems preceding and contemporaneous with it in a manner that is reproduced by Köhler's poem-making.

At the same time, the ways in which we can approach Köhler's poems are also emphatically plural. Thus the interrelationality invoked by "sie" might be imaginable in terms of the *Odyssey*'s origins as poetry for a not-yet-literate culture, a form of storytelling in bound speech which gathers together the bard or rhapsode and those listening into an oral/aural community in which, as Ong argues, "learning or knowing means achieving close, empathetic, communal identification with the known"[10] or, as Köhler's invocation of the Muse puts it, generates "ein geteiltes erwidertes ungehöriges / beisein in dem wir sind" (that togetherness shared reciprocal im / proper in which WE are) ("01 MUSE : POLYTROP," *Niemands Frau* 11). Such a togetherness or "beisein" creates, we note, a state of affairs in which the possession of property is not clearly defined and regulated (as signalled by the word "ungehörig" which I've translated as "im / proper" but suggests simultaneously "inappropriate" and "belonging to no one"). Transferred to poetry, this idea of not belonging to anyone, or, put differently, belonging to all, implies a different notion of authorship from the one that has come to dominate our understanding of that term, that of the singular originator of radically new work, the culturally lionized "er." Instead, Köhler's text, full of allusions to other, older texts and poems, albeit self-evidently an original work, insists on poetry as a Great Web, a continuous retranslation and retransmission of voices from the past in which the current poet plays a part for a time, one amongst a plurality of transhistorical practitioners, a "sie." Recollecting the oral tradition of poetry recited before an assembled group, listening, too, might belong to us all rather than just to each of us individually, and it is striking that Köhler weaves into her poems many phrases from other poets' work (as well as phrases from films and other forms of popular culture) that have become part of collective speech.[11]

Alternatively, "sie" might be imaginable in terms of a duality, a mutuality, the relationship of two equal but different subjects who don't insist on their separate interests but join forces to create something beyond themselves, a possibility addressed by Köhler's "SIRENS" poem:

"Ich" & mehr
als eins bin ich selbander DIE
("Sirenen" nennt er es) ICH BIN
MIR GLEICH die fremde ist mein
double mein teil sie hält mich
aus halt ich sie weiss ich mich
zu lassen was hält ist abstand
& ich halt ihn lieber als dass
ich flöge auf dieses angebinde

"I" & more than one I am
selfother ("Sirens" he calls it)
I AM INDIFFERENT TO MY
SELF & she the stranger is my
double a part of me is in her
keeping if I'm in her keeping I
can let my self go & keep it &
the distance I'd rather keep
than flying into this security

("13 SIRENEN," *Niemands Frau* 47)

This poem, voiced by a Siren "ich" (I) who is in relation to "die fremde" (a feminine-inflected "stranger" or "alien," though "die fremde" could equally mean a "foreign terrain"), suggests the possibility of a form of plurality that does not subsume the subjectivities participating in it. "Selbander" is an archaic German adverb meaning "as a pair" or "two at a time": the word is used in this poem to pluralize the "I," splitting her off from herself to create a "second self" or "double" who is, nonetheless, also a "stranger." The relationship configured between them in the poem suggests both closeness and distance. On the one hand, "die fremde" is "mein teil," which might mean it/she is "my moiety" as well as "my part," and she/it also "hält mich aus," meaning she/it "keeps me," "supports me," also "tolerates me," which allows the "I" to "let [her] self go." On the other hand, the poem insists on the distance between them, a distance necessary perhaps for relationship to be possible. The dynamic of this doubleness is intriguingly complex and quite different from the relationship configured in the poem between the "I" and Odysseus, the poem's "er," who, observing the speaking or singing "I" from a distance, sums her/it/them up with a pluralizing name: "'Sirenen' nennt er es" ("Sirens" he calls it).[12]

More than configuring a form of subjectivity that is not particularly vested in the "I" and is capable of generating a complex form of interrelationship with an other who is also in a sense a self, the "sie" might also, since the Sirens' song has a long history of association with the power of poetic speech, conjure up the multiple possibilities of poetry itself. Poetry thrives on dynamic and polyvalent meaning, as opposed to forms of language intent upon capturing and holding fast a singular and incontrovertible sense of what is meant – such as the languages of science, of the law, and of the academy. The important thing to realize about this poetry is that where language is polyvalent, not univocal, relationship is required to make sense of it. For example, what you (if I were writing in German, I'd have just addressed you as "Sie") might make of Köhler's deliberately and consciously created polyvalences would in all probability be different from what I make of them; the choices you or I make in how we read the lines say something about who you or I are and what interests we have, how we stand vis-à-vis the data of reality. I can't decide for you, it is up to you to create a relationship of your own to these texts. This means, incidentally, that my authority as an authority (as a scholar of contemporary German literature, for example) is taken away from me by this Siren speech; I'm no longer the master of meaning. This raises the question of whether the sort of authority which is conventionally attributed to the scholar or expert can really hold up in the face of these poems (or indeed in the face of any polyvalent literary text). Shouldn't the notion of authoritative speech, which underpins academic publishing as well as lecturing (consider the "syntax" of the lecture theatre, with a sometimes raised lectern at the front and an audience grouped below, receiving the authoritative word), be replaced by a different, more communicative concept: dialogue perhaps? Might we in fact need to do knowledge a different way? Is that what being a "sie" rather than an "er & sie" might entail?

In fact, as Köhler's poems remind us through their frequent allusions to quantum physics, knowledge is already being done in a different way. As Margaret Littler has demonstrated, Köhler's *Niemands Frau* poems challenge the principles of classical logic and Newtonian physics, suggesting instead isomorphisms between poetry and the "unpredictability of matter at the subatomic level" which is central to quantum mechanics and its acknowledgement of "the coexistence of multiple possible worlds."[13] In a sense, the perspective on the data of reality that lays claim to a standpoint outside of what is being observed, that of the objectifying "er," and the correlative form of narrative that insists upon the standpoint of the "er," his singular story, the one thread pulled from the Great Web, is the perspective of an outdated science and an outdated way of recounting reality as it is now understood. In quantum mechanics, the observer has no outside standpoint but is acknowledged as part of the system under observation whose responses to the data of reality alter what is seen: in short, as science it proposes a relational model. Confronting simple mathematics with quantum calculation, old science with new, figuratively speaking the world of "er" with that of "sie," Köhler's poems appeal for a radical change in the perspective on the data of reality. Taken at their word, the poems open up a prospect of no longer insisting on the sovereign individual subject and his linear modes of narration, inheritance, calculation and grammatical proposition. Applying the "quantum" approach to Homer's text already demonstrates how such a change in perspective recovers the network of interrelated female figures who act upon Odysseus' story and the multiple threads of relationship that bind them and him together, a quite different reading from the familiar plot-based one that emphasizes the epic tale of the singular heroic individual.

Where, though, does this leave the feminine singular "sie" in which this volume has a vested political interest and which, after all, is frequently visible in Köhler's lyric persona's negotiations with the figures derived from the *Odyssey*? I think as follows: as the plausibility of the lines about the "er" that occur in *Niemands Frau* indicates, the contemporary male individual subject continues to have a greater investment in the retention of what I have described here as an outdated form of subjectivity than does the female individual subject, because to be an "er" still brings with it the advantages of a certain kind of social power and status. History also dictates that it is more difficult to perceive the masculine subject as one among many, as a "sie." The classical autonomous masculine subject, inheritor of authority in the patriarchal line, whose aspiration is to achieve mastery, is still a pervasive social model, indeed so pervasive that many professional women today choose to model themselves in accordance with it. Nonetheless, the female individual "sie" carries with her the association with a different gender history and the inheritance of alternative, contrasting culturally symbolic values. This was argued as long ago as the 1970s when the poststructuralist feminist writings of Hélène Cixous and Luce Irigaray sought to challenge the "glorious phallic monosexuality"[14] to which the male subject is culturally and socially trained in favour of the plurality of the "sex which is not one." "In this way, 'man' becomes equated with the binary system underpinning Western metaphysics and 'woman' with a multiplicity that has the potential to supersede the strictly oppositional system of Self versus Other."[15]

As Köhler's invocation of the possibilities of "sie" singular and "sie" plural to read across into one another suggests, "sie" has/have a greater political energy, the potential to renew how we perceive and think of ourselves in relation to our unfolding realities – provided we are ready to embrace that potential for change and act with a degree of collaboration with one another, even in difference.

disclosure statement

No potential conflict of interest was reported by the author.

notes

1 Barbara Köhler, *Niemands Frau. Gesänge* (Frankfurt/Main: Suhrkamp, 2007). Page references will be given in parentheses following quotations, preceded by the poem or section title where relevant. Quotation of poems from Barbara Köhler's *Niemands Frau* is by permission of Suhrkamp Verlag AG Berlin.

2 "Cyclops, you asked my name, and I will tell it: give me afterwards a guest gift as you promised. My name is Nobody. Nobody, my father, mother, and friends call me" (*Odyssey* IX, ll.364–67, trans. A.S. Kline, available <http://www.poetryintranslation.com/PITBR/Greek/Odyssey9.htm> (accessed 16 Apr. 2016)).

3 The first modern author to argue that the *Odyssey* was written by a woman was Samuel Butler in *The Authoress of the Odyssey* (New York and Bombay: Longmans, 1897). Andrew Dalby argues the case for both the *Iliad* and the *Odyssey* having been written by a female rather than a male author in *Rediscovering Homer: Inside the Origins of the Epic* (New York and London: Norton, 2006). Nineteenth-century Homeric scholars were divided on the question of Homer's authorship. While the Unitarians argued that the epic poems display such artistry and unity that they must have been the work of a single poet, the Analysts (including Johann Gottfried Jakob Hermann and Karl Lachmann, who elaborated upon Friedrich August Wolf's hypotheses in his *Prolegomena* of 1795) argued that the texts handed down were a compilation of multiple poems by many authors.

4 On "oculocentrism" and the gaze, see Luce Irigaray, *Speculum of the Other Woman*, trans. Gillian C. Gill (Ithaca, NY: Cornell UP, 1985) 47–48. On woman's preference for touch, see Irigaray, *This Sex Which Is Not One*, trans. Catherine Porter with Carolyn Burke (Ithaca, NY: Cornell UP, 1985) 26ff. On "scopophilia" in Freud and the substitution of touch by the male possessive gaze, see also Elisabeth Bronfen, *Over Her Dead Body: Death, Femininity and the Aesthetic* (Manchester: Manchester UP, 1992) 102.

5 Rebecca May Johnson, "*Niemands Frau* as a 'Minor Translation' of the *Odyssey* from 'er' to 'sie'" in *An Odyssey for Our Time: Barbara Köhler's Niemands Frau*, ed. Georgina Paul (Amsterdam and Atlanta, GA: Rodopi, 2013) 71–87 (81).

6 See "Excursus I: Odysseus or Myth and Enlightenment" in Max Horkheimer and Theodor W. Adorno, *Dialectic of Enlightenment: Philosophical Fragments*, ed. Gunzelin Schmid Noerr; trans. Edmund Jephcott (Stanford: Stanford UP, 2002) 35–62.

7 Walter J. Ong, *Orality and Literacy: The Technologizing of the Word* [1982] (London and New York: Routledge, 2002) 45.

8 See Helmut Schmitz, "The 'nachtseite des abendlands'. Barbara Köhler's *Niemands Frau* and the Dialectic of Enlightenment" in Paul, *An Odyssey for Our Time* 139–61 (142):

> Western philosophy and Western science are marked by the exclusion of the feminine and the exclusion of the body in the positing of the scientist as distanced observer. Feminist critiques of the order of knowledge have pointed towards the gendered codification of this order from its inception.

9 Christos C. Tsagalis, *The Oral Palimpsest: Exploring Intertextuality in the Homeric Epics* (Cambridge, MA and London: Harvard UP, 2008) xii.

10 Ong, *Orality and Literacy* 45.

11 See my essay "Different Voices: Other Poets in Barbara Köhler's *Niemands Frau*, with a Special Study of the Significance of T. S. Eliot's *The Waste Land*" in Paul, *An Odyssey for Our Time* 185–210 (esp. 189–90).

12 The English translation of the "Sirens" poem cited here was prepared (partly in dialogue between poet and translator) for a reading by Barbara Köhler in Cambridge in 2001, when we read the German and the English consecutively, as is the custom with bilingual readings. In 2011, at a reading in Oxford, we prepared an orchestrated version, with some short segments read consecutively in one language then the other, but the greater part of the poem read simultaneously: as a "duality duetting," as one phrase in the translation has it. The experience was electrifying, both for the audience and for us as readers. In this way the content of the poem became a performance of different subjectivities – and different languages – bodied forth as two selves in something that both was and wasn't unison, with the German and English overlapping in a fascinating revelation of the differences between the languages, and occasionally a word and its translation directly coinciding. We found ourselves being what the words were saying.

13 Margaret Littler, "Strange Loops and Quantum Turns in Barbara Köhler's *Niemands Frau*" in Paul, *An Odyssey for Our Time* 163–84 (172).

14 Hélène Cixous and Catherine Clément, *The Newly Born Woman*, trans. Betsy Wing; intro. Sandra M. Gilbert (Manchester: Manchester UP, 1986) 85.

15 Georgina Paul, *Perspectives on Gender in Post-1945 German Literature* (Rochester, NY: Camden, 2009) 53.

Georgina Paul

aliki krikidi

THEY

Anne Ploin, 15 December 2016, gouache and watercolour on paper, 42 × 62 cm. © Aliki Krikidi.

Rebecca Ellenby, 25 November 2016, gouache and watercolour on paper, 42 × 31 cm. © Aliki Krikidi.

Rebecca Ellenby, 25 November 2016, gouache and watercolour on paper, 30 × 35 cm. © Aliki Krikidi.

Rebecca Ellenby, 6 December 2016, gouache and watercolour on paper, 61 × 42 cm. © Aliki Krikidi.

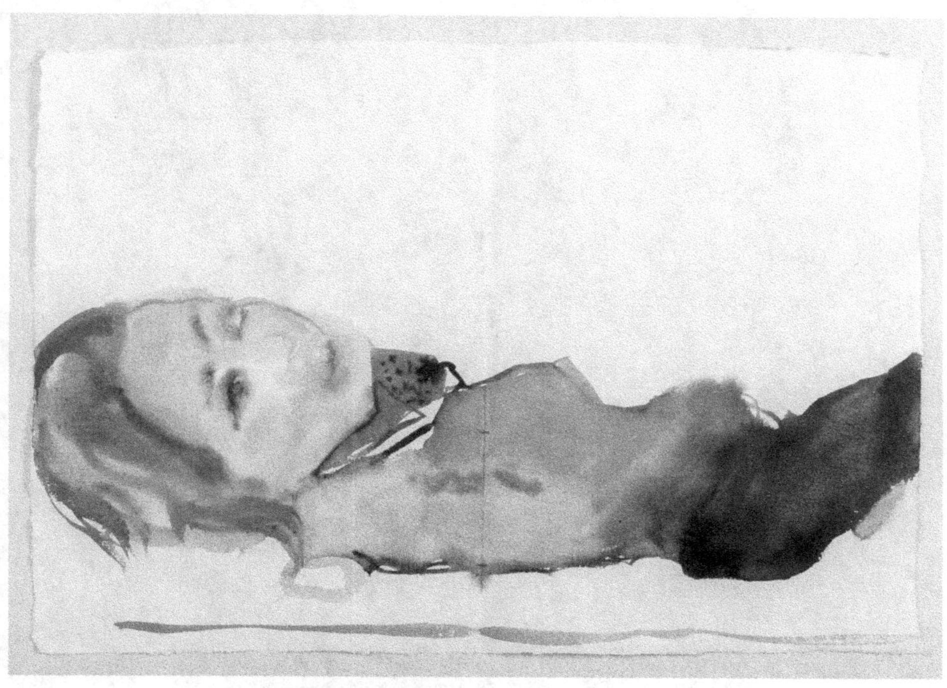

Rebecca Ellenby, 6 December 2016, gouache and watercolour on paper, 42 × 62 cm. © Aliki Krikidi.

Hannah Massie, 5 December 2016, gouache and watercolour on paper, 35 × 30 cm. © Aliki Krikidi.

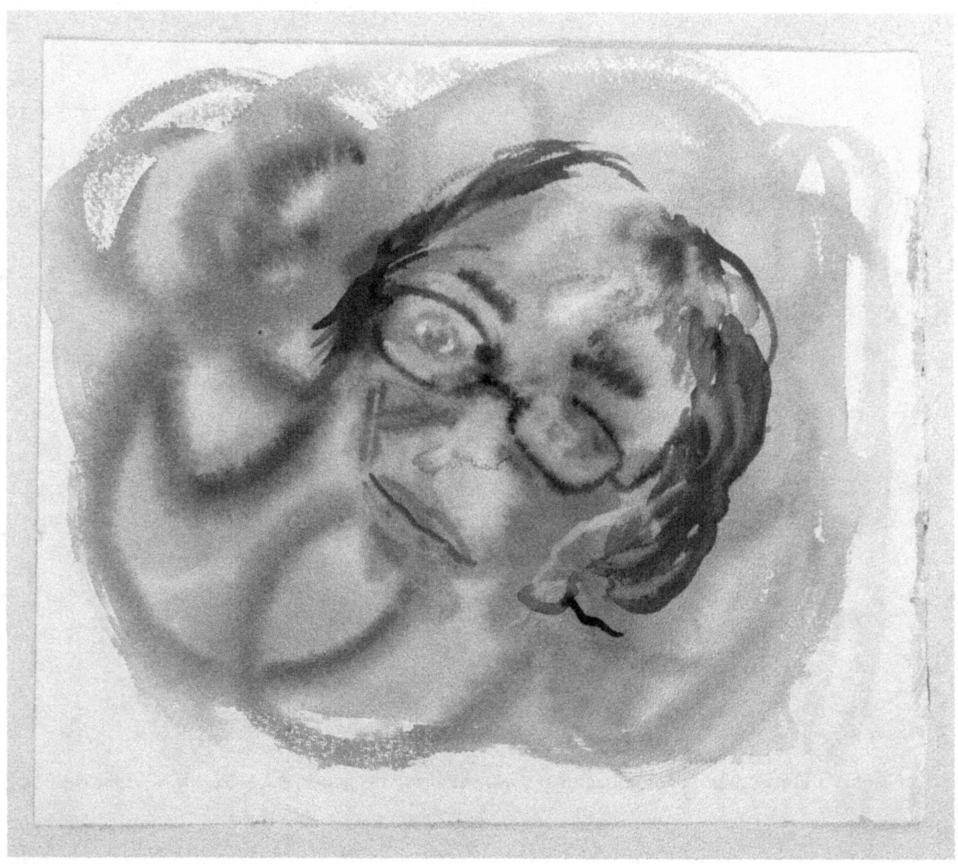

Hannah Massie, 5 December 2016, gouache and watercolour on paper, 30 × 35 cm. © Aliki Krikidi.

Rebecca Ellenby, 2 December 2016, gouache and watercolour on paper, 42 × 62 cm. © Aliki Krikidi.

They, 2 December 2016, gouache and watercolour on paper, 62 × 42 cm. © Aliki Krikidi.

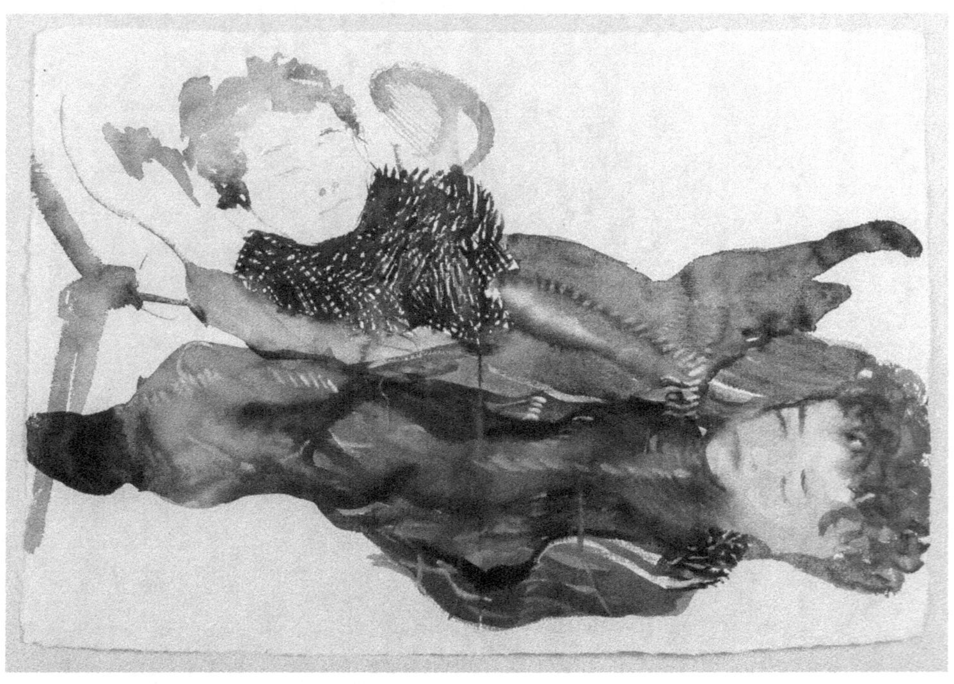

Anne Ploin, 15 December 2016, gouache and watercolour on paper, 42 × 62 cm. © Aliki Krikidi.

I encounter the bidirectional transformation of the complex to its elements and of the subjective to its imaginary composition at the core of my work process. I am fascinated by the ephemeral power of this bidirectional transformation and the elicited emotions and interpretations.

In these glimpses into transgender transition and non-binary gender identity, the colour and form journeys reflect the narrative of transformation. The departure from the binary and the journey to the interconnected parts of the whole, the adventure of reshuffling the identity foundations and exploring the "blind alleys of imaginary experience" towards a transtemporal Real.

Aliki Krikidi

lauren grodstein

GENDERED EXPECTATIONS

writing counter to my gender

In my career as a writer, I have published three novels, each from the point of view of a man – once in the first-person and twice in the third-person perspective. Of course, just because I've published three novels doesn't mean I've written only three novels. I have – like many novelists – a few complete and half-complete novels asphyxiating in a drawer in my office. But the published novels, the most successful novels, and the novels I was happiest writing (as they felt the freest to write, and the most satisfying during the production) were novels in which I inhabited, in the strange multiple-personality way that writers have, a man.

This is, I think, unexpected. When we go to the bookstore, we usually expect books by female authors to have female protagonists, and male authors to have male protagonists. My favorite writers when I was a student – writers who are still among my favorite – tend to stick to their genders: Phillip Roth, Vladimir Nabokov, and John Cheever's protagonists tend to be male, while Alice Munro and Lorrie Moore, for the most part, write women. They do so notably and beautifully, and they teach, by example – deliberately or not – that writers write best when they write protagonists who are, demographically, close to themselves.

This is sometimes the case. But this is not always the case.

My first novel, *Reproduction is the Flaw of Love* (a title that felt clever when I thought it up), was written in a fit of desperation. I had already published a short story collection, and knew that the realities of publishing wouldn't let a non-famous literary writer attempt another one – this was in the early 2000s, when new writers were allowed one story collection, but one only (these days they might not even be allowed that). The only thing I could hope to publish, if I were to publish again, was a novel. So I sat down at my desk and attempted to do this thing that seemed frightening, if not impossible, even though I had trained in both university and graduate school to do it, and even though it had been the only thing in my life I had always wanted to do. Still, to write 300–400 narratively cohesive pages, in well-formed sentences, that told the story of characters that a stranger might find engaging, and that also created a plot that felt both surprising and inevitable – the very idea of doing this seemed almost impossible. I began scrolling through everything I had learned about plot and character development in graduate school, to see if any of it would help me in my panic. When none of it did (which was a shame, considering the money I'd invested) I started going through all the old writerly axioms I'd heard in my life, thinking maybe one of them would be of service, but the only one I could really remember was write what you know.

Write what you know! Unfortunately, I didn't know a thing.

So I took stock of my surroundings. Maybe there was something I didn't *realize* I knew? I was a twenty-five year old living in a small apartment in Brooklyn, surviving on spaghetti and cigarettes. Perhaps there was a plot in this? I knew that other writers had taken on the young woman-in-Brooklyn-distress theme (and many of them, for example Lena Dunham, are still having a go at it) so why couldn't I? It was what I knew – sadly, it was all I knew.

But the novel wouldn't come. In fact, in attempting to recreate myself, and what I knew, and what I could see and touch with my own body, I found whatever spark that's necessary to create fiction so stifled I could barely get out a page. There was nothing about me that was novel-worthy – or, if there was, it was so familiar to me I couldn't see it.

Novel-making is intoxicating because it allows us to imagine the other, gives us license, in fact demands that we step outside ourselves to inhabit someone else. And so the very act of locking myself inside myself was taking away the very *freeing* thing that creating fiction is supposed to do. Moreover, it wasn't any fun.

So I took out a few pages I had written – some nonsense about walking down a Brooklyn street in a Mets cap, smoking a cigarette – and decided, very tentatively (for this was something that none of my friends in graduate school did, that very few of my favorite novelists ever did) to turn the "she's" into "he's." As I did so, I started molding the sentences gently around the new gender of the protagonist: what would *he* notice as he walked down the street, as opposed to what *she* might notice? The hip women's clothing stores and what they sold – much of it would be invisible to him, as the he I was imagining was a baseball-cap wearing sort, normatively heterosexual, a major fan of New York City's major league sports. He would notice that pretty girl, and probably that one too. He would not indulge in a long inner monologue about the nanny yelling at the child, but he would spy the man over there, the one who looked like his father, the father who died at a diner, the father who did his best by him even after he messily divorced his mother ... and so on ...

And in that act – which wasn't so renegade, really, or even very difficult – in that act of rewriting a few pronouns, I ended up being able to free myself to fully imagine another character, another human being. Which is the joy and the liberty and the reason, perhaps, to undertake the whole fictional enterprise. I kept at it, and eventually I wrote the novel which became *Reproduction is the Flaw of Love*. It tells the story of one Joel Miller, a young Brooklynite whose girlfriend may or may not be pregnant, and as he reckons with possible fatherhood he reckons with his entire life. (The entire story takes place in the time it takes to take a pregnancy test, but since I wrote the book in the early 2000s, you could still find one of those old chemistry-set type of tests, which allowed me to slow down the narrative rhythm of the thing.) I built the plot into the backstory of the novel, which was an abbreviated biography of Joel Miller, a young man whose father did in fact messily divorce his mother, and also had a complicated relationship with both his parents, a best friend who looked out for him, an ex-girlfriend he missed and a current girlfriend he felt ambivalent about. I delved into each of these relationships with the liberty of my imagination, as I was now untethered to a protagonist who mirrored myself. Of course, I gave Joel Miller some of my own experiences and a lot of what I knew: Joel and I lived in the same place, grew up in the same places, took childhood vacations to the same town. But I also gave Joel Miller all the dimensionality I was capable of, divorced from my own history or biology. I was able to do that because he was a man and I was not.

And what I learned from doing this was that the hardest thing I have to do as a novelist – the thing that will keep my reader's interest, the thing that will keep my *own* interest, and the thing that is the very ground upon which I want my stories to stand – is to create an entirely different, entirely other three-dimensional person. Fiction (at least the sort of fiction I'm most interested in reading and writing) begins with other people. To this end, I remind my writing students that the best writers really like other people, even if they find it exhausting to be around them, because in other people is the clay out of which you mold your own people. Your own characters. You need to listen to what people say. You need to know the patterns in which they speak. You need to understand what certain people like and why they are that way, what certain people fear and why – and if all of these people are, in the end, just *you*, then almost certainly your fiction will begin to feel stale, a little tired, a little uninspired. A little bit boring. If you only write characters based on yourself, you are closing down your most fertile ground, and shutting down your stories almost before they are written.

Do all authors perform this way, stripping their work of all autobiography? Of course not. But all authors should be able to, should they want to.

What writers should do, must do, is imagine the three-dimensional other. Writers need to make that other seem as real, to the reader, as the reader's mother. Writers need to make that other so true that the reader will agree to undertake the strange, almost transgressive act of treating your fiction as truth: of believing your *lies*. And in order to create that other, writers need to feel free to imagine every part of him or her. Gender is just one aspect of a character. Because the writer is charged with fully imagining another human being – and because all human beings are comprised of many things beyond gender – gender is, itself, simply one of the many aspects of a character the writer must be unafraid to imagine. Gender is not the entirety of another character, as some readers and critics assume, when the author is of the opposite gender. Instead, gender is one of the many traits that compose a character, and a writer who can create someone of another race or occupation or age in a compelling, honest way must also be able to write someone of another gender honestly and compellingly. If not, is the writer really capable of that fundamental thing she's charged with, writing another human being into reality?

The novel I published after *Reproduction* – not the next one I wrote, a 700-page monstrosity that took years to die, but the next one I published – was written from the first-person point of view of a middle-aged male physician who is having difficulties micromanaging the life of his twenty-something son the way he wishes he could. The novel, *A Friend of the Family*, represents my most critically successful book as well as my best seller, and I'm proud of it. *I was unsurprised, however, when critics responded to the book with comments about the protagonist's gender, and the unlikelihood that I (a woman) would write about this character (a man).* I wrote in the first person, and that, I believed, was what critics responded to; more than once I was called a "ventriloquist." There was a sense of surprise that a young woman would dare adopt the voice of a middle-aged man, much less do so successfully, as though the imagining of a young woman couldn't approach middle-aged male truth.

Yet what I found most interesting about that is that very few critics mentioned the many scenes which took place (again, in the first person) in a doctor's office, despite the fact that I have no license to practice medicine, or the many other scenes that showed our protagonist interacting with his son, despite the fact that when I wrote the novel I was childless. Again, the ability to imagine another gender becomes privileged, in a way, above all the other essential pieces of character a novelist has to imagine, which is not only strange, but somehow stifling.

Because truly, when you allow yourself to create another gender, what you are saying is:

I am trying to erase myself. I am not writing myself in this novel; I am not protecting myself in this novel (by, say, writing a character who is just like me, only a little bit better looking, or just like me, only really wealthy). I am not thinly veiling my autobiography, and I am not looking to rewrite my autobiography but with a happier childhood. I am creating someone else. I am attempting to fully imagine someone else.

The novel I am working on now, my fourth, is the first one written from the point of view of a woman. After three novels written from a man's point of view – the most recent one, about a male biologist (the protagonist) and his female student, was published in 2013 – I feel confident enough in my imagining to know that just because I am writing about a woman I will not be inadvertently writing about myself. I have had enough practice, over the decade and a half I've been writing, of *imagining somebody else in her entirety. I've also had enough life experience, I hope, and have met enough other people, that I am able to synthesize what I know of others into a character who is herself.*

When we imagine character, we are basing our imaginations on that which we have experienced – even if we try to imagine that which is the opposite of what we experienced. We embroider; we embellish; we spin out possibilities rooted in what we have observed on this earth. And when we completely divorce what we imagine from what we've observed, we tend to create characters who aren't "believable," because they don't behave in ways that readers recognize as human (this applies even when characters are space invaders, or house plants). All of what we imagine is rooted, fundamentally, in what we know. And so it is up to the writer to expand upon what she knows, to learn as much as she can, and to push her own prejudices, sloppy thinking, habits, and preconceptions away so that the characters she creates feel real and human and true. The best imaginings come from the ability to see clearly.

Which is why, regardless of gender and my best efforts, I can't help but exist in my characters. I do my best to strip myself of myself in order to write someone else, but to do so entirely would be impossible. I am who I am, and I am also someone attempting to be someone else. This is the writer's paradox, and the best part of the job.

disclosure statement

No potential conflict of interest was reported by the author.

Lauren Grodstein

kirsty gunn

WRITING MEN IMAGINING WOMEN

Ray knew.
Something in the smell, or the quick bits of sun flicking in and out of shadows down in the bush. Something in the wet smell there, of leaves going bad, but fresh growth, too, coming from under them, in little seeds under the damaged twigs, flowers even …
He knew, there, down at the Reserve that morning, with the shift of heavy air like a body of air pressed close against him and the shade and light amongst the trees a pattern he wore as a mask on his own face.
[…]
[…] he knew alright. Francie was back. It was like he tasted the knowledge. She was back there amongst the sweetness, in the leaves, in the smell. At last, after all this time, she'd come home. (*Featherstone* 33, 34)

He feels exhausted. He needs to go to bed. Tomorrow he'll make the call, tell Anna and his mother – what? That he will leave? Stay? Say he'll come back to London but later? Or stay on, but if so, how long will he have to stay? Days? Weeks? He can't imagine any of this. Can't think about it. Can't think any of it through. Realises, in the thickness of his tiredness and his whisky, that he doesn't even know what he is going to do this minute, this second, let alone tomorrow, anything else […]
[…]
So he's not sleeping in there […] Someone – Margaret?
Has gone in there and placed his case by the bed, turned down the covers. Turned on a little lamp. Someone –
Helen?
Has been in here. In his father's old room and prepared it for him. Knowing he'll be coming here. Knowing he'll be tired. Imagining him … Pushing open the door […]
[…]
He needs to lie down.
To think that Helen's been here. To think that she knew.
That he'd end up here. That she'd turned back the covers for him in that way …
Oh, Helen, Helen – but he wants to close his eyes …
[…]
Please.
Helen.
If he prayed, he'd be praying now.
To think he's supposed to finish this day here. In his father's old room. With Helen somewhere in the House. (*The Big Music* 170, 171)

In the two sections of text above, the first from a book I published in 2002 and the second from my most recent novel, that came out eleven years later, I see that I have long been interested in writing male characters and showing their worlds, from their point of view.

I meet them first in my imagination, these men, as they've taken body and voice in front of me, have introduced themselves to me, if you like, and then I start to inhabit their minds, start to see out through their eyes, hear the way they might hear. My hope is that in writing them, in finding ways for them to be themselves on the page, a part of us, as we read, might become them. That the Ray we've just met, someone barely able to hear the conversation going on around him so troubled is he by memory and emotion, is someone inside ourselves, that we don't so much read about him, as read from within him. There he is, I want the reader to feel, turning with thought and desire yet being sure to hold himself steady, upright, to be in control: "There was the shift of someone beside him," I write, it appears shortly after the passage above:

> one of the women moving a bag from one hand to another and he realised at that moment he hadn't heard anything anyone was saying.
> "Ray?"
> He'd listened maybe, but he hadn't heard.
> "What's that?" he said now, and the effort of speaking the two words was like wrenching himself out of himself, so tightly had he been holding his face impassive, his arms so tightly folded against his chest to keep his loud heart in.
> [...]
> *Francie ...*
> Ray pressed in his arms to himself.
> *Francie ...*
> And harder he pressed them, against his body, as if to stop his heart. (*Featherstone* 35, 37)

Then there with Callum, too, in the second extract, my hope is that the reader, like him, becomes bleary with whisky and tiredness, hearing the ragged phrases of the past that come back in snatches of memory and imagination to disturb his sense of purpose and his will:

> He wants to leave this room, he must leave it. He doesn't belong here. Not in this room of his father's that Helen's been to before him, with his jacket and his case.
> [...]
> When he's supposed to be here for his father, and none of this about Helen, but about his father, and he's supposed to be here for his father, and he's had too much to drink and he's tired and he must leave this room, please, he must get out of this room ...
> But she's been here before him, Helen. She's turned down the bed.
> [...]
> *What are you doing here?*
> Remember?
> [...]
> Her looking at him with those steady eyes of hers. (*The Big Music* 171–73)

Both these books – *Featherstone* and *The Big Music* – also begin with men and their worlds, not the men we've just met now, in these extracts, but other men, old men, alone with their thoughts. One is in a garden, one on a remote hilltop. "He looked up and thought: *I know you*" is the first line of *Featherstone* (3). "Is what there is to begin with ..." appears on the opening page of *The Big Music*, "With this image of a man, born eighty-three years ago down out of these same hills" (3). And both the books, after opening through that portal of the singular, male protagonist placed in the centre of his known, "owned" world, then spread wide out into worlds inhabited by other men, and, of course, by women.

There's Francie, whom Sonny, the old man in his garden thinks he has just seen, and Helen whom Callum can't stop thinking about ... Both of whom exert enormous charge over events and characters, and, whether absent or present in the text, are able to influence the narrative and shape it – even down to the look and texture of the words on the page. Both of their names, for example, often appear in italics and in repetition, like a kind of a pulse. Both characters arrive on the page surrounded by white space, or find themselves in a separate section of text, or on new lines in a paragraph. And yes, these women are deeply connected to and, in the end, responsible for the drive of all events that push the books through what we might call the story, what I prefer to call the world of the book,[1] and bring it to its final pages; they are key to the texture and experience of the narrative overall.

So, in many respects, none of these stories of mine about men and their lives would be stories at all were it not for the women in their stories – but that's the subject for another paper. Enough to say for now that though, yes, I am referring here to shaping a story, or an aspect of a story, from a male point of view, nevertheless I want also to alert readers to the fact that, as well as creating a way of looking out at events from Ray's and Callum's perspective, the process of writing, of imagining characters and then of reading them, is actually more broken open than that. Being sensitive to how one might be seen by others, after all, is also necessarily part of what it is to be human and social, and "Being-in-the-world" (as Heidegger puts it in *Being and Time*) would be an aspect of any work of fiction that has ethical as well as aesthetic fundaments, tending to permit other viewpoints that come from outside a single range of vision. And so the male point of view, then, I seem to be suggesting, in terms of my own fictional project, may be rather more multiveillant than first appears, have rather more a complex and fluid meaning than the rigidity of the term, its sense of usefulness as a directive, say, in creative writing classes, might imply.

Close readers of the first extract here would have observed that phrase "shade and light amongst the trees a pattern he wore as a mask on his own face," for example. Already, there's an aspect of an "other" to Ray's singular, obsessive view of things. It's the sensation of the patterning of dark and bright on his face, perhaps, that he feels, that indicates the seeing of it, by the reader, as a mask, which then in turn is given to him to wear. There's a flickering from inside to outside that reflects the flickering of dappled sunlight itself – again, something I hope the reader might feel and see, to be both inside and outside Ray, and so to have his point of view deepened by a sort of double-vision.

Another example, in the second extract, is the fracturing of Callum's singularity, of his character, by memory, so that his own voice and sensibility is cut up into pieces:

> Remember?
> *What's your name? How old are you?*
> Her looking at him with those steady eyes of hers.
> *My name's Callum. I'm nine.*
> And him looking back at her, remember. But also not able to look. (*The Big Music* 173)

In Callum's case, the problem of a singular point of view – the impossibility, really, of his maintaining it – is made explicit in his remembering of his lover, thoughts coming back to him of when she was a girl. It's impossible for him to stay focused – on getting himself to bed, in getting some sleep – because her presence in his mind, and *her* point of view – the memory of her looking back at him! – gets in the way of that singular activity. It's the kind of singular activity, I may add, of perceiving the world as a singular white male of a certain background and type may want to perceive it, that's expressed in most novels that are published today – their stories laid out in the kind of straightforward terms that can be easily managed, so: He then wondered if, or, After that he thought he must, etc. etc. – all in order that the character may be doing one certain thing at a certain time before going on to the next; endless points of action and thought following along the plot's relentless line to its fixed conclusion.

So yes, I am suggesting that breaking open the gaze, to another kind of possibility, to another kind of writing that allows for the power of something else, beyond the perception of the protagonist, is an interesting thing to do, that it complicates reading, that it enriches the idea of a singular experience and charges it with the possibility of something multiple and shared that crosses gender lines and releases a text belonging to male and female characters and readers equally, rendering an experience that is both known and familiar and new and inexplicable to all. As Woolf in her Diary wrote about *The Waves*, "We are somehow successive and continuous," "Larger and more complex than each of the individual's own memories."[2]

Might this be speaking, I wonder, this ungendering of narrative, to Irigaray's idea of the sexuate, the blurring of subject and object that may occur in life as in a story? Might this be what it is, *parler femme*, as she has it, to bring together a male and female gaze on the page, to encounter in our reading both (*Speculum de l'autre femme*)? Certainly I know, as a writer, that I am not breaking any rules of narrative "finish," which is how I describe responsibility to the unity and truth of a fictive project,[3] by suggesting that there is really no such thing as point-of-view – because, of course, we must hold onto all we have learned from Henry James and so on, Stendhal and Ford and Woolf herself; we must maintain vigorously the awareness of how much can be seen and known when we are telling stories from the perspectives of our characters. I myself am fiendishly particular about such details and reject novels and short stories wholesale if they don't pay attention to who said what and why, who knew what and why ... [4]

No, we must write properly – and those of us who are interested in free direct narrative have to pay attention to getting all our characters just right, making all of them individuals so that they see the world and relate it from their point of view in their individual way. Yet within that boundary what infinities may occur! And to have expressed that sense of possibility, the multiveillance, again, that opens out through the visor of singular point of view ... To have access to that "larger and more complex" of Woolf's ... To me, this is the adventure of novels, stories. It's how they might change our own way of seeing, perhaps change society too.

For that male point of view ... The *relentlessness* of the male gaze ... This is a feature of our life that, as I am always aware, as a feminist, is not only to be overcome in the way we express our preferences in reading and in life but also may be subdued, the political force of it disarmed, through the processes by which we make our books. So I create, as you may see in the characters of the examples I've given here, a male gaze that is unable to hold a female gaze. For how strong is it, that unwavering stare of the ten-year-old Helen, how bright the presence of the revenant Francie. In that way I hope that by allowing for the interruption of the male gaze I destabilize it, that by presenting within a story about men a woman with her own ineffable gaze I interrupt all the old ways of generic seeing. Instead of the man imagining what he will do to the woman, then, it is rather a case of his imagining what she may do to him.

To conclude, as I began, with two more quotes, one taken from a text by the mighty D.H. Lawrence – and we couldn't get more of a male point of view than Lawrence – and another from *The Big Music*, from that same section, the same night, this time Callum waking from sleep in his father's room after a troubled evening. The first shows the male point of view in all its glorious masculinity, and I write that with no sense of irony; I adore Lawrence and his gazing males! They have a quality that I would hope runs through any of the male characters I write, that I might only get them down on the page so as to be as various and textured as Lawrence gets them ... ! And the second extract shows that kind of man, I hope, and beholden to his particular point of view, but tilted, shifted from it, by his intra-gazing, may we call it, by his looking at a woman who looks back.

I wonder if there's a quality in both that indicates the pleasures and interests of allowing the two kinds of approach to writing and reading male characters? That we may see them both as discrete yet somehow simultaneously ... That by imagining men who allow themselves to be looked at by the women they are looking at we might enjoy the variance and multiplicity of both points of view; the complexity of the worlds of both sexes held fast within the covers of a book, captured within the focus and attention of our own reading gaze.

"The way of living is to answer to one's wants," Lawrence writes in "On Being a Man." He goes on:

> Not "I want to light up with my intelligence as many things as possible" but "For the living of my full flame – I want that liberty, I want that woman, I want that pound of peaches, I want to go to sleep, I want to go to the pub and have a good time, I want to look a beastly swell today, I want to kiss that girl, I want to insult that man."

Instead of that we talk about some sort of idea. ("On Being a Man")

Callum's eyes start open. In the middle of the dark after dreams – such dreams! Has he woken?
[…]
he is aware that someone is there, really there in the room with him, but not from the dream.
Someone.
"Are you okay?" she whispers.
He turns, and she is there, a shadow beside him, in the dark.
"It's me" she says.
Though he can barely see her.
His hand goes up, instinctively, to touch her face.
[…]
Then she takes his hand and puts it to her face. He can't see her. It's been … How long? Twenty years? Since she was last near him? Twenty years? Longer. It's been for ever.
"Helen?"
And he can't see her.
"Shhh … " She kisses his palm, the soft insides of his hand.
"Shhh … "
He can't see her.
Though she leans down to him, he can't. Still he can't see her.
"Helen –"
"Shhh … "
Though he still can't see her.
"Shhh … "
Still …
Can't …
Still …
"I'm here with you now" Helen says. (*The Big Music* 174–75)

disclosure statement

No potential conflict of interest was reported by the author.

notes

1 This phrase comes with reference to and in honour of Gabriel Josipovici's great *The World and the Book*, a work that has been of enormous influence and help in understanding and defining my own writing life.

2 Woolf, *The Diary of Virginia Woolf*, Friday 4 Jan. 1929, 3: 128.

3 I lecture and speak informally at a variety of literary events about the importance of "narrative finish," as I call it, which is how I describe responsibility to the unity and truth of a fictive project or alternatively "integrity of the picture plane" – to borrow a term from my sister, the painter Merran Gunn, who in turn uses it to read paintings – that one section of a work may be as complete and thought through and executed as any other. Some of these talks are available online – and one essay in particular, "On Style and Content," can be found at <www.edinburghworldwritersconference.org> and in a subsequent publication, *The 21st Century Novel – Notes from the Edinburgh World Writers' Conference*.

4 The minute you have a character acting outside him- or herself, speaking in a way they wouldn't or claiming deeper knowledge of something they could not claim to understand or know (all those children who talk as though they were literary novelists! All those women who speak and relay their experiences in full unbroken paragraphs of dialogue! All those men who have become suddenly omniscient in the middle of a first-person point-of-view novel and for no reason now know everything about everyone who inhabits the story with them! I could go on and on …), is the minute that, for me, no matter how deep that book's themes, how riveting its story, it goes into the bin.

bibliography

Gunn, Kirsty. *The Big Music*. London: Faber, 2012. Print.

Gunn, Kirsty. *Featherstone*. London: Faber, 2002. Print.

Heidegger, Martin. *Being and Time*. 1927. Trans. John Macquarrie and Edward Robinson. Oxford: Blackwell, 1967. Print.

Irigaray, Luce. *Speculum de l'autre femme*. Paris: Minuit, 1974. Print.

Josipovici, Gabriel. *The World and the Book*. Stanford: Stanford UP, 1971. Print.

Lawrence, D.H. "On Being a Man." *Reflections on the Death of a Porcupine and Other Essays*. Ed. Michael Herbert. Cambridge: Cambridge UP, 1988. 211–22. Print.

The 21st Century Novel – Notes from The World Writers' Conference. Ed. Jonathan Bastable and Hannah McGill. Edinburgh: Edinburgh UP, 2015. Print.

Woolf, Virginia. *The Diary of Virginia Woolf*. 5 vols. Ed. Anne Olivier Bell. London: Hogarth, 1977–84. Print.

Kirsty Gunn

Index

Note: Page numbers followed by "n" refer to endnotes.

For Product Safety Concerns and Information please contact our EU representative GPSR@taylorandfrancis.com
Taylor & Francis Verlag GmbH, Kaufingerstraße 24, 80331 München, Germany

www.ingramcontent.com/pod-product-compliance
Lightning Source LLC
Chambersburg PA
CBHW081355090726
47908CB00011B/2682

* 9 7 8 0 3 6 7 3 3 6 6 5 3 *